THE SHAPING OF OUR WORLD
A Human and Cultural Geography

THE SHAPING OF OUR WORLD

A HUMAN AND CULTURAL GEOGRAPHY

W. A. Douglas Jackson
University of Washington

John Wiley & Sons
New York   Chichester   Brisbane
Toronto   Singapore

For Kay
and
In memory
of
three beloved Afghan hounds,
Dodon, Rucidon, and Buzz

Library of Congress Cataloging in Publication Data

Jackson, W. A. Douglas (William Arthur Douglas), 1923–
   The shaping of our world.

   Includes indexes.
    1. Anthropo-geography.   2. Man—Influence on nature.
I. Title.

GF41.J325 1985   304.2   84-7518
ISBN 0-471-88031-0

Printed in the United States of America

10 9 8 7 6 5 4 3 2 1

Preface

The world we inhabit, as exhibited in patterns of human activity—settlement and occupance of area or place, movement, association, territorial organization, economic endeavors, and communication—is one largely of our own creation. No single scientific discipline or point of view can adequately or satisfactorily explain the diversity of these patterns. Geographers are ideally suited for the study of such patterns, but extensive borrowing from other disciplines has contributed significantly to the development of geographic insight.

The geographic perspective is spatial or territorial in the way in which it organizes its thoughts about human activity patterns, but anthropologists, economists, political scientists, sociologists, and other social scientists have much to tell about human behavior and motivation. Moreover, research into the nature and performance of humankind has moved in other directions where the talents of linguists and psychologists, for example, have been brought to bear; some of their findings have enriched the assumptions and conclusions of geographic research. But in this reaching out to other disciplines and fields of study, the geographer has not ignored the contributions of history and of historians, for how else could geography gain the perspective of time and change?

This book focuses on the world created by humankind, as expressed in the ways people have in effect dealt with the world. Human geography is the geography of humankind; cultural geography is the geography of human expression, inventiveness, and expectation. Only a fine line divides the two subfields and it is a division that need not concern us here. Both human and cultural geography find ultimate expression in the landscape, which while a part of the earth's physical whole has, nevertheless, been modified by human will and endeavor.

The Industrial Revolution, beginning about the mid-eighteenth century in England, has been a catalyst for the enormous transformation of the modern landscape of humankind. There have been massive movements of people, different settlement patterns have been created, new forms of energy have come into use—and these developments have in total greatly altered traditional values, uses of resources, and human associations. This revolution continues to play out its themes, in somewhat modified form, throughout the world today.

The patterns on the earth, however, are not solely the product of the Industrial Revolution. They represent a composite of forces and factors that reach deep into history. An understanding of the modern landscape requires that we do not reject the past. Rather, we must be aware of it, and attempt to identify its more important legacy. But we must not stop here. Within our modern world, however complex and confusing the patterns, however difficult the task of assessing relationships among phenomena, there are forces propelling the activities of humankind into new spatial forms as yet dimly seen, if seen at all. The incredible speed with which the communication (or electronics) revolution has descended on us is ushering in a geography that will see old patterns yielding to new as the landscape succumbs to further change. To say that humankind is always coming out of the past and moving into the future is to suggest simply that a degree of tension accompanies the compression of time people are forced to live with. And this tension is a feature of life in the United States no less than in South Africa, Poland, Vietnam, Saudi Arabia, El Salvador, or any other place on earth. A change in the pulse of life in the United States is felt all over today's world.

Because of the component of fast change, this book begins with a reminder that humans have not only created the environment in which they live, their milieu, but they have also attempted to be at home in it, to experience it. Although humankind is apart from nature, it remains very much a part of nature. From earliest times, people have sought to understand the relationship between nature and culture, the milieu in which they live. Culture, the product of a rapidly developing mental capacity and the remembrance of past experience, has shaped our patterns of thought, expression, and activity so much that culture components, such as language and religion, in turn shape behavior and other cultural processes.

Humankind divides the earth and its resources, though it is not a very just or equitable distribution. Inequity is the basis of much political activity whether conducted by national or international associations or by jurisdictions that have immediate effect on daily lives. Associations that are more specifically social in objective, though not exclusively so, reflect also how we feel about each other and the extent to which we include or exclude. Our group standards often exclude our sharing with the less privileged.

Cities have been the focus of much human energy since earliest times. A new type of city emerged with the Industrial Revolution, and changing forms of energy, transportation, and the Electronics Revolution may fashion still newer city types. The impact of humankind's identification and usage of the earth's resources have also led to profound variations spatially in the realm of agriculture and food production. But the modern burdens placed on resources raise pertinent questions of how humankind will fare in the future. Populations are steadily growing and multiplied needs and wants place additional pressures on familiar patterns and places. What the balance will be no one can foretell, although on the basis of what is known, it is certain that the future will hold more of today's stresses. Nor can we say how population growth will guard the earth's environment from further jeopardy and the human habitat from shantytown. We can attempt only to provide an assessment of the shape of our world and how it came to be this way.

It is to these themes that this book is directed. It does not attempt to introduce students to every term or concept used by human and cultural geographers. Rather, it seeks a synthesis, and one that is the product of historic forces, as a means of helping students comprehend the larger world they inhabit.

Acknowledgments

To these colleagues throughout the land and abroad who made critical suggestions as the manuscript of this book progressed, I am deeply grateful. None was more generous in support than Kit Salter, to whom I owe a special debt. His sensitivity to the goals of the book were always evident in the reviews that he prepared.

Joyce Barnum, of the Reference Division, Suzallo Library, University of Washington, was everything that a reference librarian should be: painstaking, thorough, and always patient. John and Helen Sherman provided invaluable cartographic assistance, especially in the development of the maps. Sally Kostal, formerly of Goodyear Publishing Company, knew how to be supportive when, at times, words of encouragement were sorely needed.

I must also speak of friends and associates. They were near during the formative stages of the book and at a critical period of illness, and they offered, as well, much-needed and creative distraction at other times: Noel McGary, Douglas Fleming, Michael Talbott, Alfred Schweppe, Nané Brennen, and Kay Baillargeon.

The following must be thanked for their contributions in reviewing the manuscript: Martyn J. Bowden, Clark University; Gary Fuller, University of Hawaii; Peter J. Hugill, Texas A & M University; Warren Hultquist, California State University—Sacramento; Karl Raitz, University of Kentucky; Michael M. Swann, University of Nebraska; and Joseph Velikonja, University of Washington. Naturally, the responsibility for errors of commission and omission are mine.

Many persons have contributed to the final appearance of the book. I am especially indebted to Maura Grant for her ability to provide many of the photos that have illuminated the spirit and thrust of the text. At John Wiley and Sons, Miriam Navarro, senior production supervisor, gave dedicated attention to bringing text, maps and photos together, and for her I have nothing but admiration. Finally, Katie Vignery, my editor, has been a source of inspiration and encouragement; and it is to her that I express my thanks.

Finally, the opportunity to complete the manuscript as a scholar-in-residence at the Rockefeller Study and Conference Center (Villa Serbelloni) at Bellagio, Lake Como, Italy, in August–September 1983, is one that will always be cherished.

W. A. Douglas Jackson

Contents

Expanded Contents

Introduction

The whole speculative impulse and systematic zeal of traditional philosophy from Aristotle to Hegel was directed at first toward an exhaustive treatment of the relationship between man and nature. Later, it moved toward the relationship between man and man, and still later to the relationship between man and history. But philosophy ignored the "human environments," the reality that for centuries represented the concrete world in which we made our anguished efforts to live, cohabit, and survive.

Tomás Maldonado,
Design, Nature, and Revolution, 1972

"Space" is the basic organizing concept of the geographer (Whittlesey, 1954, p. 28). But, this word can be "a treacherous philosophical word" because of problems of interpretation and definition (Blaut, 1961, p. 1). Given this difficulty, then, geographers must distinguish their field of study from the endeavors of other social and natural scientists by the kinds of questions they ask about the world around. These may best be described as questions pertaining to relationships and associations between phenomena that are distributed over the surface of the earth. Understood in this manner, geography can rightfully be called a spatial science.

This focus on relationships and associations has underlain geographic inquiry from earliest times. Such questions, moreover, may be studied for the past as well as for the present. This broad time perspective brings geographic study close to history. Historians, however, are primarily concerned with the record of human activity over a given period of time. Geographers, on the other hand, study human-activity patterns in a spatial context whatever the period of time. Above all, they recognize that because activity patterns are not set for all time, relationships and associations are always in a state of flux, "a coming out of the past and a going into the future."

THEMES IN GEOGRAPHY

As we know from the texts of early Greek observers, the basis of geography was the quite ordinary human curiosity about the earth and the people known to live on it. We need not concern ourselves here with a precise dating of the origins of this interest or of geography as a recognizable field of study. The Greek scholars of the sixth century B.C. and later, especially the group of philosopher-naturalists, certainly laid the foundations of a rational, as opposed to a mythologic or religious, inquiry into the order

they believed underlay the structure of the universe. But, it had to wait until the work of Eratosthenes (c. 276–196 B.C.) before the term geographer came into use.

Since that early period, geography as an identifiable body of knowledge and interpretation has been subjected to the shifting currents of philosophical thought and marked by significant regional cultural orientation. Much of what was once contained within the broad rubric of geography (meaning in the classical sense earth description) has broken away to constitute more specialized fields of study, especially in the natural sciences. Among these breakaway fields are astronomy, meteorology, and geology.

As for the narrowing focus of geographic study, it, too, has been subjected to changing emphases, both as knowledge of the earth and its inhabitants has grown and as perceptions of humankind's place have changed. From the middle of the nineteenth to the early part of the twentieth century, especially in Western Europe and the United States, the nature of the relationship between humans and the earth's physical environment was a dominant theme in geographic writing. Whether this relationship was expressed in terms of environmental control or influence or in terms of the restraints imposed on the capacity of humans to see or to take advantage of opportunities or possibilities inherent in the environment, the *human-environment theme* was and has remained, although somewhat modified today, an integral part of geographic thought and writing.

Overlapping the period in which human-environment relationships drew scholarly attention was another period when the study of regions was important (Whittlesey, 1954). An interest in observable differences among peoples and places has been part of the geographic field since the Greeks made a point of drawing attention to them. However, the study of regions and their differences assumed a major place in Western geography in the early decades of the twentieth century.

This interest in regional or areal differentiation (Hartshorne, 1959), however, created, for a subsequent generation of geographers, significant philosophic and methodological difficulties. The emphasis on differences led to the conclusion that every region or landscape was unique. This, in turn, prompted the criticism (after World War II) that regional geography afforded some excellent portraits of segments of the earth's surface, but it did not lead to any underlying body of theory to advance knowledge of the processes involved in shaping patterns on the earth's surface. On the other hand, geographers, engaged in dividing the earth's surface into regions, found that the criteria they chose for identifying regions were not necessarily accepted by all colleagues because of highly subjective methodologies. However, geographers continued to hold an interest in regions and the differences that places exhibited in their physical and cultural content (Fleming, 1973).

What the foregoing discussion suggests is that, since World War II, there has been a tendency to break with older traditions in geography and to advance a perspective on the field that demands definition and investigation along stricter lines. To emphasize their search for a new focus of study, many of the postwar generation of geographers termed their field the "new geography." What intrigued this new generation was the notion that there are principles that govern human spatial behavior and that these principles are generally applicable over the earth's surface (Abler et al., 1971). According to these objectives, the field of geography has been clearly identified as a social and behavioral science.

Even though they may recognize that some features of the earth's surface are due to unique causes—that is, an association of phenomena unlike any other association—geographers of the behavioral school have emphasized the generality of human experience, whatever the cultural heritage, wherever the location on the earth. Essential to this emphasis, then, has been the need to define human activities in spatial terms and to recognize a causal relationship between spatial structure and spatial process. "People generate spatial processes in order to satisfy their needs and desires and these processes create spatial structures which in turn influence and modify geographical processes" (Abler et al., 1971, p. 60).

The remarkable strides made by contemporary geography to develop a methodology that would permit precise measurement of geographic phenomena have been accomplished by intense interest in a number of subthemes. The 1950s and 1960s saw studies of economic regionalization (an interest shared with European and, especially, Soviet bloc countries) and of central place. Almost parallel in time was the growth of interest in innovation diffusion as a spatial process, a topic that had already received much attention in Sweden.

In the 1960s, the civil rights movement drew attention to the contribution of blacks to American life and to the fact that, a century after emancipation, blacks in the United States continued to face a multitude of social barriers that, upon inspection, revealed themselves in the spatial structure of society. In Great Britain, concern with questions of inequality and inequity produced a trend in geographic thinking that was inspired by, and drew heavily on, Marxist notions of conflict and exploitation. A similar concern in the United States spawned a group of geographers who found expression in a "radical" publication, called *Antipode*.

The larger awareness that grew out of the civil rights movement and the war in Vietnam was accompanied by a concern for humankind's general impact on the environment. This shift in interest among some geographers was stimulated by what was coming to be called the environmental crisis. Geographers in the United States had to a large degree thrown out their interest in the physical environment with the "new geography" of the postwar period. Now, they found that the natural and biologic sciences had moved quickly to tackle the problems that suddenly seemed to command attention. These were dominated by the growth of population; the expansion of cities, industries, and the automobile; the apparent depletion of natural resources; and the deterioration of the environment in general.

The behavioralist emphasis in modern geography, which now can be seen in perspective, was part of a movement within the social sciences generally. This brought a reassertion of interest in the human condition and to a fuller geographic treatment of it. Some geographers had never been fully convinced of the validity of some of the claims made for the "new geography"; others had rejected behavioralism because they found that it denied a realm of human knowledge to which they were especially committed, namely the intuitive. Basic to this school of geography, which called itself humanistic, was the recognition that geographers are not merely detached observers of phenomena "out there," but that they are very much part of the process of observation and analysis. Whether they admitted it or not, the geographers' perceptions of the world colored their analysis.

Humanistic studies, in general, have found expression in a broad range of topics: concern for humanity as a whole and for those who have been excluded from full participation in society; concern for society and the values that shape human behavior and the landscape; and, ultimately, concern for the individual in society and his or her fuller personal development through the expansion of awareness of the world and his or her agency for the creation of a more humane world. Above all, humanistic studies have reaffirmed an interest in landscape studies.

THE SEARCH FOR COMPREHENSION AND UNDERSTANDING

There is a widespread desire on the part of students in a world that is subject to forces that cause major changes in every field of human endeavor to come to grips with them. They want to understand, first of all, what has gone into producing the world and the patterns of relationships and associations that they have been taught to identify. Second, they want to understand the nature of the forces that are subjecting these patterns to change and modification. Above all, they want to know if they really are powerless to have any positive input into the course of events that shape and reshape their world. They are concerned, in the final analysis, as to how they can remain human when they seem powerless to have any impact on events and institutions that seem to demean their humanity as well as how they can find meaning in the world through a structuring of the mass of information with which they are bombarded daily.

Zelinsky has written that "genuine progress in human welfare, ultimate success in the prolonged struggle to become fully human, and most immediately evading disaster of a truly major magnitude for man and most of his fellow passengers on Spaceship Earth, may well hinge upon the promptest sort of corrective action" (Zelinsky, 1970, p. 498).

Geography and its subfields of human and cultural geography may not be the single discipline that will shed light on all the problems facing mankind and offer solutions, but "it is hard to imagine any workable therapy that excludes it" (Zelinsky, 1970, p. 498).

But, geography and the study of geography require something of the student in return. Young students of the field need, above all, to become aware of themselves in society. They need also to be aware of the values by which their society lives. Buttimer has stressed, with considerable feeling and conviction, that "to possess a system of values means that one wants and is convinced that the world ought to have a certain structure" (Buttimer, 1974, p. 38). Values influence our choice of alternatives and patterns of activity. Values, Buttimer emphasizes, make our actions intentional and impose responsibility. Such a notion has concerned thinkers from Plato onward, but no one has put it more aptly, nor more poetically, than William Wordsworth:

> Happy is he who lives to understand, not
>   human nature
> only, but explores all nature,—to the end that
>   he may
> find the law that governs each.
> (The Excursion, Book 4, 1814)

REFERENCES

Abler, Ronald et al. *Spatial Organization: The Geographer's View of the World.* Englewood Cliffs, N.J.: Prentice-Hall, 1971.

Blaut, J. M. "Space and Process." *Professional Geographer* 13 (July 1961): 1–7.

Buttimer, Annette. *Values in Geography.* Commission on College Geography. Resource Paper No. 24. Washington, D.C.: Association of American Geographers, 1974.

Fleming, Douglas K. "The Regionalizing Ritual." *Scottish Geographical Magazine* 89 (December 1973): 196–207.

Hartshorne, Richard. *Perspective on the Nature of Geography.* For the Association of American Geographers. Chicago: Rand McNally, 1959.

Whittlesey, Derwent. "The Regional Concept and the Regional Method," pp. 19–68. In *American Geography: Inventory and Prospect.* P. James and C. F. Jones, eds. For the Association of American Geographers. Syracuse, N.Y.: Syracuse University Press, 1954.

Zelinsky, Wilbur. "Beyond the Exponentials, the Role of Geography in the Great Transition." *Economic Geography* 46 (July 1970): 498–535.

1
Landscape, Experience, and Sense of Place

We shall not cease from exploration
And the end of all our exploring
Will be to arrive where we started
And know the place for the first time.

T. S. Eliot, "Little Gidding," 1942

While man's sense of time has diminished, his sense of space seems to have expanded . . . . He has a command of it, both in microcosm and macrocosm, that would have amazed the ancients; but in filling it he is tending to become personally dissociated from it; it is too big and he is too small.

Geoffrey and Susan Jellicoe,
The Landscape of Man, 1975

Key Ideas

1. The term landscape initially encompassed all of the phenomena that gave distinctiveness to any given region—an association of both physical geographic features and the human imprint.

2. Although not all geographers would agree that the study of landscape in its totality is the principal goal of geography, the landscape remains a central focus of geographic interest.

3. There is little that can be experienced in life without a spatial reference. Some of these references are identifiable marks on the landscape; others we carry in our heads.

4. In contemporary America, there is a strong desire for roots, in large part because the landscape with which we are familiar is undergoing change and familiar reference points are lost.

5. Environment and place are not interchangeable words. An environment is an association of factors drawn from both natural and cultural components of life. Place, in the sense of experienced space, is a piece of the whole, which we claim by thoughts and feelings.

6. Perception is the means whereby we take into our experience the world around us, but our mind serves as a filter. We tend, therefore, to see only what our position or culture permit us to see.

7. The European image of the New World had a profound effect on the way European immigrants transformed the wilderness into a habitable homeland. The Puritan immigrants wanted to create a new Zion where their way of life would prevail and what they considered evil would be pushed aside.

8. If images play a role in the shaping of the world we know, this human capacity can be used consciously to plan the kind of landscape in which we would want to live.

9. One way in which humans have projected their images of the world onto the landscape has been in planning the layout of gardens.

10. The garden—a perfect habitat for man? Some writers have suggested that the garden is the perfect landscape to satisfy human needs, but it can only be achieved by a complete transformation of the earth's surface.

LANDSCAPE AND REGION

Many years ago a distinguished geographer named Carl Sauer drew the attention of students to the importance of the human landscape in the study of the world around them (Sauer, 1925). The term *landscape,* to Professor Sauer, was a comprehensive one; in it he included all of the phenomena that contribute to giving any particular segment or region of the earth's surface its distinct characteristics, whether that region be in southern California or in New England. Landscape, thus, meant land shape, and the shape of any region was based on the association of both its physical geographic features as well as the imprint of human occupance—that is, as defined by house types, settlement patterns, roads, and so on. In the final analysis, though, landscape, as seen by Sauer, represented the contribution of peoples to the shaping of the environment in which they lived.

The concept of landscape was not new with Sauer; it had long been expressed in the writings of European geographers. Moreover, keen observers from the time of the ancient Greeks had long been aware of the differences that existed between segments of the earth's surface and had written about them. What Sauer did for American geographers was to provide an intellectual framework for studying and understanding these differences (Wagner and Mikesell, 1962).

Since Sauer's early work, the landscape emphasis in geography has been modified to accommodate changing geographic interests, including the relationship of humans to the environment, humankind's role in changing the surface of the earth, perception studies, and "sense of place" (English and Mayfield, 1972).

Not all geographers would agree that the study of landscape in its totality should be the principal goal or focus of research. Many have selected individual elements of human behavior in the landscape, such as urban characteristics, settlement patterns, transportation routes, and so on, for analysis and have found this path more satisfying. These geographers feel that by restricting the scope of study in this fashion, it is possible to formulate concepts that contribute to a larger body of geographic theory. Still, whatever the parameters, because geography is an earthbound spatial science, in the final analysis landscape remains at the core of all geographic study.

People shape their world, create their homes and habitat, and partition the earth's surface. In the process, as their experience grows and matures, they, too, are changed. Mountains, valleys, plains, water bodies, and other elements of the *natural environment* play a role in the way humans transform the earth; but as the human drama has been played out over thousands of years, these physical features have been modified, even as the drama develops its subplots and variants. The landscapes of the earth are the consequence of this interplay between the natural fundament and the strivings of the human race. Or, as has been stated elsewhere, landscape is the geographic expression of a myriad of human decisions (Abler et al., 1971).

Different groups of people have had different ways of settling the land, of organizing their activities, and of fixing boundaries. The variations in the human imprint are visible everywhere. The differences from one landscape to another, from one region or place to another, are the expressions of cultural development.

THE EXPERIENCE OF PLACE

Geographers have also become interested in *experienced space,* that is the way in which people perceive and experience landscape or place and the effect that this encounter has on human attitudes and behavior.

The interest in the way people perceive landscapes and the relationships between phenomena in the landscape has tended to broaden the horizon of geographic inquiry (Box 1–1). One facet of this broader interest is found in the study of *mental maps* (Gould and White, 1974). Research has shown that people carry images of places in their heads, and these images play an important role in how they behave. The process whereby these mental images is recorded on paper, or mapped, is known as *cognitive mapping* (Downs and Stea, 1977) (Figs. 1–1, 1–2). The awareness of the cognitive process has led geographers into perception studies and studies of behavior patterns as shaped by mental images.

Human experience and the experience of landscape, or spatial experiences, are intimately connected (Hall, 1959). Nothing is experienced in the course of a lifetime without a spatial reference or a pivot. Perhaps this is the basis of the suspicion sedentary people have of

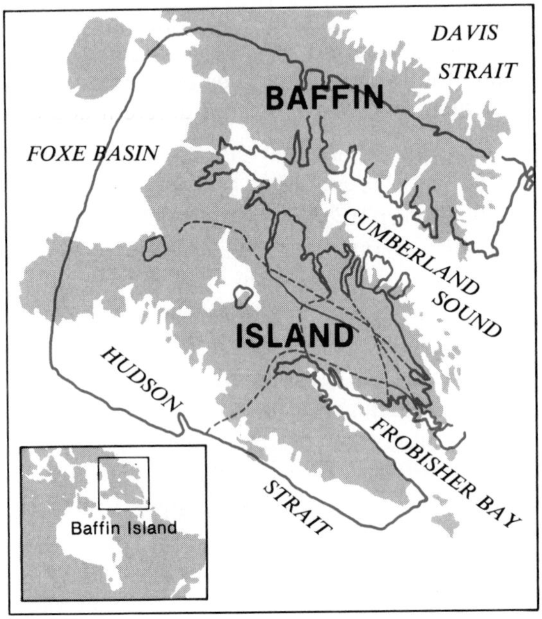

Figure 1–1

In recent years geographers have developed an interest in maps of the mind, or mental maps. These are the maps that people carry about in their heads—of their neighborhood, community, city, state, or country. Often such maps may bear a striking resemblance to reality, but they may also entail a quite substantial degree of distortion. Early hunting-gathering peoples, who ranged over a wide territory in search of game, gained a remarkable knowledge of their area. Their mental maps, if recorded, would have shown major reference points that were essential to the life and survival of the group. The superimposition of an Inuit (Eskimo) representation of the island we know as Baffinland on a contemporary map reveals the degree of accuracy attained by a native pictorialist.

(Pfeiffer, 1977)

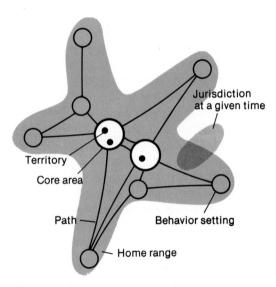

Figure 1–2

For hunting-and-gathering purposes, a somewhat complex social organization is needed, thus, the image of territory might include many meaningful spatial demarcations. Moreover, through such demarcations, the hunters, as in the case of the Australian aborigines, are linked to the land, their place.

Home range defines the usual geographic limit of regular aboriginal movements and activities; the core area is the space most commonly used and inhabited; the territory is the space that is owned and defined by an individual or group and recognized as distinct from that of others; and jurisdiction allows for use or ownership of territory for a limited time according to agreed rules.

(Rapoport, 1977).

BOX 1–1

Topophilia: A Love of Place

One of the most important studies of the role of perception and imagery in geography is entitled *Topophilia:* A Study of Environmental Perception, Attitudes, and Values (1974) by Yi-Fu Tuan. The term *topophilia* means a love of place and is derived from the Greek words *topos* meaning a place and *philos* meaning loving. Topophilia, Tuan states, "is the affective bond between people and place or setting," (p. 4). Clearly, Tuan has a deep love of place himself and a keen sensitivity to the way in which perception and imagery affect human behavior, both at present as well as in the past.

Human beings "take in the world" through their senses—by seeing, touching, hearing, and smelling. All these senses provide information about the world. The process of perceiving the world is one that employs all the senses simultaneously, and the information potentially available to an individual is clearly immense. In daily life, obviously, much of what can be taken in is simply excluded or filtered out, otherwise the senses become overloaded.

Perception, according to Tuan, is "a reaching out to the world," which begins in early childhood. As a child grows and moves about—touching, seeing, hearing, and smelling—he or she learns about the reality of the objects in the immediate environment. At an early age, the child also begins to be governed by themes that are transfigured or that offer a modified version of the larger world, the world of the adult that has been sensed or learned about. As the child continues to grow, activities are increasingly governed by the values handed down by parents or cultural values. The learning about the world is, thus, altered by culture. The consequence is that children in different places or settings throughout the world come to view the reality of the world differently. Perceptions of the world vary with groups as well as with individuals. Human beings both individually or in groups tend to perceive the world with "self" as center. The images that are formed of reality confirm this, especially when groups or individuals attempt to impose their images on the landscape.

One example of this collective self-centeredness or *ethnocentrism* is the Chinese. Historically, China thought of itself as the center of the world. For thousands of years, the Chinese lived in a secluded world, at the heart of which were fertile plains. By the fourth century B.C., Tuan states, the population of the lowland might already have reached 25 million, with a culture essentially free of outside influence. To the east lay the sea; in all directions, population densities sharply declined. Little wonder, then, that the Chinese came to think that they stood at the center of the world. In their image of the earth, therefore, they conceived of a succession of zones around the center, which they designated imperial center, and which required different degrees of control because of perceived attributes (Fig. 1–3).

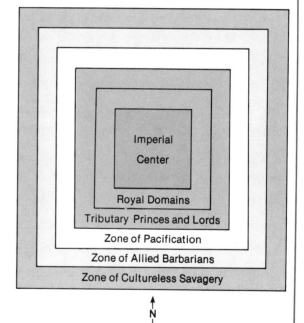

Figure 1–3

The traditional Chinese view of the world, dating back to the fifth century B.C., was ethnocentric, that is, China and especially the historic core of China was perceived as being at the center of the world. Surrounding the imperial center were zones that suggested dependency on the center, a frontier, and zones of inferior culture and barbarism.

dropouts, nomads, gypsies, and even migrants. In their movement, the last-named groups seem not to have any firm attachment to any one place, and sedentary people find this lack disturbing. It is by no means true that humans can experience place only by standing still or remaining fixed in one spot. Migrating peoples may carry a sense of place in their heads, even if their concept of place tends not to coincide at all times with the geographic reality of settled peoples.

In a significant study entitled "Torah as Movable Territory," Emanuel Maier (1975) notes that Jews throughout history have carried with them the traditions by which they remain and are identified as Jews. Many, but not all Jewish beliefs, are embodied in the Torah. The Torah traditionally has consisted of the first five books of the Old Testament. These books are accepted as containing the substance of divine revelation. Presented by Moses to the Israelites during their period of wandering in the Sinai Peninsula after the exodus from Egypt, the Torah served as a guide and a kind of blueprint. Thereafter, the Israelites carried this knowledge with them when they finally crossed the Jordan River and entered the land they believed was promised them. The Torah together with other documents on law and behavior have provided Jews ever since, wherever they were, with a sense of relationship to the God of their Fathers, a sense of community with each other, and a sense of attachment to the promised land. This knowledge has given Jews a kind of cosmic sense of place, which has been the envy of others.

If all human activity has a spatial dimension, then the experience of place may be considered a necessary condition of human existence. The human desire or need to leave an imprint on the land is inextricably related to survival *and* the search for identity because both are associated with place. The study of history is a study of the human search for meaning, and one way in which this has been expressed is in the creation

of coordinates or reference points on the surface of the earth. These reference points may symbolize the limits of a hunter's territory, or they may be associated with religious aspirations, or they may be used simply to find one's way around or to navigate. Thus, for different culture groups with different needs, places, and associated reference points may take on different but very special meanings. Consider the importance of Jerusalem to Jews, Christians, and Muslims alike or the importance of Greenwich, England—through which the prime meridian passes—to ocean navigators or even land surveyors.

THE NEED FOR ROOTS

To have a sense of place or to develop images of places that allows one to feel at home wherever one has settled, is, in effect, to experience the feeling of being rooted, or of having roots (Tuan, 1975). Human life may exist anywhere on earth, but living—in the sense of participating and experiencing—presupposes the use of imagination, of the senses, and of memory. Not all experiencing may be pleasant. But, the fullest possible use of faculties, allows humans to find a place that is really a personal *cosmos*. The process is not unlike turning a house into a home; in some instances it may work, at other times it may not. The image of home, however, remains.

In contemporary American culture, there is a strong desire for roots, for recapturing or preserving images that remind us of home, warmth, security, comfort. Part of this desire is expressed in concern for the rural countryside as a result of urban encroachment. Rural images remain strong in the United States, even though very little of the cherished way of life read about in history and novels or seen in paintings actually remains. Rapid material changes wiped out old landscape features and destroyed old reference points. Perhaps Americans can never recapture what has or what they think has been lost—but they retain their images nevertheless.

In intercontinental migrations, people often attempt to select—if given the opportunity—a place for settlement whose characteristics remind them of the place they have left. Immigrants into the United States from Scandinavia in the nineteenth century showed a preference for New England, Minnesota, the upper Northwest, and the Pacific Northwest. These regions reminded them of the places they were familiar with in the old country.

Migrating peoples, too, may name their new settlement, as happened in frontier America, after the place they left. Sometimes the name reflects hopes and expectations. Consider, for example, the naming of Salem, Massachusetts, by the Puritan founders in 1626. Salem is a word of *Semitic* origin meaning peace, and one motive for the first settlement of New England was to secure freedom from the religious intolerance the Puritans had experienced in England.

To lack a sense of place may be to suffer personal anxiety, as may be the case if one is deprived of home and familial associations. Experiments have been conducted on human subjects, depriving them of spatial experience, that is, not allowing them to know where they are. Sensory deprivation, such research has shown, leads to disorientation, hallucination, or drowsiness. Persons who suffer extended periods of disorientation are unable to see or recognize an extension of their self to place. They are, in effect, cut off.

If this experience lasts for any length of time, which is possible for people suffering emotional or physiological problems, society may step in and disallow this kind of confusion by placing such people under medical care or in mental institutions. A clear perception of space seems to be deeply relevant to the basic need for internal cohesion, mental health, a sense of security and direction, and a feeling of relationship with the world around one.

ENVIRONMENT VERSUS PLACE

The use of the term *place* in the sense of experienced landscape should not be confused with *environment*. Environment and place are not interchangeable words, and the difference is substantial. An environment is a framework, an association of elements drawn from the physical and cultural components of life, such as landforms, vegetation, seasons of the year, streets, buildings, and so on. The environment sustains life and assists in the biologic and social maturation of human beings; such elements are *environing factors*. Place, or a sense of place, on the other hand, nourishes people beyond sustenance. The catalyst that converts any location on earth with its environmental elements into a "place" is the process whereby people sense or experience it. A place is a piece of the whole, a segment of the earth's totality, claimed by thoughts and feelings. Not all people will experience place in quite the same way or with the same degree of intensity. Moreover, there is no unanimous agreement as to what people see or feel or imagine. Still, a certain consensus seems to emerge from these different views, which are at one level shared by most, if not all, members of the community.

SPACE, IMAGES, AND SYMBOLS

Human beings are symbol-using creatures. Language is the premier example of that (see Chapter 7). As a result of their perceptions of landscapes, humans are also image-making creatures. However, people do not simply react to what they perceive, like animals taught to respond to the sound of bells. The process is more complex than that. In the act of perceiving, the mind selects or filters out what is being taken in by the senses. Here culture plays a large part. Because of their cultural heritage, people tend to see only what they have learned to see or been taught to see. Consider, for example, what the Russian word kremlin conjures up in the minds of Americans. Yet, geographically speaking, the word, which means fortress or walled enclosure, was a common enough phenomenon in cities throughout medieval Europe. However, the Moscow Kremlin has assumed a sinister quality because of the events of modern history and politics that we have been taught to associate with it.

The processes of making images and of storing them in the mind are complex. The images are interesting not only in themselves, but also because they mould the patterns that humans create on the earth's surface. Andrew Clark, a distinguished historical geographer, has recommended that geographers give more attention to this aspect of the field, particularly where images and image making of the past affect present and future behavior patterns (Clark, Foreward to Blouet and Lawson, 1975). Equally important is the need to study ways in which images change because, like culture generally and values in particular, images may be or may become distorted and difficult to change.

Human beings are dynamic creatures struggling individually and collectively for survival. To survive, they must orient themselves to their surroundings. They must measure and mentally order the visual impacts or perceptions of their setting. Obviously, they must communicate their findings to each other for group acceptance, understanding, and mutual reinforcement. Humans assert themselves on planet Earth by means of their senses and their thinking processes as well as by their activities. Through structuring their earth (land), humans gain a sense of control. However, this is not an action that is done only once. Each new sensory perception may create new horizons, new reference points, a new beginning for further activity. The process of mentally shaping and reshaping the Earth, and mankind's place in it, goes on continually. In *What Time Is This Place?*, Kevin Lynch (1972) notes that images

must be flexible, in harmony with external reality, and, above all, in time with man's own biologic nature. Whereas images may afford some degree of psychic security, people must keep open to change and modification.

THE IMAGE OF AMERICA

A significant set of images grew out of the European discovery of America. These images were to have a considerable influence on the European impact on the New World. The Renaissance, which flourished in Europe roughly from the end of the Crusades to Columbus's voyages of discovery, had been a period in which human horizons were greatly expanded.

The ancient Greek geographers, whose works had been rediscovered by Western Europe during the Renaissance, had written that it was possible to travel from Spain to the Indies (meaning the East Indies) by sailing westward. Aristotle had stated that the sea was shallow and calm a few miles out from Gibraltar (the Pillars of Hercules); and Plato had made reference to a mythical Island of Atlantis, which had been submerged beneath the sea. Moreover, St. Brendan the Navigator had ventured from Ireland into the Atlantic in the sixth century A.D. and had probably reached both Iceland and the Azores. At any event, islands west of Spain and North Africa discovered by St. Brendan appeared on a medieval map published by Bartolomeo Pareto in 1455. But that was not the end of European voyages and myth making. They continued through the centuries up to 1492, filling up the map with shapes and sizes that bore little resemblance to reality.

Europeans, therefore, were primed, from fact, legend, and myth, for the emergence of something new far to the west (Chiapelli, 1976). Perhaps their imaginations were stimulated much as modern generations have been excited by the adventures of Buck Rogers, the tales of Martian landings on earth, and *Star Wars*. Certainly radio, films, and television have stretched imaginations, broadened mental horizons, and allowed Americans to anticipate and absorb the reality of moon voyages and space travel.

Thus, in a way, prior to actual contact, the "American experience" had already begun in the minds of Europeans, and images and impressions, once having taken hold in society, hung on tenaciously. Old impressions were slow to die, even when confronted with the hard evidence that actual contact with the New World provided. It was not until 1507, for example, that a map showed the various islands explored on the far edge of the Atlantic joined into a single landmass (Honour, 1975). And it was only in 1522 that the new continent was seen to be distinct from Asia. This was a far cry from what Columbus had recorded of his discovery in 1493. He thought he had reached the Spice Islands described by Marco Polo and others, often in lavish and absurd accounts. Moreover, his description of the islands fused "two pre-existing ideas—those of a fabulous Orient and an idealised Europe," so that what he wrote was made understandable in imagery familiar to educated Europeans of the time (Honour, 1975, p. 2).

The Puritan Image of America

It is a characteristic of the human mind that it can anticipate the future as well as draw from past experience. A sense of place may represent not only images derived from the past, but also images that project into the future. Because of this capability, images are important not only to present behavior patterns, but also they may serve as determinants of future behavior patterns, as we will see.

The Puritans who settled New England in the seventeenth century left the Old World voluntarily and with a strong sense of mission. They were intent on establishing in the New World a new Zion, another Jerusalem. To them it was readily apparent that they were part of God's elect. "God sifted a whole Nation," said William Stoughton (1632–1701), first Lieutenant Governor of the Massachusetts Bay Colony (from approximately 1695–1701), "that He [might] send choice Grain over into this Wilderness" (S. G. and M. S., 1670, p. 19).

Armed with such convictions, the Puritan immigrants were deeply desirous of fulfilling scriptural prophecy by transforming the wilderness into a place for the elect of God (Williams, 1962). Their feeling harked back to their image of the Garden of Eden and revealed a conscious bias against the realm of nature! They saw the wilderness as an enemy, opposed to the spread of God's kingdom. As for the natives and the wild beasts of the forest, they, too, were thought to be associated with evil. To fight the wilderness and push back the forests were not only necessary for physical survival, they represented a moral and Christian imperative as well.

Anticipations of creating an earthly paradise in New England were abruptly frustrated by the reality of their situation. First of all, the forest was interminable—it stretched farther than the imagination could carry it. Puritan settlements were kept relatively close to each other, but proximity also bred enmity and hostility. In the struggle for survival, there was a great and visible decay of godliness, despite the imposition of a rigorous church discipline. Moreover, within the settlement, suspicions of neighbors led to indiscriminate accusations that subsequently flared in 1692 in the Salem witch trials. But, long before this, conflicts led to complaints about land and its scarcity, which prompted an exodus and a founding of new towns, such as occurred in the Connecticut River Valley in the 1630s.

The causes are by no means clear, but it is evident that New England gave birth to several kinds of landscapes. Boston and Salem took on a rigid social pattern that was considerably different from that which emerged in the Connecticut Valley (Miller, 1956). Frontier experience dictated that each settlement in the wilderness would create its own Zion landscape in its own way.

Romantic Images and Frontier Necessities

"Appreciation of the wilderness began in the cities" (Nash, 1967, p. 44), and this was no less true of the image of colonial America that emerged in the drawing rooms of Europe. Eighteenth-century Europe saw the new world pioneer in the romantic image of a man of nature. For American frontiersmen, however, the circumstances were altogether different. Survival meant altering nature and this was more important than any philosophy that made them part of nature's realm.

American pioneers had scarcely gotten to know their new land before they had begun to alter it. Within a century and a half, they had colonized the Atlantic coast and had penetrated the Appalachians. A belief in the future, a *belief in inevitable progress,* which was in part derived from their Christian faith, literally undercut America's wilderness landscape, just as the Revolution of 1776 had severed ties to the British crown (Novak, 1976). As Alexis de Tocqueville (1805–1859), a French observer of the American experience, wrote in his second volume of *Democracy in America:* "In Europe people talk a great deal of the wilds of America, but the Americans themselves never think about them; they are insensible to the wonders of inanimate nature and they may be said not to perceive the mighty forests that surround them till they fall beneath the hatchet. Their eyes are fixed upon another sight: the American people views its own march across these wilds, draining swamps, turning the course of rivers, peopling solitudes, and subduing nature. This magnificat image of themselves does not meet the gaze of the Americans at intervals only; it may be said to haunt every one of them in his least as well as in his most important actions and to be always flitting before his mind" (1960, vol. 2, p. 74).

Consequences and Reaction

The Puritan image of mission was tempered with time, and the romantic image was overcome by practicality. Henry David Thoreau (1817–1862) might mourn the trees he missed like human beings, but he nevertheless used the axe to make himself a dwelling at Walden Pond near Boston. Throughout the eighteenth and nineteenth centuries, the pioneers armed with axe and gun, moved ever westward, destroying and building, and altering the landscape. As the American landscape artist and poet Thomas Cole (1801–1848) noted in his poem, "The Complaint of the Forest":

> All then was harmony and peace—but man
> Arose—he who now vaunts antiquity—
> He the destroyer—amid the shades
> Of Oriental realms, destruction's work began.

The wilderness that had made the New World unique and that such writers as Ralph Waldo Emerson (1803–1882) and others in the growing cities of the East had come to appreciate was nearing its end about the middle of the nineteenth century. When this fact was finally realized, there was only just enough time and trees left to establish the artificial enclaves known as parks. As civilization in America spread westward to embrace the Rockies, nature had to be enclosed if it were to be preserved. Yellowstone National Park was created in 1872 as the first of a system that today consists of 285 units: 37 national parks and 248 national monuments, recreation areas, wilderness areas, historic sites, and coastal areas. But even these preserves cause problems: their popularity and high attendance conflict with the desire to prevent overuse and misuse.

American Utopias

The Puritan attempt to create a paradise in the New World was not the only example of the impress of image on the wilderness landscape. Indeed, from 1663 to 1858, there were altogether some 138 settlements whose aims were the creation of a perfect society (Fig. 1–4).

The discovery of the New World stimulated the publication in Europe of a number of works that attempted to portray *the* ideal landscape

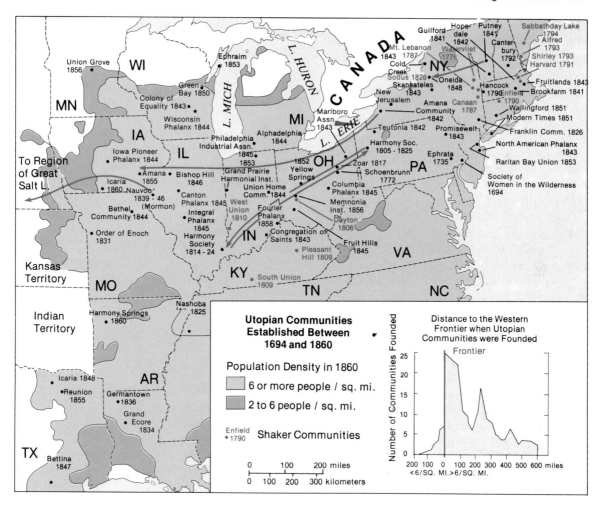

Figure 1–4

Frontier America was especially conducive to the formation of utopian settlements where men and women sought to work out principles that would lead to a harmonious society. One of the earliest involved Dutch Mennonites who, in 1663, settled at Lewes, Delaware. Among the more important were the Ephrata Community in Pennsylvania, founded in 1732; the Rappite communities of Harmony, Harmonie, and near Pittsburgh Economy (1803–1825), Brook Farm (1841–1847) at West Roxbury, Massachusetts, which stressed education and drew the attention of Nathaniel Hawthorne; the Oneida Community, founded in 1841 at Putney, Vermont, by John Humphrey Noyes, and subsequently moved to Oneida, New York—a continuation of Brook Farm without its flaws; the Amana Colony in Iowa; and the Hutterites, who still flourish in the United States and Canada and have planted colonies in Paraguay and Great Britain.

In the 1960s, there was a revival of communal living in both Europe and the United States, involving diverse groups of people who were known as hippies. Communal activities, including gardening and handicraft work, were among the stated goals of such associations.

and community. The most important work of this type was Sir Thomas More's *Utopia* (1516), and it was More who coined the word, deriving it from the Greek *ou* (not) and *topos* (place), meaning no place. More (1478–1535) set his *utopia,* where Christian communism is practiced, on an imaginary island below the equator. More's book, which implied that the ideal society was realizable if people wanted it, was immensely popular in England and Europe throughout the sixteenth century (Porter and Lukermann, 1976). Thus, it should not surprise that Europeans saw in the wilderness environment an excellent opportunity to start afresh and create utopian communities. One of the more interesting was that founded at Harmony, Pennsylvania, in 1803, under the leadership of George Rapp (1757–1847), a German religious thinker who had broken with Lutheranism.

In 1814, the community, with 800 members, was moved further west to Harmonie on the banks of the Wabash River in Indiana. Rapp surrounded the settlement with extensive plantings of vines and shrubs to symbolize the difficulty in reaching the state of true harmony. A town was laid out, and the streets were lined with goldenrain trees imported from the Far East. Dome-shaped in growth and known for their handsome foliage and unusual seed pods, these trees ensured that Harmonie was different from other frontier settlements. Because marriage within the community was discouraged, the colony could only grow by recruitment of incoming German immigrants. The colony continued to grow until 1820, but its inability to recruit labor subsequently led to its decline. In 1825, the settlement was purchased by Robert Owen (1771–1858), a Welsh-born socialist, and renamed New Harmony. Rapp immediately founded a new colony, called Economy near Pittsburgh in Pennsylvania, but it declined with his death in 1847.

Unlike other utopian socialists, Owen was a man who had gained considerable experience managing the New Lanark cotton mills in Lanarkshire, Scotland. Owen wanted to create new communities where families could have their own living spaces and where children would subsequently be raised by the whole community. Owen believed that human character was formed by external circumstances and for that reason wanted to ensure that members of the community were subjected to the proper influences from earliest years.

Thus, his purchase of thirty thousand acres at New Harmony was a step in the formation of a new self-contained community. Cooperative rather than communist in its structure and responsibilities, New Harmony sponsored a number of first in American history, all understandably associated with education: the first kindergarten, the first trade school, the first free library, and the first community-supported public school. The colony failed to prosper, however, because there was a good deal of internal conflict over the form of government and the role of religion. Owen quit the settlement in 1828, losing his financial investment; he returned to England where he died in 1858.

Of all the attempts to translate the wilderness into a place of spiritual meaning none was more important, nor enduring, than that of the Mormons, who constituted the Church of Jesus Christ of Latter-Day Saints. Founded by Joseph Smith (1805–1844) in New York State, the new religion offered a hope of salvation that appealed to many Americans and immigrants. Moving westward in stages, the Mormons founded settlements in Ohio, in Illinois, and in Missouri, the latter being designated Zion by Smith himself. In 1839, a new settlement was established at Commerce, Illinois, which was renamed Nauvoo, a community that quickly reached a population of twenty thousand. From the structures that survive, it is clear that Nauvoo had many of the features of an eastern American town, both classical in architecture and stately in appearance. Smith's teachings and the practice of polygamy led to his arrest and murder in 1844.

In 1847–1848, a majority of the Mormons elected to follow the leadership of Brigham Young (1801–1877) to Utah, where a site had been selected for a new settlement. Historians have described the Mormon migration as the best organized movement in American history. Religiously motivated, the Mormons' singular image of a cohesive, orderly community in the west made this frontier experience unique. In effect, a whole culture was removed to the basin of the Great Salt Lake where, within three months of settlement, its population reached nearly two thousand.

The great migration was a symbolic act for it placed a group of people, not unlike the Puritans of a century earlier, in a new world where they believed they had an opportunity to create a new society free of the difficulties they had experienced in the past in the eastern United States. They set out consciously to design a better community and a better future. Moreover, remoteness of location, at the time well beyond the line of American frontier settlement, offered the advantage of implementing the principles of an orderly cooperative society without outside interference.

The Mormons, however, were to find that their goals of a new Zion—and a State of Deseret (1849)—were to come in conflict with the secular statist views of the U.S. government. Some of their practices, beliefs, and goals would have to be sacrificed to the thrust of national policies. Still, much was retained of the original commitment, and it survives to the present.

Because of low precipitation, averaging 10 to 12 inches annually, water was critical to the new community. Much of the good farmland flanked the streams that drained the enclosing mountains. The scarcity of agricultural resources led to a high degree of cooperation, especially evident in the allocation of land and in the development of irrigation facilities, that was less common among more individualistic settlers. As Brigham Young stated: "[It] is a good place to make Saints and it is a good place for Saints to live; it is the place that the Lord has appointed, and we shall stay here until he tells us to go somewhere else" (cited in Arrington and Bitton, 1979, p. 113).

The central feature of the Mormon landscape was to be the Great Temple, begun in the 1850s (Fig. 1–5). Located in the heart of the Salt Lake City, the structure drew its inspiration initially

Figure 1–5

The Mormon Temple, constructed of native granite, stands impressively in Temple Square, the symbolic center of Salt Lake City and of the Mormon religion. Designed under Brigham Young's direction, it is a six-towered edifice, rising in its highest tower to 210 feet. Surmounting the tower is a statue, in hammered copper, of the angel Moroni of the Book of Mormon. The Temple was built between 1853 and 1893. Nearby stands the Mormon Tabernacle, home of the famous Tabernacle Choir, a large oval auditorium capable of seating 8,000 people. It was constructed between 1863 and 1867.

Source: Porterfield-Chickering/Photo Researchers.

from New England church design and the temple built in Nauvoo by Joseph Smith. In its final form, however, it rose massively above the community, its carved granite towers reminiscent of the surrounding mountain peaks.

Surrounding the Great Temple, the land was laid out in 135 ten-acre blocks, each divided into eight home lots of one-and-a-quarter acres each. Wide streets (135 feet) followed the cardinal points of the compass, each named for its direction and distance from the Great Temple.

Following the initial settlement at Salt Lake, other settlements were made in other parts of the basin. An active missionary policy, both in the United States and Europe, drew many immigrants to the new Zion. And with that, a Mormon Corridor was created—a stretch of territory leading from the Utah settlements southwestward toward California.

THE USE OF IMAGE IN CITY PLANNING

Just as imagery has played a role in the historic process of shaping the American landscape and some of its values, it is recognized by geographers and planners that imagery can be used consciously to plan not only settlements, but even the future habitat of humans. Planners can help fashion a better landscape if they first give attention to what a people want and dream about. This notion has been captured in an appropriate statement by Professor J. Wreford Watson, "The geography of any country lies in the dreams of its people; in what they see in it, and want from it, and make of it. Thus, the geography carried in the mind moulds the geography on the ground" (1970, p. 71). What better justification can be provided for the study of geography and landscape!

Kevin Lynch (1971), in an attempt to appreciate the role of images in the lives of people who live in cities, has analyzed the central areas of three entirely different American cities: Boston, Jersey City, and Los Angeles. Interviews with inhabitants in each city led to certain conclusions as to how a city might be structured to promote *imageability,* that is, the capacity to stimulate image building in people. By imageability, Lynch decided that a city that is "well-formed, distinct and remarkable" would invite the eye and the ear to greater attention and participation. He recommended that this could be promoted by concentrating on five forms: paths, edges, landmarks, nodes, and city districts. Paths, roads, or lines of movement provide the means whereby the entire city can be ordered. Edges, or boundaries, delineate one part of the city from another. Landmarks provide reference points. Nodes include squares, parks, and plazas, which should be well defined and partially enclosed. City districts represent subdivisions of urban space with a distinct character that marks them off from the rest. Clearly, Lynch noted, these forms play a major role, stimulating the two-way process between observer and the external physical shape upon which a planner can operate.

Many European cities have inherited a human dimension from the past when central structures designed to serve other functions and needs were not disturbed either by the Industrial Revolution or, to any great degree, by the automobile. Walking streets, squares, boundaries established during urban growth, and historic landmarks attract and please the American tourist. They are less familiar in North America where the rectangular grid, the industrial expansion of the nineteenth century, and the massive demands of the automobile have left other human needs behind. Still, whether through municipal initiative or private enterprise, efforts have been made in American cities to recapture some of the spirit of the past by preserving heritage structures, such as marketplaces, original city cores, and old waterfront warehouses, that stimulate the imagination.

THE GARDEN AS PLACE

As people seek meaning or reference points in an association with earth space, they also, as we have already seen, project their wants and aspirations onto the landscape in tangible or symbolic forms (Thacker, 1979). Almost all major world cultures since the origins of farming have attached a special meaning to spaces that have been set aside as gardens. Gardens, depending on their setting, might contain various kinds of vegetation, such as small fruit trees, vegetables, herbs, or flowers, but they usually were seen as places where human beings could find pleasure, security, comfort, or peace of mind. Whatever their size, gardens in a very real sense have represented segments of earth space where another dimension of life could be experienced. It has been said that every garden is a replica, a representation, an attempt to capture some ideal. From age to age and from one part of the earth to another, the garden and its structure have varied, yet at the same time the garden has retained a quality or a capacity to transform life that has a universal acceptance.

Oriental Gardens

The Oriental garden (and landscape painting) emphasized the lowly place that humans were seen to occupy in the nature of things. But, they were designed to appeal to the imagination and to enhance the lives of those who owned them. Their basic elements—rocks, water, gnarled trees, dwarf plantings, and flowers—had symbolic meaning as well as artistic merit. When arranged together, they reflected the beauty of nature as well as its power (Keswick, 1978).

In Japan, the earliest landscape gardens are associated with the arrival of Buddhism from Korea in the sixth century A.D. Chinese cultural influence is evident at a somewhat later period, especially in Japanese architecture. Japanese aristocrats thereupon became interested in creating gardens that would enhance the setting of their dwellings. They wanted their gardens to reflect the beauty of the scenery they saw around them (Itoh, 1973). This effect was achieved by carefully balancing the basic elements of nature and drawing frequently on the surrounding landscape, a concept known as *shakkei,* or borrowed landscape. (Fig. 1–6).

Although there were many types of gardens, such as those adorning temples, teahouses, or private dwellings, the Japanese garden format tended to be idealized, with the result that garden art was carried into the realm of the abstract. In this respect, Japanese gardens differed from Chinese gardens. The latter strove to convey both the lack of symmetry or orderliness in nature *and* its spontaneity. It was the presence of these qualities in the Chinese garden landscape that inspired the English *Romantic gardens* of the eighteenth century.

Classical Greek and Roman Settings

The ancient Greeks, whose writings reveal that they loved the natural beauty of the landscape—the airiness of the sky, the shape of the mountains, and the interplay of mountains and sea—recognized in specific settings places for the worship of particular deities. There, the Greeks erected temples or public structures, lavishing great care on their beauty. Greek literature abounds in references to sacred groves, parks, and gardens, but the garden as a feature of upper-class villas seems to have come late in Greek history. Although there is little tangible evidence today of what these gardens were like, they seem generally not to have been closed off from the world as Oriental gardens were. In the Greek way of perceiving the world, there was no barrier between inner and outer, no division between the human realm and the realm of nature.

Although influenced by Greek design, the Romans seem, nevertheless, to have had more structured garden spaces and in their city dwellings to have enclosed them. The entrance to an upper-class dwelling, for example, was through an *atrium,* which was closed to the street and often, but not always, without a roof. After the atrium, a narrow passage led into a gardenlike space, usually open to the sky, which was surrounded by columns that supported the dwelling and its rooms. In this manner, the Romans combined their feeling for outdoor space with their desire for privacy. The landscape tastes of the Romans were more formal than the Greeks

Figure 1–6

In general, there are two broad categories of Japanese gardens. There are gardens that borrow landscape, that is, they incorporate distant scenery as part of their overall design (Itoh, 1973). The Japanese use the word *shakkei* for borrowed landscape, which means literally a landscape captured alive. The other type of garden, shown here, is the courtyard garden, of which the teahouse garden is a variant. Courtyard gardens may encompass very small spaces and yet give a sense of place that is completely in balance and perspective. In the teahouse garden, stepping-stones, lanterns, and water basins constitute important features of the cultural landscape.

(*Source:* Joseph Conder, *Landscape Gardening in Japan*. Tokyo, 1893, p. 56. [Published by Kelly & Walsh, Yokohama, Shanghai, Hong Kong, and Singapore.])

and the layout of open spaces and rooms in a Roman dwelling showed it. However, the rural villa with its gardens set in the rolling landscape of the Italian peninsula was usually more relaxed in style and layout.

This influence, above all, was clearly observable in the geometric layout of Persian gardens. Persian carpet design still depicts such symbolism. In the Dry World, the garden was seen as a place of escape from a sunbaked hostile environment. With well-laid-out paths and watercourses that nourished a rich vegetation of trees and flowers and sustained exotic birds, including the peacock, the classical Persian garden stood in stark contrast to the barren landscape outside (Fig. 1–7). Most of the great gardens, which were private, were set in inclined areas outside cities and made use of water in lavish fashion.

The Impact of the Garden of Eden

For Western cultures, the most deeply meaningful representations of the garden concept is to be found in the account of the Garden of Eden in Genesis. The garden is portrayed as paradise on earth, where earth's first human inhabitants lived free of toil and care. According to Genesis 2:8, "Then the Lord God planted a garden in Eden to the east and there he put man whom he had formed. The Lord God made trees to spring from the ground, all trees pleas-

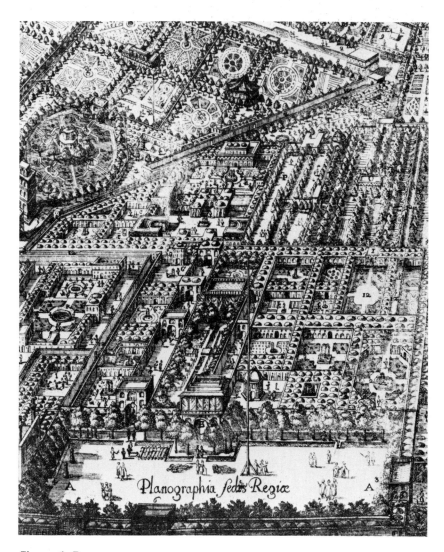

Figure 1-7

Garden imagery is the primary source of nature imagery in Persian literature. There are many reasons for this. A major source of inspiration was the paradise garden as described in the Koran, the holy book of Islam. At the same time, the existence of splendid gardens, such as that enclosed within the royal palace grounds of Isfahan, the ancient capital of Persia (Iran), stirred the imagination. Always, however, in the literary descriptions of the garden, there was an interplay of the divine and the worldly. Like European gardens of the medieval period, Persian gardens were enclosed. Even so, the Persian poet always sought to bring together humankind and nature, not leave them divided.

(Macdougall and Ettinghausen, 1976).

ant to look at and good for food; and in the middle of the garden he set the tree of life and the tree of knowledge of good and evil.''

Moreover, Genesis 2:10 affords an additional bit of information that was to have an impact not only on garden design, but on mapmaking

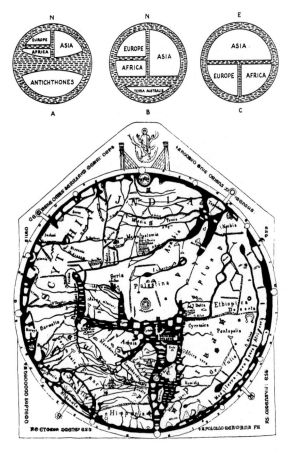

Figure 1–8

Most medieval maps were variants of the OT or T map, of which there were three early types. One (A) showed an eastern hemisphere divided into Europe, Asia, and Africa, and a southern unknown landmass. Another (B) showed a residual continent, *terra australis*, otherwise unknown at the time. A third (C) presented the known world only. The Hereford map c. A.D. 1280 (D) placed Jerusalem at the center with a heavenly paradise lying beyond India. The Don (Tanais) River, the Nile, and the Mediterranean Sea formed a T, with a peripheral ocean framing the margin of the entire map.

(After Singer et al., eds., 1957, Vol. 3, pp. 519–520.)

as well (Fig. 1–8): "There was a river flowing from Eden to water the garden, and when it left the garden it branched into four streams." A

garden divided into four parts by water, thus, became a recurring theme in medieval garden design.

Medieval Christians, understandably, also tended to envisage paradise—both the earthly one and its heavenly counterpart (Fig. 1–9)—in the form of a garden (Pearsall and Salter, 1973). For this reason, from about A.D. 800 to 1200, the garden in Christian imagery possessed two distinct components: a segment or representation of earth space and an almost impenetrable wall enclosing it (Fig. 1–10). Indeed the word paradise, from the Persian *pardes* via the Greek *paradeisos*, means park and, in this context, a walled enclosure. The porticoed garden court of

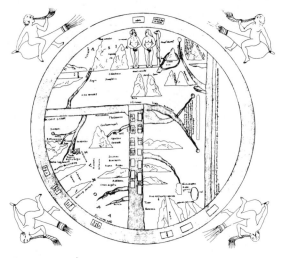

Figure 1–9

Many of the maps created in Europe that have survived from the early medieval period are highly fanciful, combining both knowledge of the earth gained from geographic observation and mythology. The Garden of Eden was often portrayed on such maps, being set in the Middle East. A map of the world of A.D. 900, however, shows Eden far to the east of Babylon. Around the circumference of the map are four wind blowers who release the winds of the earth.

(Brown, 1960, p. 31.)

Figure 1–10

The medieval image of the expulsion of Adam and Eve from the Garden of Eden was usually rich in symbolism. In this woodcut, the Garden of Eden is shown surrounded by a wall, not unlike that surrounding a medieval monastery or church courtyard. The garden is rich in vegetation, but the world beyond the wall is seen as a forbidding wilderness.

(From the *Buch der Chroniken* [*Nuremberg Chronicle*], 1483. [Leipzig: Hartmann Schedel, fac. 1933.] Courtesy Rare Book Collection, University of Washington Libraries.)

early Roman Catholic basilicas or churches was often called *paradisus.*

In medieval Europe, generally, the cloister (or the castle) garden was invariably walled. It symbolized civilization; beyond the wall lay the countryside, the *pagus,* which was little more than an unpleasant and uninteresting waste. There, according to common biblical illustration, lurked the forces of evil; its inhabitants under the influence of evil forces.

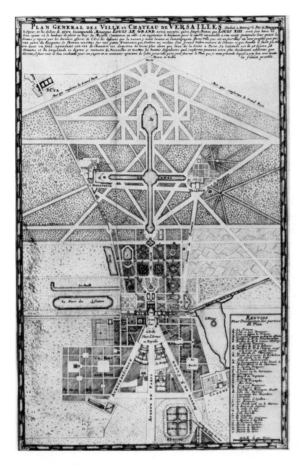

Figure 1–11

Landscape design in Europe in the late seventeenth and early eighteenth centuries was greatly influenced by France. The French sense of organization of space along geometric lines, as shown on the palace grounds at Versailles and at the town of Nîmes, was adopted by the Austrian monarchy for palace gardens in Vienna and by the Russians both in the layout of St. Petersburg (now Leningrad) as well as in the gardens at Peterhof, a royal residence on the Gulf of Finland. Until the modern age, there may have been no greater assertion of man's dominance of nature than this imposition of straight lines on the landscape.

(From *Recueil des figures, groupes, thermes . . . et autres ornements de Versailles* [Amsterdam: Pierre Mortier, 1795]. Courtesy Rare Book Collection, University of Washington Libraries.)

The European Renaissance Garden

A new feeling for space came with the *Renaissance,* whose influence spread northward out of Italy beginning in the fourteenth century. The Renaissance also brought a new image of man, which affected garden design. In Italy, Renaissance gardens, not unlike the ancient Greek or Roman, were clearly made for human enjoyment, and they were designed to add dignity to living. Descending terraces, sculptured out of the hillsides and planted with statuesque evergreens, were congenial to a quiet walk, with waterworks delighting the stroller's senses and refreshing the mind. The terraced landscape of Tuscany north of Rome is today reminiscent of this age of garden exuberance.

The European Formal Garden

By the seventeenth century, the European image of the enclosed garden as an island in a threatening wilderness was at last exploded by the emergence of science and mathematics. Straight lines drawn across the landscape proudly attested to a new sense of how space should be organized. No better example of the geometric garden is to be found than at Versailles, designed in the eighteenth century to salute the growth of *monarchical centralism* in France. Versailles is lavish, and the waterways and formal gardens were intended to glorify the Sun King, Louis XIV (Fig. 1–11). This French sense of how space should be organized, symbolizing the image of a confident human race striding somewhat arrogantly onto center stage, spilled throughout Europe. Even city planning—in Paris itself, Potsdam, and St. Petersburg (now Leningrad)—followed suit, but the concept did not stop there. It was transposed to the United States and exemplified in the layout of Washington, D.C. Finally, the grid, a great symbol of symmetry, was imposed on the prairies and plains of North America.

The English Romantic Garden

The outpouring of feeling that occurred in the latter two-thirds of the eighteenth century, particularly among the upper classes in England, produced a new garden image. In England, where little had remained of pristine nature, the gentry, partly inspired by the Chinese landscape, turned to beautifying their estates in a fashion that has left its imprint even today (Fig. 1–12). Several other factors also entered into the outpouring of feeling for nature in England. The landscapes of the French painter Claude Lorrain (1600–1682) were at the height of fashion. To English country gentlemen who liked to walk, Lorrain's work seemed to represent the

Figure 1–12

One of the most remarkable developments in England in the eighteenth century was the softening of the formal garden design that had characterized much of European landscape design. The straight lines and geometric structure that had been preferred in the layout of gardens on the Continent were abandoned as the gentry plunged into a "partnership" with nature to create "natural" landscapes. Not only did the garden designers see themselves working with nature, but also they achieved a kind of conscious spontaneity in their efforts to outdo nature.

(From John and Josiah Boydell, *The Seats of Nobility and the Gentry* [London, n.d.]. Courtesy Rare Book Collection, University of Washington Libraries.)

ideal landscape. Many people also possessed a Claude-glass, which was a convex mirror through which the countryside was viewed, giving it a soft mellow tinge, like that of Lorrain's work. In any case, love of nature—whatever that meant to the eighteenth-century Englishman—became a passion, almost a religion.

To use a phrase of the poet Alexander Pope (1688–1744), the English country garden was adapted "to the genius of the place, and the beauties not forced into it, but resulting from it" (Malins, 1966, p. 26). Nostalgia for the past—another facet of the *Romantic Movement*—also led to the discovery of ruins. Gothic vaulting—or what was left of it in some decaying churchyard—suggested, in particular, parallels with the intersecting branches of a forest glade. Where ruins did not exist, they were promptly created to achieve the desired effect. Such a picturesque interplay of the natural and the classical subsequently stimulated the passions of both poets and landscape painters.

The planned spontaneity of the English garden stood in sharp contrast to the existing, more formal gardens of European princes, but the former also appealed to continental rulers. In central Warsaw today, despite the destruction of World War II, a central park, known as the Saxon Garden, retains its design, which is in the English romantic garden style (Fig. 1–13).

The Garden—A Perfect Habitat for Man?

The garden, then, affords one example of meaningfully structured space, and, whatever culture it appeared in, was prompted by an image of place. Paul Shepard (1967), the *ecologist,* may be correct when he states that the garden is the perfect habitat, but it can only be achieved by transforming the surface of the earth (p. 114). Its sharpest expression is to be found in public parks and recreational areas. These must be protected, preserved, and, wherever possible, expanded.

EPILOGUE

Landscape is a geographic concept that entails an association of features of both the physical geographic and human geographic reality. We, as geographers, identify it and study it.

There is another aspect to landscape, however, that has drawn the attention of geographers. This aspect has more to do with the way people perceive and experience landscape, the way people create places that have meaning for them.

This chapter has introduced this notion to students at the very beginning of the book because there can be no truly significant study of the outer world, the world out there, without an awareness of the inner world, the capacity that people have to take in through their senses what they see, learn, and know about the world we usually designate the "real world." But the experience of the world out there is filtered through our individual and collective cultural heritage. Thus, in effect, the world is a myriad of places—we map these places, but we also carry images of these places around in our heads.

The images that we carry can have an effect on behavior patterns, and so they can, when identified, play a role in shaping our world. Images played an important role in the founding of settlements in the New World and contributed to the shaping of American culture, values, and experience. It is important, then, in the study of geography, as in any other human endeavor, that we be aware of the role of the subjective, the cognitive or perceptual, in our living in the world.

APPLICATION OF IDEAS

1. Through the tendency to form images and mental maps, an important component of geographic study, human beings are able to relate to the world around them by creating a sense of

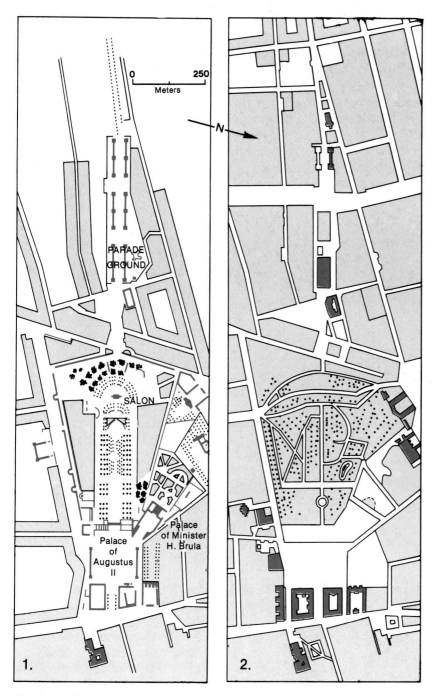

Figure 1–13

The Saxon Garden (Ogród Saski) was established near Warsaw in 1713–1748 by the Saxon King of Poland, August II. The plan of the garden was originally in the formal French style. Until 1797 the garden remained the property of the Saxon royal family, after which the city of Warsaw took it over. In 1816-27, the garden was redesigned, but in the English style which had become popular on the continent.

(*Source:* W. Kalinowski, *Zarys historii budowy miast w Polsce do polowy XIX wieku* [Torun: Poland 1966].)

place, a primary function of which is to create stability and relatedness.

2. Throughout history, humans have attempted to modify the landscape to suit their own needs. Some of these efforts have reflected the needs to express a relationship to a supreme being or to nature. Still other efforts, such as the imposition of straight lines, or the grid pattern, on the landscape, have suggested a newfound mastery. To what extent does the American landscape reflect one or all of these tendencies? How important, do you think, is the study of these human impositions for understanding the present landscape, say, of India or England or Japan?

3. Some scholars have suggested that imagery and the imagination are tools that humans may use, together with their accumulated knowledge and understanding, to create a better world for all to live in. How can this be done? How practicable in a changing world do these attempts seem to be? How do planners try to deal with such problems? What kind of landscape would you like to see emerge if you were a planner?

KEY WORDS AND PHRASES

atrium
belief in inevitable
    progress
centralism
cognitive mapping
cosmos
ecologist
environing factors
environment
ethnocentrism
experienced space
imageability
mental maps

monarchical
natural environment
pagus
place
Renaissance
Romantic garden
Romantic Movement
Semitic
sensory deprivation
shakkei
topophilia
utopia

QUESTIONS FOR FURTHER DISCUSSION

1. How do you account for the human tendency to create a sense of place?

2. How does the human tendency to create a sense of place differ from the notion of territoriality? In what way are there similarities?

3. Peter Gould and Rodney White draw attention to the fact that all of us tend to carry around in our heads images of places, or mental maps. Are you aware of your own mental maps? What are your images, for example, of Siberia, Amazonia, the state in which you live, or your country of origin?

4. In what way does environment differ from place as discussed in this chapter? Are you aware of the differences in the two as understood in your own experience?

5. What images or symbols are important to you? For example, what image do you have of the differences among the peoples of Eurasia or Africa? Can you identify on a map the countries of Asia and Africa? Are you aware of the extent to which the media—or even textbooks—use images to convey their message?

6. How have culture generally and religion or ideology in particular contributed to the differences demonstrated in the form of the garden in human history? In what way do you see the garden as a transformation of, or imitation of, nature?

7. Why do you think that various images of America persisted in the European mind, even though geographic discovery and accumulation of knowledge showed that the images were distorted? Have these early European images of America survived among Americans? (If so, give examples.)

8. Dreams of founding utopian communities on the American frontier were prevalent in the nineteenth century. Why did the frontier environment attract the utopians? Why do you suppose that utopian notions were common to

many Russian writers and thinkers in the nineteenth century?

9. What facts of history and geography might account for the different perceptions of the frontier as experienced by settlers in the United States and in Ontario (Upper Canada) in the nineteenth century?

10. Do you think that the concept of imageability, as used by Kevin Lynch, is a useful one in thinking about or planning cities or neighborhoods or even houses? What problems might this concept present?

REFERENCES AND ADDITIONAL READINGS

Abler, Ronald, et al. *Spatial Organization: The Geographer's View of the World."* Englewood Cliffs, N.J.: Prentice-Hall, 1971.

Abramovitz, Anita. *People and Spaces, A View of History Through Architecture.* New York: Viking Press, 1979.

Allen, Richard, ed. *A Region of the Mind: Interpreting the Western Canadian Plains.* Regina, Can.: University of Saskatchewan, 1973.

Arrington, Leonard J., and Bitton, Davis. *The Mormon Experience, A History of the Latter-Day Saints.* New York: Alfred A. Knopf, 1979.

Berndt, R. M. "Territoriality and the Problem of Demarcating Sociocultural Space," pp. 133–161. In *Tribes and Boundaries in Australia.* Nicholas Peterson, ed. Canberra: Australian Institute of Aboriginal Studies, 1976.

Bowden, Martyn J. "The Great American Desert in the American Mind: The Historiography of a Geographical Nation," pp. 119–148. In *Geographies of the Mind: Essays in Historical Geosophy in Honor of John Kirtland Wright.* David Lowenthal and Martyn J. Bowden, eds. New York: Oxford University Press, 1976.

Briggs, Asa. "The Sense of Place," pp. 79–97. In *The Fitness of Man's Environment.* (Smithsonian Annual 2.) Washington, D.C.: Smithsonian Institution Press, 1968.

Brown, Lloyd A. *The Story of Maps.* New York: Bonanza Books, 1960.

Cantor, Jay. "The New England Landscape of Change." *Art in America,* 1 (January–February, 1976): 51–58.

Chiapelli, Fredi, ed. *First Images of America: The Impact of the New World on the Old* (2 vols.). Berkeley and Los Angeles: University of California Press, 1976. (See especially vol. 2, sect. 8, "The New Geography.")

Clark, Andrew. "Foreword," pp. ix–xiv. In *Images of the Plains: The Role of Human Nature in Settlement.* Brian W. Blouet and Merlin P. Lawson, eds. Lincoln: University of Nebraska Press, 1975.

Downs, Roger M., and Stea, David. *Maps in Minds. Reflections on Cognitive Mapping.* New York: Harper & Row, 1977.

Duncan, Susana. "Mental Maps of New York." *New York* 19 (December 1977): 51–62.

English, Paul W., and Mayfield, Robert C., eds. *Man, Space, and Environment.* New York: Oxford University Press, 1972.

Gould, Peter, and White, Rodney. *Mental Maps.* Baltimore, Md.: Penguin Books, 1974.

Greenwood, Michael. "Myth and Landscape: An Introduction." *Artscanada* Issue No. 222/223 (October–November 1978): 1–8.

Hall, Edward T. *The Silent Language.* Greenwich, Conn.: Fawcett, 1959.

Honour, Hugh. *The European Vision of America.* Cleveland, Ohio: Cleveland Museum of Art, 1975.

Houston, James M. "The Concepts of 'Place' and 'Land' in the Judaeo-Christian Tradition," pp. 224–237. In *Humanistic Geography. Prospects and Problems.* David Ley and Marwyn S. Samuels, eds. Chicago: Maaroufa Press, 1978.

Huth, Hans. *Nature and the American: Three Centuries of Changing Attitudes.* Berkeley and Los Angeles: University of California Press, 1957.

Huxley, Anthony. *An Illustrated History of Gardening.* New York: Paddington Press, 1978.

Itoh, Teiji. *Space and Illusion in the Japanese Garden.* New York and Tokyo: John Weatherhill, 1973.

Johnson, Douglas. "Nomadic Organization of

Space: Reflections on Pattern and Process,'' pp. 25–47. In *Dimensions of Human Geography. Essays on Some Familiar and Neglected Themes.* Karl W. Butzer, ed. Research Paper No. 186, Department of Geography, University of Chicago, 1978.

Keswick, Maggie. *The Chinese Garden. History, Art and Architecture.* London: Academy Editions, 1978.

Kline, Marcia B. *Beyond the Land Itself. Views of Nature in Canada and the United States.* Cambridge: Harvard University Press, 1970.

Kreisel, Henry. ''The Prairie. A State of Mind.'' *Transactions of the Royal Society of Canada* 4, 6 (1968): 171–181.

Kuspit, Donald B. ''19th-Century Landscape: Poetry and Property.'' *Art in America* 1 (January–February 1976): 65–71.

Lee, David R. ''In Search of Center.'' *Landscape* 21 (Winter 1977): 33–37.

Lowenthal, David. ''Geography, Experience and Imagination: Towards a Geographical Epistemology.'' *Annals of the Association of American Geographers* 51 (1961): 241–260.

———. *Environmental Perception and Behavior.* Research Paper No. 109, Department of Geography, University of Chicago, 1967.

———. ''Past Time, Present Place: Landscape and Memory.'' *Geographical Review* 65 (1975): 1–36.

———. ''The Place of the Past in the American Landscape,'' pp. 89–118. In *Geographies of the Mind: Essays in Historical Geosophy in Honor of John Kirtland Wright.* David Lowenthal and Martyn J. Bowden, eds. New York: Oxford University Press, 1976.

Lowenthal, David, and Bowden, Martyn J., eds. *Geographies of the Mind: Essays in Historical Geosophy in Honor of John Kirtland Wright.* New York: Oxford University Press, 1976.

Lynch, Kevin. *The Image of a City.* Cambridge: MIT Press, 1971.

———. *What Time Is This Place?* Cambridge: MIT Press, 1972.

Macdougall, Elizabeth B., and Ettinghausen, Richard, eds. *The Islamic Garden.* Dumbarton Oaks Colloquium on the History of Landscape Architecture 4, Washington, D.C., 1976

Maier, Emanuel. ''Torah as Movable Territory.'' *Annals of the Association of American Geographers* 65 (1975): 18–23.

Malins, Edward. *English Landscaping and Literature 1660–1840.* London: Oxford University Press, 1966.

Matthews, John P. ''The Canadian Experience,'' pp. 21–30. In *Commonwealth Literature: Unity and Diversity in a Common Culture.* John Press, ed. London: Heinemann, 1965.

McHarg, Ian. *Design with Nature.* Garden City, N.Y.: Natural History Press, 1969. (Especially see the chapter, ''On Values,'' pp. 67–78.)

Miller, Perry. *Errand into the Wilderness.* New York: Harper & Row, 1956.

———, ed. *The American Transcendentalists. Their Prose and Poetry.* Garden City, N.Y.: Doubleday, 1957.

Naef, Weston J., and Wood, James N. *Era of Exploration: The Rise of Landscape Photography in the American West, 1860–1885.* Boston: New York Graphic Society Books, 1975.

Nash, Roderick. *Wilderness and the American Mind.* New Haven, Conn.: Yale University Press, 1967.

Norberg-Schulz, Christian. *Existence, Space and Architecture.* New York: Praeger, 1971.

Novak, Barbara. ''The Double-Edged Axe.'' *Art in America* 1 (January–February 1976): 44–50.

Oliver, Paul, ed. *Shelter, Sign and Symbol.* Woodstock, N.Y.: Overlook Press, 1977.

Pearsall, Derek, and Salter, Elizabeth. *Landscapes and Seasons of the Medieval World.* Toronto, Can.: University of Toronto Press, 1973.

Perl, Jed. ''The Vertical Landscape: 'In the Redwood Forest Dense'.'' *Art in America* 1 (January–February 1976): 59–63.

Perrin, Peter. ''Robin Mackenzie: The Sense of Site.'' *Artscanada* Issue No. 214/215 (May–June 1977): 2–11.

Pfeiffer, John. *The Emergence of Society.* New York: McGraw-Hill, 1977.

Porter, Philip W., and Lukermann, Fred E. ''The Geography of Utopia,'' pp. 197–224. In *Geographies of the Mind: Essays in Historical Geosophy in Honor of John Kirtland Wright.* David Lowenthal and Martyn J. Bowden, eds. New York: Oxford University Press, 1976.

Rapoport, Amos. "Australian Aborigines and the Definition of Place," pp. 38–51. In *Shelter, Sign and Symbol*. Paul Oliver, ed. Woodstock, N.Y.: Overlook Press, 1977.

Samuels, Marwyn S. "The Biography of Landscape. Cause and Culpability," pp. 51–88. In *The Interpretation of Ordinary Landscapes*. D. W. Meinig, ed. New York: Oxford University Press, 1979.

Sanford, Charles L. *The Quest for Paradise: Europe and the American Moral Imagination*. Urbana: University of Illinois Press, 1961.

Sauer, Carl O. "The Morphology of Landscape." *University of California Publications in Geography* 2 (October 1925): 19–53.

Shepard, Paul. "The Artist as Explorer." *Landscape* 12 (Winter 1962–1963): 25–26.

———. *Man in the Landscape: A Historic View of the Esthetics of Nature*. New York: Ballantine Books, 1967.

Singer, Charles, et al., eds., *A History of Technology*, Vol. 3. New York, London: Oxford University Press, 1957.

Slotkin, Richard. *Regeneration Through Violence. The Mythology of the American Frontier, 1600–1860*. Middletown, Conn.: Wesleyan University Press, 1974.

Smith, Henry Nash. *Virgin Land: The American West as Symbol and Myth*. New York: Random House, 1950. (Vintage)

Sopher, David E. "The Structuring of Space in Place Names and Words for Place," pp. 251–268. In *Humanistic Geography. Prospects and Problems*. David Ley and Marwyn S. Samuels, eds. Chicago: Maaroufa Press, 1978.

———. "The Landscape of Home. Myth, Experience, Social Meaning," pp. 129–152. In *The Interpretation of Ordinary Landscapes*. D. W. Meinig, ed. New York: Oxford University Press, 1979.

Stoughton, William. *New England's True Interest*. 2nd ed. Cambridge, Mass.: S.G. and M.S., 1670.

Taft, Robert. *Artists and Illustrators of the Old West, 1850–1900*. New York: Crown, 1953.

Thacker, Christopher. *The History of Gardens*. Berkeley and Los Angeles: University of California Press, 1979.

Tocqueville, Alexis de. *Democracy in America*, Vol. 2. New York: Alfred A. Knopf, 1960.

Tuan, Yi-Fu. *Topophilia: A Study of Environmental Perception, Attitudes, and Values*. Englewood Cliffs, N.J.: Prentice-Hall, 1974.

———. "Images and Mental Maps." *Annals of the Association of American Geographers* 65 (1975): 205–213.

———. "Place: An Experiential Perspective." *Geographical Review* 65 (1975): 151–165.

———. "Geopiety: A Theme in Man's Attachment to Nature and to Place," pp. 11–40. In *Geographies of the Mind: Essays in Historical Geosophy in Honor of John Kirtland Wright*. David Lowenthal and Martyn J. Bowden, eds. New York: Oxford University Press, 1976.

———. *Space and Place: The Perspective of Experience*. Minneapolis: University of Minnesota Press, 1977.

———. "Sacred Space: Explorations of an Idea," pp. 84–99. In *Dimensions of Human Geography: Essays on Some Familiar and Neglected Themes*. Karl Butzer, ed. Research Paper No. 186, Department of Geography, University of Chicago, 1978.

Tuveson, Ernest Lee. *Redeemer Nation. The Idea of America's Millenial Role*. Chicago: University of Chicago Press, 1968.

Wagner, Philip L., and Mikesell, Marvin W. *Readings in Cultural Geography*. Chicago: University of Chicago Press, 1962.

Wallace, Noel M. "Living Sacred Sites," pp. 125–127. In *The Preservation of Australia's Aboriginal Heritage*. Robert Edwards, ed. Canberra: Australian Institute of Aboriginal Studies, 1975.

Warkentin, John. "Time and Place in the Western Interior." *Artscanada* Issue Nos. 169/170/171 (Early Autumn 1972): pp. 20–37.

———. "Discovering the Shape of Canada." *Artscanada* Issue No. 188/189 (Spring 1974): pp. 17–35.

Watson, J. Wreford. "Image Geography. The Myth of America in the American Scene." *Advancement of Science* 27 (September 1970): 71–79.

Williams, George H. *Wilderness and Paradise in Christian Thought*. New York: Harper & Bros., 1962.

2

Culture: Evolution and Diffusion

Wonders are many, but none,
  none is more wondrous than man.
Man moves over the grey sea
  using the wind and the storm,
  daring the depths and surges.
Even the eldest of all the gods—
  Earth, inexhaustible Earth—
man masters her
  with yearly ploughs that turn and return
  and the steady step of the horse.
Language and thought
  light and rapid as wind,
man has taught himself these, and has learnt
  the ways of living in town and city,
  shelter from inhospitable frost,
  escape from the arrows of rain.
Cunning, cunning is man.
Wise though his plans are,
  artful beyond all dreaming,
they carry him both to evil and to good.

Sophocles, *Antigone,* c. 441 B.C.

Key Ideas

1. Culture is the accumulation of learned experience and is transmitted, in part, from generation to generation and diffused from one group to another over the earth's surface.

2. An important component in cultural evolution has been the development of a complex system of language communication.

3. Much of cultural development took place in fertile river valleys, such as the Tigris-Euphrates, the Nile, the Indus, the Hwang Ho (Huanghe), as well as in fertile lowlands in Meso-America.

4. When human groups are slow or fail to respond to environmental changes or revolutionary changes in their technological capabilities, they are experiencing a culture lag.

5. Although culture is an essentially conservative phenomenon, it can undergo change, through innovation and the spatial diffusion of innovation.

6. Spatial diffusion is the process whereby the innovation is spread or carried over the earth's surface.

7. Not all peoples or areas are equally receptive to innovation. Barriers inhibit the penetration of new ideas and, depending on the degree to which they block passage, they are known as absorbing or permeable barriers.

8. Cultural landscapes have long interested the geographer, who has seen them both as products of tangible human imprint as well as a reflection of human values and aesthetics.

CULTURE AND GEOGRAPHY

The study of cultural processes within a spatial context has long had a special interest for geographers, but because of its very breadth and complexity, "culture" has never had a closely knit structure. Even definitions of cultural geography have not been easy to reach. According to Wagner and Mikesell, cultural geography is the application of the idea of culture to geographic problems (Wagner and Mikesell, 1962).

In spite of the difficulties posed by the field, there have been a number of recurring themes that have drawn the attention of geographers. Among these are: the components of culture, such as language, religion, institutions, material objects, and so on; the evolution of culture; culture areas and landscapes; and cultural diffusion.

In recent years, there has been a sharp upsurge of interest in the field, in part reflected in landscape studies, research in innovation diffusion, concern for aesthetics and values, and environmental perception.

HOW SUPERIOR ARE HUMANS?

Human beings have long believed themselves superior to other living creatures. Not only have some religious beliefs reinforced this attitude, but material accomplishments attest to human's skills, imagination, organization, and energy. Moreover, some animals have been kept for thousands of years in positions of dependence, their biologic evolution directed to satisfy human wants and needs. Still other animals have been regarded as fair game to be preyed upon for amusement by the heavily armed sportsman or wanton hunter.

Bronowski (1973) believes that what makes humans different from all other creatures on earth is language. Language, he states, is the distinctive feature that humans alone possess: "Language as we use it," Bronowski writes,

"has something of the character of a hunting plan, in that (unlike animals) we instruct one another in sentences" (p. 45). (See Chapter 7 for a discussion of language and communication.)

That magnificent human bastion, however, is now being challenged in research undertaken on chimpanzees. Chimpanzees, laboratory testing shows, can learn and use a human language—notably *Ameslan,* the sign language of the deaf. Researchers argue that although human linguistic and mental abilities are clearly greater than those of other *primates* (that order of creatures to which man and the apes belong), they are greater only in degree, not in kind. However, apes cannot create a sentence, even if they do learn many isolated symbols (Fig. 2–1).

THE NATURE OF CULTURE

A Diary and a Blueprint

Culture, the accumulation of learned experience, is transmitted from one generation to another and over earth space from one group to another. In a sense, culture is the guardian of human activities on earth. This means that each generation can build on what has gone before without having to start all over again. Not every group, therefore, must go through the same pattern of experience to reach a comparable goal; one group can learn from another.

Culture is both a diary and a blueprint; through eons of time, generations of mankind have left something behind—a "book of instructions," which we all inherit for our use. Viewed in this way, the term culture pertains to the very essence of human existence. Among all the creatures of the animal kingdom, humans are unique in their capacity to create and sustain culture. Modern science shows that it is possible to teach and train chimpanzees, but these primates bear no traces of culture-creating capacity.

Figure 2–1

Let's make no mistake about it—it is humans who study and classify life and material phenomena on earth, not the other primates. Ongoing research tells us more about apes and chimpanzees than we knew previously, but the fact remains that the research has been initiated by humans.

(*Source:* Robert A. Wallace, *Biology: The World of Life.* Goodyear, Santa Monica, California, 1978.)

The dominant cultural mode through the millennia has undergone many changes. Widespread hunting was gradually replaced in favorable areas by pastoral activities or farming. Since the mid-eighteenth century of our era, many peoples (beginning first in Europe) have come to embrace industrial manufacturing. But, for the world as a whole, the pattern of development represents a mosaic.

Some groups in remote parts of the globe, such as the Inuit of northern Canada, continue to hunt much as their ancestors did thousands of years ago. Others, as in less accessible parts of the humid tropics, employ farming practices little changed from generations past. In places like Mongolia and the drier parts of Southwest Asia, pastoralism continues to be the way of life of groups who resist the pressures to turn to crop cultivation and to settle in permanently fixed communities. Still others, however, crowd into cities, as in the industrialized world; increasingly, in what has come to be called the Third World, the developing countries face integration into a new way of life that characterizes much of the developed world.

The human diary, then, is an interesting one; it can tell us generally from where we have come. In some cases, it may even serve as a blueprint, suggesting what patterns may emerge in the future. Prediction, however, is not an easy task. The mushrooming of human technology has enhanced our capacity to modify the world around us, and earlier or traditional ways of life, values, and relationships have been greatly challenged. Changes in technical capacity tend to bring a direct and rapid response in human economic-activity patterns. For example, the development of the supertanker made possible not only larger volumes of petroleum shipments, but also greatly altered long-standing global directions of flow. Political patterns, on the other hand, are not so readily modified by changes in technology. Wars are often fought, at least initially, with the weapons of the past. Today, highly sophisticated missile devices are capable of bringing devastation to any spot on the globe, as the Falkland Islands conflict in 1982 demonstrated; yet society clings to nineteenth-century concepts of territorial sovereignty.

The Emergence of Modern Human Beings (*Homo sapiens sapiens*)

The Australopithecines

Initial *hominization,* that is the appearance of humanlike creatures, seems to have taken place between 3 and 4 million years ago. At that time, several types evolved in eastern and southern Africa. Among these were a number of short creatures, no taller than a preteenage boy, of the *genus* or family known as *Australopithecus.* These creatures walked in a stooped but somewhat upright manner, and they lived on the ground.

By about 2 million years ago, the branch leading to modern humans was represented by possibly two types. One was robust, with a massive face and strong facial muscles, essentially a vegetarian and a grubber of roots. Scientists now think that this robust vegetarian died out about two hundred fifty thousand years ago. The other type, slender in build and about four

feet tall, was most likely a hunter, for samples of teeth indicate *carnivorousness,* suggesting that meat was the predominant component of the diet. This type became extinct at an early period, or possibly was replaced by a larger, stronger creature. It is not certain if any of these early creatures migrated to lands beyond Africa—a continent that had undergone relatively fewer geological and climatic changes than the other continents—but it seems possible that groups crossed into Eurasia sometime beginning around seven hundred thousand years ago. Other than that they may have used pebble tools, we have no evidence of material culture.

Homo erectus

The fossilized bones discovered in Java in 1891 and in China (at Choukoutien [Zhoukoudian] near Peking [Beijing]) in the 1920s, together with similar fossilized remains subsequently unearthed in other parts of the Old World, are now regarded as belonging definitely to humanlike creatures, but of a much later period than the *australopithecines* mentioned above.

These creatures, of the genus known as *Homo erectus* because they walked erect, also fashioned crude stone tools (*Lower Paleolithic* or *Old Stone Age* culture) and possibly knew how to create fire. *Peking man* (the name given to the fossil remains in China), in particular, seems to have used fire in caves as far back as four hundred thousand years ago for heating, cooking, and protection against the attack of animals (Box 2–1).

The wide geographic distribution of *Homo erectus* suggests an *adaptive capacity* not possessed by the earlier australopithecines because the former could live and hunt under a greater range of environmental conditions. Still, during the early Ice Ages (*Pleistocene epoch*) when ice covered mountains and the northern part of Eurasia, *Homo erectus* remained restricted to more temperate areas of the Old World (Table 2–1).

Homo sapiens neanderthalensis

An immediate precursor of modern humans emerges up to two hundred thousand years ago. This prototype is named *Homo sapiens neanderthalensis* (*Neanderthal man*). The name is derived from a skull unearthed in 1856 in the Neander Valley near Düsseldorf, in what is now the Federal Republic of Germany.

Neanderthal man was for a long time depicted as a brutish, fearsome creature because of his flattened head, extremely prominent brow ridges, and receding chin. Now, as knowledge of human origins has been pushed backwards in time, this image has been altered. A comparison of the skull of Neanderthal man with the skulls of earlier creatures has suggested that the former was not as primitive as was once thought. For that reason, the Neanderthal is now included in the human family. Over the past century, many other fossils, animal bones, and handworked tools have been uncovered in Africa, Asia, and Europe, suggesting that Neanderthals were also widely dispersed. The cave at Le Moustier in southern France—where a great diversity of flaked stone tools, bone points, and spearlike, sharpened animal ribs have been found—has given its name to local Neanderthal culture (i.e., *Mousterian*). A number of Neanderthal burial sites suggest some degree of social organization and possibly a religious consciousness.

Homo sapiens sapiens

Neanderthal man flourished in Europe some seventy-five thousand years ago, during the Third Interglacial and into the Fourth Glacial Period. Before the last advance of the ice had come to a halt, some thirty-five thousand years ago, the Neanderthals had presumably become extinct. The sole *hominid* survivor of the period was *Cro-Magnon man*, who is recognized as a member of the genus *Homo sapiens sapiens*. Nomadic hunters, the Cro-Magnons migrated into Europe from the Middle East. They occupied the coastal areas of the Mediterranean and scattered inland to what was then the *tundra*, the treeless barrens on the southern margin of the retreating glaciers in Europe.

The cave paintings in France and Spain suggest that these new people had developed a way of life that was different from the habits of the

---

BOX 2–1

The Two-Hundred-Thousand-Year-Old Dwelling

The cave at Zhoukoudian located some 30 miles southwest of Beijing, China, is unlike any other dwelling place on earth. Discovered by scientists in the early 1920s, the limestone cave appears to have been continuously occupied for some two hundred thousand years (Rukang and Lin, 1983). From a careful examination of fossil-bearing deposits, which rest layer upon layer on the bottom of the cave, it is evident that the first inhabitants, *Homo erectus pekinensis*, or Peking man, moved in about four hundred sixty thousand years ago. Generations followed generations until the entry to the cave collapsed about three hundred thousand years ago, burying it. Thereafter, the dwelling place was abandoned and all but forgotten, except by the local population.

It is from the cave deposits that scientists have learned that Peking man was a hunter, catching both large and small game. His diet, however, also consisted of grains he had collected. The knowledge that he possessed about fire enabled him to warm himself during the cold and to cook his food. Peking man possessed tool-making skills and even had a degree of social organization that regulated his group.

Fossil study places the origin of *Homo erectus* at about 1.5 million years ago. Thus, the inhabiting of caves, such as the one at Zhoukoudian, seems to have been a development that occurred at a much later date in the dawn of the human record.

Table 2–1

Prehistoric Time Period in the Emergence of Modern Human Beings

This table is a generalized record of the evolution of life on earth from earliest times down to the beginnings of the Neolithic period or New Stone Age culture, about 8,000 to 10,000 years ago. *Homo erectus,* the first truly erect creature, appeared about 1.5 million years ago, but the fashioning of stone tools, some of the first material evidence of cultural evolution, was already underway. Early *Homo sapiens* date to about 200,000 to 250,000 years ago, whereas in Europe, Neanderthal man appeared about 100,000 years ago. Modern man, Cro-Magnon type, appeared in Europe some 25,000 years ago.

Geologic Era	Cultural Era		Time Period
			Billions of Years Ago
Precambrian earliest era	N O N E	4.9 4	Creation of Earth Formation of the ancient seas First life: single-celled algae and bacteria appear in water
			Millions of Year Ago First oxygen-breathing animals appear
		800	Primitive organisms develop interdependent specialized cells
		600	Shell-bearing many-celled invertebrate animals appear Evolution of armored fish, first animals to possess backbones
Paleozoic (period lasted 370 million years)	N O N E	400	Small amphibians venture onto land, colonization of land areas Reptiles and insects appear
		320	Thecodont, ancestor of dinosaurs, arises Age of dinosaurs begins
Mesozoic (period lasted 165 million years)		130	Birds appear Mammals live in shadow of dinosaurs (proliferate in the Tertiary period) Age of dinosaurs ends
		80	
Cenozoic/Tertiary (period lasted about 65 million years)		60	Prosimians, earliest primates, develop in trees
		40	Monkeys and apes evolve
		20	
		10	*Ramapithecus,* oldest known primate with apparently manlike traits, evolves in India and Africa
		8	
		6	Fragmentary fossils of hominids, closest primate ancestor to man found
		4	Oldest known remains of hominids from Awash Valley in Ethiopia (Afar Ape-man)
		3[a]	
Quaternary (Lower Pleistocene)	Lower Paleolithic Oldest period of Old Stone Age	2	Spectacular finds of hominid forms in East and South Africa (australopithecines)
		1	*Homo erectus* spreads through temperate zone of northern hemisphere
			Thousands of Years Ago
(Middle Pleistocene) Middle period of most recent epoch		800	*Homo erectus* in China, Java, Europe, and North Africa
		600	
		400	Artificial shelters made from branches; evidence of use of fire found in caves near Peking (Beijing)
		200	*Homo sapiens neanderthalensis* emerges

Reported Advances of Ice

↑ Acheulian ↓

Table 2–1 *(continued)*

Geologic Era		**Cultural Era**		**Time Period**	
(Upper Pleistocene) Latest period of most recent epoch	Last Ice Age	Middle Paleolithic Middle period of Old Stone Age	↑ Mousterian ↓	80	Neanderthal type in Europe
				60	Burials in Europe and Near East suggest belief in afterlife, cult of the dead
					Woolly mammoths hunted by Neanderthals in Europe
					Cave bear becomes focus of cult in Europe
		Upper Paleolithic Latest period of Old Stone Age		35	Cro-Magnon people reach Europe
					Hunters cross from Asia over land bridge to populate New World and reach Australia via Southeast Asia
					First artists decorate walls and ceilings of caves in France and Spain
			Magdalenian	30	Figurines sculpted for nature worship
				20	Invention of needle makes sewing possible
					Bison hunting begins on Great Plains of North America
Holocene		Mesolithic ↑ Middle Stone Age		10	Bow and arrow invented in Europe
Present epoch		Neolithic (New) Stone Age			

[a] Recent evidence points to creatures walking upright about 3.6 million years ago.

Source: Data drawn from various sources, for example, Jean-Claude Fisher and Yvette G. Valy, *Fossils of All Ages* (New York: Grosset & Dunlap, 1978), and publications of Time-Life Books.

Neanderthals. They had become considerably more skilled in the making of stone and bone tools, they could draw and paint with considerable skill and imagination, and they had developed speech, which certainly hastened the formation of social groups and the development of culture.

The warming trend in the earth's climate that occurred about eight to ten thousand years ago meant the extinction of many mammals that had long roamed the earth—the woolly mammoths, giant wolves, and cave bears, as well as reindeer and horses in North America. These climatic changes were accompanied by movements of people that resulted in a fundamental redistribution over the surface of the earth. New invaders from the Near East and south-central Asia brought to Europe advances in the art of tool making and a more highly developed social structure. Among these human beings were groups that were by now essentially agriculturalist. Waves of migrants—like a series of pulsations dating possibly from forty thousand years ago—had crossed the narrow Bering Straits that separate Asia from Alaska (either by island hopping or over a dryland bridge) and had found their way from the Old World to the New World. At the same time, other members of the human species had reached the peripheral regions of the earth, the Pacific islands and Australia.

THE EVOLUTION OF CULTURE

The Tempo of Culture Change

Some 3 million years had passed after the first appearance of East and Central African australopithecines before modern human beings appeared. Contrasted with historical time, biologic evolution, as Table 2–1 suggests, was extremely slow, but in the case of the hominids, many scientists believe that it occurred more rapidly than for most other forms of life. Whether or not one accepts the evidence of biologic evolution, the evidence of cultural evolution cannot be rejected. And it occurred over a relatively short space of time. Cave art probably does not predate thirty-five thousand years; the events of recorded history begin only about 5000 B.C. The most phenomenal changes in human culture, however, have occurred within the past two hundred years. Advances in our knowledge of electronics are ushering in a computer age, which already is beginning to reshape patterns of behavior and learning that should have dramatic cultural consequences.

Importance of Communication

What was it that brought about this phenomenon that enabled human groups to take not just one step forward, but two or three steps building up to a run? We do not know fully the answer to this question (Box 2–2). Clearly, however, a major prerequisite for *culture change* has been the development of a means of communication. The main imprinting forces in

---

BOX 2–2

Environmental Change, Human Evolution, and Cultural Adaptation

One of the leading American geographers in the study of human and cultural evolution is Karl W. Butzer.

The period when hominids, or humanlike creatures, first emerged in Eurasia, according to Butzer, was a critical climatic threshold (1977). It was near the beginning of the Pleistocene, a period that has been marked by extreme climatic variations. These changes have been associated with repeated periods of *glaciation,* or glacial advances and retreats, in the higher latitudes of the northern hemisphere.

The last glaciation, known in the United States as the Wisconsin, began about seventy thousand years ago. It was at that time that *Homo sapiens sapiens* began to replace more archaic hominid forms, such as the Neanderthal type.

Essential to this development, Butzer believes, was an unequal distribution of life-supporting resources over the earth's surface. Some areas possessed resource opportunities to support size-able clusters of people, whereas other and intervening areas did not. The sharp fluctuations in climate associated with glacial advances had a decided effect on the ability of people to survive. The stresses that occurred in the relationship of people to their environment led to human adaptation, to migration, or to death. "Environmental changes triggered cultural responses," writes Butzer, "that favored biological evolution, which in turn affected the biological capacity for culture" (1977, p. 584).

This intricate feedback, therefore, was one between the evolution of the brain, invention, and improved manual skills as well as more complex speech habits and social organization.

One aspect of this development was the entrance of *Homo sapiens sapiens* into Europe (Cro-Magnon type) about thirty-five thousand years ago and the subsequent migrations into North America from Asia and into Australia from Southeast Asia. Another aspect was the appearance of brilliant artistic expression as well as the use of plants and animals that ultimately led to their *domestication,* or controlled development and use, thus, affording the historic hunter with an alternative food base.

culture transfers are symbolic, with language playing a particular role (Haggett, 1975). We do not know what the languages of early peoples were like. But, the advances displayed in the art of tool making by the peoples who experienced the *Neolithic* or *New Stone Age* revolution depended principally on their ability to exchange ideas with other members of their group or with neighboring groups. People first had to talk, then, through a steadily improving faculty of speech, communicate their new techniques and discoveries to others. Sound values were attached to the pictorial symbols; subsequently, forms of writing came into existence.

The Hearths of Civilization

There is no evidence of writing as such before the rise of *civilization* (organized civilian life) in the *culture hearths* of the Old World (Table 2–2). These birthplaces of civilization lay principally in fertile river valleys, such as the Tigris-Euphrates in Mesopotamia (Iraq), the Nile in Egypt, the Indus (Pakistan), and the (Huanghe) Hwang Ho in China. The birth of civilization was marked by the appearance of the city, a settlement type that first took shape about 3500 B.C. in Sumer, in southern Mesopotamia. The first known examples of writing are from Sumer; they are on clay tablets dating back to at least 3000 B.C.

This new pattern of urban life—associated with the clustering of peoples, a surplus of locally produced foodstuffs, commodity exchange, and so on—required that records be kept. The records were kept in ancient Egypt as well, and like those of Sumer, they were pictorial, or *hieroglyphic*. Later, in Egypt though not in Sumer, sound values were attached to the pictorial symbols.

When cities emerged in the Americas millennia later, the art of writing remained unknown in the Inca world. But in Meso-America, on the other hand, a system of hieroglyphics developed and was used by the Mayans.

CLASSIFICATION OF CULTURE

Julian Huxley (1887–1975), the English biologist, in a comparison of biologic and cultural evolution, has proposed a convenient model for categorizing culture. He identifies three constituent components: *mentifacts, sociofacts,* and *artifacts* (Haggett, 1975). In our discussion so far, we have already referred, albeit indirectly, to these three components.

Mentifacts are the most tenacious of the components of a culture, but they cannot be seen. They lie in the realm of ideas and are of the mind. Included in this category are religious beliefs, ideologies, legends, folklore, magic, attitudes toward nature, and views of the universe. Artistic ideas and styles are also part of human mentifacts.

Sociofacts pertain to those aspects of culture that place people in society. Among these are the structures and systems that link individuals to family and kinship groups, to educational and political institutions, to religious structures and organizations, and to all other associations that are found in society.

Those aspects of culture that have a material basis in group behavior are included among the artifacts. The artifacts of human use of the earth are the pots and pans—the pottery—of everyday living, types of clothing and bodily adornment, housing, tools and implements, the layout of cities and farm fields, forms of transportation, and other tangible evidence of human behavior.

The Huxley model is a convenient one, but it warrants some thought. Some scholars prefer a categorization of culture simply into material and nonmaterial. The material culture includes the artifacts mentioned above. But, like the human imprint on the landscape, it is seen as the direct result or product of overt action, a product of available technology. On the other hand, the nonmaterial culture is thought to apply to behavior per se. It represents man's intellectual capacity to effect change. After harvesting the wild upland grasses growing in Asia, for exam-

Table 2-2
Culture Hearths and Cultural Evolution from the Paleolithic to the Neolithic or New Stone Age

Culture Hearth	20,000 to 10,000 B.C.	10,000 to 8000 B.C.	8000 to 6000 B.C.	6000 to 4000 B.C.	4000 to 2000 B.C.	2000 B.C. to Birth of Christ	Birth of Christ to A.D. 100+
Population Growth	---------->More Than 8 Million			---->About 100 Million	---->About 250 Million		---->350 Million
Near East	Early villages of hunters-gatherers. Early domestication of the dog.	Sheep domesticated c. 9000 B.C.	Jericho—oldest known settlement. Wheat and barley cultivated, goats domesticated, 6200 B.C. Copper used in Mediterranean trade.	Earliest irrigation 5500 B.C. First steps toward writing on clay tablets.	First city, Uruk, 3500 B.C. Egyptian trading ships in Mediterranean.	Phoenicians develop alphabet. Iron spreads throughout Europe.	Birth of Mohammed, 570 A.D.
Nile Valley	Possible domestication of sheep in North Africa.			First farming villages in Egypt, 4500 B.C. Livestock herding in Sahara, 5000 B.C.	Writing in Egypt, 3000 B.C. Pyramids, 2700 B.C.		Trade routes across Sahara.
Indus Valley				Earliest domesticated animals; sheep, goats, pigs, cattle, 5500 B.C. Earliest farming villages, 4000 B.C.	First cities of Indus Valley. Chickens and elephants domesticated. 1900 B.C.		
Far East			Earliest pottery in Japan. Cultivation of soil in Thailand.	Earliest farming villages in China, 5000 B.C. Early writing, ca 4000 B.C.	Rice cultivated 3000 B.C. Silk moth domesticated. Farming villages in Thailand. Early Bronze Age tools.	First cities in China, 1800 B.C. Buddha in India. Confucius in China. Great Wall completed, 200 B.C.	First city in Vietnam.

Source: Pfeiffer, 1977, pp. 42–43.

ple, the early agriculturalist realized that the seed of grasses might be planted; thus, after what must have been a long period of trial and error, the cultivator was born. The growth in output of foodstuffs that occurred in the centuries following supported ever larger concentrations of people.

CULTURE LAG

When groups of human beings are slow to respond mentally (and psychologically) to changes in their spatiophysical environment—as must have been the case many times in the past—they experience a *culture lag* (Box 2–3). During such a period, if there is no accommodation to the new situation, the group may be subjected to considerable stress and confusion. On the other hand, there may be a receptivity to ideas introduced by other groups that permits a refashioning of patterns of behavior, institutions, and so forth, to reflect the new realities. In other words, people may attempt to overcome the lag between their cultural equipment and the challenge of the new. In so doing, they may prepare themselves for further change. In modern democratic societies, politics is the major theater where many of these adjustments take place, however slowly.

History records many instances where civilizations have risen and subsequently declined. The inability of Roman leadership to adapt its urban institutions to the demands of a spatially enlarged realm, embracing many diverse peoples throughout much of the Mediterranean basin, may have been a major factor in the fall of the Roman Empire. (Of course, this brief assessment has the advantage of hindsight and the reasons underlying the collapse of Roman civilization were undoubtedly more complex.)

The Resistance of Pastoral Peoples to Change

Pastoral peoples present a special problem for modern governments, whether in Africa, Asia,

BOX 2–3
The Case of the Ik People

A contemporary example of a people who seem doomed to extinction is that of the Ik who live in East Africa. The Ik, although as intelligent as any culture group, appear to have reached the limits of adaptability. They do not respond in a positive manner to a change that has occurred in their existence for reasons not clearly understood by outside observers (Turnbull, 1972).

Originally, the Ik were a wandering people who lived by hunting and gathering. Before World War II, they were encouraged to give up their nomadic way of life and settle in a confined mountainous region in northeastern Uganda that borders on Kenya and the Sudan. The Kidepo Valley, to the west of this area, was full of game throughout the year, and this land had formed the Ik's principal hunting ground. But, at that time, it was taken over as a national park, and the Ik were excluded from it (Fig. 2–2).

Game are not plentiful in the Ik's new permanent environment—indeed, the region had been only a temporary resting point in the traditional annual nomadic cycle. Some crop cultivation takes place, but the climate is droughty—on an average of once every four years the rains fail. When the fields ripen, the Ik take only what they can consume. There are no storage facilities, and what is left in the fields may rot before it can be eaten. For this reason, starvation has cut deeply into the ranks of the Ik.

As a result of their inability to sustain themselves, the level of village or social life among the Ik has deteriorated below the bare minimum. Ik family ties have weakened, and the people now appear devoid of love, kindness, and tenderness. Because a family offers no economic advantage, no effort is made to sustain it, and children are turned out by their mothers at the age of 3. From 3 until 13, children band together for survival. At 13, they assume adulthood and fend for themselves.

The Ik could hunt on the plateau below them, but hunting requires a degree of cooperation that no longer is found in the tribe. Since malnutrition and hunger have lowered energy levels, the Ik seem to be resigned to death.

The Ik may not be unique in facing such a dilemma. Other hunting or pastoral peoples in Africa may face a similar situation, particularly if they occupy remote areas deemed suitable as animal preserves or national parks. The creation of a park in the high Simen Mountains of northern Ethiopia, north of Gondar, has been stubbornly opposed by the pastoral tribes who live there. The confiscation of traditional lands and relocation to lower elevations outside proposed park boundaries will pose crucial problems for these Ethiopian peoples, demanding the choices that survival requires.

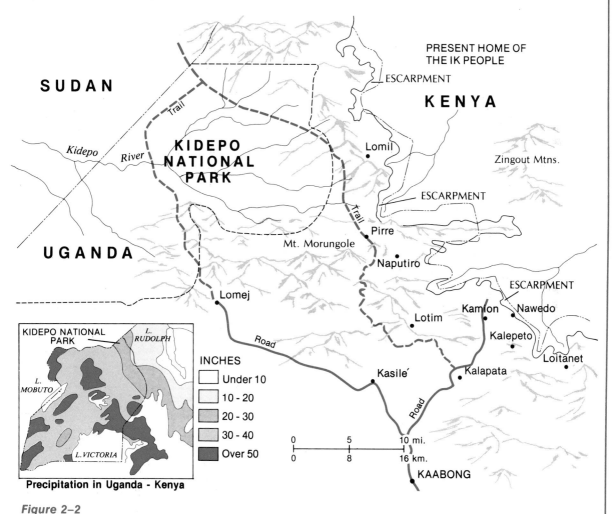

Figure 2–2

The present homeland of the Ik is confined primarily to the escarpment and dry uplands in northeastern Uganda, to the south of Kidepo National Park, overlooking the droughty grasslands of northwestern Kenya. Villages are found between Mount Murungole in the northwest and Loitanet in the southeast. The Kidepo Valley, which was once the hunting grounds of the Ik, is closed to them.

or elsewhere. Because herdsmen must seek out pasture and water for their flocks and herds, their way of life is built around seasonal migration. But, in their migrations, they frequently run up against the boundaries of a new political order.

The search for space by Kazakh pastoralists, a Turkic people who have lived for centuries in Turkestan in the heart of Asia, for example, symbolizes the plight of such migratory peoples. When sovereignty over the area was divided between Russia and China in the nineteenth century, the Kazakhs found their traditional grazing lands cut in two.

Russian settlement west of the international boundary sent Kazakh pastoralists fleeing into Chinese Turkestan in 1916. Many fled again into

China in the early 1930s when the Soviet Union attempted to *collectivize* Kazakh herds. A reverse flow of Kazakh refugees into the Soviet Union occurred in 1949–1950 when the Chinese Communist forces reached northwestern China. In 1962, when the Chinese imposed *collectivization* on their territory, thousands of Kazakhs fled from China into the Soviet Union as well as over the Himalayas into India and Pakistan.

Although sporadic border crossings may still occur, the Kazakh herdsmen, whether in the Soviet Union or in China, have no alternative but to settle and allow their traditional way of life to be restructured into a sedentary mode of existence. A similar development has occurred in the Mongolian People's Republic. Mongol

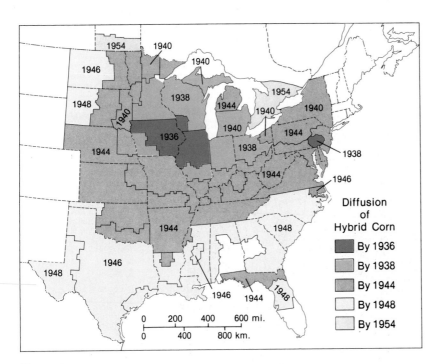

Figure 2-3

The diffusion of hybrid corn in North America began with its initial acceptance by farmers in Iowa and Illinois in 1936. Within a decade, its cultivation was widespread throughout the midwestern United States. By the late 1940s and early 1950s, it had penetrated into southwestern Ontario and even into Manitoba. Besides altering the agricultural economy, this new strain of corn changed American eating habits, with beef becoming a predominant staple food.

nomads have been forced to settle on the land in permanent camps. Elsewhere their traditional felt tents, or yurts, have been replaced in the larger centers, like Ulan Bator, with state-built high-rise apartment houses.

The odds against the survival of traditional pastoralism in those parts of the globe where it is still practiced are high. It remains to be seen how effectively these peoples—the Kazakhs, the Mongols, the Bedouins of southwest Asia, and the cattle herders of East Africa, among others—can adapt to the changes that are being forced on them.

PROCESSES IN THE FORMATION OF CULTURE

Although the nature of culture—its guardianship of the continuity of the spatial patterns of human existence—is essentially conservative, the cultures of peoples have been modified through the adoption of new ideas or techniques. In this spatial process, the role of *diffusion* or *innovation diffusion* has been seen by geographers to be of fundamental importance (Brown, n.d. [a]).

The Role of Innovation in Culture Change

Innovation is the process whereby a new idea, new item, or a new technique comes into existence and is subsequently accepted by a community. Innovation may constitute nothing more startling than a simple invention, but if approved or adopted, its effect can be accumulative. The evolution of stone cutting tools from the Old Stone Age into the New Stone Age, for example, must have represented an accumulation of inventions that at the time they were individually fashioned may have caused only slight modifications. Their ultimate consequence, however, was to make hunting more

Figure 2–4

Mycenae, an *acropolis* (citadel) on a rocky hill southwest of Corinth, in Greece, was founded by non-Greeks about 2900 B.C. Still standing is its famous Lion Gate, which is capped by a beam of massive rock.

(*Source:* W. A. Douglas Jackson.)

Figure 2-5

The great Inca city of Machu Picchu in Peru lies in ruins, attracting only tourists. Remnants of its architecture, built in the late fifteenth century A.D., are reminiscent of the massive ruins of ancient cities in the Mediterranean basin, such as those of Mycenae.

(*Source:* Carl Frank/Photo Researchers.)

efficient, increase the food supply, and improve the conditions of life. Consider the impact of the development of new strains of hybrid corn in the United States in the late 1930s. Crop patterns were altered, leading to the strengthening in the Midwest of the feed base for livestock raising, which greatly influenced American eating habits (Fig. 2–3). Similarly, the introduction of *"miracle" wheat* and rice in the developing countries in the 1960s and 1970s improved their capacity to feed themselves.

Innovation is linked to time and to place, being very much dependent on the existing content of a people's culture. Inventions occurring at different places and times may resemble each other, although they may not have the same cultural roots or effects. The dome was devel-

oped by the Romans from the arch, but it was also invented independently by the Eskimos for their igloos. The beam that formed the entrance to the stone structures of the Inca cities of Peru was identical to that of the temples and palaces of ancient Greece, which had appeared at a much earlier period (Figs. 2–4, 2–5). On the other hand, the culture hearths of the Middle East produced script, but at the time of the Spanish conquest when Inca civilization collapsed, nothing comparable to even Egyptian hieroglyphics had developed in the Inca Empire. Nor did the Inca possess the wheel before the advent of the Spaniards, even though their terraced fields were irrigated with engineering skill and ingenuity. Printing had been discovered in China by the end of the second century

A.D.; typography was extensively developed in Korea by the middle of the thirteenth century. At the time, this technology was still unknown in Europe. The Chinese also learned to make paper, and by the middle of the eighth century the technique had been transferred to the Arabs through contact in central Asia; but papermaking in Europe, learned from the Arabs, dates only from the late thirteenth century. On the other hand, Johannes Gutenberg, who lived during the first half of the fifteenth century, is generally credited with the invention of the printing press, an idea that had never been conceived in the Far East (Fig. 2–6).

Among peoples of similar or related cultures, parallel inventions are often common. Because constituent elements in culture are shared by many peoples, the record suggests that if one person does not invent something new another is likely to do so. For example, the basic elements necessary for the development of the telephone were generally known by the 1830s. On February 14, 1876, Elisha Gray (1835–1901) and Alexander Graham Bell (1847–1922) both made applications for American telephone patents (Fig. 2–7). Elisha Gray had approached the problem of transmitting several telegraph messages over the same wire at the same time through electricity. Bell, in contrast, had searched for a solution to the problem through acoustics. Each, however, had arrived at the concept of harmonic telegraphy at the same time. Gray's claim to the invention of the telephone was denied in favor of Bell's, largely because Gray had failed after his application to test his device successfully. Bell, however, accomplished this three days after filing his application, and his patent was subsequently upheld in the courts of the United States. The Bell System was one of the most important innovations in modern times, making possible more rapid transmission of information from people to people, person to person.

Another example of parallel discoveries within a given culture may be found in the development of the concept of *natural selection,*

Figure 2–6

No invention was more effective in contributing to the peaceful diffusion of ideas than that of the printing press. Until the middle of the fifteenth century, the only books available in Europe were those that had been written by hand, often elaborately designed and executed with great care. The development of the printing press and movable type, made it possible to put books within reach of the common people. The illustration shown here is of an early screw-down press in operation.

(From *Claudius Ptolemaeus Cosmographica.* Rome: 1478. [Amsterdam: Theatrum Orbis Terrarum. 1966. Fac. Newberry Library Copy, 1937.] Courtesy Rare Book Collection, University of Washington Libraries.)

the natural process tending to preserve forms of animal and plant life best adapted to the conditions under which they live. As Charles Darwin (1809–1882) was preparing his ideas on natural selection for publication in 1858, he found suddenly that Alfred Russell Wallace (1823–1913) had already reached similar conclusions based on his own observations. This competition pushed Darwin to publish immediately (1859)

Figure 2–7

Alexander Graham Bell was born in Edinburgh, Scotland, in 1847 and died in Nova Scotia in 1922. At an early age, he became interested in his father's efforts to devise a system of speech for the deaf. In the 1870s, he set to work to develop the telephone, which he patented in the United States in 1876. This innovation had a profound effect on cultures all over the world.

(*Source:* Culver Pictures, Inc.)

his *On the Origin of Species,* which became the classic work on evolution and natural selection.

Many other discoveries, including those pertaining to electricity, radio, and flying, occurred almost simultaneously in the United States and in other countries, such as Germany, Italy, France, England, and Russia. Persistence in pursuing the success of the invention usually has been the basis on which an individual's research has been recognized and accepted.

Some of the innovations leading to new patterns of belief or living may have taken a long time to incubate and to surface. There may have also been discrete revolutionary moments

when a totally new idea has burst on the world with deep cultural implications. This certainly has been true of some of the scientific discoveries, such as those advanced by Isaac Newton (1642–1727) and Albert Einstein (1879–1955). Their theories in their time revolutionized views of the universe.

Diffusion

Culture change through the spatial diffusion of innovations assumes that a process that geographers call *spatial interaction* has taken place. This means simply the spread or dissemination of new ideas, techniques, or items, from one group and from one place to another over the surface of the earth (Box 2–4). The diffusion of these innovations depends essentially on flows (Kariel and Rosenvall, 1983).

Diffusion, thus, presupposes some form of contact. It is difficult for new ideas or techniques to spread if peoples live in isolation. Throughout history the most effective means whereby spatial diffusion has occurred has been through migrations, wars and conquests, and trade. The spread of Christianity throughout the Old World and into the New World is a good example of the spatial diffusion of new ideas.

In modern society where the facilities for communicating widely over vast distances have become more intense, the diffusion process may occur through a series of nonpersonal or impersonal contacts. By means of the telephone, television, radio, and the newspaper, the products of advertisers are brought into people's homes with reminders that life-styles can be enriched and lives made fuller if only the listener, the viewer, or the reader adopts or purchases the items being advertised.

The spatial diffusion process may be defined in a variety of ways, but geographers generally identify several types, the most common being *expansion diffusion* and *relocation diffusion* (Fig. 2–8). In expansion diffusion, one might imagine the spread of an idea or item from place to place and from group to group so that the area of impact and the number of people subject to impact become steadily larger. A review of the history of Islamic expansion through the Arabian peninsula and across North Africa or into the Tigris-Euphrates Valley suggests the process of expansion diffusion.

Relocation diffusion is applied to the spatial process involving bodily movement of people (and ideas and techniques) from one place to another. The transference of New World crops, such as corn and potatoes, to the Old World occurred when the Spaniards in the sixteenth century carried samples back to Spain. Generally, however, relocation diffusion may be applied to many migrations whereby people have moved from one place to another and have carried the innovation with them.

Because the diffusion process may in reality entail a combination of types, one needs first to understand the situation before attempting to identify any one example. The spread of a contagious disease, like the smallpox that swept through the New World with European contact, is an excellent illustration of a variant of expansion diffusion, namely *contagious diffusion*. The process whereby an innovation may filter down through a society or community, suggesting water cascading over rocks, might be termed *cascade diffusion*. Where ideas are transmitted through leapfrogging from person to person within a preexisting hierarchic structure, the term *hierarchic diffusion* is used. The transmission, moreover, may be either upward or downward through the hierarchy. Obviously, this type of diffusion is an important phenomenon in political activities. The personal appeal by radio or TV from the White House allows the president to reach the people without going through all the tranmission links of the political system. On the other hand, letters directed to congressional leaders from members of constituencies is a way of leapfrogging, or bypassing, channels that permits the flow of information upward from grass roots levels.

The Absorbing Barrier

The purpose of an *absorbing barrier* is to function with respect to innovation diffusion much as a sponge soaks up water. Any barrier that halts or deflects the penetration of an innovation operates as an absorbing barrier. Soviet authorities, for example, have in the past regularly jammed radio transmission from the capitalist world so that Soviet peoples would not be exposed to what are officially deemed to be harmful western ideas or ideologies. Restrictions on trade and travel may seek to achieve a similar result.

It is seldom that any barrier erected by humans has functioned in a total manner. Broad expanses of desert, seas, and high mountains have in the past effectively impeded human movement, but whether human or natural, such boundaries cannot prevent a certain degree of seepage. Even the Soviet attempts to insulate its peoples have not been successful and news items, music styles and western clothing, including blue jeans, penetrate the Soviet Union from the Western World. When a boundary fails to halt spatial diffusion, it may be considered to be a *permeable barrier*. Obviously, some boundaries are more permeable than others. The Canadian government, for example, has taken steps to reduce the impact of U.S. culture on Canadians by requiring foreign-owned magazines, published in Canada, to contain a specific amount of material pertaining to Canadian affairs. Despite these and other attempts to lessen the volume of foreign news inundating Canadians, Ottawa has recognized that in a democratic society it cannot prevent Canadians from viewing television or radio programs originating south of the border, from enjoying films from the United States, or from visiting friends and shopping in the United States (Box 2–5). For Canada, the cost of ensuring the growth of a Canadian point of view in a land stretching from west to east over five thousand miles is a high one.

A

a. The Initial Stage

b. A Later Stage

B

a. The Initial Stage

b. A Later Stage

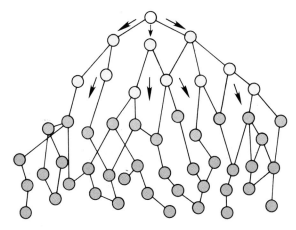

Figure 2–8

(A) Expansion diffusion. (B) Relocation diffusion.

(*Source:* Gould, 1969, p. 4.)

(C) The process of hierarchical diffusion.

(*Source:* Gould, 1969, p. 6.)

BOX 2–4

Torsten Hägerstrand and His Contribution to Diffusion Studies

The interest of American geographers in the spatial processes of diffusion was stimulated by the work of the Swedish geographer Torsten Hägerstrand at the Royal University of Lund. Hägerstrand's first substantial contribution, *Innovation Diffusion as a Spatial Process,* was originally published in Sweden in 1953.

Hägerstrand's work was concerned with the spread of several agricultural innovations in central Sweden, such as bovine tuberculosis controls and subsidies for the improvement of grazing. These case studies were accompanied by general studies of the spread of postal-checking services and the introduction and diffusion of the automobile in Sweden.

In the latter case, Hägerstrand found that the automobile was first introduced into Sweden from Europe south of the Baltic in the 1890s. By 1906, usage of the new form of transport was widespread enough to require the passage of government regulatory legislation. The legislation required registration of all automobiles and a count was kept for every year thereafter. Hägerstrand's study of the diffusion process covers the years up to 1933 (Fig. 2–9). Clearly in the period studied, the diffusion of automobile ownership throughout Sweden was impressive.

In the spatial diffusion process, Hägerstrand recognized the importance of six essential elements. The first of these is the area or environment in which the process develops or takes place. The second element refers to time, that is the length or period of time during which the diffusion process occurs. The third element is the item being diffused, whether material or tangible or nonmaterial or ideational. The remaining three elements in Hägerstrand's model relate to the ensuing spatial patterns formed in the diffusion process—the different places of origin, the destination, and the directions that the item being diffused follows.

Hägerstrand was also responsible for developing another concept, *innovation waves.* In "The Propagation of Innovation Waves" (1952) as well as in his subsequent *Innovation Diffusion as a Spatial Process,* Hägerstrand likens certain aspects of the diffusion process to the action of waves on the Swedish coast. He noted that Scania, or Skåne, the region of Sweden nearest the continent (Denmark), was often the first to receive new items from the rest of Europe. The introduction of the automobile for example—together with other innovations that crossed the narrow straits into Scania—were likened to waves that roll in from the sea, hence "innovation waves."

Hägerstrand's writing had a strong influence on diffusion studies not only in Sweden, but also elsewhere, including the United States. With the acceptance of his work, modifications of his model were made. Among the more useful American studies on innovation diffusion, the works of Peter Gould (1969), Richard Morrill (1965), and Laurence Brown (n.d.) might be cited.

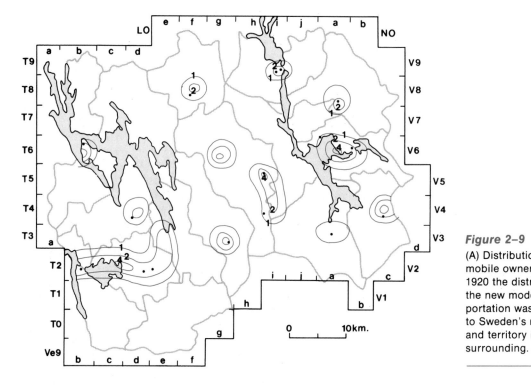

Figure 2–9

(A) Distribution of automobile owners, 1920. In 1920 the distribution of the new mode of transportation was confined to Sweden's major cities and territory immediately surrounding.

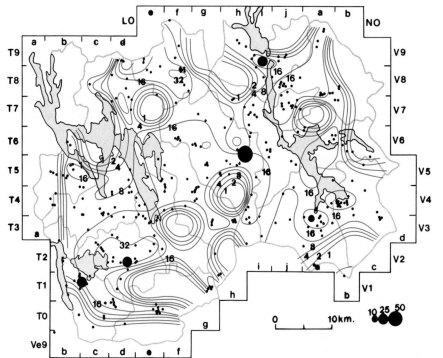

Figure 2–9

(B) Distribution of automobile owners, 1933. By 1933 the number of automobile owners in Sweden had grown as the new mode of transportation had been accepted. The waves of diffusion are increasingly evident.

If peoples accept innovations, they may also reject them. Generally, the degree of acceptance tends to weaken the greater the distance from the point of origin. Canadians living at Churchill on Hudson Bay may be less inclined to adopt a new item seized on more readily by compatriots living in Toronto. When this occurs, the geographer speaks of *distance decay*. Christianity was ultimately accepted by many diverse groups throughout the world, but European missionaries in the New World frequently found that conversion meant accommodation and a mixing of traditional theology with local practices. If it takes ever-increasing time for the acceptance of an innovation at ever-greater distance from the point of origin, then one may speak of both distance *and* time decay, or *time-distance decay*.

CULTURE AREAS AND CULTURAL LANDSCAPES

Through the evolution of *culture traits* or characteristics together with the roles of innovation and spatial diffusion, different groups of people living in different territories have produced areas of common culture, or *culture areas*. All culture areas possess spatial attributes in common, even though their physical geographic characteristics may differ widely (Wagner and Mikesell, 1962). Some of these spatial attributes may be identified as follows: (1) cores or culture hearths, (2) pathways of communication or diffusion, and (3) territory over which a group sharing common traits is distributed.

The Arab-Islamic culture area came into being with the establishment by Mohammed, the Prophet, of Mecca and Medina in western Arabia as the culture hearth of the new Islamic civilization. The trade routes, linking oases and river valleys, formed the pathways whereby armies and traders carried the essence of the new culture throughout the Middle East and North Africa. Ultimately, the territory of the

BOX 2–5

The Spatial Diffusion in Canada of News from the United States

Canadians frequently claim that they know more about what happens in the United States than the republic's citizens know about Canadian events. This complaint is rooted in a variety of geographic considerations. First, Canada, although the second largest country in the world in terms of territory, has only a tenth of the population of the United States. Moreover, the boundary between the two countries is one of the longest unfortified borders in the world, with the bulk of the Canadian population living within a few hundred miles of it. Sharing for the most part a common language, the United States and Canada share also a democratic tradition that has permitted the free flow of peoples and ideas.

Studies of Canadian newspapers have revealed that the press devotes a fairly large proportion of its news space to events in the United States (Kariel and Rosenvall, 1983), ranging from a third to over two thirds of all foreign news. Within that range, three categories of news items seemed most appealing to Canadian editors: sports, political and economic events and developments, and human-interest stories.

Clearly, these items help create Canadian awareness of the United States and contribute to the formation of images and mental maps. These, in turn, influence Canadian attitudes toward the republic and their continued receptivity to information originating south of the border. When considered alongside Canadian access to TV and radio programs originating in the United States, together with the U.S. films that play throughout Canada, it can be seen why some Canadians are deeply concerned about the diffusion of American culture in Canada.

The French-speaking population is insulated from much of this information flow because their language serves as a barrier. News items from the United States must be translated into French, and the cost places a burden on the French-language newspapers, which they themselves must carry.

new culture area came to stretch from the Indus to the Atlantic and from the Mediterranean to the Sahara Desert. However, although the core has remained intact through the centuries, even though the capitals of the Islamic empire moved from city to city, the boundaries of the culture area have fluctuated. Spain was lost in the west, but in the east, Islam subsequently penetrated into the Balkans and deep into Asia. The further from the Arabian culture hearth the Islamic armies marched, time-distance decay lessened the impact of the Arab language. At the same time, the rise of sectarianism within Islam, notably in Mesopotamia and Persia (Iran), led to modifications in the unity of Islamic belief.

What this example suggests is that culture areas entail a certain degree of homogeneity, or uniformity, but a variety of causes may lead both to boundary modifications and to the formation of trait variations.

The *cultural landscape,* a somewhat more concrete phenomenon than culture area, pertains to human occupance or imprint within a territory, leading to what is termed a *culture region.* The cultural landscape, or the culture region, includes the components of culture—the mentifacts, sociofacts, and artifacts—that have found territorial expression. On the one hand, it may represent the visible or tangible evidence of human occupance and use. Yet the mere compilation of objects in the landscape may not necessarily add up to "cultural landscape." Only where the compilation is "marked by historical perspective and an understanding of cultural and natural processes" (English and Mayfield, 1972) does the "cultural landscape" truly come into focus.

The tangible facts of observation must be linked to the broader themes of human endeavor, for example, the role of fire in landscape change, the intrusion of humans into the life of plants and animals, the development of agricultural systems, settlement patterns and the rise of the city, the development of new forms of energy, transportation, and so on.

EPILOGUE

Although difficult to define, cultural geography can be seen to be a field whose ultimate goal is an understanding of the processes whereby cultures change, culture areas take shape, and cultural landscapes are formed. Central to these processes is the concept of spatial relationships and interactions, the means whereby innovations come into existence and are adopted and diffused over the surface of the earth from group to group and place to place.

Reflection on the way in which culture evolves, contributes to the formation of culture communities and areas, and leads to an imprint in the landscape offers the student the opportunity to understand better the origins and nature of his or her own culture.

At the same time, the cultural landscape has become for many geographers a reflection of values, echoing religious thought, perspectives on nature, and human attitudes in general. The works of landscape painters, of novelists and poets, and even of musicians, have been used in attempts to convey something more than is afforded by the tangible. Such cultural landscapes are aesthetic landscapes, and they owe much to individual perception.

APPLICATION OF IDEAS

1. The principal difference between humans and the other primates is the capacity of the former to create and transmit culture. Language is an important component of culture.

2. The biologic evolution of humanlike creatures occurred over millions of years. *Homo sapiens* in the form of Neanderthal man appeared about two hundred fifty thousand years ago, but there was no substantial change in the way of life until the development of cultivation about ten thousand years ago. Cultural evolution has taken place within a shorter time span—recorded history dating from about 3500 B.C. with the development of the city.

3. Civilization arose within a relatively short span of time in a number of centers in the Old World—widely scattered from the Nile Valley to China. Civilization did not emerge in the New World until several thousand years later, but even though New World civilizations bore strikingly similar features to those of the Old World, they differed in some important aspects.

4. One convenient classification of culture identifies three categories: mentifacts, artifacts, and sociofacts. Such a division enables us to examine differing cultures in an objective way.

5. Culture lag is an important concept that pertains to the ability of a community to adapt to changing circumstances. Adaptive communities are alert to possibilities of new ideas, inventions, or innovations to help them survive. The record of many past societies suggests that decline and fall have been associated with an inability to change.

6. Innovation is the process whereby a new item, an invention, comes into existence. Culture is built on a massive record of innovations, or inventions.

7. Innovation diffusion is the process whereby an item, an invention, or an idea, is disseminated or diffused over space. There are many differing types of spatial diffusion that have an impact on daily life.

8. Culture areas are important to an understanding of world patterns, but they are not permanent.

9. The cultural landscape is a more concrete concept than culture area; it pertains to, and is reflected in, human use of segments of earth space, or regions.

KEY WORDS AND PHRASES

absorbing barrier
adaptive capacity
Ameslan
artifact
australopithecines
Australopithecus
carnivorousness
cascade diffusion
civilization
collectivization
collectivize
contagious diffusion
Cro-Magnon man
cultural landscape
culture
culture area
culture change
culture hearth
culture lag
culture region
culture traits
culture transfers
diffusion
distance decay
domestication
expansion diffusion
genus
glaciation
hierarchic diffusion

hieroglyphic
hominid
hominization
Homo erectus
Homo sapiens neanderthalensis
Homo sapiens sapiens
innovation
innovation diffusion
innovation waves
mentifact
"miracle" wheat
Mousterian
natural selection
Neanderthal man
Neolithic period (New Stone Age)
Paleolithic period (Old Stone Age)
Peking man
permeable barrier
Pleistocene epoch
primates
relocation diffusion
sociofact
spatial interaction
time-distance decay
tundra

QUESTIONS FOR FURTHER DISCUSSION

1. What do you think the statement, "culture is the guardian of human activities on earth" implies? Do you agree? Is this an overstatement?

2. What is different about the cultures of urban Americans and bush natives of Amazonia? In what way will the culture of urban Americans ultimately transform the culture of bush natives? How long do you think it will take? What stresses and tensions do you think the bush natives will experience?

3. Why is language an important means of communicating culture? Are the messages being transmitted always received and accepted by the receiver? What problems might the receiver experience in understanding the communications?

4. Little is known of the motives that compelled early humans to paint pictures on the walls of remote recesses of caves. What do such pictures tell you about these people? What do you think was the impact on culture of the pictures?

5. Julian Huxley provided a convenient model for categorizing culture. How precise are the boundaries between the components of culture? How might you determine, say, the mentifacts of past ages?

6. Culture lag is an interesting concept because it helps us understand the failures of peoples to adapt to new circumstances. Is there danger that modern industrial societies might experience a culture lag should they fail to respond to the challenges posed by the limits of the earth's fossil fuels? Compare such a future society to the situation of the Ik.

7. Why have hunters and pastoralists resisted attempts to settle them in one place?

8. Is the process of spatial diffusion always or entirely a one-way street? What, if anything, might happen to a group that is in the process of disseminating new ideas or techniques to another group? What is the nature of the feedback? Does the spatial diffusion of new ideas or techniques necessarily contribute to general progress or advancement? Or can there be serious side effects?

9. What do scientists believe about the evolution of modern human beings? When did initial hominization take place? What does this mean? At what period can we say cultural evolution begins? When have the most significant changes occurred in the human diary?

REFERENCES AND ADDITIONAL READINGS

Bowden, Leonard M. *Diffusion of the Decision to Irrigate: Simulation of the Spread of a New Resource Management Practice in the Colorado Northern High Plains.* Research Paper No. 97. Department of Geography, University of Chicago, 1965.

Brown, Laurence A. "Diffusion Research in Geography. A Thematic Account." *Studies in the Diffusion of Innovation.* Discussion Paper No. 53. Department of Geography, Ohio State University, n.d. (a).

———. "The Innovation Diffusion Process in a Public Policy Context." *Studies in the Diffusion of Innovation.* Discussion Paper No. 58. Department of Geography, Ohio State University, n.d. (b).

Bronowski, Jacob. *The Ascent of Man.* Boston: Little, Brown, 1973.

Butzer, Karl W. "Environment, Culture and Human Evolution." *American Scientist* 65 No. 5 (1977): 572–584.

———. "Cultural Perspectives on Geographical Space," pp. 1–14. In *Dimensions of Human Geography. Essays on Some Familiar and Neglected Themes.* Karl W. Butzer, ed. Research Paper No. 186, Department of Geography, University of Chicago, 1978.

Cameron, R. "The Diffusion of Technology as a Problem in Economic History." *Economic Geography* 51 (1975): 217–230.

Cartwright, Frederick F. *Disease and History.* New York: Thomas Y. Crowell, 1972.

English, Paul Ward, and Mayfield, Robert C., eds. *Man, Space, and Environment: Concepts in Contemporary Human Geography.* New York: Oxford University Press, 1972.

Farb, Peter. *Humankind.* Boston: Houghton Mifflin, 1978.

Fischer, Jean-Claude, and Valy, Yvette G. *Fossils of All Ages.* New York: Grosset & Dunlap, 1978.

Gould, Peter R. *Spatial Diffusion.* Resource Paper No. 4, Commission on College Geography, Association of American Geographers, Washington, D.C., 1969.

Gould, Peter, and Tornquist, Gunner. "Information, Innovation and Acceptance." *Lund Studies in Geography.* Ser. B, No. 37 (1971): 148–168.

Hägerstrand, Torsten. "The Propagation of Innovation Waves." *Lund Studies in Geography,* Ser. B, No. 4 (1952): 1–20.

————. *Innovation Diffusion as a Spatial Process.* Chicago: University of Chicago Press, 1967. (Originally published in Sweden, 1953).

Haggett, Peter. *Geography: A Modern Synthesis,* 2nd ed. New York: Harper & Row, 1975.

Hall, Edward T. *The Silent Language.* Greenwich, Conn.: Fawcett, 1959.

Jordan, Terry C., and Rowntree, Lester. *The Human Mosaic. A Thematic Introduction to Cultural Geography,* 3rd ed. New York: Harper & Row, 1982.

Jung, Carl G. *Man and His Symbols.* New York: Doubleday, 1964.

Kariel, Herbert G., and Rosenvall, Lynn A. "United States News Flows to Canadian Newspapers." *American Review of Canadian Studies* 13 (Spring 1983): 44–65.

Leighly, John, ed. *Land and Life. A Selection from the Writings of Carl Ortwin Sauer.* Berkeley: University of California Press, 1963.

Morrill, Richard. "Migration and the Spread and Growth of Urban Settlement." *Lund Studies in Geography,* Ser. B, No. 26 (1965): 1–208.

Pfeiffer, John E. *The Emergence of Society. A Prehistory of The Establishment.* New York: McGraw-Hill, 1977.

Rogers, E. *Diffusion of Innovations,* 3rd ed. New York: The Free Press, 1983.

Rukang, William, and Shenglong, Lin. "Peking Man." *Scientific American* 248 (June 1983): 86–95.

Sauer, Carl O. "Plants, Animals and Man," pp. 34–61. In *Man and His Habitat.* R. H. Buchanan, Emrys Jones, et al., eds. London: Routledge & Kegan Paul, 1971.

Turnbull, Colin. *The Mountain People.* New York: Simon & Schuster, 1972.

Wagner, Philip L., and Mikesell, Marvin W. *Readings in Cultural Geography.* Chicago: University of Chicago Press, 1962.

3

Culture and Its Relationship to Nature

To start with, we are what our world invites us to be, and the basic features of our soul are impressed upon it by the form of its surroundings as in a mould. Naturally, for our life is no other than our relations with the world around.

José Ortega y Gasset, *The Revolt of the Masses,* 1932

Key Ideas

1. As a species *Homo sapiens* is part of the realm of nature. But humans are apart from nature in the sense that they are aware of their separateness and that they have a life unlike other animals.

2. When geographers have employed the term environment they meant primarily the physical setting. Today, it is convenient to think of the environment as follows: the potential environment, the effective or operational environment, and the perceptual or perceived environment.

3. Environmental attitudes reflect the legacy of the past, but attitudes alone do not determine how people will interact with their physical setting.

4. Modern geography traces its origins to the nineteenth century, particularly to the work of a number of German scholars, Karl Ritter, Alexander von Humboldt, and Friedrich Ratzel.

5. Publication of *On the Origin of Species* by Charles Darwin marks an important turning point in the history of science and of geographic thought.

6. In the United States, Ellen Churchill Semple and Ellsworth Huntington were early exponents of environmentalism.

7. In France, in particular, there was a strong reaction to the emphasis that geographers were placing on the role of the environment.

8. Nature today is accepted as a complex set of processes that dominate the natural world as studied by the whole array of natural scientists, that is, the biologist, botanist, meteorologist, and so on.

INTRODUCTION TO THE THEME OF ENVIRONMENTAL RELATIONSHIPS

Interest in the relationship between natural events and human experience is one that seems to be as old as recorded history. Ancient texts, for example, often make references to unusual earthly or celestial happenings, especially where the dimensions were such as to provoke great wonder or anxiety and fear. The Greeks, we know, became very much aware of their world and were impressed with the differences they saw both in *natural environments* and in the behavioral patterns of the peoples who inhabited them.

Although a curiosity about nature and the possible relationship between nature and culture pursued mankind through the ages, it was not until the middle of the nineteenth century that this theme became a focus of the emerging field of geography. And it remains a basic theme of modern geography, although the geographer's understanding of the role of nature, or the natural environment, in human affairs has undergone many shifts of emphasis.

This chapter is designed to review, in abstract manner, the way in which different broad culture groups might have viewed nature and the world around them; it also seeks to outline the evolution of the human-environment concept within the geographic literature.

In the manner in which people shape their world, it should be kept in mind that every generation tends to define its own problems in different ways. Every generation probably feels that its life has been oppressed and disturbed by mistakes inherited from past generations (John H. Storer cited in Detweiler et al., 1973). It is always easy to place the blame for misfortune on others, especially our forefathers. Yet we should always keep in mind that underlying the experience of every generation is a process involving a continuous change of ideas. Whatever mistakes past generations may have made, succeeding generations also benefit from the steady accumulation of knowledge and information as to how to live a better life.

The problems that the present generation faces differ from those of the past only in degree. To a large degree, these problems are rooted in culture and in the relationship between culture and nature. It is to this relationship that attention must be given.

A PART OF NATURE: APART FROM NATURE

Homo sapiens as a species *is part of* the realm of *nature*. This statement does not deny human uniqueness but testifies to the fact that, like other living creatures, people grow and mature, age and die (Fig. 3–1). On the other hand, our species *is also apart from* nature. Through the workings of the mind, humans are aware of themselves and of their separateness, and they are conscious of the fact that they have a life unlike other animals. Humankind alone is constantly enriched by experience that is turned into knowledge. People work consistently, too, with images for the human mind is endowed with imagination. People associated in groups and communities create symbols that they attempt to convey to others through language. This sharing of symbols forms the foundation of culture and culture groups.

The question of the relationship between culture and nature is one that has concerned thinkers since the earliest recorded times. It continues to intrigue geographers and other scientists today, especially because humans have seemingly gained an ascendancy over nature through the development of a complex technology. Yet the human race persists in behaving as it did before it gained the means to threaten its own existence by extensive destruction of the life-sustaining elements of the earth.

Figure 3–1

The Peaceable Kingdom by Edward Hicks (1780–1849) shows the harmonious state of man in nature. Some 80 versions of this work were painted by Hicks, an American Quaker.

(Courtesy of the Worcester Art Museum, Worcester, Massachusetts.)

In the years following World War II, geographers in the United States placed a growing emphasis on the study of the spatial patterns of human behavior, thereby neglecting not only the traditional branch of their discipline that dealt with the physical components of the earth's environment, but also the environmental question as a whole. During the past decade, however, there has been a rekindling of interest in the environment that has permitted geographers to join other scientists in the pursuit of solutions to environmental problems that concern us all. In doing so, geographers have taken a new look at how culture affects the habitat that humans are creating for themselves.

CULTURE AND ENVIRONMENT: AN INTERACTIVE PROCESS

Culture—the sum total of learned experience—is an essential attribute of humans. It is the characteristic that enables them to adapt to hot deserts and arctic tundras, to farm the soil and to live in cities, to travel in spaceships to the moon and to explore the ocean depths. At all times, there is an ongoing interactive process that relates people to the world around them.

The science of *ecology* (from the Greek *oikos*, meaning house, and *logos*, meaning thought) is the study of the relationships between plant and animal organisms and their physical environment. The term *ecosystem* was coined some forty years ago by a botanist, A. G. Tansley, to describe the situation where this complex network of relationships forms a functioning whole in nature.

Under the term *cultural ecology,* the geographer has long been interested in the interplay between the patterns of human activity and the environment in which they occur. In the past, however, when geographers used the term environment, they meant primarily the physical setting; today, it usually is given a wider meaning. We have come to think of environment as the sum total of all the forces within the world with which all life interacts. The *environment* has been defined as the aggregate of all the external conditions and influences affecting the life and development of an organism. In the case of humans, these external conditions—apart from the physical setting (which in any case has been modified through the centuries)—are the expanding cities, the social and political systems of society, and other objects and facets of human inventiveness, in short, cultural experience and creativity.

To grasp fully the circumstances and complexities of human behavior on earth, we have to consider this totality of environment and some other factors as well. These factors may be categorized as what man *is*—that is, humankind's physical, biologic, and mental endowments and humankind's aptitudes, talents, and drives.

In our study of humans, we must remain aware that they and their activity patterns are the consequence of a whole array of forces, or factors, of both culture and nature. We still have much to learn about the intricacies, both biologic and nonbiologic, of the human-environment relationship, particularly as this relationship has changed or developed through time. We believe that all people are created equal, but appearances tell us that no two are made exactly alike. There is variety as well in individual behavior patterns. It is clear that

with each step we take toward understanding people, we find that the horizon expands and that there is more than we need to know.

In any given study of human-environment relations, the analysis will undoubtedly give more weight to some factors, less to others, and ignore still others. Necessity compels selectivity, whereas the selection itself reflects the interest and training of the analyst who is also part of the relationship. The scale or level of generalization of a study influences selectivity as well. It is possible to study the environment of a given individual, of a given population, or of a given community and in each case the concept of the environment may differ.

TYPES OF ENVIRONMENT

Because of some of the difficulties mentioned above, it seems more convenient and useful to think not in terms of the physical or nonphysical environment, but rather of types of environment that cut somewhat differently across human experience and performance. These may be designated the *potential environment,* the *effective* (or *operational*) *environment,* and the *perceptual* (or *perceived*) *environment* (Fig. 3–2).

The potential environment may be defined as all the components of the environment (both physical and cultural) that are "real" to people as well as those of which they are not aware together with the biologic heritage that affects human existence and behavior.

The effective or operational environment consists of those components that have a direct or recognizable bearing on human activities or situations. Modern American urban dwellers, for example, function under an array of environmental components—such as high-rise office buildings, supermarkets, automobile congestion, polluted air, and social, legal, and political constraints—that affect their behavior

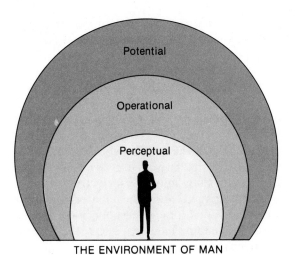

Potential

Operational

Perceptual

THE ENVIRONMENT OF MAN

Figure 3–2

Geographers have offered many different schemes to classify humankind's environment, and the distinctions between these environments are not easy to define. According to J. Sonnenfeld, the whole environment that is external to man is seen as the geographic environment (Sonnenfeld, 1972). (In the diagram this is shown as the potential environment.) This geographic environment includes the sum total of the components of the environment, physical as well as cultural, known and unknown to man. Within this larger framework is the operational environment in which man operates (and of which he is not always fully aware). The perceptual environment falls within this sphere and represents a still more restricted environment, one based on learning and experience. (Sonnenfeld recognizes a still narrower environment, not shown here—a behavioral environment derived largely from individual behavioral patterns.)

patterns. These components are very different from those that prevail in a Bangladesh village. Moreover, a different sociocultural heritage and different living conditions will cause Americans to view or perceive the world in a way that is foreign to the Bangli. Thus, each group has a unique perceived environment that is reflected in differing responses. A young Bangli girl who marries at 10 will recognize that she must bear as many male children as possible to help sustain her should her husband die and leave her a widow because in traditional Muslim society women do not work. Such a problem is alien to the Americans' perceptual field.

This introductory study attempts to survey human attitudes and activity patterns on earth largely in terms of the operational and perceptual environments of mankind.

THE IMAGERY OF NATURE

The Shaping of Environmental Attitudes

Modern living patterns change so rapidly for the members of a highly industrialized society that people very quickly tend to forget their roots. Manners and customs handed down from generations that lived on the soil often seem incomprehensible and irrelevant to contemporary men and women. Yet these origins are not totally forgotten, even though we may not see clearly the meaning of residual symbols.

Such is the case with many of our views of nature. We need to be aware of the historical legacy of these views because the bits and pieces that have come down to us, although far from intact or consistent, have contributed to the shaping of the variations in attitudes toward the natural environment that different culture groups exhibit today. Contemporary Americans have been called "the children of the *Enlightenment*," meaning that they are the products of the intellectual revolution of the seventeenth and eighteenth centuries and that they are heirs to the belief in progress and to the notions of man and nature that were advanced during those centuries. Because progress has come to mean the material advance that is associated with economic growth and economic growth is a product of cultural interaction with natural support systems, then it is important to understand how we and others view nature and how those views have been altered.

Attitudes alone, of course, do not determine the way people will interact with the natural environment. Groups whose beliefs would have them treat the world as a sacred place may still turn their surroundings into a wasteland. Good intentions alone are not sufficient; they must be fortified with accurate knowledge of the ecosystem and of nature and its realm. Some understanding of the human record should help as well.

Early Mythmaking

Knowledge of the human species and of the earth as human's habitat is of very recent origin. Prehistoric people had little basis for an objective understanding of either complex phenomenon. Their movements over the land were restricted to distances they could wander on foot. The seas stretched off into the vast unknown, and in any case, most navigators did not dare venture far from the shore. From archeology, we know that from about forty thousand years ago, people whose body appearance and physiology were much like that of modern humans spread over the earth, later forming communities that became fixed settlements, cities, city-states, and empires; but until nearly a thousand years after the birth of Christ, it is likely that no single individual had ever seen more than a tiny segment of the earth's surface. Neither were the general wanderings recorded nor fully comprehended in relationship to other earth events or human activities.

In spite of these limited horizons, humans possessed a curiosity that often compelled them to think beyond the observable and to wonder about the universe and their place in it. Unable to interpret phenomena in terms of disciplined thought, such as history and geography, humans invented fantasies, myths, and legends to satisfy their thirst for understanding. Such imaginings were fanciful and often complex, as they are among many geographically isolated, nonindustrial peoples today. But these world views served—and continue to serve—as a means whereby individuals or the group could find meaning and direction in daily activities and in societal relationships.

Perhaps more than any other phenomena, the rhythms of nature reflected in the sequence of seasons, the rise and fall of the waters of the river, and the position of the sun and the moon in the heavens arrested human attention.

Because survival often depended on the regularity of nature, this interest is not surprising. For eons of time, prehistoric man was a hunter-gatherer, relying on edible roots and plants or on the hunt for food. When livestock raising developed in various parts of the Old World, the herdsman needed succulent grasses to nourish his flocks. In areas where cultivation became regularized, the availability of water and a knowledge of when to sow and when to reap were important in staving off the anxiety and fear that must have been a characteristic of life in many communities. Widely disseminated throughout early Middle Eastern civilizations are the tales of the marriage of heaven and earth, which sent rain to fertilize the soil; and from the rise and fall of the Nile in Egypt came the earliest agricultural calendrical observances.

Except for local hills, tablelands, or mountains that were seen to rise above the lowlands and valleys, common experience indicated that the earth was flat. A spear thrown at a fleet-footed deer was seen to curve downward, but the reason was entirely unknown. If one ventured from familiar places into the vastness beyond, common sense warned that there would be no return, for out beyond was the edge of the earth. The earth, too, in larger perspective, seemed to be at the center of everything, for was it not the solid platform about which the sun, the moon, and the stars could be seen to move?

The World Views of the Hunter

To the members of a culture based on hunting, all the phenomena in the world around seemed alive. That is how a Pitt River Indian in northeastern California contrasted his attitudes with those of Anglo-Americans: "White people think everything is dead" (Shepard, 1967). Because of a devotion to scientific inquiry, modern man finds it difficult to appreciate this relationship that hunting peoples have felt for their world or to see any value in it that can still be applied to life today. The hunter saw the natural world as sharing human qualities (a belief known as *animism*) and consequently treated natural phenomena as sacred events or objects of respect or worship. Such an attitude was widespread and dominant in prehistoric times and survived into historical times in the Mediterranean world, in South and East Asia, and among native Americans. Harvey Cox (1966), in *The Secular City*, has attempted to describe the rootedness of the hunter—whom he calls *presecular man*—in nature:

> Presecular man lives in an enchanted forest, its glens and groves swarm with spirits. Its rocks and streams are alive with friendly or fiendish demons. Reality is charged with magical power that erupts here and there to threaten or benefit man. Properly managed and utilized, this invisible energy can be supplicated, warded off, or channelled. If real skill and esoteric knowledge are called into play, the energies of the unseen world can be used against a family foe or an enemy of the tribe. (p. 19)

The hunter found a powerful weapon in *magic*. It helped the individual or the tribe to rely on innate strength to meet the difficulties and dangers of the hunt, but it was more than that. The use of arts, charms, or incantations allowed the hunter to believe that humans could affect the course of events in the way they desired. Through the use of magic, moreover, the hunter related to the larger world. It was, indeed, the hunter's way of expressing beliefs about the larger cosmos and in a reliable established order of nature that could be manipulated for the benefit of the tribe.

The phenomenon of *totemism* made it possible for the hunter to incorporate the creatures of the natural world into tribal territory and life. The hunter endowed innumerable beings with

significance and a place in nature. In this way, there seemed to be an organic unity to the landscape. But as Diamond Jenness, the Canadian anthropologist who has studied the beliefs of the Ojibwa people of northern Ontario, has pointed out (cited in Levi-Strauss, 1970):

> To call these beings supernatural slightly misinterprets the Indians' conception. They are a part of the natural order of the universe no less than man himself, whom they resemble in the possession of intelligence and emotions. Like man, too, they are male or female, and in some cases at least may even have families of their own. Some are tied down to definite localities, some move from place to place at will; some are friendly to Indians, others hostile. (p. 37)

Some of the most dramatic examples of this aspect of tribal life may be found among the natives of the Pacific Northwest Coast of North America. These peoples, most notably the Haida Indians of the Queen Charlotte Islands, were skilled carpenters, boat builders, and carvers, but these skills tended to be suppressed after European contact (Box 3–1) (Figs. 3–3A, 3–3B).

As far as modern man is concerned, magic and totemism were based on an erroneous concept of how natural forces in the universe operate. The different way that hunting groups perceived that natural world is difficult for industrial society to comprehend fully.

Cultivation Transforms Perspectives

As cultivation of the soil developed in various parts of Asia some eight to ten thousand years ago, important variations in the way nature was viewed took place. Because farmers relied on their planted crops for food, the earth's fertility became of primary importance. Thus, group rituals and ceremonies came into existence for the purpose of stimulating fertility. The feminine principle in nature was identified and emphasized; earth became the Great Mother—hence, Mother Nature—and sacrifices to her were believed to help ensure a bountiful harvest. The

BOX 3–1

Magic and Totemism Among The Native Americans of the Northwest Pacific Coast of Canada

Before the arrival of Europeans, the native tribes of the Pacific Northwest Coast of Canada lived in village communities that usually faced the sea. The first impression that one would have had on approaching by boat was of a mass of poles, richly decorated, rising above a series of wooden structures. The latter were known as longhouses to the Salish tribes and as big-houses to other tribes along the coast. These houses were massive, multifamily dwellings. They ranged from 30 feet in width to about 100 feet in length and rose to some 40 feet in height. Massive posts and frames cut out of cedar supported the sloping plank roof and walls. Many of these posts were carved or painted as was the door in front, which provided access to the dark interior of the house.

On the poles that towered above the dwellings, the totems of the owner and his wives were carved and painted, often in brilliant hues of black, red, and blue-green. Birds or animals representing supernatural spirits were carved as family totems, or crests; they served to indicate the close relationship that the family or clan had with these spirits. The totem was the means whereby this relationship could be identified. At the same time, it was a way of proclaiming the status within the tribe of the family that owned it. In this meaningful way, each pole reminded the family of the mysterious power possessed by the spirits thus represented, but at the same time, it served to assuage anxiety and promote collective harmony. Some villages boasted more than sixty of these monumental carvings.

None of the longhouses survives today. Thanks to the efforts of Christian missionaries, many of the poles were cut down and burnt; to the Christian mind, they suggested paganism. Other poles were stored in museums. After a period of government prohibition, totem carving is once again permitted, and the art is being recaptured.

Figure 3–3A

The totems shown were found on Vancouver Island, British Columbia; they combine both animal and human features. Standing outside the dwellings of the village, the handsomely carved poles linked families to their community and to nature and were representative of the cosmology of the Haida.

(Photo by George Thornton Emmons, 1910. Courtesy Photography Collection, University of Washington Libraries.)

Figure 3–3 B
Skidigate beaver pole was printed on canvas by Emily Carr (1871–1945) about 1942. A Canadian artist, Carr spent much of her artistic career capturing in oils the life and lore of Canada's Pacific Northwest Coast Indians. The intensity with which she experienced the tall Pacific forests and awe-inspiring totems is clearly revealed through strong color and broad dramatic brush strokes.

(Courtesy of the Vancouver Art Gallery, Vancouver, British Columbia.)

masculine principle was represented by vegetation, which, following the seasons, flourished in summer and died in winter, to be awakened again in the spring. The cult of the Great Mother and her dying and reviving partner became the basis of many Middle Eastern religions. With regional variations, the concepts of female and male in nature were worshipped under the names of Ishtar and Tammuz in Mesopotamia, Isis and Osiris in Egypt, and Astarte and Adonis in Syria and Palestine. In classical Greece, dying vegetation was represented by a female (Box 3–2).

Although the origins are ancient, the folk beliefs of many Hindu villagers in modern India include the worship of Mother Earth, a great goddess whose marriage with other gods (depending on the locality) is celebrated in festivals and religious observance. Reverence for all forms of life is part of these beliefs. This not only contributes to the worship of fertility, but also to the population problem with its dire pressures on India's farmland and resources.

The Coming of Urban Civilization

With the appearance of cities in Mesopotamia and Egypt some time in the fourth millenium B.C., humankind's view of the natural forces in life tended to expand, whereas the gods, whose original identity lay in natural or cosmic phenomena, took on identities that divorced them from their source. Somewhat later in classical Greece, the gods assumed attributes that were essentially human, showing a capacity for love and hate, jealousy and revenge.

The word *civilization* is derived from the Latin *civis,* meaning civil. A civilian or civilized person was a citizen, one who lived in a city (Fig. 3–4). The growth in population of urban centers brought into existence new institutions designed to allow society to regulate itself, to organize the use of the land, and to carry on warfare. With these changes, often came a priest-king. He assumed responsibility for communicating with the gods, often being considered as a god himself or as descended from a god. In Egypt, the pharaoh was regarded as the son of Ra, the sun god, and the prevailing belief was that after death his existence would continue at another level. For this reason, giant pyramids were built on the banks of the Nile to house the dead and form a link between present and future. After elaborate embalming, the pharaoh was buried with his possessions and retainers for use in the next life.

At the heart of some of the early urban communities in Mesopotamia, there was often a structure—like the skyscraper in the modern metropolis—that reflected humankind's determination to leave a mark on the landscape. In Mesopotamia such a structure was known as a *ziggurat,* a structure that reminds one of the biblical Tower of Babel. At the top of the ziggurat was a shrine, and from that high point, humans could examine the heavens and determine seasonal or astrological guidelines for farming and other activities (Fig. 3–5).

The Orient, Harmony with Nature

Perhaps because of the geniality of the environment—luxuriant forests and a wide variety of plants, a productive soil, and a strikingly impressive interplay of upland and valley morphology—the Chinese were infused with a deep sense of their relationship to nature from earliest times. They believed that all natural phenomena had emerged from the bowels of the earth and, therefore, they tended to worship natural objects.

The Chinese ruler, unlike the priest-king of Mesopotamia and the pharaoh of Egypt, was not a divinity, but after his death, he did become an object of worship, and sacrifices were offered to his departed spirit. Royal tombs, like those near the ancient city of Hsian (Xien), were elaborate affairs.

Many early rites and beliefs were systematized into the moral or ethical code of *Confucianism* in the fifth century B.C., but *Taoism,* which originated somewhat earlier, afforded the Chinese a mystical view of nature unknown in the Mediterranean basin. Taoist beliefs urged people to adapt their daily lives around the patterns observed in nature, in a kind of surrender to forces beyond human control.

Confucian goals were equally lofty, but the mystical component was almost totally absent.

BOX 3–2
Mythology and Geography in Ancient Egypt and Greece

The Egyptian god Osiris was especially symbolic of the region's geography. Initially a nature god, Osiris was a vegetation spirit that died and was reborn, a cycle that was unending. As such a spirit, he represented the grain, the vines, and the trees. However, he was more than that. He was also the Nile, which rose and fell each year, and he was the rays of the sun that faded at dusk over the desert in the west to reappear more brilliantly at dawn in the east. The juxtaposition of *arable* or farmland and desert in Egypt was also symbolized in the struggle between Osiris and his jealous brother Set, who represented the desert, dessicating winds, and darkness.

Osiris was wed to his own sister, Isis, whose fertile lands were annually made productive by the flooding of the river. It was she who helped spread the agricultural culture by teaching women to grind grain, spin flax, and weave cloth. In spring and autumn, great festivals were held in Egypt in honor of Isis, many of which survived right up to the Christian era.

In classical Greece, the notion of fertility reappears in the tale of Demeter and her daughter Persephone. Carried off to the underworld by Pluto, Lord of the Dead, Persephone leaves Demeter to grieve at the loss of her daughter. Demeter in her sorrow permits nothing to grow in the earth's parched and crumbling soil. Zeus, the supreme god of the Greeks, becomes afraid that humans might starve and, so, compels Pluto to restore Persephone to her mother for at least two thirds of the year. When Persephone returns, the Greek landscape turns green as grain begins to grow, reflecting Demeters's joy. However, when Persephone returns to the underworld, the vegetation again withers, symbolizing the onset of winter. To the Greeks, the two goddesses personified grain, and at Eleusis near Athens, secret rituals were carried out on their behalf.

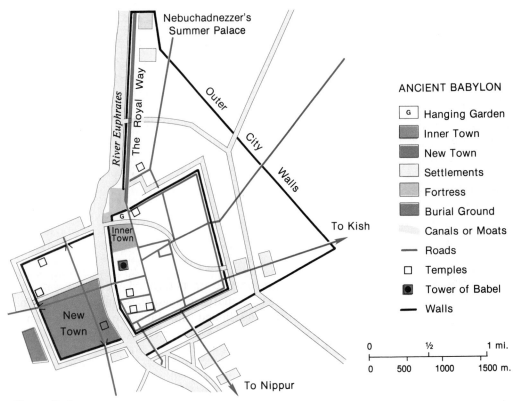

ANCIENT BABYLON

- G Hanging Garden
- Inner Town
- New Town
- Settlements
- Fortress
- Burial Ground
- Canals or Moats
- — Roads
- □ Temples
- ◉ Tower of Babel
- ━ Walls

Figure 3–4

The site of Babylon, about 55 miles south of Baghdad, dates back to the fourth millenium B.C. Like most ancient Mesopotamian cities, Babylon was built of dried clay bricks which, over centuries, have been reduced through erosion to mounds of dirt. Entrance into the city was via the Ishtar Gate, which opened into a boulevard known as the Royal Way, through which passed all the great processions of the time. The Royal Way paralleled the Euphrates river, allowing visitors to reach the city by boat. The shift in the course of the Euphrates to the west away from the Royal Way was one of the causes of the decline of Babylon.

(From Oates, 1979, p. 148)

Confucius advocated the establishment of a government of superior men whose cultivated minds would result in behavior patterns that showed concern for others and, at the same time, were ritually correct. Through the practice of such rites, men's spirits would be joined. This, in turn, would lead to harmonious relations among all humankind. Correct behavior, according to Confucius, would contribute to world harmony.

Mencius, or Meng-tzu (371?–?289 B.C.), who was the second sage of China after Confucius, amplified the teachings of the master (Dobson, 1963). Mencius continued to assert high principles of government, but he also advocated the conservation of resources. Mencius pointed out, "The people are the most important element in a nation; the spirits of the land and the grain come next; the sovereign counts for the least."

Figure 3-5

The ziggurat, a temple tower, seems to have been a common feature of the early cities of Mesopotamia. In Assyrian, the word was *ziggurratu*, from *saqaru*, meaning to build high. The temple tower of Babylon reminds one of the biblical Tower of Babel described in the Old Testament.

(*Picture Credit:* Georg Gerster/Rapho/Photo Researchers, Inc.)

Despite a unique sensitivity to landscape beauty and a somewhat passivist nature philosophy, early Chinese civilization, nevertheless, quickly developed the technical skills to subject the environment to significant modification. The kind of rational inquiry into nature that took place among the peoples of the eastern

Mediterranean, however, was little known to the Far East.

Japanese feelings about nature were not too dissimilar from the Chinese, but this is not surprising because in many respects early Japanese culture was a historical offspring of the Chinese. The first major cultural infusion from the mainland came during the T'ang dynasty (A.D. 618–906) in China, when the Chinese conception of nature was still in a formative stage. The Japanese way of life during that period was centered around a vague collection of beliefs that, above all, recognized humans as an integral part of nature. *Homo sapiens* was so much a part of the environment that there was no word in Japanese for nature.

In short, much of the traditional Japanese perspective on nature was really an intuitive feeling that pervaded the entire society. This feeling linked the Japanese with the world around them and made them aware of it. Belief in spirits together with imported concepts of harmony with nature as espoused by the Taoists remained a component of Japanese thinking down to the impact of the West. Indeed, although industrialization has forced significant modifications in Japanese thought, a residue of primitive folk beliefs probably remains in the makeup of the Japanese to this day.

Greek Speculative Philosophy

The development of objective inquiry in the Greek world in the sixth century B.C. was remarkable, especially if contrasted with the speculative philosophy of the rest of the known world (Parkes, 1959). Many of the notions about the earth and the universe that had been passed down from generation to generation began to be questioned. The motive was simple curiosity. The concepts these Greek thinkers developed were not necessarily new; the Egyptians and the Babylonians had already accumulated a considerable amount of knowledge of the universe. With their extraordinary curiosity, however, the Greeks wanted to understand in a systematic way why things happened the way they did. To pursue this goal they first had to divest themselves of many of the traditional mythologies. In all early civilizations, what we call astronomy went hand in hand with astrology, superstition, myth, and primitive forms of religion. What was unique about the Greek questioning was that it represented the first attempt in human history to explain observable phenomena in terms of uniform naturalistic laws of causation.

This line of thinking began with Thales (634?–?546 B.C.) of Miletus, a Greek city on the coast of Asia Minor south of the site of Troy. The setting was right for speculative thought which was, as Aristotle (384–322 B.C.) pointed out several centuries later, the product of an age already provided with the necessities for well-being and leisure.

These Greek thinkers from the sixth century B.C. onward had an invaluable scientific tool in geometry, which they developed into a useful intellectual instrument. It is not clear whether Thales and his immediate disciples conceived of the earth as anything other than a cylinder. They did, however, believe it to be in motion, although they could offer no explanation of the fact. By about 540 B.C., Pythagoras was able to maintain that the earth was spherical, a concept subsequently confirmed by Aristotle, who observed that the shadow cast by the earth during lunar eclipses is always circular (Box 3–3).

The Greeks believed that the entire universe, the whole realm of nature, behaved in an orderly way, thus, they also came to believe that man was part of this orderly totality. Although all men were shaped from the same mold, the Greeks recognized that human motivations varied. These differences, they believed, were due to the influence of the natural environment (Box 3–4).

The Medieval World View

Differences between peoples of the kind that caught the attention of the ancient Greeks did

---

BOX 3–3

The Experiment of Eratosthenes of Alexandria

A deep, dry well and a keen eye brought about one of the most remarkable discoveries in the third century B.C. The eye was that of a North African Greek, named Eratosthenes (275?–?194 B.C.), who became head of the library in the city of Alexandria, the impressive port built by Alexander the Great near the mouth of the Nile. Eratosthenes was an inquisitive man. He was aware that the angle at which the sun's rays hit the earth varies from place to place. In Syene (now Aswan), an Egyptian upriver town some 5000 *stadia* (500 miles) south of Alexandria, the sun's rays at noon on the day of the summer solstice (June 21) were observed to shine directly down a well shaft to light up the bottom. On the same date at noon in Alexandria, Eratosthenes knew that the sun was not directly overhead, for the sun's rays cast a shadow. Using a simple geometric calculation, Eratosthenes was able to show that the difference in angle of the sun's rays between Syene and Alexandria was about one fiftieth of a circle. Multiplying 5000 *stadia* by 50, Eratosthenes advanced the first recorded close approximation of the earth's circumference—250,000 *stadia* or about 25,000 miles. (The modern measure of the circumference of the earth at the equator is 24,902 miles and the mean diameter is 7917 miles.) Although this was an outstanding achievement, Eratosthenes's calculations were subsequently ignored, forgotten, or lost. When Columbus set out for the Indies, he knew, as did all master seafarers of the medieval period, that the earth was round, but he had no idea how large it was.

BOX 3-4

**Preservation of Ancient
Views on the Relationship of
Peoples and Their
Environments**

Near the end of his work on *Politics,* Aristotle drew some remarkable conclusions about the relationship between climate, people, and political organization. He wrote:

> Those who live in a cold climate and in Europe are full of spirit, but wanting in intelligence and skill; and therefore they retain comparative freedom, but have no political organization and are incapable of ruling over others. Whereas the natives of Asia are intelligent and inventive, but they are wanting in spirit, and therefore they are always in a state of subjection and slavery. But the Hellenic race (i.e., the Greeks), which is situated between them, is likewise intermediate in character, being high spirited and also intelligent. (p. 271)

The writings of Aristotle together with those of other ancient Greek thinkers were among the first Greek texts to be translated into Arabic over a thousand years later. In this way, classical notions of the influence of the physical environment on human behavior found their way into texts of early medieval Arab geographers. Ibn-Khaldun (1332–1406), born of an Arab family that had migrated from Muslim Spain to Tunis, was one who wrote of the influence of climate on society and institutions.

These early notions of a cause-and-effect relationship between the physical environment and human behavior may strike us as simplistic today. However, when Europe "discovered" the classics during the Renaissance, Greek ideas were revived and later contributed to geographic thought in Europe and America in the nineteenth century. It was during the Renaissance, too, that the works of Ibn-Khaldun became known to Europeans.

not interest medieval European Christendom. Speculation about the universe or the natural environment was not encouraged. Ironically, the views of Aristotle and Ptolemy were accepted by the church and any attempt to question them was seen as heresy. Aristotle, in particular, had become almost a Christian saint. His notions of a hierarchically structured earth-centered universe were widely accepted among Christian theologians. However, it was not so much from Aristotle that the Church's *cosmogony,* or view of the universe, was derived, but rather from the Alexandrian, Ptolemy (Claudius Ptolemaeus) (Fig. 3–6).

Ptolemy (A.D. 73?–?151) developed earlier Greek ideas about the universe into a unified system through his great work, the *Almagest.* According to the *Ptolemaic system,* the earth was the fixed center of the universe about which the heavenly or celestial bodies revolved in concentric circles, each turning on its own axis. On the perimeter of the universe, in the eighth and last sphere, were the fixed stars set like diamonds in a tiara. The fixed orderliness of this geocentric system fitted the structure of feudal society very well (Chenu, 1968). "There was a place for everything (and everyone) and everything (and everyone) was in its place" might have been taken as a motto of the medieval church. As Arnold, the twelfth-century abbot of Bonneval (near Chartres) in France, pointed out:

> God distributed the things of nature like the members of a great body, assigning to all their proper places and names, their fitting measures and offices. Nothing is confused in God, and nothing was without form in primordial antiquity; for physical material, as soon as it was made, was forthwith cast into such species as suited it. (Chenu, 1968, p. 9)

In addition to accepting the universe as a closed and unchanging system, the church also regarded it as having been created, once and for all, in perfection (Fig. 3–7). The chronology of Creation as outlined in Genesis in the Old Testament was accepted as essentially a true and

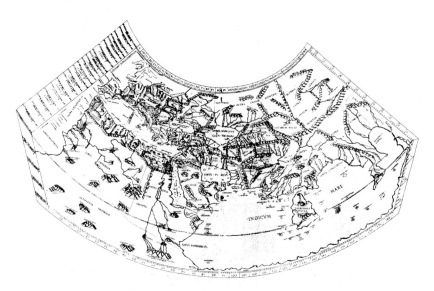

Figure 3–6

Ptolemy's explanation of the movement of the celestial bodies remained for fourteen centuries the basis of astronomy and of church teaching. His principal scientific work, *Great System of Astronomy* (more commonly known as *Almagest*), comprised 13 volumes. The *Almagest,* written initially in Greek, was subsequently translated into Arabic in the ninth century and from Arabic into Latin in the twelfth and thirteenth centuries. It was not until the fifteenth century that European scholars returned to the original Greek.

Ptolemy was also deeply interested in geography, and he provided the basis for the modern system of latitude and longitude. The Ptolemaic map displays an incredible amount of geographic knowledge, although Ptolemy's view of the world—from our vantage point— was considerably distorted. The Mediterranean world is sharply outlined, as is the Black Sea. Africa beyond the coastal region remains an unknown quantity, as does the configuration of India and East Asia beyond.

(From *Claudius Ptolemaeus Cosmographica.* Rome: 1478. [Amsterdam: Theatrum Orbis Terrarum, 1966. Fac. Newberry Library copy, 1937.] Courtesy Rare Book Collection, University of Washington Libraries.)

literal history of the origins of the world. It even came to be believed that Creation had occurred about 4000 B.C. and that there had been little change in the earth since the beginning, or at least since the Flood. The medieval perception of the realm of nature embraced all physical, observable phenomena plus the world of spirit, which included angels as well as souls. Nature, therefore, was not usually contrasted with the affairs of mankind, but rather with the *supra-natural* (i.e., above nature), in terms of what happens naturally as opposed to what happens as a result of divine intervention in human history. It was believed that God was pleased with his creation but that nature, like man, who has been expelled from paradise, was not perfect; in time, as God's plan unfolded, nature would be transformed into its ideal state (Box 3–5).

Christianity derived much of its basic nature ethic from Judaism. The Old Testament had depicted nature as a lower order of creation, given as a trust to mankind with accountability to God. Moreover, God manifested Himself to man through physical or natural phenomena:

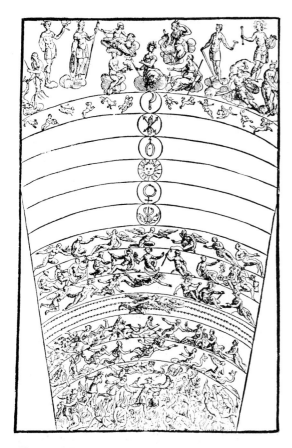

Figure 3–7

Mythology and a belief in the earth as the astronomical center of the universe combined to create an image that, although modified by Christian theology, remained meaningful to European minds until the sixteenth century. At the core of the scheme was the fiery sphere of Hades, beyond which were the spheres of water, earth, and air. Above these were the heavens of the moon, followed by the planets of Mercury, Venus, the sun, Mars, Jupiter, and Saturn. The latter planet was believed to contain the symbols of the zodiac. Above Saturn or the arch of the heavens was the dwelling place of the different powers—six male gods and six female godesses—that controlled the universe.

(From Manley P. Hall, *An Encyclopedic Outline of Masonic, Hermetic, Quabbalistic and Rosicrucian Symbolical Philosophy.* [San Francisco: 1928.] Courtesy Rare Book Collection, University of Washington Libraries.)

the "voice" of God was heard in thunder, the "hand" of God was felt in pestilence, and so on. This biblical view of nature, however, was much modified by the early medieval period in Europe. The concept of the imperfection of nature had been transformed into the notion that untamed nature was possessed of evil and, where it was not ignored, had to be overcome.

The Renaissance and the Rise of Modern Science

Because of the church's power in medieval Europe, it took great courage to challenge ecclesiastical authority. However, in the latter part of the fifteenth century, about the time Columbus set out for the Indies, there was a man who was preparing to do just that. Born in 1473 in Torun on the Vistula River, in what is now Poland, Nicolaus Copernicus (d. 1543) studied at the famous medieval universities of Cracow and Bologna (Fig. 3–8). Then, through the assistance of an uncle, he became a canon of the church. His real interest, however, lay in the workings of the universe. In his great work *De revolutionibus orbium coelestium* (*On the Revolutions of the Celestial Bodies*), he challenged the accepted foundations of heaven and earth (Bronowski, 1973).

First, Copernicus contended that the universe is not geocentric: the earth (and, thus, by inference, man) does not lie at the center of the universe. Like other heavenly bodies (Copernicus did not call them planets), the earth revolves around the sun, making one annual orbit as it rotates on its axis. Copernicus also concluded that the universe is far larger than generally had been believed. Al-Farghani, a ninth-century Arab astronomer, had provided a set of calculations that gave the distance from the earth to the farthest reaches of the universe at about 65 million miles, and calculations such as these survived until Copernicus's time. Today, we know that the earth is even farther than that from the sun. Indeed, the length of time that it would take to reach the star nearest to earth,

BOX 3–5

"In the beginning God created the heavens and the earth"

The Genesis account of the origins of the earth and of mankind, according to many Christian biblical scholars, contains several variants (compare Gen. 1:1–2:4a and 2:4b–3:24) but remains, in any case, divinely inspired. In Gen. 1:1–2:4a, God creates the earth, night and day, all creatures, and finally mankind. Mankind is created in the image of God, is blessed, and enjoined to "be fruitful, multiply, fill the earth and conquer it." God is pleased with his work and rests on the seventh day.

In the following variant, the paradise account (Gen. 2:5–3:24), God creates a garden into which he places man. Seeing that it is not good for man to be alone, he fashions woman. In this account, too, man participates in the giving of meaning to the world around because God brings the animals and birds to man "to see what he would call them." Thus, in a very symbolic way, man takes part in the act of creation. However, because both man and woman violate God's injunction by eating of the fruit of the tree of the knowledge of good and evil that stands in the middle of the garden—a deed God has expressly forbidden—they are driven from the garden, and a curse is placed on the serpent that encouraged the eating of the fruit as well as on the soil that nourished the tree.

Somewhat later, in Gen. 6:5–13, God becomes aware of the extent of human wickedness on the earth, regrets having made mankind, and sees that even the animals, the reptiles, and the birds of heaven have been corrupted. God sends a flood upon the earth, but one good man (Noah) and his family together with representatives of all other living things are preserved. When the waters recede, Noah's ark comes to rest, it is emptied, and all living things are enjoined to be fruitful and multiply on the earth. God establishes a covenant with mankind wherein he promises never again to destroy all living creatures. However, he makes man morally responsible for his fellow man and for the sanctity of human life.

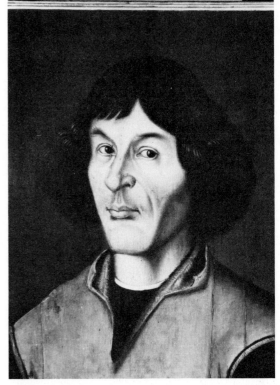

NICOLAVS COPERNICVS.

Figure 3–8

The Renaissance produced men of great versatility, such as Leonardo da Vinci (1452–1519) and the scientist Copernicus. Like other Renaissance men, Nicolaus Copernicus derived many ideas from ancient Greek texts, including the notion that the earth possibly was in motion. (This copy of his portrait hangs in the town hall at Torun, Poland, his place of birth.) What Copernicus contributed to Western civilization was a new image of the world, a new view of the cosmos that shook the very foundations of church-dominated Western Europe, which clung to the Ptolemaic version. His contemporary, Martin Luther (1483–1546), derided the findings of Copernicus by saying that Copernicus wanted to prove that the Earth goes around the Sun and the Moon as if someone sitting in a moving wagon or ship were to suppose that his vehicle were at rest and the Earth and the trees were moving past him.

(*Source:* Polish Agency Interpress Photoservice)

which is four light-years away, would be equivalent to more than the whole of our written history, perhaps even as long a time as the whole existence of *Homo sapiens* on earth. (And then there is the time it would take to return to earth!)

Although Copernicus's ideas had an influence on the subsequent development of science, they initially met with substantial opposition. To the church these ideas were, indeed, heresy. Still, as years passed, the revolt against the Ptolemaic earth-centered system gained momentum, chiefly in the work of Galileo Galilei (1564–1642) (Fig. 3–9). His *Dialogue Concerning the Two Great Systems of the World* was published in Italian in 1632. In the *Dialogue,* he discussed the two quite different images of the universe, or cosmogonies: the geocentric, put forth by Ptolemy, and the heliocentric, proposed by Copernicus. Although Galileo tried to be objective in his presentation, he did not fool the church; he was brought before the Inquisition and forced to recant. Galileo dealt another crushing blow to the orthodox view when his 30-power telescope led to the discovery of Jupiter's satellites and spots on the sun. In the Ptolemaic system, the heavenly or celestial bodies were supposed to be spotless, eternal, and perfect (Fig. 3–10).

Following the work of Johannes Kepler (1571–1630), a scientific theory concerning the origins of the earth replaced the concept of a created, fixed, and static cosmos. For the first time, the concept of evolution was applied to the universe, and Kepler's laws became the basis of modern astronomy. In the centuries that followed, the concept of evolution would be applied to the geologic history of the earth, to living organisms, and then, within the past century, to man himself.

Because of Copernicus, Galileo, and others, the notion of the universe as closed and finite was destroyed. This revolution led to the development of new perspectives on nature and on human dignity as well. The Renaissance, which flowered first in the Italian city-states, stimu-

Figure 3–9

Galileo, who was born in Italy, studied the classics, theology, music, art, and medicine before turning to mathematics and physics. When Galileo learned that a telescope had been invented in the Netherlands (1609), he built one himself and soon observed imperfections and irregularities on both the sun and the moon as well as four moons encircling Jupiter. At that time, the Copernican theory—that the earth was not the center of the universe but moved around the sun—had few adherents. But after Galileo's *Dialogue* was published in Italian, lay people were able to understand what the Copernican controversy was all about. It was for this reason that Galileo was brought before the Inquisition in 1633 and placed under house arrest.

(*Source:* Culver Pictures, Inc.)

lated an interest in nature and an awareness of its beauty, which not only found expression in the gardens of Renaissance villas, but also enabled man to look outward on the physical world with hope. The Renaissance so altered the type of questions asked by thinkers that the German philosopher Immanuel Kant (1724–1804) declared that "a new light flashed on all students of nature." These changes ultimately were to have a devastating impact on society at

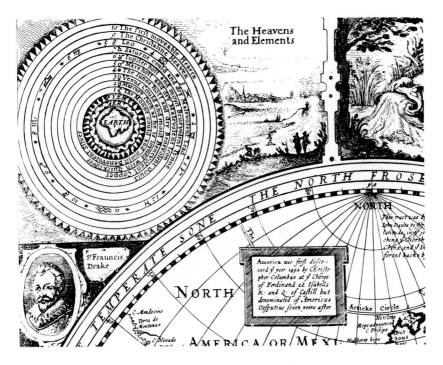

Figure 3–10

A segment of a map published by John Speed of London in 1627 shows the earth at the center of the universe surrounded by a belt of air (aer) around which is a belt of fire (fyer). The moon, whose path is around the earth, is described as "could and most Benevolent Silver." Beyond the moon's orbit are the orbits of Mercury and Venus. Then comes the sun, which is described as "hott and dry Benevolent Could." Beyond the outer planets, such as Jupiter and Leo, are the "Christaline Heaven" and "The First Moveable Heaven." Copernicus and Galileo were to destroy completely this system by insisting (and proving) that the earth was a minor celestial body moving around the sun.

(John Speed, *A Prospect of the Most Famous Parts of the World.* London, 1627. [Amsterdam: Theatrum Orbis Terrarum, 1936.] Courtesy Rare Book Collection, University of Washington Libraries.)

large as well as on Europe's religious and political organization.

In the seventeenth century, men became increasingly intrigued with machines—however impractical many of them may have been—and began to perceive of God as a creator who had set the earth "machine" in motion and remained its ruler. Just as observable scientific laws governed the functioning of a clock, so specific laws were believed to account for the apparent orderliness in the universe. The task of science, therefore, became the study of these laws to determine how nature works (Fig. 3–11).

The scientist wanted not only the knowledge to be gained from the discovery of natural laws, however. He saw, as Francis Bacon (1561–1626) observed in his book *Novum Organum* (1620), that such knowledge afforded the key to power, to the ultimate mastery of nature (Leiss, 1974). "We must in truth," said Bacon, "dissect nature; we must hound her because she hides her secrets from us. Knowledge and not faith is the means whereby the world of nature

Figure 3–11

The "marvels of nature" were a big attraction to early eighteenth-century society. Museums of natural history as such did not exist, but this woodcut suggests how many of nature's oddities were presented to the curious public. Society also was made aware of nature's variety through the writings of scholars, such as John Amos Comenius (1592–1670), Jean Jacques Rousseau (1712–1778), and Benjamin Franklin (1706–1790).

(*Théâtre des Merveilles* from *Description abrégée des planches, qui representent les cabinets et quelques-unes des curiosités contenuës dans le Theatre des Merveilles de la nature de Levin Vincent* [Haarlem, The Netherlands, 1719]. Courtesy Rare Book Collection, University of Washington Libraries.)

is revealed to us." Knowledge of the workings of nature and mastery over it were not goals to be achieved simply for exploitative reasons. Armed with a knowledge of the laws of nature, Bacon believed, society could better adapt itself to them, and in this way, progress could be achieved.

By the eighteenth century, this interest in natural law was translated into a concern for the natural rights of the individual in a society still governed by a monarchical political structure modeled after the medieval view of the universe. The pursuit of natural rights—the achievement of which, it was believed, would liberate people from unnatural constraints—was a premise that underlay both the American and French revolutions. In a modification of this premise, Karl Marx (1818–1883) argued that freedom from the exploitation of a class structure, outmoded by the forces of progress, would usher in a society where ultimately humans would neither exploit nature nor their fellow human beings.

A belief in progress is inherent in a number of traditional religions, notably Judaism and Christianity, but an essentially moral or spiritual progress was initially envisaged. In the seventeenth and eighteenth centuries, this original concept of progress lost ground as society turned to the promise of material progress through science. Indeed, science has been referred to as the religion of the nineteenth and twentieth centuries.

THE CULTURE-NATURE RELATIONSHIP IN MODERN GEOGRAPHIC THOUGHT

Nineteenth-Century Roots

Geographic thought over the past century and a half—the life span of what may be described as modern geography—has tended to parallel the development of European, and later American, philosophy and scientific theory. For the most part, geographers today have adopted a balanced understanding of the humans-nature dialogue, one not unlike that held by most natural and social scientists. This is not to say that earlier geographic statements of this relationship (which emphasized the physical environment) are of no interest to us or that they have entirely passed into history. There are still social scientists and historians who, when referring to geographic factors, think of them almost exclusively in terms of physical geography.

Modern geography can trace its roots to western Europe, in particular to Germany in the first half of the nineteenth century (Freeman,

1961). Exploration, the colonization of new lands, and scientific discovery were opening up the globe at a rate unprecedented in human history. Europe, the home of modern science, was "discovering" the world. Surveys, atlases, and cartographic representations of the earth were filling in details that had long remained unknown to the European mind.

Karl Ritter and Alexander von Humboldt

As geographic knowledge grew, efforts were made to organize it into some kind of meaningful structure. Among the early efforts were those of the German-born Karl Ritter (1779–1859) (Fig. 3–12) and Alexander von Humboldt (1769–1859) (Fig. 3–13). Both men were keen observers of the world around them, although Ritter scarcely left Europe, whereas von Humboldt traveled the globe.

Ritter has often been called the founder of *regional geography:* his *Erdkunde* or *General Comparative Geography,* although incomplete, was published in 19 volumes from 1817 to 1859. The work dealt for the first time in history with large earth regions. Humboldt's *Kosmos,* published in 6 volumes and atlas between 1845 and 1861, was a more systematic treatment of earth phenomena.

Ritter tended to focus principally on humankind and, although he believed that a reciprocal relationship existed between humans and earth, his approach tended to foster the growth of *environmentalism,* that is, the influence of the environment on human activities, in geographic thought. Humboldt was particularly interested in the realm of nature; his travels carried him far afield and he observed a broad array of phenomena in differing earth environments. He developed a respect for the unity of nature, believing as a scientist that it could be subjected to rational systematic inquiry. The task of geography, said Humboldt, is to investigate the relationship between organic life and the inorganic surface of the earth. Although he was aware that inanimate creation had an influence on the animal and vegetable kingdoms, he was too careful a scientist to advance any overall hypothesis concerning this relationship.

Charles Darwin and
His Influence on Geographic Perspective

Both Ritter and Humboldt died in 1859, the year that *On the Origin of Species* by Charles Darwin (1809–1882) was published. Thus, this date marks a turning point in the history of science and of geographic study. It should be noted that 1859 was the year in which Karl Marx (1818–1883) published his first book on economic theory, a study that was to have a considerable impact on subsequent geographic thought.

As a young man in 1831, Darwin had sailed aboard the HMS *Beagle* on a circumnavigation of the globe. From this voyage and additional years of study, he documented a theory of natural selection that was to shake up the entire Western world. A reading of Thomas Malthus's *An Essay on the Principle of Population,* published in 1798, also suggested to him how, in an

Figure 3–12

Educated in Germany, Karl Ritter first taught history in Frankfurt before becoming a professor of geography at the University of Berlin in 1820, a post he held for forty years. As a student, Ritter had been taught to be aware of the relationships between things in his immediate vicinity, beginning with his house and school. That early interest led him to study relationships over the entire earth. The first volume of his monumental *Erdkunde* or General Comparative *Geography,* published in 1817, dealt with Africa. In 1819 he published a volume on Asia. These volumes had a great impact on the geographic thinking of the time and led to his appointment at Berlin.

(*Source:* Culver Pictures, Inc.)

Figure 3–13

From his earliest years, Alexander von Humboldt had shown an interest in natural science. By 1792 he had completed his formal education and thereafter he began a professional career that involved a position in government followed by a lifetime of world travel, writing, and lecturing. He enjoyed the company of learned thinkers, including Ritter and Goethe. His six-volume work, *Kosmos,* was a truly remarkable synthesis of knowledge of the world. His contributions to geology and plant geography as well as to general geography stand as a major turning point in the history of scientific exploration.

(*Source:* German Information Center.)

overcrowded world, a natural selection of adaptations was possible. Darwin saw that inheritable variance was a factor in evolution and in the adjustment of species, but he could not account for the source of this variance, which we have since come to know as a function of mutation.

Geographic writing after 1860 owes much to its German and European practitioners, but it is certain that Darwin, the British biologist, added a dimension that had hitherto been lacking. Darwin's emphasis on time and change contributed to the emergence of a time-perspective in human geography (Stoddart, 1966). Darwin's notion, too, of ecology (of the interrelationships between living things and their environment) advanced the geographer's interest in human-environment relations.

Environmentalism in Geographic Thought

The geographers known as environmentalists believed that the physical environment was an active, although inanimate, participant in the activities of humankind. They held that the environment contained within it the guidelines that affected or determined the direction that human-activity patterns would take (Box 3–6).

Among the German geographers influenced by Darwin's evolutionary theory was Friedrich Ratzel (1844–1904), who also had training in biology. In his major work, *Anthropogeographie* (vol. 1, 1882; vol. 2, 1891), Ratzel attempted to show how the distribution of man on earth had been more or less controlled by natural forces. His writing shows a deterministic bias, but it would be a mistake to classify him only as an environmentalist.

In the United States, among the better known supporters of the environmental thesis were Ellen Churchill Semple (1863–1932) and Ellsworth Huntington (1876–1947).

A student of Ratzel, Semple sought to introduce his ideas to American geographers. Her classic work *Influences of Geographic Environment* was published in 1911. There, in a tone suggestive of an animistic, purposeful nature, she wrote (p. 1):

> Man is a product of the earth's surface. This means not merely that he is a child of the earth, dust of her dust; but that the earth has mothered him, fed him, set him tasks, directed his thoughts, confronted him with difficulties that have strengthened his body and sharpened his wits, given him his problems of navigation or irrigation, and at the same time whispered hints for their solution.

Although Semple's environmentalism was broadly physical geographic in conception, she took pains to disassociate herself from a strict determinist position. Huntington, on the other hand, was committed to the idea that climate played a major role in the development of civilization and human destiny.

In 1915, in *Civilization and Climate,* Huntington wrote (p. 3):

> Climate is fundamental by reason of its vital influence upon the quantity and quality not only of man's food, but of most of his other resources; it plays a large part in determining the distribution and virulence of the parasites which cause the majority of diseases; and through its effect upon human occupations, modes of life, and habits, it is one of the main determinants of culture.

Huntington recognized the role that "the slow processes of biological variation and selection" played in creating differences among living organisms, but climate remained the "more fundamental in the sense that it is the cause rather than a result of . . . other factors."

In *Mainsprings of Civilization,* Huntington's final work (published in 1945), it was clear that he had given a great deal of thought to the thesis that he had proposed three decades earlier. Although the influence of climate on civilization remained his central concern, Huntington sought to soften his earlier emphasis. In discussing the relationship between health, physical vigor, and human progress, he shied away from too direct a statement (pp. 237–238):

Good health and high civilization obviously go together. Each . . . helps the other. Physical vigor seems to be one of four foundations without which civilization cannot make progress; civilization, in turn, is one of three chief factors in giving people health and vigor. The foundations of civilization are (1) innate capacity; (2) a physical environment with sufficient natural advantages to maintain a rising standard of living; (3) a cultural inheritance to serve as a basis on which to build; and (4) sufficient vigor so that the other three conditions are well used. Some people insist that abundant natural resources are necessary if civilization is to reach a high level, but Iceland, Nor-

---

BOX 3–6

The Marxist Perspective on Nature

Although nineteenth century geographic theory held that the environment determined the general character of human-activity patterns, Marx arrived at a different conception of the forces shaping human activity and, thus, the course of history. Marx believed that the relationship between humankind and the earth environment governed the stages in the development of society and the socioeconomic system. But, for Marx, the *mode of production,* or the way people make a living, determined the general character of the social, political, and spiritual processes of life, not the earth environment.

Nature, or the natural environment, for Marx, was a totality. In this totality, there is a conscious, active, sensate, modifying agent—the human species—and an unconscious, inorganic, insensate, inactive element—that part of nature external to man. The two cannot be separated, however; they are both part of an encompassing unity and progress.

Still, from the beginning of history, according to Marx, humankind struggled with that part of nature that is external (Marx, 1964). This struggle is necessary for humankind to satisfy basic needs for housing, clothing, and food—in short, to survive. Throughout the course of this struggle, which is the historical record, humankind transforms its relationship to nature or the natural environment. At the same time, humankind is transformed.

According to Marx, this transformation takes place through the central role of human labor. Labor is the prime expression of life; it is a process in which both humans and nature participate; and it is in its application that change is brought about both in the external world as well as in humans themselves. The change, however, has a negative impact on humankind and especially on those who are compelled to work. The change in reality is one leading to a separation between humankind and nature. It produces an *alienation* from nature, which results in a fragmenting of the internal structure of society. The break with nature and the destruction of societal unity occur when workers are separated from the product of their labor.

This alienation, according to Marx, is characteristic of socioeconomic conditions under capitalism. The product of human labor belongs to the factory owner and comes to possess a value that is greater than the labor that went into producing it. The difference between the two yields the capitalists their profit. Labor is thereby exploited.

Marx's goal was that of overcoming alienation. He believed that the integration of the human personality would result. With this would come freedom, unity, and harmony among peoples. But to achieve these desirable ends, capitalism would have to come to an end.

way, Switzerland, and New England all indicate that if people are sufficiently vigorous and intelligent, handicaps along this line can be overcome. The three chief factors in giving people health and vigor are (1) innate biological endowment; (2) a physical environment which is favorable in relation to climate, food, and disease; and (3) a cultural tradition in which the arts of medicine, nutrition, sanitation, and hygiene, as well as trade and transportation, have made good progress.

Geography as Human Ecology

A variation on the human-environment theme was offered by Harlan Barrows (1877–1960), a professor of geography at the University of Chicago and, in 1922, president of the Association of American Geographers. In an address to the association, he stated what he believed would be the future goal of geographic study (Barrows, 1923). "Geography," he said, "will aim to make clear the relationships existing between natural environments and the distribution and activities of man" (p. 3). Barrows urged that geographers view the human-environment question in terms of "man's adjustment to environment, rather than from that of environmental influence" (p. 3). It is clear that Barrows wanted to minimize the danger of attributing to the environment an active, causative, or determining role.

Both sociology and geography are interested in human populations, but sociology, Barrows said, deals largely with the cultural relations among humans. Geography, on the other hand, is concerned with the surface manifestations of man's occupancy. The geographer, according to Barrows, begins with what we ourselves see. Still, his definition of geography as *human ecology*—the study of the adjustment of people to their environment—did not entirely elevate the central focus of geography from natural environmentalism.

The Possibilist Reaction

The notion that society is not free to choose, which was implicit in the environmentalist stance, brought a reaction from geographers trained more in history than in the natural sciences. This was especially true in France where geographers did not deny the essential interrelation of all phenomena on the earth's surface, but recognized the role of human initiative and ingenuity as more important in the establishment of spatial-activity patterns. They believed that the earth and its elements were not to be considered as the starting point of study; rather, their conceptual framework in geography began with the needs and capabilities of human beings. Nature does not act on the needs of humans, the French geographers argued, but rather it is humans who, choosing two or three out of several means of satisfying their needs and by clinging obstinately to what they have chosen, act in the long run on nature.

Geographers, like Lucien Febvre (1878–1956), Paul Vidal de la Blache (1845–1918), Jean Brunhes (1869–1930), Isaiah Bowman (1878–1950), and Carl Sauer (1889–1975), who placed the emphasis on the human role in the culture-nature relationship, were known as *possibilists* (Taylor, 1957). The possibilists did not claim that *Homo sapiens* could be free of all physical environmental constraints, but they did reject the concept that portrayed nature as an active determinant in human affairs. On the other hand, they did not believe that humans were omnipotent. Humans only have freedom, the possibilists asserted, to choose among the possibilities and the opportunities that are open to them and of which they are aware.

Challenge and Response

The British historian Arnold Toynbee (1889–1975) interpreted the possibilist thesis in a slightly different way. In keeping with his dynamic view of history, Toynbee saw the events leading up to the rise and fall of civilizations as *challenge and response*. "Challenge-and-response," he wrote, "resembles cause and effect only in standing for a sequence of events. The character of the sequence is not the same.

Unlike the effect of a cause, the response to a challenge is not predetermined, is not necessarily uniform in all cases, and is therefore intrinsically unpredictable'' (Toynbee, 1972, p. 97).

A social group, according to Toynbee, may or may not respond to the challenge of the environment by making changes in its traditional way of doing things or in its culture. If it does not respond, it may be deprived of certain resources and opportunities for survival. Of course, inability to respond—to find alternate sources of energy when needed, to eliminate salts from irrigated farmland, or to improve on diet—may be the result of a lack of technological capability, ignorance, or even insufficient will. If the group does not, or cannot, respond, it may decline as a group and ultimately become extinct. If it does respond, it may improve—or at least preserve—its adaptation to and domination of the environment. Of course, a society can, and often does, make a wrong response.

Not all scholars will agree with the Toynbee thesis, seeing it, perhaps, as too simplistic a summary of an infinitely more complex process. It provides, however, another way of viewing the complex relationship between mankind and the physical world.

THE MARRIAGE OF SCIENCE AND TECHNOLOGY

The cultural and environmental changes of the twentieth century—a consequence of the late nineteenth-century marriage of science and technology—have taken modern humans far beyond all previous levels of material achievement. These vast changes have brought us into a world where the limits to what man can do seem to be basic physical, geographic, or economic limits. Humankind, it has been suggested, may be approaching a kind of structural maturity where the capacities and activity patterns that are developed and achieved in the next few decades may constitute the structures

and limits that will determine or characterize human organization of the earth for a long time to come. We live in a crucial period.

Scientific and technology advances have brought about an immense increase in economic wealth, first in Europe, then in the United States and Canada, then in Japan, and subsequently in other parts of the world. The success of the Industrial Revolution has come to be measured almost exclusively in terms of gross national product and in quantities of goods and services rather than in the quality of human relationships. For most of the inhabitants of the industrialized parts of the globe, human life—often at costs to other life systems and the physical environment—has been made more comfortable, healthier, longer, and richer in experiences.

Yet in the introduction to a book entitled *Where the Wasteland Ends* (1972), Theodore Roszak asks:

Why, in our time, have societies well endowed with industrial plenty and scientific genius turned uglier with totalitarian violence than any barbarous people? Why does the moral blight of nationalist bigotry and the disease of total war continue to haunt the children of the Enlightenment, more oppressively now than in the age of Voltaire? Why do nihilism and neuroses brood over what we please to call the "developed" societies, taking as great a toll of human happiness as gross physical privation in the third world? (p. XXVIII).

Modern civilization has produced technological marvels capable of altering natural landscapes forever; indeed, modern civilization is the product of that technology. The "machine in our garden" has replaced much of the sheer physical energy that governed humankind's activities just a few centuries ago. Since the turn of the twentieth century, technology has dominated human life to a degree never before known, even in the hydraulic civilizations of ancient Mesopotamia, Egypt, and China. Man's relationship to man has been greatly changed and man's relationship to nature has been subjected to severe stress.

Lest we think that this kind of transformation is simply a reflection, or a product, of the capitalist mode of production and exploitation, we need only look at what the "spoils of progress" have wrought on the Soviet Union landscape. Public or state ownership of the means of production has not spared the USSR from some of the worst effects of environmental disruption. It is clear that the cause lies not so much in sociopolitical organization as it does in population growth and expansion, industrialization, urbanization, mismanagement, and waste. These phenomena obviously are to be found increasingly the world over.

THE CALL FOR A NEW ENVIRONMENTAL ETHIC

The manifestations of change in the environment and the implications of further environmental despoliation have given rise to a number of calls for a new ethic, one based less on the mastery or conquest of nature and more on the theme of harmony.

The conservation movement that emerged in the United States in the middle and the latter half of the nineteenth century was principally concerned with finding the means for halting the destructive trends apparent in the human race's use of the earth. Since World War II, the new naturalists (if they may be called that) have been principally interested in achieving a change in human values. Organizations, such as the Sierra Club and Greenpeace U.S.A., help to focus attention on many of the environmental problems. Although founded in 1892 by John Muir (1838–1914), the naturalist, to preserve the scenic beauty of the Sierra Nevada and similar areas, the club today campaigns actively against the disruption of natural ecosystems. Greenpeace U.S.A., a younger organization, founded in 1979, claims a membership of at least one hundred thousand. An activist, although nonviolent, protest group, Greenpeace U.S.A. members believe that verbal protests against imperiling environmental quality are not adequate. The organization has taken the lead in opposing the disruption of the life of endangered species.

Scholars in the West have contrasted the aggressive Western attitudes toward nature with the historic passivity of the Orient. They imply that this aggressiveness is rooted in the Judeo-Christian heritage. Aldo S. Leopold, one of the first to call for a change in our environmental ethic, believed that conservation was getting us nowhere "because it is incompatible with our Abrahamic concept of land. We abuse land because we regard it as a commodity belonging to us. When we see land as a community to which we belong, we may begin to use it with love and respect" (1949, p. viii).

The ecologist Ian McHarg, on the other hand, draws attention to the fact that, in Genesis, man is regarded as exclusively divine. From this premise, Western man has come to believe that all other creatures and things occupy a lower and generally inconsequential status. Man, by virtue of his assumed uniqueness, should assert dominion over all living creatures; he is enjoined by God to subdue the earth (McHarg, 1969). The historian Lynn White has argued in a somewhat similar vein (White, 1967). Our ecological problems, he states, derive from "Christian attitudes towards man's relation to nature which are almost universally held not only by Christians and neo-Christians but also by those who fondly regard themselves as post-Christians" (p. 1206).

Although these arguments possess some degree of truth, they are not the whole truth. The industrialized world, predominantly (but not entirely) Christian in origin, has become a technological society that is like a behemoth which has spread its tentacles to most of the regions of the globe. However, it was the content of the revolutions in thought in Western Europe since the Renaissance and in modern America since the Civil War as well as in technology that have led us to our newly "conquered" environment, with all its attendant problems.

The call for a new ethic, however, needs to be viewed in terms of societal needs, perhaps practical needs. Conservation groups have done a splendid job of educating the general public and, above all, the corporate leaders of industry. Such leaders today generally acknowledge the legitimacy of environmental concerns, although they continue to bridle at restrictions and regulations imposed in the 1970s. The narrowing of differences between groups opposed to further economic development that threatens environmental balances and industrialists has been a step toward moderation and broader concern. But, there remains a tendency for the pendulum to swing. In the 1980s, with the encouragement of the conservative administration in Washington under President Ronald Reagan, the pendulum has tended to swing away from the environmentalists. It may take another period of confrontation, as the United States witnessed in the 1960s, to bring humankind back into balance with nature.

The Quality of Life

There is a tendency among many of us to be passive about the world we inherit. We tend to think that because of the complexity of the world, there is little we can do to have any significant impact on it, and we have a tendency also to take the world around us for granted. What we forget, is that the world we live in is very much one of our own creation, of our own realization. As inhabitants of a segment of the earth's surface, we contribute to the shaping of the environment in which we live, and at the same time, we contribute to our own personal growth and awareness. We contribute to the making of our world and we enrich our own lives in the process. It is with this enrichment that the term *quality of life* is associated.

As was pointed out by Nicholas Helburn (1982), in an address to fellow geographers, quality of life has two meanings: one personal, the other environmental—or one internal, the other external. The first pertains to pleasant personal experience, such as hiking in the countryside, mountain climbing, or listening to music; the other involves life in a given region or in a place where one has the opportunity to do the things one likes. Thus, personal satisfaction and the setting in which one can enjoy life go hand in hand.

In the promotion of these goals, geographic learning has an important role to play. We need to learn about our external world. However, quality of life as a desirable goal cannot be achieved simply by formal study. We need to reflect on what we learn, enjoy it, interpret it, and truly become aware of the world around and of ourselves in it. In this way, we live in the world and find meaning.

EPILOGUE

The contemporary scientific view of nature obviously owes much, in one way or another, to earlier patterns of thought and endeavor. There is a difference, however, between the modern perspective and that of the eighteenth or nineteenth centuries. Nature is seen today as neither an organism nor a machine. Rather, nature is accepted as a complex set of processes that dominate the natural world as studied by the biologist, the physicist, the ecologist, the meteorologist, the pedologist, the botanist, and other natural scientists.

The relationship between the natural realm and the world of human affairs, moreover, is seen as equally complex. This relationship keeps changing because both human society and nature are constantly changing, although changes in nature are seldom evident to the naked eye. The interaction between a dynamic nature, on the one hand, and a society equipped with an advanced science and an ever-more-powerful technology, on the other hand, has produced an environment on earth that is new. This ongoing and increasingly complex interaction gives rise to fears and anxieties about the future of humanity as well as the challenges it must meet if life is to endure. This interaction, in the final analysis, affords an essential core of geographic study.

Earlier civilizations—Egyptian, Greek, Roman, Chinese, and others—accumulated a vast amount of information about the world around them. Much of what they accumulated was passed on through tradition and learning. Some of the notions of the early thinkers were correct and useful, and many of them accomplished many astounding feats. However, a great deal of what they believed was totally erroneous, and it was interwoven with myth, superstition, and folk stories. Although we have gained from past experience, it will be only through a continued pursuit of knowledge that we can rise above both past misconceptions and the constraints of the present that prevent us from achieving the full potentiality for all life on earth.

APPLICATION OF IDEAS

1. There is a tendency to blame previous generations for many of the problems that we face today; however, we have inherited a positive legacy as well—the learning and experience of the past, which we can use to solve present problems.

2. Humans are a part of nature, in that, like all living things, they are subject to the laws of nature. But, humans are also culture-creating beings who are affected by the culture they create. The relationship between nature and culture is an interactive one.

3. There are different ways of viewing the environment. The differences are important and contribute to an understanding of the interactive process.

4. Throughout history, humans have viewed the world around them, the potential environment, from their own cultural vantage point.

The legacy of these views has contributed to our attitudes toward the environment. Of course, attitudes alone do not determine the way people will interact with the environment.

5. Scientific views concerning the environment began largely with the Renaissance in Europe. One major step was the challenge to the traditional notion of the universe as earth centered. This challenge literally contributed to shaking the foundations of the medieval world order.

6. Modern views of nature or of the environment are based on a recognition of complex processes at work, together forming part of a whole. Pieces of this whole are studied by the biologist, ecologist, and other scientists.

7. Geographic theory in the nineteenth century owed much to past learning, but it passed through several phases. Geographers today are interested in the environment as part of their field of study because they have become aware that humans make major contributions to the shaping of the habitat in which they live, whether for good or for ill. Moreover, through an integrative approach is it not possible for geographers to make a substantive contribution to contemporary human-environment problems?

KEY WORDS AND PHRASES

alienation
animism
arable (farm) land
challenge and
　response
civilization
Confucianism
cosmogony
cultural ecology
ecology
ecosystem

effective
　(operational)
　environment
Enlightenment
environment
environmentalism
human ecology
magic
mode of production
natural environment
nature

operational
  (effective)
  environment
perceptual
  (perceived)
  environment
physical
  environment
possibilists
potential

environment
presecular man
Ptolemaic system
quality of life
regional geography
supranatural
Taoism
totemism
ziggurat

QUESTIONS FOR FURTHER DISCUSSION

1. In what way do you think the notion that "man is apart from nature" is true? What patterns of human activity tend to reject this notion today?

2. What are the important components of your effective (operational) environment? How do they differ from those of your perceptual environment?

3. What types of new archeological or other finds are steadily altering our knowledge of the earth and of humans? Give some examples.

4. To what extent do you think that knowledge of early civilization has value for us today? What are some examples?

5. An attempt to find rational explanations for natural phenomena developed among Greek thinkers in the sixth and fifth centuries B.C. Why do you think that no comparable development occurred in Oriental thinking?

6. Why did the medieval church find the views held by Ptolemy concerning the universe so compatible with its teaching? Who ultimately brought about a transformation of Ptolemy's views? What effect did this transformation have on the way in which the universe and earth were viewed?

7. How can Francis Bacon's observations of the way in which humankind was to approach nature be applied by modern critics of environmental deterioration?

8. What was the contribution of Charles Darwin to geographic thinking?

9. Define the term possibilism. How does this framework of analysis compare with the notion of challenge and response as explained by Arnold Toynbee?

10. What does quality of life mean to you? Give examples of how you think you can enhance the quality of life of your community, of your place, or of your existence.

REFERENCES AND ADDITIONAL READINGS

Allen, John L. "Lands of Myth, Waters of Wonder: The Place of the Imagination in the History of Geographical Exploration," pp. 41–62. In *Geographies of the Mind. Essays in Historical Geosophy in Honor of John Kirtland Wright.* David Lowenthal and Martyn J. Bowden, eds. New York: Oxford University Press, 1976.

Aristotle. *Politics.* (Trans. B. Jowett.) Oxford: Clarendon Press, 1938.

Barrows, Harlan. "Geography as Human Ecology." *Annals of the Association of American Geographers* 13 (1923): 1–14.

Bronowski, J. "The Heavens Were Brought Down to Earth by Copernicus the Humanist." *Smithsonian* 4 (April 1973): 40–48.

Brown, Lloyd A. *The Story of Maps.* New York: Bonanza Books, 1960.

Campbell, Joseph. *The Masks of God: Creative Mythology.* New York: Viking Press, 1970.

Chenu, M-D. *Nature, Man, and Society in the Twelfth Century.* Chicago: University of Chicago Press, 1968.

Clark, Kenneth. *Landscape into Art.* Boston: Beacon Press, 1961.

Cox, Harvey. *The Secular City,* rev. ed. New York: Macmillan, 1966.

Detweiler, Robert, et al. *Environmental Decay in Its*

Historical Context. Glenview, Ill.: Scott, Foresman, 1973.

Dobson, W. A. C. H. *Mencius: A New Translation Arranged and Annotated for the General Reader.* Toronto, Can.: University of Toronto Press, 1963.

Dubos, René. *So Human an Animal.* New York: Charles Scribner's, 1968.

——. *Reason Awake. Science for Man.* New York: Columbia University Press, 1970.

——. *A God Within.* New York: Charles Scribner's, 1972.

Eiseley, Loren. *The Invisible Pyramid.* New York: Charles Scribner's, 1970.

——. *The Star Thrower.* New York: Times Books, 1978.

Eliade, Mircea. *The Sacred and the Profane. The Nature of Religion.* New York: Harcourt, Brace & World, 1959.

English, Paul W., and Mayfield, Robert C., eds. *Man, Space, and Environment.* New York: Oxford University Press, 1972.

Farrington, Benjamin. *Greek Science.* Harmondsworth, Eng.: Penguin Books, 1953.

Freeman, Thomas Walter. *A Hundred Years of Geography.* London: Duckworth, 1961.

Glacken, Clarence J. "Reflections on the Man-Nature Theme as a Subject for Study," pp. 355–371. In *Future Environments of North America: Transformation of the Continent.* F. Fraser Darling and John P. Milton, eds. New York: Natural History Press, 1966.

——. *Traces on the Rhodian Shore. Nature and Culture in Western Thought from Ancient Times to the End of the Eighteenth Century.* Berkeley and Los Angeles: University of California Press, 1967.

——. "Man Against Nature: An Outmoded Concept," pp. 127–420. In *The Environmental Crisis: Man's Struggle to Live with Himself.* Harold W. Helfrich, ed. New Haven, Conn.: Yale University Press, 1970.

Graves, Robert. "Introduction," pp. V–VIII. In *New Larousse Encyclopedia of Mythology.* London: Prometheus Press, 1959.

Helburn, Nicholas. "Geography and the Quality of Life." *Annals of the Association of American Geographers* 72 (1982): 445–456.

Hewitt, Kenneth, and Hare, F. Kenneth. *Man and Environment. Conceptual Frameworks.* Resource Paper No. 20. Washington, D.C.: Commission on College Geography, Association of American Geographers, 1973.

Huntington, Ellsworth. *Civilization and Climate,* 3rd ed. New Haven, Conn.: Yale University Press, 1924.

——. *Mainsprings of Civilization.* New York: John Wiley, 1945.

Jackson, John G. *Man, God, and Civilization.* New Hyde Park, N.Y.: University Books, 1972.

Leiss, William. *The Domination of Nature.* Boston: Beacon Press, 1974.

Leopold, Aldo S. *A Sand County Almanac, and Sketches Here and There.* New York: Oxford University Press, 1949.

Levi-Strauss, Claude. *Totemism.* Boston: Beacon Press, 1963.

——. *The Savage Mind.* Chicago: University of Chicago Press, 1970.

Lowenthal, David. "George Perkins Marsh on the Nature and Purpose of Geography." *Geographical Journal* 126 (1960): 413–417.

Marx, Karl. *The Economic and Philosophic Manuscripts of 1844.* D. J. Striuk, ed. New York: International Publishers, 1964. (First English translation 1932).

McHarg, Ian. *Design with Nature.* Garden City, N.Y.: Natural History Press, 1969.

McKinley, Daniel. "The New Mythology of 'Man in Nature,'" pp. 351–362. In *The Subversive Science.* Paul Shepard and Daniel McKinley, eds. Boston: Houghton Mifflin, 1969.

Needham, Joseph. *History of Scientific Thought.* Vol. 2, *Science and Civilization in China.* Cambridge: Cambridge University Press, 1962.

Oates, Joan. *Babylon.* London: Thames and Hudson, 1979.

Parkes, Henry Bamford. *Gods and Men. The Origins of Western Culture.* New York: Alfred A. Knopf, 1959.

Robinson, H. Wheeler. *Inspiration and Revelation in the Old Testament*. Oxford: Clarendon Press, 1962.

Roszak, Theodore. *Where the Wasteland Ends*. Garden City, N.Y.: Doubleday, 1972.

Saarinen, Thomas F. *Perception of Environment*. Resource Paper No. 5. Washington, D.C.: Commission on College Geography, Association of American Geographers, 1969.

Semple, Ellen Churchill. *American History and Its Geographic Conditions*. Boston and New York: Houghton Mifflin, 1903.

———. *Influences of Geographic Environment*. New York: Henry Holt, 1911.

Shepard, Paul. *Man in the Landscape: A Historic View of the Esthetics of Nature*. New York: Ballantine Books, 1967.

———. *The Tender Carnivore and the Sacred Game*. New York: Charles Scribner's, 1973.

Sonnenfeld, Joseph. "Geography, Perception, and the Behavioral Environment," pp. 244–250. In *Man, Space, and Environment: Concepts on Contemporary Human Geography*. Paul W. English and Robert C. Mayfield, eds. New York: Oxford University Press, 1972.

Stoddart, D. R. "Darwin's Impact on Geography." *Annals of the Association of American Geographers* 56 (1966): 683–698.

Taylor, Griffith, ed. *Geography in the Twentieth Century. A Study of Growth, Fields, Techniques, Aims and Trends*. New York: Philosophical Library, 1957.

Tuan, Yi-Fu. *Man and Nature*. Resource Paper No. 10. Washington, D.C.: Commission on College Geography, Association of American Geographers, 1971.

———. "Ambiguity in Attitudes Toward Environment." *Annals of the Association of American Geographers* 63 (1973): 411–423.

———. *Topophilia: A Study of Environmental Perception, Attitudes, and Values*. Englewood Cliffs, N.J.: Prentice-Hall, 1974.

Toynbee, Arnold. *A Study of History* (Revised abbreviated edition). New York: Barre Publishing Co., 1972. (Weathervane Books)

Weiss, Paul. *Nature and Man*. Carbondale: Southern Illinois University Press, 1965.

White, Lynn, Jr. "The Historical Roots of Our Ecological Crisis." *Science* 155 (Mar. 10, 1967): 1203–1207.

Wright, John K. *The Geographical Lore at the Time of the Crusades: A Study in the History of Medieval Science and Tradition in Western Europe*. New York: Dover Press, 1965. (Originally published, 1925).

4
The Transformation of the Environment

To the amazement of their rude companion, three great magicians in turn caused a pile of bones to become a skeleton, then fleshed out the bony structure, and finally prepared to endow it with new life. Shaken, the simpleton cautioned, "Don't you realize that these are the remains of a tiger?"

Caught up in the frenzy of artful invention, the magicians ignored the warning. From his tree, the simpleton watched the splendid moment of rebirth and—ultimately—the consumption of the three wise men.

Panchatantra
(Sanskrit fable), unknown date

It is only the most recent, and brief, period of his tenure that man has developed in sufficient numbers, and acquired enough power, to become one of the most potentially dangerous organisms that the planet has ever hosted.

John McHale,
The Ecological Context, 1970.

Key Ideas

1. The historical record is one of increasingly effective efforts to develop technology for major earth transformations to suit human needs.

2. The earth is the product of billions of years of ceaseless change due to extensive crustal activity in the form of earthquakes, volcanoes, and other such phenomena.

3. No single environment has ever been just right for humans; yet humans lack many of the physiological endowments that help animals to survive.

4. Humans could not change their biology, so they changed the environment in which they lived.

5. The keeping of animals in captivity for human use began some ten thousand years ago, marking a significant stage in cultural and social evolution.

6. Plant domestication occurred in many parts of the Old World and, independently, in the New World as well.

7. Irrigation was an important innovation by which the output of foodstuff was regularized and increased.

8. Shifting cultivation was practiced in Europe in early times, but as population densities grew, farmers were forced to develop new systems of land management.

9. The ploughing of the grasslands was also attended by a lack of appreciation for what overcultivation might produce, especially in times of drought.

10. Competition for the fish and other resources of the sea has long been intense, but in the past, the degree of utilization ordinarily permitted the resource to reestablish itself. The future seems less certain.

A GEOGRAPHIC INTEREST

"Nowhere else in the world," writes Professor David Lowenthal, "have four centuries of civilization more thoroughly transformed the lineaments of the landscape [than in America]. Is there really one aspect of our geography that bears the slightest resemblance to that of pre-Columbian America . . . beyond the broadest configurations of peaks and plains and the most general conditions of climate?" (1953, p. 207).

Professor Lowenthal was not being critical

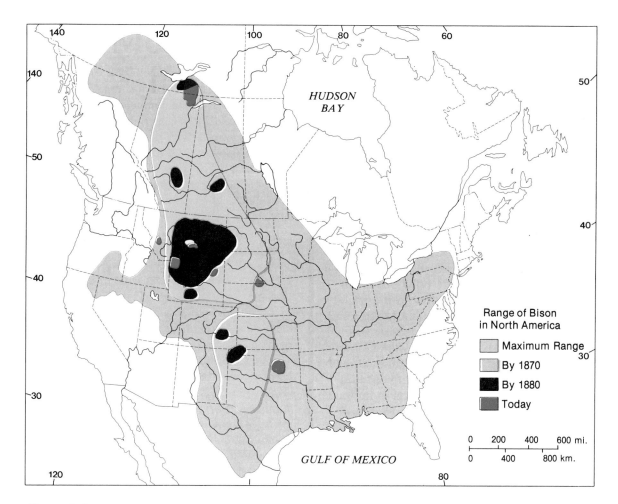

Figure 4–1

From the bison, the Plains Indians gained food, fuel, clothing, shelter, and other essentials. At the beginning of European immigration, the bison roamed widely over the interior of North America. However, their very number led to thoughtless slaughter and waste; by 1800, the bison was extinct east of the Mississippi. The hunt began in earnest, however, with the opening of the Union Pacific and Kansas Pacific railways about 1865. A northern and a southern herd were almost entirely eliminated. From the few hundred animals that survived, the present herds, about thirty thousand head, are descended.

(Dorst, 1970, p. 52).

of the transformation of America. He was simply drawing attention to one of the most dramatic modifications of environment that has occurred in human history. The tempo with which these changes took place have, however, led a restless people to commit many blunders that violated their natural heritage. Perhaps one of the most dramatic ways to illustrate the work of humans is to see what happened to the bison or buffalo that once roamed widely over North America (Fig. 4–1).

The reshaping of the earth's surface is a process that has been going on since earliest times; it is a theme that remains central to geographic study.

THE TOTAL HUMAN IMPACT

People are capable of transforming their environment to suit their needs; with few exceptions, other living organisms take their native surroundings as they find them. History is a record of humankind's increasingly effective efforts to develop the tools and techniques by which to shape its habitat. Among the methods that have been employed to achieve this goal— for better or for worse—have been fire, deforestation, the development of agriculture, an ever-increasing urban sprawl, mining and other extractive industries, and the creation of a complex technology. Singly or in association with other factors, our activities have changed vegetation and wildlife patterns, the soils, the atmosphere, and the waters of the earth—the whole earth ecosystem. Human activities are now beginning to affect outer space as well.

Until about ten thousand years ago *Homo sapiens* was similar in his hunting habits to other living creatures on earth. Humans killed to eat and to protect themselves. Family populations were small, skills were limited, and the source of energy was primarily human muscle power. Fire was probably used to drive game

into openings, but for the most part, hunters did not modify the natural environment to any appreciable degree. We have evidence of this today. Because human populations did not advance toward civilization at the same rate, remnants of these early types of culture still survive in remote, inaccessible areas of the globe. Certain tribes found in Australia, New Guinea, the Philippines, the Amazon Basin, and elsewhere are not unlike historic Paleolithic (Old Stone Age) peoples. It is true, of course, that these groups have undergone some acculturation following contact with industrial cultures, but they continue to hunt and to gather edible plants much as their ancestors have done for millennia. They are not cultivators; they do not herd; nor do they disturb the local ecology in any substantive way. Once humans began to lead more sedentary lives, they started to change the natural surroundings in many ways, a process that has continued at an ever-accelerating rate. Before we review what humans have done to modify the earth, however, we should remind ourselves of what nature has wrought.

NATURE SHAPES THE EARTH'S ENVIRONMENT

Geologists estimate that the earth is about 4.9 billion years old, if not older. Through eons of time, the surface of the planet has been moulded and shaped into the broad physical geographic configuration we know today (Fig. 4–2). The earth's landmasses and oceanic basins are in a state of constant change, although we may not always be aware of these changes (Box 4–1). Continents now separated by seas and oceans were at one time connected by land bridges. Geologic, fossil, and paleobotanical evidence suggest that millions of years ago giant supercontinents called Laurasia and Gondwana (Fig. 4–3) took shape and slowly drifted apart. The thrusting, folding, and faulting of the earth's crust have produced mountains and uplands that, over long periods of time, were planed down by the forces of erosion, only to be thrust up again. Volcanic eruptions through the earth's skin have allowed gaseous, liquid, and solid materials to pour or spew forth, forming cones or otherwise modifying the face of the earth. Periodic jarring in the earth's rocky crust has set in motion the powerful forces we know as earthquakes (Fig. 4–4), and the subsequent seismic waves (incorrectly called tidal waves or *tsunami*) have submerged islands and coastal lowlands. Such phenomena might explain the Greek legend of Atlantis, a lost continent that disappeared into the sea.

Through this long period of crustal activity, climates have also changed. When there was a strong warming trend in the climate, lush vegetation and awesome, diverse types of animal life, such as giant reptiles of the Mesozoic era (100 to 250 million years ago), flourished. Cooling periods, the most recent being the Pleistocene that dates back 1 million years, led to the formation of immense ice sheets that periodically covered much of the polar portions of global landmasses and mountains (Fig. 4–5). Now advancing, now retreating, these vast glaciers chiseled, gouged, ground, and cracked the rock to form gravel, sand, and, ultimately, soil. To the work of the ice have been added the pelting and sculpturing blows of wind and rain and the powerful eroding action of running water. Finally, these great forces of nature have been supplemented by the influential but less

---

BOX 4–1

Earth: The Home of Humankind

The 600-million-mile sweep that the earth takes around the sun occurs every 365½ earth days, but its path is not a perfect circle. It is an ellipse, and a wiggly one at that. The earth's average 92.9 million-mile distance from the sun varies by 3.1 million miles during the course of a year. It is not, however, the nearness of the earth to the sun but the tilt of the earth's axis toward the sun that accounts for the seasons. The succession of the seasons is the result of the earth's journey around the sun.

The earth in orbit rotates on its own axis, but that rotation is also irregular. These irregularities are caused by the earth's only natural satellite, the moon, which exerts a strong influence on the earth. The gravitational force of the moon lifts the waters on the earth's near side and this pull produces the tides, a phenomenon that slightly unbalances the earth's spin. Lunar pull is so strong that scientists have said that the North American continent may bulge six inches when the moon is overhead.

Scientific discoveries have confirmed the fact that man inhabits a minor planet bound to an ordinary star (our sun) on the periphery of one galaxy in a universe that numbers billions. Yet of all the planets that conceivably could support human life, the earth is the one we know of that does. The earth's interior and its skin, its atmosphere and its climate, and even the way it behaves in space—all of these factors combine with other features and attributes to create an environment in which life flourishes. Until the probes of Mars and other planets prove otherwise, the earth remains truly the wonder of the universe.

A

B

C

D

Figure 4–2

(A) Mount St. Helens before and after. (B) Bryce Canyon. (C) Glacial scouring of the Canadian Shield. (D) Grand Canyon.

Picture Credits: (A) Jack Leffler/Sky Eye. (B) Joe Munroe/Photo Researchers, Inc. (C) W. A. Douglas Jackson. (D) Photo Researchers, Inc.

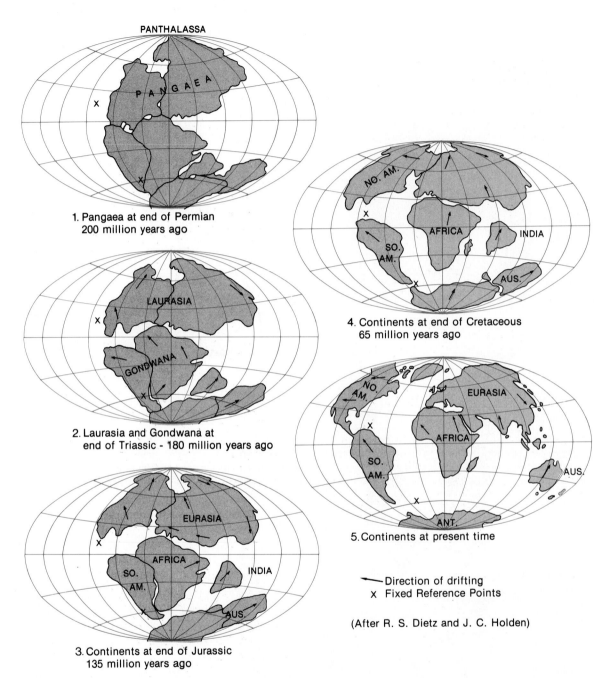

1. Pangaea at end of Permian
   200 million years ago

2. Laurasia and Gondwana at
   end of Triassic - 180 million years ago

3. Continents at end of Jurassic
   135 million years ago

4. Continents at end of Cretaceous
   65 million years ago

5. Continents at present time

— Direction of drifting
X Fixed Reference Points

(After R. S. Dietz and J. C. Holden)

Figure 4–3

The theory of continental drift was first proposed by Alfred Wegener (1880–1930), a German geophysicist and meteorologist. Wegener hypothesized that the present continents on the surface of the globe were part of one original landmass some 200 million years ago. Gradually, the landmass separated and drifted apart. According to this hypothesis, the continents are still in the process of shifting; a major "break" in North America for example, occurs in the San Andreas fault in California. The theory of continental drift helps to explain much of the history of the earth and why the continents are at present the way they are. Wegener's principal work, *The Origins of Continents and Oceans,* was first published in German in 1915. An English translation appeared in 1924.

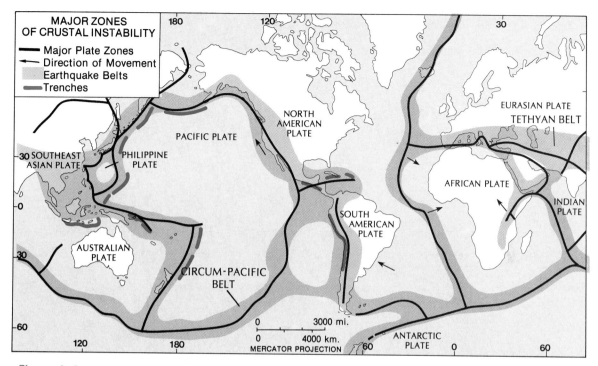

MAJOR ZONES OF CRUSTAL INSTABILITY
— Major Plate Zones
← Direction of Movement
Earthquake Belts
Trenches

Figure 4–4

Major zones of crustal instability are found where the tectonic plates of the earth's crust come together. One of these extends from the mid-Atlantic eastward through the Mediterranean, Anatolia, Iran, and the Himalayas to Southeast Asia. A mid-Atlantic zone stretches from north of Iceland to the Antarctic. The most active zone today is the one that girdles the Pacific Ocean, including the San Andreas fault, and that accounts for about 80 percent of present earthquake activity. The high mountains along the western side of the Americas are due to the pressure of the continents against the Pacific plate.

dramatic role of vegetation, the activities of other forms of life, and, above all, of humankind itself.

HUMANKIND AS SUPERSCULPTOR

Apart from the massive upheavals of nature, humans have also been capable of causing substantial changes on the surface of the earth and in the earth's environment generally. In the course of historical time, the human population has made tremendous modifications in its habitat. Humankind's influence is felt today throughout the globe. For a long time, the human capacity to effect change was negligible because populations were small and technical equipment modest. Early peoples stood in awe of the forces of nature and were aware of their own impotency before them. Indeed, to placate nature or to manipulate it, humans fashioned simple, then more complex, systems of magic and worship to satisfy their need to understand, to allay fears, and to afford some sense of direction.

As humankind's cultural and technological achievements grew, however, the capacity to

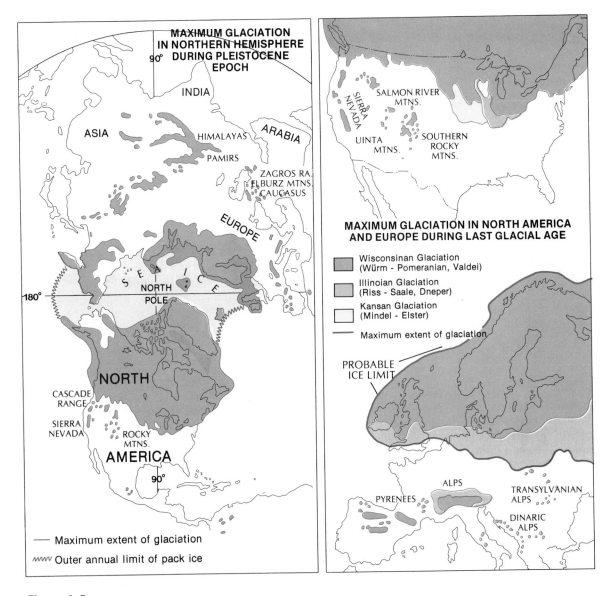

MAXIMUM GLACIATION IN NORTHERN HEMISPHERE DURING PLEISTOCENE EPOCH

INDIA

ASIA

HIMALAYAS

ARABIA

PAMIRS

ZAGROS RA.
ELBURZ MTNS.
CAUCASUS

EUROPE

SEA ICE

NORTH POLE

180°

NORTH

CASCADE RANGE

SIERRA NEVADA

ROCKY MTNS.

AMERICA

90°

— Maximum extent of glaciation

〜〜 Outer annual limit of pack ice

SIERRA NEVADA

SALMON RIVER MTNS.

UINTA MTNS.

SOUTHERN ROCKY MTNS.

MAXIMUM GLACIATION IN NORTH AMERICA AND EUROPE DURING LAST GLACIAL AGE

Wisconsinan Glaciation
(Würm - Pomeranian, Valdei)

Illinoian Glaciation
(Riss - Saale, Dneper)

Kansan Glaciation
(Mindel - Elster)

— Maximum extent of glaciation

PROBABLE ICE LIMIT

PYRENEES

ALPS

TRANSYLVANIAN ALPS

DINARIC ALPS

Figure 4–5

Although glaciation affected parts of the earth's surface in early times, the term Ice Age is usually applied to the Pleistocene era. Northern Eurasia experienced three major glacial advances, but there were four in North America together with many minor readvances. Glaciers also formed in mountainous regions.

During periods of glacial advance, the level of the seas fall, creating land bridges between islands and landmasses. Moving ice acts as a powerful erosional force, transporting debris, including large boulders, great distances. The scouring of the earth's surface by ice disrupts older drainage patterns and gives rise to a pockmarked landscape, such as that found on the Canadian Shield west of Hudson Bay. Wasting continental glaciers also leave debris spread across vast areas (ground moraines) or piled up into hills and ridges (terminal or lateral moraines). Debris is also carried away from the glacier by meltwater streams, which may form broad spillways draining into glacial lakes.

effect change also expanded (Mumford, 1970). People gained the wherewithal to modify both physical and nonhuman biotic conditions. In time, there even came the possibility of directing human evolution. Now postindustrial society has at its disposal the means to destroy much or all of life on the planet Earth (Dorst, 1970).

No single environment has ever been just right for humankind. Humans are not bound to one spot. They have, ever since the appearance of *Homo sapiens* at least, modified habitat to suit needs. If we compare humans anatomically to other creatures, we recognize that they share with monkeys and apes certain important advantages that are not to be found in other living species. Normally, humans walk in an upright position, with hands free for other tasks; humans can also produce a variety of sounds that form the basis of a detailed and elaborate communication system. Above all, humans possess an important quality that no other primates have: the gift of imagination. It is this characteristic together with experience and acquired skills that has produced culture. No monkey or ape has ever written a symphony, built a city, or devised a means of journeying to the moon. Still, in spite of these attributes, humans lack many of the physiological endowments that help animals to survive. Humans are vulnerable—without clothes or protective covering—to climatic extremes. They have no natural weapons for defense or attack. Above all, they are not highly specialized within any given environmental situation. Because humans could not change these biologic traits, they learned to change their environment. They used their knowledge and intelligence to fashion tools and other devices to secure food and to protect themselves, to clothe themselves against inclement weather, to shelter themselves, and to develop fire. Some writers have suggested that in part the history of our species should be envisaged as a struggle against the environment. This struggle has had its effect on the human population as well as serious consequences for other living systems (Fig. 4–6).

THE USE OF FIRE

In the ancient Greek play *Prometheus Bound* by Aeschylus (525–456 B.C.), the giant Prometheus first brings fire to the people on earth. As a result, Prometheus earns the enmity of the gods to whose level humankind can now raise itself (Box 4–2). Whether *Homo erectus,* some four hundred thousand years or more ago, made the first fires out of curiosity or mischief, for warmth or protection, we cannot say. We do know, however, that throughout history, fires—both naturally occurring and artificially or accidentally induced by people—have led to major modifications in the earth's vegetative cover. It is quite likely that most, if not all, vegetation regions on the earth have at one time or another been altered by fire. Human-made fires have contributed to the broad extent of temperate grasslands and tropical savannas where one might be inclined to expect forests.

Early hunters, whatever their views of the spirit world, employed fire to drive their prey out of the forests. Later, shepherds and herdsmen burned over areas to extend and improve pastures. Professor Charles Davis has drawn attention to this phenomenon as he witnessed it in northeastern Australia (Davis, 1959). He observed that the purpose of burning, as it was employed by Australian cattlemen, was to extend "the grazing after the last rains" or to make "the new growth available as early as possible when the new rains arrive" (p. 555) (Box 4–3).

Fire as a tool for environmental modification gained even greater impact with the expansion of crop cultivation, particularly in forested regions. Among early farmers—as, indeed, among pioneer settlers throughout the world— the trees were cleared and burned to allow crops to be grown. Until the rise of the indus-

A

B

C

D

E

Figure 4–6

(A) Log skid, Vancouver, British Columbia. (B) Land fill in Inland Sea of Japan. (C) Farm in southwestern Saskatchewan. (D) Bingham Canyon Mine, Utah. (E) Terraced hill in Taiwan.

Picture Credits: (A) Historical Photography Collection, University of Washington Libraries. (B) W. A. Douglas Jackson. (C) Department of Natural Resources & Industrial Development, Regina. (D) Kennecott Copper Corp./ Photo Researchers, Inc. (E) Fritz Henle/Photo Researchers, Inc.

trial city in the nineteenth century, perhaps no other facet of human culture led to such drastic changes in the environment as did the burning of forest vegetation to clear the land for farming.

DEFORESTATION

Alongside destruction of the forests through burning is human modification of them through use. The need of wood for housing, shipbuild-

---

BOX 4–2

Prometheus the Firegiver

The ancient Athenians developed an interesting myth pertaining to the manner in which humans acquired a knowledge of fire. According to the story, Zeus—the supreme god, the symbol of authority in both the universe and in society—had determined to withhold fire from mortals. The Titan, Prometheus, who loved humans, stole the flame from Hephaestus, the god of fire, and brought it to earth and taught its art to man. Angered by this deed, Zeus sent Hephaestus to capture and punish Prometheus. For his misdeed,

Prometheus was doomed to be chained to Mount Caucasus and to have a vulture daily consume his liver. There Prometheus was to remain, despite his torture and pain. But Prometheus continued to defy Zeus. Finally, the prisoner was rescued by Hercules, who killed the vulture and broke the chains.

Since the sixth century B.C., the Greek naturalists had been presenting a new understanding of nature based on observation rather than mythology. By the fifth century B.C., when Aeschylus, the greatest of the Greek dramatists, told the legend in *Prometheus Bound*, this "enlightenment" had begun to gain such a hold on the Athenians that it threatened traditional beliefs and cults. Aeschylus's drama, therefore, served as a warning against allowing human intelligence to grow at the expense of traditional social stability, symbolized by the order imposed by the age-old gods (Figure 4–7).

Figure 4–7

The legend of Prometheus had a profound impact on Renaissance thought in Europe. The illustration shown here is from a 1547 edition of the works of Vitruvius, a first-century B.C. Roman architect. As evident from the illustration, Vitruvius speculated—contrary to the Promethean ideal—that it was man who tamed fire and that it was not a gift of the gods. Here the Roman architect shows both men and beasts in the background fleeing in fear from a forest fire as others in the foreground utilize fire without fear.

(*Source:* Marc Vitruve Pollion. *Architecture ou Art de bien battir.* Paris: 1547. [Reproduced by Gregg Press, Ridgewood, N.J., 1964.])

ing, fuel, and, later, paper, have compounded the transformation of the vegetative cover brought on by the hunter, the herdsman, and the farmer. Both North China and the Mediterranean Basin were very early denuded of trees to make way for other uses. Professor Marvin Mikesell has carefully documented the deforestation of the mountains of Lebanon, where once grew extensive stands of cedar, fir, juniper, and oak (Mikesell, 1969). The cedars of Lebanon were widely prized for their durability, and they constituted an important early component of Mediterranean maritime trade via Tyre and Sidon. It is also well known that Solomon obtained timber from Lebanon for his temple in Jerusalem.

In Europe, extensive deforestation did not really begin until the medieval period. Then, it gradually spread from the Mediterranean northward and from the Atlantic eastward into Russia. Deforestation was also a component of medieval thought for the forest was identified with paganism if not savagery. This kind of thinking, which had an economic basis as well as definite religious overtones, was carried in later centuries by European immigrants—especially those of Puritan stock—to other parts of the world, notably to North America.

In the twentieth century, many countries in the industrialized world, including the United States, have made an effort to reforest the land, not only to preserve an important commercial resource, but also to guard against soil erosion. In the developing countries—especially in the tropics where forests are extensive—deforestation has proceeded at a rapid pace, not only to satisfy domestic needs for wood and fuel and to create additional farmland for growing populations, but also to earn additional necessary hard currency from timber exports to pay for imports of manufactured foods, fertilizers, and other needed items. The impact of such extensive forest cutting, however, is widespread and the repercussions are serious. Not the least of the tragedy is the loss of an environment that supports a wide array of bird and wild animal life.

BOX 4-3
Fire and the Landscape

The fires of nature have since the beginning been an integral part of the earth's ecosystem. They never devastated landscapes. Natural fires, in fact, led to the formation of total ecological regions, or *biomes,* that represented the right combination of plant and animal life (climax associations) in the right environment to allow humankind to develop (Pyne, 1982).

With the introduction of human-made fires, the cutting of forests, and the ploughing of the soil, natural balances began to change. Natives of North America discovered that the burning of their woods each fall usually resulted in lusher vegetation the following summer. Such burnt-over areas were easier to penetrate and to hunt in. Humans, generally, however, had a poor comprehension of the role of fire in the formation of ecosystems so that their fire-making habits were often more destructive than constructive. Today, controlled burnings are widely accepted as an integral part of land management. Indeed, the U.S. Forest Service has become aware of a dual responsibility that it possesses in the 188 million acres of federal land it manages. Some fires must be suppressed, but some must be cheered on, including the lightning fires in remote forest areas.

DOMESTICATION OF ANIMALS

The keeping of animals in captivity began some ten thousand years ago and reflects not only a major intrusion into the existence of other living creatures, but also a significant stage in the path of human social evolution. The domestication of animals presupposes a social medium: a certain level of social complexity is necessary before the keeping of animals on a wide scale is possible (Isaac, 1970) (Fig. 4–8).

There are many theories that attempt to ex-

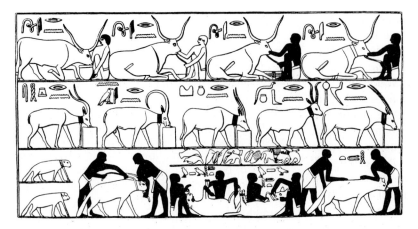

Figure 4–8

There is a wide array of pictorial representation on the tombs of ancient Egypt that not only afford some insight into how Egyptians lived and made war, but also how they sought to advance their culture. In this illustration from a tomb at Saqqara, Egypt, dating to about 2500 B.C., attempts to domesticate various animals are shown.

Domesticated cattle are shown in the top illustration, but the middle frame suggests efforts to tame various types of antelopes, shown with collars around their necks. At the bottom, hyenas are portrayed, but the Egyptians gave up on the domestication of these wild animals and stuffed them instead.

(*Source:* Singer et al., eds., 1957, vol. 1, p. 341).

---

plain the origin of *domestication*. Almost all of these are based on the notion of purpose. People needed certain animals, it is suggested, and, therefore, contrived to tame them. This view can encompass the theory of a religious origin—animals used as sacrifices—as well as that of economic need—animals required for meat and skins. Whatever its origin, it is certain that domestication proceeded slowly for the simple reason that animals also remained available through hunting and trapping.

The first animal to pass under human dominion was the scavenger dog. In the latter part of the Paleolithic period, dogs may have been used in hunting. Certainly, there is evidence for this use from about 12,000 B.C. Dogs were also eaten, although they were never considered a major source of food in the Old World.

Archeological excavations have placed the domestication of hoofed animals tentatively at about 9000 B.C., although the finding of bones does not necessarily imply domestication. Cer-

tainly, it seems reasonable to assume that at this stage of human habitation, life had become somewhat more sedentary. The remains of goats and sheep, with characteristics suggesting domesticated breeds, together with the remains of dogs and pigs have been found in Middle Eastern excavations dating to 7500 B.C. (Fig. 4–9).

For the domestication of cattle, a settled existence, at least in the early stages, was a prerequisite. A long-horned animal, believed to be the ancestor of modern cattle, ranged throughout the forested regions of Europe, North Africa, and southwestern Asia from earliest times to the seventeenth century (Fig. 4–10). Remains of a short-horned type have been found in settlements in Central Asia (Turkestan) dating back some five thousand years. Of equal antiquity are the prehistoric cave drawings of herdsmen and cattle in the Sahara, hinting at both a wetter climate and domestication (Simoons, 1971). The earliest date for cattle domestication has now been placed at 6500 B.C. in Greece. The domesticated humped cattle of India have been dated back to about 2500 B.C. This phenomenon seems to have been repeated many times throughout the Old World, and the same pattern also may have been true of pigs.

The last group of animals to be domesticated comprises those that were used as beasts of burden, although they also may have served as a source of meat and milk among many peoples. The horse is believed to have been tamed in southern Russia about 3000 B.C. The domestic donkey dates from about the same time in Egypt, whereas the water buffalo was known as a domesticate in India by about 2500 B.C., if not earlier. The one-humped dromedary was tamed about 2000 B.C. and the two-humped Bactrian camel possibly around 1500 B.C. Among the bedouin or nomadic tribes of Arabia, the camel is a major source of milk, with milking camels remaining at the head of the herd.

The fact that not all culture groups moved from a hunting-gathering economy to the herding of animals was not necessarily due to the harshness of the environment or the backwardness of the people. Australia, for example, had no animals suitable for domestication before European contact, other than the dingo (a type of wild dog). The Americas also were almost destitute of such animals—apart from the llama, alpaca, guanaco, and bison—until the Spaniards brought horses and cattle from the Old World. On the other hand, in northern Eurasia, the reindeer was probably herded at a very early date, with the herders adapting themselves to the migration of the animals.

CROPPING THE SOIL

About ten thousand years ago, at approximately the same time that domestication of animals began, the planting of crops and the working of the soil was underway, but no one really knows how this change began (Braidwood,

1960). The process was slow, as hunting-and-gathering cultures adapted to the more sedentary life needed for the domestication of animals and plants.

Certainly, the process was more complicated than has traditionally been assumed (Sauer, 1956). It was thought that the Middle East was the scene of man's first enduring attempt to harvest crops and to cultivate the soil. New evi-

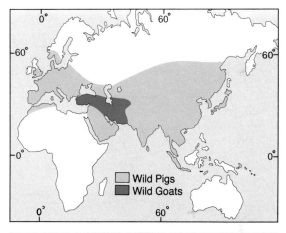

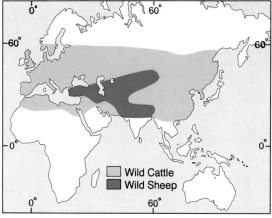

Figure 4–9

The ancestors of major Old World domesticated animals ranged widely over Asia. Pigs and cattle were at home from the Atlantic to the Pacific. Sheep and goats were generally more restricted to central and southwest Asia.

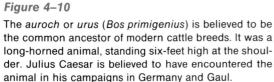

Figure 4–10

The *auroch* or *urus* (*Bos primigenius*) is believed to be the common ancestor of modern cattle breeds. It was a long-horned animal, standing six-feet high at the shoulder. Julius Caesar is believed to have encountered the animal in his campaigns in Germany and Gaul.

(A) A statue of the head of a sacred cow was found in the tomb of Tutankhamun (1361–1352 B.C.) in Egypt. The horned head apparently represented Hathor, the goddess of the Theban necropolis, who was often shown as a cow emerging from a papyrus swamp. The illustration shown here is a porcelain reproduction, courtesy of the Boehm Studios, Trenton, N.J. The original is in the Cairo Museum. (B) Long-horned cattle in Hungary photographed by the author.

dence from Southeast Asia, however, suggests that inhabitants there were growing plants quite as early as in the Middle East. The earliest evidence of the cultivation of vegetables comes from Thailand, where legumes were used and possibly cultivated as early as 9000 B.C. Research elsewhere may confirm still other important agricultural hearths. Certainly, plant domestication occurred in China, especially in the north, and possibly even in Taiwan and Japan (Grigg, 1974). Moreover, several root crops were probably domesticated in the tropical lowlands east of the Andes in South America, their cultivation spreading into the Amazon basin some time after 7000 B.C. From South America, the cultivation of these root crops—sweet potato, manioc, and arrowroot—diffused into the Caribbean islands and Central America. West Africa may also have been a setting for domestication when the native yam and the oil palm tree came into use at an early date (Fig. 4–11).

In the Middle East, the cultivation of grains most likely began in semipermanent communities located on uplands overlooking river valleys (Fig. 4–12). Modern Iraq and Iran have some of the most ancient sites, which offer the best evidence of a succession of events, but southeastern Turkey and adjacent regions are important as well. Wheat and barley were among the first food crops to be selected for use in this region, but they differ substantially from modern varieties. Wild wheat, however, can still be found in abundance on the uplands and hills of the Middle East; wild barley is more widely found over Western and Central Asia (Fig. 4–13). At a much later date, maize (corn) underwent a similar evolution in the New World (Johannessen, 1970).

In time, these Middle Eastern farmers, along with their animals came down from the uplands to utilize the river valleys where water was more readily available. Two agricultural sites, at M'lefaat and Jarmo in Iraq, represent the oldest settled agricultural villages ever to be studied in detail. Both date back to about 5000 B.C.; M'lefaat may even be older.

From Mesopotamia, crop cultivation may have been carried to other areas. Quite possibly, predynastic Egypt received its initial stimulus to cultivate crops from the Tigris-Euphrates region, and this may have been true also of Harappa and Mohenjo-Daro in the Indus Valley. There is evidence to suggest that about 3500 B.C. agriculture was practiced in the uplands of Baluchistan, with farmers moving down into the valley of the Indus River about 3000 B.C. (Grigg, 1974).

IRRIGATION AGRICULTURE

After these early farmers moved to the river valleys to utilize water for their crops, new forms of socioadministrative organization, based on irrigation, vastly altered the relationship between humans and the physical environment. Improvement in agricultural techniques, both through irrigation agriculture and the breeding of improved livestock, gradually led to an increase in food production.

Irrigation, like the process of domestication itself, did not suddenly emerge as a developed technology. In its crudest form—digging of shallow ditches to divert water from streams into nearby plots—it probably was practiced by some of the earliest farmers. But an irrigation economy came to include much more than this. It allowed farmers to decide when water was needed to supplement the natural supply of rainfall (and how much), it permitted them to drain surplus water from the fields, and it made possible for them to benefit from flooding (and the depositing of fresh silt) without suffering devastation. At its most sophisticated level, the practice of irrigation entailed the construction of complex systems of canals, aqueducts, dams, sluices, and embankments. To achieve such facilities, a high degree of social organization, a large labor force, and cooperation and leadership were essential. As Karl A. Wittfogel has shown, an elaborate structure of nonhydraulic public works—(cities, defense walls, and roads together with religious and political structures) were required if the society based on irrigation farming was to be governed and protected (Wittfogel, 1957).

In the broad Tigris-Euphrates lowland and subsequently in the other river valleys of the Old World, the irregular nature and extent of flooding during the high-water period meant that water management had to be carried out on a large scale or not at all (Box 4–4). The sheer scope of the undertaking—the large engineering works, the size of the necessary labor force, the digging and moving of soil—suggested that the problem could be solved only by utilizing all available labor, voluntary or slave. The planning and direction of the works had to be vested in central authority. The resulting social organization on a mass scale not only accomplished the project, but also produced both a governing class and class differentiation.

Settlements grew—not only to make large-scale irrigation possible, but also because irrigated land produced surplus food to support a nonfarm population. In southern Mesopotamia, mounds have been uncovered that date to the fourth millennium B.C. They have revealed temples, palaces, and market sites together with remnants of dwellings made of uniformly moulded clay bricks. Copper and bronze implements also date from this time. These settlements were definitely not just farming communities whose inhabitants were wholly

Figure 4–11

The Russian geographer-geneticist N. I. Vavilov (1887–1943?) identified nine centers of origin of cultivated plants. Some centers of plant domestication, such as those for barley, coincided with early culture hearths in Mesopotamia, the Eastern Mediterranean, South Asia and the Far East, and in the Americas. However, other grains, such as corn (maize) (tropical America) and sorghum (Africa), originated outside the above culture hearths. Root crops originated in the Americas as well as in Southeast Asia.

MESO-AMERICA
Beans
Cacao
Chili
Maize
Squash
Manioc (Cassava)
Potatoes
Pumpkin
Sweet Potatoes
Tobacco
Tomatoes

ANDEAN HIGHLANDS
Beans
Maize
Manioc (Cassava)
Potatoes
Pumpkin
Sweet Potatoes
Tobacco
Tomatoes

occupied in tilling the soil or raising livestock, although they may have contained a number of farmers. These cities were religious centers, administrative centers, trading marts, and centers of artisan enterprise. They represented a new kind of phenomenon and their existence was supported by the agricultural surplus produced by the ever-growing surrounding farming population.

The need to predict and plan for the most auspicious times to till, plant, and harvest also led to humankind's first attempt to understand the seasons. It was in Ur, around 3000 B.C., for example, that wise men determined that the year comprised 365¼ days. The timing and consequences of seasonal changes and uniformities were also codified. Thus, environmental modification, a growing sociocultural complexity, and an increase in knowledge went hand in hand.

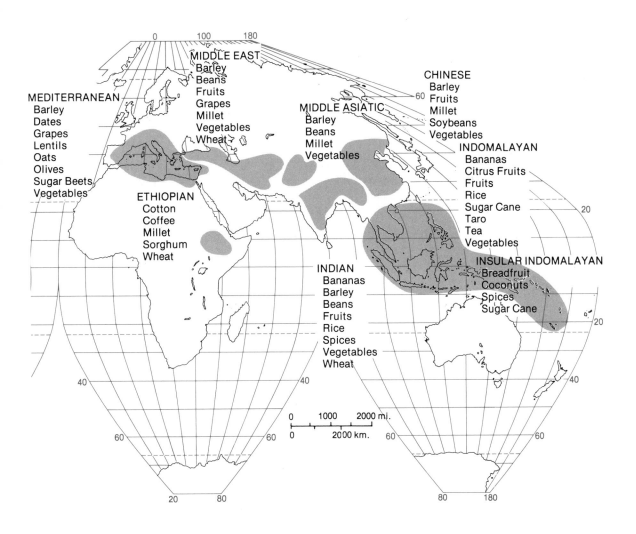

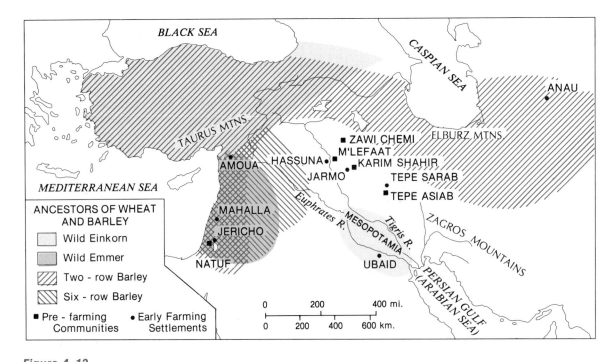

Figure 4-12

The wild grasses that were the ancestors of wheat and barley grew widely in the uplands from Turkey to Iran. Archeological evidence reveals that a number of early agricultural communities arose in the hills above the Tigris-Euphrates Valley. It is possible, too, that a primitive form of irrigation may have been practiced from an early date. Subsequently, however, the farmers moved into the lowlands where the water supply was more plentiful and assured.

SHIFTING CULTIVATION

Outside the fertile alluvial river valleys, farmers may initially have adopted a system of cultivation that has been described variously as shifting cultivation, *slash-and-burn agriculture,* or *swidden farming* (Struever, 1971). This system entails the temporary use of plots produced by the cutting back and burning off of the vegetative cover. *Swidden* is an old dialect word from northern England, meaning burned clearing. Each geographic region, however, has its own term for the practice: *caingen* in the Philippines, *ladang* in Indonesia, *djum* in India, *chitemene* in parts of Africa, and *milpa* in Meso-America.

Under ideal conditions, shifting cultivation not only preserves the natural ecosystem, but also permits the transformation of a natural vegetative cover into a harvestable one. Such an effort entails hard physical labor, as the early pioneers in the eastern forests of North America soon discovered, but not necessarily a large labor force.

The clearing and burning off of the forest releases into the soil mineral nutrients that were locked up in the vegetation. In tropical areas, where the soils have been heavily leached, crops draw heavily on the potash released into the earth so that the completeness with which the vegetative cover is burned is crucial. Some loss of nutrients occurs in the process, but the

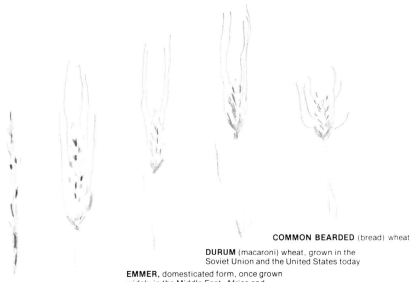

COMMON BEARDED (bread) wheat

DURUM (macaroni) wheat, grown in the
Soviet Union and the United States today

EMMER, domesticated form, once grown
widely in the Middle East, Africa and
Europe

EINKORN, domesticated form, once
grown widely in Europe and Asia Minor

WILD EINKORN, once found widely
dispersed in the Middle East

Figure 4–13

Two of the earliest forms of domesticated wheat were einkorn (*Triticum monococcum*) and emmer (*Triticum dicoccum*). Einkorn was grown throughout Turkey and Europe; emmer was widespread in the Middle East and North Africa. *Triticum timopheevii,* another early type, had no common name. Modern wheats were derived from some of these early species, both through hybridization in the wild and by scientific breeding. *Triticum durum,* often known as macaroni wheat, is grown widely in southern Russia and in western Siberia. At the turn of the nineteenth century, it was brought to North America, where it subsequently became an important grain in Minnesota. *Triticum aestivum,* a cross between emmer or macaroni wheat and goat grass, is a common bread wheat.

ultimate food benefit to the farmer is obvious. It has always been thought that shifting cultivation provides for subsistence only, but surpluses may result under careful management, especially because such fields are rarely planted to single crops.

Where conditions are less than ideal, on the other hand, forests may be destroyed without substantial benefit to the farmer. The clearing and firing of the forest may open up the soil to erosion and general deterioration. The original tree cover may be replaced with scrub vegetation. In temperate lands, the rate of forest replacement is slow so that without additional input, such as fertilizers, crop yields may be poor. In the humid tropics, the forest may quickly recover, but even there, shifting cultivation must follow a locally determined, well-defined pattern, if the population is to be fed. Shifting cultivation in tropical areas supports today some fifty million people.

Early European Agriculture

In Europe, early agriculture, some five thousand years ago, was mainly of the shifting or swidden type. In the Danube Valley, for example, stone axes and fire were used to reduce the oak forests. In the clearings, a second growth of grasses and trees helped restore the soils if livestock were not left to feed in the fields. The use and spread of the ox-drawn plough may have been instrumental in establishing agriculture on a permanent basis, following the initial period of slash and burn (Grigg, 1974). Where livestock subsequently became an important component in the farm economy, as cattle did in Western Europe and sheep and goats did in the Mediterranean, cleared forestland was rapidly transformed into grasses and heath. The stock ate the grasses and clovers that sprang up, and they trampled or ate the shoots of trees as soon as they appeared above ground. Such practices led to the destruction of both the vegetative cover and of the soil itself. The slopes of the Mediterranean lands were already severely eroded by winter rains, even before the Christian era.

The spread of farming into forests and grasslands is an excellent example of the progressive modification of the earth's environment by humans, but such defoliation should not be judged too harshly (Darby, 1956). The history of agriculture in Europe, especially since the medieval

---

BOX 4–4

Egypt: The Gift of the Nile

The Greek historian Herodotus (485?–?425 B.C.) noted that Egypt was "a gift of the Nile." Because the population of Egypt is concentrated along the 675 miles of the river between Aswan and the Mediterranean, one can in truth state that Egypt is the Nile. Without the waters of the Nile, the narrow ribbon of green that parallels the river would yield entirely to the dusty brown of the encompassing desert. Unlike the Tigris and Euphrates, the Nile undergoes regular periods of high and low water. By May, the level of the river is at its lowest point and the soil is parched and dry. But by June, the spring rains that have poured down on the Ethiopian Plateau far to the south have flooded the banks of the Nile downstream. Rich in vegetative matter, minerals, and potash, the river deposits a layer of rich humus over farmlands. It was for this reason that the river banks in ancient times were described as the Black Land to set them off from the desert, which was the Red Land. The god Osiris, held in high esteem in ancient Egypt, was associated with the Nile and the fertile soil, but the waters sometimes failed to come and famine would result. The need to keep records of the river's rise and fall may have contributed to the development of Egyptian hieroglyphics. In any case, the productive agriculture of the valley gave rise to a rich and flourishing civilization and sustained it for several thousands of years. (Fig. 4–14).

Apart from the Nile, there are no other major waterways draining the land. Outside the valley, cultivation is not possible without supplemental supplies of water. Thus, the Nile silt, which constitutes the present-day cultivated area of Egypt, is the only area where extensive cropping is possible. Such a rich resource, however, must support population densities of twenty-five hundred per square mile. Settlements are large and range in size from thirty-five thousand to over three hundred thousand—their livelihood derived largely from agriculture, which employs up to half the total population. The building of the Aswan High Dam, completed in the 1970s, was designed to expand the irrigated area by up to 1.5 million acres. But Egypt's population of 45.9 million (1983) continues to grow at a rapid rate (over 3 percent), thus robbing the country of the benefits accruing from the reclaimed crop area.

period, is one that suggests the achievement of a viable balance between humans and the land. Because some of the best farmland had been occupied from a very early date, farmers were compelled to work out systems of land use that entailed steadily improved crop rotation systems and, where possible, a well-managed crop-livestock economy. Land reclamation, especially the drainage of marshlands, was also an important feature of the medieval farm economy, particularly in England, the Netherlands, and later in Italy (Fig. 4–15).

DIFFUSION OF EUROPEAN FARMING METHODS

When European farming methods were carried to other parts of the world where agricultural resources seemed unlimited, notably in North America, the immigrant farmer often lost sight of the need to maintain a balance with nature. Settlers in humid, eastern North America found a forested environment not too dissimilar from that which they had left in northwestern Eu-

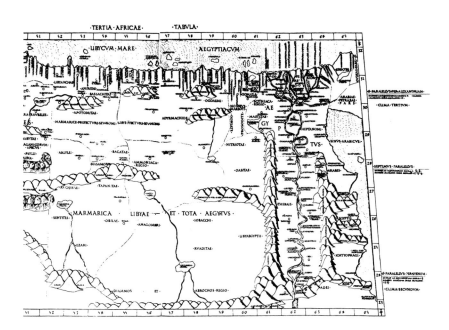

Figure 4–14

Ptolemy's map of Egypt, prepared sometime during the middle of the second century A.D., shows not only the great interest he had in attempting to determine latitude and longitude, but also, and more important, that he was a keen observer of the world around him.

Here it is evident to mapmaker and reader alike that Egyptian civilization was concentrated in the valley of the Nile, judging by the number of towns and cities identified. The vast western interior is shown as sparsely settled, save for the Mediterranean coast. A modern map of Egypt would reveal a similar pattern of distribution.

(*Source: Claudius Ptolemaeus Cosmographica.* Rome: 1478. [Amsterdam: Theatrum Orbis Terrarum, 1966. Fac. Newberry Library Copy, 1937.] Courtesy Rare Book Collection, University of Washington Libraries.)

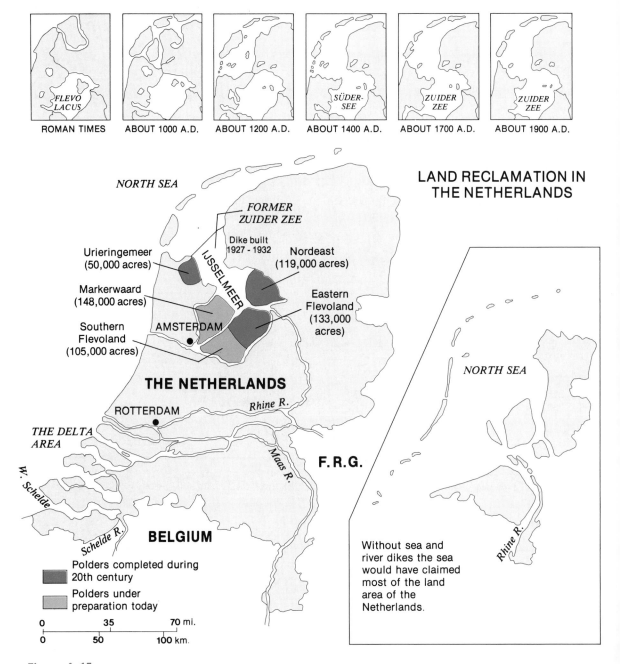

| ROMAN TIMES | ABOUT 1000 A.D. | ABOUT 1200 A.D. | ABOUT 1400 A.D. | ABOUT 1700 A.D. | ABOUT 1900 A.D. |

FLEVO LACUS — *SÜDER-SEE* — *ZUIDER ZEE* — *ZUIDER ZEE*

LAND RECLAMATION IN THE NETHERLANDS

NORTH SEA

FORMER ZUIDER ZEE

Dike built 1927 - 1932

Urieringemeer (50,000 acres)

IJSSELMEER

Nordeast (119,000 acres)

Markerwaard (148,000 acres)

Eastern Flevoland (133,000 acres)

AMSTERDAM

Southern Flevoland (105,000 acres)

THE NETHERLANDS

ROTTERDAM

Rhine R.

THE DELTA AREA

Maas R.

F.R.G.

NORTH SEA

W. Schelde

Schelde R.

BELGIUM

Rhine R.

■ Polders completed during 20th century

▨ Polders under preparation today

| 0 | 35 | 70 mi. |
| 0 | 50 | 100 km. |

Without sea and river dikes the sea would have claimed most of the land area of the Netherlands.

Figure 4–15

One of the best examples of European drainage schemes may be seen in the attempts to wrest the submerged coast of the Netherlands from the sea.

In the Netherlands, the project entailed the reclamation of about five hundred thousand acres in five separate land areas, known as *polders,* with the formation of a freshwater lake known as Ijsselmeer. Between 1927–1932 a 20-mile-long dike was erected across the Zuider Zee, cutting off the proposed Ijsselmeer. Work then proceeded on the Urieringermeer polder and the Nordost (North East) Polder. After World War II, work was completed on East Flevoland. Markerwaard and South Flevoland have yet to be reclaimed.

Figure 4–16

Not all Europeans created farmland in the New World by clearing the forests. The French settlers along the shores of the Bay of Fundy, who came to be known as Acadians, created farmland by draining the coastal marshes. The technology was brought from Poitou, France, where freshwater marshes had been drained and used for farming. In Acadia, the technology was adapted to the salt marsh tidal flats of the Fundy shore, where crops were raised both for livestock and human consumption.

This illustration of dike building on the flats south of Fort Beauséjour, in what is now southern New Brunswick, is by the Toronto artist, Lewis Parker (dates unknown).

(Photo courtesy of the Historical Resources Administration, Village Historique Acadien, Caraquet, New Brunswick, Canada.)

rope, but the vastness of the new resource base kindled an unbridled optimism. The fertile land offered, probably for the first time in human history, the promise of almost continuous growth in agricultural production. The demand for land and for a homestead, which was to become part of the American dream, was accompanied by a creed of maximization of agricultural output.

"What constantly forced the nation's agriculture toward ever greater output," one writer notes, "was a growing hunger in the American belly—not only for food and fiber, but for what they could buy" (Worster, 1979, p. 94).

In the heady days of early expansion, the forest stands were reduced, but the unregulated cutting subsequently led to the loss of millions of acres of commercial timberland and the destruction of countless acres of good farmland (Fig. 4–16). The clearing of magnificent stands of white pine in central Ontario in the mid-nineteenth century, in part to satisfy American and

British naval demand, eliminated a resource that has never been restored. Sadly, too, the immigrants who were offered farms in the area by private land companies found after a period of backbreaking toil that the land was ill suited to agricultural pursuits.

When the new Americans moved out onto the prairies of the West, they were ill prepared, in both experience and understanding, to manage the fertile but drought-prone, fragile soils of the grassland environment. At any rate, failure in one area could be followed by a new stake so long as the frontier was "out there." But, the closing of the frontier in the early decades of the twentieth century was not accompanied by a basic change in farm philosophy.

The creation of a granary of global significance in the heart of the North American continent stood out as a tribute to the endurance and fortitude of American and Canadian prairie farmers. But, their continual expansion of cropland in violation of agronomic principles contributed to the drought cycle and the dust bowl of the 1930s. Millions of acres of topsoil were blown away, darkening cities at noon (Figs. 4–17, 4–18). The ideology of the prairie farmers was of an indefinitely expanding universe, but they did not see that they were fast approaching, under the technology available to them, the limits to growth.

Even today, according to *The Global 2000 Report to the President* (1982), extensive wind and water erosion of U.S. soils has led the Soil Conservation Service to conclude that to sustain production at present levels, soil losses (through erosion, not urban expansion) must be cut in half. The report concludes that the outlook is not promising.

In Russia, a similar pattern of misuse occurred in the nineteenth and twentieth centuries as settlers began filling up the *steppe* or grasslands of southern and Asiatic Russia. Misuse of the prairies was intensified by the rapid growth of the rural population, strip farming in European Russia, and overextension into the droughty steppes of Asiatic Russia.

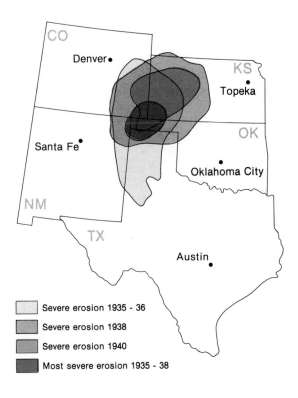

Severe erosion 1935 - 36

Severe erosion 1938

Severe erosion 1940

Most severe erosion 1935 - 38

Figure 4–17

Extent of Area subject to severe wind erosion, 1935–1940.

(*Source:* Adapted from Worster, 1979, p. 30.)

After the Revolution of 1917 and following the enforced collectivization of peasant holdings after 1928, the Stalin regime, in its haste to increase output, paid little heed to the warnings of soil scientists as it pushed farming deeper into the dry prairies. The results were predictable, forcing the regime to slow down. However, when Khrushchev came to power in 1953, he, too, wanted a victory on the land and his program called for the ploughing of up to 100 million acres of land for grain, in part at the expense of necessary fallowing and soil moisture (Goldman, 1972). When dry years occurred, dust storms were common and the exposed prairie yielded up millions of acres of fine-grained topsoil.

Figure 4–18
Western Kansas, April 14, 1935—Black Sunday.
Picture Credit: Photo Researchers, Inc.

DESERTIFICATION: THE MARCH OF THE DESERTS

Serious as are the problems that face prairie farmers in temperate lands, they pale alongside the ecological collapse of the savanna grasslands of the *Sahel* in northern Africa. The Sahel, a region of varying width on the southern side of the Sahara Desert, stretches from the Atlantic Ocean in the west to the Horn of Africa in the east.

The peoples of the Sahel are divided among a series of newly independent states that once belonged, although not exclusively, to the British and French empires. Included are such countries as Sudan, Chad, Niger, Mali, and Upper Volta. Their peoples are engaged principally in raising cattle, sheep, and goats on the coarse savanna grasses that are part of the region's natural vegetation. Crop cultivation is practiced on a limited scale.

In 1968, a drought set in that lasted six years. The searing heat and dry winds brought Saharan characteristics from the north. Vegetation dried up, water holes ran dry, and livestock perished. In Mali, more than 90 percent of its cattle, sheep, and goats were dead by 1974. As *The Global 2000 Report to the President* states (1982, vol. 1, p. 33): "Desertification does not necessarily mean the creation of Saharalike sand deserts, but rather it includes a variety of ecological changes that destroy the cover of vegetation and fertile soil in the earth's drier regions, rendering the land useless for range or crops."

The growing pressure of population on the land in Africa and the heavy emphasis on livestock raising, an economy that had been expanded—rather unwisely as it turned out—to capitalize on foreign markets, had led to severe overgrazing. The problem was compounded by

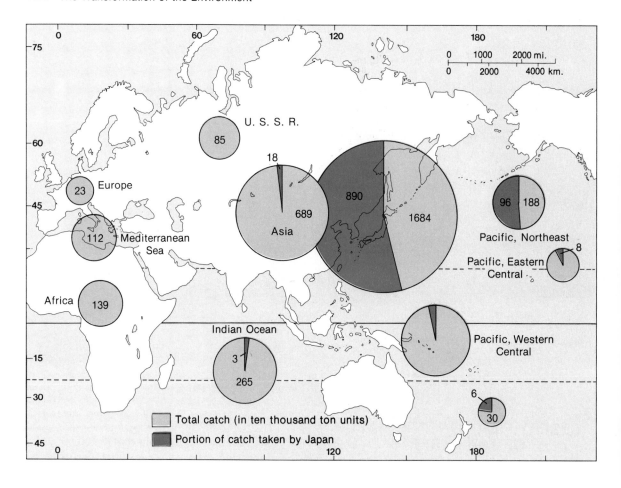

the existence of political boundaries, dating from the 1950s and 1960s, that restricted freedom of movement of the herds. Moreover, the production of crops, such as cotton and peanuts for export, reduced the amount of land given over to domestic food production. Thus, when drought struck, malnutrition, starvation, the loss of livelihood were the consequences.

The Sahel crisis raised the level of world interest in the problems of *desertification*. In 1977, an international conference was convened in Nairobi, Kenya. There, the results of human folly were enumerated: the earth's productive land has been reduced by about fourteen million acres per year and rates of desertification are expected to expand some 20 percent by the year 2000. With deserts on the march, the conference recommended a list of conservation measures—long known to specialists—namely, soil conservation, the planting of windbreaks and shelterbelts to conserve soil moisture and reduce erosion, water conservation, and improved livestock range management (Worster, 1979). The unsettled political status of much of the Sahel, however, makes the implementation of any of these measures on anything but a limited scale doubtful in the forseeable future.

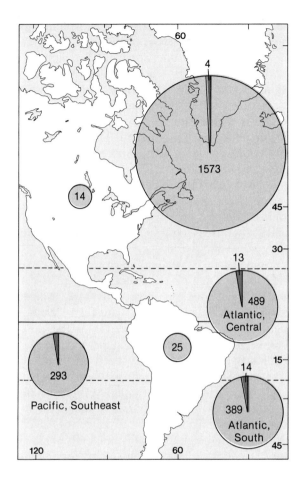

Figure 4–19

The importance of the North Atlantic and northern Pacific fisheries are clearly evident in this map of world catch. The North Atlantic fishery is dominated by the northern European countries. Japan, as is to be expected, depends heavily on Pacific waters for the bulk of its catch. Japanese fleets have become increasingly wide ranging, but the extension of economic zones to 200 miles restricts their range of operation.

COMPETITION FOR THE SEA'S RESOURCES

Approximately one half of the world's fish resources are found in four areas: the North Pacific, the Atlantic from New England to Labrador, the North Atlantic between Iceland and Norway, and off the coast of Peru. Newer fishing grounds, however, are being opened off the coasts of South America and South Africa and in the Indian Ocean.

The habits and living conditions of marine life vary greatly. Some species—cod, haddock, and pollack for example—are *demersal*, that is,

they feed off the bottom of the seabed. Others, known as *pelagic fish*—herring, mackerel, salmon, tuna, shad, pilchard and so on—swim close to the surface. Salmon and trout are *anadromous,* that is, they return generation after generation from the sea to freshwater to spawn and to die; others, such as eels, migrate from freshwater to spawn in the sea.

The Baltic and North seas have been centers of large herring fisheries since the eleventh century when they served as the foundation of the economies of Baltic city-states and the trading association known as the Hansa. When the herring left the Baltic in 1413 for reasons unknown, the Hansa cities suffered a severe blow. During the medieval period until the reign of Louis XIV, fish were a mainstay of the diet of Catholic Europe. At least 166 days a year, including Lent, were set aside for partial fasting—fish could be eaten but meat, poultry, and eggs could not. Large-scale exploitation of the Atlantic cod fisheries began with the voyage of John Cabot to Labrador in 1498. During the sixteenth and seventeenth centuries, hundreds of European vessels, mainly from France and Portugal, annually reached the Grand Banks, where cod were caught, dried, and shipped back to the Old World.

Fish have also played an important role in the diet of the Japanese and Chinese since earliest times, although fishing in the Orient has tended to be restricted to coastal waters. The indigenous peoples of the North Pacific coasts depended on fish, as did such peoples as the Solomon Islanders in the South Pacific who attached initiation rites to fishing.

Since World War II, new fishing grounds have been opened in the Southern Hemisphere and new species of fish have been harvested. Accompanying this development has been a decline in the catch of some of the more common species because of overfishing. Greater attention also is being given to deep sea fishing, particularly for krill, a shrimplike creature found in great abundance in the Antarctic Ocean. However, depletion of krill stocks will undoubtedly affect the primary source of food of most whale species.

World Fish Catch

From 1950 to 1970, the world fish catch jumped from 16 million tons to a phenomenal 70 million tons (Fig. 4–19). Thereafter, it leveled off, and declined in some areas. For example, in the early 1970s, the Peruvian anchovy fishery industry collapsed because of overfishing. The pressure on the fishing grounds, however, has remained intense. Food from the sea accounts

for 10 percent of the world's total protein consumption and 20 percent of the world's animal protein consumption. Sonar and helicopters make it possible to track shoals; and factory ships, some weighing as much as about 40,000 tons, often are equipped with a device that operates like an enormous vacuum cleaner, sucking up all forms of marine life. The fishing fleets of the Soviet Union and of Japan, in particular, have grown immensely. The former has developed what can best be described as floating fishing cities capable of accommodating up to some thirty thousand persons. These include mother ships, factories, and transports; highly mobile, they range the world over.

Some estimates would suggest that the marine harvest can be raised to an annual 200 to 300 million tons of species not yet utilized by humans. Jacques-Yves Cousteau (1910–) believes, however, that because of the rapacious nature of modern fishing methods, the total marine life has already been substantially reduced. Under careful management, an upper limit of 100 million tons annually may be the prospect of the future. To sustain such a target, every effort must be made to reduce the effects of pollution and guard against oil spills, such as those accompanying the wreck of the *Torrey Canyon* in 1967 and of the *Amoco Cadiz* off the coast of Brittany, France, in 1978, which have greatly elevated concern for the sea's continued productivity. In addition, as humankind turns increasingly to the seas for oil, blowouts at drilling platforms, such as have occurred in the Ekofisk field in the North Sea and in the Ixtoc I field in the Gulf of Mexico, open up a whole new area of concern.

In recent years, the bulk of the fish have been harvested by sixteen countries. Of these, however, Japan, the Soviet Union, mainland China, Peru, the United States, and Norway have accounted for over 50 percent (Fig. 4–20). Japan ranks as the leading fishing nation, followed by the USSR (Box 4–5). Many of the developing countries, where the need for animal protein is

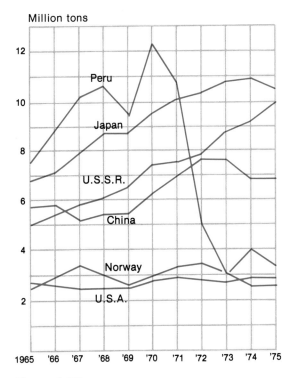

Figure 4–20
Peru occupied first place in world fisheries catch until about 1970 when the anchovy fishery industry collapsed. Since then, Japan has been the world's number one fishing nation. The USSR is its nearest competitor.
(*Source:* Japan Fisheries Association, 1975; Food and Agriculture Association of the United Nations, 1982.)

great, are either landlocked or cannot afford the investment required to sustain a modern fishing industry. In recent years, countries, such as India, South Korea, Thailand, Indonesia, the Philippines, and Vietnam, have been taking a larger share, but their combined harvest is less than that of the USSR (which harvests over 9 million metric tons).

It is ironic that only about half of the global catch is edible; of that, no more than 10 percent is usable protein. Some of the species taken, such as mackerel, pollack, and sardines, are considered low grade and go primarily into the production of pet food and cattle feed.

Whaling

Whaling, like the slaughter of buffalo on the western plains of North America, provides a notorious example of human exploitation of the earth's resources. The hunting of whales dates to about 1600 B.C., but whaling as a commercial enterprise began when the Basques in northern Spain in the eleventh century A.D. started to harvest whales from the waters of the Bay of Biscay. By the sixteenth century, the whaling industry was concentrated off Newfoundland, and whale oil was in great demand for European lamps. In addition, whalebone was used in the manufacture of European girdles. By 1697, the industry had grown so large that some two thousand whales were killed off the coast of Spitsbergen by Dutch, Norwegian, and English whalers.

As it grew, the industry became more efficient—and more devastating. In the late nineteenth century, the harpoon gun was used for the first time. After that innovation became widely accepted, the whalers roamed the seas in search of whales, transferring from the North Atlantic to the Southern Hemisphere where stocks were more plentiful. Factory ships that reduced the whales to oil at sea were another innovation that led to a great expansion of hunting. Whales could be hauled on board ship to allow for flensing and cutting, and the wastes could be dumped overboard. By 1930–1931, Antarctic waters were host to 41 floating factories. In 1933, the 28,907 whales that were caught produced 2,606,201 barrels of oil.

So severe was the depletion of whale stocks in general and of some species in particular that international agreements limiting the catch became essential. However, with World War II, whaling virtually ceased. "That time of turmoil for people," as *The Limits to Growth* points out, "was a time of peace for whales" (Meadows 1972, p. 152).

After World War II, an International Whaling Commission, with 17 participating countries, was set up to regulate the whale harvest,

BOX 4–5

Japan Searches for Food from the Sea

Japan is heavily dependent on the world's seas to feed its population. Before World War II, fish counted for at least 15 percent of the total food consumed in Japan. Today, with an annual per capita consumption of 148.6 pounds, Japan's dependency on fish greatly exceeds that of all the other major industrial countries in the world; fish provide almost 50 percent of the animal protein in the Japanese diet. In fact, the per capita fish consumption in Japan exceeds that of the USSR, the United States, and Great Britain combined (Table 4–1).

In recent years, Japan has landed over 15 percent of the world fish catch. Of its total harvest, coastal fisheries have tended to account for a fourth of this catch, but because of the spread of industrialization and urbanization in Japan and the resultant pollution of local fishing grounds, coastal fishing has tended to level off. In the Inland Sea, wastes from ships and from the land have accumulated at its bottom, and the steady buildup of sludge has all but destroyed traditional fisheries. Nevertheless, the Inland Sea provides increasing amounts of low-grade fish, such as sardines, cutlass fish, and mackerel, that enter from the ocean.

More than 87 percent of Japan's fish catch comes from waters within two hundred nautical miles of shores. Japanese fleets harvest tuna in the Pacific, Atlantic, and Indian oceans; skipjack tuna in the Central Pacific; salmon in the North Pacific; pollack in the eastern Bering Sea and around Kamchatka; cuttlefish in the northwestern Atlantic, northern Pacific, and off New Zealand; and mackerel in the East China Sea and off New Zealand. Japanese fleets also have participated vigorously in the king crab harvest in Alaska waters. To meet domestic demand for sea bream, squid, and octopus, Japanese fleets are forced to go as far as Africa. Japan also has made efforts to develop the fishing grounds off Mexico and South America.

Thus, the adoption of the 200-mile economic zone stands to reduce Japanese take from the coastal waters of other states and threatens the Japanese diet.

At the same time a new North Pacific Fisheries Convention under negotiation between Canada, the United States, and Japan will restrict Japanese salmon fleets to 175° W longitude. The new line, if recognized, should help conserve North American salmon stocks and afford a boost to Canadian and American fishermen. Japan, in turn, would net only salmon of Asian origin. In exchange for its agreement, Japan will be granted more favorable quotas for other species to be taken within the 200-mile zone of Pacific America.

To offset the loss of fish from distant fishing grounds, the Japanese government has begun a campaign to popularize consumption of low-grade species and to expand fish farming in coastal waters. In 1975, for example, some 15 million tons of salmon, trout, carp, and eels were harvested. Similar experiments are being applied to prawns and other forms of shellfish. Although such attempts are encouraging signs, the potential for serious problems should not be underemphasized.

Table 4–1

Annual per Capita Consumption of Fish and Shellfish for Human Food by Selected Countries 1975–1977 (average in pounds)

Country	Average Pounds	Country	Average Pounds
Japan	148.6	USSR	63.3
Iceland	147.3	France	48.9
Hong Kong	111.3	Canada	40.1
Korea (ROK)	104.3	Great Britain	38.1
Norway	103.6	United States	35.1
Portugal	85.1	Bangladesh	22.9
Spain	77.8	South Africa	15.4
Denmark	77.4	Zaire	13.7
Philippines	73.0	India	7.0
Sweden	71.6		

Source: National Fisherman. *The American Fisheries Directory and Reference Book*, 2nd ed. Camden, Maine: National Fisherman, 1981, pp. 92–93.

set limits to the catch, and protect the whales from extinction. Even so, 57,891 whales were killed in 1966. They yielded, however, only 60 percent of the oil produced in 1933, suggesting that larger whales, particularly of the blue and fin type, had been driven to the brink of extinction. About 80 percent of the catch is presently from Antarctic waters.

Other Resources from the Seas

The resources of the seabed represent a new kind of frontier for humans. Life on earth began in the sea, and it is to this realm that humans are returning for many of the resources needed for the modern era. Supremacy over nature has always been linked to technology and skills. In the past, the vastness of the seas has presented seemingly insurmountable obstacles. Except for the taking of salt, humans have been almost powerless to exploit the resources of any but the most shallow areas. Now, however, advanced technology will be increasingly employed to extract valuable natural resources from the seabed.

Oil and Gas

Until recently, offshore drilling for oil and gas was restricted to relatively shallow waters. This was true off the coast of California, in the Gulf of Mexico, in the Caspian Sea near Baku, and in Lake Maracaibo in Venezuela. By 1953, however, drilling had taken place into water of a depth of 300 feet, and within a decade semisubmersible rigs made it possible to drill to greater depths. By 1964, one sixth of the earth's total output of oil and gas came from offshore wells (Table 4–2).

When it was determined late in the 1960s that there were extensive pools of oil and natural gas under the North Sea, a new era opened in the offshore industry. Then, by the late 1970s, it became possible to drill to depths of 15,000 feet,

Table 4–2

Offshore Production of Oil Relative to Total Output, by Major Regions, 1982 (thousands of barrels)

Region	Offshore	Total
Middle East	1,497	4,581
North America	405	3,610
Africa	259	1,623
Latin America	1,096	2,255
Asia Pacific	581	961
Western Europe	973	1,085
Others, including Soviet bloc	65	5,279
Total	4,876	19,394

Source: American Petroleum Industry. *Basic Petroleum Data Book. Petroleum Industry Statistics 3* (3), 1983, Sec. 4, Table 1a; Sec. 11, Table 2. Washington, D.C.: American Petroleum Institute, 1983.

a phenomenon that drew attention to the potential utilization of oil and gas believed to underlie the Beaufort Sea in Canada's Arctic region.

The rapid development of technology in the oil and gas industry suggests that the largest reserves of these important resources may be found not only in the sedimentary basins of the continental shelves, but also even in ocean depths. For this to happen, however, more than advanced technology will be required. Because it is possible that by the late 1980s, a third of the world's oil and gas output may come from beneath the seas, agreements at an international level will have to be worked out.

Coal and Minerals

Coal has long been mined from under the sea, but using shafts that begin on land. As the demand for energy sources increases, a step-up in coal mining under the seas undoubtedly will occur. The seabed is rich in minerals as well as coal, and their exploitation is also a certainty. Copper, nickel, zinc, gold, silver, and manganese—these are some of the treasures to be found on the ocean floor.

Nodules of manganese oxides that continually accumulate on the deep ocean floor have been known since the voyage of HMS *Challenger* in 1873–1876; however, the scientific community showed little further interest in the find until late in the 1950s. The seabed of the Pacific west of Mexico is believed to be especially rich in these nodules. As the technology for underwater mining has become increasingly adept at this difficult task, extensive seabed mining has become a very real possibility. However, because many of these nodules lie on deep ocean floors beyond the 200-mile limit of any country, the question of how to develop and to share these resources is one that has yet to be resolved by the nations of the earth.

The Need for Agreement

Henry Wadsworth Longfellow (1807–1882) in his poem, "The Building of the Ship," refers to the water bodies of the earth as:

> The dim, dark sea, so like unto Death,
> That divides and yet unites mankind!

When human beings gained the navigational skills to venture out onto the earth's seas and oceans, they opened up a medium to speed contact and improve communication. Yet, at the same time, this contact over the seas has not always been in the spirit of friendliness. Humankind has fought over perceived maritime advantages—trade routes, fisheries, and, more recently, mineral resources on or under the seabed. Today, agreements on how the sea and its wealth are to be divided among the nations of the world seem as elusive as ever, although, in varying degrees, the entire human population is dependent on the earth's bodies of water. It is that dependency that unites humankind, but unfortunately a clear realization of what this means has not been fully grasped by all.

EPILOGUE

The measure of the human transformation of the earth is difficult to gauge. Moreover, the changes brought about by humans in the past century and a half have been more profound than anything attempted in the previous millennia of history.

That impact is even more extensive than suggested in this chapter. The growth of population, industrialization, and the rise of the city, which are discussed in subsequent chapters, have also made their contribution. Pollutants have been added to the atmosphere, climates have been modified, water bodies have been poisoned, and natural landscapes have been ripped apart and rearranged to suit new demands.

Although it is easy to emphasize the destructive role that humankind has played in changing the face of the earth, that role needs to be viewed in perspective. Human ingenuity has produced many innovations that have benefited humankind. A growing awareness of the finite nature of things may lead humankind into greater caution and less willingness to sacrifice the natural fundament to the same reckless degree that was shown in the past.

APPLICATION OF IDEAS

1. Give some thought to the many ways in which we have transformed the American environment since the first European immigrants reached the Atlantic seaboard. David Lowenthal suggests that the tempo and magnitude of change have been truly incredible compared with other lands and cultures.

2. Until some almost cataclysmic happening in nature, such as the eruption of Mount St. Helens in 1980, we tended to think of the earth as being relatively stable and to forget the magnitude of the forces that have shaped the surface of the planet. Humankind, however, has also been a significant contributor to environmental modification. Can you think of other ways—other than those identified in the chapter—that we have transformed our habitat?

3. One of the major turning points in the transformation of nature's realm came with the domestication of plants and animals. To what extent do you think diffusion might have accounted for this phenomenon occurring in a number of places over the earth? What arguments can you give for independent innovation in many of the different regions of domestication?

4. What were the consequences of the development of irrigation agriculture? How does irrigation agriculture differ from shifting cultivation: note that the latter survives in many tropical areas of the globe today and can be an ecologically successful system. What may ultimately bring about the demise of shifting cultivation? What alternatives are there to slash-and-burn agriculture?

5. Consider the many ramifications of the marriage of science and technology? Why had this union not occurred before the Industrial Revolution? What are its implications for your life?

6. Assuming the industrialized world needs a new environmental ethic, how is this goal to be realized? What can you do to bring it about?

KEY WORDS AND PHRASES

anadromous	shifting cultivation
biome	slash-and-burn
demersal	agriculture
desertification	steppe
domestication	swidden
pelagic fish	swidden farming
Sahel	tsunami

QUESTIONS FOR FURTHER DISCUSSION

1. Why was the ability of early humans to transform their habitat limited? Can you cite, however, instances where the landscape was significantly modified?

2. Why has no single environment ever been just right for mankind? Can you cite geographic evidence to support this statement?

3. Why did the knowledge of fire gain such importance in human legend? What do you think human life was like without it?

4. In China, the deforestation of the land contributed to the expansion of crop cultivation. In the Mediterranean basin, timber was an important component of trade. Explain why there was this difference.

5. Traditionally, scientists believed that the Middle East was the cradle of crop cultivation, although perhaps not exclusively. Today, it is believed that there were a number of major centers (and a number of minor centers) where the cultivation of crops occurred indigenously and diffusion played a less important role in the geographic development of farming. How do you account for the emergence of this new theory? What conclusions about mankind can be drawn from it?

6. What circumstances might have led to the development of irrigation agriculture? How did this development alter patterns of human organization and activity?

7. Shifting cultivation, an early form of crop cultivation, is still practiced in some parts of the globe today. Why has it survived in some places and disappeared in other regions? What are its advantages and disadvantages?

8. To what extent did European farming methods affect attitudes toward, and use of, the forests of Anglo-America? Of prairie soils?

9. What sources, statistical or otherwise, would you want to check to gain some appreciation for the extent of the transformation of the landscape in America since 1800?

10. How are world fisheries to be maintained at present levels? What needs to be done to ensure wise use of the other resources found in the ocean's environment?

REFERENCES AND ADDITIONAL READINGS

American Petroleum Institute. *Basic Petroleum Data Book. Petroleum Industry Statistics 3* (3). Washington, D.C.: American Petroleum Institute, 1983.

Bell, Daniel. "Technology, Nature and Society." *American Scholar* 42, (1973): 385–404.

Braidwood, R. J. "The Agricultural Revolution." *Scientific American* 217 (1960): 130–148.

Brown, Harrison. "Technological Denudation," pp. 1023–1032. In *Man's Role in Changing the Face of the Earth.* William L. Thomas, Jr., ed. Chicago: University of Chicago Press, 1956.

Butzer, Karl W. *Environment and Archeology. An Introduction to Pleistocene Geography.* Chicago: Aldine, 1964.

Darby, H. C. "The Clearing of the Woodland in Europe," pp. 183–216. In *Man's Role in Changing the Face of the Earth.* William L. Thomas, Jr., ed. Chicago: University of Chicago Press, 1956.

Davis, Charles. "Fire as a Land-Use Tool in Northeastern Australia." *Geographical Review* 49 (1959): 552–560.

Detwyler, Thomas R., and Marcus, Melvin G. *Urbanization and Environment* Belmont, Calif.: Duxbury Press, 1972.

Disch, Robert, ed. *The Ecological Conscience. Values for Survival.* Englewood Cliffs, N.J.: Prentice-Hall, 1970.

Dorst, Jean. *Before Nature Dies.* Boston: Houghton Mifflin, 1970.

Food and Agriculture Association of the United Nations. *Commodity Review and Outlook: 1981–82.* FAO Economic and Social Development Series No. 22 Rome: FAO, 1982.

Gerasimov, I. P., et al., eds. *Natural Resources of the Soviet Union: Their Use and Renewal.* San Francisco: W. H. Freeman, 1971. (English edition edited by W. A. Douglas Jackson.)

The Global 2000 Report to the President. Vol. 1. New York: Penguin Books, 1982.

Goldman, Marshall I. *The Spoils of Progress. Environmental Pollution in the Soviet Union.* Cambridge: MIT Press, 1972

Grigg, David B. *The Agricultural Systems of the World: An Evolutionary Approach.* London: Cambridge University Press, 1974.

Harden, Garrett, and Baden, John, eds. *Managing the Commons.* San Francisco: W. H. Freeman, 1977.

Harlan, Jack R. "The Plants and Animals that Nourish Man." *Scientific American* 235 (1976): 88–97.

Harris, D. R. "New Light on Plant Domestication and the Origins of Agriculture: A Review." *Geographical Review* 57 (1967): 90–107.

Heichelheim, Fritz M. "Effects of Classical Antiquity on the Land," pp. 165–182. In *Man's Role in Changing the Face of the Earth.* William L. Thomas, Jr., ed. Chicago: University of Chicago Press, 1956.

Issac, Erich. *Geography of Domestication.* Englewood Cliffs, N.J.: Prentice-Hall, 1970.

Japan Fisheries Association. *Fisheries of Japan, 1975.* Tokyo: Japan Fisheries Association, 1975.

Johannessen, Carl L., et al. The Domestication of Maize: Process or Event?" *Geographical Review* 60 (1970): 393–413.

Leighly, John, ed. *Land and Life. A Selection from the Writings of Carl Ortwin Sauer.* Berkely and Los Angeles: University of California Press, 1963

Leopold, Aldo. *A Sand County Almanac.* New York: Oxford University Press, 1949.

Lewis, Pierce F., et al. *Visual Blight in America.* Resource Paper No. 23. Washington, D.C.: Commission on College Geography, Association of American Geographers, 1973.

Lowenthal, David. "George Perkins Marsh and the American Geographical Tradition." *Geographical Review* 43 (1953): 207–213.

———. *George Perkins March: Versatile Vermonter.* New York: Columbia University Press, 1958.

Manners, Ian R., and Mikesell, Marvin W., eds. *Per-*

spectives on Environment: Essays Requested by the Panel on Environmental Education. Publication No. 13. Washington, D.C.: Commission on College Geography, Association of American Geographers, 1974.

Marsh, George Perkins. Man and Nature or, Physical Geography as Modified by Human Action. Cambridge: Harvard University Press, 1965. (Belknap Press) (Originally published, 1864).

McHarg, Ian. Design with Nature. Garden City, N.Y.: Natural History Press, 1969.

Meadows, Donella H., et al. The Limits to Growth. New York: Universe Books, 1972

Meinig, D. W. "The Continuous Shaping of America: A Prospectus for Geographers and Historians." American Historical Review 83 (1978): 1186–1217.

Mikesell, Marvin. "The Deforestation of Mount Lebanon." Geographical Review 59 (1969): 1–28.

Mumford, Lewis. The Myth of the Machine. The Pentagon of Power. New York: Harcourt Brace Jovanovich, 1970.

Nash, Roderick. The American Environment. Readings in the History of Conservation, 2nd ed. Reading, Mass.: Addison-Wesley, 1976.

National Fisherman. The American Fisheries Directory and Reference Book. 2nd ed. Camden, Maine: National Fisherman, 1981.

Pyne, Stephen J. Fire in America. A Cultural History of Wildland and Rural Fire. Princeton: Princeton University Press, 1982.

Roszak, Theodore. Where the Wasteland Ends. Politics and Transcendence in Postindustrial Society. Garden City, N. Y.: Doubleday, 1972.

Russell, Richard J. "Environmental Changes Through Forces Independent of Man," pp. 453–470. In Man's Role in Changing the Face of Nature. William L. Thomas, Jr., ed. Chicago: University of Chicago Press, 1956.

Sauer, Carl O. "The Agency of Man on the Earth," pp. 46–69. In Man's Role in Changing the Face of the Earth. William L. Thomas, Jr., ed. Chicago: University of Chicago Press, 1956.

Scarlott, Charles A. "Limitations to Energy Use," pp. 1010–1022. In Man's Role in Changing the Face of the Earth. William L. Thomas, Jr., ed. Chicago: University of Chicago Press, 1956.

Sears, Paul B. "The Processes of Environmental Change by Man," pp. 471–486. In Man's Role in Changing the Face of the Earth. William L. Thomas, Jr., ed. Chicago: University of Chicago Press, 1956.

Shepard, Paul. Man in the Landscape: A Historic View of the Esthetics of Nature. New York: Ballantine Books, 1967.

Simoons, Frederick J. "The Antiquity of Dairying in Asia and Africa." Geographical Review 61 (1971): 431–439.

———. "Contemporary Research Themes in the Cultural Geography of Domesticated Animals." Geographical Review 64 (1974): 557–576.

Singer, Charles, et al., eds., A History of Technology, Vol. 1. New York: Oxford University Press, 1954.

Stewart, Omer C. "Fire as the First Great Force Employed by Man," pp.115–133. In Man's Role in Changing the Face of the Earth. William L. Thomas, Jr., ed. Chicago: University of Chicago Press, 1956.

Struever, Stuart, ed. Prehistoric Agriculture. Garden City, N.Y.: Natural History Press, 1971.

Tuan, Yi-Fu. "Discrepancies Between Environmental Attitude and Behavior. Examples from Europe and China." Canadian Geographer 12 (1968): 176–191.

Udall, Stewart L. The Quiet Crisis. New York: Avon Books, 1964.

Wegener, Alfred. The Origin of Continents and Oceans. New York: E. P. Dutton, 1924.

White, Lynn. "The Historical Roots of Our Ecological Crisis." Science 155 (1967): 1203–1207.

Wiener, Philip P., and Noland, Aaron, eds. Roots of Scientific Thought. A Cultural Perspective. New York: Basic Books, 1957.

Wittfogel, Karl A. Oriental Despotism: A Comparative Study of Total Power. New Haven, Conn.: Yale University Press, 1957.

Worster, Donald. Dust Bowl. The Southern Plains in the 1930s. New York: Oxford University Press, 1979.

5

The Shaping of World Population Patterns

Heaven cannot help being high, the earth cannot help being wide, the sun and the moon cannot help going round, and all things of the creation cannot help but live and multiply.

Chuang Tzu (369–286 B.C.),
The Book of Master Chuang

The explosive growth of the human population is the most significant terrestrial event of the past million millennia. . . . No geological event in a billion years—not the emergence of mighty mountain ranges, nor the submergence of entire subcontinents, nor the occurrence of periodic glacial ages—has posed a threat to terrestrial life comparable to that of human overpopulation.

Paul Ehrlich,
The Population Bomb, 1968

Key Ideas

1. World population began its upward trend about A.D. 1650. This turning point was brought about by a number of factors, all of which added up to an improvement in living conditions.

2. The sharp upward curve has shortened the doubling time of world population.

3. Although world totals increase, there remain major regional variations. These are due to a variety of factors.

4. The dramatic increase in the population of the nonindustrialized world after World War II was due to the introduction of lifesaving drugs and medical care.

5. The result of high birthrates is that the developing countries, with a decline in deathrates, are only halfway through the demographic transition.

6. There are three principal areas of high population density: East Asia, South Asia, and Europe. Additional heavy concentrations of people are found in parts of Southeast Asia and east-central North America.

7. Average population density tells us nothing of the way in which people cluster within a region or of the settlement pattern or of the culture.

8. High population densities in northwestern Europe and the northeastern United States are based on urbanization.

9. Some thinkers have not believed that unlimited population growth was necessarily the cause of human misery. Some saw it as a decided economic advantage.

10. Thomas Malthus was one of the first to draw attention to what unrestricted population growth might mean.

POPULATION GEOGRAPHY

The study of population lies at the core of human geography. Because human geography focuses on the use to which humans make of the earth's resources, it is clear, then, that understanding of certain characteristics of population groups or communities is necessary. Indeed, there are a number of specific questions concerning population that are of immediate interest to the geographer.

These questions pertain to the way in which world and regional populations have grown, how large the numbers are, and what we may expect of them in future based on past and present trends. At the national level, census data contain much of this kind of information, but their range and usefulness are confined within national territorial boundaries. In addition to numbers, the geographer is also interested in the distribution of population, the patterns that population groups have formed, and what those patterns may be like in the future.

Finally, population geography also includes a concern for densities, with the degrees of concentration within given areas of the world's population groups. A study of density patterns reveals much about how a people live, what resources they must draw on to survive, and the level of their technical development.

A HYPOTHETICAL WORLD POPULATION CLOCK

Imagine a giant clock towering over a hypothetical landscape marking the passage of time. Imagine, too, that the clock contains age-old computers that record every addition to the world's population every hour, with totals provided for every day and every year.

Over thousands of years, the clock computers have recorded a very slow but steady increase in the number of new inhabitants to our hypothetical landscape. At least, that would

---

BOX 5–1

The Population Clock

Charles Babbage (1792–1871), idiosyncratic nineteenth-century English mathematician and inventor, had a fetish for accuracy. After reading the celebrated line, "Every moment dies a man/every moment one is born," written by the poet Lord Tennyson, he wrote to the latter: "It must be manifest that if this is true, the population of the earth would be at a standstill." His proposed change: Every moment dies a man/every moment 1$\frac{1}{16}$ is born (cited in the *Christian Science Monitor,* 1978).

We are more precise in our measurements today. In Washington, D.C., a research organization, called the Population Reference Bureau, announced in 1976 that world population had

reached the 4 billion mark, on March 21, 1976, at 7:30 P.M. EST. By the end of 1983, it had climbed to over 4.67 billion.

The Population Reference Bureau maintains an outdoor digital clock on a downtown Washington street that records the estimated growth of the world's population. Another clock, in the Department of Commerce building, records the growth of the population of the United States. It announces that there is a birth every 10 seconds, a death every 16 seconds, an immigrant (a legal immigrant) every 81 seconds.

What does this mean for the United States? It suggests that were it not for immigration, the population of the United States would grow very slowly. Every year, however, some 400,000 new immigrants enter the country, with perhaps another 1 to 2 million illegal entries, mainly from Latin America.

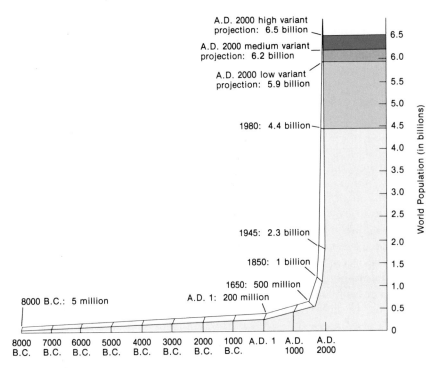

Figure 5-1

In 1650, the total world population amounted to upwards of 500 million. By 1850, it had doubled, reaching over 1 billion. Although Europe's population grew after 1650, climbing significantly after 1750, the growth of Asia's population is assumed to have been fairly substantial in earlier centuries. By 1850, it is clear that Asia had already begun to surge ahead of the rest of the world.

(Adapted from Woytinski and Woytinski, 1953, chap. 2.)

have been the case until about A.D. 1650. Thereafter, the recording of new births would begin to suggest a more rapid tempo of increase, a tempo steadily quickening every year. By the mid-1980s, with the entire computer printout in front of us, we would have become aware that over the past two hundred years there had been a sharp upward surge in the number of inhabitants our landscape contains, which as you have guessed is planet Earth (Box 5-1).

For 1984, we would learn that for every hour the clock strikes, the population of the earth has grown by a little over 10,000, and for every day about 250,000. This means that over the past year up to 92 million persons have been added to the earth's total number of inhabitants, or the equivalent of the combined populations of the New England states together with New York, Pennsylvania, Ohio, Texas, and California.

This phenomenon of rapid increase—the single most important fact about population in the world today—has been described as the *population bomb* or the *population explosion* (Ehrlich, 1968). It means that world population in terms of numbers has been increasing at a truly alarming rate.

What is the cause of this phenomenon? How long will it continue? What does this growth mean in terms of living space and resource use? How is the world to deal with this challenge? The answers to these and other questions are sought in the sections and chapters that follow.

In attempting to understand this challenge, it

is useful to see population growth in historical context, for an understanding of the present cannot be had without examining some aspects of past human behavior.

WORLD POPULATION GROWTH: A.D. 1650 TO THE PRESENT

Any attempt to understand the implications of contemporary population growth must take into consideration the time span involved and the nature and level of prevailing social, cultural, and economic conditions.

Up until about A.D. 1650, world population growth had been slow (Box 5–2). At the beginning of the Christian era, world population may have reached 250 million (Ehrlich and Ehrlich, 1970). By 1650, about the time Galileo died in Europe, the 250 million had grown to 500 million, but it had taken over a thousand years to do so. At midcentury, a turning point seems to have been reached (Fig. 5–1). A gradual improvement in living conditions in many parts of the world—in China, Japan, as well as in Europe—undoubtedly contributed to the upward turn (Zelinski et al., 1970).

However, in the following century, world totals grew rapidly to over 700 million and reached more than 1 billion by 1850 (Table 5–1). If these estimates are reasonable, such growth would indicate a global *rate of natural increase* of about 0.3 to 0.4 percent between 1650 and 1750, rising to 0.5 percent in 1800, and to 0.8 percent after that. The increase continued until post-World War II when the rate of natural increase reached 2.0 percent or more. By 1983, it had dropped to about 1.7 percent, suggesting that some lowering of the rate was taking place.

The Rate of Natural Increase

The rate of natural increase is determined by comparing the number of live births with the number of deaths. In the seventeenth and eighteenth centuries, both *birthrates* and *deathrates*

BOX 5–2
Estimating Past Populations

Knowledge of world and regional trends in population growth in the distant past is based to a large extent on inference, on what can be gleaned from an assortment of historical documents and records, and on guesswork. We know that population counts, usually for administrative and tax purposes, took place in the ancient Middle East, the Roman Empire, and China. But these records must be used with care.

Source materials for later periods improve and a clearer picture emerges, at least for western Europe. From the *Domesday Book,* completed in A.D. 1086 during the reign of William the Conqueror, one can arrive at an estimate of between 1 and 1.25 million for the population of England, about the size of the population of Maine in 1983. Indeed, on the basis of the *Domesday Book,* the British geographer Henry C. Darby, made a detailed study of the geography of England as it was in the middle of the eleventh century (Darby, 1977). By 1377, when a poll tax was levied in England, the population had grown by an additional 1 million, to about the size of the state of Arkansas in 1983. However, the Black Death, or plague, which reached England in 1348, may have taken up to 1.5 million lives. In any case, the *demographic* problems of England corresponded with those on the Continent. Between 1346 and 1361, the fearful plague took an estimated 24 million lives, or about a fourth of the total population of Europe.

We can only guess at the population of Asian countries during the medieval period. Living conditions there were even worse, it is believed, than in Europe. Still, surveys and records were kept, especially in China where documents drew the attention of Marco Polo when he arrived in Beijing in 1275. He had seen nothing like them in Europe. Even so, because of the way the counts were taken, such records can only be used suggestively. Estimates of the number of people elsewhere in the world have no value whatsoever.

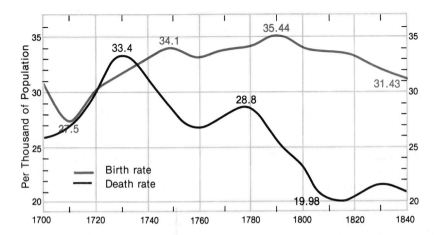

Figure 5–2

Church records are one of the better sources of information on births and deaths in England because a regular census did not occur until the mid-nineteenth century. The birthrates and deathrates shown here are obviously estimates, but they do reflect a generally accepted pattern. In 1700, both birthrates and deathrates were relatively high. The rise in deaths in the early part of the century was due to smallpox and other diseases, but as living conditions began to improve toward the end of the century, mortality dropped abruptly. The birthrate remained high and, if anything, during the early decades of the Industrial Revolution, actually climbed. By the early part of the nineteenth century, the number of births per 1000 of the population had begun to decline.

world wide were high so that the gap between the two was not large. Many children were born; many people died at an early age. However, as deaths began to decline in some parts of the world at the end of the eighteenth century and birthrates remained high, there was a rise in the rate of natural increase. The drop in mortality, especially in Europe, was associated with the general disappearance of both plague and famine and an improvement in diet.

Population growth, like the interest on a savings account, increases exponentially, that is, the larger the deposit, the greater the compound interest. With a decline in mortality, the demographic curve tends abruptly upward as the gap between births and deaths widens. This pattern was evident in England between 1700 and 1810, especially as counts and later censuses began to make the change apparent (Fig. 5–2) (Box 5–3). An awareness of this phenomenon together with a belief that the earth's ability to feed expands arithmetically alarmed a number of Europeans as early as the eighteenth century. One of the foremost was the English clergyman and writer, Thomas R. Malthus (1766–1834).

Associated with this evidence of population increase were two equally important phenomena: one pertained to the lengthening of the human life span (Fig. 5–3), the other to the shortening of the time it took for population to double (Box 5–4).

WORLD REGIONAL POPULATION TRENDS

Variations

Even though world population grew through the centuries, it is evident that there were major differences in rates of increase from place to

Figure 5–3

At birth, early man in Europe, about 25,000 years ago, could expect to live on an average slightly over 29 years, but it is possible some survived to the age of 40, judging by the fossil skulls unearthed. Cro-Magnon types, which resembled modern humankind, probably fared better. But, it took the development of agriculture and the advance of technology to boost living standards and lengthen human life expectancy, as in the Bronze Age, which lasted from about 2000 B.C. to 1000 B.C.

By the fourteenth century, an Englishman might expect to live beyond the average of 38 years, but a man in his 50s and 60s was still relatively rare. It has only been since the nineteenth century that people could expect to live—at least in the industrialized countries of the West—to be at least 60. Today 74 years is the average in the United States.

BOX 5-3

The Origin and Value of the Census

The first attempts at systematic enumerations of population and resources got underway in the seventeenth century. *Mercantilist* Europe needed to know what its overseas colonies contained. In 1666, the French made a survey of their colony on the banks of the St. Lawrence—New France.

The first regular census (from the Latin, meaning count) of a European state, however, was carried out in 1749–1750 when Sweden initiated the practice, but the compilation was incomplete. 1790 marked the year of the first census of the United States, required by a provision of the Constitution, and it was conducted every ten years thereafter. France and England had systematic counts in 1801, but the first reliable census of the United Kingdom was that of 1841. The British instituted ten-year censuses of India in 1871, and Russia got around to its first (and only) census of the empire in 1897. Soviet censuses have followed irregularly in 1926, 1939, 1959, 1970, and 1980.

The modern census does not necessarily present a wholly accurate or comprehensive picture of a territory's inhabitants. From 1954 to 1982, there had been no official census of China, and Western scholars had found the earlier one of 1953 to be less than satisfactory. Soviet censuses often convey more information on Soviet life by what is not included than what is. Procedures for conducting counts vary from country to country; they are often colored or distorted by national policy and economic and strategic considerations. Such differences and inadequacies in census materials should be kept in mind when comparing countries around the world.

place. These differences—then as now—were due to variations in culture, social structure and values, levels of economic development, political stability, and health care. The historical record of regional variations contributes to an understanding of present world differences.

Estimates of past trends in the population diaries of Asia, Africa, and South America are, at best, poor guesses. Certainly, in some areas, there was substantial growth. There was also at times substantial population migration. The picture that emerges for Europe, however, is clearer. Moreover, it was the emigration of Europeans to relatively sparsely occupied lands of the globe that helped shape in subsequent centuries the patterns of growth elsewhere.

In 1650, Europe probably had between one fifth and one fourth of the earth's inhabitants. By the middle of the twentieth century, the demographic importance, or the population weight, of Europe had declined to less than one fifth of world population. On the other hand, the European occupation of the Americas and Oceania raised their totals to over 10 percent of present world population. Africa today has 10 percent of the total, but the astounding fact is that Asia remains the most populous continent, claiming over 50 percent of all the people on earth.

THE DECLINE OF EUROPEAN DEMOGRAPHIC WEIGHT

Despite the upswing in Europe's population after 1650, smallpox, one of the worst killers after the plague, swept away more than 60 million lives in the seventeenth century (Fig. 5–4). Tiny Iceland, in 1707 alone, lost a third of its inhabitants. However, by the end of the century, a combination of factors led to a decline in European mortality and with that occurred Europe's population explosion (Table 5–2). England was one of the first to experience these changes.

Demographic Transition During European Industrialization

In the early stages of industrialization in mid-eighteenth century England, the deathrate began to decline, despite the harsh living conditions that accompanied the rise of the factory. This decline was to a large extent the result of an improvement in the survival rates of infants, who received better care in cities and towns than had been the case in villages.

As industrialization proceeded and the movement from the countryside to the city in-

---

BOX 5–4

Doubling Times of World Population

The upward turn in the rate of population increase led to the emergence of a startling phenomenon. The span of time in which the earth's population doubled was shortening. It took two centuries (from 1650 to 1850) for doubling to occur. Doubling occurred again between 1850 and 1930, but the time span was shortened to 80 years. Since 1930, the doubling time has contracted still further. In March 1976, the world population clock struck 4 billion, and it is possible that it may reach 8 billion in 2020.

Date (A.D.)	World Population	Approximate Time Required for Population to Double
1	250 million	1,600 years
1650	545 million	200 years
1850	1,171 million (1 billion)	80 years
1930	2,103 million (2 billion)	46 years
1978	4,219 million (4 billion)	41 years
2020	8,000 million (8 billion)	39 years

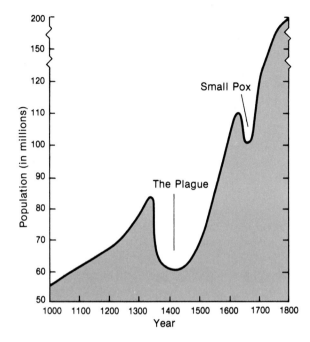

Figure 5–4

In Europe during the medieval period, population grew as the quality of life improved because of increases in the output of foodstuffs. However, the effects of the plague in the fourteenth century and smallpox in the seventeenth century are clearly evident because they cut deeply into the upward trend.

Table 5–2
Estimated Increase in the Population of Some of Europe's Political Territories and Regions (1700–1850)

Territory or Region	1700 (millions)	1800 (millions)	1850 (millions)	Percent Increase 1700–1800	Percent Increase 1700–1850
France	19.0	27.3	34.9	43.6	83.6
Germany	15.0	24.3	35.4	62.0	126.0
Russia	12.0	30.9[a]	61.6	157.5	413.3
Italy	11.0	18.1	23.6[b]	64.5	114.5
United Kingdom[c]	6.7	10.5	23.2[d]	56.7	246.2[e]
Spain	6.0	10.5	15.5[f]	75.0	158.3

[a] Part of this increase was due to the territorial expansion of the Russian Empire.

[b] Estimates for 1848.

[c] Includes England, Wales, and Scotland.

[d] Data for 1861.

[e] Percent increase 1700–1861.

[f] Data for 1857.

Source: Adapted from R. R. Palmer, ed., *Atlas of World History* (Chicago: Rand McNally, 1957), p. 193; Jerome Blum, *The End of the Old Order in Rural Europe* (Princeton N.J.: Princeton University Press, 1978), chap. 12.

creased throughout the nineteenth century, the number of births began to drop. The traditional agrarian way of life had been based on the large family, which was a necessity for farming. As people settled in urban areas, children were seen to be of less practical value. In addition, housing was scarce and the larger the family the greater the difficulty in providing for it—at least

until the children themselves had reached working age. In the towns and cities, the new tendency was to delay marriage or consciously have fewer children. This decline in the birthrate together with the decline in the deathrate that had already occurred led to a slowing down in the rate of natural increase. By 1900, it was clear that a new social ethic based on smaller families had come into existence in England as well as in those countries on the Continent that had undergone industrialization.

The drop in the deathrate as industrialization got underway began Europe's *demographic transition*. The decline in the number of births completed it (Fig. 5–6). In the early decades of the twentieth century, the dramatic upsurge in population numbers that had characterized Europe's previous century came to a halt. The *population profile*, or structure of the population, changed.

Demographic transition in Scandinavia has been well documented (Fig. 5–7). This region is not the most industrialized in Europe, but it has become highly urbanized. As its population left impoverished rural areas in the nineteenth century, the process that was to sharply change the

Figure 5–5

Although the population of the British Isles had grown rapidly in the early part of the 19th century, the rate of increase slowed by the end of the century as birth rates declined. Still London, the center of Britain's political, economic, and social life continued its upward growth. Horse-drawn carriages and busses, shown here in 1890 on the Strand, one of London's more famous streets, contributed to the impression of congestion as well as of bustle and activity.

Source: The Bettmann Archive.

Figure 5–6

The demographic transition can be seen in the changing profiles of the population of the United Kingdom and the United States. In 1871, the U.K. profile was broadly based, showing high birthrates and a significant proportion of the population under the age of 15. Some 70 years later, after two world wars, the birthrate had dropped as the population had aged. By the 1960s, the population had aged further as the number of people in the age bracket from 20 to 50 years had declined. Comparison with U.S. profiles over the same period shows a similar trend. By 1970, the population structure of the United States had changed dramatically from the 1870s. The narrower base reveals the drop-off in birthrates, whereas the bulge in the adolescent age group reflects the postwar baby boom. The depression of the 1930s was accompanied by very low birthrates, which accounts for the narrow "waist" in the 30 to 39 age bracket.

demographic structure of Scandinavia began. Between 1850 and 1930, mortality dropped from 20 to 12 per 1000; at the same time, births declined from 32 to 18 per 1000. Subsequently, births and deaths fell still further. By 1980 in Norway, Sweden, and Denmark, the birthrate

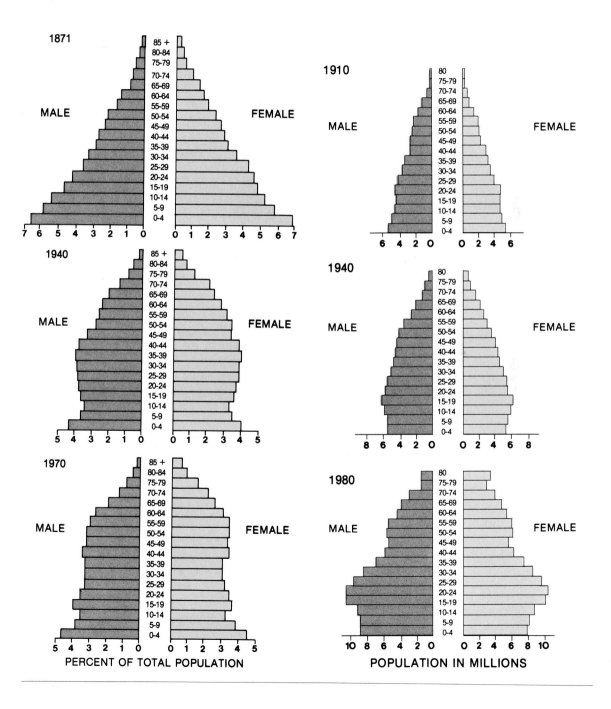

PERCENT OF TOTAL POPULATION

POPULATION IN MILLIONS

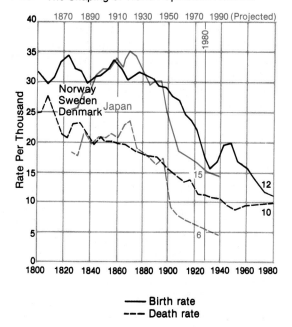

— Birth rate
--- Death rate

Figure 5–7

During the latter part of the nineteenth century, the birthrates of the Scandinavian countries—Norway, Sweden, and Denmark—fluctuated. Then the number of births began to fall dramatically after 1910, plummeting again after 1950. During the same period, the number of deaths also fell. It is interesting to compare these rates with those of Japan where industrialization began in the latter decades of the nineteenth century. Since 1900, Japanese birthrates and deathrates have dropped quite fast.

stood at 12 per 1000, the deathrate at about 10 per 1000, giving a rate of natural increase of about 0.2 percent. The pattern of change was similar in France and, in time, came to characterize much of Europe.

DEMOGRAPHIC TRANSITION IN THE UNITED STATES

After the founding of the Republic, the population of the United States grew rapidly. From 6.4 million in 1800, it climbed to 45 million in

1876. Immigration contributed significantly to growth, but early marriage and large families were a predominant characteristic of early nineteenth-century America. The rate of natural increase at the time has been estimated at a phenomenal high of about 3.0 percent—a rate that is considered explosive when it occurs today (e.g., in Kenya with 3.9 percent and in Algeria and El Salvador with 3.2 percent each).

In 1790, about 5 percent of the population was classified as urban, that is, inhabitants living in centers of 25,000 or greater. Throughout the nineteenth century, and particularly after the Civil War, the proportion of urban dwellers grew. At the same time, the rate of natural increase declined until in 1900 it stood at about 2 percent. Population growth remained rapid, however, but this was principally because of the very large influx of immigrants—now largely from eastern and southern Europe—after 1880. From 1860 to 1920, the rural population of the United States declined from 80 percent to about 50 percent of the total as cities grew. In 1910, the urban population represented 45.7 percent of the total, but over the next decade, it climbed to 51.2 percent. By mid-1980s, about 75 percent of the population of the United States may be regarded as urban. The birthrate stands at 16 per 1000 with a deathrate of 9 per 1000, resulting in an annual rate of natural increase of 0.7 percent. Moreover, the U.S. Census Bureau in 1983 stated that although the population of the United States between 1980 and 1982 had grown by 5 million, a sharp increase had occurred in the age group over 65 years. Indeed, the number of people 65 years and up, which reached 2.4 million in 1982, had climbed 9.1 percent since 1980.

Similar patterns have been recorded for Japan and the Soviet Union, suggesting that the factors that bring about demographic transition and the subsequent aging of the population are associated with the social accommodations made in an industrializing, urbanizing society regardless of ethnic culture or ideology.

THE POPULATION EXPLOSION IN THE NONINDUSTRIALIZED WORLD
Causes of the Explosion

It was only after the smoke had cleared from the battlefields of World War II that world leaders and population experts began to be alerted to the problems posed by the rapid growth of world population. Relative stability in population matters had been achieved in the industrially developed countries, but elsewhere in the world, evidence of great population instability came into sharp focus (Fig.5–8) (Table 5–3).

When introduced into countries where 80 percent or more of the population lived in the countryside, the new miracle drugs, notably penicillin and streptomycin, together with the application and use of insecticides, such as DDT, quickly altered the age-old balance between life-supporting and death-delivering forces. The high mortality or deathrate in the nonindustrialized world was brought under control with amazing speed. In Sri Lanka (formerly Ceylon), for example, there were 22 deaths per 1000 in the late 1940s, but by 1954 that had been cut to 10 per 1000 and in 1983 to only 6 per 1000 (Fig. 5–9). Major victories in tropical lands were achieved over yellow fever, cholera, smallpox, and other highly contagious diseases and parasitic growths. A spectacular change in the human environment had occurred for people living in such lands. Birthrates, however, remained high because of cultural and social pressures. This combination of factors, as in Europe in the late eighteenth century, permitted population totals to turn sharply upward.

Since 1945, the populations of Africa, Latin America, and Asia as a whole have doubled (Demeny, 1974). Prevailing rates of growth in these areas have far exceeded the global average (Table 5–4), and only limited success has rewarded efforts to dampen traditionally high birthrates (Fig. 5–10). Such areas are, for the

Table 5–3
Population Trends: Developed and Developing Countries, 1983

	People (million)	Crude Birthrate (per 1000 population per year)	Crude Deathrate (per 1000 population per year)	Annual Rate of Natural Increase (percent)
World	4,677.0	29	11	1.8
Developing Countries	3,514.0	38	12	2.1
Africa	513.0	46	16	3.0
Asia (except Japan)	2,611.0	30	11	1.9
Latin America (excluding temperate areas)	346.0	31	8	2.4
Developed or Industrialized Countries	1,158.0	15	10	0.6
United States	234.0	16	9	0.7
Japan	119.0	13	6	0.7
Europe	489.0	14	10	0.4
USSR	272.0	19	10	0.8
Others: Canada, Australia, New Zealand, Latin America (temperate)	93.0	19	8	1.0

Source: *1983 World Population Data Sheet.* (Washington, D.C.: Population Reference Bureau, April 1983.)

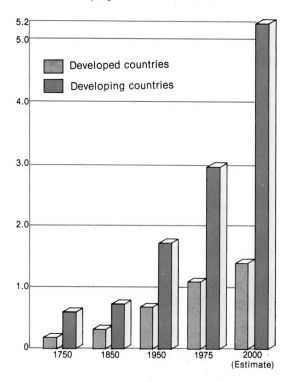

Figure 5–8
The rapid upsurge in the population of the nonindustrialized countries relative to that of the developed, or industrialized, parts of the world became clearly evident after World War II. By 1975, almost two thirds of the world's population lived in countries where agriculture formed the basic means of subsistence. By the year 2000, it is possible that some four fifths of the world's population will continue to live on a basis of agriculture because birthrates remain high and population growth as a whole exceeds the rate of economic development.

Figure 5–9
In Sweden, the birthrate declined in the latter half of the nineteenth century as rapidly as the deathrate. In Sri Lanka, however, when the deathrate began its decline (as early as 1918 but precipitously after 1940), the birthrate remained high. It was the difference between the two rates that gave Sri Lanka high rates of natural increase in the 1960s. Today, Sri Lanka's birthrate (29 per 1000) compares with that of Sweden in 1900. Sri Lanka's deathrate, however, is lower than that of Sweden today owing to the high percentage of the population under 15 and the sharp decline in infant mortality. Of Sweden's population, 20 percent is under 15 but 16 percent are over 65.

most part, only halfway through the demographic transition.

Critical Problem Areas

Africa's average birthrates and deathrates of 46 and 17 per 1000 produce the highest rates of natural increase in the world. Kenya's rate of natural increase of 4.1 percent in 1983 is the highest in Africa and creates a difficult dilemma

for a developing country. In parts of Meso-America and the Caribbean islands, the situation is almost as alarming. Birthrates as high as 47 per 1000 (Nicaragua) are offset by deathrates of up to 11 per 1000, causing a rate of natural increase of up to 3.6 percent. In countries with massive population reservoirs—such as India, Pakistan, and Bangladesh—measures to control the upward surge have had little impact. In India, national policy has consistently favored a slower population growth; family planning has contributed to some decline in births, but the achievement has been concealed by a falling deathrate. In 1983, India's rate of increase stood at 2.1 percent, indicating the possibility of

Table 5–4
Demographic Statistics of Range of Nations Showing Rates of Natural Increase in Percentage, 1983

	Rate of Natural Increase	Birthrate	Deathrate
Kenya	4.1	5.4	1.3
Honduras	3.5	4.5	1.0
Zimbabwe	3.4	4.7	1.3
Algeria	3.2	4.6	1.4
Ghana	3.2	4.8	1.6
Guatemala	3.2	4.2	1.0
Egypt	3.1	4.3	1.2
Morocco	3.1	4.4	1.3
Uganda	3.1	4.6	1.5
Costa Rica	2.5	2.9	0.4
Venezuela	2.8	3.3	0.5
El Salvador	2.6	3.6	1.0
Malagasy Republic	2.6	4.5	1.9
Mexico	2.6	3.2	0.6
Upper Volta	2.6	4.8	2.2
Sri Lanka	2.2	2.8	0.6
India	2.1	3.6	1.5
Colombia	2.0	2.8	0.8
Taiwan	1.8	2.3	0.5
Chile	1.6	2.2	0.7
China	1.5	2.3	0.8
Hong Kong	1.2	1.7	0.5
Singapore	1.2	1.7	0.5
Australia	0.9	1.6	0.7
Japan	0.7	1.3	0.6
United States	0.7	1.6	0.9
France	0.5	1.5	1.0
Belgium	0.1	1.3	1.1
Italy	0.1	1.1	1.0
Luxembourg	0.1	1.2	1.1
United Kingdom	0.1	1.3	1.2
Sweden	0.0	1.1	1.1

Source: 1983 World Population Data Sheet. (Washington, D.C.: Population Reference Bureau, April 1983.)

Table 5–5
Changing Birthrates and Deathrates in India 1901–1983

Census Year	Total Population (millions)	Birthrate	Deathrate	Rate of Natural Increase (%)
1901	236	46	44	0.2
1911	249	51	43	0.8
1921	248	49	48	0.1
1931	276	46	36	1.0
1941	313	45	31	1.4
1951	357	39	27	1.2
1961	439	40	21	1.9
1969	537	43	18	2.5
1978	635	34	14	2.0
1983	730	36	15	2.1

Source: Various sources, including *1978 World Population Data Sheet* (Washington, D.C.: Population Reference Bureau, 1978); *1983 World Population Data Sheet* (Washington, D.C.: Population Reference Bureau, April 1983).

ing as rapidly as that of other parts of Asia (e.g., India). At that time, it was assumed that the birthrate was above 35 per 1000 and that this rate would only decline very slowly by the 1970s. Government efforts to bring China's growth under control, particularly by prohibiting early marriages, increasing social pressure on married couples, and abortion, however, have been effective, especially in cities. Hence, the rate of increase may have fallen to about 1.5 percent. This decrease is remarkable in view of the fact that 80 percent of China's population still live in villages. Even if this rate is correct for the country as a whole, population growth could reach more than 1.2 billion people in the year 2000.

Taiwan, however, illustrates what can be done given more favorable economic growth conditions. There, the introduction of improved health care has been associated with substantial agricultural reform and massive inputs of capital from abroad to spur industrialization. Taiwan's deathrate (1983) of 5 per 1000 is one of the lowest in the world, but with births at 23 per

a doubling of its population (730 million) in 33 years (Table 5–5)!

China's population characteristics remain something of an enigma. One fifth of the globe's inhabitants, possibly 1024 million people (1983 estimate) live in China, but Western experts disagree on trends and totals. During the 1960s, the population of China was thought to be grow-

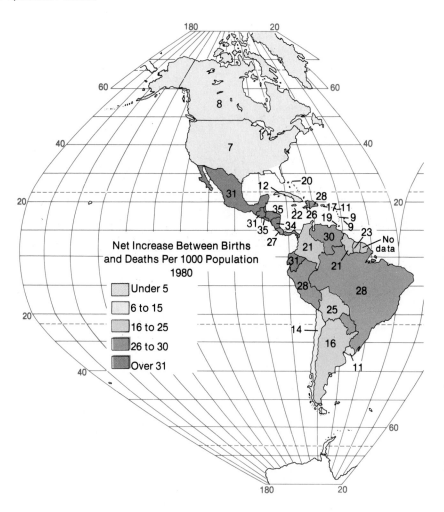

Net Increase Between Births and Deaths Per 1000 Population 1980

- Under 5
- 6 to 15
- 16 to 25
- 26 to 30
- Over 31

1000, its annual growth rate of about 1.8 percent is sustained by the fact that 32 percent of its population is under 15 years of age.

The Profile of an Exploding Population

Populations that grow rapidly are broadly based, that is, the young constitute a large proportion of the total. India is a classic example, as is Pakistan (Fig. 5–11) and many other lesser developed countries. In 1983, Pakistan had an estimated population of 95.7 million; Bangladesh—formerly East Pakistan—had 96.5 million. If present trends prevail, both countries will double in about 25 years. Such phenomenal growth, based on a rate of over 2.7 percent, is the inevitable result of having populations in which about 45 percent of the total is under 15 years of age. In industrially developed countries, the ratio of persons under 15 is usually between 20 and 25 percent.

Life expectancy at birth in the lesser developed countries, however, is still substantially

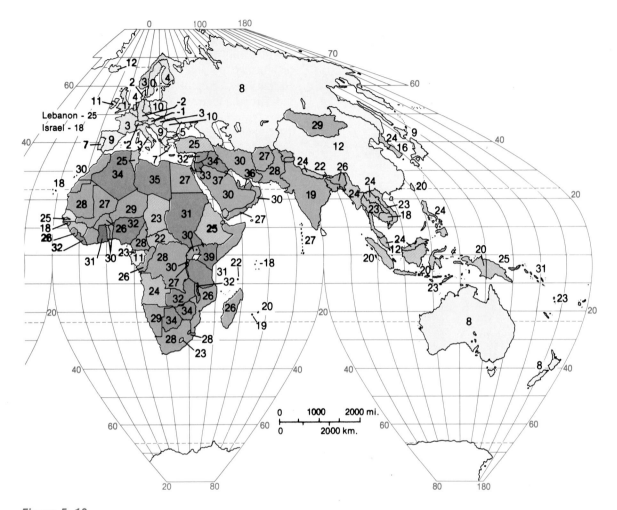

Figure 5–10

In many lesser developed countries, the rates of natural increase remain high because of high birthrates and rapidly declining deathrates. With few exceptions, these areas face severe problems of assuring employment to the thousands who enter the labor pool each year, of housing the migrants who regularly leave the villages for the cities, and of providing sufficient food.

In the Meso-American country of El Salvador, for example, the labor force grew from 650,000 in 1950 to 1.25 million in 1975, with projections showing it expanding to 3.2 million by the year 2000. Clearly, the volatile politi-

cal situation in that Latin American country is based to a large extent on the inability of thousands of workers to find gainful employment. And this is especially true in the agricultural sector where land tenure is restrictive, holdings small, and society stratified.

It has been estimated that Latin America's labor force of about 100 million will almost double by the year 2000. The problem is hemispheric in scope, and the underlying causes defy immediate solution.

(*Source: 1980 World Population Data Sheet.*)

less than in the industrialized countries. In Sweden, life expectancy at birth is 75 years, in Japan 76, and in the Unites States 74. By contrast,

it is about 50 in India, and only 47 in Bangladesh. In parts of West Africa, life expectancy at birth is as low as 43.

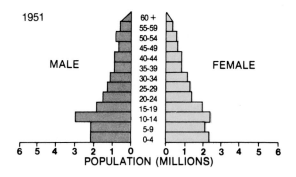

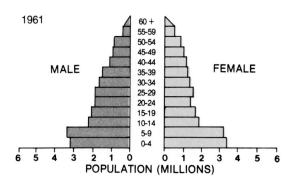

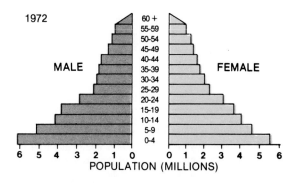

Figure 5–11

Pakistan is an example of a country undergoing rapid population growth because of persistently high birthrates and declining deathrates. Because its population is broadly based, with nearly half of the total under age 15, growth will continue to expand rapidly unless something is done to control the birthrate.

(*Source:* Adapted from "Pakistan: A Demographic Report," *Population Bulletin*, 29 (1973), pp. 10–11.)

A significant feature of the population structure of a country—apart from the question of growth—is the proportion that is economically productive or will be so in the future. In the Indian subcontinent, there are millions of young mouths to feed, deflecting investment away from economic growth. Indian census data for 1981 have shown a population increase of nearly 25 percent over the past decade. This alarming situation has jolted India's governing officials and has spurred new calls for intensified planning efforts. But, this is a difficult undertaking in a country where there is a strong reverence for life and any mechanical means to limit the number of children a family might have is widely abhorred. The truth is, however, that in 1981 India had 12 million more people than the government had projected, bringing the country's total to 688.6 million at that time.

For China, population growth there, in practical terms, means that jobs for 20 million young people must be found each year. That's how many reach working age annually, even though population growth in China has been reduced to only 11 million per year. The young people were born during China's baby boom in the 1960s.

DENSITIES

If the earth's more than 4 billion inhabitants were distributed evenly over the surface of the globe, the density would average about 2 persons per square mile. Such a statistic might be helpful on a television quiz program, but otherwise it is meaningless. Humans are essentially land animals and have not yet chosen to live on or under the seas, which comprise most of the earth's surface. If the population were spread evenly over the earth's land surface, average density would rise to about 53 persons per square mile, the current density in the United States. However, this statistic, like the one

Figure 5–12

A striking feature of the population of developing countries where the rate of natural increase remains high is its youthfulness. This is especially evident whenever mass demonstrations or rallies occur, as shown here in

Beijing, China, with thousands of students assembled in the capital's major square, known as Tien An Men.

Picture Credit: Paolo Koch/Rapho/Photo Researchers, Inc.

above, is interesting but not very helpful to an understanding of how population groups live. Rather, because of the irregular nature of the land surface and its differing capacities to sustain life as well as for reasons of culture, history and tradition, humankind has formed large concentrations in certain regions, whereas other vast areas remain with only a handful of people.

High-Density Regions

There are three principal areas of substantial concentration: East Asia, South Asia, and Europe (including the central part of European Russia) (Fig. 5–13). There are additional heavy

concentrations in parts of Southeast Asia and in the east-central part of North America. Finally, there are significant but smaller clusters of population in Africa, in the Caribbean area, in South America, and on the southwest coast of the United States. Some of the regions of high density also have high rates of population growth—this is particularly true in the tropics—but this phenomenon is by no means universal.

The greater part of the human population has chosen to live in the lowlands, coastal plains, and river valleys of the world, particularly where climatic conditions are generally temperate. People tend to avoid regions lacking in moisture or in warmth, but regions subject to

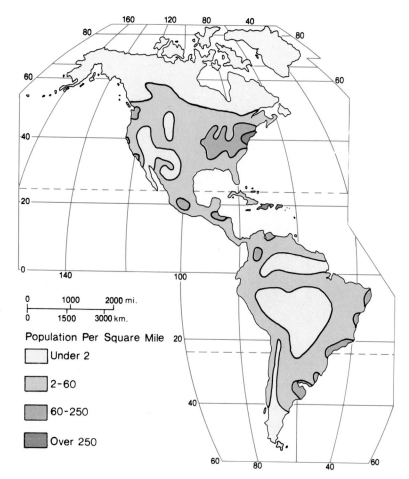

Figure 5–13

The continents with high population concentration are Asia, Europe, and North America. However, the nature of that density varies with degrees of urbanization, arable land, overall economy, and culture. Vast parts of the globe remain sparsely occupied because they are most extreme in their physical environmental characteristics—that is, cold, dry, hot, wet, mountainous, and frequently inaccessible.

Population Per Square Mile

- Under 2
- 2–60
- 60–250
- Over 250

excessively high temperatures and humidity do not widely attract them either. In the frozen polar wastes, the vast interiors of the northern continents, the rugged uplands, the inaccessible swamps, the broad and expanding deserts of the subtropics—wherever a high degree of specialization is required to sustain life—population is thinly spread. Where native cultures are present in such areas, a low level of domestic technology has made it impossible for them to modify their habitat to any substantial degree, and they have responded in a manner that ensures survival but little more.

Broad physical environmental factors, then, account for the basic patterns of human distribution. They do not, however, account for the variations in human behavior that occur within each environment. Culture and levels of technical equipment clearly play an important role.

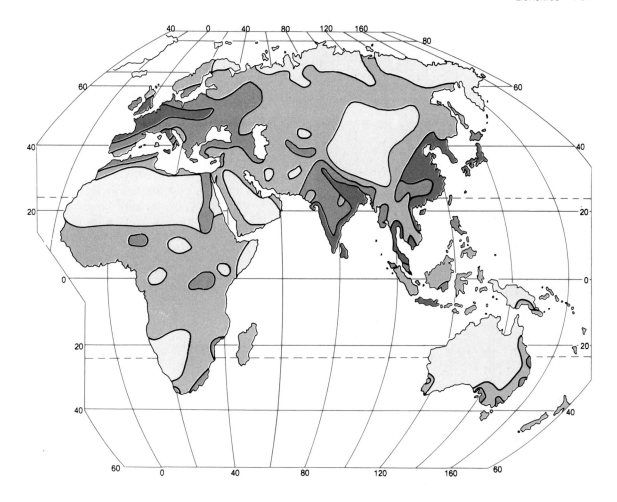

Density in Context

The Concept

The concept of density is ordinarily associated with distribution. Used alone, however, density tells us little because it is a relative term and should always be regarded as such. The concept may be used in many ways, even to mislead. Before World War II, the Nazis used the notion of overcrowding in Germany—of a dynamic people pressing against its political boundaries—to confuse the Western powers and to justify the need for additional *living space,* or *lebensraum,* which was to be obtained at the expense of Germany's neighbors.

A major weakness in the concept of density is that it does not take into consideration the potential of a region to support its population. Average density alone tells us nothing of the way in which people cluster within the region, the pattern of settlement, the way in which they make a living, or their culture. Density needs to be associated with more than numbers of people and territory; it must be seen in the context of its own particular enviroment and its social and demographic situation (Fig. 5–14).

Supporting High Densities

The high densities of northwestern Europe and of the northeastern United States—well over 1000 persons per mile^2—are based on urbanization. They are sustained at their present high level because they can count on the resources of vast areas that lie beyond their borders. To survive, however, these regions must trade. On the other hand, the 39 million inhabitants of Egypt crowd together in a similar density along the banks of the Nile. Most of them depend entirely on the land they till and the water made available for irrigation. If the water supply were cut off, millions now existing at subsistance levels would surely starve unless additional quantities of food were brought in from abroad. The High Dam on the Nile at Aswan has been built to guarantee additional water to the farmers of Egypt, but if Egypt's population continues to increase at 3.1 percent per year, the advantages of the new storage reservoir will most assuredly be lost. Any increase in output through an expansion of irrigation will be absorbed without permitting significant savings. In certain economic conditions, even what seems an exceedingly low density may be too high. A density of 2 per mile^2 among hunting peoples of northern Canada may be excessive if the game on which they have traditionally depended becomes severely depleted by outside hunters or disease or if the migratory routes of the herds are disrupted by pipelines or similar monuments of the predominant industrial culture of most of North America.

Figure 5–14

In Hong Kong, the hillside shanties that housed refugees from China in the 1960s have largely been replaced with high-rise apartment dwellings, a substantial investment on the part of the Hong Kong government. The Chinese are inveterate shopkeepers and craftsmen, and it is this ability to work that has helped support the British colony's population, which grew from an estimated 3.3 million in mid-1962 to over 5 million in 1983. Its per capita gross national product in U.S. dollars ($5460) exceeds the world average ($2754) and, with the exception of the oil-producing nations in the Middle East and Japan, is one of the higher figures in all of Asia.

Picture Credit: W. A. Douglas Jackson, 1967.

Impact on Health and Well-being

Some contemporary scientists are concerned about high desities for reasons other than the *carrying capacity* of the region (Calhoun, 1969). The results of research on rodent and other animal behavior have suggested to some biologists that there are limits to the extent living creatures—and by inference humans—can absorb the impact of high density without developing markedly pathological patterns of behavior. Some sociologists believe that people who live in too close contact with others, mainly in urban areas, will develop intergroup conflicts owing to the friction of their highly diverse cultures, languages, religions, values, and life-styles. They fear that conflicts such as these in the burgeoning industrial cities of the world will cause more human misery by the twenty-first century than will the absolute increase in population itself.

THEORIES CONCERNING POPULATION GROWTH

As the ramifications of unrestricted world growth have slowly penetrated the human consciousness, the population problem has assumed some of the dimensions of an *Orwellian*[1] *nightmare*. In terms of resource utilization, food supply, improvement in the quality of life, and preservation of the natural environment, the human race faces a challenge of monumental proportions. Yet the relationship between population growth and the earth's capacity to support it is a theme that has haunted humans since earliest historical times.

Various ancient schools of philosophy in China, including the Confucian, considered the implications of a rapid growth in population. The Chinese believed that such growth might reduce output per worker, depress the level of mass living, and foster conflict and instability. The Chinese also gave some thought to the

question of an optimum limit for a population engaged in agriculture.

In the Mediterranean region, there were at least two approaches to the question of population. In the third and fourth centuries B.C., Greek writers, such as Plato and Aristotle, considered the problem in a somewhat abstract manner. Their concern was with the relationship between size of population and life within the ideal state. The early Hebrew thinkers, on the other hand, placed a great deal of emphasis on God's injunction to man to multiply and subdue the earth. Some modern ecologist have laid the blame for much of Western man's aggressiveness toward nature on this biblical injunction. However, although the doctrine of the medieval Christian Church was essentially in favor of high birthrates, the preservation of virginity outside marriage and of celibacy within marriage were considered higher ideals than procreation. (In fact, the Roman Catholic Church was not a proponent of large families until the nineteenth century.)

The mercantilists, an influential group of policymakers and writers in Europe between the sixteenth and eighteenth centuries, were especially interested in population growth, but not because they were devout inheritors of the Judaeo-Christian tradition. Rather, they saw a significant relationship among markets, foreign trade, and more people. Migration to the colonies, although initially believed to be a drain on the mother country, nevertheless gained favorable attention because the colonial association was a complementary one: as population grew and spread over the colony, markets for the manufactured goods of the mother country expanded and, in turn, more raw material could be made available for the factories of the motherland.

These mercantilist views also brought opponents, among whom was Thomas Malthus (1766–1834) (Fig. 5–15). Rapid population increase and the resulting diversion of too large an amount of productive resources to human consumption, according to Malthus, were the

[1] George Orwell (1903–1950) was a British author who published two books that gained wide recognition, *Animal Farm* (1945) and *Nineteen Eighty-Four* (1949). These novels are satirical, the latter, in particular, depicts a completely totalitarian world where the human dimensions of life are grossly distorted.

Figure 5–15
Thomas R. Malthus was a clergyman and a professor of history and political economy. His doctrine regarding population growth was elaborated in his *An Essay on the Principle of Population,* which was published anonymously in 1798. The work aroused bitter opposition, which led Malthus to revise the text, provide more evidence, and publish a second edition in 1803. The renowned economist Adam Smith (1723–1790) had developed an optimistic view of society and progress. Malthus, on the other hand, saw life as a grim and difficult struggle for survival. The only remedy, according to Malthus, was to ensure that the birthrate be kept under control so that population numbers did not outrun the earth's ability to support human life.

Picture Credit: Mary Evans Picture Library/Photo Researchers, Inc.

flicts. In a later edition of his essay, Malthus argued in favor of "moral restraint" as a curb on fertility through the postponement of marriage and smaller families.

Karl Marx (1818–1883), while looking at the residual effects of industrialization in Britain and other European countries, did not see population growth as a problem for concern at all. For him, the question was simply one of assuring that all workers were rewarded equally for their labor. Poverty and its attendant ills, he argued, were simply products of the capitalist mode of production, which was based on the exploitation of the masses. Under a socialist economy, where the means of production are owned by the people, everyone shares in the profits. As industrialization proceeds, he argued, the communal wealth increases. Moreover, he believed a planned system of economic development would ensure a wise use of resources for the good of all. In his view, population increase was not a problem if economic growth were directed in a productive way.

Marxian views on population are still generally upheld in the Soviet Union. In any case, the Soviet Union is characterized by a low rate of population growth. Because the rate in the Soviet Union has fallen to 0.9 percent, Soviet officials are very much aware that the decline has reduced the size of the labor force. Manpower is very much needed to guard the country's extensive borders, they feel, and to develop the resources of Siberia. Moscow does not have an official population policy, but some Soviet theorists are inclined to favor a stimulation of fertility, especially among the European segment of the population, to build a large labor force in the future. In East Germany and in other Soviet bloc countries, the regimes have offered incentives for having larger families with some degree of success.

In the United States many people became aware of the problem of overpopulation only with the publication of *The Population Bomb* by Paul Ehrlich in 1968. Since then, concern for the quality of life in the United States together

principal causes of mass poverty. He foresaw that certain controls, which he called *"misery and vice,"* would ultimately come into operation to limit growth. By misery, Malthus meant disease, starvation, and related ills; under vice, he listed war, social convulsions, and other con-

with a concern for the preservation of the environment has led one group of citizens to press for *zero population growth,* a population equilibrium where the number of births balances the number of deaths. But by 1983, when the rate of increase was 0.7 percent, even the United States still remained a long way from such a goal.

Such groups draw on the *Malthusian* premise and may be identified as *neo-Malthusian.* They accept the concept that there are limits to the earth's capacity to support unlimited population growth. They fear the consequences to the whole earth ecosystem if continued stress is placed on it. They argue that rates of population growth must be brought down.

Among the more widely known supporters of this thesis are the authors of *The Limits to Growth* (Meadows et al. 1972), which predicted dire consequences within a century if certain steps were not taken immediately to curb both population growth and the consumption of resources. At the Worldwatch Institute in Washington, D.C., an organization created to focus attention on world problems, the chief spokesman, Lester R. Brown, has followed a comparable thesis, which at times has seemed even frightful. "What we must now recognize," he has written (Brown, 1974, p. 16), "is that continuing population growth, even at a moderate rate, will henceforth aggravate virtually all of the important economic, ecological, social, and political problems facing mankind."

Western intellectual response to the implications of world population growth has by no means been uniformly of the same school of thought however. Ester Boserup, an agricultural economist who worked for some years in India and other Asian countries, has taken a position that is the opposite of the neo-Malthusians (Boserup, 1965). She wants to know, first of all, how changes in agricultural conditions affect the demographic situation. Subsequently, she argues that population growth is not a threat but rather a precondition of agricultural development and technological expansion. She be-

lieves that an ever-improving technical base will promote an increase in agricultural productivity as a result of population. Finally, she concludes, "in many cases the output from a given area of land responds far more generously to an additional input of labour than assumed by neo-Malthusian authors" (p. 14). The increase in grain production under the Green Revolution from the early 1960s onward would tend to support her thesis.

Still, the warnings implicit in the writings of Malthus and his modern followers are worth heeding, simply because the challenges faced by mankind are staggering in their complexity, and there is much more that we need to know before we undertake major programs, the consequences of which may cause further imbalance between population growth and the earth's resources.

EPILOGUE

Can the nonindustrialized or developing countries reduce their rates of population growth so that they can lessen the stress such growth places on their societies and move ahead with economic development? What steps must be taken to achieve such goals?

The experience of the Western industrialized countries offers a model whereby rates of natural increase were reduced as industrialization and urbanization proceeded. However, it took up to a century for most of the West (including Japan) to pass through the demographic transition where the pressures of hitherto rapid population increases were reduced. Moreover, these countries could draw on world resources, much of which were contained within colonial empires, to satisfy the requirements of industrialization. Furthermore, they could send both their surplus populations and the output of their factories abroad, relieving pressures at home. The prospects in the mid-1980s for the rest of the world are not encouraging.

In the Western industrialized countries, the population is aging. Indeed, the rate of natural increase, particularly evident in the case of Sweden, is approaching zero. The industrialized countries have enjoyed the benefits of a relatively high standard of living because of their economic growth, but, increasingly, the cost of providing health care and other services to sustain senior citizens falls heavily on the youth and those of working age. In many European countries, 15 percent of the population is over 64 years of age. In the United States, the problem is reflected in increases in social security deductions from workers' paychecks and concern for future funding of such pensions.

APPLICATION OF IDEAS

1. A startling phenomenon of the modern world is the continuing upward surge in total population, sometimes called the population explosion. This trend upwards is due to continuing high birthrates and, since World War II, declining deathrates.

2. Actually, the population explosion pattern describes the developing countries, rather than the developed, or industrialized, countries. The latter began their demographic transition over 150 years ago, with a decline in deathrates subsequently to be followed over a century with a fall in birthrates. This transition is associated with industrialization and urbanization.

3. The hope is that the developing nations, where deathrates have fallen, will imitate the European model and experience a decline in birthrates. However, population pressures on scarce resources are already so acute that the Malthusian prediction shows evidence of working itself out. Population growth may be followed by Malthus's "misery and vice."

4. Many of the countries with high birthrates and high rates of natural increase are also char-

acterized by high densities. There is a fear that these high densities will create not only social problems, but also pathological behavior patterns.

5. Severe policies had to be implemented in China to reduce the rate of natural increase. It is questionable if a democratic country, like India, could follow China's example, given also the reverence for life that exists among India's peasant population.

KEY WORDS AND PHRASES

birthrate	"misery and vice"
carrying capacity	*neo-Malthusian*
deathrate	Orwellian nightmare
demographic	population bomb
demographic	population explosion
transition	population profile
lebensraum (living	rate of natural
space)	increase
Malthusian	zero population
Marxian	growth
mercantilist	

QUESTIONS FOR FURTHER DISCUSSION

1. What does the term demographic transition mean? What must occur for it to be fully realized?

2. How do you account for the significant decline in Britain's (or Scandinavia's) deathrate in the nineteenth century?

3. What were the reasons for the rapid population growth of the United States during and immediately after the Revolutionary War period? What brought about the decline in the deathrate in the United States? What precipitated the decline in the birthrate?

4. What is meant by the term population explosion as used to describe recent and current demographic trends? What has brought about the sharp increase in world population?

5. What continents (and countries) have rates of increase that significantly surpass the world's average annual rate of increase?

6. It has been reported that, although mainland China's total population is over 1 billion, its birthrate has fallen significantly over the past 15 years. How do you account for this seeming discrepancy?

7. What is so alarming about a population profile that resembles a broadly based pyramid? What can be done about such a problem? How long do you think it would take to reach a more desirable population age structure?

8. Why did thoughtful opinion in Western Europe concerning Europe's (and the world's) demographic picture become more optimistic toward the end of the nineteenth century? Did this optimism prove Thomas Malthus wrong?

9. Marxists generally have not viewed the growth of population in the same terms as other Western population specialists. Why do they not view the question of an increase in numbers with great concern? Why do some Eastern European Communist states seek to increase their own numbers by natural means?

10. What does a regions's population density tell you? What does density alone not tell you? What factors other than simple density must be taken into consideration in determining the quality of life of any given people?

REFERENCES AND ADDITIONAL READING

Blum, Jerome. *The End of the Old Order in Rural Europe.* Princeton, N.J.: Princeton University Press, 1978.

Borgstrom, George. *The Food and People Dilemma.* North Scituate, Mass.: Duxbury Press, 1973.

Boserup, Ester. *The Conditions of Agricultural Growth. The Economics of Agrarian Change Under Population Pressure.* Chicago: Aldine, 1965.

Braudel, Fernand. *Capitalism and Material Life 1400–1800.* New York: Harper & Row, 1975. (Colophon Books)

Brown, Lester R. *In the Human Interest. A Strategy to Stabilize World Population.* New York: W. W. Norton, 1974.

Calhoun, John B. "Population Density and Social Pathology," pp. 111–118. In *Science, Conflict and Society. Readings from Scientific American.* San Francisco: W. H. Freeman, 1969.

Cartwright, Frederick F. *Disease and History.* New York: Thomas Y. Crowell, 1972.

Cipolla, Carlo M. *The Economic History of World Population,* 7th ed. Harmondsworth, Eng.: Penguin Books, 1978.

Clarke, John I. *Population Geography,* 2nd ed. Oxford: Pergamon Press, 1972.

Coale, Ansley J. "The History of the Human Population." *Scientific American* 231 (1974): 40–51.

Darby, Henry C. *Domesday England.* Cambridge: Cambridge University Press, 1977.

Davis, Kingsley, "Population," pp. 101–110. In *Science, Conflict and Society. Readings from Scientific American.* San Francisco: W. H. Freeman, 1969.

Demeny, Paul. "The Populations of the Underdeveloped Countries." *Scientific American* 231 (1974): 148–159.

Demko, G. J., et al. *Population Geography: A Reader.* New York: McGraw-Hill, 1970.

Dubos, Rene. *Man Adapting.* New Haven, Conn.: Yale University Press, 1969.

Ehrlich, Paul R. *The Population Bomb.* New York: Ballantine Books, 1968.

Ehrlich, Paul R., and Ehrlich, Anne H. *Population, Resources, Environment, Issues in Human Ecology.* San Francisco: W. H. Freeman, 1970.

Freedman, Ronald, and Berelson, Bernard. "The Human Population." *Scientific American* 231 (1974): 31–51.

Glas, D. V., and Grebenik, E. "World Population, 1800–1950," pp. 60–138. In *The Cambridge Economic History of Europe,* Vol. 6. H. J. Habakkuk and M. Postan, eds. Cambridge: Cambridge University Press, 1965.

Hardin, Garrett, ed. *Population, Evolution and Birth Control,* 2nd ed. San Francisco: W. H. Freeman, 1969.

Hardin, Garrett, and Baden, John, eds. *Managing the Common.* San Francisco: W. H. Freeman, 1977.

Johnston, R. J. "Population Distributions and the Essentials of Human Geography." *South African Geographical Journal* 58 (1976): 93–106.

Kosinski, Leszek. *The Population of Europe.* London: Longman, 1970.

Kostanick, Huey Louis, ed. *Population and Migration Trends in Eastern Europe.* Boulder, Colo.: Westview Press, 1977.

Lerner, I. Michael. *Heredity, Evolution and Society.* San Francisco: W. H. Freeman, 1968.

McGaugh, Maurice E. *A Geography of Population and Settlement.* Dubuque, Iowa: William C. Brown, 1970.

McNeil, William H. *Europe's Steppe Frontier, 1500–1800.* Chicago: University of Chicago Press, 1964.

Meadows, Donella H., et al. *The Limits to Growth.* New York: Universe Books, 1972.

Palmer, P. R., ed. *Atlas of World History.* Chicago: Rand McNally, 1957.

Revelle, Roger. "Food and Population." *Scientific American* 231 (1974): 160–171.

Schnell, George A. and Monmonier, Mark S. *The Study of Population. Elements, Patterns, Processes.* Columbus, Ohio: Charles E. Merrill, 1983.

Science, Conflict and Society. Readings from Scientific American. San Francisco: W. H. Freeman, 1969.

Shepard, Paul, and McKinley, Daniel, eds. *The Subversive Science. Essays Toward an Ecology of Man.* Boston: Houghton Mifflin, 1969.

Trevelyan, G. M. *English Social History. A Survey of Six Centuries Chaucer to Queen Victoria.* London: Longmans, Green, 1942.

Westoff, Charles F. "The Populations of the Developed Countries." *Scientific American* 231 (1974): 108–121.

Woytinski, W. S., and Woytinski, E. S. *World Population and Production. Trends and Outlook.* New York: Twentieth Century Fund, 1953.

Wriggins, W. Howard, and Guyot, James F. *Population, Politics, and the Future of Southern Asia.* New York: Columbia University Press, 1973.

Zelinski, Wilbur. *A Prologue to Population Geography.* Englewood Cliffs, N.J.: Prentice-Hall, 1966.

Zelinski, Wilbur et al. eds. *Geography and a Crowding World.* New York: Oxford University Press, 1970.

6
Migration

People are crossing national boundaries to-day in unprecedented numbers. Migrant workers in Europe, the United States, and Canada currently total more than twenty million. . . . This is half as many as emigrated from Europe to North America in the great nineteenth- and twentieth-century movement of people, yet this new migration has occurred in only thirty years.

Elsa M. Chaney
"Migrant Workers and National Boundaries: The Basis for Rights and Protections," 1981

Key Ideas

1. In recent years, the world has seen many people uprooted from their homelands, wandering over land and sea in search of a new place to settle.

2. Grave as the problem of the uprooted is, it is only one chapter in the refugee crisis. In 1980, it was estimated that some 16 million persons throughout the world were refugees or displaced persons.

3. Migration is an historic process that is as old as humankind itself.

4. Many people move, but a migrant is a person who moves between communities, and in the United States over county boundaries.

5. There are many reasons why people migrate. Migration has, on the one hand, been associated with a push-pull mechanism. Behavioralists tend to see every decision to move as based on a rational process. Perhaps, to understand the motives for migration, one should see in it human responses to major dislocations or transformations in regional geographic structures.

6. Europeans afford a good example of people migrations that are the result of major changes in their way of life.

7. Europeans migrated in two principal directions: from the countryside to the city, and from Europe to other parts of the globe.

8. The shaping of modern America was due to several migrations that occurred during the nineteenth century, among which were the westward movement, the rural-urban migration, the migration to the suburbs, and the movement of southern blacks into northern cities.

9. After World War II, the migration westward, particularly to California, quickened. Since 1970, there has been a substantial migration from North to South.

10. Accompanying the national movement of population in the United States has been, since 1970, a decided urban-rural flow of people, a reversal of a trend that was predominant over the preceding 150 years.

MIGRATION AS A GEOGRAPHIC PHENOMENON

The patterns and spatial structures that humankind creates on the earth's surface are the result of human goals and aspirations in every realm of endeavor. Such patterns are not permanent, however, but subject to change; one of the compelling factors for change is the movement of peoples.

Migration, as a geographic phenomenon, is of interest not only to geographers, but also to other social scientists. The conclusion of World War II saw major dislocations of populations in Europe, which drew the attention of specialists in East European affairs. In recent years, geographers have tended to focus on specific population movements, often of a domestic or regional nature, leaving the global canvas to others. This chapter serves to introduce the student to some of the movements of population in the world, especially where they have been or are seen to be of major proportion and significance.

THE AGE OF THE UPROOTED

The Tragedy of the Boat People

When the North Vietnamese Communists took over South Vietnam in 1975, many thousands of people began to leave their homeland and seek refuge elsewhere. As supporters of the old regime in the South, these Vietnamese feared economic hardship and in some cases even persecution. Four years later, as political relations between Vietnam and China worsened, thousands more were compelled to migrate, mainly because they were of Chinese origin—*overseas Chinese,* whose families had been resident in Indochina for centuries. Fearing for their lives, this new wave of migrants paid for passage in boats they hoped would take them to friendly, receptive countries. It was for this reason that they came to be called the boat people.

If lucky and their boats did not sink, the refugees reached camps in Thailand, Malaysia, Indonesia, and Hong Kong. There, some attempt was made to relocate them in different countries around the world. Altogether, since 1975, at least 1 million people have fled Indochina, abandoning homes not only in Vietnam, but also in neighboring Laos and Cambodia. Thousands have been resettled in the United States, Canada, France, Australia, West Germany, and Great Britain. But thousands more continue to languish in camps because the host countries lack the resources to take them in as residents and the international community has not yet found them new homes.

As one French official at a refugee processing center in Bangkok, Thailand, said with despair: "They just never stop coming and will continue to do so until the political atmosphere changes."

The World Refugee Crisis

Grave as this problem is, it is only one chapter of the world's refugee crisis. Refugees are by no means confined to the Southeast Asia region. In the early 1980s, it was estimated that there were 16 million refugees and displaced persons in the world as a whole. The Indochinese, obviously, constitute only a small portion of the total number of refugees (Table 6–1).

Peoples are in flight from the Horn of Af-

Table 6–1
Refugees and Displaced Persons, 1980 (by region of origin)

Asia	7,292,500
Africa	4,045,200
Middle East	3,312,500
Latin America	1,085,300
Europe	229,750
World Total	15,965,250

Source: *Christian Science Monitor,* November 18, 1980.

rica—from Ethiopia as well as from neighboring Somalia, where one in every three inhabitants is a refugee (Fig. 6–1). They are fleeing also from the semiarid wastes of Chad in Central Africa for fear of persecution and of the Libyan army, which invaded from the north. Thousands are pouring into Pakistan from Afghanistan ahead of the probing thrusts of the Soviet Red Army. And nearer the United States geographically, people take to boats from Cuba and Haiti in search of a better life beyond the Caribbean. Nor is the movement restricted to groups of people who are identified as refugees. Thousands of Mexicans annually cross the border into the United States without official permission as they seek employment and funds to support their families and themselves.

The modern world has witnessed some of the most dramatic movements of people in human history. They are dramatic because they entail large numbers of people moving within a short period of time over large sections of the earth's surface. This century has become, indeed, the age of the uprooted, the century of homeless people (Fig. 6–2).

This phenomenon, the migration, or mass movement, of humanity, has been a major factor in the shaping of our world. And, most likely, it will continue to shape the world of the future.

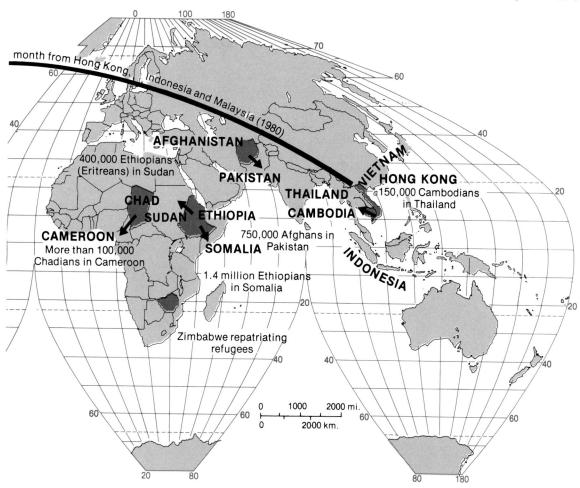

Figure 6–1

Never before in human history have so many people in different parts of the globe, voluntarily or involuntarily, left their homes in search of a new life elsewhere. Such migration often means hardship and deprivation. A new twist to migration has been given by governments anxious to be rid of "surplus" or unwanted population. The displacement of ethnic Chinese in Southeast Asia and the migration of Cubans in 1980, for example, were both stimulated by respective governments to remove persons considered undesirable for ethnic, economic, social, or ideological reasons.

(*Source: Christian Science Monitor,* May 28, 1980.)

WHY DO PEOPLE MIGRATE?

A Historic Phenomenon

Migration, as a process of moving from one place to another over earthspace, is a phenomenon that is as old as humankind itself (Bouvier, 1977). In its totality, the story of the human race is in large measure the story of human wandering, of overcoming the *tyranny of space,* that is, overcoming the vast distances between places of which humankind has taken possession (Brown and Neuberger, 1977). From the beginning, there was the spreading out of peoples from the cradles of early hominization and from the later civilizations in Africa and Asia. Early migrations were undirected, and people moved in the several directions of the compass. Migrant paths often crossed as regions of the globe filled with inhabitants, forcing still another migration and the search for a new place to settle (Box 6–1).

Throughout recorded history, migrations have also been associated with invasions. Arab armies, for example, carried the message of Islam across North Africa in the eighth century A.D., extending both the sphere of the faith and the language space of the Semitic people. From still earlier times, southern Russia, the Danubian Basin, and even western Europe felt the thrust of invaders from Asia. One of the last great invasions originating in Central Asia was

that of the Mongols who swept over the Russian steppe in the thirteenth century. Remnant peoples, such as the Tatars, may still be found in European Russia.

What Is a Migrant?

Why people move is a recurring question that intrigues geographers as well as other social scientists. But, before this question can be tackled, it is necessary to determine what a migrant is.

There are two types of population movement. One occurs within the same community and involves a move from one neighborhood to another. Few people in the United States live out their lives in the house in which they were

Figure 6–2
The exodus from Vietnam. Facing incredible hardships at sea and an uncertain future on land, refugees from Vietnam, nevertheless, were prepared to risk everything to find a new home. This boatload of migrants, 2,700 on board, reached Manila Bay in The Philippines only to be told they could not get off until a host country was prepared to accept them. The heat contributed to exhaustion, which was compounded by the abominable living conditions aboard ship.

Picture Credit: J. P. Laffont/Sygma, 1978.

born. In the 1950s and 1960s, for example, approximately one in five households changed places of residence every year (Biggar, 1979). But, most of these movers were not migrants.

According to the Bureau of the Census, anyone who moves across a county boundary is a migrant. Within the context of this definition, therefore, the United States saw about 40 percent of its population move across county lines between March 1975 and March 1978 (Biggar, 1979). However, intercounty movement within a large metropolitan area may entail only a change of residence within the same spatial community. In the broader canvas, such movers may not be considered migrants.

A more workable definition of migrant, then, may consider only movement between communities, that is, (1) from one metropolitan area to another, (2) from a metropolitan area to a nonmetropolitan area, (3) from a nonmetropolitan area to a metropolitan area, and (4) from a rural area to another rural area over a county line. Movement within these parameters, then, may be deemed migration, and it would entail intranational as well as international flows of people.

The Causes of Migration

The Push-Pull Mechanism

One convenient way in which to think of migration is to visualize a *push-pull mechanism* at work (Brown and Neuberger, 1977, pp. 171–173). According to this concept, people are "pushed" out of their homes or the areas in which they live and are "pulled" to new homes in other areas. Lack of economic opportunity; political, ideological, or religious oppression or persecution; or general dissatisfaction with the conditions of living are among the factors pushing people to move or migrate. The desire for greater economic opportunity; the dream of greener pastures elsewhere; the search for *amenities,* that is, a materially better life-style; or freedom are among the forces pulling people

to new places (Long and Hansen, 1979). Ullman, in particular, saw the role of amenities associated with the climate and living conditions in California as a major factor in "pulling" migrants to the West Coast after World War II (Ullman, 1954).

Useful as the push-pull mechanism is as a

BOX 6–1

Migration to Outer Space

It is generally assumed by most historians and economists that the frontier in Russia and the frontier in the United States, two countries that had experienced substantial movements of population over their surfaces, had been closed by 1910. What this means is that there was no longer any substantial amount of readily available or accessible land suitable for the creation of new farms and farming communities.

Since then, a major direction of migration throughout the world has been into the cities: first into the industrial cities of Europe, the United States, Japan, and Russia, and second into the cities of the Third World. Major international relocations of people have been associated with these two phenomena—the migration to the frontier and rural-urban migration.

But what of the future? Where will people go who wish to or must migrate? A number of scientists believe that in the twenty-first century, thousands if not millions of people may be living in outer space. These scientists see colonies in outer space, such as satellite farms, factories, and power stations, as possible solutions to many of the problems facing earth inhabitants.

The successful flights of the reusable space shuttle in the 1981–1983 period offer the possibility of shuttles of people moving daily to space stations. Certainly, manned space shots by the end of the 1980s should become routine, and space will become permanently occupied by at least a few men and women in orbit.

basis for explanation, it is probably too simplistic a concept to account for all the diverse motives that underlie an individual's decision to migrate. Even for many of the world's refugees, the precise cause of the migration is not always readily apparent.

The Behavioralist Interpretation

Behavioralists, those who seek an empirical basis for understanding human-activity patterns, assume generally that migration occurs as a result of decisions made by individuals or groups in the light of what they perceive the world to be (White and Woods, 1980). Further, it is assumed that underlying these decisions is a belief that the act of migration will ultimately enable migrants to satisfy better their needs and desires in other places. According to the behavioralists, people make rational decisions about their lives. "Important within the analysis of why migration occurs is the perception of spatial differentiation of opportunities—the idea that different geographical locations offer different levels of potential well-being to various sections of the human population" (White and Woods, 1980, p. 7).

Within this conceptual framework, it is possible to categorize migrants as active, sequent, or passive according to the motivation determining their choice of destination (Walter, 1980). Active migrants are those whose decision to move is based on a desire to improve their living conditions elsewhere. The decision is theirs, although they may not have full information on their planned destination. Sequent migrants are followers, those whose decision to migrate is based on some degree of familiarity with the destination of active migrants. They choose to join those who have gone before. Passive migrants make no positive choice of their own but join others at their request.

The Pilgrims were active migrants. Once established, they were followed by other Puritans. Subsequent migrations of both sequent and passive migrants reinforced a pattern pioneered by others.

The first wave of Irish migrants to England during the Industrial Revolution was toward the centers of heavy manufacturing near the coast of the Irish Sea. In time, these immigrants fanned out into other parts of England. Since the 1930s, sequent migrants from Ireland followed, settling in those secondary areas known to have received an earlier generation of Irish (Walter, 1980). In this way, Irish settlement in England moved away from the industrial centers on the coast.

The Need for a Broad Geographic Perspective

The behavioralist interpretation of the causes of migration seems to overlook many of the wider ramifications of population movement. What needs to be determined, of course, are the numbers of people migrating and the distances they move. Variations in regional development are more likely to have an influence on how people make a choice, especially where they perceive that they can improve on the conditions of their livelihood. This factor, undoubtedly, was important in drawing countless millions to the shores of North America in the nineteenth century even though they found on arrival that the streets were not paved of gold. For countless others, the changing conditions of life at home that involved major revisions in the structure of the economy may have been motivating factors in their decision to leave (Safa and DuToit, 1975; Todd, 1980). Until the early decades of the twentieth century, the movement of peoples toward the frontiers of global settlement reflected major transformations in older economies (McNeill and Adams, 1978, p. 7). And, contemporary migration, however disrupting it may seem, is another manifestation of a worldwide shift from a rural agrarian, or agricultural, economy to an urban industrial one (Safa and DuToit, 1975).

MIGRATIONS OWING TO CHANGING SOCIOECONOMIC CHANGES

Europeans as Migrants in the Eighteenth to the Twentieth Centuries

Europeans over the past two centuries afford a classic example of a migrating people whose world was undergoing a major transformation. They moved in two well-defined directions: into the factory towns and cities within Europe and into relatively empty lands in other parts of the world.

Rural-Urban Migration Within Europe

Even before the steam engine or the power loom had been invented, the principal cities of Europe had experienced growth. By the seventeenth century, largely because of their expanding centralized royal or princely functions and commercial growth, cities like London, Naples, Milan, and Paris—despite periodic fires, the plague, and other problems—had each increased their population size to over 100,000. London led with 250,000, but Naples was not far behind with 240,000. Paris had grown but then declined in size owing to internal political instability. Rome, Palermo, Lisbon, Antwerp, and Amsterdam also had all reached 100,000 (Braudel, 1973) owing principally to rural-urban migration.

At the end of the eighteenth century, London, Paris, Naples, Madrid, and Constantinople (Istanbul) were Europe's largest cities, London having reached 860,000 inhabitants, followed by Paris with 670,000. Between 1700 and 1820, the population of greater London doubled—to over 1 million—with much of the increase caused by the unfailing stream of migrants from the countryside. During the nineteenth century, these large capital cities continued to draw people from the rural areas, but from the middle of the century onward, an increasing number of migrants settled in the new factory towns spawned by the Industrial Revolution.

Free internal migration within Europe did not cease with the Industrial Revolution. As the economy of many Northern European states expanded during the 1960s and 1970s, thousands of workers were drawn from countries in the Mediterranean Basin and from the Middle East. By 1975, there were almost 6 million migrant workers in eight northern continental European countries, at least a third of which had been attracted by the booming economies of West Germany, France, and Switzerland. For families back home—in Italy, Turkey, Yugoslavia, and North Africa—the worker migration meant substantial remittances, reaching up to $24 billion in 1980, which made possible improvements in these families' standard of living. By the 1980s, however, recession in the industrialized countries compelled a cutback in migration, even forcing many workers to return to their native lands. Still, the use of foreign labor to do "dirty jobs" in the cities and factories of northern Europe remains an important opportunity for southern workers.

European Colonial Emigration

However significant internal movements of population were in Great Britain and on the Continent, the most impressive direction of flow was beyond the boundaries of Europe itself (Fig. 6–3). In the century and a half before the American Revolution, over 1 million persons left northwestern Europe for overseas colonies in the New World. By 1763, the French colony on the banks of the St. Lawrence River had grown from a relatively small group of settlers to over 60,000 persons. The settlements on the Atlantic seaboard to the south were predominantly English in origin, but there were colonists from continental Europe as well. For a short time, the Dutch had held Manhattan, and in 1638, Swedes had reached the Delaware. In 1681, a group of Quakers under William Penn

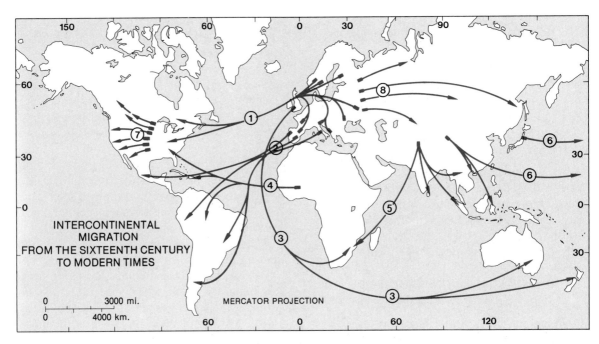

150 60 0 30 90

60

30

INTERCONTINENTAL
MIGRATION
FROM THE SIXTEENTH CENTURY
TO MODERN TIMES

0   3000 mi.
0   4000 km.

MERCATOR PROJECTION

60 0 60 120

Figure 6–3

From the sixteenth to the twentieth centuries, millions of people migrated across the globe. In this movement, one can distinguish about eight main directions of population flow. The greatest migration in terms of numbers of people entailed the exodus from Europe to North (1) and South America (2). An offshoot of this transatlantic movement was that which originated in Great Britain and terminated in the southern hemisphere (3), in southern Africa (3), and in Australia and New Zealand (3). For the most part, this European migration was a free migration, although the earliest settlers in Australia were exiles in the British penal system.

The migration, albeit under forced conditions, of Africans to the Americas (4) is a major chapter in the resettling of peoples and a phenomenon that has contributed much to American culture. In addition, through the cen-

turies, countless numbers of people from South Asia migrated to Africa and Southeast Asia (5) (6). The Chinese migration to Southeast Asia produced the overseas Chinese, Chinese who had migrated but were still considered citizens of China. Still other Chinese came to the United States and Canada (6) to work in the building of the western railroads. The migration of Japanese to the West Coast of the United States and Canada (6) as well as to Brazil in the pre-World War II period, is also important.

Finally, the migrations of Russians across northern Asia (8) and of Anglo-Americans across North America (7) are also among the world's great migrations, although they did not entail to any extent the crossing of national boundaries.

settled in Pennsylvania, to be followed to the New World by religious groups from Germany. At the end of the eighteenth century, the reorganization of rural landholdings occasioned by the enclosure movement in Scotland sent thousands of Scotch-Irish to the Pennsylvania frontier (Fig. 6–4).

Migration from Great Britain to the colonies began under the auspices of various charters and enterprises, some with professed religious and social goals, others almost purely economic. Between 1607 and 1680, Parliament, believing England overpopulated, officially sanctioned emigration to the New World. After

Figure 6–4

The Pilgrim Fathers. Throughout history there have been many reasons why people have migrated. The first English settlers in New England in 1620 came to North America to find a more abundant life together with religious freedom. Of those who sailed on the "Mayflower" one-third were staunch Puritans, the rest being hired to protect the interests of the London Company which financed the pilgrimage.

This illustration shows a group of Pilgrims embarking in The Netherlands prior to joining the "Mayflower".

Picture Credit: Mary Evans Picture Library/Photo Researchers, Inc.

1680, the adoption of *mercantilism,* a policy that endorsed government regulation of the economy to strengthen state power, frowned on further population drain—at least initially. This, in turn, slowed emigration, except for groups, like the Quakers, of which England would just as soon be rid. The shortage of labor that was a feature of colonial life, particularly where plantation agriculture had become established, encouraged, however, another kind of transatlantic movement—the shipment of black slaves from Africa.

Migration from Mediterranean lands to the Americas developed more slowly than that from northwestern Europe, mainly because the Spanish and Portuguese colonies in the New World were seen as sources of wealth to be transported home rather than as opportunities for resettlement of population from the Old World.

Europeans also found their way to other parts of the world. In 1652, a band of Dutch soldiers landed at the tip of southern Africa. Later (after 1688), they were joined by French *Huguenots,* or Protestants, and Germans. After 1820, English settlers arrived, the Dutch colony having fallen under British control. British emigrants also colonized the antipodes, reaching New South Wales (Australia) in 1788 and New Zealand after 1825. The aboriginal population of Australia may have been about 300,000 at the time of European contact, but disease, warfare,

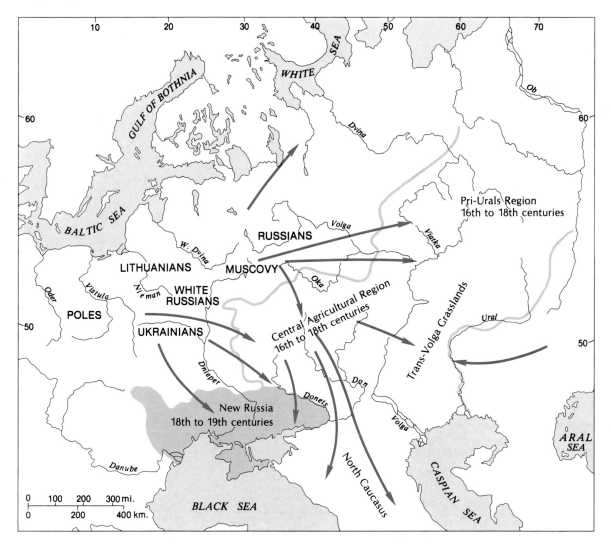

Figure 6–5

One of the more interesting features of the population geography of Russia was the migration and resettlement of Moscovites (Russians) and Ukrainians in the black-earth country south of the Oka River. From the sixteenth to the eighteenth centuries, these Slavic peoples pushed south and southeastward, stopping the raids of the Tatars from the Crimea and ultimately occupying the lands along the coast of the Black Sea. Known as New Russia, this region quickly filled with migrants in the eighteenth and nineteenth centuries, spilling over—about the time of the emancipation of the serfs in 1861—into the North Caucasus. Thereafter, the tide of internal migration was principally toward Siberia.

and displacement from traditional hunting grounds cut deeply into these numbers. By 1840, when British sovereignty was established in New Zealand, the Maori, one of the more numerous of the indigenous peoples of Oceania, totalled about 250,000, but their number fell to fewer than 50,000 by the end of the nineteenth century. If the greater Oceania population stood at 2 million in the eighteenth century, there was undoubtedly a sharp decline through the nineteenth century with increasing European contact. Thereafter, improvements in the standard of living led to population increases, but few natives of full-blood survive.

Russian-Ukrainian Migration

Throughout the seventeenth and eighteenth centuries very few peoples from eastern Europe participated in overseas settlement. The largest of the European countries, Russia, was busy creating a colonial empire that was attached by land to its own political hearth in the principality of Muscovy. The latter had been established in 1148 on a hill overlooking the Moskva River. Following a period of political expansion that led to the consolidation of Muscovite power in Central Russia, Russians began to colonize the relatively empty lands to the south and east (Fig. 6–5).

Russian peasants had first begun to migrate southward in the late fifteenth and early sixteenth centuries (McNeill, 1964). Wretched farming conditions in the region around Moscow—associated with poor soils and a harsh climate—together with the imposition of serfdom drove many peasants to steal across the Oka River in search of a freer and more bounteous life in the black-earth parkland and grassland belts to the south. At that time, the vast rolling upland to the south of Moscow was only sparsely occupied. The political boundaries of the Moscow, or Muscovite, principality had been pushed steadily toward the Caspian Sea, but north of the Black Sea the open countryside remained the domain of bands of wandering Turko-Tatar horsemen, remnants of the once powerful Empire of the Golden Horde, the Mongol state that had dominated much of central and southern Russia from the thirteenth century onward. Its weakening by the end of the fifteenth century was an invitation to Russian expansion and colonization.

Between 1509 and 1521, the Russians built a defensive line across the land, its pivot being the kremlin, or fortress, of Tula. This line was designed to protect both Moscow and the frontier settlements as well. When in 1571–1572, the Tatars broke through, laid waste the countryside, and sacked Moscow, the Russians ordered the building of additional fortified lines to the south of the Tula line to ensure greater security. Behind these fortifications, the settlers filled up the land, and then pushed deeper southward.

When the Black Sea coastal area fell under Russian control after a war with the Ottoman Turks at the end of the eighteenth century, the Tatar threat was finally eliminated, and migrants from the north poured southward into what came to be called New Russia. By the end of the nineteenth century, densities of up to 200 persons per square mile or more were achieved. Groups of Germans, Serbs, and Bulgars also settled in New Russia along with the Russians and Ukrainians.

Russian penetration of the North Caucasus had begun as early as the sixteenth century, but it was not until the middle of the nineteenth century, that peasant colonies were organized there. After the emancipation, or freeing, of the peasants from feudal obligations to landlords in 1861, movement to the North Caucasus became a free and spontaneous migration.

When the free lands in the North Caucasus were occupied, land-hungry peasants turned to Siberia. Explorers from Muscovy had reached the Pacific coast of Asia as early as the first half of the seventeenth century, to be followed by fur traders, missionaries, and administrators. Russian settlements and posts were established. The tsarist government then took to establishing fortified lines across Siberia—against the nomadic Turkic people in the dry steppe of Central Asia and against other potentially hostile peoples, including the Manchus (the native inhabitants of Manchuria) and the Chinese in the Far East. Between 1892 and 1897 the Trans-Siberian Railroad was built eastward from the Urals across Siberia, opening up vast areas of virgin grassland for settlement. The population of Siberia in 1863 was estimated at 3.4 million. During the next two decades the numbers of migrants reaching Siberia rose to 10,000 a year (Treadgold, 1957). With the opening of the railway, up to 100,000 persons per year reached Siberia. Between 1905 and 1913 some 3.6 million settlers crossed the Urals, with up to 758,000 in 1908 alone. By 1910, however, the good land had been claimed. Altogether, from 1885 to 1914, some 4.4 million persons had resettled in Russia's Asiatic territories (Demko, 1969). With the closing of the frontier, migration to Siberia has been into the cities primarily.

Later European Overseas Migration

The peopling of Siberia (and Asiatic Russia generally) by Russians and Ukrainians took place largely within a few decades. Because of the large numbers of people involved, it came to be called the *Great Siberian Migration*. In comparison, however, over 65 million Europeans migrated overseas in the period from approximately 1850 to 1950 (Table 6–2). Of these emigrants, more than half entered the United States directly (Table 6–3). Over 5.5 million went to Canada, an additional 5 million reached Brazil, and some 3 million went to Australia and New Zealand.

In the early nineteenth century, migrants to the United States—from England, Ireland, Germany, and Scandinavia primarily—were largely of the farmer-peasant class. During the 1840s and 1850s, the economic and social level of the migrants tended to decline. The Irish who arrived had been impoverished and forced off the

land by the potato famine; there were also destitute weavers from Great Britain and Germany whose trades had been rendered obsolete by the new machines of the Industrial Revolution. After 1860, however, it was less the "push" from Europe and more the "pull" of job prospects in the United States that led to transatlantic movement. Toward the end of the century, the flow from a Prussianized and increasingly militaristic Germany reached a peak, and an increasing number of migrants of peasant origin arrived from eastern Europe. From 1900 to World War I, Italy, the Balkans, Russia and other countries in east-central Europe provided the bulk of the Europeans crossing the Atlantic. Since World War II, many of the Europeans who have migrated to the United States have come from countries dominated by the Soviet Union.

The American Impact of European Immigration

In historical perspective, the migration of Europeans to the Americas has transformed the population face of the New World.

It is estimated that there were some 10 to 12 million natives living in the Americas early in the seventeenth century. These figures seem exaggerated, however, and may be more appropriate to the time of European contact and conquest a century earlier. In many cases, the arrival of the Europeans brought military defeat to native states and empires. At the same time, the rapid diffusion (contagious diffusion) of diseases (especially smallpox) that were carried over from the Old World decimated the population. In Meso-America and South America in particular, the native population declined sharply.

The Inca Empire of Peru, after a period of impressive territorial expansion (1438–1493), had about 4.5 million inhabitants when the Spanish conquest occurred in 1532. Over the next century and a half, the territory's popula-

Table 6-2
Average Annual Emigration Overseas from Europe, 1846-1963
(thousands)[a]

Countries	1846-1890	1891-1920	1921-1939	1940-1945	1946-1963
Europe total	377	910	366		585
British Isles	180	161	106		162
Germany[b]	76	30	36		92
Sweden, Denmark, Norway	26	35	14		12
France, Switzerland, Netherlands	16	14	9	World	87
Italy	31	246	68	War II	111
Austria, Hungary, Czechoslovakia[c]	14	145	15		—
Russia/Poland, Lithuania, Estonia, Finland[d]	8	118	44		—
Spain and Portugal	26	139	55		71
Other	—	22	19		50

[a] Data refer to gross emigration. The number of returnees was sometimes quite large so that in certain cases net emigration differed quite substantially from gross emigration.

[b] Within contemporary boundaries.

[c] Until 1920, Austro-Hungarian Empire.

[d] Until 1920, Russia; after 1920, Poland, Lithuania, Estonia, and Finland (without Russia).

Source: W. D. Borrie. *Trends and Patterns in International Migration Since 1945, UN World Population Conference,* Belgrade, 1965. WPC/WP/474, p. 42. Table based on United Nations and International Labor Organization data adapted from Leszek A. Kosinski, *The Population of Europe.* London: Longman, 1970, p. 57.

Table 6-3
Emigration from Europe into the United States in the Years, 1820-1966[a]
(thousands)

Years	Europe Total	Great Britain	Ireland[b]	Germany[c]	Scandinavia	Austria[d] Hungary Czechoslovakia Yugoslavia	Italy
Total	35,220.9	4,728.8	4,706.8	6,862.9	2,468.0	4,491.4	5,058.0
1820-1850	2,199.7	370.3	1,042.4	594.8	17.0	—	4.8
1851-1870	4,517.9	1,030.9	1,349.9	1,739.1	151.1	7.8	21.0
1871-1900	10,568.3	1,626.9	1,480.8	2,676.3	1,271.0	1,019.4	1,015.0
1901-1920	12,512.6	867.4	485.2	485.4	707.8	3,046.9	3,145.4
1921-1940	2,825.1	359.7	233.8	526.3	209.5	246.5	523.3
1941-1960	1,950.1	344.1	84.3	704.4	81.8	151.1	243.2
1961-1966	647.2	129.5	30.4	136.6	29.8	19.7	105.3

[a] 1820-1867: alien passengers arrived; 1868-1891 and 1895-1897: immigrant aliens arrived; 1890-1894 and since 1898: immigrant aliens admitted. Before 1906, country from which aliens came; thereafter, country of last permanent residence.

[b] Comprises Eire and Northern Ireland.

[c] Includes part of Poland in 1899-1919 and Austria 1938-1945.

[d] Data for Austria and Hungary since 1861, including both part of Poland 1899-1918 and Romania until 1918; excluding data for Austria 1938-1945; Serbia and Montenegro reported since 1899.

Source: Data of the U.S. Immigration and Naturalization Service, cited in Leszek A. Kosinski, *The Population of Europe.* London: Longman, 1970, p. 64.

tion fell to less than 1 million. The Aztec Empire from its base in the valley of Mexico had come to embrace about 75,000 miles^2 in Mexico and Central America. When Hernando Cortez arrived in 1519, it may have had a population of some 5 million. By the middle of the seventeenth century, smallpox, measles, and typhus had taken a substantial toll on the population, reducing it to about 1.3 million.

North of the Rio Grande, the native population may have totaled 1 million in 1500. Of these, almost three fourths lived in what is now the United States. The highest population densities were in the Southwest and included areas occupied by the Pueblo people. Here, as elsewhere in the Americas, European contact brought about a decline in the native population, although those who inhabited the Southwest were less affected than those who lived east of the Mississippi and on the plains.

In spite of the immigration of Europeans, the native people remain an important component of many Meso-American and South American countries today.

The Slave Trade

Until well past the middle of the nineteenth century, much of Africa south of the Sahara remained unknown to European empire builders. European contact was confined principally to coastal areas, although the major rivers had facilitated some European penetration inland. African civilizations dated back to the fifth century B.C., but of African kingdoms and tribal complexities, Europeans knew little. For them Africa was the "dark continent."

Over the past century, that image of Africa has changed, but because of the lack of native records, estimates of past population totals for Africa remain highly questionable. As in other continents, populations were not fixed. Africa experienced periods of tribal migrations that resulted in the pattern of tribal distribution that confronted Europeans on contact. By the 1650s, for example, Bantu peoples migrating

southward through eastern Africa had reached the territory later to become the Transvaal and the Orange Free State in South Africa. Their migration toward the Cape of Good Hope occurred just as Dutch settlers were planting their first colony there. In West Africa indigenous political units had come and gone, peoples had migrated, and from across the Saharan desert, Islam had penetrated the region to establish cultural ties between West Africans and the Middle East.

One of the principal elements in the contact of non-Africans with Africa was the slave trade. Along the eastern coast of Africa as far south as Mozambique, Arab traders from the Middle East had dealt in slaves as early as the fourteenth century. Europeans entered the trade toward the end of the sixteenth century. Most of the Africans destined for the New World, however, were taken from the west coast of the continent (Nigeria, the Gold Coast, Gambia, Sierra Leone, Liberia, the Ivory Coast, the Congo, and Angola), although some originated in the east in Mozambique and the Sudan. The Africans forced into exile represented many different languages, customs, and ways of life (Fig. 6–6). In colonial Anglo-America, much of this heritage was repressed as families and friends were permanently separated through sale and purchase. In South America, slaves were usually kept together according to homeland tribes, thus preserving something of traditional African life. Out of the irreversible conditions of the Afro-American experience emerged a unique cultural expression, found in spiritual life, music, and artistry.

We may never know how many millions of Africans were removed from their native habitat. Severe labor shortages on plantations in the Americas caused a substantial increase in slaving as the eighteenth century passed. By 1776, there were about 500,000 slaves in Anglo-America, a number that reached 767,000 in the United States in 1790. In Brazil, an initial attempt to harness the native Indian population on farms and in mines failed, and a massive

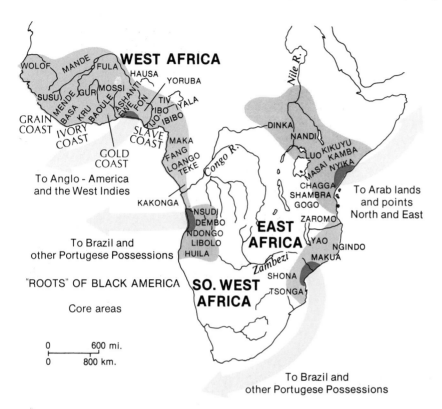

Figure 6–6

The African regions that figured prominently in the slave trade to the Americas included the present states of Guinea, Ivory Coast, Ghana, Nigeria, and Zaire on the west coast, and to a lesser extent, Mozambique on the east. The captured people came from a variety of tribes and different language groups and had little in common. Blacks from East Africa, south of the Horn, had long been associated with Arab traders and had been carried back to Arabia and neighboring areas.

importation of Africans ensued. By the end of the eighteenth century, of Brazil's estimated total population of 3 million, there were at least 2 million slaves and free blacks.

This enslavement and transportation no doubt demographically affected the peoples left in Africa. But we cannot know for certain what changes occurred in population totals there. Estimates suggest a decline between 1650 and 1850, but the transmission of European diseases also may have been a major factor in the taking of African lives.

TWENTIETH-CENTURY INTERNATIONAL MIGRATION

The twentieth century has already been referred to as the century of homeless people. It has earned that name. The resettlement of peoples across the globe during the sixteenth to the twentieth centuries pales in comparison with the record since World War I. No discussion of refugees and migrations would be complete without some reference to the dislocations that began roughly 60 years ago.

First, following the Greek-Turkish War of 1921–1922, about 1 million Greeks were forced to leave Turkey and resettle in Greece. The antagonisms between Greeks and Turks surfaced many times after that, but the most disruptive period was the Turkish invasion of Cyprus in 1974. That event resulted in the migration of the Greek Cypriot community into the western half of the island, leaving the eastern half to the Turkish Cypriot community.

During and after World War II, not only were many people forced to flee before invading or occupying armies, but also populations were exchanged as postwar boundaries were redrawn to reduce the size of minority populations (Kosinski, 1970). The Soviet occupation and incorporation of neighboring territories, such as independent Latvia, Lithuania, and Estonia; eastern Poland; eastern Romania; the Karelian isthmus (from Finland); and so on, resulted in the transfer to Soviet rule of about 20 million people.

In South Asia, the partition of the Indian subcontinent in 1947–1948 resulted in the two-way migration of 18 million Hindus from East and West Pakistan and Muslims from India. The creation of Bangladesh out of East Pakistan in 1971 made refugees, albeit of a temporary nature, of some 10 million persons, the bulk of whom were cared for by India (Fig. 6–7). In East Asia, the success of the Communists in China in 1949 drove upwards of 2 million people to Taiwan, an offshore island, and an additional 2 million or more reached Hong Kong, causing grave housing problems there.

In the Middle East, the creation of the state

Figure 6–7

Bangladesh refugee camp. The war between India and Pakistan in 1971 that culminated in the secession of East Pakistan and its creation as the independent state of Bangladesh created enormous dislocation of peoples. Millions were forced out of their villages to take refuge in other parts of Bangladesh or in India.

This relief camp of 36,000 people was set up in Dacca, the capital of Bangladesh, to take care of Bihari refugees.

Picture Credit: Bernard Pierre Wolff Photo Researchers, Inc.

of Israel in 1948 caused a wholesale exodus of Palestinian Arabs into neighboring Arab countries, notably Jordan. The survival, despite many reverses, of the Palestine Liberation Organization (PLO), until 1982 concentrated in Lebanon, is in no small measure due to Palestinian resentment at the loss of homes and farms to the immigrant Israelis.

The European scene was again disturbed in 1956 when the Hungarians revolted against Soviet occupation and, failing to gain their freedom, sent over 200,000 persons into Western Europe and ultimately on to the United States and Canada. Up until the erection of the Berlin Wall in 1961, some 3.7 million East Germans found asylum in West Germany, draining the eastern state of much of its young talent.

In Africa, the granting of independence to former colonies was not necessarily accompanied by peace and security for all the people. Countless numbers crossed boundaries to rejoin tribes or to avoid persecution. The struggle for independence in Zimbabwe (formerly Southern Rhodesia) and the conflicts in Uganda, in Angola, in the Horn of Africa, and in the *Sahel* (southern Sahara) are but continuing sagas of the search for new equilibrium in that continent.

Finally, the revolution led by Fidel Castro in Cuba began one of the greatest intrahemi-

---

BOX 6–2

The Impact of Latin American Immigration on the United States

In the United States, Hispanics number anywhere from the official count of 12 million to the unofficial estimate of 20 million. The common 2000-mile-long border with Mexico defies complete control. With a birth rate of 3.3 percent, a death rate of 0.8 percent, Mexico's population of 69.3 million (1981) is expected to double in 28 years. Mexico's per capita *gross national product* (GNP), the total value of output and services per person, is only a tenth of that of the United States. Population pressure—the search for a decent livelihood—has forced thousands of Mexicans, therefore, to cross into the United States in search of work.

In view of these stark realities, what does this portend for the future population characteristics of southern states or for the United States as a whole? Federal funding has been created in the United States to help assimilate these Spanish-speaking newcomers (Pifer, 1979). Indeed, Spanish-English bilingual education has already tapped two thirds of the monies allocated for providing instruction to all new non-English-speaking immigrants. However, there is a difference here with past practice. Traditionally, English has been the medium of instruction in the United States. This was a major factor in the creation of the *melting pot,* the assimilation of immigrants in the nineteenth century. But, the introduction of other languages, notably Spanish, into the classroom, has caused concern. Bilingual instruction is designed to be an educational measure; but some segments of American society view with alarm the possibility that bilingualism will become a permanent feature of American life in the future. In the case of the Hispanics, the fear of American society is that it will provide them with a strategy to realize social, political, and economic aspirations that run counter to historic Anglo-American goals for the country.

Can the United States, which was able to assimilate through its classrooms and other established institutions in the past, also assimilate this large and most likely continuing influx from Latin America? What will the United States be like in half a century?

spheric migrations in the Americas. Between 1960 and 1971, some 750,000 Cubans, over half of whom settled in the United States, were to be followed in 1980 by thousands more who came by boat to Florida. In 1980–1981, boatloads of Haitians also crossed the Caribbean in search of sanctuary and a better life in the United States (Box 6–2).

INTERNAL MIGRATION IN THE UNITED STATES: NEW TRENDS

The shape of the United States as it appears in the second half of the twentieth century could not have evolved without the enormous spatial mobility of its population. The nineteenth cen-

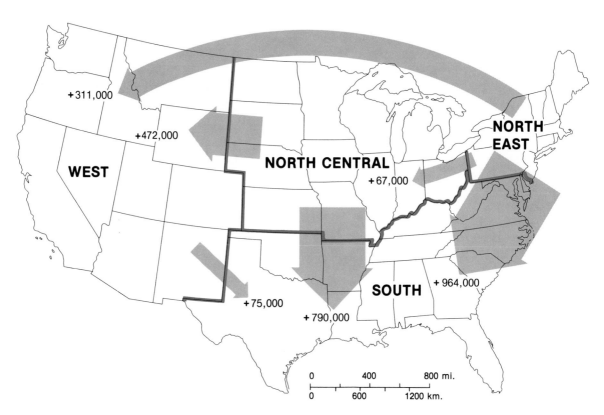

Figure 6–8

Since 1970, there has been a pronounced exodus of people from the northeastern and north-central states into the West and the South. So dramatic has the increase in the numbers of migrants to the South become, that the migration has been described as a Sunbelt migration.

Between 1970 and 1975, the Northeast suffered a net loss of 1.3 million inhabitants, which grew to 1.5 million in the period 1975–1980. The north-central states declined by 2.4 million in the overall period 1970–1980. On the other hand, the South showed a net gain in population of 1.8 million in 1970–1975 and 1.76 million in 1975–1980. In the decade, the West gained 1.6 million inhabitants.

(*Source:* Berry and Dahmann 1977, fig. 40; *Statistical Abstract of the United States: 1981,* p. 13.)

tury had witnessed the conquest of a continent and the peopling of the vast territory lying west of the Appalachian Mountains. By mid-century the migration to the frontier was accompanied also by a rural-urban movement as the young cities of the Northeast, and subsequently the Midwest, developed a base in manufacturing. With the turn of the century, and especially after the adoption and diffusion of the automobile, came the migration into suburbs. And this movement was further aggravated as immigrants from Europe and the southern parts of the United States flowed into the central districts of the sprawling cities of the North.

But, the map of the United States reflects additional trends—although rooted, in part, in past patterns of migration—that represent new sets of decisions and aspirations among the population.

The Migration to the West and the South

The movement westward, particularly where the principal destination of the migrants was California, quickened after World War II. During the two decades following the war, California received an average of 1000 migrants a day (Biggar, 1979). In the 1960s, California added 2.1 million inhabitants to its population as a result of a net in-migration from other parts of the country.

In the 1970s, the trek westward gained a new momentum when the census of 1970, confirmed in 1980, revealed that a significant exodus from the northeastern and north-central states was underway. People were continuing to move westward in considerable numbers, but a still larger migration was now underway to the

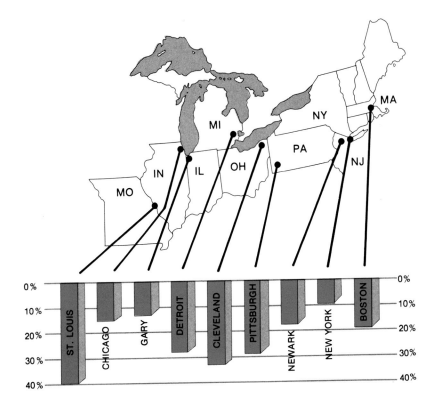

Figure 6–9

The census of 1980 has confirmed what earlier trends suggested, namely, a flow of people out of the older states of the north into southern and western states. Although blacks have shown a tendency to move from northern cities to the south, many of the migrants have been nonpoor seeking a better lifestyle.

(*Source: Christian Science Monitor*, January 15, 1981.)

South, in what came to be called collectively the migration to the *Sunbelt* (Fig. 6–8).

After the 1980 census, it had become clear that of the areas of the United States experiencing the most rapid growth over the preceding decade were those providing a wide range of amenities. Among the latter were facilities or opportunities for outdoor recreation and a pleasant climate or natural beauty. What this development suggests is not simply a desire to leave regions of the countries where the winters are relatively long and cold—the so-called *Frostbelt,* or *Snowbelt*—for those regions of greater sunshine—the so-called Sunbelt—but individual decisions to seek out areas capable of satisfying specific life-style goals.

More specifically, this migration has been directed toward seashores, inlets, lakes, rivers, mountainsides, ski resorts, hunting preserves, and other like places. Access to the amenities afforded by these geographic locations are, of course, believed to exist in the South and the West, principally in Florida and Texas, but also in Idaho, Colorado, Wyoming, Nevada, Arizona, New Mexico and, to a lesser degree, in California (Fig. 6–9) (Box 6–3).

Although this migration contains a reverse flow of blacks from northern cities to southern localities, the bulk of the migrants to the Sunbelt states has been made up mostly of the non-poor. Among these have been senior citizens seeking retirement in areas deemed attractive; professionals whose jobs have been dispersed from older areas of the country into areas possessing facilities for outdoor recreation; and younger people attracted by the growth of an economic base that has taken shape initially to service the retirees (Fig. 6–10).

The Exodus from Large Metropolitan Areas

Associated to a significant degree with the migration to amenity-rich states has been an exodus from large metropolitan areas into nonmetropolitan areas. Indeed, the census of 1980

BOX 6–3

Internal Migration in the United States: Unpredictable and Sometimes Reversible

Texas, Arizona, Colorado. It comes as no news that these are growth states and will continue to be for years to come.

But, says a new report by a prestigious Harvard University-Massachusetts Institute of Technology (MIT) study group, so are Vermont, Iowa, and Kansas.

Vermont, Iowa, and Kansas?

These states, and several others in the so-called frostbelt, are enjoying a resurgence that defies the conventional wisdom that all cold-weather states are losing population uniformly, according to the study. Likewise, it finds that not all Sunbelt states are growing alike. Indeed, such glamour states as California and Florida are not matching the growth rates of some of their less obvious neighbors.

The study, *Regional Diversity: Growth in the United States, 1960–1990* (Jackson et al., 1981), maintains that it is simplistic to chart population and economic trends by dividing the country only into Sunbelt and frostbelt regions. Rather, it finds, there are subgroups within each of these broad regions—all of which do not perform alike.

Based on their findings taken from 1980 U.S. census data, authors Gregory Jackson and his associates of the Joint Center for Urban Studies, say there are actually four categories of states: fast-growth, decelerating, resurgent, and no-growth (Jackson, 1981). All of the Sunbelt regions will continue their growth. . . . But it is equally clear to us that three of these regions—East South Central, West South Central, and Mountain—will continue very fast growth. The study projects that growth to take place at a 26 percent rate over the next 10 years. The other Sunbelt regions, South Atlantic and Pacific, they say, will grow less fast—probably at a 10 percent rate.

As for the frostbelt, . . . a resurgent New England (especially its three northernmost states) and the West North Central region also will grow at a rate (10 percent) that distinguishes them from the Mid-Atlantic and East North Central regions, which actually will experience negative growth (minus 3.8 percent) between now and 1990.

Source: Quoted in the *Christian Science Monitor,* October 30, 1981.

confirmed that for the first time in over a century, the pattern of rural-urban migration had been reversed. This migration, moreover, has not entailed simply a move to the suburbs. Rural counties not adjacent to an urban one are now growing faster than urban counties. The U.S. Bureau of the Census has found that the desire to leave cities is stronger than the concern over higher gasoline prices. Moreover, the movement out of metropolitan areas seems to have speeded up since the gasoline crunch of 1973–1974 when queues at service stations became a daily phenomenon. In the 1970s, for example, the Philadelphia metropolitan area lost 2.2 percent of its population. Between 1970 and 1980 Boston lost 136,000 inhabitants, and Detroit 82,000 inhabitants (Fig. 6–11) (Table 6–4).

Implications of Contemporary Migration Trends

Political Implications

The shift in population away from the traditional economic core in the Northeast and Midwest has encouraged a process of homogenization in American politics. What this means is

Figure 6–10

The Strip at Miami Beach. Miami Beach, Florida, symbolizes the good living and the search for the sun, attracting the young and the not so young year round. Prior to 1912, Miami Beach was a mangrove swamp. Subsequently the area was dredged to make an island, and a causeway was built linking it to the mainland. Today the entire oceanfront is lined with high-rise hotels and condominiums.

Picture Credit: Georg Gerster Photo Researchers, Inc.

Table 6–4
Changing Frostbelt Urban Populations in Large Metropolitan Areas (in thousands)

City	1960	1970	1980	Percentage Change 1970–1980
Boston	2,688	2,899	2,763	−4.7
Chicago	6,221	6,977	7,102	+1.8
Cleveland	1,909	2,064	1,899	−8.0
Detroit	3,950	4,435	4,353	−1.9
Jersey City	611	608	557	−8.4
Newark	1,833	2,057	1,965	−4.5
New York	9,540	9,974	9,120	−8.6
Philadelphia	4,343	4,824	4,717	−2.2
Pittsburgh	2,405	2,401	2,264	−5.7
St. Louis	2,144	2,411	2,355	−2.3

Source: Statistical Abstract of the United States: 1981, pp. 18–20.

that the liberal-conservative gap within the several regions of the country is narrowing and most likely will continue to narrow. Migration to the Sunbelt is not necessarily producing a Sunbelt conservatism, winning over the liberals among the migrant population. Rather, the in-

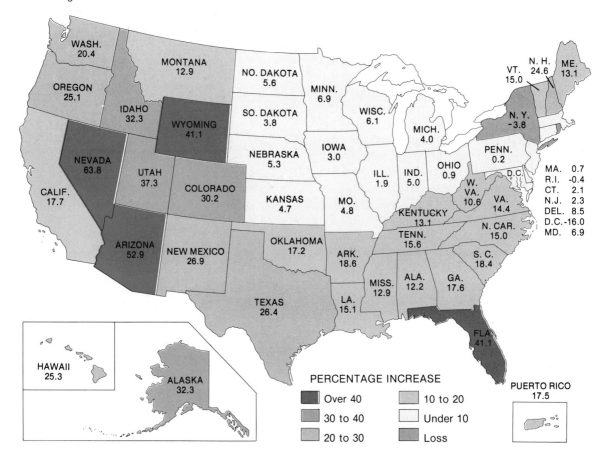

Figure 6–11

Although the population of the United States in the decade 1970–1980 grew by over 11%, many states increased the number of their inhabitants far in excess of the national average, notably Nevada, Arizona, Florida, Wyoming, and Utah. Other states, particularly in the Northeast and the north-central parts of the country, increased by considerably less than the national average. New York State, Rhode Island, and the District of Columbia declined in population during the decade.

flux of northerners into southern and western states may lead to a significant reduction in the differences between liberal and conservatives.

On the other hand, the increase in the number of inhabitants in southern and western states will be immediately reflected in the reapportionment of congressional seats. Western and southern congressmen will simply possess more political clout than they have had hitherto (see Table 6.5).

The Constitution requires seats in the House to be apportioned on the basis of population, according to the decennial census. Because the number of seats in the House remains constant at 435, the population shift required a reshuffle of House seats. In 1980 Florida picked up 4 seats, Texas 3 and California 2. New York lost 5; Illinois, Ohio, and Pennsylvania lost 2 each. In all, 11 states in the South and West gained 17 seats at the expense of 10 largely

Table 6–5
Population Change, 1970–1980,[a] by States (in thousands)

	1970[b]	1980[b]	Percent Change		1970[b]	1980[b]	Percent Change
Ala.	3,444	3,891	+12.9	Neb.	1,485	1,570	+ 5.7
Alaska	302	400	+32.4	Nev.	488	799	+63.7
Ariz.	1,775	2,718	+53.1	N.H.	737	921	+24.9
Ark.	1,923	2,285	+18.8	N.J.	7,171	7,364	+ 2.6
Calif.	19,975	23,669	+18.4	N.M.	1,017	1,299	+27.7
Colo.	2,209	2,890	+30.8	N.C.	5,084	5,874	+15.5
Conn.	3,032	3,107	+ 2.4	N.D.	617	654	+ 5.9
Del.	548	596	+ 8.7	N.Y.	18,241	17,557[c]	− 3.7
D.C.	756	638[c]	−15.6	Ohio	10,657	10,797	+ 1.3
Fla.	6,791	9,739	+43.4	Okla.	2,559	3,026	+18.2
Ga.	4,587	5,464	+19.1	Ore.	2,091	2,632	+25.8
Hawaii	769	965	+25.4	Pa.	11,800	11,867	+ 0.5
Idaho	713	945	+32.5	R.I.	949	948[c]	− 0.1
Ill.	11,110	11,419	+ 2.7	S.C.	2,590	3,119	+20.4
Ind.	5,195	5,491	+ 5.6	S.D.	622	690	+ 4.2
Iowa	2,825	2,914	+ 3.1	Tenn.	3,926	4,591	+16.9
Kan.	2,249	2,363	+ 5.0	Texas	11,198	14,228	+27.0
Ky.	3,220	3,661	+13.7	Utah	1,059	1,461	+37.9
La.	3,644	4,203	+15.3	Vt.	444	512	+15.3
Maine	993	1,125	+13.2	Va.	4,651	5,346	+14.9
Md.	3,923	4,216	+ 7.4	Wash.	3,413	4,130	+21.0
Mass.	5,689	5,737	+ 0.8	W.Va	1,744	1,950	+11.8
Mich.	8,881	9,259	+ 4.2	Wis.	4,417	4,706	+ 6.5
Minn.	3,806	4,077	+ 7.1	Wyo.	332	471	+41.8
Miss.	2,216	2,520	+13.7	P.R.	2,712	3,196	+17.9
Mo.	4,677	4,917	+ 5.1	**Total**	**203**	**226**	**+11.3**
Mont.	694	787	+13.4				

[a] 1980 estimates as of July 1, 1980.

[b] Totals include population living abroad and in the territories.

[c] Indicates population decrease.

Source: Christian Science Monitor, December 18, 1980; Statistical Abstract of the United States: 1981, p. 9.

northeastern and midwestern states. Clearly, a shift in political power in the United States is underway.

Economic Implications

The decline of many of the older industrial cities in the Northeast and Midwest, with their loss of population and jobs to the Sunbelt or the suburbs, has given city leaders cause to reex-amine the nature and function of their municipalities if they want to survive. They recognize that they will never again be the factory towns they once were, offering unskilled production jobs to blacks or newly arrived immigrants. What the future will bring remains to be seen. The creation of new jobs based on skills will offer one direction for the cities to go. At the same time, major changes in energy-consumption patterns will lessen disadvantages now pos-

Figure 6–12

Sunbelt settlement. A new housing development outside Phoenix, Arizona, is laid out so as to imitate Florida in the desert. The escape from the inclement weather and the problems of the big cities of the Northeast, however, frequently results in the creation of new problems in the Sunbelt—surburban congestion, heavy reliance on the automobile, a high degree of conformal living and, in the desert, an uncertain water supply.

Picture Credit: Georg Gerster/Photo Researchers, Inc.

sessed by northern cities. Finally, as the problems of pollution, crime, and urban deterioration are tackled, many would-be migrants may awake to the fact that a move to an ever-growing South and West may result in more problems for the individual than it resolves (Fig. 6–12).

EPILOGUE

Internal and international migrations are not a new phenomenon. They are, in fact, as old as the human race itself. It was widespread movement that led to the peopling of the earth's surface, leading to cultural and racial mixing. What is unusual about contemporary migration is not so much its phenomenal scale but that the directions that have prevailed for several centuries have been reversed.

Industrialization in Europe was greatly facilitated by the shedding of excess rural populations in a major flow to cities and industrial areas. But, this dislocation of population also produced a strong flow to peripheral, and mostly transoceanic, areas—to the Americas, to Australasia, and even to Africa. Nineteenth-century America, in the grip of its own industrial transformation, witnessed a movement to cities *and* an even more dramatic movement into its vast western interior. Russia and the

Soviet Union experienced similar patterns of migration.

In the United States at present as well as in a number of other industrialized countries, the predominant movement of population is away from the crowded metropolitan areas into smaller cities and even the rural countryside. At the same time, at the international level, there is a pronounced flow from the lesser developed to the industrialized countries, whether as refugees in flight or migrants seeking a better life.

In the nineteenth century, migrants to the United States hailed principally from Europe. In recent decades, the shift has been toward Latin America; peoples of Hispanic origin now constitute a fast-growing minority, adding a strong new element to the American population mix.

APPLICATION OF IDEAS

1. The twentieth century has seen mass migrations on a large scale, and these migrations have caused much misery and dislocation. However, they should be viewed as part of the process whereby humankind has shaped its world.

2. Definitions are sometimes difficult to arrive at in a way that satisfies every scientist, but migrants are more than just movers. What criteria would you suggest be employed in arriving at a meaningful definition of a migrant?

3. Behind the dislocation that migration entails may be seen broad geographic patterns, among which are major transformations in older regional economies.

4. Contemporary migrations, at least at the world level, may be seen as a broad shift from agrarian to industrial economies.

5. In the United States, recent data suggest that a major factor in internal migration has been the desire to enjoy a more relaxed lifestyle, one capable of providing the amenities that the nonpoor (at least) seek.

KEY WORDS AND PHRASES

amenities	melting pot
behavioralists	mercantilism
Frostbelt	overseas Chinese
Great Siberian	push-pull mechanism
Migration	Sahel
gross national	Snowbelt
product (GNP)	Sunbelt
Huguenot	tyranny of space

QUESTIONS FOR FURTHER DISCUSSION

1. Do you think the notion of push-pull is useful in reviewing the history of European migration? Cite countries where you think the "push" was a more powerful force than the "pull."

2. How do you account for the increase in urban population in Europe before 1800? Did in-migration play a major role in this growth? Why?

3. Why did English mercantilist philosophy oppose migration to the colonies? Do you think that mercantilism was a contributory factor in the development of the transatlantic slave trade? If so, explain how.

4. By what method did settlers from Muscovy proceed southward through the grasslands toward the Black Sea? To what extent did this migration contribute to the present distribution of Russians and Ukrainians?

5. What was the major country of origin of European emigrants in the period 1846–1890? Why? In the period 1891–1920? Why? What shift in geographic origin occurred among European emigrants to the United States between 1820 and 1920? Why?

6. Why are the estimates of Africa's population before 1900 at best only uncertain guesses? What significant effects did the slave trade have on Africa's estimated numbers?

7. Looking beyond the human tragedy often associated with the migrations of the present, can you identify major world changes that may underlie the shifting of population?

8. What were the major directions of nineteenth-century migration in the United States? Compare these patterns of migration with those occurring in Europe and Russia.

9. Were you to consider migrating, what factors would enter into your decision to move or not to move? How important would lifestyle be?

10. What are the implications for the United States of both immigration patterns and internal migration patterns?

REFERENCES AND ADDITIONAL READINGS

Beaujot, Roderic P. *Canada's Population: Growth and Dualism.* Population Bulletin 33(2). Washington, D.C.: Population Reference Bureau, 1978.

Berry, Brian J. L., and Dahmann, Donald C. *Population Redistribution in the United States in the 1970s.* Washington, D.C.: National Research Council, National Academy of Sciences, 1977.

Biggar, Jeanne C. *The Sunning of America: Migration to the Sunbelt.* Population Bulletin 34(1). Washington, D.C.: Population Reference Bureau, 1979.

Bouvier, Leon T., et al. *International Migration: Yesterday, Today, and Tomorrow.* Population Bulletin 32(4). Washington, D.C.: Population Reference Bureau, 1977.

Braudel, Fernand. *Capitalism and Material Life, 1400–1800.* New York: Harper & Row, 1973.

Brown, Alan A., and Neuberger, Egon, eds. *International Migration. A Comparative Perspective.* New York: Academic Press, 1977.

Clarke, John I. *Population Geography.* Oxford: Pergamon Press, 1965.

Davis, Kingsley. "The Migrations of Human Populations." *Specific American* 231 (1974): 93–105.

Demeny, Paul. "The Populations of the Underdeveloped Countries." *Scientific American* 231 (1974): 148–159.

Demko, George J. *The Russian Colonization of Kazakhstan, 1896–1916* (Uralic and Altaic Series, Vol. 99). Bloomington: Indiana University Press, 1969.

Greenwood, Michael J. *Migration and Economic Growth in the United States.* New York: Academic Press, 1981.

International Migrations and Immigrant Settlement. Ottawa: Department of Manpower and Immigration, 1975.

Jackson, Gregory, et al. *Regional Diversity: Growth in the United States, 1960–1990.* Boston: Aukurn House, 1981.

Jackson, J. A., ed. *Migration* (Sociological Studies No. 2). Cambridge: Cambridge University Press, 1969.

Kosinski, Leszek A. *The Population of Europe.* London: Longman, 1970.

———., ed. *Demographic Developments in Eastern Europe.* New York: Praeger, 1977.

Kosinski, Leszek A., and Prothero, R. Mansell. *People on the Move: Studies on Internal Migration.* London: Methuen, 1975.

Kostanick, Huey Louis, ed. *Population and Migration Trends in Eastern Europe.* Boulder, Colo.: Westview Press, 1977.

Long, Larry H. *Interregional Migration of the Poor: Some Recent Changes.* Current Population Reports (Special Studies P–23, No. 73). Washington, D.C.: U.S. Department of Commerce, Bureau of the Census, 1978.

Long, Larry H., and Hansen, Kristin A. *Reasons for Interstate Migration.* Current Population Reports (Special Studies P–23, No. 81). Washington, D.C. U.S. Department of Commerce, Bureau of the Census, 1978.

McNeill, William H. *Europe's Steppe Frontier, 1500–1800.* Chicago: University of Chicago Press, 1964.

McNeill, William H., and Adams, Ruth S., eds. *Human Migration. Patterns and Policies.* Bloomington: Indiana University Press, 1978.

Morrison, Peter A., and Wheeler, Judith P. *Rural Renaissance in America? The Revival of Popu-*

lation Growth in Remote Areas. Population Bulletin 31(3). Washington, D.C.: Population Reference Bureau, 1976.

Pifer, Alan. Bilingual Education and the Hispanic Challenge (Annual Report). New York: Carnegie Corporation, 1979.

Safa, Helen I., and DuToit, Brian M. Migration and Development. The Hague: Mouton, 1975.

Schnell, George A., and Monmonier, Mark S. The Study of Population. Elements, Patterns, Processes. Columbus, Ohio: Charles E. Merrill, 1983.

Statistical Abstract of the United States: 1981. Washington, D.C.: Bureau of the Census, 1981.

Thomas, Brinley. Internal Migration and Economic Development. New York: UNESCO, 1961.

Todd, Daniel. "Rural Out-migration and Economic Standing in a Prairie Setting." Transactions, Institute of British Geographers (New Series) 5 (1980): 446–465.

Treadgold, Donald W. The Great Siberian Migration: Government and Peasant in Resettlement from Emancipation to the First World War. Princeton, N.J.: Princeton University Press, 1957.

Ullman, Edward L. "Amenities as a Factor in Regional Growth." Geographical Review 44 (1954): 119–132.

Walter, Bronwer. "Time-Space Patterns of Second-Wave Irish Immigration into British Towns." Transactions, Institute of British Geographers (New Series) 5 (1980): 297–317.

White, Paul, and Woods, Robert. The Geographical Impact of Migration. London: Longman, 1980.

7

Language, Communication, and the Landscape

Throughout the earth men spoke the same language, with the same vocabulary. Now as they moved eastwards they found a plain in the land of Shinar where they settled. . . . "Come," they said, "let us build ourselves a town and a tower with its top reaching heaven. . . ." Now Yahweh came down to see the town and the tower that the sons of man had built. "So they are all single people with a single language!" said Yahweh. "This is but the start of their undertakings. There will be nothing too hard for them to do. Come, let us go down and confuse their language on the spot so that they can no longer understand one another."

Genesis 11:1–8
Jerusalem Bible

Spoken words are the symbols of mental experience and written words are the symbols of spoken words.

Aristotle (384-322 B.C)
On Interpretation, Book 1, Chapter I

Key Ideas

1. Language is the conveyor of ideas. To understand other people, one needs to understand the ideas communicated by language.

2. Humans have had a variety of experiences over the surface of the earth, and this experience is shared through communication.

3. Peoples in different communities are inclined to interpret the expressions of other cultures through the filters of their own traditions and experiences.

4. The study of place-names, tangible symbols of people's goals and aspirations, is a fascinating one, especially in the United States. Place-name study is known as toponymy.

5. Where a common language is spoken, a distinct community of language takes shape.

6. A community of language will occupy a segment of earthspace within which there is frequent social contact and interaction.

7. Some three to four thousand languages are spoken on earth, but a very small number of languages are spoken by the majority of the earth's population.

8. The world's languages are usually grouped into principal language families.

9. Lingua franca is the name given to a language that serves as a widespread medium of communication where there is a multiplicity of tongues.

10. The sharing of experiences through a common language means the sharing of values, and through close interaction an ethnic community may emerge. A language space thus may be an ethnic space.

11. At some stage in development, an ethnic community becomes a national community, although the differences between the two are hard to define.

THE IMPORTANCE OF LANGUAGE TO THE GEOGRAPHER

Geographers are very much aware that population patterns and distributions are characterized by a diverse number of languages, but the geographic interest has seldom been expressed beyond listing languages according to broad family associations over generalized areas. At its simplest level, language corresponds to, and reflects, the experience of a people, an experience that a people have shared with each other over a period of time. A geography of languages should convey something of the diversity of human experiences, but it is extremely difficult for any one field of study to achieve this with any degree of satisfaction.

On the other hand, geographers have made a substantial contribution to *toponymy,* the study of place-names. A place-name may not tell us much more than who the founder of a settlement was, but it is possible through the study of place-names to learn something of the original community as well—where the people came from, perhaps what language they spoke or what religious beliefs they held, and so on.

In any event, as we study what language is, we soon realize how important it is to understand how people think and feel about the world around them and how their expressions of thought and feeling have helped shape the world we live in.

LANGUAGE AS COMMUNICATION ABOUT COMMON EXPERIENCE

To speak to another person is to try to communicate. It is an act of mutual involvement or of making something common, for the words communication and common have the same Latin root. When we speak to another person, we attempt to establish a common ground of experience so that we can understand what is being said. Language or the use of words, thus, implies that there is a pattern of experience that both persons readily perceive. In its simplest expressions, language corresponds to simple or elementary experiences that the speaker and the listener have in common. With that basis established, language can be extended or rendered somewhat more complex as the experiences become more diversified.

If I travel throughout the United States and report to a group of American students on what I have seen and heard, they should have little difficulty understanding what I am talking about. However, if having traveled widely in India, I return to relate what I have learned of Hindu religious experiences, my American audience may not entirely grasp the subtleties of what I am trying to convey. My stay-at-home audience will in all likelihood hear my lecture in terms of their own local experience. English is the medium in which I am communicating, but the lack of understanding is based on our widely different experiences. There is treachery in language because understanding requires not only a knowledge of words, but also a grasp of the ideas and concepts behind the words.

Language as a Conveyor of Cultural Phenomena

Words are essentially symbols for the features of a culture. When we speak, we transmit our experience by creating and transferring symbols; speaking is the vocalization of the symbols of culture. The more varied the collective experience, the richer the vocabulary of the language and the greater the mosaic of symbols. Because culture is what people in a community absorb, language is the means whereby the content of culture is disseminated.

Language, above all, is a conveyor of ideas (E. Hall, 1959) (Fig. 7–1). If the ideas of one group of people are grasped by another, even where different languages are spoken, understanding is achieved. In Switzerland, for exam-

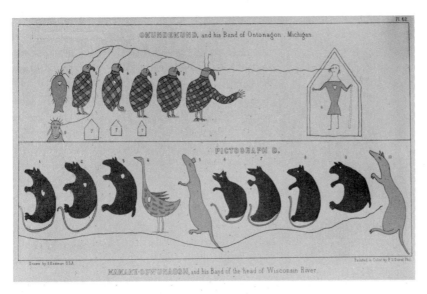

Figure 7–1

The Amerindians used pictographs to convey messages. These examples illustrate both the creativity and vitality of this form of communication.

The upper pictograph represents a message of friendship sent by chief Okundekund and his band of Ontonagons to the president of the United States, the figure shown in the house (The White House.) The chief is identified by the two lines rising from his head; the four warriors behind him belong to the eagle totem. The fifth warrior is a member of the catfish totem. The figure at lower left is evidently also an important chief. Harmony and peace are suggested through the device of connecting the eyes. The sketch of three houses suggests the willingness of the people to adopt the customs of the white men.

(*Source:* Henry R. Schoolcraft. *Historical and Statistical Information Respecting the History, Condition and Prospects of the Indian Tribes of the United States.* Philadelphia: Lippincott, Gambo, 1851–1857. Vol. 1, p. 418.)

ple, four different languages are spoken; yet the Swiss have had a long history of common association and understand each other well enough to form a separate community of people distinct from the larger European nations around them. This phenomenon is what the political scientist Karl Deutsch calls *complementarity* (1953); it is an essential component in the growth of ethnic awareness and nationalism, a topic discussed later.

Language and World View

Because words are symbols of culture, language—if we study it thoroughly—can tell us something of a people's collective experience and of their world view. We may even find evidence of these culture symbols in the land-scape. They may show up in the location of churches, mosques, and synagogues; they may be evident in the location and care given to cemetaries; they may appear in house types and the layout of farmsteads; or they may simply be revealed in the spelling and use of road signs.

However, because human communities scattered over the surface of the earth have different and varied experiences in differing geographic environments, words of common usage in one language may convey a different meaning in another.

Wilhelm von Humboldt (1767–1835), the elder brother of Alexander von Humboldt, the geographer and naturalist, was one of the first students of language to stress the significance of language study. Working with materials that his brother brought back to Prussia from his world travels, the elder Humboldt suggested that sounds and words afforded insight into the character and perspective of a people. The real difference between languages, he recognized, was one of *Weltansichten,* or world perspectives. Language, he believed, was a living and dynamic form of expression that sheds light on human experience.

This attribute of a language may be seen in the following example. Among the Hebrews in biblical times, there was no word equivalent to our English word nature. The only way this concept—that is, the underlying forces of the universe—could be rendered into Hebrew, as evident in the books of the Old Testament, was to say "God" or "Yahweh". When a particular phenomenon in place or time was to be described, it had to be portrayed in *anthropomorphic,* or human, phrases, such as the voice of God in the thunder or the burning bush, or the hand of God in the onset of pestilence or famine. The Greeks living at the same time across the Mediterranean would not have understood such symbolism. Neither would the Chinese, who from earliest times felt a close kinship with nature but did not have the concept of a single god as the Hebrews did.

What these examples tell us is that people in different cultures—and this is true of any period in history—are concerned about different phenomena or problems. They have different systems of thinking about them, and as we study foreign languages, we become increasingly aware of this. Some languages simply have difficulty expressing ideas readily communicated by others.

THE LANGUAGE BARRIER

Communities are inclined to interpret the expressions of other cultures through the filters of their own traditions and experiences. The great British playwright, George Bernard Shaw (1856–1950) once said that England and the United States were two countries separated by the same language. The experience of two En-glish-speaking peoples in different geographic environments, where contact was dependent on the speed and frequency of oceanic voyages, created diverging modes of expression. These different modes, with intonations, accents, gestures, and so on, are contained within the languages we describe today as English English and American English.

As a new nation fashioned out of successive waves of immigrants, the peoples of the United States tended during the great *melting pot* years of the past century to turn their backs on the "old country." They wanted to be Americans and to be part of the American commonality, sharing equally and fully the American experience. But, this American experience has made it difficult for, say, German-Americans, Russian-Americans, Japanese-Americans, and others to understand the subtle (and sometimes not so subtle) changes that have taken place in the culture and speech of the peoples of familial homelands. A society where advertising and the media have made astounding efforts to reach Americans in every part of the country, nevertheless, has difficulty comprehending the evolving hopes, aspirations, philosophies, and problems of those kin who never migrated. The American school system, unfortunately, has paid little attention to the languages of other culture groups. The shortage of Farsi (Persian) speakers in the U.S. embassy in Tehran, Iran, in 1979–1980, undoubtedly contributed to the barrier that prevented embassy personnel from gaining the necessary sensitivity to Iranian domestic problems that led to the overthrow of the shah and the attack on the embassy. During the Vietnam involvement more than a decade earlier, few universities in the United States offered the relevant language instruction that might have facilitated efforts to understand the plight of the Vietnamese, whether South or North. A conscious and costly effort is essential if the United States, which seeks to be the leader of the Free World, is to develop the capacity to lead with compassion and sensitivity to the just needs and the goals of other peoples.

In short, to grasp all that languages can convey to us about other peoples' cultures and patterns of thought, we must advance beyond thinking of speech as mere words or sounds. As former Indian prime minister Jawaharlal Nehru (1889–1964) once stated:

> If we seek to understand a people, we have to try to put ourselves, as far as we can, in that particular historical and cultural background. . . . It is not easy for a person of one country to enter into the background of another country. So there is great irritation, because one fact that seems obvious to us is not immediately accepted by the other party or doesn't seem obvious to him at all. . . . But that extreme irritation will go when we think . . . that he is just differently conditioned and simply can't get out of that condition. . . . One has to recognize that . . . countries and peoples differ in their approach and their ways, in their approach to life and their ways of living and thinking. In order to understand them we have to understand their way of life and approach. If we wish to convince them, we have to use their language as far as we can, not language in the narrow sense of the word, but the language of the mind (Nehru, 1950, pp. 58–59).

LANGUAGE AND SOCIAL BEHAVIOR

Careful linguistic research suggests that language can reveal facets of human social behavior. This association is revealed in America in studies that relate speech dialect to land settlement and migration patterns. Linguistic research in South Carolina, for example, has shown that the patterns of dialectical differences have had less to do with the origin of the settlers and the physiography of the territory than with clearly identifiable patterns of social behavior, especially class status (Fig. 7–2) (Box 7–1).

In South Carolina, the Tidewater, with its historic cultural centers at Georgetown, Charleston, and Beaufort, was settled initially by peoples from southern England. North of the Santee River, which enters the Atlantic between Georgetown and Charleston, the land was settled later by Scotch-Irish. Peoples of German and German-Swiss origin tended, in time, to predominate south of the Santee. Even

though the Tidewater English represented a minority of the European population of South Carolina, some of their speech characteristics came to be widely accepted throughout the entire region (McDavid, 1964).

Linguists have found that the spread of these characteristics was due to the movement inland from the Tidewater of the socioeconomic system associated with the English, namely, the plantation system with its slave population. Moreover, inland settlements, especially those founded near the *fall line* (where the rivers descended onto the coastal plain from the piedmont of the Appalachian Mountains) tended to function as cultural outposts of Charleston. With the marketing of up-country cotton through Charleston and other ties between the two regions, Charleston served not only as the economic node of the colony, but also as the social focus. The attitudes and the speech of the Charleston elite became marks of status even inland on the South Carolina frontier where the geographic environment was totally different. Before the Civil War, many up-country and frontier leaders, like John C. Calhoun (1782–1850), even adopted and championed the interests of the large slaveholders of the coastal plain. Prestige values and their acceptance among the people of different ethnic origin and patterns of living seem in this case to have been the factor that influenced the spread of Tidewater pronunciation.

Place-Names in the Landscape

Place-names, an obvious expression of language in the landscape, provide another example of how word usage reflects social values. Wilbur Zelinsky has illustrated this phenomenon in his study of the spread of classical town names in the United States during the late eighteenth century (Zelinsky, 1955, 1967). Toponymy, the study of place-names, has become a science in itself (Wright, 1929). In America, there is almost a wearisome repetition of European counterparts: 27 Manchesters, 21 Romes, 19 Viennas, and so on.

Foreign or essentially ethnic place-names in

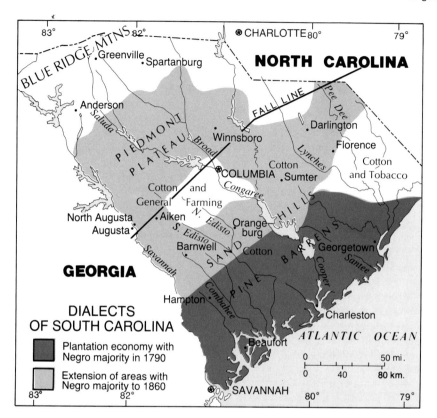

Figure 7–2

Social values are often associated with language, dialect, or pronunciation. The speech of South Carolina is a good example of this kind of relationship. The Tidewater of South Carolina extends inland for about 30 miles, and it was here that the first English culture centers were established in colonial times. Plantation agriculture became a basic feature of the region. Inland from the Tidewater is a belt of pine barrens that was not suited to the plantation and where small-scale farming was the standard practice. Plantation life was aristocratic in tradition, and the speech patterns and the values associated with that way of life spread inland to be adopted by nonplantation, non-English settlers in the coastal plain and in the up-country piedmont as well.

(*Source:* McDavid, 1964.)

America have tended to retain and reflect their European origin longer than other cultural elements transferred from the Old World. As Isaac Taylor wrote over 100 years ago, "Successive bands of immigrants may forget their mother tongue, and abandon all distinctive national peculiarities, but . . . the names which, on their first arrival, they bestowed upon the places of their abode, are sure to remain upon the map as a permanent record of the nature and extent of the original colonizations" (cited in Kaups,

1966, p. 378). Such place-names are associated with pioneers and first settlers only.

(Salem, a Semitic word meaning peace, is found as a place-name in many parts of the United States. With biblical origins, it was first applied to an English colony in New Jersey at a Quaker settlement in 1694; in New Hampshire in 1750; in Virginia in 1768; in Ohio in 1801, another Quaker settlement; in Illinois in 1813; in Oregon in 1840; and, finally in Missouri in 1845.)

LANGUAGE ORIGINS

It is not known when language originated. But, at some point millennia ago, hominid cries became human sounds and, if they remained in one location, humans gained the capacity for words. It is possible that when early humans lived as simple hunters, there was but one language on earth. As human experience broadened through time and Paleolithic culture gave

---

BOX 7–1

Language Choice, Culture, and Social Status

Where a choice is possible, the use of one particular language by a group of people can tell us much about the users. As geographer Sarah K. Myers has observed, the study of language use is especially valuable for the human geographer because in many cases it is language that defines and delimits culture areas. The use of a language, too, is an indicator of social status.

Dr. Myers explored these facets of human geography in a study of language shifts among migrants in Lima, Peru (Myers, 1973). This study deals particularly with language use by a migrating people. It attempts to determine "how much and in what context Quechua-speaking migrants from the Andean highlands use Spanish in Lima, Peru's capital and *primate city* [*italics added*] or leading city." Myers confirmed that shifts in the use of language, from Quechua to Spanish, are sensitive indicators of the processes of culture change, a conclusion that might be explored in other contexts.

Similar studies undertaken among minority groups in the United States, ethnic or otherwise, provide insight into the way such groups view themselves and their status within the larger society. The black subculture, for example, has developed a language all of its own that helps those who use it to satisfy their need for expression (Ley, 1974). City street gangs, too, have an idiom that conveys little to middle-class groups unless some effort has first been made to understand the function of the language style.

Social class, occupation, ethnic association, and place of residence are some of the factors that impinge on language use. Sex is another social factor that is significant, and sociolinguists have attempted to show how sex differentiation in language occurs (Thorne and Henley, 1975).

Although male dominance is built into many cultures, it is especially evident in the culture of English speakers. In English, for example, the male is associated with the universal, the general, the subsuming: God, chairman, man. The female is more often excluded or is identified as the special case, that is, chairlady. Words associated with males, moreover, tend to have positive connotations, conveying notions of power, leadership, or prestige. By contrast, female words are more often negative, convey weakness or inferiority, immaturity, or softness.

In American society, if a male uses what are generally thought of as female expressions, he is described as effeminate, which implies unmanliness or something less than manliness. If a female uses terms generally associated with male expression, she may be thought of as lacking in femininity, but this does not carry quite the disapproval that is directed toward the male who crosses the line of expression.

Without necessarily endorsing all new idioms of expression, American society as a whole might gain much through a better understanding of how and why people within given situations rely on specific terms, dialects, or languages. Not only would such an awareness deepen our comprehension of the infinite variety of cultural expression of which humans are capable, but also it would allow us to understand how vital a role language has played in our efforts to take possession of, and humanize, the landscape.

way to Neolithic, language—having first developed local variations—evolved into many forms of speech that made communication difficult. The biblical story of the Tower of Babel symbolized this stage in cultural evolution.

How many languages have ever been spoken in the past is impossible to ascertain. Many languages, including the Coptic in ancient Egypt, have vanished, leaving only a trace. Still, others have left no trace at all. Some languages, such as Tasmanian, disappeared as their speakers died out. Some have lost ground to more aggressive cultures, as Gaelic and Breton, both old Celtic languages, retreated before the peoples who came to speak English and French. Basque, a language spoken in the Pyrenees of northern Spain and southern France, may be the sole survivor of the languages spoken in Europe before the Indo-Europeans arrived.

LANGUAGE AND COMMUNITY SPACES

Where a common language is spoken, there will exist a distinct community of language or a language space. Ordinarily, such a community will share a common segment of earthspace within which frequent social contact and interaction have taken place.

If for some reason social interaction among peoples inhabiting a region weakens, then differences in expression may occur. Variations in word usage or intonation may lead to the formation of *dialects*. This is evident in England, where population mobility in the past was relatively low. It is true also of Germany. Even in the United States, striking differences in pronunciation between a long-time resident of New England, a Texan, a southerner, and an Appalachian hill farmer persist even to the present.

In Baghdad, Iraq, it was common for Christian Arabs to speak one dialect when talking among themselves but, when in a mixed Christian-Muslim group, to resort to the general Baghdad dialect. (This practice of using two or more variants of the same language is known as *diglossia*.)

If there is protracted separation among groups or social interaction ceases altogether, as it must have done among the earth's early hunting populations, distinct languages develop. The larger the earthspace and the weaker the pattern of social interaction within it, the more likely it is for broad variations to occur.

A pre-Columbian map of North American languages shows large language spaces throughout the Great Plains where small hunting bands roamed over relatively large territories. On the Atlantic and Pacific coasts, the language spaces were smaller in area but greater in number, suggesting that they possessed resources sufficient to sustain their populations without the need for a wide-ranging search for food.

The Slavic peoples who occupied the forests and grasslands of what was to become Russia probably spoke a common language with dialectic variations. However, the differences that developed between Great Russian, spoken in forested Muscovy, and Ukrainian (a Slavic word meaning on the frontier), the language that formed in the forest-grasslands to the southwest, were due to the experiences of the two peoples in differing natural and socioeconomic environments. Speakers of Great Russian tend to think of Ukrainian as only a dialect of Russian and not a separate language, much to the annoyance of Ukrainians.

When people migrate from their homeland, they are often likely to keep intact the language of the period of migration than are those who remain behind. In the new environment, the language may undergo changes as patterns of living are transformed, but these differences will not parallel those occurring in the homeland. The speech of the Ozarks, for example, comes closer to that of Elizabethan England than does the language used today by newscasters and commentators at the British Broadcasting Corporation in London (Box 7–2).

BOX 7-2

The Survival of Elizabethan English in the Ozarks

The life of Elizabeth I (1533–1603) preceded only by a short time the period of early settlement in America. During the next 150 years, various types of English then spoken in the British Isles were carried to the colonies. Although they have disappeared from standard English English, many of the features of these dialects can still be found in the United States. Indeed, the patterns of speech that had a significant effect on the development of American dialects can be traced to the language variations brought to early colonial settlements.

Shakespeare's prose, written between 1590 and 1616, seems to have reflected a cultivated use of Elizabethan English, especially that spoken in and around London. On the other hand, the style of the King James Bible, published in 1611, affords some insight into a rather elegant form of speech or writing characteristic of the preceding century. Expressions of English carried to the colonies possessed some of these characteristics. The comparable form of speech that has survived among isolated communities in the Ozark Mountains in Missouri has an exuberance and forcefulness that have long disappeared from standard English, even in the United States. Scores of words in daily use in the Ozarks, for example, are no longer used elsewhere (Allwood, 1964). The verb to stink, which *Webster's New World Dictionary of the American Language,* College Edition (1964) defines as "to have a strong, unpleasant smell," is used in the Ozarks as simply "to give off an odor" (which was the word's original meaning). Hence, it is possible to say, "It sure stinks beautiful." Whenever polite expression is required, whether in the United States or the United Kingdom, present custom would be to avoid the use of the word stink altogether. Other obsolete words that are still found in the Ozarks are buss, meaning to kiss; bespoke for engaged to be married; and dauncy, for fastidious about food.

MAJOR LANGUAGES AND PRINCIPAL LANGUAGE FAMILIES

Although there are between three and four thousand languages presently spoken on earth, a very small number of languages are spoken by the greater proportion of the world's total population. There were 250 million people living on the globe two thousand years ago. By contrast, at present some 400 million people speak English as a first language and many more may use English on certain occasions. No single language in the world is spoken by more people than is Mandarin Chinese (Table 7–1).

It is the sum total of the usage of a language that determines whether a language is considered major. In the past, such a claim may have been advanced for Sanskrit, Greek, Latin, Persian, and Chinese. Since World War II, because they have become the media of international trade, scientific exchanges, and general communication, English, French, German, Spanish, Portuguese, Italian, Russian, Arabic, Chinese, and Japanese fall into this category. Among these, English is employed most frequently, but such may not necessarily be the case in the future.

The world's languages, if some variations are allowed, also may be grouped into *principal language families:* Indo-European; Hamito-Semitic; Sino-Tibetan; Malayo-Polynesian; Dravidian; Japanese, Korean, and Vietnamese; Ural-Altaic; Mon-Khmer and Munda; Caucasian; and so on. Only a few of the languages referred to here are used outside a local area.

EUROPE-BASED LANGUAGES

Most of the languages of Europe belong to the Indo-European family. Forms of Indo-European speech are believed to have originated among peoples inhabiting the grasslands of Eurasia. One branch of the family spread north-

Table 7–1

**Principal Linguistic Families and Languages Based on 1983 Estimates
(20 Million Speakers or More)**

Linguistic Families and Languages	Estimated Number of Speakers (millions)	Principal Areas of Use
A. (I) Indo-European		
Germanic		
English	397	United Kingdom, United States, Canada, Australia, New Zealand, other members of British Commonwealth
German	119	Germany, Austria, Switzerland, Luxembourg
Dutch and Flemish	20	The Netherlands, Belgium
Romance		
Spanish	251	Spain, Mexico, Argentina, Chile, and other parts of former Spanish empire
Portuguese	151	Portugal, Brazil, parts of Africa
French	107	France, parts of Africa, Quebec
Italian	62	Italy, Switzerland
Romanian	23	Romania
Slavic		
Russian	274	USSR
Ukrainian	42	Ukraine SSR
Polish	39	Poland
Serbo-Croatian	20	Yugoslavia
(II) Indo-Iranian		
Persian (Farsi)	28	Iran, Tadzhik SSR
(III) Indo-Aryan		
Hindi	254	India
Bengali	151	Bangladesh, West Bengal (India)
Urdu	72	Pakistan
Punjabi	68	Punjab (India and Pakistan)
Marathi	57	Maharashtra (India)
Gujarati	34	Gujarat (India)
Oriya	27	Oriya (India)
B. Hamito-Semitic		
Arabic	155	North African countries, Middle East
Hausa	22	Nigeria, Central and West Africa
C. Sino-Tibetan		
Chinese (Mandarin)	726	China
Cantonese	55	South China
Wu	51	Chekiang (Zhejiang), Kiangsu (Jiangsu) (China)
Min	42	Fukien (Fujian), Taiwan
Thai	39	Thailand
Burmese	26	Burma
Hakka	23	South China
D. Malayo-Polynesian		
Malay-Indonesian	115	Indonesia, Malaysia
Javanese	49	Java
Tagalog	26	Philippines
E. Dravidian		
Telugu	60	South India
Tamil	59	South India, Sri Lanka
Kannada (Kanarese)	32	South India
Malayam	31	South India
F. Japanese, Korean, Vietnamese		
Japanese	118	Japan
Korean	60	Korea
Vietnamese	45	Vietnam

Table 7–1 (continued)

Linguistic Families and Languages	Estimated Number of Speakers (millions)	Principal Areas of Use
G. *Ural-Altaic*		
Turkish	45	Turkey
H. *Lingua franca*		
Swahili (Bantu)	30	Tanzania, Kenya

Source: *The World Almanac & Book of Facts 1983*. New York: Newspaper Enterprise Association, 1983, p. 206.

westward into Europe. The other branch, consisting of two divisions—Indo-Iranian and Indo-Aryan—was carried southeastward through the Iranian plateau into the Indian subcontinent.

The Indo-European languages of Europe consist of three principal subgroups: Germanic, Romance, and Slavic (Table 7–2). Each subgroup includes a number of closely interrelated languages. Within the Germanic are found German, English, Dutch, and the Norwegian, Swedish, and Danish languages. The Romance subgroup includes Italian, Portuguese, Spanish, French, and Romanian. The principal Slavic languages are Russian, Ukrainian, Polish, Czech, Serbo-Croatian, and Bulgarian.

Beginning in the sixteenth century, when the great age of European discovery was underway, many of these European languages were carried to other parts of the globe (Fig. 7–3). English-language spaces were created in North America, Australia, New Zealand, and in parts of Africa, Asia, and the Pacific islands. Spanish, Portuguese, and French also reached the New World and Africa and Asia as well. The French-speaking people of Quebec, the Acadians of Canada's Atlantic provinces, and the Cajuns (a corruption of Acadien) of Louisiana are descendants of the first migrants from France to the New World. Much of Meso-America and South America use Spanish and Portuguese because they were reached first by navigators from Spain and Portugal. Dutch traders and explorers carried their language to the Caribbean; to southern Africa, where it is known today as Afrikaans; and to the islands of southeast Asia. German and Italian unity were not achieved until late in the nineteenth century so that their colonial activity, principally in Africa, was short-lived, making permanent transplant of their respective languages difficult. Unable to advance westward into Europe, Russian speakers pushed across the Urals and reached the Pacific by the middle of the seventeenth century, settling in Pacific North America shortly thereafter. Russian place-names, such as Alaska's Sitka and Baranof Island as well as Russian River, California, remind us of the former Russian presence in North America. Russian is the official language of all of northern Asia, although the diversity of native languages is substantial.

Europe possesses a number of additional languages that do not belong to the three principal subgroups. Among these are Greek, Celtic (the language of the Welsh, the Gaelic peoples of Ireland, Scotland and Brittany), Baltic (Lettish [Latvian] and Lithuanian), and Albanian (whose people are predominantly Muslim). Southern Russia also claims a number of Armenians, but their homeland is traditionally associated with the upland plateaus of Asia Minor.

Table 7–2

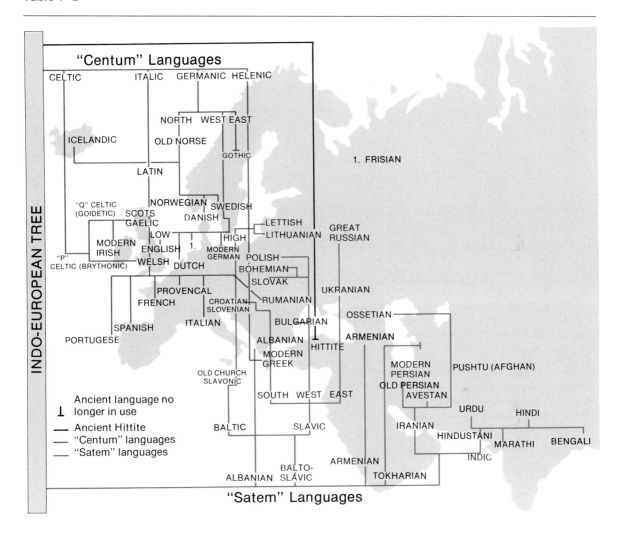

The Indo-European Family

The proliferation of the languages in the Indo-European family was a long process. Some languages came into existence quite early and have survived until the present. Others, such as Hittite and Gothic, died out at a very early time—Hittite about 1000 B.C., and Gothic about A.D. 400. The Tokharians (or Tocharians) whose language disappeared around A.D. 1200 were a people of substantial culture who had lived in Central Asia from earliest times to the medieval period in European history. Indo-European languages, for linguistic purposes, are usually divided into two groups: the Centum, represented by the peoples of Western Europe, and the Santem, which includes many of the languages of Eastern Europe and the Indo-Iranian and Indo-Aryan groups of South and Southwestern Asia.

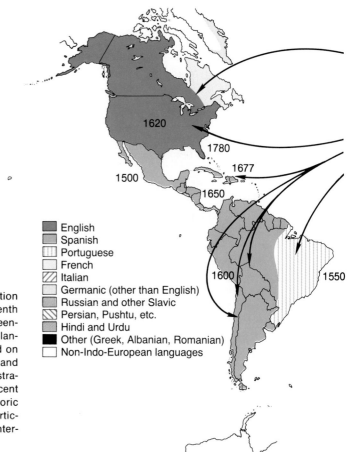

Figure 7–3

A great wave of Europe-based language migration began with the Age of Discovery in the fifteenth century, although Norsemen had reached Greenland and Canada at an earlier period. The languages of western Europe were superimposed on the Americas, on parts of Africa, on South and Southeast Asia, and on Oceania (including Australia). In many areas, native peoples have in recent years begun to strengthen the use of their historic languages, but the Indo-European tongues, particularly English, afford convenient vehicles for international communication.

Asia-Based Languages

South and Southwest Asia

Of the languages spoken in the vast area stretching from the Persian (or Arabian) Gulf to Bangladesh and from the Tadzhik SSR (a republic of the Soviet Union) to the Indian Ocean, the principal ones belong to two associated divisions of the Indo-European family: Indo-Iranian and Indo-Aryan.

The Indo-Iranian includes the languages of the Tadzhiks and the Iranians (i.e., Farsi) as well as of the Pushtu (or Pashto) of Afghanistan and the Baluchis of Pakistan. Kurdish speakers, who occupy the plateau of southwestern Turkey, northeastern Iraq, and northwestern Iran, also belong to this group. Because of their demands for national identity and autonomy, they are subjected to continuous oppression from the Turks, Iraqis, and Iranians over whose territory they stretch.

Of the Indo-Aryan group, the Hindi language is the most widespread, especially in the Indian subcontinent. It is, along with English, the national language of the Indian Union. Drawing much in the way of literary expres-

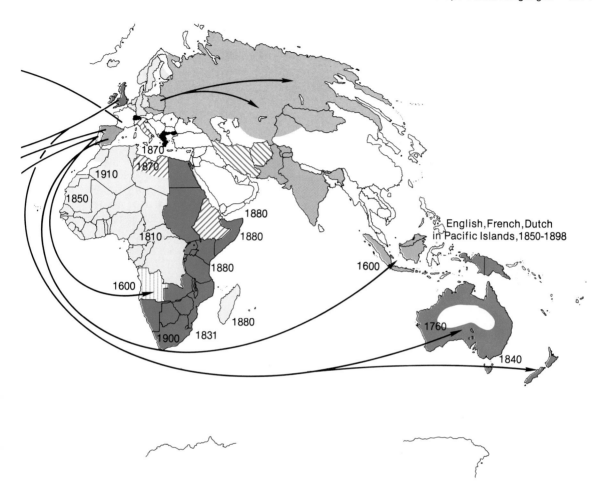

English, French, Dutch in Pacific Islands, 1850–1898

sion from ancient Sanskrit, including its alphabet, Hindi has been closely associated with Hindu and Buddhist religious experience and culture.

Hindi, and the closely related languages such as Marathi, Bengali, Bihari, and others, are found primarily in the northern two thirds of India (Box 7–3). Urdu is similar to Hindi, but many of its phrases are adapted from Arabic, whose alphabet it employs. Urdu is the official language of Pakistan and its literary traditions stem from Islam (Fig. 7–4).

Dravidian-speaking peoples inhabit the southern third of India. There are at least 20 Dravidian languages, but four are principal and have long literary traditions. These include Telugu, Tamil, Kanarese (or Kannada), and Malayalam. Tamil speakers are found also in Sri Lanka, Malaysia, and Indonesia. Altogether there are over 180 million Dravidians in the world.

Southwest Asia and North Africa-Based Languages

The principal language family throughout much of this part of the *Dry World* is designated Hamito-Semitic (Fig. 7–5). Altogether there are

BOX 7-3

Language and Political Stress in India

The 1961 census identified 1652 different languages in India. For many of these languages, however, there are not many speakers. However, what makes unity difficult in India is that there are four principal language families:

Indo-Aryan	73 percent of the population
Dravidian	24 percent of the population
Tribal dialects	1.5 percent of the population
Tibeto-Burman	about 0.7 percent of the population

People speaking tribal dialect and Tibeto-Burman languages are found principally in the northeastern part of the Indian Union.

Of India's languages, at least 33 have over 1 million speakers each; of these, 14 are listed in India's constitution. These 14 languages account for almost 90 percent of the population; 49 languages have at least 100,000 speakers each.

In addition to this enormous complexity of speech, India has four basic scripts with numerous variations. Sanskrit, Hindi, and Marathi use the same script, known as Devanagari. The four principal Dravidian languages have their own scripts. An Iranian-Arabic script is used for Urdu and Kashmiri, found in northwestern India, and finally the Roman script is used for English.

These incredible differences led to the adoption of two official languages to serve the states of the Union of India in 1948: Hindi and English. English was the language of the administration in India for over 150 years of British rule; it remains a language in wide use among intellectuals. Because of its widespread use, it was retained to promote national unity. English is also the preferred national language of the Dravidians, who oppose the adoption of Hindi, because they fear political, economic, and social domination by Hindi-speakers.

Language politics in India is also expressed at the local level as well. Six states in northern India have adopted Hindi as their official language; six other states use their respective major regional languages as official languages. The state of Gujarat uses both Hindi and Gujarati as official languages; Orissan, on the other hand, has adopted English and Oriya. Three states, Karnataka and Kerala in the south and Nagaland in the northeast, employ English as the official language. In Jammu and Kashmir in the northwest, Urdu is the official language, but it is spoken by only a small fraction of the population. The majority speak Kashmiri, which is different from Hindi to such a degree that it has close affinities with the Indo-Iranian subgroup.

---

over 170 million members of the family. The terms Hamite and Semite are derived from two of Noah's sons, Ham and Shem, mentioned in the biblical account of the flood.

One of the oldest Semitic languages known to have been written is Akkadian (or Assyrian), a language spoken in the upper Tigris-Euphrates Valley some five thousand years ago. It employed a cuneiform script that was adapted from the Sumerians in the lower valley. Phoenician—once spoken along the Mediterranean coast—and Hebrew are also of ancient origin; it was the Phoenician script that served as the basis of the Greek alphabet. Hebrew went out of common usage before the birth of Christ, being replaced in Palestine by Aramaic, another Semitic tongue. In the twentieth century, the emergence of the State of Israel has led to a revival of Hebrew, although its form is different. For Jews who lived in the *Diaspora*, however, classical Hebrew served as the language of prayer and study.

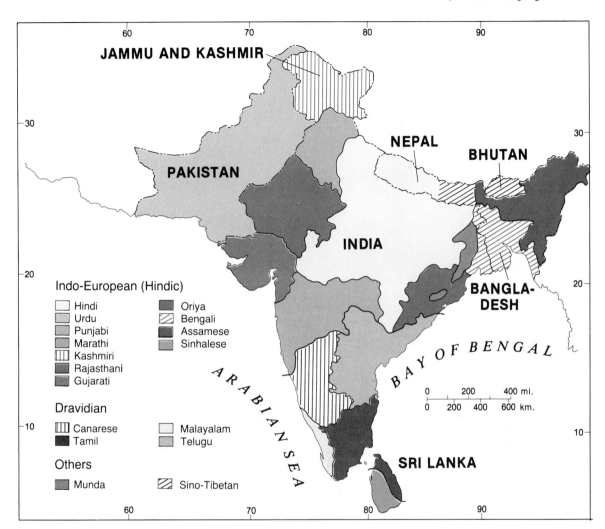

Figure 7-4

India faces both the problems of a rapidly growing population, which places great pressures on the land and other resources, and the difficulties associated with attempting to create a sense of national community, although many different languages and dialects are spoken. A major linguistic division occurs between the Hindic peoples of the north and center and the Dravidians of the south. But within both major groups, there are a number of distinct dialects, some of which are sufficiently different to be considered separate languages.

Arabic, spoken by over 150 million people, is the dominant language in the Dry World west of the Indo-Iranian and Indo-Aryan language groups. It is the primary language of Islamic civilization because its oldest and most important literary and religious text, the Koran, is written in Arabic (Box 7–4).

Amharic, the official language of Ethiopia

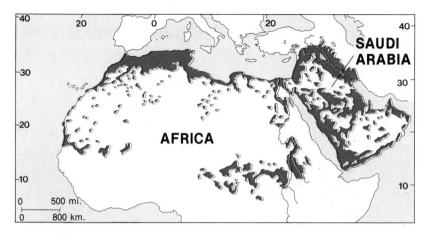

Figure 7–5

The homeland of the Semitic languages was probably central and northern Arabia. Certainly, Arabia was the center of distribution of the peoples who spoke these languages. From there, they spread—sometime before 3000 B.C.—into the Tigris-Euphrates Valley and subsequently through the Fertile Crescent and along the Levantine coast (Canaan and Phoenicia). At a somewhat later date they occupied southern Arabia and still later crossed the Red Sea into Ethiopia. The migration of Semites across North Africa occurred after the rise of Islam. Arab traders carried Arabic (and Islam) down the coast of East Africa and by sea to Southeast Asia.

spoken by about 10 million people, is also classified as a Semitic tongue, but it differs from other Semitic languages, in that its alphabet was derived from Coptic, a Hamitic language widely used in Egypt in the third century A.D. Coptic was the language of Egyptian Christians, and it was greatly influenced by Greek because the Coptic religious tradition was associated with the Byzantine Church. Although Amharic originated with Semitic invaders from southern Arabia, it was modified by the languages originally spoken in Ethiopia and those spoken by the peoples of the upper Nile.

Hamitic languages were widely spoken throughout northern Africa before the Arab conquest. Today, peoples belonging to the Hamitic family are scattered across northern Africa and reach as far south as Nigeria in the west and Kenya in the east. Among the principal members are the Berbers, principally in northwest Africa; the Galla in Ethiopia; the Somali in Ethiopia, Kenya, and Somalia, and the Hausa in Nigeria. The Hausa tongue is native to about 25 million people.

East and Southeast Asia-Based Languages

The Sino-Tibetan family includes a large number of people found in an area stretching from the Tibetan Plateau and the Himalayas northward to the Amur River and the Pacific. Vast though this area is, it is not nearly as congested linguistically as Europe or Africa; large stretches of territory are sparsely inhabited, and in the populous areas, a single-language community encompasses an incredible number of people.

The Sino-Tibetan family includes four subbranches, glaringly unequal in numbers of speakers. These are Chinese, Tibeto-Burman, Thai, and Miao-Yao.

Chinese, spoken by nearly 900 million people, consists of a number of dialects, the most important of which are Mandarin, the official tongue to the People's Republic of China; Cantonese; Wu; Min; and Hakka. Among the Tibeto-Burman subbranch are the languages and dialects spoken in Tibet, the Himalayas, and upper Burma. Thai, or Thai-Lao, is predominant in Thailand and Laos, whereas Miao and Yao are spoken by small groups in southern China.

The Japanese language space since World War II has been confined principally to the home islands of Japan. Spoken by more than 100 million, it ranks among the top 10 languages of the world. Although it adopted Chinese pictographic characters in the third century A.D., Japanese is not related to Chinese.

Korean, too, ranks as an independent language, its space largely coterminous with the political extent of North and South Korea (60 million people). Almost 1 million Koreans, however, live in China and the Soviet Union (mainly in Soviet Central Asia). The Korean alphabet, invented in 1443–1446, is unique, bearing no relationship to the scripts of either China or Japan.

Vietnamese has borrowed nearly half its vocabulary from Chinese, but it remains almost an independent tongue. Spoken by about 45 million people, its alphabet is also unique, having been devised by Catholic missionaries in the seventeenth century.

Mon-Khmer languages are spoken in Southeast Asia by almost 8 million people. The name derives from the two principal members of the family—Khmer, the national language of Cambodia, and Mon, spoken by a small number of people in Burma. The Khmer empire reached its greatest extent from the ninth through the twelfth centuries A.D. Later, Khmer space was invaded by the Thais, forcing a contraction into Cambodia, (now Kampuchea). Mon was also more widespread in the past, in part because of its early role in the diffusion of Buddhism.

Munda languages predate the Dravidian in India, but they have receded into the more remote areas of the subcontinent under the im-

pact of peoples with more advanced cultures. They number about 5 million.

Oceania-Based Languages

The Malayo-Polynesian language space stretches more than halfway around the globe, from the Malagasy Republic off the east coast of Africa, through the Indonesian archipelago, the Philippines, and across the islands of the Pacific. Its speakers number perhaps 190 million people. The Malay-Indonesian branch is the principal division; it includes Indonesian, Javanese, Tagalog (spoken in the Philippines), and Malagasy. On the islands that dot the Pacific Ocean, hundreds of Malayo-Polynesian languages are spoken, including Maori, Samoan, Tongan, and Tahitian (all Polynesian); Figian (Melanesian); Chamorro Gilbertese, and others (Micronesian).

Northern Eurasia-, Central Asia-, and the Caucasus-Based Languages

The Ural-Altaic languages occupy a broad belt of territory across Eurasia from Finland in the northwest and Turkey in the southwest to eastern Siberia and the Pacific in the Far East. Because of significant differences within the classification, the subgroups are often treated as separate language families.

The Uralic languages, largely (but not entirely) confined to the northern extremity of the landmass, have approximately 20 million speakers, the most important being the Finnic group (Finns, Estonians, Mordvins, Mari, and Komi) and the Ugric group (mainly Hungarian). The Samoyeds (or Lapps) of the Far North are included in the Uralic family, although their language is almost an independent one. In the Soviet Union, the alphabet of the Uralic peoples is Cyrillic, although Estonian, like Finnish and Hungarian, still uses the Latin alphabet.

The Altaic languages, spoken by some 80 million people, are thought to have originated in

BOX 7-4

Arabic and the Sense of Arab Brotherhood

Until the death of Mohammed in A.D. 632, Arabic was spoken only in Arabia and not even in all parts of that vast, arid, half-inhabited peninsula. After Mohammed made Islam the dominant religion of the region, the newly converted Arabs embarked on a conquest of a major part of the world.

Although Islamization and Arabization started out together, Arabic ultimately lagged behind spatially as Islam made converts well beyond the Dry World. But, within the Dry World, Arabic overcame many of the languages spoken at the time. In the Fertile Crescent, Arabic replaced Aramaic and Hebrew; in Egypt it confined after A.D. 997 the use of Coptic to the small Christian community. However, Arabic did not succeed in supplanting the Indo-Iranian languages of Persia (Iran) or Afghanistan—nor Kurdish in Kurdistan, Turkish in Turkey, or Turkic in Central Asia. For centuries, too, the Berbers and other Hamitic peoples of North Africa resisted the new language.

But, within the Arabic-speaking countries, there has been a pervading consciousness of being part of one nation, the "Arab nation," irrespective of the number of political units or socioeconomic groups into which this larger nation is divided. Even in conflict, the feeling persists among Arabs that, however bloody or painful the disagreement, the conflict will pass and peaceful reconciliation will occur. Above the divisions lies the awareness of an all-Arab national unity or brotherhood.

In the creation of this feeling of common identity, the Arabic language has been the most potent factor. Arabic is a unifying force in a way that perhaps no other language on earth is. Arabic is not only the medium of expression of an "Arab nation," but also of an "Arab family" (Fig. 7-6).

It is the use of Arabic that defines and determines membership in this national family. Linguistic identity, moreover, has achieved a precedence over religious differences, although this may be less true at present than in the past, as evident from the communal strife in Lebanon.

Arabic, to many Arabs, is the best and most beautiful of all languages. In its rhythm, music, and logic, many Arabs take great pride.

the Altai Mountains of western Mongolia. The family consists of three subdivisions: Turkic, Mongolian, and Tungusic.

The Altaic peoples originally seem to have been woodland-based hunters, but in the sixth century A.D., a Turkic group—probably already distinguishable from the Mongolian—created an empire stretching from China to the Black Sea. Later, this group splintered, only to fall under the domination of the Mongols in the twelfth and thirteenth centuries.

Peoples speaking Turkic languages include the Turks of Turkey, who account for more than half of all the speakers, and the Turko-Tatars, mainly in the Soviet Union. Constituent members of the latter group are widely scattered—along the Volga, primarily as remnants of the once-powerful Golden Horde; in the Urals; in the Caucasus Mountains; in the Soviet republics of Central Asia; in southern Siberia near the Altai Mountains; and in northeastern Siberia in the Lena Valley. Another group, known as Uigurs, numbers about 4 million in northwestern China, but only one hundred fifty thousand in the neighboring USSR.

The Mongolian group inhabits principally the drier upland part of south-central Siberia, adjacent Outer Mongolia (Mongolian People's Re-

Figure 7-6
The market place has served as a place for the exchange of goods and ideas since earliest times. This vegetable market in Turpan in the Xinjiang-Uighur Autonomous Region of China is interesting because, in addition to its permitting a display of local produce, it also reflects the linguistic diversity of the region. The sign on the wall contains characters in Chinese and Arabic script, advertising the presence of a market.

Source: Tia Schneider Denenberg/ Photo Researchers, Inc.

public), and the neighboring districts of China. In the early seventeenth century, Mongolian language space was extended westward when a Mongol group, known as the Kalmyks, migrated to the mouth of the Volga, where they are found today. Tungusic peoples are spread over a vast area of northeastern Siberia, but their numbers are not significant.

Members of the Caucasian language family consist primarily of Georgians at the east end of the Black Sea and of peoples speaking dialects in the rugged Caucasus Mountains. The term Japhetic has often been applied to this family, evolving from Japheth, the third son of Noah.

Altogether about 5 million people speak one of the approximately 40 Caucasian languages.

Other Language Spaces

Among the remaining peoples of the globe, there are language and dialects in use that defy general classification. Among the Native Americans some 25 linguistic families have been identified (Fig. 7–7). The complexity is similar in Africa. Apart from the Hamito-Semitic languages of the north, three main linguistic groupings have been recognized. These are the Khoikhoi (Hottentot-Bushmen) of Southwest

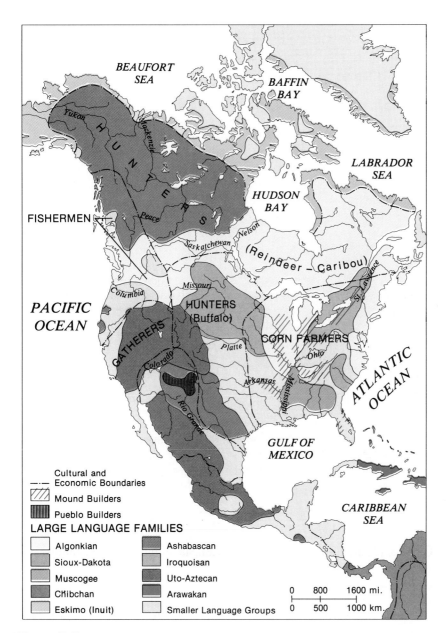

Figure 7–7

The native peoples of North America belong to a number of different language groups. The last migrants from Asia, the Eskimo, or Inuit (as they are called in Canada), still occupy the northernmost reaches of the continent and are distinct from American Indians generally. The latter, who came in one, possibly two, waves of migration from Asia, may be arranged for convenience into seven large groups. The Athabascan peoples occupied the far northwest and the Mackenzie and upper Yukon river valleys. These tribes were primarily hunters of the forest, although some pursued the caribou out into the open barrens. To the southeast of the Athabascan and south of the Inuit were the Algonquins (Algonkians), wandering bands of Indians who fished on the coasts and hunted in the forests. The peoples who lived to the south, the Iroquois tribes, practiced agriculture as well. They occupied the St. Lawrence Valley and the fertile lowlands around the lower Great Lakes.

Africa; the Niger-Congo group, including the Bantu, south of the *Bantu line,* which stretches from the Cameroons to Kenya; and the Chari-Nile, which includes the Nubian (Nile) and Nilotic languages (Nuer, Masai) of East Africa (Fig. 7–8).

Finally, throughout Asia and other parts of the world there remain remnants of other extremely old languages, spoken only by small groups of people, such as the Ainu of northern Japan, the Chukchi of eastern Siberia, the Australian aborigines, the Papuans, and the Eskimo-Aleuts.

Lingua Franca

Where there is a multiplicity of languages that makes communication difficult, one language may be used by several communities for specific purposes. This is true of English in the Indian subcontinent as well as elsewhere. In the past, however, other languages have had this function. Sogdian, a Central Asian language, served as a medium of communication during the first millenium between the Indo-Iranian world and the Far East; it played a major role in commerce and in the early diffusion of Buddhism. Greek and Latin have had similar roles in the Mediterranean. Greek reached into Southwest Asia and into North Africa, whereas Latin replaced many of the local languages of the basin in both administration and trade. It was the widespread use of Greek and Latin that contributed much to the spread of Christianity.

Lingua franca is the name given to languages whose universality invites this special function. The term means literally "the language of the Franks," a derivative commonly used at Mediterranean ports in the medieval period. Consisting chiefly of Romance words drawn from Italian, Spanish, and French, it also incorporated Greek and Arabic.

In the modern world, certain regional languages have also gained special favor. *Swahili*—more correctly called Kishwahili, from the Arabic word meaning coastal—developed among Arabic-speaking settlers of the East African coast beginning about the seventh century A.D. Although Swahili has been modified by the introduction of Arabic words, it is still classified as a Bantu language. Swahili subsequently was carried inland by Arab traders and its space expanded greatly. Before World War I, the Germans adopted Swahili as the language of administration in their East African colony of Tanganyika. It has since become the national language of Tanzania and the official language of Kenya besides English. Swahili is spoken by some 30 million people.

Pidgin and *creolized languages* also have come into existence to bridge the gap between peoples. A pidgin, which is a mixture of other languages, has no native speakers, even though it may be widely used, as English pidgin is in Papua New Guinea today. Pidgin becomes a creolized language when its use spreads and it is adopted as a mother tongue by the subordinate language group. Although rarely written, such a language serves as a useful medium of communication. This has been true of the French *Creole* spoken in Louisiana and the West Indies.

Language Space as Ethnic Space

The sharing of experiences that takes place within a community where people can talk to

---

Figure 7–7 (continued)

The Plains Indians consisted of a number of tribes who spoke distinct languages, although sign language became a convenient device for communication. The Indians of the Pacific Coast depended heavily on the sea for survival, agriculture was entirely unknown along the northern part of the coast. The rest of North America north of the Rio Grande, apart from Muscogee in the southeast, was occupied by numerous small brands. Finally, Meso-America was the center of the Aztec and Mayan civilizations with their high degree of cultural attainment.

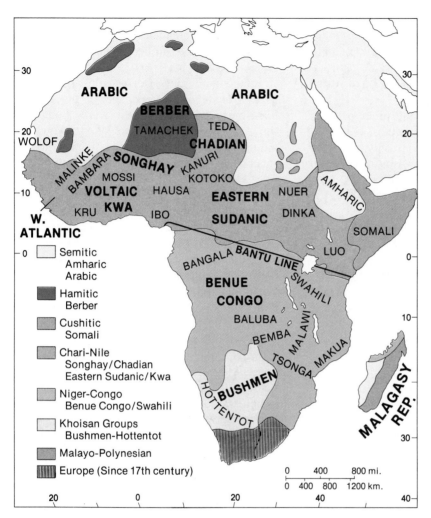

Figure 7–8

The demarcation known as the Bantu line divides the Bantu people (Niger-Congo languages) from the Chari-Nile group that dominates central Africa from the Atlantic to the Ethiopian highlands. To the north of the Chari-Nile stretches a broad band of Arabic speakers, with surviving and scattered pockets of an older language group, the Hamites. Pushed into the drier, more inhospitable parts of southern Africa are descendents of the Khoikhoi (Hottentot—Bushmen) who speak a Khoisan language.

each other, understand each other, and trade with and serve each other means the sharing of sociocultural values. Through this kind of close interaction, an *ethnic* community may emerge. This is especially true if there is a sharing of common space and usually, but not always, a common language. Thus, a language space may be an *ethnic space* as well.

In the formation of an ethnic community, people become conscious of themselves as different from other groups, and whatever real differences there are become reinforced by group attitudes and values.

As an ethnic community takes shape, if there is one common language, the language itself tends to become a phenomenon of value. In that case, the language becomes the very trademark of the ethnic community; it becomes the symbol of *ethnicity* (Deutsch, 1953). For example, one of the major goals of the Parti Québécois, which came to power in the Canadian Province of Quebec in November 1976, was to ensure that French remain the language of the province. Once in power, party leaders took official steps through legislation to achieve the desired goal. The fear had been that, if increasing numbers of people in Quebec were forced to learn English, ultimately the French-Canadian culture and way of life would disappear from the banks of the Saint Lawrence.

The characteristics of ethnicity are also interesting to observe because they provide evidence of the way a people think of themselves. The Old Testament affords some insight into the ethnicity of Hebrews for example. This minor Semitic tribe, which came out of the desert to conquer much of Canaan, was a remarkably ethnocentric one. The Hebrew notion of a special relationship with God as "the Chosen People" together with the belief in a "Promised Land" made these people supremely conscious of themselves as unique, with a special role to play in the history of the peoples of the earth. Such ideas set the Hebrews apart from other Semitic peoples in the Fertile Crescent and may have been a factor that contributed to the resentment non-Jews felt toward Jews in the many centuries following their exile from Jerusalem.

The common awareness that is associated with ethnicity plays a large part in cementing a people together, in creating ethnic spaces, and in determining the perception they have of themselves and of the world around them. Language plays a major role in establishing membership in, and identification with, the group.

This principle is evident in the differences that have emerged over the past seven centuries between Hindi-speaking and Urdu-speaking groups in South Asia. Hindi and Urdu, as was noted earlier, are both Hindic languages, but the alphabets are different. What is important, however, is that they signify two different communities and ways of life, one Hindu, the other Muslim.

Ethnicity and Nationality

Examples of the forging of national groups along ethnic lines are to be found in Europe's historic record. In *Nationalism and Social Communication*, Karl Deutsch notes that when the Finnish people migrated from the countryside to the towns, they became aware of the differences between themselves and the Swedish settlers on the coast. By coming together in the towns, the Finnish country people gave birth through social interaction and communication to a new entity that was Finnish. The nineteenth century was one that in effect witnessed the Finnization of the territorial space that came to be identified as Finland (Deutsch, 1953).

From this and other studies of Europe, Deutsch has identified the stages in the formation of an ethnic and, subsequently, a national community. As an ethnic community develops and its differences from other communities grow, it becomes conscious of itself as representing a totally distinct people. With formal organization or some form of control, the ethnic group is moulded into a *nation*. As a basis for political organization, the *nation-state* gained acceptance in Europe during the nineteenth century, and the premise that nations had the *right of self-determination,* or independence, became an accepted principle in the Treaty of Versailles in 1919 following World War I (Fig. 7–9). By then the imperial order of Europe, imposed by Russia, Austria-Hungary, Germany, and the Ottoman Turks, had collapsed, and the

Figure 7–9
Because of the historic intermixing of Germanic and Slavic peoples in eastern Europe, the language map of central Europe on the eve of World War I was a complex mosaic. In 1919, the Treaty of Versailles made an attempt to give the ethnic groups national territories, but the drawing of boundaries created major difficulties. Although there was some interwar migration of peoples, the language map remained a complex one until World War II when forced migrations tended to bring national groups together. The historic presence of Magyars (Hungarians) and Romanians further complicated the spatial arrangement of peoples in eastern Europe because the Hungarians belong to the Ugric language group and the Romanians, the Romance language group.

nations of Europe were demanding recognition. International boundaries were redrawn—both then and later, after World War II—and millions of people were compelled to migrate from one national space to another because it was recognized that political space and national space should be one and the same thing.

Manipulation of Language and Ethnicity

Ethnicity can be manipulated and many multinational states today often resort to this tactic as a device to control their minorities. Governments of such states can play off one ethnic group against the other. Manipulation

Figure 7-10
In societies where information is subjected to close governmental supervision, large poster boards are placed at convenient places throughout the city and countryside where people can read what a controlled press permits. One of these large boards stands at Tian-an-men, the gateway to the Forbidden City in Beijing, China.

Source: Paolo Koch/Rapho/Photo Researchers, Inc.

may occur by altering the alphabet of a minority people or by adopting other restrictive language or linguistic policies; such practices have been used in the USSR (Box 7–5) and in China (Fig. 7–10).

Ethnicity, Nationality, and Bilingualism

Language and ethnicity tend to be associated on a one-to-one basis: one language, a distinct ethnicity or *nationality*. However, an ethnic iden-

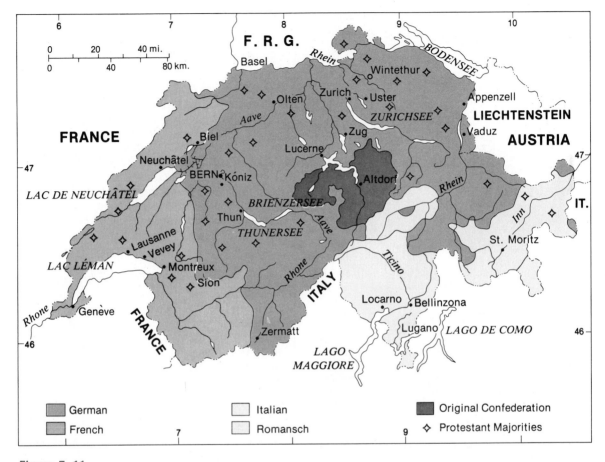

Figure 7–11

Forest cantons owing allegiance to the Austrian Habsburgs controlled the main passes through the Alps from Germany to Italy in medieval times. Their language was a Germanic one. After their union in 1291 and the defeat of the Habsburgs in 1315, the forest cantons were joined by other cantons—including some that spoke French, Romansch, and Italian—to form the Swiss Federation that exists today.

tity may emerge even where more than one language is the basis of daily expression.

Americans have achieved a kind of ethnic identity, based on Anglo-Saxon origins, through the process of socializing or assimilating the millions of peoples who have migrated to the United States from all parts of the globe. In the political development and geographic expansion of the country, the different peoples mingled so that, for the most part, there were no subordinate ethnic spaces to compete with the larger all-American one. Even on the Indian reservations, the nearest thing in the United States to ethnic or tribal spaces, official policies—at least until recently—encouraged the study of English and the neglect of tribal dialects and lore.

Switzerland, on the other hand, is a classic example of a place where different language groups exist side by side (French, German, Ital-

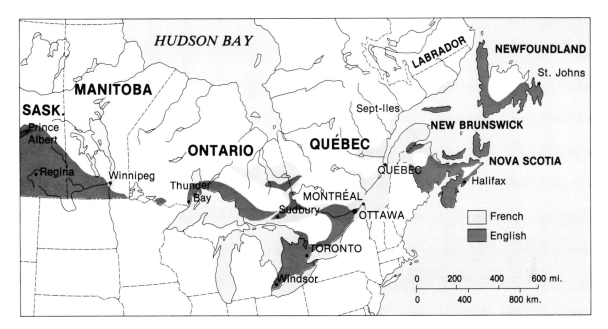

Figure 7–12

The bulk of Canada's French-speaking population lives in the Province of Quebec and is heavily concentrated in the lowland along the lower Saint Lawrence River. There are smaller but important French-speaking communities in Canada's Atlantic provinces as well as in eastern and northern Ontario. Still smaller communities are found in the provinces of western Canada, with the principal cluster near Winnipeg in Manitoba.

According to general estimates, less than 30 percent of Canada's population is of French origin (descendants of seventeenth-century immigrants), 47 percent British, and the remaining 23 percent other nationalities. English and French are the official languages of the country, but the provincial administration of Quebec has insisted that French alone serves as the language of government, business, and elementary education in that province. A reason for this action is to insure that the French language survives in North America.

ian, and Romansch), but the language spaces make up one essential ethnic community—Swiss. The Swiss, whatever their language, accept the language differences to assure the preservation of the Swiss Federation (Fig. 7–11).

Effective Transmission Networks

Where ethnic survival is a goal and national and political stability are essential, but where national societies are spatially *bilingual*, what is needed is the creation of an effective transmission network that democratically transcends language differences. Without such a cohesive

mechanism, there is little to halt the trend toward ethnic tensions. Moreover, ethnic tensions, such as exist in Canada between those who identify as Québécois and those who call themselves Canadians and in Belgium between the French-speaking Walloons and the Flemish (Figs. 7–12, 7–13), aggravate problems in the economy. If unresolved, such tensions can lead to separation and the further political fragmentation of the world. Such a trend could be disastrous, especially in Africa with its vast number of tribal dialects, even though the task of forging stable communities within boundaries imposed historically by Europeans at times seems insurmountable.

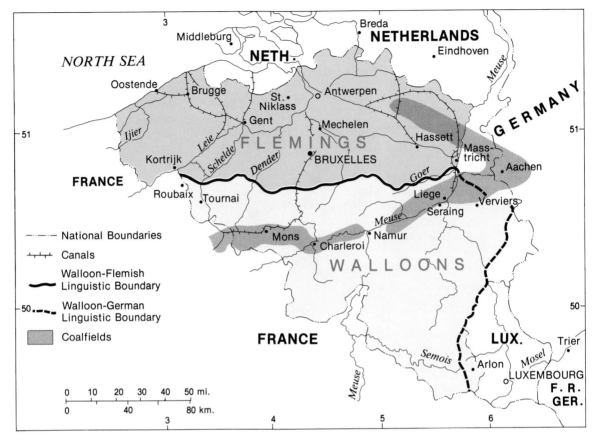

Figure 7–13

Belgium's population consists of two ethnic groups. Approximately 3.5 million French-speaking Walloons live in southern Belgium, whereas in the north are found 5.5 million Dutch-speaking Flemings. Constitutional crises have occurred in Belgium in recent years in part because of Walloon fears of being dominated culturally and economically by the Flemish. In 1980, an autonomy plan established separate parliaments for each region. However, no decision was taken with respect to the future status of (Brussels) Bruxelles, the capital, in a newly federated state. Brussels has a population of about 1 million, the majority of whom speak both Flemish and Walloon.

EPILOGUE

The existence of a correlation between culture and language has long been recognized. However, few studies have been undertaken by geographers to demonstrate this correlation in a spatial context. There has been a tendency, especially among English-speaking peoples, to take language for granted, and this sad truth is reflected in the widespread lack of interest shown in the languages of the rest of humankind. The relationship between language and culture, however, should constitute a basis upon which an understanding of cultural differences and cultural expressions should be built. No one has stated this premise more succinctly than the linguist-anthropologist Edward Sapir (1884–1939) (cited in Patai, 1983):

> Human beings do not live in the objective world alone, nor alone in the world of social activity as ordinarily understood, but are very much at the mercy of the particular language which has become the medium of expression for their society. . . . The fact of the matter is that the "real world" is to a large extent unconsciously built upon the language habits of the group. No two languages are ever sufficiently similar to be considered as representing the same social reality. The world in which different societies live are distinct worlds, not merely the same world with different labels attached (p. 68).

APPLICATION OF IDEAS

1. Words are the symbols of culture and the vocalization of these words is the basis of communication and cultural transmission. Knowledge of the language of other peoples helps in the understanding of their cultural aspirations.

2. Not only is language an expression of a people's collective experience, but also there is a tendency among humans to interpret the expressions of other cultures through the filters of their own traditions and experience. Perhaps the real differences between languages and peoples lies in their *Weltansichten,* or world perspectives.

3. Where a common language is spoken, there will exist a distinct community of language, or a language space. In any event, a common language generally develops in an area where there is frequent, friendly, or positive interaction among peoples. Altogether, some three to four thousand languages are spoken, but only a small number of languages are spoken by the greater proportion of the earth's population.

4. The earth's languages may be grouped in principal language families within which there are many subdivisions. Lingua franca, pidgin,

and creolized languages are important because they serve special purposes.

5. The sharing of experiences through a common language leads to the formation of ethnic communities that may ultimately come to form national communities.

KEY WORDS AND PHRASES

anthropomorphic	lingua franca
Bantu line	melting pot
bilingual	nation
complementarity	nationality
creole	nation-state
creolized language	pidgin
dialect	principal language
diaspora	family
diglossia	right to
Dry World	self-determination
ethnic	Swahili
ethnicity	toponymy
ethnic space	Weltansichten
fall line	

QUESTIONS FOR FURTHER DISCUSSION

1. Why is the question of language an important one for the geographer? What difficulties does the study of language pose?

2. What can language tell us about a people's culture, their perception of nature, the relationships of one people to another? Without a knowledge of Russian, how well do you think you could determine what the Russians, collectively, actually think?

3. What does Karl Deutsch mean when he uses the term complementarity? Why do people who use the same language fail at times to understand each other?

4. In what way can language define culture areas? Give examples from Eurasia, Africa, and an American city.

5. What can the study of place-names tell us about the origins of a people or of the region's early history? Give examples from the United States, England, and Africa.

6. How widespread is the usage of Mandarin Chinese in the modern world? Where do the majority of its speakers live? How extensive are the use of English and Russian? Where do most of the speakers of these languages live?

7. How extensive is the Hamito-Semitic family? To what other phenomenon of culture is the distribution of members of this family closely, although by no means entirely, associated?

8. What are the origins of the term lingua franca? How does lingua franca differ from pidgin and creolized languages?

9. In what way are language, ethnicity, and nationality related? Is language always the basis or the only basis of community awareness? What other cultural factors might contribute to differentiation among peoples?

10. Do you think extensive study of foreign languages would help you become a more effective citizen of the world community? Give examples of ways that your behavior or activity patterns might be altered.

REFERENCES AND ADDITIONAL READINGS

Allwood, Martin S. *American and British. A Handbook of American-British Language Differences.* Published privately, 1964.

Baugh, Albert C. *A History of the English Language.* New York: Appleton-Century, 1935.

Baugh, Albert C., and Cobb, Thomas. *A History of the English Language,* 3rd ed. Englewood Cliffs, N.J.: Prentice-Hall, 1963.

de Carvalho, C. M. Delgado. "The Geography of Languages," pp. 75–93. In *Readings in Cultural Geography.* Philip L. Wagner and Marvin M. Mikesell, eds. Chicago: University of Chicago Press, 1962.

Deutsch, Karl. *Nationalism and Social Communication: An Inquiry into the Foundations of Nationality.* New York: John Wiley, 1953.

Eastman, Carol M. *Aspects of Language and Culture.* San Francisco: Chandler & Sharp, 1975.

Gleeson, Patrick, and Wakefield, Nancy, eds. *Language and Culture.* Columbus, Ohio: Charles E. Merrill, 1968.

Hall, Edward. *The Silent Language.* Greenwich, Conn.: Fawcett, 1959.

Hall, Joseph Sargent. *Smoky Mountain Folks and Their Lore.* Asheville, N.C.: Great Smoky Mountains Natural History Association, 1960.

Hymes, Dell. *Language in Culture and Society. A Reader in Linguistics and Anthropology.* New York: Harper & Row, 1964.

Katzner, Kenneth. *The Languages of the World.* New York: Funk & Wagnalls, 1975.

Kaups, M. "Finnish Place Names in Minnesota: A Study in Cultural Transfer." *Geographical Review* 56 (1966):377–397.

Kerr, Elizabeth M., and Aderman, Ralph M. *Aspects of American English.* New York: Harcourt, Brace & World, 1963.

Krauss, Robert M., and Glucksberg, Sam. "Social and Nonsocial Speech." *Scientific American* 236 (1977): 100–105.

Kurath, Hans. *A Word Geography of the Eastern United States.* Ann Arbor: University of Michigan Press, 1949.

Ley, David. *The Black Inner City as Frontier Outpost.* AAG Monograph Series No. 7. Washington, D.C., American Association of Geographers, 1974.

Lind, Ivan. "Geography and Place Names," pp. 118–128. In *Readings in Cultural Geography.* Philip L. Wagner and Marvin W. Mikesell, eds. Chicago: University of Chicago Press, 1962.

McDavid, Raven I., Jr. "Linguistic Geography and Toponymic Research." *Names* 6 (1956): 65–73.

———. "Postvocalic *r* in South Carolina: A Social Analysis," pp. 473–482. In *Language in Culture and Society. A Reader in Linguistics and Anthropology.* Dell Hymes, ed. New York: Harper & Row, 1964.

Myers, Sarah K. *Language Shift Among Migrants to Lima, Peru.* Research Paper No. 147. Department of Geography, University of Chicago, 1973.

Nehru, Jawaharlal. *Visit to America.* New York: John Day, 1950.

O'Barr, W. M., and O'Barr, Jean F. *Language and Politics.* The Hague: Mouton, 1976.

Patai, Raphael. *The Arab Mind,* rev. ed. New York: Charles Scribner's, 1983.

Reed, Carroll E. *Dialects of American English,* rev. ed. Amherst: University of Massachusetts Press, 1977.

Sapir, Edward. *Culture, Language and Personality,* ed., D. G. Mandelbaum. Berkeley: University of California Press, 1970.

Schmandt-Besserat, Denise. "The Earliest Precursor of Writing." *Scientific American* 238 (1978): 50–59.

Steward, George R. *Names on the Land: An Historical Account of Place-Naming in the United States.* New York: Random House, 1945.

Swadesh, Morris. *The Origin and Diversification of Language.* Chicago: Aldine-Atherton, 1971.

Thorne, Barrie, and Henley, Nancy, eds. *Language and Sex. Difference and Dominance.* Rowley, Mass.: Newbury House Publishers, 1975.

Wagner, Philip L. "Remarks on the Geography of Language." *Geographical Review* 48 (1948): 86–97.

The World Almanac & Book of Facts 1983. New York: Newspaper Enterprise Association, 1983.

Wright, John K. "The Study of Place-Names," *Geographical Review* 19 (1929): 140–144.

Zelinsky, Wilbur. "Generic Terms in the Place Names of the Northeastern United States." *Annals of the Association of American Geographers* 45 (1955): 319–349.

———. "Classical Town Names in the United States. The Historical Geography of an American Idea." *Geographical Review* 57 (1967): 463–495.

8
Religious Values in the Landscape

As the forehead of Man grows broader, so do his creeds;
And his gods they are shaped in his image, and mirror his needs;
And he clothes them with thunders and beauty, he clothes them with music and fire;
Seeing not, as he bows by their altars, that he worships his own desire;
And mixed with his trust, there is terror, and mixed with his madness is truth.
And every man grovels in error, yet every man glimpses a truth.

Don Marquis (1878–1937),
The God-Maker, Man

A meridian decides what is the truth.

Blaise Pascal (1623–1662)
Pensées, Sec. 4, No. 282

Key Ideas

1. In Western industrialized societies, there is a tendency to overlook the importance of religious values in the landscape, yet religion is an active force, shaping the lives of many people in other parts of the world.

2. Religion represents the human attempt to come to terms with the powerful forces that affect human life, including the knowledge that humans are mortal.

3. The practice of religion has been associated with the symbolic marking off of both time and space.

4. Most of the world's major religious systems originated in Asia. Some have remained highly localized, others have striven for universalism.

5. Hinduism, the predominant religion of India, is an amalgam of different expressions.

6. Buddhism originated in India and is the religion of much of Southeast Asia; it plays an important role in East Asian life.

7. China really has no formal religion as such, but from earliest times, Taoism and Confucianism have played a major role in Chinese life and thought.

8. Shintō is essentially a Japanese phenomenon; it represents an accumulation of ancient myths and feelings.

9. Judaism is totally unlike the religions of East and South Asia, in that it is first of all monotheistic and represents a new concept of God in the world.

10. Christianity emerged from Judaism, but it developed features that differed significantly from Judaism. One of its features was its missionary zeal and claim to universality.

11. Major divisions within Christian ranks occurred with the development of Constantinople; another occurred in Europe during the Renaissance.

12. The American Christian experience was shaped by the American environment and, above all, by the frontier.

13. Islam, whose hearth was Arabia, is a monotheistic religion based on the teachings of a book, the Koran. Its diffusion was rapid.

THE IMPORTANCE OF RELIGION

In Western industrialized societies, with their focus on material accomplishments, there is a tendency to overlook the important impact that religious values have had—and continue to have—in the shaping of our world. This tendency is largely due to the enormous role that modern technology plays in our daily lives. Through world news media coverage, however, we are periodically reminded that we in the Western world pay too little attention to a phenomenon that continues to shake many countries and affect the behavior patterns of many people.

Geographers have long been interested in the role that religious values have played in the shaping of the landscape (Isaac, 1961–1962; Sopher, 1967; Zelinsky, 1961). However, the role that religion plays today in the daily lives of many millions of people has tended to be underplayed.

For many people, the religion in which they are raised is considered the *only* religion. Not only do they not take any deep interest in the religions of others, but also they often look on them as being in error, if not downright false. Ignorance, intolerance, and discrimination have all too often been associated with religious beliefs, and we can see the consequences of these attitudes at work throughout the world today.

Europe in the sixteenth and seventeenth centuries was marked by terrible religious wars and, although the scale of conflict has lessened, religious values with strong political overtones mark daily life in various parts of the globe even today. The competing forces native to the beleaguered state of Lebanon, for example, have their roots in historic religious communities, both Christian and Muslim. Under the Turkish Ottoman Empire before World War I, such communities were virtually self-governing in a system known as the *Millet System.* Today, each struggles to avoid being overwhelmed by the other. Lebanese Shiites, who are believed to constitute a majority among Lebanese Muslims, have become increasingly more powerful and even attack other Muslims. Conflicts between Christians and Muslims have led to widespread killings in the past decade.

The emergence of Pakistan as an independent state in 1947 was both an expression of the strength of Islam in the Indian subcontinent where Hindus dominated and a reaction to the disintegration of Muslim rule that had prevailed there under British imperial control in the nineteenth century. The overthrow of the Shah of Iran in 1979 was in no small measure due to a fundamentalist response to the forces of modernization that threatened traditional values and a way of life. The rallying cry of Islam, *Allahuakhbar,* meaning God is great, echoes louder today in Muslim countries than it has for centuries.

In their dealings with the Islamic countries, Christians are generally unaware that to Muslims the world is divided into two distinct camps—believers and nonbelievers. There may be differences within the camp of believers, but Muslims tend to view the Christian West as permissive and self-indulgent. On the other hand, the Christian countries have remained ignorant of the basic premises of Islamic law, its origins, content, and values. Today, the interest of the Western world in Islamic countries, especially in the Middle East, is tarnished by the need for oil and a concern for geopolitical advantage.

Lack of understanding associated with religious differences is by no means confined to Muslim-Christian relationships. The struggle in Northern Ireland is one that has at its core a demand for universal equal rights, but it is waged between communities that are primarily divided by religion, the Protestant establishment and the Catholic minority. Religious segregation permeates not only employment, but also the classroom.

In the United States in recent years, there has been a strong revival of interest in traditional Christian values, and this has been expressed in attempts to strengthen the family, opposition to the Equal Rights Amendment (ERA), opposition to abortion, and a request for the institution of daily prayers in the classroom. Christian groups, of a *fundamentalist* persuasion, drawing inspiration and values from the Bible, have sought to spread their views through the medium of television and in campus ministries. The so-called Moral Majority represents a group of citizens who have directed this revival into the political arena, especially at the federal level.

WHAT IS RELIGION?

At the heart of all religions, whatever their expression—worship of the sun, sky, or mountains; the reverence for tribal originators or family ancestors; the belief in an omniscient god–lies the human attempt to come to terms with the powerful forces of nature that indiscriminately affect human life, including the knowledge that *homo sapiens,* like all living creatures, is mortal. It entails, therefore, an acceptance of revelation that comes from above and beyond nature (the *supranatural*); a belief in either spirits (*animism*), divinities (*polytheism*), or a single god (*monotheism*); and a recognition of a sacred realm in life as opposed to a nonsacred or secular realm. It is, in short, a total reaction to life.

Before studying religion's impact on the shaping of our world, it is necessary to define the term. There is, unfortunately, no commonly accepted definition; theologians, philosophers, sociologists, and psychologists treat it differently, with each definition reflecting a vocational and specialized interest (Sopher, 1967). Perhaps it is best to think of religion as a collective name for a variety of human experiences associated with the search for the meaning of life (James, 1902/1958).

Most, if not all, religions have statements of belief—often enshrined in authoritative books or documents—and a ritual or ceremony. They may, if organized, have an administrative structure with priests and clergy. The practice of religion may affect many facets of group behavior, from dietary habits or the location of buildings to the perception of space, and a religion's relationship with the land or with nature may have many ramifications (Tuan, 1976). On the other hand, religion may be an entirely personal phenomenon, a guide to individual behavior and ethical concern. In the final analysis, this latter facet of religion may be the more important one in human life, but it is with group beliefs and their spaces that the geographer is concerned.

RELIGIOUS SYMBOLISM

Symbols play an important role in the development and practice of religion, and some have even been imposed on the landscape. Animal paintings on cave walls—certainly possessing a magical if not a religious significance—go back to the Ice Age. Art, music, and architecture have traditionally been closely associated with religion. The peoples of Mesopotamia translated their gods into the sky in the shape of animals that still survive as the signs of the zodiac. Greek mythology was full of animal symbolism, which in altered form and meaning played an important role in Christianity (the fish and the lamb, for instance).

The circle, found in many religions, is as old as religion itself and is said to represent the integrated self, the totality of human life in its relationship to the larger world. The stone circles at Stonehenge and Avebury in England are believed to date back to Neolithic ceremonials when such monuments may have been used to observe events in the sky. In the Zen Buddhist sect, the circle represents enlightenment and symbolizes human perfection. For Christians, the central symbol of their faith is the cross;

Celtic Christianity imposed the circle on to the cross.

SACRED TIME AND SPACE

The practice of religions has also been associated with the symbolic marking off of both time and space. Many festivals and holidays (holy days), although secularized, or commercialized in much of the Western world, have an origin in religious experience. In the religions of many ancient cultures, time was viewed as circular. Thus, early humans, in the annual celebration of certain feasts, were asserting a belief in the renewal or regeneration of the world. As Mircea Eliade, an historian of religion and sacred space, points out, with each new year time was reborn or began again, that is, the world was created anew (Eliade, 1959). Although Western civilization came to see its world as moving toward some ultimate goal, aspects of this circular view of time remain. The Christian Easter did not become an established institution until the second century A.D., but its annual recurrence finds a parallel in earlier pagan spring-fertility festivals.

Similar to the notion of sacred time is the concept of sacred space—a place set apart from routine daily activities that embodies human spiritual aspiration (Sopher, 1967). A sacred place may be found in nature—and many pre-Christian cults in the Roman Empire had such places, but a sacred place may also be a temple, church, synagogue, mosque, or even a city.

In the past, high places or large rocks were often thought to possess special religious significance. It was there that people could reach out to, or be touched by, the divine. Moses received the Ten Commandments on Mount Sinai after leading the Israelites out of Egypt. Solomon's Temple subsequently was built on a mount in Jerusalem, and a western retaining wall built by King Herod to support a new temple on the site

of the old, known as the Wailing Wall, remains a deeply significant place for Jews today. One of the holiest places for Muslims in Jerusalem is the Dome of the Rock, built in A.D. 691, which contains the rock where, it is said, Abraham offered to sacrifice his son Isaac to God and from whence Mohammed ascended to heaven. The Kaaba in Mecca is a building venerated because of the Black Stone embedded in one of its corners; it annually draws millions of pilgrims from all over the Muslim world.

Because Jerusalem has deep historic significance for Jews, Christians, and Muslims, any activity by one group that disturbs the balance brings an immediate reaction, if not conflict. But, the antagonism may cut across different lines as well. In 1981, for example, members of a zealous, ultraorthodox Jewish sect—who opposed on religious grounds even the founding in 1948 of the state of Israel—attempted to halt archeological excavations on the site of the City of David (built about 1000 B.C.) just outside the present walls of old Jerusalem. Their claim was that under Jewish law, graves—none of which have actually been found—may never be disturbed, even a millennium later. What this opposition suggests is a growing division within Israel itself between the deeply religious community and the nonorthodox and secular population. This split may be as potentially dangerous for Israel as any perceived Arab threat.

Despite the fact that mountains or high places were, in ancient times, often possessed of the image of the holy, this was not necessarily true in later times. In Europe during the early medieval period, mountains aroused passionate dislike because they were regarded, ironically, as *less* than holy. Because mountains had a "wartlike appearance," they appeared to many people as an affront to a symmetrically minded creator, whom they believed could only have called into being a smooth, spherical globe. Although Petrarch in the fourteenth century was the first European known to climb a mountain (Mount Ventoux in the Alps) for the joy of discovery, mountains continued to be regarded, even until the late seventeenth century, as "uncouth, inhospitable, freezing and unfruitful," and their inhabitants, "in all respects, below humanity" (Piggott, 1976, p. 113).

This sense of the sacred remains an important component in the lives of millions of people today, especially in places such as India. Here, the Ganges River, a number of cities, and many specific temples possess a truly sacred dimension. In the Western world, however, such reverence for a place has become detached from religion and greatly transformed. In the modern state, the birthplaces of presidents, the tombs of military or other heroes, and similar historic places have taken on a shrinelike quality, but their purpose is to enhance loyalty to the nation rather than to a god or gods. The modern civic center, domed stadium, or concert hall, with their elaborate communication systems, can assemble vast crowds to hear a visiting evangelist, but the space itself is totally devoid of the religious sense. A campaign against religions is a feature of Soviet policy, but the tomb of Lenin, the founder of the Soviet State, draws thousands regularly to Red Square in Moscow, much as the mummified saints in the catacombs of the Pecherskiiy Monastery in Kiev attract the Christian faithful.

MAJOR RELIGIOUS SYSTEMS

Most of the world's major religious and ethical systems originated in Asia (Fig. 8–1). A number of these are strongly ethnic in outlook and for that reason have remained largely among the peoples with whom they originated. This is true of Hinduism, the Chinese beliefs encompassed by Taoism and Confucianism, and Shintō in Japan. Three of the major religions—Buddhism, Christianity, and Islam—are universalist, in that they have spread far beyond their hearths

and gained widespread appeal (Kaufmann, 1976). Judaism, which is both a religion and a culture, attempted at one time to make converts, but missionary activities ended with the destruction of the Temple in Jerusalem by the Romans in A.D. 70.

South Asian Hearths

Hinduism

The origins of *Hinduism* are complex, but the name derives from a region in northwestern India through which the Sind River flows. The oldest sacred writing of Hinduism is the *Rig-Veda,* parts of which may date to 1500 B.C. The term Hinduism probably originated with Muslim invaders of the eleventh century A.D.; they called the land they were invading Hindustan and the religion of the people Hinduism (Sopher, 1967).

As a faith, Hinduism is an amalgam of religious expressions that range from the worship of spirits in nature to that of many gods and from a belief in a single personal god to an exalted form of mysticism. Although not a coherent religion, Hinduism has its texts, temples, and shrines. The essential spirit of Hinduism seems to be to live and let live—in many ways, this viewpoint has permeated almost all aspects of Hindu life. Indeed, it may be India's undoing because reverence for life has been a major factor in India's high birthrate. Government attempts to lower the birthrate by tampering with the procreative process have produced widespread opposition and antagonism.

THE FORMATION OF HINDUISM

Hinduism reflects the accretions of successive waves of invaders from the northwest dating back many thousands of years. Each group brought with it different religious practices, and it was from many of these traditions that Hinduism evolved. The earliest peoples to penetrate the subcontinent carried with them a number of fertility *rites,* involving the cult of the tree and female deities. Later invaders brought the worship of animal-headed deities and the animal-vehicles on which every major Hindu deity rides (Figs. 8-2, 8-3). Serpent spirits and the Hindu concept of reincarnation, or *transmigration of souls* from one body to another, probably also originated at this time.

The Dravidians, arriving about 3000 B.C., superimposed a new language, still found on the Deccan Plateau of south India, and reinforced many of the older deities. It is possible that the founders of the great cities of Harappa and Mohenjo-Daro in the Indus valley were Dravidians.

The Aryans, seminomadic cattle herders and cultivators from a less fertile region, swept into the subcontinent about 1550 B.C. Their language was an Indo-European one and their gods had names not unlike those of the Greeks. The *Sanskrit* texts, the *Vedas* and *Upanishads*, originated with these peoples. The *Vedas* contain over a thousand hymns to be used at sacrifices to the gods, which are dominated by powerful male gods associated with the heavens. The greatest Vedic deity is Indra, who is both a weather god and a war god.

THE CASTE SYSTEM

Following the last great wave of Aryan invaders there emerged in the subcontinent a complex, all-embracing system of social organization known as *caste*. Because caste was rooted in Hinduism, it had a religious basis, but relationships between castes were hierarchically determined and tended to reflect socioeconomic units or occupations.

As historically constructed, there were four main components of the hierarchy. At the top of the societal body were the priests or Brahmans; they taught the Vedas and performed certain religious functions (Fig. 8-4). Representing the arms of the body were the warriors; they fought the enemies of, and gave gifts to, the Brahmans. Tradesmen, bankers, and gentlemen farmers constituted the body's trunk, producing wealth for the Brahmans. Those who toiled with their hands made up the feet.

However, unlike the members of the body, there were those who were considered to be outside. These people were "impure," and, thus, were the *untouchables*. They were outcastes (outcasts) and prohibited from participating in any of the Hindu rituals.

When India became independent in 1948, the caste system was abolished, but after some three thousand years of practice, socioeconomic differentiation of the population based on caste lines has been slow to disappear.

HINDUISM AND THE LANDSCAPE

Throughout Hindu Asia, the gods are never far from humans, with the result that Hinduism permeates all facets of life. Moreover, the natural features of the landscape, such as trees, hills, mountains, and rivers, all possess a spiritual quality. Hinduism imposes no conscious design on the landscape, but Hindu temples articulate a larger and symbolic view of nature and of the universe (Michell, 1977). Hindu temples have incorporated elements from Buddhism so that the uniquely Hindu element is often concealed. The great temple, however, tends to represent a Hindu vision of the world in miniature. It is in and through the temple with its often exaggerated and highly ornamented images that the divine component in life is made evident to, and approachable by, humans.

Hinduism, thus, has a strong link with nature. The great Hindu festivals, for example, suggest major episodes in the Indian biologic or seasonal calendar. The festival at the time of Rathajatra is especially colorful as it celebrates the transition from the droughty season to the rainy season when vegetation turns green. It symbolizes the eternal rhythm of nature—birth, decay, and rebirth. Hinduism is also organized around important centers of pilgrimage, such as Puri on the east coast of India, which annually draws large crowds of people to the festival of Rathajatra.

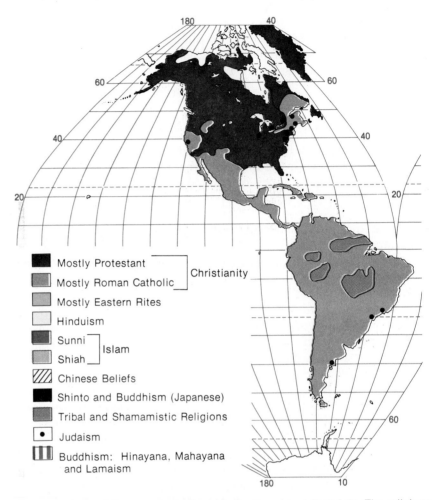

Figure 8–1

The present distribution of the main religions of the world is due to many of the great events of the past.

With the exception of Buddhism, the religions of East Asia have had significance primarily in the countries of origin. Buddhism, emerging in India, was dif-fused through Southeast and East Asia. The religions of Southwest Asia, Judaism, Christianity, and Islam have also spread far beyond their hearths. Islam was carried by armies and traders to Africa and Spain in the west and to the islands of Southeast Asia in the east.

An ancient Hindu belief about the natural world that has survived the centuries is associated with dietary habits and the veneration of the cow (Box 8–1). The cows of India are sacred; most Hindus will not eat the flesh of cattle, and the government has been forced to impose a ban on cow slaughter. Hence, the animals wander at will, even on busy urban streets. In 1972, India had 237 million cattle, including 58 million buffaloes. If present trends continue, India will have by the end of the century about 400 million cattle, which will increasingly strain the country's limited resources.

For Hindus, no river is holier than the Ganges, and a dip in it washes away all sins. Benares, on the Ganges, is one of the most sa-

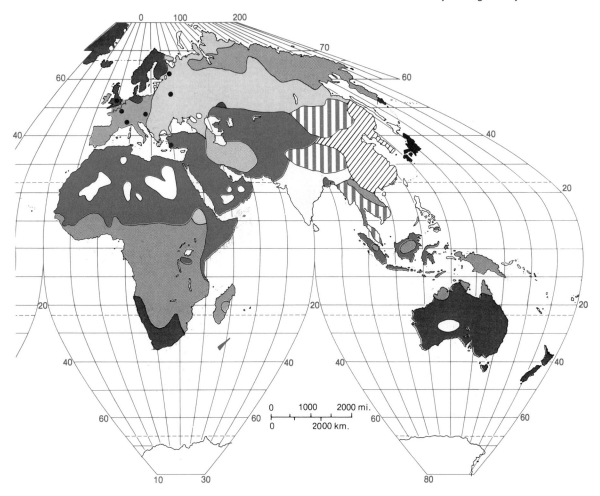

Judaism, which arose in the Middle East, was dispersed to the surrounding lands when Jews were forced into exile. Christianity, spreading from the Middle East across the Mediterranean and Black seas to Europe (and Russia) was carried subsequently by emigrants to the New World of the Americas, southern Africa, Oceania, and Siberia.

cred of Hindu cities. Death in the city, it is believed, takes one to heaven.

Jainism

The term *Jainism* derives from *Jina,* which means conqueror and pertains to those persons who have achieved spiritual liberation or enlightenment.

Jainism arose in India in the sixth century B.C. in protest against traditional Vedic rituals and caste. Jainists believe that there were 24 founders, or *tirthankaras.* Little is known of early doctrines, but the concept of *ahimsa,* or protection of all living creatures, remains at the

Figure 8-2

Different cultures have produced different conceptions of the earth. In one Hindu conception, the earth took the form of a stupa, pyramidal in shape, which was held up by elephants, whose movements were the causes of earthquakes. The elephants stood on a huge turtle, believed to be an incarnation of the god Vishnu; the turtle, in turn, was entirely surrounded by a cobra, which symbolized water. Greek and Hebrew conceptions of the earth also gave a prominent place to water.

Source: From Arthur Beiser and the Editors of Time-Life Books, *The Earth* (Life Nature Library, 1970).

Figure 8-3

The Hindu god Shiva, the most important of the incarnations of Vishnu, typifies both destruction and reproduction. He resides on Mount Kailas, the northern peak of the Himalayas, and, as god of regeneration and of justice, he is armed and performing the cosmic dance, a dance that ends in the destruction of the universe.

Courtesy Eugene Fuller Memorial Collection, Seattle Art Museum.

core of modern belief. Its expression is nonviolence and equality.

Like Hinduism from which it sprang, Jainism has its religious festivals, fasting periods, pilgrimages, and shrines, the latter erected at sites marking the principal events in the lives of the 24 founders. Among Jainists, the caste system, although not totally ignored, was never as clearly marked as in Hinduism. Certainly, it was never adhered to by Jainist monks in monastic life.

Sikhism

Sikhism, a relatively new religion in India, dating to the fifteenth and sixteenth centuries A.D., began essentially as a bridge between Hinduism and Islam. Its founder, Guru Nanak (1469–1539) preached against fanaticism and intolerance as well as against the caste system and reliance on ritual. The "one" god in whom the Sikhs believe is the abstract principle of truth.

The murder of several succeeding gurus by

PRIESTS
AND
LEARNED MEN

SOLDIERS
AND RULERS

MERCHANTS
AND
FARMERS

LABORERS
AND CRAFTSMEN

the Moghul emperor of India fostered a history of bloody hatred between Sikhs and Muslims. As a result, the tenth and last guru, Gobind Singh (1666–1708), succeeded in transforming the Sikhs into the best fighting force in the subcontinent, a development that subsequently served the British well both in India and in campaigns elsewhere. Basically, Sikhism seems closer to Islam than Hinduism, but over the centuries, it has tended to incorporate many Hindu rites and practices, including an acceptance of the caste system and the taboo against eating beef. When South Asia was partitioned into India and Pakistan in 1947, the Sikhs elected to remain in India, where they later (1966) were given a federal state of their own, the Punjab, within the Indian Union.

In the great Sikh center at Amritsar stands the Golden Temple, a structure noted for its simplicity and beauty and a tribute to Sikh organization and application. There are about 10.5 million Sikhs in India, but pilgrims of many faiths find their way to the Golden Temple.

Buddhism

Origins and Early Diffusion

It was at Buddh Gaya in northeastern India that Siddhārtha Gautama (c. 563–c. 483 B.C.), the Buddha, was born. Legend reports that in search of enlightenment, he resolved to sit in meditation under a Bodhi tree (*Fiscus religiosa*)

Figure 8–4

The earliest name for caste was *varna,* meaning color, and skin coloration may have been a factor in the evolution of the caste system. Originally the upper three strata of Hindu society were light skinned, the lowest stratum, dark. Each caste had its own *dharma* (or religion of the caste), which, in effect, contained the obligation to discharge the responsibilities of the caste. Thus, the lowest castes were bound there for eternity with no escape possible. Not even death offered hope of salvation because the Hindu belief in reincarnation meant rebirth at the same status or a worse status.

until he experienced "awakening." When this occurred, he became a Buddha, an enlightened one. Buddh Gaya, in modern Bihar state, remains one of the holiest of Buddhist sites.

Buddhism, the religion that grew out of the teachings of Gautama Buddha, remains essentially a religion of detachment or nonactivity. Striving for a freedom from all worldly cares, Buddhism urges an acceptance of the inevitability of cause and effect and the recognition that nothing is permanent (even the Buddha must die!).

Unlike Hinduism, Buddhism became a great missionary religion. The Buddha himself sent out missionaries. However, no man deserves more credit for the early diffusion of Buddhism in India than Asoka, who became king of northern India about 275 B.C. (al Faruqi and Sopher, 1974). After a bloody campaign to conquer the Indian coast along the Bay of Bengal, he adopted Buddhism and dispatched missionaries to Syria, Egypt, North Africa, and Macedonia as well as throughout India. Although Buddhism profoundly affected Indian culture, it later lost ground and was absorbed by Hinduism. Still, in recent decades the number of Indian Buddhists has been increasing, owing mainly to conversion of persons of low status. Moreover, in tribute to the Indian origin of Buddhism, the modern Indian state has adopted as it symbol Asoka's lion, marking the place of Buddha's first teaching.

Buddhism reached Sri Lanka (Ceylon) in the third century B.C., from where it spread to Burma, Thailand, and Indochina. The landscape of Burma is also dotted with thousands of impressive pagodas and temples, notably at Mandalay and Pagan. Even though Buddhism reached the islands of Southeast Asia, Indonesia is almost entirely Muslim (except for the island of Bali, which remains Hindu) (Fig. 8–5).

BOX 8–1

The Indian Belief of Ahimsa

There is a traditional Indian prohibition against killing a living creature, known as *ahimsa,* but it is not practiced with uniform zeal. As Gary S. Dunbar (1970) points out, Jains and Buddhists practice *ahimsa* almost consistently, Hindus apply it somewhat selectively, Muslims are not bound by it, and animists and Christians scarcely heed it at all.

"Over the years" Dunbar notes, "the animals have learned who their friends are. They can sense not only the difference between an Indian and a European (the turban is an emblem of mutual toleration while the hat means trouble), but somehow they manage to detect doctrinal differences as well. Almost overlooked during the mass migrations in the Punjab after the partition of India and Pakistan in 1947 were the migrations of some animal species: *nilgai* [a large antelope] were seen crossing into India following their Hindu protectors, and wild pigs scurried into Pakistan for safekeeping" (pp. 24–25).

Ahimsa is based on respect for all life, including animal life, and it remains as one of the cardinal virtues of Indian humanity. Above all, it involves the protection and veneration of the cow. Not all Hindus, however, regard the eating of beef an abomination; nor are all Hindus strictly vegetarians.

BUDDHISM AND THE LANDSCAPE

The most distinct symbols of Buddhism in the landscape, in India as elsewhere, is to be found in the stupa, an architectural symbol of the imagined structure of the cosmos. Early stupas were little more than earthen burial mounds, but with the death of Buddha, they acquired a deeper religious significance when his ashes were distributed to stupas in the principal cities of India. It is a great hemispherical structure, built of stone and brick, crowned with a platform (Fig. 8–6). Other stupas are found throughout the Buddhist world.

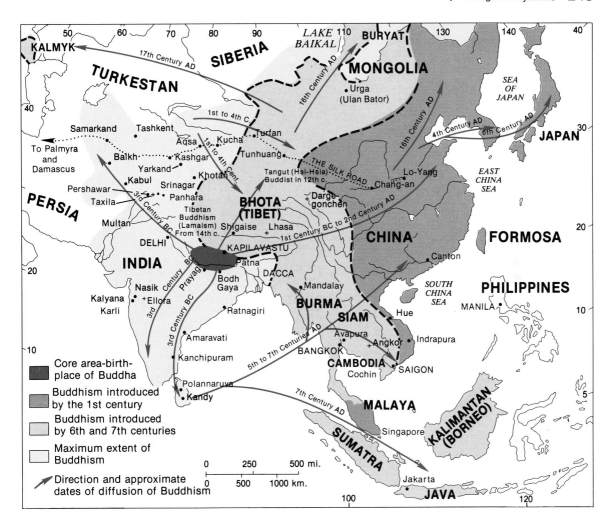

Figure 8–5

From its hearth in northeastern India, Buddhism spread southward in the third century B.C. to Ceylon (Sri Lanka). From Ceylon, Buddhism was diffused to Burma and to the other lands and islands of Southeast Asia. The more conservative form of Buddhism (Theravada or Hinayana) tended to predominate, although the Khmer temples in Cambodia reflect a Mahayana influence. On the other hand, the Mahayana form predominated in East Asia. Buddhism may have reached China as early as the second century B.C., but there is no conclusive evidence to prove it. Certainly, by the first century A.D., Buddhism existed on Chinese soil. From the fourth to the sixth centuries, it spread to Korea and Japan. Buddhist missionaries also carried the doctrine into Central Asia (Turkestan), where it remained influential from the first to the eighth centuries. Tibet became Buddhist in the seventh century, from there Buddhism reached Mongolia.

Figure 8–6

Sanchi is a village about 23 miles northeast of the city of Bhopal in central India. Its stupas (or burial mounds) date back to the reign of Emperor Asoka in the third century B.C. The Great Stupa at Sanchi is probably the finest of its type. Not only does its structure have cosmic meaning, but also it suggests the power of humankind through the symbols thereby created.

Source: Louis-Frederic/Rapho/Photo Researchers, Inc.

The Buddhist notion of the relationship of humankind to the universe is represented diagrammatically by the *mandala,* which has constituted a blueprint for religious architecture. This magical diagram shows Buddha at the very center of the cosmos, surrounded by four mythical Buddhas seated at the four cardinal points of the compass. To reflect this concept, stupas frequently had gates on their four sides—at the north, south, east, and west. The stupa of Borobudur on the island of Java is probably the finest of this type in the Buddhist world.

REGIONAL VARIATIONS IN BUDDHISM

In its long history, Buddhism, like Christianity, underwent many changes, assumed diverse forms, and generated many philosophies. The emergence of two distinct schools, however, brought major differences in religious expression.

Southeast Asia
Theravada Buddhism, also known as *Hinayana Buddhism,* is the more conservative of the two schools, its teachings being closer to those of the Buddha. Found today across Southeast Asia, Hinayana Buddhism places a strong emphasis on monasticism as the route to salvation.

East Asia
Mahayana Buddhism, as early as the fifth century A.D., also spread through Southeast Asia and Indonesia, making converts in Cambodia and Vietnam. Many of the famous Khmer temples in Cambodia, especially at Angkor, were built by Hindus and Mahayana Buddhists.

Figure 8–7

The stone statue of Buddha on Mount Sogri in South Korea is the tallest statue of Buddha in the world. It was constructed between 1939 and 1963 on a temple site that was first developed in A.D. 533 shortly after Buddhist scriptures were brought to Korea from India.

Picture Credit: W. A. Douglas Jackson, 1973.

However, Mahayana Buddhism won its greatest number of converts in China, Korea, and Tibet. It tends to focus on mythology, devotional worship, and metaphysics.

Far Eastern Hearths

East Asia represents an entirely different world from South Asia and, since earliest times, its philosophic or religious systems have taken another course. India is concerned with its gods, metaphysics, and caste. China has experienced little of this, and this has been true to some extent also of Japan. Certainly Taoism, Confucianism, and Shintō have had nothing of the content of Hinduism. The early Chinese, in fact, were profoundly skeptical of religions. Even so, when Buddhism penetrated the Far East, it found ready acceptance, especially in Japan. In China, like so much of the foreign influence that reached that country, Buddhism was ultimately engulfed by traditional Chinese beliefs. Indeed, this characteristic of Chinese culture inhibited the entrenchment of Communist ideology in China after the 1949 revolution.

By the first century A.D., Buddhism became widely known in China and was promoted in northern China by its rulers. Chinese architects began to translate the Indian stupa form into the pagodas that were to dot the Chinese landscape. In the south, it was the educated classes who were drawn to Buddhism when they discovered a deep affinity between Buddhism and Taoism.

By the ninth century, Buddhism was firmly established throughout China. However, persecution followed in the tenth century and the monasteries and temples were destroyed. Buddhism did not disappear from China however; it fused with native cults.

From the fourth to the sixth centuries A.D., Buddhism spread from China to Korea (Fig. 8–7) and to Japan, where it soon merged with Shintō. One of the most impressive settings in Japan is Nara, the old capital (A.D. 710–793), with its many Buddhist temples and sculptures (Fig. 8–8).

One of the many different schools and types of Buddhism that developed in the Far East was Ch'an, which later became Zen in Japan. It has survived to the present largely because it ceased to be a foreign, Indian doctrine, and became Chinese and subsequently Japanese. Authoritarian, demanding discipline and training;

delighting in the moment, but seeking a detachment from the world; fostering a keen aesthetic sense—these are some of the attributes of Zen that have attracted many followers—even in the Western world.

Tibet and Mongolia

Tibetan Buddhism, found also in Mongolia and among the Kalmyks near the mouth of the Volga, does not fit strictly into either of the above categories. Buddhism first reached Tibet in the seventh century A.D.; there a fusion with the indigenous Bon cult, a form of *shamanism*, took place. The cult abounded in demon worship, sorcery, magic, and the rite of human sacrifice. Buddhism absorbed the temples and

Figure 8–8

The Great Image of Buddha, the largest bronze image of Buddha in the world, is seated in the Daibutsuden, the largest wooden structure in the world, in the Tōdai-ji Temple, Nara, Japan. The temple dates to the eighth century A.D., although the Daibutsuden has been de-

stroyed by fire and rebuilt many times. The present structure dates to 1709. The figure of Buddha is 15-meters (49.2 feet) high, with one ear measuring 2.7 meters (8.8 feet).

Source: W. A. Douglas Jackson, 1977.

priests, but the more sinister elements disappeared from the religion.

Tibetan Buddhism is unique in its hierarchy of monks *and* its belief in the transmigration of souls. At the top of the hierarchy sits the Dalai Lama, a reincarnation of the preceding Dalai Lama, who was enthroned in the Potala in Lhasa. In the seventeenth century another office, that of the Panchen Lama, was established and theoretically it has possessed more power than that of the Dalai Lama. In the political events occurring after 1950, the Panchen Lama secured the support of the Chinese Communists and, when the latter took over Tibet, the Dalai Lama fled to India, where he resides today. He remains, however, spiritual leader of Tibet's estimated 6 million Buddhists.

Late in the sixteenth century, Tibetan Buddhism spread into Mongolia, although Buddhism from China had reached the Mongols at an earlier date. However, in Communist Mongolia today, the temples are closed and the prayer wheels are silent (Fig. 8–9). This may also be true of Tibet, which has been fully incorporated into the Chinese People's Republic.

Taoism

ORIGINS AND AFFINITY WITH NATURE BELIEFS

Taoism was part of the early folk faith of the Chinese; it represents an accretion of ideas dating to the sixth century B.C. Its name originates with the *doctrine of the tao* set forth by Lao-tzu (c. 604–c. 531 B.C.). The word *tao* defies exact definition, although it has commonly been translated as the way. Lao-tzu's teachings emphasized a return to nature and, associated with that, a need for spontaneity, humility, yielding, gentleness, and emptiness.

Figure 8–9

The Gandan Monastery, Ulan Bator, Mongolian People's Republic, was an outpost of Tibetan Buddhism. For the most part, the monasteries of Mongolia are closed, and the prayer wheels are silent, except when visitors are shown the site.

Source: W. A. Douglas Jackson, 1959.

In stressing the unity of nature, Taoist philosophers also made it clear that they considered nature to be independent of human standards (Needham, 1969). This relativism required that humankind refrain from making ethical judgments about nature. To the Taoists, man was *not* the measure of all things, as the following parable so aptly demonstrates:

> If a man sleep in a damp place, he gets lumbago and may die. But what about an eel? And living up a tree is frightening and tiring to the nerves. But what about monkeys? What habitat can be said to be "absolutely right"? Then men eat flesh, deer eat grass, centipedes enjoy small worms, owls and crows delight in mice. Whose is the "right" taste, "absolutely"? Monkeys mate with apes, bucks with does, eels consort with fishes, while men admire great beauties such as Mao Chhiang and Li Chi. Yet at the sight of these women the fish plunged deep into the water, birds flew from them aloft, and deer sped away. Who shall say what is the "right" standard of beauty? In my opinion, the doctrines of benevolence and righteousness and the paths of right and wrong are inextricably confused. How could I discriminate among them? (quoted in Needham, 1969, p. 49).

Because Taoism lacked a specific doctrine, it readily absorbed many popular beliefs and practices, and later it afforded a fertile ground for the absorption of Buddhist ideas.

Confucian Ethics

ORIGINS

K'ung Fu-tzu or Confucius (551/552–479 B.C.) was the greatest of Chinese philosophers and educators. Unlike those of the Taoist philosophers, which combine philosophy and religion, Confucius's teachings were largely devoid of the spiritual or mystical element. He was concerned rather with the problems of this world and human behavior. Desirous of order and stability, Confucius seems to have believed that the true purpose of government—in contrast to the political conditions in China at the time—was to ensure the welfare and happiness of its citizens. The Taoists retreated into a world of relativism, but the Confucianists believed that

every human was potentially capable of determining what is good and acting on it. Theirs was essentially a human-centered world.

IMPACT ON THE LANDSCAPE

Ancient China—within which both Taoism and Confucianism had roots—venerated the earth as the expression of the great forces of creation. This is especially evident in the design and layout of ancient cities, which symbolized in miniature the known world. Because the earth was believed to be square, the cities, in turn, were square. This was true of all the important imperial capitals in Chinese history, except for Nanking (Nanjing) and Hanchow (Hangzhou). To some extent this image was repeated in provincial capitals and other major cities. The cities as well as the dwellings within them were oriented exactly to the cardinal directions so that gates and windows might receive the earth's "magic currents." It is not surprising, therefore, that it was the Chinese who invented the compass.

Shintō

ORIGINS

Early Japanese culture borrowed heavily from China, but *Shintō* was a native phenomenon. The term Shintō was coined in the sixth century A.D. and applied to native beliefs to distinguish them from Buddhism, which was introduced from China. Early Shintō was probably not even a religion but just a set of intuitive feelings about the world. With the adoption of Chinese writing, Shintō myths and lore were recorded in two books, the *Kojiki* (records of ancient matters) and the *Nihongi* (chronicles of Japan), which became the chief documents of the religion. Shintō can be translated as the way of the gods, and its central concern is with "pollution" and "purification."

Prior to World War II, Shintō became the basis of a state cult associated with emperor worship, inspiring fanatical loyalty and devotion among the Japanese military. A number of shrines were administered by the state and designated as places for worship for all the people irrespective of religious faith. After the war, this form of state Shintō was abolished and the administration of these shrines was separated from the state. At present Shintō remains alive in Japan, although not especially robust.

IMPACT ON THE LANDSCAPE

A Shintō shrine, a marvel of simplicity in a small compound, may be detected by the gate, known as a *torii,* which is set at the entrance (Fig. 8–10). These shrines have drawn heavily on Buddhism, often combining statues of Buddha with traditional Japanese symbolism. If any simple division between Buddhism and Shintō

may be made, it is that Shintō has given its attention to life on earth, whereas Buddhism is concerned with life after death. Marriage ceremonies, the birth of children, and their years of childhood growth are celebrated at Shintō shrines (Fig. 8–11). A Shintō priest, too, has the duty of blessing the site for a new dwelling. Buddhism, on the other hand, plays a role in the funeral service.

In ancient Japan, reflecting the early influence of Chinese culture and art forms, urban space and temple grounds were organized to create a microcosmic image of a larger view of the world. This was especially true of Kyoto—named Heian-kyō, the Capital of Peace, when it was founded in A.D. 794—which followed the same general plan and mathematical exactness

Figure 8–10

The Itsukushima or Miyajima shrine is an ancient Shintō shrine near Hiroshima, Japan. Noted for its beautiful setting, the shrine is situated on an island and can be reached by ferry from Hiroshima. Its *torii,* made of camphor wood, rises out of the sea about 500 feet from the shore. As is characteristic of many Shintō shrines, this one contains several statues of Buddha.

Source: Courtesy of George Kakiuchi, 1975.

Figure 8–11

In Shintō, worship consists of obeisances, offerings, and prayers. Obeisance takes the form of a humble bow; the offerings presented before the altar are primarily food and drink; and the presentation of offerings is usually accompanied by prayers. Throughout the Japanese countryside are found small wayside shrines that the people use in the practice of their religion.

Source: Courtesy of George Kakuichi, 1975.

as Ch'ang-an, the capital of T'ang China from A.D. 618 to 907 (Chang, 1970). The evil influences believed to come from the northeast were diverted by the Kamo River and rendered ineffective by the placing of a temple on Mount Hiei, precisely to the northeast. The imperial palace was located at the northern end of the city, with a broad avenue leading from the palace gardens to the southern gateway of the city. This great central avenue divided the rectangular plan into two equal parts. A similar design was applied in the older city of Nara, although

little remains today to identify the original outline.

Southwest Asian Hearths

Judaism

ORIGINS

Judaism is so unlike the religions of South and East Asia that its origins among a lowly group of Semitic seminomads over four thousand years ago still evokes profound amazement. Its truly novel and distinctive concept of YHVH (Yahveh, Yehovah, or God) has exerted a decisive influence on Western thought and culture ever since (Arberry, 1969).

The Old Testament, recorded over a period of a thousand years, is the central document of Judaism around which its liturgy is developed. What is unusual about the book is that it presents a totally new concept of God in the world: it is entirely monotheistic. Moreover, it affords a revolutionary new concept of humans: man is created in the image of a God who transcends nature; thus, man is raised out of nature but endowed with a supranatural dignity. Unconcerned with God before the Creation, the Old Testament portrays the notion of a God working through history, where a Chosen People, the Jews, in a Promised Land, serve as the chief vehicle of that history (Ben-Gurion, 1966). Chief concerns of the Old Testament are ethical morality, righteousness, and social justice.

MAJOR STAGES IN THE
EVOLUTION OF JUDAISM

Although tracing origins back to Abraham, who came from Ur (now in Iraq), the tribes of Israel came together with the Exodus from Egyptian exile over three thousand years ago. Following a period in Sinai, when the distinctive features of their religion took shape, the Israelites burst into Canaan through Jericho and subsequently formed a kingdom about 1020 B.C., its most colorful leader being David. The first temple around which religious life was organized was built by King Solomon on a hill in Jerusalem. The kingdom subsequently divided into two parts: Israel, with its capital at Samaria, and Judah, with its capital at Jerusalem, in the south.

In the eighth century B.C., Assyria advanced on Israel and Samaria fell. Judah survived until 587 B.C. when King Nebuchadnezzar of Babylonia captured Jerusalem, destroyed the Temple, and carried its people back to Babylon. Thereafter, the Jews lived in exile until the emergence of a conquering Persian empire made it possible for them to return to Jerusalem.

Jewish religious life thereafter centered on a rebuilt Temple (538–516 B.C.) and with the texts and writing known as the Torah. Exile had demonstrated how deeply rooted and widespread the Jewish faith had become. Exile, moreover, had also scattered the Jewish population, and Jews continued to live outside the homeland in what came to be called the *Diaspora*. A significant number of Jews remained in Babylon, but in time, Egypt came to hold the largest Jewish population outside Judah. Moreover, under the influence of other cultural traditions, notably Greek (Hellenic), Judaism took on new attributes. Jewish identity, which had once been associated with territory, was modified as Jews spread throughout the Mediterranean basin. By the time of Roman rule, there may have been close to 3 million Jews in the world, with large colonies in Asia Minor, Syria, Babylonia, and Egypt. Some 50,000 Jews lived in Rome (Fig. 8–12).

The dispersal of Jews led to conversions of non-Jews to Judaism, a phenomenon that lasted for several centuries. The destruction of Jerusalem and the Temple (which had been rebuilt in the first century B.C. by King Herod the Great) by the Romans in A.D. 70, following a succession of Jewish revolts and wars, dealt the Jewish community there a severe blow. The subsequent adoption of Christianity as the official religion of the Roman Empire and the restrictions imposed on Jewish worship, forced Judaism to withdraw into itself. The persecution that accompanied the Jews from Palestine to England over the next fifteen hundred years or more required that they simply stand fast in their traditions and laws. Their subsequent contribution to the intellectual life of Western Europe was substantial, and in the *ghettos* and villages of Eastern Europe, a rich folk culture took shape—colorfully portrayed in the musical comedy *Fiddler on the Roof*. However, a yearning for Jerusalem accompanied most Jews wherever they settled and lived, even though their lives came to be deeply rooted in their new environment.

JUDAISM TODAY

The Holocaust eliminated Judaism as a European religion. Now, the three major centers of Judaism's distribution include the United States (some 6 million), the Soviet Union (about 3 million), and Israel (2.5 million). Although Jews constitute only a relatively small portion of the population of the United States, their role in the American community is substantial. American political leaders are mindful of their Jewish constituents when forced to make decisions concerning the State of Israel.

A major problem facing Jews everywhere is associated with the preservation of identity. In the United States, the decline of sectarianism has tended to reduce the religious content of that identity, although Orthodox Jewish communities survive in most cities. In the Soviet Union, the government has not only banned the teaching of Judaism and Jewish culture to the young, but also has sought to wipe out any Zionist aspirations or hopes for emigration. In Israel, a secular nationalism has taken root that remains in conflict with the traditional religious community, which is strongly supported (in 1983) by the Israeli government.

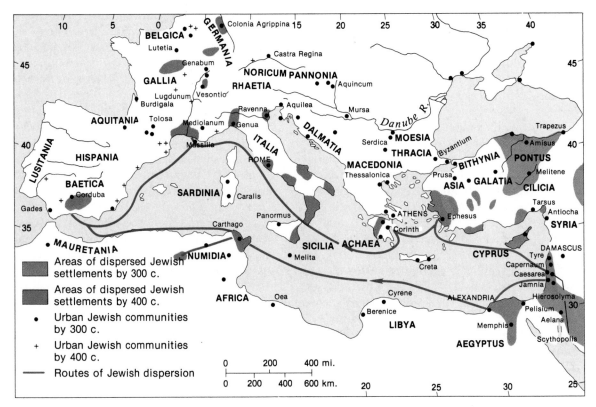

Figure 8–12

Even before the Babylonian captivity in the sixth century B.C., Jews were widely scattered throughout the Middle East from India to Ethiopia. In the following centuries, the number of Jews in the Diaspora increased as they came increasingly under Greek influence. Alexandria, the port city of Egypt, and Antioch in Syria became major centers of Jewish concentration. During the Roman period, and especially after the destruction of Jerusalem and the Temple in A.D. 70, the Jewish communities living beyond Palestine grew substantially in numbers and by the fourth century A.D. may have totaled anywhere from 3 to 6 million. Jews played a prominent role in the early trading history of Arabia and Central Asia, forming the religion of the elite in the Khazar Empire in southern Russia in the tenth century. It has been suggested that the Jews who settled in eastern Europe were descendants of the Khazars, but this theory is not widely accepted.

Christianity

ORIGINS AND DIFFUSION

The cultural hearth of Christianity was Palestine under the Romans and its religious setting was Judaism (Stone, 1973). Its origins, like those of most religions, were humble and unpromising. However, at a very early stage in its development, from a Jewish sect to a religion claiming *universality,* it came in contact with Greek or *Hellenistic thought,* which was to exercise a profound influence on its character and content. The Mediterranean world at that time was dominated by Rome, but the language of learning was Greek. Christianity represents a fusion of many ideas and concepts, seemingly contradictory, and for this reason scholars usually describe it as *syncretic.*

Traditional Jewish hope had been nationalistic in character. Jews looked for a restoration of the ancient kingdom of David under a Davidic king, the Messiah. Jesus, the central figure of the new faith, offered, on the contrary, the promise of eternal life in the kingdom of heaven, God's kingdom, which was at hand. The great majority of the Jews refused to accept this interpretation of the Messiah. Jesus's disciples, maintaining that he had arisen from the dead, carefully preserved their traditions about him. Missionaries went out to Jewish communities in the cities at the eastern end of the Mediterranean. However, as the new faith spread, it underwent significant changes.

Instrumental in promoting a broadened interpretation of the faith was Paul, a Hellenized Jew and a Christian convert. His preaching took him to the marketplaces of many Graeco-Roman cities. Paul's letters to the Christian communities, the gospels detailing Jesus's life, and the written traditions of the Jerusalem community came to form much of the New Testament. The latter was added to the Old Testament to constitute the Christian Bible.

Christianity spread rapidly along the administrative and trade routes of the Roman Empire (al Faruqi and Sopher, 1974) (Fig. 8–13). In A.D. 313, Christianity was officially recognized in Rome as the religion of the empire, but divisions appeared that reflected basic differences between Latin and Greek traditions. These differences came to a head with the death of Emperor Constantine, who had established Constantinople as the capital of the Roman Empire in the East.

THE EAST-WEST DIVISION OF CHRISTIAN SPACE

By the fourth century, three major bishoprics emerged in the Christian world—Rome, Antioch, and Alexandria. To these were added Jerusalem and Constantinople. However, because the empire was balanced between two great cultures, Greek and Roman, the *Greek rite* tended to dominate in the East, whereas the *Latin rite* prevailed in the West. The Bishop of Rome, claiming preeminence through St. Peter, attempted to assume primacy over the entire church, but his claims were contested by the other bishops.

This cultural division in Christian earthspace came to a head finally in 1054 when four Eastern patriarchs severed their ties with Rome. The break became truly decisive in 1204 when the Fourth Crusade, in an attempt to impose the Latin rite, succeeded in capturing and looting Constantinople. Unlike the authority of the Bishop of Rome in the West, which was for the most part the only effective authority after the collapse of Roman civil administration, *Eastern (Orthodox) Christianity* never came together in a tightly knit organization. The Patriarch of Constantinople was recognized as spiritual leader in the East, but the other bishops remained autonomous (Box 8–2). Still, as Orthodox Christianity spread into Eastern Europe, it found itself competing with Roman Catholicism, which created diverse religious problems. When the Turks (who were Muslims) conquered Constantinople in 1453, many of the Orthodox churches in the Middle East lost their importance. As the rulers of the tiny principality of Muscovy in central Russia gained in stature and territory, they laid claim to the Orthodox heritage, their ecclesiastics proclaiming Moscow the *Third Rome*, after Rome and Constantinople.

Estimates place the number of Orthodox Christians in 1983 at anywhere from 150 to 250 million people; the disparity is the result of a lack of data on the number of Christians in the Soviet Union. Other large congregations of Orthodox believers are found in Romania (18 million); Greece (15 million); in other Balkan countries, such as Yugoslavia and Bulgaria (18 million); and in North America (6 million).

From earliest times there were other, smaller Christian groups in the East whose beliefs and practices kept them apart from either Catholicism or Orthodoxy. These include the Coptic

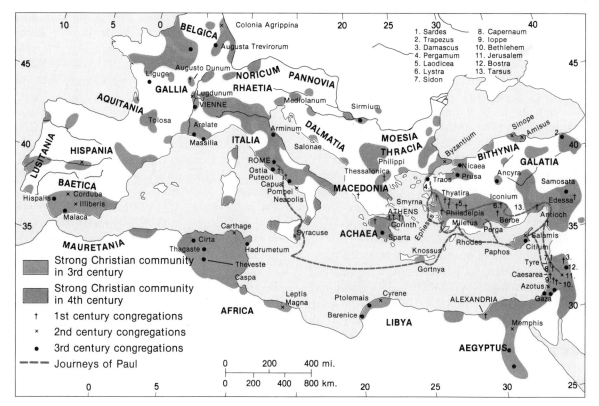

Figure 8–13

Christianity became the official religion of the empire of Constantine in A.D. 313, but long before this time, Christian communities had sprung up throughout the Mediterranean Basin. Around A.D. 112, Pliny, the governor of Bithynia on the south coast of the Black Sea, reported to the Roman Emperor Trajan that Christians were to be found in the region. Even before that time, Christians had reached Rome, where they were persecuted under the Emperor Nero (A.D. 64). Sometime around A.D. 170, there were Christians in Gaul and in North Africa. Christianity also penetrated Arabia via the trade routes.

Church of Egypt and Ethiopia, whose pope was banished in 1981 to a desert monastery by the Egyptian government, presumably for stirring up religious unrest between Muslims and Copts; the Armenian Church; and the Jacobite Church of Syria, Iraq, and India.

THE CRUSADES

Christianity spread into Europe throughout the Middle Ages and became so firmly established that European Christians—between 1096 and 1291—launched the Crusades against the Muslim Saracens, who had gained possession of much of the Holy Land. The successful creation there of Crusader states, predominantly French in origin, reestablished the church's physical ties with Jerusalem and the Levantine Christian population. Contact over the Mediterranean, too, pushed forward the frontiers of trade by creating a demand in Europe for oriental products, such as spices and perfumes. For

BOX 8-2

The Vatican and the Papacy

One of the most powerful religious institutions in the world is the *papacy,* collectively the system of central authority and government of the Roman Catholic Church. At its head is the Bishop of Rome, known to Roman Catholics as the Pope. The headquarters of the papacy is for the most part confined to Vatican City, a unique, independent state, that embraces less than a square mile of territory. Although the Vatican is situated on the right bank of the Tiber River in the heart of Rome, the capital of the Italian republic, the Vatican possesses greater influence in the world than does Italy itself. St. Peter's Square and Basilica, the papal palace, museums, administrative offices, a post office, and gardens, are among the Vatican's attractions.

Although the seat of authority of the largest branch of Christianity, Vatican City is all that is left of the once-extensive Papal States, which stretched across Italy from medieval to modern times and were ruled by the popes.

The Bishop of Rome first began to claim a preeminent position in the Mediterranean world for his office in the third century A.D. This claim was based on the tradition that St. Peter, one of the disciples closest to Jesus, had been designated as "the rock" upon which the church would be founded. He was crucified and buried in Rome, presumably on the site over which St. Peter's Basilica ultimately rose. The Bishop of Rome also claimed primacy from his association with the administrative center of the historic Roman Empire,

which was soon to crumble under the attacks of tribes originating in east-central Europe.

Other bishops of the church contested these claims. The most determined opposition came from the Bishop of Constantinople, the city created by Emperor Constantine as the capital of the Roman Empire in the East. In 1054, when the split between East and West became final, the Bishop of Rome quickly gained an ascendancy in the Western world. For centuries thereafter, the papacy exercised not only religious leadership throughout western Europe, but also temporal power, power superior to any other prince or king of the time.

Internal disputes weakened the papacy in the fourteenth and fifteenth centuries, which was followed by the rise of Protestantism and the formation of national churches in the sixteenth century. In 1870, when the Papal States were forcibly annexed to the new Kingdom of Italy, the papacy lost its temporal power, save its possession of the Vatican, confirmed in the Lateran Treaty in 1929 between the Italian government and the papacy. An enunciated claim to *infallibility* (without error) in matters of faith and morals in 1870 gave the pope an added religious aura.

Church unity has become a major objective of many Christians. The role of the papacy and, above all, its claim to infallibility remain, however, major obstacles to close association for non-Catholic Christians.

all of the waste associated with the Crusades, especially in human resources, these expeditions gave Europeans a greater awareness of the world outside. What is more, they succeeded in putting western Europeans back in touch with the ancient learning of Greece as preserved by the Muslims.

THE REFORMATION

The next important milestone in Christian history occurred in the sixteenth century. The means of communication in Europe were revolutionized in 1453, the year the Gutenberg Bible was printed in Latin. The diffusion of the works of Copernicus and other scientists soon followed. At about this time, princes and kings, with a new awareness of self, challenged the authority of the pope. But even more crucial was the challenge to church tradition found in the teachings of Martin Luther (1483–1546). The *Protestant Reformation* divided Western Europe into warring camps (Fig. 8–14). New interpretations of the Bible followed, to be quickly disseminated throughout the Protestant world. John Calvin (1509–1564) in Switzerland proclaimed the Bible the sole and final authority for Christians and the Calvinist movement spread to the Netherlands; to Scotland, where it was adapted by John Knox; and to England, where, in the Puritan movement, it led to the conflict with the king and the establishment of colonies in the New World (New England).

Catholicism reached the New World initially through the Spaniards, Portuguese, and French, but the religious diffusion from Great Britain and northwestern Europe was essentially Protestant in character.

Isolated in southern Africa, the Dutch Reformed Church developed an ethic of its own that contributed to the formation of a new culture, the Boer or Afrikaner.

CHRISTIAN MONUMENTS ON THE LANDSCAPE

The modern world contains many architectural monuments that date from past ages of great religious concern and strife. Rich in symbolic decoration and design, they tell us much of the Christian pursuit of salvation. They also reveal (at least until the thirteenth century) the scope of the Christians' rejection of nature's realm, even though it was often in wild places—such as the deserts of the Middle East, the inaccessible mountaintops from the Caucasus to the Alps, and the dark forests of Russia and northern Europe—where monks and penitents sought refuge for contemplation and meditation (Box 8–3).

BOX 8–3
The Rise and Role of Monasticism

Monasticism was an early feature of Christianity; in Western Europe, from the sixth to the tenth centuries it was dominated by the Benedictines. Their most famous monastery was in southern Italy at Monte Cassino, a hill that rises to over 1700 feet. Monte Cassino had been founded by Saint Benedict in 529 on the site of a temple of Apollo.

In time, other orders appeared in Europe, such as the Cluniacs (910), the Cistercians (1098), the Franciscans (1209), and the Dominicans (1215). The Cistercians, because of a commitment to arduous labor, often undertook the reclamation of marshes and wastelands. Through their enterprise, they came to play an important role in the economic life of medieval Europe, especially in the development of the English wool trade and in the expansion of crop cultivation in eastern Europe. The Dominicans played an active role in the leadership of the medieval church, whereas the Franciscans taught in the universities, keeping alive some of the learning of the past.

The Christian world in eastern Europe, despite the vicissitudes of politics and war, retained its Byzantine model. In market towns and villages, onion-shaped domes, often golden in color, rose over stone structures designed with narrow window slits that seemed to suggest physical separation from the world outside (Fig. 8–15). In western Europe, especially north of the Alps, a breakthrough in architectural style in the twelfth and thirteenth centuries led to the vaulted arch, which made possible the Gothic cathedrals that soar majestically upward (Jellicoe and Jellicoe, 1975).

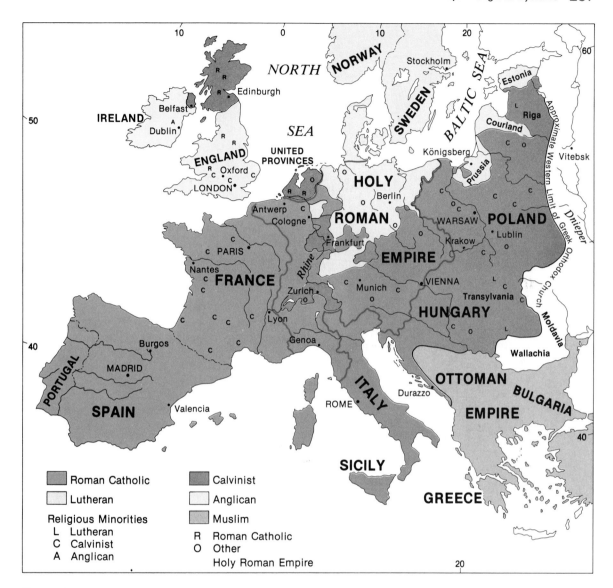

Figure 8–14

The split with Rome that occurred in England under Henry VIII together with the religious reformation led by Martin Luther on the continent created important divisions within medieval Europe. For the most part, northern Europe—including the Baltic countries, northern Germany, and part of Switzerland—joined England and Scotland in the Protestant camp. Mediterranean Europe, west of the jurisdiction of the Orthodox Church and the Ottoman Empire, remained Roman Catholic.

Figure 8–15

The Church of the Intercession (Pokrov Bogoroditsy), located by the Nerl River on the outskirts of the city of Vladimir, is a fine example of twelfth-century Orthodox or Byzantine architecture in Russia. The structure is now a museum.

Source: W. A. Douglas Jackson, 1976.

The American Religious Expression

Many factors have shaped the development of religion in the United States, not the least have been religious freedom and church-state separation. Within this context *sectarianism*—the splintering of denominations into sects and the formation of new sects—has flourished. The original founders of most of the Thirteen Colonies brought with them the religious forms of the Old World; in nine of the colonies, they established a single church (Carroll, 1979). Nineteenth-century immigrants, from Catholic and Lutheran Europe, added further diversity. However, the freedom that Americans experienced together with the leveling effect of the frontier, the divisions between North and South caused by the Civil War, and the expansion of industry and cities led to a burgeoning multiplicity of religious statements that was totally an American phenomenon.

Early in the eighteenth century, beginning in New England, Calvinist churchmen seeking escape from the formal exercise of religion began to stress the religion of the heart and the need for an immediate experience of salvation. As a result of this "awakening," a folk, or frontier, religion came into existence by the end of the century. An important feature of this folk religion was the camp meeting (Hill, 1980).

These camp meetings stimulated emotionalism, leading in turn to the protracted camp meeting, or revivalism. Although led initially by the older denominations, such as the Congregationalists (in New England), the Methodists, and the Baptists, the revivalists took a new form in serving the needs of people of lesser means. The older denominations became increasingly oriented toward the more securely established citizenry.

The Pentecostal Movement

During the nineteenth century, the earlier evangelical trend gave way to the *Pentecostal Movement*. The Pentecostals taught that all Christians should seek a postconversion religious experience called baptism with the Holy Spirit. The term Pentecostal was inspired by the belief that the seventh day after Easter was the day of the resurrection of Christ when the 12 disciples, meeting in Jerusalem, began to speak in languages unknown to them, a gift known as *glossalalia*.

The roots of the modern movement, however, date to January 1, 1901, when, in Topeka, Kansas, a Bible student experienced spirit baptism and began speaking in tongues. Most Pentecostals thereafter declared that glossalalia was the initial evidence of being spirit baptized, or "born again."

Topeka did not become the focus of the movement, but Pentecostalism spread throughout the country, accompanying migrants (relocation diffusion) to the larger cities, such as Los Angeles, Chicago, and St. Louis. Pentecostal services often began in tents, but as attendance grew, they moved to larger buildings, sometimes located in fashionable parts of the city. Aimee Semple McPherson (1890–1944) opened her Angelus Temple in Los Angeles in the 1920s. This foreshadowed dozens of temples, tabernacles, and revivalist centers that grew up in American cities. Some temples even launched ambitious overseas missionary programs.

Revivalism appealed to the immigrant, to the poor, and particularly to women, in part because it was the one religious movement in the United States in which women could fully participate. As black migration to the North increased, revivalist meetings proved popular, beginning in storefront churches.

Among the Pentecostal groups, one of the more important has been the Assemblies of God, founded in 1916–1917 in Hot Springs, Arkansas. Combining traditional theology with the new revivalist experience, the Assemblies of God became the fastest growing Pentecostal sect in the United States. By the 1960s and 1970s, Assemblies of God had lost the fervor of the earlier Pentecostalists, but missionary activity remained important. In 1981, it has been estimated that there were some 35 million adherents in the world, embracing a high percentage of the Protestant population of Catholic countries, for example, Italy, France, and the Latin American countries. Inroads have been made in Africa and among Christians in the Soviet Union. Between 1970 and 1980, membership in the United States increased by 1 million, thus reaching 1.6 million in 9562 churches.

MORMONISM

The United States also became the hearth of a variant of Christianity, namely the Church of Jesus Christ of Latter-Day Saints (also known as the Mormon Church), with a membership in 1981 of 2,706,000.

Founded in Palmyra, New York, in 1830, *Mormon* beliefs are based on the revelations of Joseph Smith (1805–1844). He claimed to have had visions and to have discovered golden tablets on which the Book of Mormon was recorded. This work is believed by Mormons to be a document from pre-Columbian America that records the relations of the inhabitants of pre-Columbian America with God. According to the Book of Mormon, America was settled by Hebrews who came to the Western Hemisphere in three migrations and whose descendants, the Indians, were darkened by their having fallen away from God.

In 1831, Smith led his small band of adherents to Kirtland, Ohio. From there, the Saints (as they were called) moved first to Independence, Missouri, then to Nauvoo, Illinois, on the Mississippi River. For a few years the community prospered and Zion (as the settlement was called) seemed well on its way to becoming a state within a state. Opposition developed in the region, however, in part because of the practice of polygamy. In 1844, a mob murdered Smith. In 1846–1847, under the leadership of Brigham Young (1801–1877), the greater part of the Saints left Nauvoo and migrated westward, coming to rest in the basin of the Great Salt Lake. There, through cooperation and community effort, the Mormons built their desert Zion.

In succeeding years, additional agricultural settlements were planted along the *Mormon Corridor* that leads southwestward toward California (Fig. 8–16). In 1849, the settlers came together to form the State of Deseret, but the U.S. Congress responded by creating the Utah Territory in 1850. A short period of tension and conflict ensued, although during the 1850s the territory continued to grow and prosper. By 1865, some one thousand miles of irrigation canals crossed the land. When admission to the Union occurred in 1896, Utah had been wrested

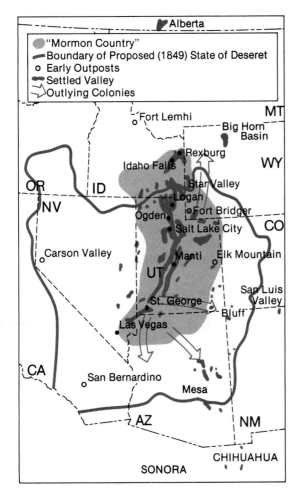

Figure 8–16

The Mormon community, established by Bringham Young in Utah in 1846, spread out from Salt Lake City to include a settlement along a Mormon Corridor that ran southwestward to California.

from the desert, its agricultural prosperity a testament to what the hard work and cooperation of a determined people can achieve.

AMERICAN RELIGIOUS PLURALISM

Protestantism long held a privileged position in the United States, but in the decades after World War II, that could no longer be considered true. Immigration from Catholic countries has eroded the Protestant majority which, in any case, is divided into liberal and conservative, or fundamentalist, denominations; in some instances, it is divided between North and South. About 60 percent of the U.S. population regards itself as Protestant, 27 percent as Roman Catholic. Persons of Jewish faith constitute about 2 percent of the population; all others, including Muslims, about 4 percent. Some 7 percent of Americans have no religious preference.

Christianity's Efforts at Universalism

Although Buddhism and Islam both have raised a claim to universal validity, no other world religion has succeeded in realizing this objective to the degree that Christianity has. Through overseas expansion of the European political and cultural systems as well as a vigorous missionary activity, Christianity became a truly global phenomenon. In the twentieth century, the missionary work of a number of American Protestant sects has been particularly impressive. The Mormon Church, too, has garnered members from beyond the boundaries of the United States, making significant inroads in Latin America.

But apart from conversion, the worldwide dominance of the Western work code has led to widespread acceptance of the Christian calendar, with its seven-day week and the work-free Sunday. Christian festivals, such as Christmas, are also observed in many lands where the prevailing beliefs, as in Japan and Taiwan, are non-Christian.

Islam

THE MEANING OF ISLAM

The word *Islam* has several different meanings. In one sense, it refers to the universal religion conveyed to humankind by a series of prophets—Abraham, Noah, Moses, Jesus, and Mohammed—each of whom carried a message from God. To Muslims, the last prophet, Mohammed, is the greatest and the book he brought, the Koran, completes and supersedes all previous revelations. In a wider sense, the word Islam denotes the whole rich civilization that grew up as a result of the diffusion of Islamic teachings (Arberry, 1969).

In the modern world, over 600 million persons share the heritage of Islam. Although the Arab peoples are predominantly Muslim, such diverse groups as the Turks, the Persians, the peoples of Afghanistan, Pakistan, Bangladesh, and Indonesia also, in the course of history, embraced the faith. About 10 percent of the total population of both India and China are Muslims. Some 35 million Muslims inhabit the Soviet Union, especially in the southern regions and along the Volga River. In recent years, there has been a growth of Islam among the black population of the United States, best exemplified in the conversion of the boxer, Cassius Clay, who became Muhammad Ali.

ORIGINS

When Mohammed was born about A.D. 570 in Mecca in Arabia, the Semitic Arab peoples had not yet entered history. Rather, they had lived on the periphery of the great civilizations of Greece, Rome, Persia, and Byzantium. Mecca, itself, was the focus of caravan routes that crossed the desert, and the religion of the people was associated with worship of a Black Stone, the Kaaba. Both Judaism and Christianity had penetrated the desert with the camel caravans and had made converts in the oasis towns (Lewis, 1976).

Mohammed, experiencing his "call" at the age of 40, made few inroads among the local Meccan merchants, who feared a loss of trade if their tradional religious base was destroyed. As a result, Mohammed "fled" to Medina to the north, in A.D. 622, in a move called the *hejira*. This event marks the beginning of the Muslim

calendar. In 630, he captured Mecca, incorporating into Islam the rituals of the Kaaba and the practice of pilgrimage.

When Mohammed died in 632 in Medina, his followers had overrun all of the Arabian peninsula, and one condition of the area's political submission was conversion to Islam.

The Koran is unlike the Bible. Its central theme is monotheistic, but this concept is not presented in the storylike manner that characterizes much of the Old and New Testaments. Because of the beauty of expression, the Koran is especially suited for reciting aloud. Islam has no priesthood or complicated theology. Possibly, for these reasons, it has appealed to many peoples, especially in Africa where it is winning converts even today. Apart from prayer and fasting, it requires every Muslim to make a pilgrimage, or *hajj*, at least once in a lifetime to the holy cities of Mecca and Medina (Fig. 8–17).

When the Jews in Medina failed to accept the new faith, Mohammed required that his followers pray in the direction of Mecca rather than Jerusalem as had been the custom; the Sabbath (Saturday) was replaced by Friday as the day of prayer; Ramadan, the month of fasting, was introduced to replace the Jewish holy day of Yom Kippur, the Day of Atonement; but the prohibition against eating pork and blood was retained (Box 8–4).

Because Jews and Christians were "people of the Book," Islam did not view them in the same way it did idolators. When the Muslims conquered an area, therefore, the choice between conversion or death was something that only pagan Arabs had to face. Women were given special protection by being placed in *purdah* (Fig. 8–18); slavery was preserved, although many of its features were less harsh than was later practiced in the American South. In the realm of literacy and artistic expression, Islamic scholars and designers made important contributions. For a period of time, in the early medieval period, Islamic scholars founded major centers of learning.

Figure 8–17

Muslims are enjoined to make a pilgrimage (hajj) to Mecca at least once in their lifetime. The most venerated spot to Muslims is the Kaaba, a cubelike structure in the midst of the courtyard of the Great Mosque (Haram al-Sharif, or noble sanctuary). It is the focus of Muslim devotion and the direction reference point that all believers must face during prayers. The shrine—by tradition built by Adam and rebuilt by Abraham and his second son, Ishmael—contains a sacred Black Stone. The Black Stone was venerated in pre-Islamic times; in Islam, the circling of it (seven times) forms an essential part of the ritual performed by the pilgrim.

The pilgrimage begins every year on the 7th and ends on the 10th day of the last month of the Muslim year. Before the pilgrims enter Mecca, they don white garments and refrain from cutting their hair or their nails or shaving until the ceremony ends. Up to 1 million persons a year enter Saudi Arabia for the purpose of visiting Mecca, the Holy City.

For Shiah Muslims or Shiites, Kerbala in Iraq constitutes a place of special importance to which the Shia make pilgrimages.

Source: Photo from Manley P. Hall, *An Encyclopedic Outline of Masonic, Hermetic, Quabbalistic and Rosicrucian Symbolical Philosophy* [San Francisco, 1928]. Courtesy Rare Book Collection, University of Washington.

EARLY TERRITORIAL EXPANSION

Following Mohammed's death, despite conflict over the succession, the Arabs were unified and inspired by a faith that gave them a sense of pride and mission. In rapid succession, they conquered Syria, Palestine, Iraq (in 637), Persia (637–644), and Egypt (640–642). Within 100 years Islam had been carried across North Africa (640–698), into Spain (711), and into south-ern France, where it met its first defeat (Battle of Poitiers, 732). It penetrated Anatolia, the Caucasus, and Central Asia (651–715), and it reached the Indus Valley via Persia and Afghanistan (661–715) (al Faruqi and Sopher, 1974) (Fig. 8–19).

The conflicts that arose after Mohammed's death led to the transfer of the seat of power, the *caliphate* (from the Arab word *khalīfah*, meaning deputy of Mohammed), from Medina

BOX 8–4

Ramadan and the Requirements of Islam

Islam is free of elaborate ritual. Adherence to the faith requires acknowledging the oneness of God and Mohammed as God's messenger. This is the first of the five pillars of the faith. The others are: prayers five times a day facing in the direction of Mecca; the observation of Ramadan, the ninth month in the Muslim calendar, as dictated by Mohammed in the Koran; annual almsgiving; and a pilgrimage to Mecca at least once in a lifetime.

Ramadan begins in late spring with the first sighting of the new moon; it continues until the next new moon is sighted. During that time, all Muslims over 18 years of age must abstain from food and drink from dawn until dusk. As with Christmas, Ramadan is supposed to be a time for good will. Gifts may be exchanged and money is given to the poor. Nowhere is Ramadan celebrated more intensely or strictly than in Saudi Arabia. Here, Ramadan requires the firing of cannons twice each day, once at sunset when fasting ends, and again at dawn when fasting begins.

cent are Shiites, and they are found in a majority in Iran (94 percent of the total Muslims), neighboring Iraq (60 percent), and Bahrain (55 percent).

The *Sunnis*, who represent the great majority of Muslims, predominate in the remaining Muslim countries of the Middle East, North Africa, and South Asia. They accept the historical order of the first four caliphs and their elected successors as the true and rightful line of authority. The Sunnite caliphate survived into the

Figure 8–18

Muslim women wear a burka, or chodor—a light-weight black covering—when going out in public. The burka is commonly seen on the streets of many modern cities in the Middle East as well as in the countryside.

Photo courtesy of Frank Koontz, 1976.

to Kufa in Iraq, to Damascus in Syria, and subsequently in A.D. 762 to Baghdad, the City of Peace, on the Tigris River. Baghdad became the seat of power of the Abbasid dynasty, but with the passage of time, the Islamic empire ceased to be Arab led, as leadership passed to Persians and Turks.

SECTARIANISM

The early dynastic struggles led to the emergence of the *Shiah* sect. The Shiites considered Ali, the husband of Mohammed's daughter Fatima, the rightful successor to the caliphate, believing that authority should remain in the family. Of the world's Muslims, about 14 per-

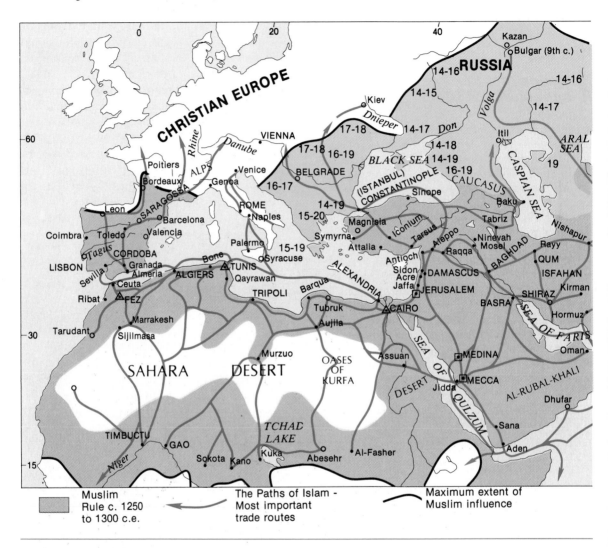

Muslim
Rule c. 1250
to 1300 c.e.

The Paths of Islam –
Most important
trade routes

Maximum extent of
Muslim influence

twentieth century under the Ottoman Turks when, in 1924 under Kemal Atatürk (1881–1938), the first president of the Republic of Turkey, it was abolished.

Although the caliphate no longer exists, the King of Saudi Arabia has the role of preserving and watching over the holy cities of Medina and Mecca and of facilitating the pilgrimage of the faithful once they reach his kingdom.

As the 1978–1979 revolutionary movement in Iran showed, Shiism in Iran is bound up with nationalism and a rejection of Western values.

Events demonstrated, too, that Shiite religious leaders, or *mullahs,* can command enormous prestige, because their religious judgments are given the status of Islamic law. In the Sunni faith, the sacred law of Islam was codified in the tenth century. The pronouncements of contemporary Sunni leaders, thus, lack the binding authority of the Shiite *mullahs.* Perhaps the greatest difference between the two groups is to be found in the emotionalism with which Shiite Muslims observe the death of Ali's son, Hussein, in A.D. 680 at the hands of the Omayyad

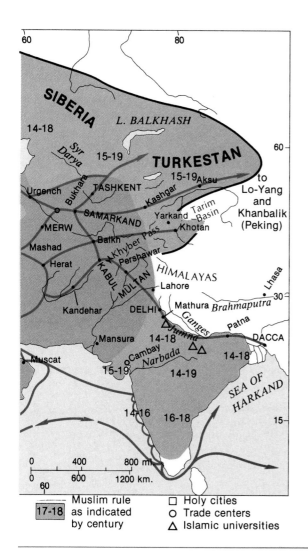

Figure 8–19

Mohammed died in A.D. 632, and within a very short time, Muslim Arab armies had overrun most of Arabia as well as all of Mesopotamia, Palestine, Syria, Persia, and Egypt. Within the next century, Islam had been carried along the North African coast. By 711, Spain was in Muslim hands and France had been penetrated, but the march was halted at Poitiers in 732. In the East, the Muslim faith had reached the Caucasus, Central Asia, Afghanistan, and northern India. With the exception of France and Spain, this vast territory remains today predominantly Muslim.

caliphate. This emotionalism was evident during the attack on the American Embassy in Teheran, Iran, in 1979.

Several other sects grew out of the Shiah movement, the most important being those of the *Druze* and the *Baha'i*. The Druze, found today in small communities in Israel, Lebanon, and Syria, disassociated themselves from traditional Islam. The Baha'i faith, which won a considerable number of converts in North America during the early part of the twentieth century, developed in Iran after 1850. Its

founder, Baha Allah, emphasized universalism and pacifism; his tomb is located in Haifa, Israel. The Baha'i faith has been banned in revolutionary Iran, and members of the sect have been persecuted and executed.

DIFFUSION OF ISLAMIC INFLUENCE

In the ninth century, with the expansion of trade and navigation, the diffusion of Islamic thought and culture reached its widest extent, well beyond the Dry World. Traders from the

Persian (or Arabian) Gulf reached the west coast of India, Ceylon, Malaya, and the islands of Southeast Asia. In Malaya and Indonesia, Islam replaced Hinduism and Buddhism in all but the island of Bali. Converts were made in the southern Philippines. In the mid-tenth century, Muslim ships reached Canton, where a considerable Muslim colony grew up. It is possible that the Muslims also reached Korea and Japan. A slave trade was developed with the east coast of Africa.

Muslim traders also penetrated overland and deep into Eurasia. Converts were made among the nomadic Turkic peoples of the steppe. There were Muslim troops in the Khazar Khanate (whose leaders were of the Jewish faith) at the mouth of the Volga, and a mission from Baghdad in the tenth century converted the Bolgars, who lived upstream near the modern Soviet city of Kazan. Muslim coins have been found in Scandinavia and even in Britain. In northwestern China, the Dungans, an ethnic Chinese group, remain Muslim to this day. Invading Mongols (the Golden Horde) established a Muslim state in central-southern Russia in the thirteenth century. A twelfth-century Muslim kingdom was established in India later (in the sixteenth century) under the Mongol-Turkic Timurids and became the Moghul Empire. In eastern Europe, Muslim Turks invaded the Balkans, conquered Constantinople in 1453 (Box 8–5), and subsequently pushed to the very gates of Vienna before being stopped in 1529. It was not until World War I that the native—predominantly Slavic—peoples of the Balkans succeeded in driving the Turks back toward Asia Minor, but Islam remains, especially in Albania and Yugoslavia.

IMPACT ON THE LANDSCAPE

The traditional center of Muslim religious life is the mosque, called *masjid* in Arabic, a place of gathering. Every city of importance was required to have a mosque. Although there was no universal mosque design, the interior was usually simple and unadorned. The concept of the mosque may have originated in Mohammed's house in Medina, which was believed to have been made of sun-dried bricks, with a large portico and courtyard. However, Islamic artists sought to provide relief from the dry grey-brown landscape of the world around them by coating mosques in turquoise or blue tiles, creating edifices of stunning beauty (Jellicoe and Jellicoe, 1975). The mausoleum of Tamerlane (Timur) at Samarkand in Central Asia is probably one of the most magnificent of its kind. The Taj Mahal in India is another well-known example of Muslim architecture (Fig. 8–21).

City delineation into quarters was another Islamic tradition, but this practice may have reflected kinship ties or occupational status more than any religious strictures. In early Muslim societies, ownership of land was the major source of wealth, although income gained from manufacturing and trade were also of great importance. Every town or city has its *suq,* or marketplace, and on the outskirts of oasis settlements, there were usually large *caravanserais,* large areas where animals were parked prior to a journey overland.

ISLAMIC LEARNING

During the first 150 years of the religion's existence, Islamic scholars laid the basis of Islam's cultural golden age. Through translation, the Muslims became the heirs of Greek learning, much of which was subsequently forgotten in the West until the Renaissance. In medicine, astronomy, and geography as well as the arts, the works of Islamic scholars were substantial. Muslim geographers and historians, in particular, became extensive travelers, roaming from Spain to India and beyond. Ibn-Fadlans's account of an official Abbasid mission to the Volga Bolgars in A.D. 921 provides valuable information on the Slavs and the Scandinavian Rus (a branch of which founded the Kievan Rus state). Indeed, it was in the tenth century that

BOX 8–5

Constantinople's Conversion from Christian to Muslim

The transformation after 1453 of Constantinople, the most Orthodox city in Christendom, into a Muslim city that was to serve as the capital of an expanding Turkish (Ottoman) Empire, was an event that clearly reveals the imprint of religion on the landscape. From A.D. 330 until its fall to Turkish armies, life in Constantinople was intricately interwoven with the Orthodox Church. Under its new rulers, Constantinople literally acquired a new landscape. As one writer notes (Lifchez, 1977), "A vast construction of domes and mina-

rets, marking the religious and charitable settings of the city, created a bold and sober image signifying important Muslim values translated into urban form" (p. 3). One of the most dramatic changes was the conversion of the massive sixth-century Cathedral of Santa Sophia (Hagia Sophia) into a mosque by the addition of four tall minarets. By the middle of the sixteenth century, Constantinople had become essentially a Muslim city (Fig. 8–20).

Figure 8–20

Hagia Sophia, originally an Orthodox cathedral, was first built in A.D. 532. It was converted to a mosque after the Ottoman conquest in 1453; the Christian mosaics were covered and the minarets added. It became a museum in 1938.

Source: W. A. Douglas Jackson, 1971.

Figure 8–21

The Taj Mahal, a mausoleum, is an excellent example of the beauty of Muslim architecture. It stands near Agra in India. The structure, situated in a beautifully landscaped garden, was built between 1631 and 1653 by Shah Jahan for himself and his favorite wife, Mumtaz Mahal. The octagonal building is entirely of white marble, with magnificent interior decorations.

Source: J. Allan Cush/Rapho/Photo Researchers, Inc.

Arabic geographic literature reached its zenith, including the works of Ibn-Haukal and Muqaddisi. The most brilliant of all Arab geographers, al-Idrisi, worked at the court of the Norman King of Sicily, Roger II (A.D. 1130–1154).

THE RESURGENCE OF ISLAM IN THE TWENTIETH CENTURY

The outward expression of renewed religious faith among the world's Muslims, particularly those of the Middle East, is due to many factors. One cause certainly may be found in Muslim reaction to the period of Turkish and European domination that lasted from the end of the eighteenth century up to modern times. Islamic pride and self-esteem have only begun to recover from this long period of what is seen as imperial control from outside.

The founding of Israel in 1948 tended to focus hostility—generally directed toward the U.S. and the European powers that supported the new state and Zionism whose goal is the recreation of the biblical kingdom. Rising nationalism, although causing regional divisions among Muslims, also received a powerful thrust as countries, like Iran, Iraq, Saudi Arabia, and the Persian (Arabian) Gulf states, sought to secure control over their oil resources.

The growth of wealth, especially that based on oil production, stimulated a rapid rural-urban migration and the expansion of cities. This was accompanied by the importation of Western technology and Western values, which undoubtedly triggered the strong reaction that was experienced in the Iranian Revolution and the toppling of the shah. Muslims everywhere want to share in the improved standard of living experienced in the Western world and which, in some countries, the new-found oil wealth has made possible. But the dilemma Muslim countries face is whether they can import Western technology and at the same time keep out the values that may accompany it. This problem lies at the core of the Islamic resurgence, which is essentially traditionalist. This concern is at the heart of the strong reaction of the Iranian Shiite Muslim's, but there has been a spillover into Sunni communities in the Persian (Arabian) Gulf area.

EPILOGUE

The religious experience, whatever its form or cultural content, can be seen for what it has been and remains—an experience closely associated with many facets of human life, thought, and activity. What is of interest to geographers, of course, is the extent to which religion has shaped thought patterns, expectations, symbols, and the like, that have contributed to the shaping of the human landscape in all its amazing and complex diversity.

The general lessening of sectarian and religious boundaries in the United States has tended to make us think that religion may no longer exercise the strong control throughout the world that it once did over the human mind. The landscape, wherever subjected to the processes of industrialization and urbanization, seems to be assuming a homogeneity in which the shopping mall and civic center count for more than the worship place. However, extensive travel reminds us, somewhat abruptly, that other cultures, especially in the nonindustrial world, continue to possess a strongly developed religious component. And, in some instances, it may be getting stronger, with consequences in the political and economic realm that could affect the lives of all. Moreover, even in the United States, the civic center may, too, on occasion be the focus of religious activities whenever a well-known evangelist comes to town. The attendance on such occasions suggests that even in the United States there may be a widespread attempt to reinforce the religious experience and enhance specific values that seem to be engulfed in a world of rapid scientific and technological change.

APPLICATION OF IDEAS

1. Religious values have played, and continue to play, an important role in shaping our world. This is a fact that is sometimes forgotten or neglected in Western industrialized societies, whose focus has been on material development. Clearly, in many parts of the world, religion still has a powerful influence on society.

2. Religion represents an attempt on the part of people to come to terms with the powerful forces that affect human life, but much prejudice and intolerance are also associated with religion because of the tendency for people to believe that theirs is the only true religion.

3. Religious values are evident in the landscape. In some instances, high places (or mountains), rivers, and cities are revered; in other instances, temples, synagogues, churches, and mosques have been set aside as sacred places. There has also been a tendency to mark time by holy days, or holidays.

4. The varieties of religious experience are substantial and profound. They reflect the life, history, and cultural development of a people. They frequently bear a relationship with the natural environment within which they developed, and, in turn, they have left their imprint on the world we know.

KEY WORDS AND PHRASES

animism
Baha'i
Buddhism
caliphate
caravanserais
caste
Diaspora
doctrine of the tao
Druze

Eastern (Orthodox)
    Christianity
fundamentalist
ghetto
glossalalia
Greek rite
hajj
hejira
Hellenistic thought

Hinayana Buddism
Hinduism
infallibility
Islam
Jainism
Latin rite
Mahayana Buddhism
mandala
Millet System
monasticism
monotheism
Mormon
Mormon Corridor
mullah
papacy
Pentecostal
    Movement
polytheism
Protestant
    Reformation
purdah
rite

Sanskrit
sectarianism
Shah
shamanism
Shiah
Shiite
Shintō
stupa
Sunni
supranatural
suq
syncretic
tao
Theravada Buddhism
Third Rome
torii
transmigration of
    souls
universality
untouchables
Upanishads
Vedas

QUESTIONS FOR FURTHER DISCUSSION

1. In what way does linear or progressive time differ from circular time? Give examples of expressions of these different concepts of time found in the landscape.

2. Name some ''sacred spaces'' (other than a church, synagogue, or mosque) that you are familiar with. In what way might the concept of sacred space have meaning for the organization of the human landscape in the twentieth century?

3. What do you know about the landscape and history of the Middle East that might suggest reasons for the origin of monotheism there? In what way do the monotheistic religions differ from the polytheistic religions that originated in other parts of Asia?

4. How widespread is the distribution of believers in Buddha today? Why was Buddhism largely absorbed by Hinduism, even though the former arose in India?

5. Japan traces its cultural roots to China. What then is the relationship of Shintō, a native Japanese religious phenomenon, and the religions imported from the mainland? What role does Buddhism play in contemporary life?

6. How widespread had Judaism become before the birth of Christ? How do you account for the diffusion of Jewish beliefs and practices?

7. Once established, Christianity spread rapidly throughout the Roman world, but how do you account for the endurance of the church during the difficult period when the empire itself was undergoing decline? What structures did the church adopt from the Roman experience?

8. Compare and contrast the divisions of Europe that occurred following the break between Orthodox and Catholic Christians and between Catholic Christians and Protestants. What were some of the cultural and socioeconomic factors associated spatially with these divisions?

9. In what way is Islam related to the other monotheistic religions of the Middle East? What was its effect on the peoples who occupied its hearth?

10. How far westward and northward did Islam penetrate before its withdrawal to its contemporary position? What remnants of the Islamic world remain in Europe?

REFERENCES AND ADDITIONAL READINGS

Arberry, A. J., ed. *Religion in the Middle East*. Cambridge: Cambridge University Press, 1969.

Arrington, Leonard J., and Bitton, Davis. *The Mormon Experience. A History of the Latter-Day Saints*. New York: Alfred A. Knopf, 1979.

Ben-Gurion, David. *The Jews in Their Land*. Garden City, N.Y.: Doubleday, 1966.

Carroll, Jackson W., et al. *Religion in America; 1950 to the Present*. New York: Harper & Row, 1979.

Chang, Sen-Dou. "Some Observations on the Morphology of Chinese Walled Cities." *Annals of the Association of American Geographers* 60 (1970): 63–91.

Deffontaines, Pierre. "The Place of Believing." *Landscape* 2 (1953): 22–38.

Dunbar, Gary S. "Ahimsa and Shikar: Conflicting Attitudes Toward Wildlife in India." *Landscape* 19 (1970): 24–27.

Eliade, Mircea. *The Sacred and the Profane. The Nature of Religion*. New York: Harcourt, Brace & World, 1959.

al Faruqi, Isma'il Ragi, and Sopher, David, eds. *Historical Atlas of the Religions of the World*. New York: Macmillan, 1974.

Fischer, Otto. "Landscape as Symbol." *Landscape* 4 (1955): 24–33.

Glacken, Clarence J. *Traces on the Rhodian Shore. Nature and Culture in Western Thought from Ancient Times to the End of the Eighteenth Century*. Berkeley and Los Angeles: University of California Press, 1967.

Hill, Samuel S., Jr. *The South and the North in American Religion*. Athens: University of Georgia Press, 1980.

Isaac, Erich. "Religion, Landscape and Space." *Landscape* 9 (1959–1960): 14–18.

———. "The Act and the Covenant: The Impact of Religion on the Landscape." *Landscape* 11 (1961–1962): 12–17.

———. "God's Acre." *Landscape* 14 (1964–1965): 28–32.

Jackson, J. B. "Reason and Religion in Newtonian America," pp. 153–163. In *The Interpretation of Ordinary Landscapes. Geographical Essays*. D. W. Meining, ed. New York: Oxford University Press, 1979.

Jackson, Richard H. "Religion and Landscape in the Mormon Cultural Region," pp. 100–127. In *Dimensions of Human Geography, Essays on Some Familiar and Neglected Themes*. Karl W.

Butzer, ed. Research Paper 186, Department of Geography, University of Chicago Press, 1978.

James, William. *The Varieties of Religious Experience.* New York: New American Library, 1958. (Mentor Books) (Originally published, 1902)

Jellicoe, Geoffrey, and Jellicoe, Susan. *The Landscape of Man. Shaping the Environment from Prehistory to the Present Day.* London: Thames & Hudson, 1975.

Kaufmann, Walter. *Religions in Four Dimensions. Existential, Aesthetic, Historical, Comparative.* Pleasantville, N.Y.: Reader's Digest Press, 1976.

Lewis, Bernard, ed. *The World of Islam. Faith, People, Culture.* London: Thames & Hudson, 1976.

Lifchez, Raymond. "Constantinople-Istanbul: The Making of a Muslim City." *Landscape* 21 (1977): 2–14.

Michell, George. *The Hindu Temple. An Introduction to Its Meaning and Forms.* New York: Harper & Row, 1977.

Needham, Joseph. *History of Scientific Thought.* Vol. 2, *Science and Civilization in China.* Cambridge: Cambridge University Press, 1969.

Parkes, Henry Bamford. *Gods and Men. The Origins of Western Culture.* New York: Alfred A. Knopf, 1959.

Piggott, Stuart. *Ruins in a Landscape.* Edinburgh: University of Edinburgh Press, 1976.

Read, Herbert. *Icon and Idea. The Function of Art in the Development of Human Consciousness.* New York: Schocken Books, 1965.

Smith, Timothy L. "Religion and Ethnicity in America." *American Historical Review* 83 (1978): 1155–1185.

Sopher, David E. *Geography of Religion.* Englewood Cliffs, N.J.: Prentice-Hall, 1967.

Stone, Michael E. "Judaism at the Time of Christ." *Scientific American* 228 (1973): 80–87.

Synan, Benson. *The Holiness-Pentecostal Movement in the United States.* Grand Rapids, Mich.: Erdmans, 1971.

Tuan, Yi-Fu. "Geopiety: A Theme in Man's Attachment to Nature and to Place," pp. 11–40. In *Geographics of the Mind. Essays in Honor of John Kirtland Wright.* David Lowenthal and Martyn J. Bowden, eds. New York: Oxford University Press, 1976.

Zelinsky, Wilbur. "An Approach to the Religious Geography of the United States." *Annals of the Association of American Geographers* 51 (1961): 139–167.

9
Social Forms
and
Social Spaces

Without society, and a society to our taste, men are never contented.

Thomas Jefferson (1743–1826)
Writings, Vol. 6.

Key Ideas

1. Some animals, like the orangutan, are solitary creatures, but humans are social creatures.

2. War and social tensions are frequently due to perceived differences that produce fear or anxiety in the minds of the viewers. Hence, the conflicting parties may have quite the same views of each other—a mirror image.

3. Scholars have attempted to seek out the causes of social conflict; one of the oldest examples of social conflict is that between peoples who lived on the move and peoples who lived in fixed places—the steppe versus the sown. Much of early history records the invasions of nomads—steppe peoples or barbarian tribes who have invaded settled areas.

4. Another variant of social conflict, equally as old, is that between the town and the countryside.

5. Membership in a group entails a degree of regulation. Rules and customs determine relationships within the group and between groups.

6. One of the most degrading forms of social distinction is the practice of slavery, which is as old as civilization itself.

7. The way in which people are related to the land and perceive that relationship is central to the question of social grouping and social space.

8. Feudalism was a prime example of how social division of property rights resulted in a society that was hierarchically structured and spatially restricted.

9. The Agricultural Revolution in Europe released workers from the land, who then were drawn to the new industrial towns and cities taking shape in the late eighteenth century. In the cities, the new working class found that its existence was also restricted, by place of employment, long working hours, and lack of social or economic well-being.

10. In the United States incoming groups lived in urban neighborhoods segregated from each other, but as the groups became assimilated into the American way of life, they moved into better neighborhoods and improved their social status. This pattern was true for almost all new urban residents save the blacks, who tended to concentrate in districts near the center of a city.

GEOGRAPHIC INTEREST IN SOCIAL PROCESSES AND PATTERNS

Geographers have long shown an interest in the spatial processes and structural patterns of social life, although there is no clear consensus on what the content of social geography should be. Much of this interest in recent years has focused, although not exclusively, on the cities. What seems to have become a matter of growing concern are the discriminating features of modern life, especially as evidence mounts that demonstrates the exclusion of different groups of people from participation in the full benefits that society offers. So strong has the concern for social inequalities become that some geographers would argue that social geography by definition *must be concerned* with inequalities. Inequalities represent differences, often spatial differences, and the focus of geography *is* spatial differentiation (Coates et al., 1977).

This emphasis is surely one that raises our awareness of the inequities that characterize the modern landscape, but the student needs to be aware that society from earliest recorded history has been characterized by differences, inequities, and discrimination. Where the issue draws emotional fire is when discriminatory practices in modern society run counter to our democratic hopes and expectations, to the promise of a just society.

TO BE ALONE OR NOT TO BE ALONE

For reasons not fully understood, the adult orangutan—found in the wild, principally in Borneo and Sumatra—is a solitary creature. Except to mate, the orangutan usually remains alone. In this respect, the orangutan is unlike other apes, who live in families and social groupings. Among most apes a hierarchy of relationships also determines status and role play-

ing, and these relationships help define individual and group territory. When the group becomes excessively large, the dominant males may come in conflict with each other. The losers then drift toward the periphery of the group, followed by some females and their young; secession from the main group may occur, giving rise to a new group with its own hierarchy and territory.

Like most of the apes, humans live in groups; they are social creatures (Fig. 9–1). When we say that humans are social, we mean that many of their activities entail a coming together with other men and women. There are many ways in which people come together: to live, to work, and to play. Individuals, moreover, tend to belong to a number of different groups whose purpose and goals may overlap or differ entirely. Some groups are basic and common to all peoples everywhere on earth whatever their culture. Others lack universality and are unique to specific cultures at particular periods.

COMPETITION AND CONFLICT

The Role of Perception

War, it has often been said, begins in the minds of men. With some degree of truth it could be added that conflict—or at least social tensions—begin with the perception of human differences. Whether at the local or the international level, differences between groups are often the cause of mutual suspicion, fear, or anxiety. Americans, for example, may view the leaders of the Soviet Union as villainous, power-hungry men who are determined to destroy Western democracies and to dominate the world at any cost. Russians also may have a *mirror image* or similar perceptions of American leaders—as a group of men who are dominated by Wall Street and who are determined to preserve their privileged status by manipulation of the working class and colonial peoples. Such

Figure 9–1(a)

Humans are social beings. From childhood through adulthood, humans are social beings, coming together for play, recreation, education, work, religious practices and politics. Here a group of children enjoy making soap bubbles in a New York City park.

Source: David M. Grossman/Photo Researchers, Inc.

Figure 9–1(b)

Apes are social beings. These three young apes stay together as they explore their world. Curiosity propels them onward, but uncertainty keeps them together. At maturity they may seek out mates, but they will know what their place is in the society through a well-defined pattern of relationships.

Source: Pat Kirkpatrick, National Audubon/Photo Researchers, Inc.

perceptions often impede attempts to achieve stable relationships and, whatever their degree of truth, remain a major factor in foreign affairs.

At the domestic level, group differences or the perception of them may also promote internal tensions. The latter may arise from competition for housing, jobs, or for available resources generally. Whatever its complexion, conflict or competition between groups seems to be as old as civilization itself and an enduring characteristic of human societies.

Social Darwinism

Scholars have attempted to seek out the causes of social conflict. In 1859, Charles Darwin (1809–1882) proposed a theory of biologic evolution that other thinkers subsequently extended into the realm of sociology. The British philosopher Herbert Spencer (1820–1903), in particular, drew analogies between biologic organisms and their evolution, on the one hand, and social structure and its change, on the other hand. Indeed, Spencer even anticipated some of Darwin's biologic conclusions and may have coined the phrases *"struggle for existence"* and *"survival of the fittest"* when viewing the way organisms struggle to survive. Such thinking had important consequences for social theory, giving rise to *Social Darwinism*, a concept of behavior in human society that equated social inequalities and conflict with the process of natural selection in the biologic sense.

The Class Struggle

Karl Marx (1818–1883), a contemporary of Darwin, rejected the biologic analogy. He saw the conflicts in society, especially in capitalist society, as emerging out of the struggle between

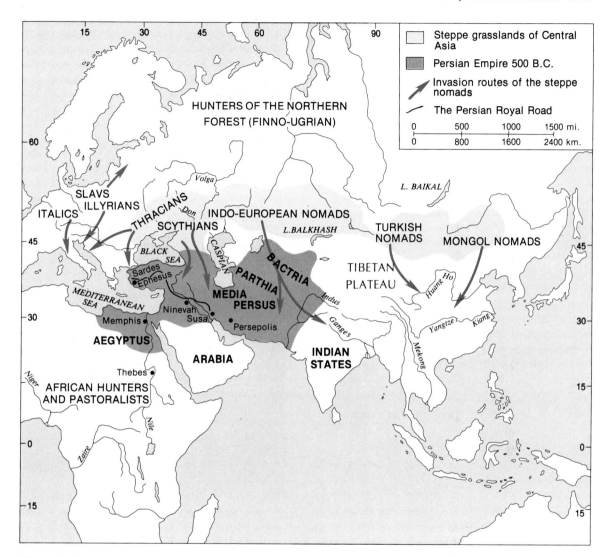

Figure 9–2

The history of the Central Eurasian grasslands records the interventions of many nomadic pastoral peoples into the lives of sedentary peoples who lived in fixed settlements and cultivated the soil. Some scholars have looked at these invasions or population movements in a somewhat systematic way.

Owen Lattimore in *Inner Asian Frontiers of China* (1940) made a significant contribution to our understanding of the development of Chinese culture through his study of the incursions of horsemen from the Mongolian steppe into northern China. He concluded that the boundary between the mounted nomads of the steppe and the farmers of China was a zone of varying width over which there was frequent interaction. This interaction between the two peoples throughout history contributed significantly to the culture of the different societies. As Lattimore himself notes (1940, p. 550), the pressure put on the people of the steppe margin by the evolution of Chinese agriculture and society helped to create the true steppe society, whereas the cycle of pastoral activity in the nomad scheme possessed a vigor that enabled the nomads to interact on the history of China with independent force.

Studies, such as that by Lattimore and by Douglas L. Johnson (1969), for example, are part of the growing literature on the frontier compiled by geographers.

classes. Marx believed the *class struggle* evolved from, and was related to, the way in which the means of production were owned or controlled. According to Marx, it was the struggle between groups or classes over the ownership of property that created the dynamic component in history. Theoretically, conflict would end only when property or the means of production were owned by all. At that stage, the exploitation of men by other men would cease, and a classless society would emerge wherein harmony prevailed.

One of the sharpest criticisms of the Marxist interpretation of conflict within society came from another German, Max Weber (1864–1920), a thinker who had considerable impact on early sociologic theory. He agreed that "the most fateful force in our modern life is capitalism," but he argued that "the impulse to acquisition, pursuit of gain, of money, of the greatest possible amount of money, has in itself nothing to do with capitalism." Throughout the world, Weber noted, "class struggles between creditor and debtor classes; landowners and landless serfs, or tenants; trading interests and consumers or landlords, have existed elsewhere in various combinations" (Weber, 1958).

Steppe Versus Sown

One of the oldest social conflicts in history is that which arose between the nomadic peoples of the grasslands (the steppe) and the peoples of the agricultural villages (the sown). *Steppe versus sown* is a struggle between people who live on the move—hunters or herdsmen—and those who till the soil in one place—farmers—peoples with totally different views of life and of each other.

Traditionally, the peoples of the steppe, conceived in popular imagery as wild and free, held farmers in low esteem. When the nomads learned to mount horses—as was the case with the Scythians (the centaur of Greek mythology) in the region north of the Caucasus some thirty-five hundred years ago—they demonstrated

their contempt and, possibly, envy by swooping down on farming settlements to pillage, burn, and destroy. The farmers saw the invaders as brutish and uncivilized, and they feared their surprise attacks (Fig. 9–2).

Figure 9–3

The building of walls was a characteristic feature of early Chinese civilization. Every Chinese city had its surrounding wall, as did every settlement of any size in northern China. The Great Wall, shown here, is over 3000-kilometers (1863-miles) long, and was designed specifically to repel the attacks of nomadic horsemen from the grasslands to the north and northwest.

Source: Georg Gerster/Rapho/Photo Researcher, Inc.

Invasions of "Civilized" Areas

The cities of the Tigris-Euphrates valleys in classical times were frequently subjected to attack by nomadic peoples. Egypt, because it was isolated by the Sinai Desert, was well insulated, at least from invasion from the east. In China, in various stages during the fourth and third centuries B.C., a Great Wall was built to keep the "barbarians," mounted horsemen who lived on the inner Asian steppe frontier, from overrunning the settled agricultural areas of the China Plain (Fig. 9–3). Much later, in the sixteenth century A.D., Muscovites built a line of defense against the attacks of horse-riding Tatars from the Crimea. Such a fortified line lay to the south of Moscow and extended to the east and west of the *kremlin* (or fortified post) erected at Tula (Fig. 9–4). Subsequently, as the Muscovites moved southward, the agricultural frontier was protected by additional fortified lines that confined the Tatars to the coastal areas of the Black Sea.

Ibn-Khaldun and the 120-Year Cycle

The Muslim historian Ibn-Khaldun (1332–1406) attempted to find an explanation for the seemingly endless conflict between steppe peoples and those of the sown. He believed that a settled farming population ultimately succumbs to the luxury and vice of the towns and, once softened, becomes an easy prey of pastoral nomads who are hardened by their difficult life on the move. The conquerors, however, soon adopt, or are assimilated to, the ways of the conquered with the result that they, in turn, are overrun by hostile migrating bands. The cycle, Ibn-Khaldun thought, repeated itself approximately every 120 years.

Figure 9–4

In the early sixteenth century, Tula became the key to the defense of the Muscovite state on the south. It was fortified with an oak wall in 1509, which was replaced by brick in 1521. As part of a fortified line, the Tula kremlin helped block the path of marauding Tatar horsemen who struck from deep in the grasslands of southern Russia.

Source: Ihor Stebelsky, 1968.

The American Frontier

In North America, the conflict between the steppe and the sown is symbolized in the confrontation between the native Americans of the plains, whose mobility and hunting grounds had been greatly expanded with the introduction of the horse by the Spaniards, and the Anglo-American pioneers whose movement westward destroyed the buffalo herds on which the Amerindians depended. The range wars between cattlemen and homesteaders in the late 1870s and early 1880s may be seen as another example of the conflict.

Town Versus Countryside

The confrontation between town and countryside is probably as old a social conflict as that between the steppe and the sown and, indeed, it may be regarded as only a variant.

The Marxist Interpretation

According to Karl Marx the antagonism between town and countryside is an ongoing phenomenon that characterizes the whole course of human history. It begins, he observed, with the transition from barbarism to civilization, from tribe to state, from locality to nation, and runs through the whole history of civilization to the present day. Some modern examples that must come to everyone's mind would suggest that the interpretation Marx gave to this phenomenon is indeed an accurate one, although the balance at present seems tipped in favor of the town or city.

CONSERVATIVE COUNTRYSIDE AND THE CHANGING CITY

The country (or rural) population, linked to the land and dependent for the most part on the natural rhythm of the seasons, has been traditionally conservative and unchanging. The towns, on the other hand, have been for the most part "like so many electric transformers" (Braudel, 1975). They have attracted the restless, have increased the tensions of living, have accelerated the frequency of exchange between people, and have ceaselessly stirred up men's minds.

FEAR OF THE CITY

The antagonism that first arose between town and country grew out of one of the oldest divisions of labor—between those who work with their hands in the soil to provide food and those who work at more specialized activities that can only be described as urban. Judging by our knowledge of Sumerian city-states, the rise of the first cities brought organized warfare. Thus, the city from earliest times has been associated with war. The countryside, on the other hand, has often been seen as a refuge. The city meant taxation, sometimes confiscation of crops; in many cultures—even the American—it has provoked negative feelings. In medieval Europe, the growth of royal power was to a large extent associated with the rise of the town and the guilds as opposed to the feudal nobility who dominated large sections of the countryside.

In recent centuries, the simple fact of population concentration has been a matter of concern to some of the more stable (and traditional) elements in society. Large agglomerations of people have been thought to be corrupting. The eighteenth century French thinker, Jean Jacques Rousseau (1712–1778), for example, expressed this notion in his novel Émile. Men, thought Rousseau, are not made to be crowded together in anthills, but scattered over the earth to till it. The more they are massed together, he said, the more corrupt they become.

The nineteenth century, with its rapid urbanization, brought a number of expressions of fear concerning the emergence of urban masses. The latter were felt to be amorphous—they seemed to lose all sense of individual identity, and in their intraurban migrations, urban workers seemed not only anonymous, but even sinister. There was, too, a suspicion that not only did people in cities lose their religious or ethical sense, but also that they had escaped the stable influences traditional society could bring to bear on rural folk. Having lost this stabilizing influence, they became—as the restless urban masses in England in the 1840s must have appeared to the gentry and middle classes—more readily subject to propaganda and to pressures that threatened the established order. Even after the social tensions of the 1840s had passed and England settled into a new prosperity, English cities continued to be regarded as centers of extreme views and expression.

Such reflections as these on the town-country dichotomy are not of academic interest only. Anyone who has followed events in the modern period will find the continued presence of age-old antagonisms. In the communizing of China after 1949, thousands of urban Chinese sought refuge in Hong Kong to avoid being resettled in rural communes. Since its victory in Vietnam, the Hanoi-based regime has displayed antagonistic attitudes toward the southern cities, regarding them as centers of essentially bourgeois, consequently morally corrupt, behavior patterns. Finally, in what must surely be one of the worst excesses in human history, the Khmer Rouge regime in Cambodia (now Kampuchea) literally disemboweled its cities and towns by forcing their inhabitants to walk into the countryside. Hundreds of thousands died in the process, and urban areas were left abandoned and in almost total ruin.

Twentieth-century urbanization in the Western industrialized countries has contributed much to overcoming the historic differences between town and countryside. It has done this by the sheer physical expansion of cities and by a cascade diffusion of urban values via the mass media. The rural way of life has also been transformed by technological breakthroughs in agricultural methods.

SOCIETAL DIVISIONS

Group Membership

Human history has been marked by the formation of a wide variety of societal divisions larger than the family, such as tribes, classes, castes, and so on. Humans seem not to be able to escape social differentiation. These group distinctions are based on a wide variety of circumstances or conditions: ethnic or racial origins, residence, wealth, noble birth, occupation, or even education. Such distinctions usually bring discrimination and sometimes physical separation.

Membership in a group imposes specific group-reinforcing attitudes and values on its constituents. Rules and customs determine intragroup and intergroup relationships and behavior patterns. If a member adopts differing attitudes or violates cherished class values, that individual will probably be ostracized within, or expelled from, the group. For example, *excommunication*—more widely used in the past than today—is a device whereby a member of a Christian church may be expelled from the society of the faithful for some heresy. The excommunicant is shunned and not allowed to participate in group rituals until the ban is lifted. Conformity and obedience remain essential to continued acceptance within a group, but some groups are clearly more demanding than others in the degree to which they require adherence to group values. The class stratification of British society in the past permeated almost every facet of life, and it was expected that members of the several classes would "know their place" in the hierarchy. Class distinctions may be less clearcut today in Great Britain than before World War II, but they are nevertheless present and color the attitudes of the Conservative and Labour parties. Status based on birth or inheritance has tended to be of considerably less importance in the United States than other criteria, such as income or racial origins. In the

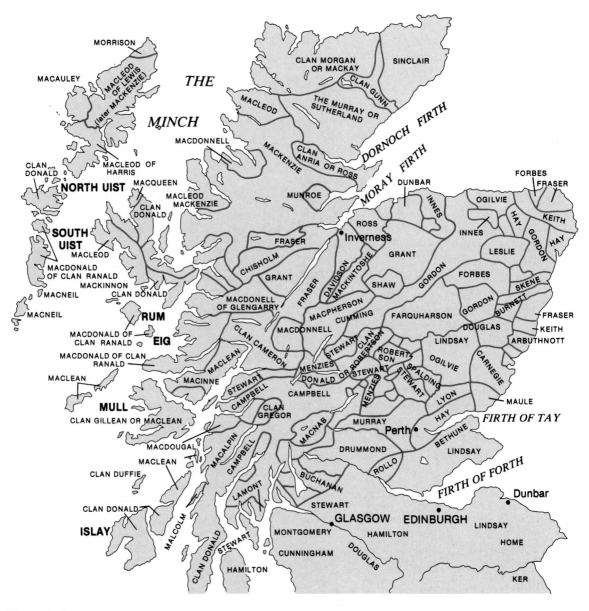

Figure 9–5

Clan organization was strengthened in parts of Scotland because the nature of the terrain led to the formation of small, detached communities living in isolation from each other. For the most part, the clan system was restricted to the Highlands, and is believed to have originated before 1000 A.D. The tribal structure was dealt a severe blow when the English defeated an uprising of the clans in 1746. The association of tartans with clan relationships is largely a creation of the eighteenth century.

Russian Revolution of 1917, the historic gentry and privileged classes were all but wiped out, and those noble persons who survived in Russia melded into the mass of the people.

Social Spaces

Social groups have their own spaces and, as among street gangs in cities, boundaries may be significant and readily identifiable. Where social groups possess distinct locations, patterns of human interaction and relationships emerge and develop—somewhat like the growth of a spider's web. The environment or the spatial component of the group enters into the creation and shaping of goals and behavior, but the process is a complex and little-understood one. Moreover, to understand the way in which a group plays out its own drama, it is necessary to have some glimpse, if possible, of how the group itself perceives its own environment or social space.

The Family, Clan, and Tribe

Nearly every human child begins life within a family, the first social group the child comes to know. (Legends will frequently have children raised by an animal, as the she-wolf suckled Romulus and Remus, who founded Rome, but the very unnaturalness of the event enhances the tale.) In time, the child becomes aware of a larger pattern of interrelationships with broader spatial dimensions based on ties of blood that place the child's immediate family within an extended family, a clan, or even a tribe. Clans, as constituted historically in Ireland and Scotland, represent a number of families claiming descent from a common ancestor and bearing a common surname (Fig. 9–5). Tribes represent similar groupings and, in addition, tend to have a common territory. The Germanic peoples who pushed against the northern boundaries of the Roman Empire from the first century A.D. onward were called tribes by the Romans, in part because they followed native customs rather

---

BOX 9–1
Tribes and Tribal Affiliations in the Arabian Peninsula

Most of the people living in the Arabian peninsula belong to one or more of the major tribes that have survived to the present. Tribal allegiance gives both character and meaning to life among Arabians, making possible a sustained loyalty to locality but allowing for the development of national feeling.

In Saudi Arabia, life traditionally was composed of villagers, townspeople, and nomads. Life in the towns and villages was not organized on the basis of tribal associations, although the administration may have been dominated by a few families. In the 1980s, such administrators tend to have a kinship relationship with the ruling family of the country, the House of Saud.

Outside the villages and towns—and the modern cities—the nomads continue a way of life that is centuries old. These nomadic people, or bedouin, constitute a fourth of the Saudi population, but their numbers are steadily declining. Still, their code of behavior and way of life continue to have a stronghold on the imagination of all the people. Within the tribe, which usually consists of a number of extended families, the chief or sheikh possesses considerable personal power. Values that are admired are those that promote group cohesion and survival. In the past, blood revenge was a law of the desert that prompted raiding against an enemy, primarily with the aim of stealing livestock. At that time, the limits of each tribal territory were carefully defined and generally comprised a summer and a winter camping ground (Fig. 9–7).

---

than state law (Fig. 9–6). Tribal associations remain important in many parts of the world even today; this is particularly true in Africa and in Saudi Arabia (Box 9–1) (Fig. 9–7).

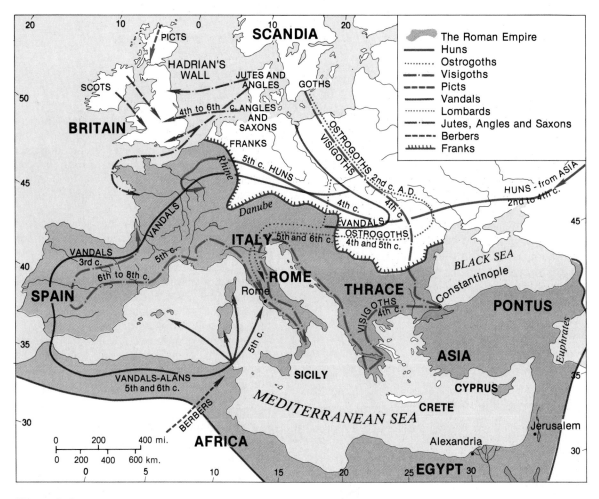

Figure 9–6

The Germanic frontier always posed a security problem for the Roman Empire. The first Germanic tribes that attempted to break into the empire were the Teutons and Cimbri in 113 B.C. Julius Caesar carried the boundaries of the empire to the Rhine and his successor, Augustus, built lines of fortifications, known as a limes, beyond the river. Still the continuous onslaught of barbaric tribes led to the ultimate breakdown of the empire. The Huns, originally from deep in Central Asia, crossed the Rhine and penetrated Gaul in 450 A.D. In 486 A.D., Gaul was conquered by the Germanic Franks, who laid the basis for a new political organization in western Europe. In the meantime, Rome was sacked by the Germanic Visigoths (in 410 A.D.) and the Vandals (455 A.D.). From the middle of the fifth century onward, the Roman Empire in the West was under Germanic domination.

Caste and Place in India

If a child had grown up in a village in pretwentieth-century India, the family would also have had membership in a socioeconomic group known as a caste. Throughout much of the long history of the South Asian peninsula, hereditary membership in a caste determined not only how the caste member would make a living but who a marriage partner would be (see Chap-

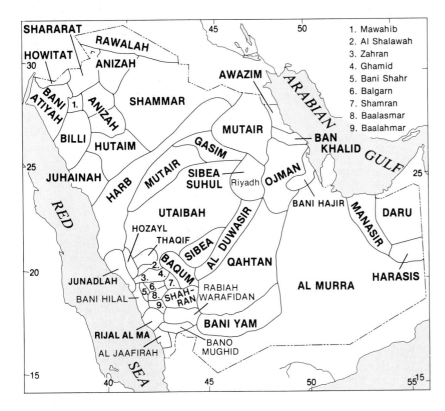

1. Mawahib
2. Al Shalawah
3. Zahran
4. Ghamid
5. Bani Shahr
6. Balgarn
7. Shamran
8. Baalasmar
9. Baalahmar

Figure 9–7

Tribal Associations in Saudi Arabia.

(*Source:* Hussein Hamza Bindagji, *Atlas of Saudi Arabia* [Oxford: Oxford University Press, 1978], p. 11.)

ters 8 and 10). Caste has been legally abolished in India, but caste attitudes still affect behavior patterns, especially in rural areas, and they determine the place within which certain groups are permitted to function.

Serfdom and Social Immobility

One of the truly unusual characteristics of modern society in general and of American society in particular is its mobility, both upward socially and outward spatially. In early medieval Europe, however, a son followed his father and a daughter her mother through the confining patterns of village life that had been constant for generations. Under early medieval land tenure, that is, *feudal tenure,* village families were bound to the land of the manor house and could be legally free only when set free by the lord of the manor, by participating in the Crusades, or by escaping to a town or a frontier region.

Under this system, the entire commmunity, from the vassals of the king downward, was subject to varying degrees of service or servitude (Fig. 9–8). In the case of the peasantry, their servitude amounted to a surrender of personal liberty. *Serfs,* or villagers tied to the land, could not be sold, but could be transferred along with the land to which they were attached. It was this fact that distinguished serfs from slaves, who were the personal property of a master.

By the fifteenth century, serfdom had almost disappeared from western Europe. The Revolution of 1789 wiped out the last vestiges of it in France. In Russia, it was terminated by a proclamation of the tsar in 1861 (Blum, 1961). Although the first half of the nineteenth century had brought a decline in the ratio of male serfs to all males in the Russian population, as late as 1851, male serfs still represented some 40 percent of the total.

Slavery

The distinctions between serfdom and slavery are fine ones. Both serfdom and slavery have meant the oppression of one segment of humanity by another. The roots of slavery are as old as civilization itself. The Code of Hammurabi, who was king of Babylon is the second millennium B.C., contains references to slavery. However, slavery is most familiar to us in the context of the European and American enslavement of Africans. Slavery as an institution was introduced into the Americas not long after Columbus's discovery. Columbus transported

king

crown vassals
(tenants-in-chief, consisting of dukes, counts, margraves, and lesser clergy)

barons
(counts and viscounts)

knights

free burghers
peasants, villeins, serfs   (townsmen)

Figure 9–8

In classical feudalism, the king was at the apex of a pyramid, and directly beneath him were the crown vassals. (Thus, the King of England who also claimed the Duchy of Normandy was considered a vassal of the French king.) The crown vassals also had their vassals, known as barons. Generally, such vassals owed their allegiance only to their immediate superior. The barons, in turn, had their vassals, the knights who constituted the backbone of the feudal armies. At the bottom of the pyramid was the mass of peasantry. The commonly accepted term used in England for a peasant, villein, was derived from the Latin *villanus*, meaning inhabitant of a village. In Europe, the use of the term serf was more widespread. As commerce grew, the feudal kings came to rely on burghers (townsmen) to combat the power of their vassals.

sugarcane to the West Indies from the Canary Islands on one of his voyages, thus laying the foundations of the plantation system in the New World.

In their colonies in the New World, the Spaniards and subsequently the Portuguese at first attempted to use the natives as workers in mines and quarries. In 1517, however, 17 Africans were sent to the royal mines on Hispaniola and found capable of doing work that Spaniards and natives were unwilling or unable to do. The sharp demand for field labor that followed the introduction of sugarcane and the enormously high mortality rate among the natives led to the growth of the African slave trade.

Following the example of the Spaniards and the Portuguese, the Dutch, French, and English also began to move Africans to the new plantations established in their West Indian colonies. In the next century, there grew up an immensely profitable and highly specialized trade across the Atlantic. Ships originating in England or in the Atlantic seaboard colonies carried trade goods to the slave coast (Gulf of Guinea) in West Africa. From there, in what is called the *middle passage*, the second part of the transaction, cargoes of Africans were transported to the West Indies. From the West Indies, sugar and molasses were shipped to England, where they found a ready market (Fig. 9–9). Vast family fortunes were created and many fine country houses in England were built on the profits from this three-way trade.

The first black "indentured" workers in what is now the United States were landed at Jamestown, Virginia, by a Dutch trader in 1619. Although slavery is often thought of as a southern phenomenon, in 1636 a human cargo from Africa reached Massachusetts. Black slave labor was employed in the construction of the Dutch West India Company's fort at New Amsterdam (New York) in 1626–1628.

Slavery was legalized in the English seaboard colonies by the latter half of the seventeenth century. At that time, the slave traders found the mainland market—especially with the ex-

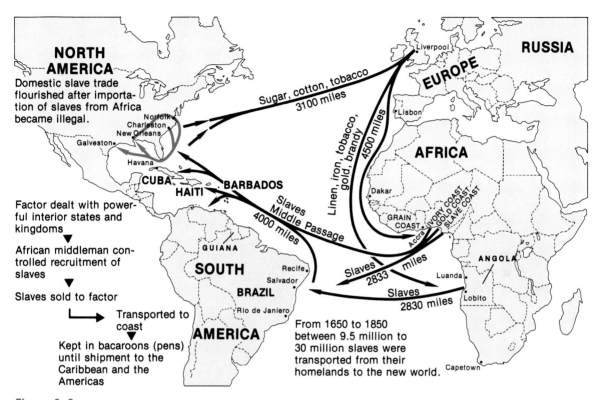

NORTH AMERICA
Domestic slave trade flourished after importation of slaves from Africa became illegal.

Norfolk
Charleston
New Orleans
Galveston
Havana

CUBA
HAITI
BARBADOS

Factor dealt with powerful interior states and kingdoms ▼

African middleman controlled recruitment of slaves ▼

Slaves sold to factor ▼

└▶ Transported to coast ▼

Kept in bacaroons (pens) until shipment to the Caribbean and the Americas

GUIANA

SOUTH

Recife
Salvador

BRAZIL

Rio de Janiero

AMERICA

Sugar, cotton, tobacco 3100 miles

Linen, iron, tobacco, gold, brandy 4500 miles

Slaves Middle Passage 4000 miles

Slaves 2833 miles

Slaves 2830 miles

From 1650 to 1850 between 9.5 million to 30 million slaves were transported from their homelands to the new world.

RUSSIA

EUROPE

Liverpool
Lisbon

AFRICA

Dakar

GRAIN COAST
IVORY COAST
GOLD COAST
SLAVE COAST
Accra

ANGOLA

Luanda
Lobito

Capetown

Figure 9–9

American slave traders, like their English or European competitors, made a triangular voyage. From northern Atlantic coast ports they carried trade goods to West Africa. There they took aboard a cargo of slaves, which they carried to the West Indies or continental American plantations before returning to their home ports. The English trader altered the route somewhat. Trade goods were carried from Britain to West Africa, where a cargo of slaves was boarded for the voyage to America. Sugar, molasses, and (later) cotton were then brought back to Britain, although not necessarily in the slave ship.

pansion of plantation agriculture (primarily tobacco and cotton) in the southern colonies—vastly superior to that of the West Indies. Vast numbers of Africans were thereafter carried to Baltimore and other Atlantic ports (Fig. 9–10). On the eve of the American Revolution, there were estimated to be over half a million slaves in the colonies, but countless thousands had died over the years in transport, their bodies dumped at sea. Up to the middle of the nineteenth century, according to some estimates, between 9.5 and 30 million Africans were uprooted and transported to the New World.

Social and humanitarian pressure in Great Britain led to the abolition of slavery in the empire between 1833 and 1843. Slave owners were granted £20 million as compensation for the loss of their property. Other European nations followed suit. In the United States, slavery together with the demand on the part of northern manufacturers for a protective tariff contributed to the sectional cleavages that rent the country in the middle of the nineteenth century. Although slavery was becoming economically unsound in the South—as well as morally reprehensible—southerners defended the institu-

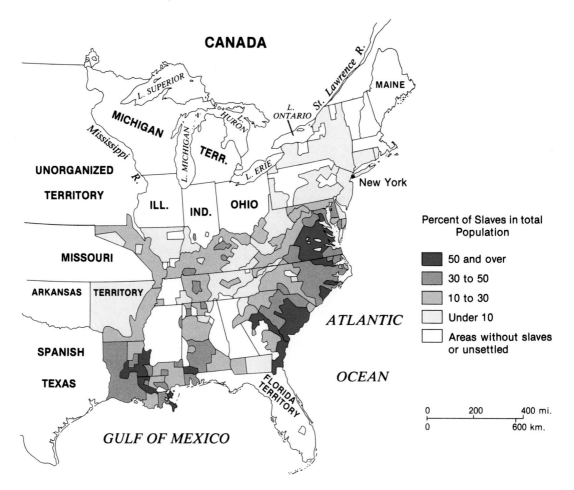

Figure 9–10

Slavery never took hold in the northeastern colonies, even though it was recognized as early as 1641 in Massachusetts and 1650 in Connecticut. At the time of the Revolution, there were only 47,000 black slaves in New England and the mid-Atlantic states. The remaining 455,000 were found in the South. When Maine was admitted to the Union in 1820 as a free state and Missouri as a slave state, slavery not only came to an end in the North but was prohibited in the Louisiana Purchase territory north of 36° 30′ (the Mason and Dixon Line).

tion as part of their way of life. The appearance in the North in the 1830s of the American Anti-Slavery Society did much to spread feeling for emancipation and racial equality. By the 1840s, a tide of abolition sentiment had begun to spread over the northern states, convincing many that slavery was a sin and had to be abolished. The Union victory in the Civil War finally brought slavery to an end. A century was to pass, however, before the civil rights movement was to give American blacks a semblance of the social equality that they hitherto had been denied. Prejudice, however, remains.

PROPERTY RIGHTS AND SOCIAL SPACES

The way in which people are related to the land—and perceive of that relationship—is central to any discussion of social grouping and social space. This notion is true of urban populations as well as of agricultural ones. Relationship to the land may be expressed in terms of property rights, which encompass the way in which land is held (land tenure), the rights and privileges that are attached to the land, and the way in which those rights are passed down from generation to generation or from person to person. In arid regions, the relationship to the land per se may not be as crucial as access to water for irrigation or the watering of livestock.

The relationship of people to land (or water) is not so much a relationship between a human being and the land itself as it is a relationship between one human being and another as this relates to the land. In such a relationship, one person has the right to transfer possession or usage of the land and has the right to exclude another from it. Property has a built-in discriminatory mechanism because it restricts. In this manner, it can give rise to social stratification and to divergent social spaces.

Marx's critique of economic development grew out of what he saw in mid-nineteenth-century Europe. Having no property rights and status, thousands of peasants in Europe were uprooted from the land in the Agricultural Revolution and were dehumanized still further by the capitalists and entrepreneurs of the Industrial Revolution. Marx, however, was not the first to see the relationship between property rights and social status. In the eighteenth century, Rousseau attributed the cause of inequality in society to the introduction of private property, but in *The Social Contract*, he wrote that what society had taken away (i.e., equality), it could also restore. Utopia, as described by Sir Thomas More in 1516, was a society where property was held in common, with everyone working only six hours a day. Utopia's inhabitants lived in model homes and raised flowers. Utopia had neither poverty nor want—nor social classes! As one European noted in comparing Utopia with his homeland (Woodruff, 1966), "I can have no other notion of all other governments that I see or know (except Utopia) than that they are a conspiracy of the rich, who on pretense of managing the public, only pursue their private ends. . . . The rich men not only by private fraud, but by common laws do every day pluck away from the poor some part of their daily living."

Rousseau's eighteenth-century image of *natural man* and the European romanticized view of the *noble savage* were based on the presumed freedom that was believed to exist where mankind was not bound by the chains of class and property, in short, by civilization. The restricted social space of the impoverished was, in such idealistic images, released in an instant for all time. Such images were predicated on limitless social spaces for all humankind. The flowering of communistic groups and societies in nineteenth-century Europe and America (including the Harmony Society in Pennsylvania and Indiana) is tangible evidence of how strong was the desire to create new societies free of spatial restriction and discrimination. Most of the attempts floundered on the bedrock of materialism and property however.

The Urban Dispossessed of the Industrial Revolution

The industrial city that emerged in England in the late eighteenth and early nineteenth centuries was a totally new phenomenon and created a new human experience. Opportunities for employment in factories or in other activities pulled thousands from the countryside, where the concurrent enclosure movement was depriving them of access to the land. These developments led to great concentrations of people in places where hitherto there had been little more than a village, if that. Asa Briggs has studied the transformation of one English town, Manchester, as a result of the development of the cotton industry, which began there in the period 1770–1790 (Briggs, 1968). The Manchester mills drew people from all over Great Britain and forced to the surface what seemed to be intractable social problems. He describes Manchester during the Industrial Revolution as a *shock city* because of

its rapid growth. The population of Manchester by 1831, according to Briggs, had increased by almost six times since 1771, and by 45 percent alone in the decade 1821–1831, the period of its greatest growth in the nineteenth century. It was the cotton industry that accounted for the phenomenal change, the "din of machinery" being the music of economic progress.

The impoverishment that small farmers, tenants, or farm laborers had endured in the countryside was now continued in the squalor of the new spatial scheme of things in which the uprooted country people had to live and die. The struggles in England and France in the seventeenth and eighteenth centuries against strong

Figure 9–11

The Industrial Revolution had a considerable impact on the geography of population, as well as the manner in which people were grouped together in the industrial cities. One feature of British industrial cities in the nine-

teenth century were the rows of brick dwellings that lined city streets, as shown in this view of enclosed backyards of London row houses.

Source: Mary Evans Picture Library/Photo Researchers, Inc.

Table 9–1
Class and Longevity in the British Midlands in the Early Nineteenth Century

Social Classification	Average Age of Death (years)	
	In Manchester	In Rutlandshire
Gentry, professional persons	38	52
Shopkeepers, tradesmen (and in Rutlandshire, farmers)	20	41
Mechanics, laborers	17	38

Source: After Asa Briggs, *Victorian Cities* (Harmondsworth, Eng.: Penguin Books, 1968), p. 101.

monarchical control had enshrined private property as an absolute right that the new commercial and artisan classes were ever ready to claim. But the lower stratum of society was excluded from these benefits of economic change and property. Nowhere was this exclusion more tangibly evident than in the new factory towns. The gulf between the rich and the poor, between the millowners and their workers, grew wide, sparking social disturbances and outright conflict (Box 9–2). Manchester was one of the most thriving cities of the new industrial order, it was also one of the most oppressive. Wages were low and hours of work were long, often extending to 12 hours or more per day. Children and wives worked to help sustain the family. The diet was inadequate and unemployment was an ever-present threat whose effects could be most severe. Disease and accidents were common and the dank living and working conditions hastened death (Table 9–1). Little wonder that the wealthy left the city to live in country houses, leaving the poor to the row houses, sewage-littered streets, and smoke-polluted air of the industrial town or city (Fig. 9–11).

Charles Dickens, the British novelist (1812–1870), has bequeathed important commentaries on the social ills that beset England during the Industrial Revolution in the nineteenth century. He was especially sensitive to the way in which the underprivileged were aware of, perceived

of, and responded to their place in the larger English social fabric. Dickens's mastery of detail helps the reader gain a better image of the social spaces of the leading characters in his plots. Fyodor Dostoevsky (1821–1881) achieved a similar effect in his novels about life in Russia.

SOCIAL CONSEQUENCES OF MODERN PATTERNS OF URBAN CONCENTRATION

The Emergence of the Shock City

At the beginning of the nineteenth century about 3 percent of the world's population lived in urban places. With the growth of trade and commerce and the expansion of administrative functions and manufacturing, the urban proportion had climbed to 15 percent by 1900. By the 1980s, some 30 to 40 percent of the world's population had attached itself to urbanized areas, although in the industrialized countries, the ratio had reached 70 percent and more.

Urbanization, with its agglomeration of peoples, has entailed a set of processes working in the landscape to transform the spatial organization of society. With its accompanying dissemination of the values, attitudes, and material attributes of a way of life we have come to call

BOX 9–2

Marx and the Social Dislocation of Industrialization

The *Chartists* were a group of people in Great Britain who sought to improve social conditions through political reform, principally through vote by ballot in equal electoral districts. Their Charter, published in 1838, came on the heels of the failure of Parliament's Reform Bill (1832) and the Poor Law Amendment Act (1834) to bring relief to the workers. Some years later, on the anniversary of the *People's Paper,* a Chartist newspaper, Karl Marx made a toast that summed up the nature of the dislocation that industrialization in its earlier stages had wrought. Marx said:

There is one great fact, characteristic of this, our nineteenth century, a fact which no party dares deny.

On the one hand, there have started into life industrial and scientific forces, which no epoch of the former human history ever suspected. . . . In our days everything seems pregnant with its contrary; machinery gifted with the wonderful power of shortening and fructifying human labour, we behold starving and overworking it. The new-fangled sources of wealth, by some strange weird spell, are turned into sources of want. . . . At the same pace that mankind masters nature, man seems to become enslaved to other men or to his own infamy. Even the poor light of science seems unable to shine but on the dark background of ignorance. All our invention and progress seem to result in endowing material forces with intellectual life, and in stultifying human life into material force. This antagonism between modern industry and science on the other hand, modern misery and dissolution on the other hand; this antagonism between the productive powers and the social relations of our epoch is a fact, palpable, overwhelming, and not to be controverted.

(Marx and Engels, 1955, vol. 1, pp. 359–360)

urban or modern, it has given rise to social phenomena hitherto unknown to a predominantly agrarian society. Because these new values and mores may be only differentially adopted within the spatial context of the city, enormous variations in social conduct result. Thus, the modern city is a complex of confusing and overlapping social spaces.

If Manchester was England's shock city in the early nineteenth century, its American counterpart could have been any eastern or midwestern city in the 1890s. Chicago is one example. There, the coming together of peoples forced to the surface social problems not unlike those of the cities of the English Midlands, but Chicago also had a typically American ingredient. The cities in the United States had drawn people not only from the farms, but also immigrants from the rural areas of Europe. The census of 1870, for example, revealed that two fifths of the populations of some of America's largest cities, including Chicago, were foreign-born. At the beginning of the twentieth century, the majority of the immigrants in the United States originated from the Mediterranean basin and eastern Europe (Italians, Russians, other Slavs, etc.). These peoples crowded into the tenements of American city wards (Box 9–3) (Fig. 9–12). There was, thus, an ethnic—and alien—component in the American city. Somewhat later, as blacks migrated from the South to the Northeast and Great Lakes regions, there was a racial component as well. Because of the complexity of the problems that surfaced in Chicago, the city constituted an ideal laboratory for the study of social organization (Fig. 9–13). The University of Chicago, through its School of Urban Sociology, pioneered the way for many later studies of social class and urban structure in America.

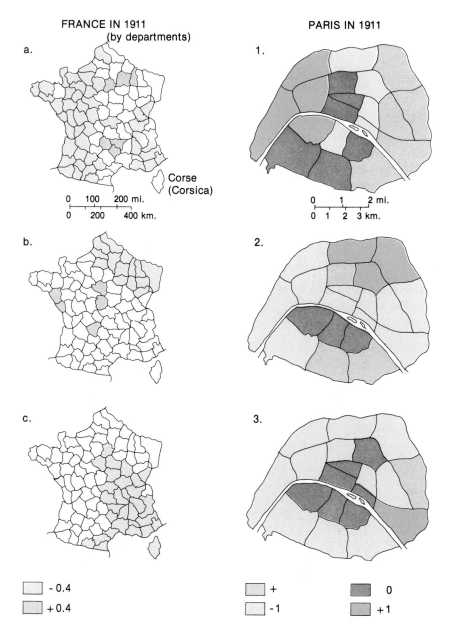

a.

1.

Corse
(Corsica)

```
0    100   200 mi.
0     200    400 km.
```

```
0    1     2 mi.
0  1  2  3 km.
```

b.

2.

c.

3.

☐ - 0.4
▨ + 0.4

▨ +
☐ -1

▦ 0
▨ +1

Figure 9–12

Residential segregation in North American cities is an historic fact; successive waves of Europeans moved into cities of the United States, and more recently Canada, usually locating in areas already settled by members of their own ethnic group. A careful study by two British geographers, P. E. Ogden and S. W. C. Winchester, has shown that residential segregation of provincial migrants has also been a factor in the growth and development of Paris, even though ethnicity was not a factor determining settlement but place of origin within France was.

Thus, their analyses of available data shows a striking correlation between the location of the sending *départements* within France and the relocation of the migrants within the *arrondissements* (wards) of Paris. That is, as (9–12 a.) (9–12 1.) reveal, migrants from the western regions of France tended to settle in the western part of Paris.

(*Source:* After Ogden and Winchester, 1975, p. 38.)

Figure 9-13

Life in a tenement in a US industrial city at the turn of the century lacked privacy. Families, often newly arrived from Europe, crowded together in single rooms, with poor ventilation and often with poor or no facilities for washing or toilet. This tenement flat is home to 7 persons.

Source: The Bettmann Archive.

Classes and Social Spaces in the American City

Almost three fourths of the population of the United States, according to the census of 1980, is classified as urban, living on slightly less than 2 percent of the nation's land. What is more, the large, sprawling urbanized areas (known as the metropolitan areas) with populations of over 1 million claim about 46 percent of the total population, a ratio, however, that has changed little since 1970.

What this enormous concentration of people—almost 150 million—provides in a spatial context is a vast system through which interaction between human beings is made possible. Unlike anything known before, the urban setting creates the possibility for more differing encounters between individuals and groups than any other pattern of settlement known to humankind. Unlike the serfs who lived out their lives for the most part in an extremely restricted physical and social space, people in the modern metropolis have opportunities for wide-ranging experiences, which should enlarge their horizons. Such is not always the case however.

A city dweller must confront many barriers and problems—and this is especially true where incomes or occupations are greatly differentiated or where racial or ethnic characteristics contribute to social separateness. Urban populations get divided according to wealth, origins, and expectations. Cities include exclusive residential neighborhoods and *slums* (or low-in-

BOX 9–3

Migrating to the Familiar

Foreign immigrants to the United States tended over the latter half of the last century to be drawn, largely through ties of family and culture, to areas (both urban and rural) already settled by earlier immigrants of similar culture (Ogden and Winchester, 1975). A comparable pattern has been shown to exist in the migration of Frenchmen from the *départements* to Paris. In 1911, for example, not only were provincial migrants segregated residentially within Paris, but the groupings in Paris reflected, at the same time, the sending *départements* (i.e., those from which the migrants came). Migration patterns are important for an understanding of group patterns and group separations, but much more work has yet to be done before the process is fully understood.

come areas), ethnic or racial ghettos and middle-class suburbs. The social distance between members of such groups and neighborhoods, even though physically contingent, is often great. Every urban landscape is a mirror of the politico-socioeconomic conditions of the society that maintains it. In the United States, the *laissez-faire,* or capitalistic, ethic has always been strong; success and social status are much sought after; and competition is an inherent element of everyday social and economic life. Differences in occupation, differences in income, differences in ethnic or racial origin, all spill over into group competition, and the latter is frequently reflected in conflict over places in which to live. In South Boston in 1975, the descendants of an earlier Irish immigration came to blows with blacks over their respective residential spaces and fears of trespass. Such outbreaks represent an extreme form of competitive bidding for the use or possession of urban land.

In the modern city, the affluent are usually better able to obtain satisfaction of their wants and needs than other urban inhabitants are. They are more likely to have access to—or even be part of—the urban power structure. Those with less money are further removed from the decision-making process and may, indeed, have no way of influencing the system, except through vocal, if not violent, group activity. Minority groups have resorted to calling attention to their plight and their frustration by rioting. They also have evolved their own territorial systems for defense and protection. The spatial segregation of minority groups represents the most extreme example of social separateness, and it is one that has often been promoted or reinforced by real estate agents or banks that are unwilling to offer loans for mortgages or neighborhood improvement in what they regard as undesirable sections of the city. This denial of mortgage money by some banks has come to be known as *redlining* or *geographic disinvestment*. It reinforces the decline in the quality of the neighboring environment (Fig. 9–14).

An area of the city that is accessible or central has many obvious advantages. Centrally located urban land, however, is high-cost land, which usually prevents the maintenance of private dwellings there. Most locations in the city center have long been preempted by banks, shops, and the like. In most American cities, especially in the Northeast—beyond the core, but within the inner city—are the dwellings of an earlier, genteel age, long abandoned by the wealthy in their flight outward. Successive waves of migrants have since occupied and subdivided these houses, but the tenants now tend to be black (Box 9–4). Beyond the decaying inner city is usually a vast grey area of houses and apartments erected in the early to middle twentieth century. Toward the periphery of the city, population densities continue their decline as the first signs of suburbia are evident.

This kind of residential delineation has contributed to many of the modern city's ills. It

Figure 9–14

Many central areas of US industrial cities that served as home to waves of immigrants at the end of the 19th century have ultimately succumbed to decay and abandon, as shown here in the South Bronx, New York City.

Painted store windows, graffiti on walls, refuse in the streets, are frequently the visible manifestations of slum development.

Source: Abram G. Schoenfield/Photo Researchers, Inc.

BOX 9–4

Segregation in British Cities

Following World War II as the United Kingdom granted independence to its many colonies in Africa, Asia, and the Caribbean, population adjustments occurred in the Commonwealth. There has been an extensive migration of ''coloured'' peoples to the industrial areas of England and Scot-

land. As a result of this influx, pockets of concentration have taken shape in many cities, especially in the Midlands (Fig. 9–15). This kind of racial concentration, long known to American cities, is a relatively new phenomenon in British cities and has triggered a great deal of uneasiness in social relationships (P. N. Jones, 1970). The riots that occurred in many English cities in July 1981 were, in part, caused by racial tensions because such a large segment of the nonwhite population remained unemployed and saw no prospect of future work.

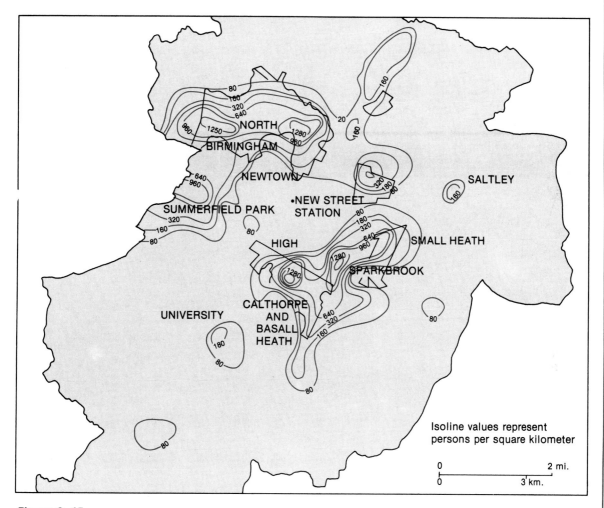

Figure 9–15

In his study of colored immigrants in Birmingham, England, in the period 1961–1966, P. N. Jones found that, once established, colored settlement nuclei continued to grow, but within a relatively restricted radius. By 1966, almost the entire central core of the city had become receptive to colored immigrants, leading to a significant increase in density. If the trend continued, Jones believed that the colored population would constitute a majority of the inhabitants; this concentration, he feared, would lead to the formation of a ghetto, an undesirable development (P. N. Jones, 1970, p. 217). The immigrants were principally from the West Indies, India, and Pakistan.

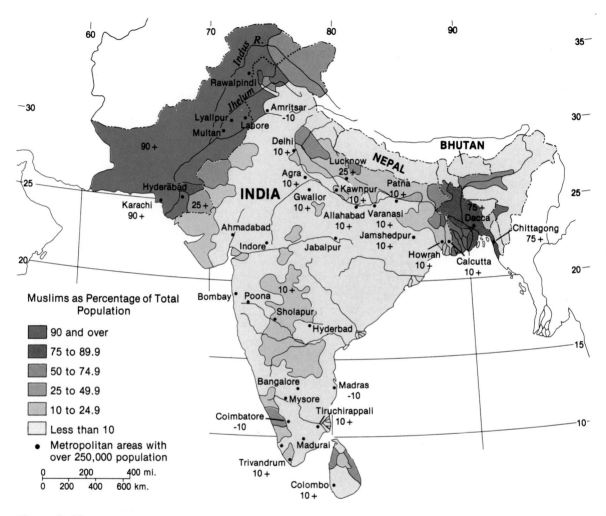

Figure 9–16

Much rioting and bloodshed accompanied the formation of an independent India and Pakistan in 1948, as Muslims sought to flee to the security of the new Islamic state (Pakistan). Today, Muslims form the predominant element in Pakistan and in Bangladesh. Substantial minorities of Muslims, however, remain in India, where they enjoy considerable freedom.

contributes to and reflects transportation patterns and problems; it affects the tax base of the city and the city's ability to provide essential public services; and it has a decided impact on the quality of schooling and raises questions pertaining to equality of opportunity.

COMMUNALISM

Even in an age dominated by science and technology, religious affiliation continues to play a role in the formation of social communities and spaces. This phenomenon of loyalty to a group

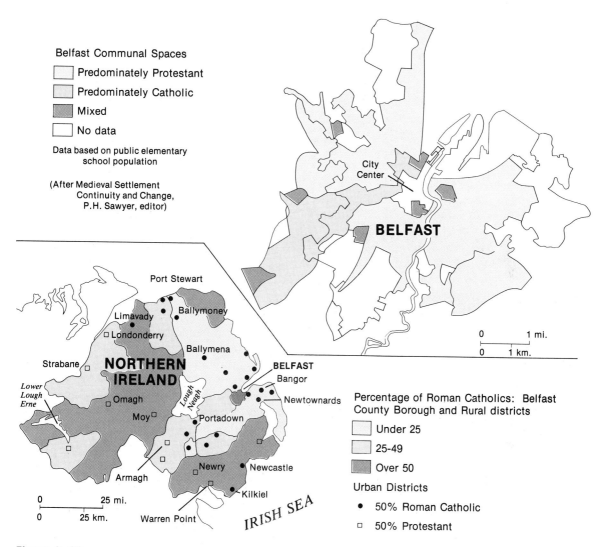

Figure 9–17

During the reign of Elizabeth I in England, Ireland began to feel the power and influence of the larger island. Then, in the early seventeenth century, beginning with the reign of James I of England (James VI of Scotland), the region was extensively colonized by Scottish and English Protestants, although the native population remained predominantly Catholic. The Protestant element in Northern Ireland is less dense in the western counties, which also tend to be less advanced economically than those of the east. Belfast is predominantly Protestant, but there are extensive Catholic neighborhoods.

based on religion is known as *communalism*. It is not doctrinal differences—such as stirred medieval minds to frenzy—that are the significant factors but the fundamental differences in beliefs, customs, and ways of life among various religious groups. These differences may be so strong as to override other class distinctions and even lead to open conflict.

In 1948, religious affiliation was the basis for the political division of the Indian subcontinent into Pakistan and the Union of India. The colonial districts along the Indus and Ganges rivers that had a Muslim majority in 1941 became the nucleus of West and East Pakistan when Britain granted independence. Many millions of Muslims continued to live in India where their religious rights were respected and tolerated, but Pakistan became essentially a Muslim state, as is the newly created state of Bangladesh (formerly East Pakistan) (Fig. 9–16).

Communalism is also the major factor in the unsettled socio-political history of Northern Ireland. Religious affiliation there is a consideration of supreme social significance. Differences between the two communities—Protestant and Roman Catholic—have created specific social spaces that are separate and distinct (Compton, 1976). Protestant neighborhoods, representing two thirds of the total population, are clearly identified by the Catholics, the minority, and the reverse holds true for Catholic neighborhoods (Fig. 9–17). The Protestants were granted land by the British government in the seventeenth century and as they gained political and economic power, the Catholics were the dispossessed.

For the most part, the Protestants are found in Belfast and in the eastern counties, but there are isolated concentrations of Catholics there as well. Londonderry (or Derry) the second largest city, has a population that is two-thirds Catholic, but the area enclosed within the seventeenth century walls is almost sacred to Protestants and jealously kept Protestant.

The conflict between the two groups is not so much over religion as such, as over civil rights and equality. The Protestants, politically, favor union with Great Britain; that is, preservation of the status quo. Catholics tend to be antiunionist, leaning toward a united Ireland—but most reject the radical goals and tactics of the Irish Republican Army, a clandestine organization dedicated to destroying the Protestant ascendancy in Northern Ireland. Ever since Northern Ireland came into existence in 1921, there has been a kind of caste system, with Protestants as the favored group. Discrimination in housing and jobs prevails (Byrne, 1980). Although both Protestants and Catholics in Northern Ireland undoubtedly face similar economic problems today, it is along religious lines that they tend to unite and act.

EPILOGUE

The patterns that humans create in the landscape reflect a variety of motivations and goals. None seem more enduring than the social patterns. Every society at every period in its evolution has created its own mosaic revealing that these patterns or spatial structures have an existence that is closely identified with the society itself.

Humans are social beings and social aggregation is the principal cause of the mosaic. Conflict is often a characteristic of society, and various interpretations of the origins of conflict have been offered. Inequalities and inequities within a society are undoubtedly a reflection of the way society doles out the benefits of membership, but inequalities and inequities are not solely associated with modern industrial or capitalistic society. Neither are discrimination and segregation the products solely of modern social organization.

If the continued existence of inequities are a disturbing element, it is largely because we have come to expect our democratic way of life to iron out differences, thus admitting all members of society to a fair share of the benefits.

APPLICATION OF IDEAS

1. Humans are social creatures who come together in groups to satisfy a variety of needs and aspirations.

2. Equally as old as the need to group is social conflict. Scholars have attempted to understand both the grouping process as well as the basis of conflict. We seem to be no nearer a solution of group tensions today than in the past. Indeed, the continued competition for available resources, for living space, and for growth and development may only enhance the danger of conflict.

3. Social groupings and social conflicts have taken a variety of forms throughout history. And we should assume that the future will bring still newer forms of association.

4. Property rights have often been the basis of social conflict because ownership of property carries with it the right to exclude and to restrict.

5. Some major examples of exclusion and restriction may be found in the institution of slavery, in medieval serfdom, in the plight of the working class in the early period of industrialization, and in urban residential segregation with its redlining or geographic disinvestment.

6. Another form of conflict is found in divisions based on religious beliefs that are expressed in terms of exclusion, lack of freedom, or lack of access to full civil rights and the opportunity to participate in the total society as evident in Northern Ireland today.

7. The affluent are able to find satisfaction for their wants, the less affluent are not. Moreover, a policy of redlining or geographic disinvestment reinforces the decline in the quality of neighborhoods and prevents the poor from finding alternatives.

8. In an age dominated by science and technology, conflicts between groups can still have a religious basis.

9. When India became independent of Great Britain in 1947, conflict between Hindus and Muslims led to the creation of the Muslim state of Pakistan. This, in turn, led to a substantial migration of peoples from the new state of India into Pakistan and vice versa.

10. Communalism is a factor in the social conflict in Northern Ireland. Although the root cause of the conflict lies in the unwillingness of

the establishment in Northern Ireland to extend full partnership to the Irish minority, the two groups—the establishment and the Irish minority—are divided principally along religious lines, Protestant and Catholic.

KEY WORDS AND PHRASES

Chartists	natural man
class struggle	noble savage
communalism	redlining
départements	serf
excommunication	shock city
feudal tenure	slums
geographic	Social Darwinism
disinvestment	steppe versus sown
Kremlin	struggle for
laissez-faire	existence
middle passage	survival of the fittest
mirror image	

QUESTIONS FOR FURTHER DISCUSSION

1. Because humans are social beings, what are some of the geographic expressions of antisocial behavior or social conflict?

2. In what ways were the notions implicit in Darwin's understanding of natural adaptation and biologic evolution carried over into the social realm? How did Karl Marx understand the nature of conflict in society?

3. How are class distinctions revealed in the modern American urban landscape? How were they expressed in the medieval European rural landscape?

4. What made the institution of slavery so widespread in the Americas? Why did it make so little headway in the English and French colonies of the northern part of the Atlantic seaboard?

5. Explain how the institution of private property has attracted social theorists interested in the sources of societal conflict. In what way is the institution used to exclude people in the modern American city?

6. Do you think the term shock city an appropriate one for such cities as Manchester, England, or Chicago, Illinois? Do you know of other cities that might qualify? What is implicit in the term shock?

7. Why did the Industrial Revolution inspire both admiration and sorrow? Include in your answer such critiques of the social-economic system as those of Karl Marx.

8. Are you aware of instances of redlining or geographic disinvestment in your neighborhood or city? Do you know of instances where banks have sought to improve run-down areas of cities?

9. In what way has communalism in India and in Ireland contributed to social divisions and even physical separation? Are the causes of the strife solely religious or are there other operative factors?

REFERENCES AND ADDITIONAL READINGS

Blum, Jerome. *Lord and Peasant in Russia from the Ninth to Nineteenth Century.* Princeton, N.J.: Princeton University Press, 1961.

Braudel, Fernand. *Capitalism and Material Life 1440–1800.* New York: Harper & Row, 1975.

Briggs, Asa. *Victorian Cities.* Harmondsworth, Eng.: Penguin Books, 1968.

Brown W. H., Jr. "Access to Housing: The Role of the Real Estate Industry." *Economic Geography* 48 (1972): 66–78.

Brush, John. "The Distribution of Religious Communities in India." *Annals of the Association of American Geographers* 39 (1949): 81–98.

———."Spatial Patterns of Population in Indian Cities." *Geographical Review* 58 (1968): 362–391.

Buttimer, Anne. "Social Geography," pp. 134–145. In *International Encyclopedia of the Social Sciences,* Vol. 6. D. L. Sills, ed. New York: Macmillan, 1968.

———. *Values in Geography.* Resource Paper No. 24. Washington, D.C.: Commission on College Geography, Association of American Geographers, 1974.

Byrne, David. "The Deindustrialization of Northern Ireland." *Antipode* 12 (1980): 87–96. (This entire issue of Antipode is given over to the problem of Northern Ireland.)

Clarke, Colin G. "Residential Segregation and Intermarriage in San Fernando, Trinidad." *Geographical Review* 61 (1971): 198–218.

Coates, B. E., et al. *Geography and Inequality.* Oxford: Oxford University Press, 1977.

Compton, P. A. "Religious Affiliation and Demographic Variability in Northern Ireland." *Transactions of the Institute of British Geographers* (New Series) 4 (1976): 433–452.

Eyles, J. "Social Theory and Social Geography." *Progress in Geography* 6 (1974): 27–88.

Johnson, Douglas L. *The Nature of Nomadism.* Research Paper No. 118, Department of Geography, University of Chicago, 1969.

Jones, Emrys, ed. *Readings in Social Geography.* London: Oxford University Press, 1975.

Jones, P. N. "Some Aspects of the Changing Distribution of Coloured Immigrants in Birmingham, 1961–66." *Transactions of the Institute of British Geographers* 50 (1970): 199–218.

Langton, John. "Residential Patterns in Pre-industrial Cities: Some Case Studies from Seventeenth-Century Britain." *Transactions of the Institute of British Geographers* 65 (1975): 1–27.

Lattimore, Owen. *Inner Asian Frontiers of China.* American Geographical Society Research Series No. 21. New York: American Geographical Society, 1940.

Lyashchenko, Peter I. *History of the National Economy of Russia to the 1917 Revolution.* New York: Macmillan, 1949.

———. *The German Ideology.* London: Lawrence and Wishart, 1970.

Marx, Karl, and Engels, Friedrich. *Selected Works* (2 vols.). Moscow: Foreign Languages Publishing House, 1955.

Ogden, P. E., and Winchester, S. W. C. "The Residential Segregation of Provincial Migrants in Paris in 1911." *Transactions of the Institute of British Geographers* 65 (1975): 29–44.

Preston, David A. "Geographers Among the Peasants: Research on Rural Societies in Latin America." *Progress in Geography* 6 (1974): 143–178.

Rose, Harold M. *Social Processes in the City: Race and Urban Residential Choice*. Resource Paper No. 6. Washington, D.C.: Commission on College Geography, Association of American Geographers, 1969.

Wallace, Donald Mackenzie. *Russia. Its History and Condition to 1877,* Vol. 2. Boston: J. B. Millet, n.d.

Weber, Max. *The Protestant Ethic and the Spirit of Capitalism*. (Trans. Talcott Parsons.) New York: Charles Scribner's, 1958.

Woodruff, A. M. "A Comparison Between Henry George and Karl Marx on Their Approach to Land Reform," pp. 2–44. In *1966 International Seminar on Land Taxation, Land Tenure, and Land Reform in Developing Countries*. Hartford, Conn.: University of Hartford, 1966.

10
Pariah
Landscapes

In society we not only live together, but at the same time we live apart, and human relations can always be reckoned, with more or less accuracy, in terms of distance.

Robert E. Park cited in Peter Jackson and Susan J. Smith, eds., *Social Interaction and Ethnic Segregation, 1981*

Key Ideas

1. The term *pariah* stems from the practice of identifying in India persons belonging to low-caste groups in Hindu society.

2. Society may reject what it deems unacceptable. Often the consequences of such rejection are mild; society may simply choose to ignore whom it considers on a different plane.

3. In some instances, however, society may banish whom it chooses, and this act of banishment may entail physical separation, isolation, or worse.

4. Among forms of isolating or segregating peoples are the spatial enclaves known as ghettos.

5. The black ghettos of American cities contain three fifths of the 11 million blacks in the United States. The largest incoming group into northern cities has, until recently, been black. The 1968 Civil Rights Act declared white and blacks equal, but discrimination in jobs and housing still hamper blacks.

6. The blacks are not the only group in America to experience life on the periphery of the larger society. The Amerindian population was never enslaved, but it lost much of its birthright owing to the expansion of European settlement and occupance.

7. Federal policies were aimed at assimilation of the natives into the larger society, especially off the reservations. But the effort to assimilate often led to dislocations because it left the Amerindians without a sense of place, without roots.

8. Apartheid is an Afrikaans word used to describe the official policy of the white South Africans toward the majority of the black and colored Africans within their midst.

9. Even though the economy and standard of living of white South Africa depend on the labor of the Bantu, the government has sought to reduce the buildup of social tensions by moving toward "independence" for these homelands—but of the four created to date, none is recognized internationally.

THE GROWTH OF GEOGRAPHIC INTEREST

Because social geography has developed a tendency to become concerned with the manner in which members of a society share, or fail to share, in the benefits of a society, some geographers have found *pariah landscapes*—spatial expressions of exclusion—to be of special interest.

During the period of the civil rights struggle in the United States in the 1960s, geographers suddenly awakened to black America and ghetto life. That interest seemed to crest, however, in the 1970s, and since then the problems facing blacks, notably the high unemployment among urban black youths, have not gained much attention. This has not been the case in Great Britain, where the expression of racial and ethnic tensions in British cities represents a relatively new geographic phenomenon. Social geographers in Britain tend, on the whole, to be in the forefront of the study of spatial expression of discrimination, but the framework of analysis tends to view the social landscape in neo-Marxist terms. This ideological inclination tends to confine the conflicts in society to those that arise under capitalism at a specific period in human development.

THE ORIGIN OF THE PARIAH

The term pariah, a word of Tamil origin, was once applied by the British to low-caste groups, or untouchables, in India. The Paraiyan were a Tamil (Dravidian) caste of low-status workers, but increasingly, other caste groups with occupations that were equally of low status came to be included. Thus, a pariah was one who, in effect, was a societal reject. The English language has assimilated the term to mean simply an outcaste or outcast.

The all-pervasive nature of the caste system has already been discussed in Chapter 8. The point that needs emphasis here is that caste in India was based on the religious idea of an indelible stain resting on certain persons and of the social notion that certain functions or activities were relegated to certain status or caste levels. Intimate association or intermarriage of peoples of higher caste with those at the bottom of the pyramid were rejected as violations of the law of purity.

ARE THERE PARIAH LANDSCAPES?

The spatial organization of human behavior patterns takes place not only because people come together in a positive way to work for specific goals. They are also shaped by people who choose not to associate. People frequently tend not to join with others because they perceive in them characteristics, features, or differences that they do not like. They reject what they deem unacceptable. Rejection may be stimulated by racial differences or differences in religion, in language, in diet, in income and social status, in education, in sex or sexual expression, and in politics. Often disassociation or nonassociation among people within society is little more than that: a kind of mutual tolerance if not acceptance. On the other hand, the desire not to associate may carry with it intense feelings of dislike, if not hatred.

The historic record affords examples where perceived differences are not only *un*acceptable to the majority, but also physical separation or segregation is the sought-after solution, unless outright genocide is practiced. The unacceptable, the rejected, are society's pariahs, and their spatial separation from society may take the form of banishment to a colony, a camp, an institution, a *ghetto,* or a *reservation.* These latter entities may be designated pariah landscapes. In some instances, it is not so much that society seeks to banish some of its members as that the leaders of the society find in these un-

Figure 10–1

Nazi concentration camps, 1943–1944. Adolph Hitler and the National Socialist (Nazi) Party ruled Germany from January 30, 1933, to the spring of 1945. Not only did Hitler turn Germany into a totalitarian dictatorship under his leadership, but also from the very first days of Nazi rule, concentration camps were set up to contain all critics of the new regime. Among those banished to such camps were Germany's Jews. As Germany expanded throughout Europe, additional camps were created to house the Jews found in the conquered territories. In such camps most of the Jews of Germany and Central Europe perished, in all nearly 6 million.

(*Source:* Gilbert, 1982, p. 168.)

fortunate people the needed scapegoats for society's ills.

The Gulag Archipelago and the Concentration Camp

The Gulag Archipelago, 1918–1956, by the Russian author, Aleksandr I. Solzhenitsyn (1918–)—now living in exile in the United States—depicts an incredible incarceration system that functions like a state within the Soviet State (Solzhenitsyn, 1974–1975). The inmates of the *Gulag archipelago* are for the most part imprisoned by the Soviet regime for what it terms "crimes against the state," meaning largely political opposition to the dictatorship. The spatial pattern of their existence is determined by a vast internal security system whose

Figure 10–2

Dachau. Prior to the Nazi era, Dachau, a small town in Bavaria, in southern Germany was noted for its natural setting, attracting artists from all over the world. Sadly it is no longer remembered for its picturesque beauty. A Nazi concentration camp, noted for its brutality, was set up in 1933. By the end of World War II, it had held more than 200,000 prisoners, over 30,000 of whom had been exterminated there. Thousands of additional persons were sent from Dachau for extermination elsewhere. Many of the survivors who greeted liberation by Allied armies were barely alive and could hardly stand up alone.

Source: Black Star

concentration camps, or slave labor camps, that were created by the Nazis in Germany in the 1930s and that subsequently spread to occupied countries during World War II were equally monstrous (Gilbert, 1982) (Fig. 10–1). In camps, like those at Dachau and Auschwitz, millions of people were imprisoned and usually put to death for no other reason than that they were identified as non-Aryans—persons of racial or ethnic origin said to be inferior to the Master Race, that is, persons of Germanic or Nordic stock (Fig. 10–2). Like the Soviet Gulag, the Nazi concentration camps with their working gas chambers and crematoria represent, without doubt, the most extreme and cruelest form of spatial banishment that a society or its leadership can devise. Sadly, in the modern age, similar camps may be found in other countries as well.

Leper Colonies

Not all banishment, however, has necessarily entailed the extreme forms practiced in modern times by the Soviet, Nazi, and other tyrannical regimes. Throughout recorded history, societies have taken or have been forced to take steps to banish groups whose existence represented a perceived and possibly a real threat to the well-being of society as a whole.

Among such banished groups were the *lepers,* people who contracted a repulsive disease that, in its final stages, led to disfigurement and death. Today, leprosy is found in hot humid or subtropical regions of the globe, but advances in diagnosis and care have made it susceptible to medical treatment. In the past, however, before the causes of the disease were known, the only course society could take was to banish lepers to isolated places or colonies. There, untreated and cut off from society, they were allowed to suffer their lives without hope and to die. Today the term leper is usually applied to anyone who is subject to societal disapproval (Fig. 10–3).

tentacles spread silently across the entire surface of the Soviet Union. Many who enter the Gulag are lost forever. Solzhenitsyn himself endured the confinement, was released, and had the courage to write about it—an activity for which he was ultimately exiled from the Soviet Union.

Not only does the Gulag outrage the sensibilities of all freedom-loving peoples, but also the

Figure 10-3

It is not known how many people are infected with leprosy throughout the world, but their numbers may reach 10 million. In the past, lepers were simply banished to isolated places because the cause of leprosy was unknown and healthy persons feared contact. Today infected persons are hospitalized and treated, allowing many to return to normal life. This situation, however, is true only where treatment is obtained early in the development of the disease.

This leposarium in Nepal is reached by a path through paddy, allowing families to visit infected relatives and friends.

Source: Morton Beeke/Photo Researchers, Inc.

Mental Institutions

In the past, society viewed the mentally disturbed with a mixture of curiosity, fear, and revulsion. For the mentally ill, ridicule, neglect, and even ill treatment were usually their due. In the medieval period, some attempts were made to deal with these unfortunate people and, indeed, in the thirteenth century, the first asylum for the insane was erected in England. Known as the Bethlem Royal Hospital, its name was soon corrupted to *Bedlam,* which, in turn, in colloquial usage came to mean an uproar. In time, Bedlam was the name given to all asylums in England. And, to insure that the Bethlem Royal Hospital was kept at a decent distance from settled London, it was moved to Moorfields in 1675 (where ravings could be heard for the price of the twopence entrance fee) and to Saint George's Fields in 1815, the location of each suggesting open spaces. In 1930, it was moved to its present location in Croydon. In colonial America, the insane were frequently auctioned off or driven from towns by court order. Not until the nineteenth century did humanitarian concern for the mentally ill begin to emerge in the Western world. However, society has yet to accept its full responsibility for providing adequate care and treatment for these people.

Retirement and Convalescent Homes

When we are young, we want to grow up or become older, but to be old—and infirm as well—in some modern societies is a highly undersirable condition (Box 10–1). Since World War II, homes for the aged or the elderly, now usually referred to as senior citizens' or con-

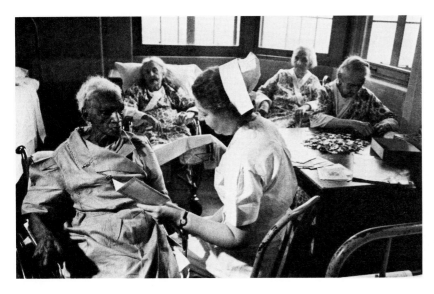

Figure 10–4

The convalescent or retirement home is not always a pleasant place to visit, even if it means seeing beloved members of families. A society that has been youth-oriented as the American society has been frequently finds it difficult to contemplate the aging process, illness, and death. Well-to-do neighborhoods in cities often have op- posed such homes on the grounds that their presence would violate the zoning code.

This geriatric ward is found in a Brooklyn (New York) city hospital.

Source: Stan Levy/Photo Researchers, Inc.

valescent homes, have become common phenomena, especially in the big cities of North America. Such places as these are symbolic of a society that has become atomized or has experienced a breakdown in familial ties (Fig. 10–4).

In the agrarian past, the grandparents or the maiden aunt remained part of the family even until death. Chinese society traditionally has held its elder citizens in high esteem and certainly the Judaeo-Christian heritage required that parents be honored. In the modern industrial society, however, the tendency has been to place the elderly and the infirm in homes that have been isolated from the family and society as a whole. Indeed, some communities fear the presence of such homes within their midst as disruptive of peaceful neighborhoods. Whatever society's intent, the occupants of such homes are robbed in their golden years of the basic ingredients of their humanity: a sense of

work, dignity, and usefulness. Where they possess sufficient financial resources, some of the elderly have participated in the Sunbelt migration, with Florida proving the most attractive destination. But, even in the retirement settings of the Sunbelt, there has been a tendency (sometimes even a desire on the part of the elderly) to segregate or to be segregated spatially.

GHETTO LANDSCAPES

The examples of pariah landscapes given thus far may seem somewhat extreme and quite dissimilar in nature and intent. Still, whether suffering the terrifying incarceration of a concentration camp system or experiencing the feeling of isolation and hopelessness in a colony or group home, the inmates are denied full access

BOX 10–1

Banishing Death

The tendency to isolate the elderly and the infirm in American society is, in part, associated with, and may be a reflection of, a much older desire to banish from consciousness that component of life known as death. "This collective national amnesia with respect to a distasteful subject," writes the geographer Wilbur Zelinsky, "is perhaps best illustrated by the astounding fact that in virtually none of our planned towns, cities, or suburbs is land set aside for the departed" (Zelinsky, 1976, p. 172). An earlier generation of observers of the American scene were even more severe in their judgment of attitudes toward death (Harmer, 1963; Mitford, 1963). At any rate, attitudes and burial practices provide many clues to the behavior patterns and customs of the living that help shape our world.

Concern for immortality seems to have become part of the human heritage since early times. However, different culture groups through the ages have approached the fact of death in different ways. In some interesting aspects, American views of the afterworld or afterlife are not greatly different from those of the ancient Egyptians. In Egypt, the embalmed bodies of the pharaohs were carefully wrapped and placed in monumental tombs—with provisions and often companions—to see them safely on the journey through the underworld. The clothing, jewelry, food, and other items entombed with the pharaoh would be required in the next life. The Greeks were less concerned about immortality, but they dispatched their fallen heroes through cremation. Among the Hebrews, the grave became an inte-

Figure 10–5 (A)
The classical American cemetery tends to be cluttered with high-rise tombstones, each a memorial to the dead.

Source: F. B. Grunzweig/Photo Researchers, Inc.

gral part of the faith. As the soul alone came to be regarded as of primary concern, the body was seen as unclean. Disposal of the dead meant burial in a cave or appropriate tomb site outside the boundaries of the settlement.

In the evolution of Christianity in Western Europe, the loss associated with death also was seen as a promise of everlasting life. But the two concepts were often in conflict. Caves were used for burial purposes, but increasingly, the sacred grounds of churchyards were reserved for that purpose. Heretics, suicides, criminals, and eccen-

trics were excluded, and their bodies were usually buried beside roads or at crossroads.

In colonial America and up to the first half of the nineteenth century, death was almost exclusively a family affair. The family washed and dressed the corpse and, in procession, carried it in a box to the churchyard, where they also saw to the actual burial [Fig. 10–5(A)]. On the frontier, the graveyard was invariably beyond the town limits, like Dodge City's famous Boot Hill. In the older cities of the eastern seaboard, there was a movement to have graveyards removed to the outskirts

Figure 10–5 (B)

In sharp contrast, the contemporary cemetery provides a park like setting, as seen at Forest Lawn Memorial Park.

Source: Bernard P. Wolff/Photo Researchers, Inc.

Box 10-1 (*continued*)

of settlement, as the New York City Board of Health urged in 1806 (Harmer, 1963, p. 119). But this recommendation had as its goal the avoidance of epidemics. New York also suggested that burial grounds be public facilities.

By midcentury, however, the picture began to change. Private enterprise made death a business and the tendency was for the cemetery to be operated for personal gain. This development required that there be an undertaker and a funeral director.

The transfer of what was once largely a family affair to hired specialists led increasingly to the desire to give the deceased a proper send-off. The anxiety associated with death encouraged persons to accept literally the spiritual metaphor that death is but a short sleep after which we awaken for an eternity. The practice of embalming became common with the beginning of the twentieth century. The wooden box became a cloth-lined coffin and, in time, an elaborate and costly casket. Funeral parlors offered slumber rooms, replacing the traditional wake at the family home. And burying grounds or graveyards became cemeteries and finally memorial parks (Zelinsky, 1976, pp. 182–183). From simple crosses in Christian cemeteries, monuments became ornate, designed to last for all time (Francaviglia, 1971, p. 507), and finally, reflecting the park or garden image, a simple slab of marble or concrete. The dead became the "dear departed," and they "passed away," "passed on," or "passed over."

Forest Lawn Memorial Park in Southern California, with its gates as massive as those of Buckingham Palace, its museum, music, and gift shop, represents both the ultimate in private enterprise and the general desire to banish the notion of death [Fig. 10–5(B)].

Finally, the patterns of social segregation found among the living were transferred to the world beyond. Cemeteries for Catholics, for Jews, for Orientals, and for blacks (in the South) ensured that in death none of the religious values that separate humans would be ignored. The victims of our international squabbles lie with honor in military cemeteries.

to that which society can offer. This is not to say that those who violate community laws or require treatment of illness and special care should not be offered institutional support. But, that other element in the human psyche that would banish those society views as a threat, a disturbance, or a nuisance requires further examination and review.

The spatial parameters of these landscapes have little in common; they may not be explicitly geographic or territorial. However, there are other landscapes, which we identify as pariah landscapes also, that are clearly spatial in their expression. These are the *enclaves* known as ghettos.

The Jewish Ghetto in Europe

When in fear or misery, humankind has sought to ease despair by crying out for a scapegoat. From early medieval times, the Jews in Europe suffered such a role. For reasons largely associated with the origins of Christianity and their failure to embrace the new faith, the Jews who clung to the way of their fathers were discriminated against and frequently persecuted.

Decrees of banishment against Jews were promulgated in England in 1290, in France in 1306, in Spain in 1492, and in Portugal in 1497 and 1506. By the middle of the sixteenth century, there were no Jews legally resident in England, France, the Netherlands, Spain, Portugal, the Scandinavian countries, or Russia. All Jews in Christian lands were concentrated in Poland and in parts of Germany and Italy. Jews who remained in Europe were often blamed when some natural calamity took place. They were held responsible, for example, for the Black Death in the fourteenth century.

The term ghetto probably originated in Italy, where from the mid-sixteenth century onward, Jews were confined to restricted spaces within cities. A similar practice was adopted in Germany and Poland. Inside their walled areas, the Jews had a considerable degree of autonomy; outside they were subject to abuse.

Figure 10–6

The Pale. The word pale means an enclosure, a territory or district that is enclosed. The Jewish Pale, or Pale of Settlement, was a region set aside in western Russia by Catherine II in 1791 to segregate spatially Russia's Jews (and the Jews brought within the empire by the partitions of Poland) from the rest of society. Within the pale, Jews were confined generally to towns and cities. At various times in the nineteenth century, they were permitted to live in other Russian cities, although under certain forms of supervision. The pale as a territorial, social, and cultural phenomenon survived until 1917.

(*Source:* Gilbert, 1982, p. 14.)

The French Revolution contributed to the breakdown of the ghetto in western Europe, although it did not wipe out prejudice. Many west European Jews gained prominence in banking, trade, and politics, not to mention philosophy and the arts, In eastern Europe, on the other hand, the ghetto survived until the twentieth century.

A 1791 law of Catherine the Great (Empress of Russia) created a special region for Jews, known as the *Pale of Settlement* or the *Jewish Pale*. This reserve was located along Russia's western frontier (Fig. 10–6). There, Jews were settled in villages where, despite official pressures, a rich cultural life developed. Similar ghettos could be found in the territories of Russia's imperial neighbors. However, even in the Pale, Jews were not free of violent attacks, such as the 1903 *pogrom* in Kishinev when 49 Jews were murdered.

Despite a period of mid-nineteenth-century liberalization in Russia, the pogrom, terrorization, and various forms of social and economic oppression in the latter part of the century forced thousands of Jews to emigrate. Many settled in the United States, some remained in Europe, and others began migrating to Palestine.

The emergence of Nazism in Germany made the 1920s and 1930s a particularly difficult time for Jews. During World War II, the Nazis established walled ghettos for Jews, often building on existing ghettos. The most notorious was the Warsaw ghetto, which was also the largest. There, between 1940 and 1943, some four hundred thousand Jews were confined and, as part of Adolf Hitler's ultimate solution to the Jewish question, annihilated to the last man and woman.

The Black Ghetto in American Cities

In the years immediately following World War II, the major sources of immigrants into the northern cities of the United States were the rural South, the economically depressed counties of Appalachia, and Puerto Rico. The largest incoming group was the black from the rural South (Hart, 1960) (Fig. 10–7).

By 1965, three fifths of the 11 million blacks in the United States inhabited the centers of large cities, commonly known as ghettos (Morrill, 1965). It was not that blacks were banished by the American majority to specific sections of cities, but that once located within them, they had difficulty moving out of them.

The 1968 Civil Rights Act declared white and black Americans to be equal, deserving of equal treatment by society at large. With respect to housing, that act did not mean that the color bar of previously all-white neighborhoods or the white suburbs would come tumbling down, but it did offer hope to the less privileged. Some blacks availed themselves of the opportunity to move from the ghettos. Between 1970 and 1977, for example, the number of blacks living in the suburbs increased by 34 percent; however, blacks still constitute only 6 percent of the suburban population compared with about 12 per-

cent of the population of the United States as a whole. For the most part then, blacks, particularly poor blacks, are compelled to live near the center of a city, which presumably is nearer to their places of employment and where public transportation is available at a relatively low cost.

Low incomes generally have made it difficult, if not virtually impossible, for most blacks, even if they so desired, to go elsewhere. In this respect, they are more confined than earlier foreign-born immigrants who moved like waves through the cities. In the 1960s, there was a substantial movement of blacks from low-paying into higher paying jobs, but this trend slackened by the mid-1970s. In 1982, the average income earned by blacks was only 57 percent of that earned by whites, after rising to 63 percent in the 1960s. About 32.5 percent of American blacks live below the official poverty line, a ratio higher than for any other group.

Among blacks in the 16-to-19-year-old age group, unemployment reached an incredible 40 percent in 1982, but not all of this problem may be attached to the decay of northern cities and their industries. The loss of agricultural jobs in the South has been a major contributing factor. If for any reason the prospects for employment in the United States worsen, as some observers in the early 1980s believed they would, young blacks will suffer even more. From 1978 to 1985, the blacks' share of the teenage labor force is expected to increase from 10 to 15 percent, resulting in a further deterioration in the black situation.

Continued immigration in the 1960s and a generally higher net reproduction rate than for the population as a whole ensured the survival of black ghettos. The black population in many cities increased at such a tempo as to cause a steady worsening of the overcrowded conditions of their social space. Some black ghettos have been expanding physically, but often not as rapidly as the black population (Rose, 1971, 1972). The consequence has been ever-increasing densities in the inner city, breeding filth,

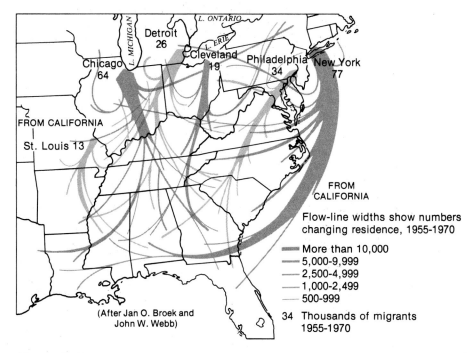

Figure 10-7

Black migration into the ghettos of northern cities gained in momentum during the early decades of the twentieth century, reaching a peak in the decade after World War II. The migration not only transformed the composition of many eastern cities (and some in the West as well), but also it entailed major readjustments for many blacks who had left rural areas to seek economic opportunity in America's fast-growing cities.

(*Source:* Broek and Webb, 1978, p. 89.)

---

destitution, despair, and crime. Some blacks, when possible, have returned to the South seeking opportunities no longer found in northern cities.

Attempts have been made to provide greater opportunities for blacks to share in the American dream through improved inner city facilities for education, through busing, urban renewal, and public housing, but the task is a monumental one. As the 1977 Annual Report of the Carnegie Corporation of New York—written by Alan Pifer and entitled, "Black Progress: Achievement, Failure and an Uncertain Future"—points out: "De facto, the United States is still two nations" (Box 10-2).

RESERVED SPACES FOR AMERINDIANS

The blacks are not the only group in America to experience a life on the social periphery. The Amerindian population was never enslaved, but nevertheless the European settlers managed to deprive the native Americans of much of their birthright (Box 10–3). Although the consciences of many whites have been stirred by the tragedies of the historic record, only in recent years have the native peoples, both in the United States and Canada, organized themselves to demand redress.

The dispossession of land that was the experience of the peasantry in Europe was paralleled to a degree in North America by the dispossession of the natives. Much of the early

---

BOX 10–2

Two Points of View: Race Relations in the United States: Further Improvement in the Status of Blacks

Despite the notion that the United States contains two nations—one black and one white—many people feel that race relations, in broad terms, have improved in the two decades since 1960. Surveys conducted in the early 1980s indicated that a large percentage of blacks saw themselves as better off than a decade earlier. Blacks, too, felt that white Americans were far more inclined to accept full citizenship for blacks measured by a willingness to vote for people qualified for high office without regard to race and to accept school and residential integration. Still, many whites continue to hold negative images of blacks. This perception of white attitudes is especially disturbing to young blacks, who feel that the same overall opportunities for employment are not open to them as for whites and that the desired equality remains an elusive thing.

THE COST OF BEING BLACK IN AMERICA

The socioeconomic cost of being black in America runs to several thousand dollars a year, according to Dr. Dan Thompson, a black sociologist at Dillard University in New Orleans, Louisiana. Clearly there are advantages to being a white American and these are evident not only in terms of job opportunities and employment, but also in access to schools and clubs. This opinion on the cost of being black arose in connection with the question of how race is defined in the United States (New York Times, September 30, 1982; July 6, 1983). In Louisiana, for example, it is determined legally by a not too precise mathematical equation. Before 1970, "a trace" of Negro ancestry made a person black in the eyes of the state—such a definition also holds in South Africa. A new law in 1970 defined that "trace" as up to one thirty-second of one's ancestry.

This question of race determination came before the courts in 1982 when a Louisiana-born woman with a "light skin" and "large dark eyes" discovered that her Louisiana birth certificate showed her as black rather than white. Her claim to being nonblack, or white, was based on the fact that, with the exception of a great-great-great-great grandmother, who was a black slave, all of her ancestors were white. Louisiana was seeking to prove, on the basis of the 1970 law, that the woman was black and had traced her geneology back 222 years. The state claimed, too, that the woman was "raised colored." The issue was resolved in July 1983, when the law of 1970 was repealed by the Louisiana legislature.

Elsewhere in much of the United States, race is simply a matter of what the parents tell the authorities at the time of registration of birth, with no questions asked. Many blacks are proud of their heritage and even though their eyes are blue and their skin fair, they remain black. Others, however, have crossed and "pass" for white. Some blacks feel that the attempt to classify American citizens on the basis of color or "blood" is not only foolish but demeaning. They would urge that the distinction be abolished. For them, it is a question of equality before the law in every respect.

contact the English settlers in the New World had with the native tribes was directed toward reducing the area of Amerindian space in a physical sense. The French in Canada were less inclined to do this because their empire was based on the fur trade and the wide-roaming native trappers and hunters were essential to its success. In the English colonies, as the coastal areas were settled, the Amerindians were pushed further into the interior, a pattern that was to repeat itself across the continent.

That policy of restriction took on a new dimension in the United States when a plan to remove the native population physically was adopted by Congress in 1830. Resettlement beyond the Mississippi was to be the fate of all the tribes. A *Permanent Indian Boundary* paralleling the 95th meridian (south of the Missouri River) was established and the eastern tribes were to be located to the west of it (Billington, 1950, p. 659) By 1840 approximately one hundred thousand natives had been transported into the new environment, where they joined the Plains Indians to form "one big reservation."

The frontier of white settlement, however, continued inexorably westward, calling for revisions of the notion of a Permanent Indian Boundary (Fig. 10–8). This was especially true in the territory that came to constitute Kansas and Nebraska in 1854. With the end of the Civil War, the pressure further increased. In 1867–1868, a commission was appointed by Congress to determine ways of removing friction between the Amerindians and Anglo-Americans, of securing the safety of overland routes, and of finding permanent homes for the native tribes. By 1876, after a series of negotiations, the Amerindians were confined to areally reduced and isolated reservations. About a decade later, the occupants of the area known as the Indian Territory were compelled to cede their tribal lands, and in 1889, this land, in what is now Oklahoma, was opened for settlement under the Homestead Act. In the northern plains, continuing confrontations led to battles, massacres, and death, but ultimately, the Amerindians were forced to yield (Fig. 10–8). In the period from 1887 to 1934, the land base of the reservations was reduced·from 138 to 48 million acres, 20 million of which were classified as semiarid land or desert.

With the natives confined to reservations, a new policy emerged that sought to transform the Amerindians by getting them to abandon their traditional cultural systems. The General Allotment Act of 1887 opened to Amerindians the possibility of private land tenure, a break with their traditional relationship to the land, but carrying with it U.S. citizenship. The Gen-

---

BOX 10–3

How the Native Peoples of North America Came to Be Called Indians

It was on August 3, 1492, that Christopher Columbus (1446?–1506) in the service of King Ferdinand and Queen Isabella of Spain, set sail across the Western Ocean, an unknown quantity to the mapmakers of the time. On October 12, he sighted and named the island of San Salvador, which he thought was a part of the Indies, a group of islands known to be off the southeast coast of Asia. Columbus's goal had been to reach those islands by sailing westward. What he had reached, although he did not know it, were the islands of the Caribbean and the New World. The native peoples that he met on San Salvador, on other islands, and on the mainland were Indians as far as Columbus knew; henceforth, they were called Indians. The islands off the southeast coast of North America were subsequently identified as the West Indies to distinguish them from the oriental Indies, which became known as the East Indies. For their part the Indians were jubilant at the arrival of these first Europeans because they believed they were "men from heaven."

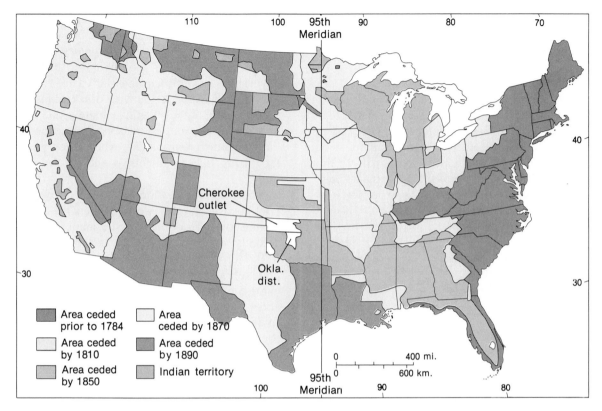

Figure 10–8

By the end of the 18th century, few Amerindian bands remained in the seaboard states. After independence, the native peoples were gradually relocated to western lands, especially west of the 95th meridian. Thereafter the migration of Anglo-Americans westward forced further native land cessions.

eral Allotment Act of 1891 permitted Amerindians to lease tribal lands to white settlers, thus further reducing their physical space. Although the United States wanted its native population to farm, it made little effort to assist in such an effort, and much of the land reserved for Amerindians was, in any case, not suited to cultivation. The process of assimilation was further encouraged by making education in English-language schools compulsory; these schools usually required children to live away from home, thus putting as much distance as possible between Amerindian children and their tribal culture (Box 10–4).

The policy of transformation did little for Amerindians, except to destroy many historic values, putting little in their place. Those who left the reservations for the city seemed even more demoralized. The encouragement that has been given in recent years by the federal government to the strengthening of native group or tribal ties is not supported by sufficient funds to stimulate economic activity. Thus, through the Red Power movement, some Amerindians have sought to bring their claims before society at large, but the ears that listen are not always comprehending or understanding. Despite the growing mobilization of native peoples to preserve and possibly recapture traditional values, some whites continue to maneuver, especially

BOX 10–4
Chief Seattle's Testimony

The Amerindian's relationship to the land was quite different than that of the settlers who forced them off it. The feeling of reverence for the earth that most native Americans held was expressed by Chief Sealth, or Seattle, as he came to be known, at a tribal assembly in 1854 (*Chief Seattle's Testimony,* 1976, pp.15–16).

> This we know, the earth does not belong to man; man belongs to the earth. This we know. All things are connected like the blood which unites one family. All things are connected.

Whatever befalls the earth befalls the sons of the earth. Man did not weave the web of life, he is merely a strand in it. Whatever he does to the web, he does to himself.

His remarks at that time also reflected the Amerindians' feelings of defeat and demoralization brought about by the U.S. government's efforts to confine the tribes to reservations.

> But we will consider your offer to go to the reservation you have for my people. We will live apart, and in peace. It matters little where we spend the rest of our days. Our children have seen their fathers humbled in defeat. Our warriors have felt shame, and after defeat they turn their days in idleness and contaminate their bodies with sweet foods and strong drink. It matters little where we pass the rest of our days (Fig. 10–9).

Figure 10–9
(A) The grave of Chief Seattle, for whom Seattle is named, at Suquamish on the Port Madison Indian Reservation, Olympic Peninsula, Washington, was badly neglected for many years, as shown here. (B) Because of this neglect, a group of interested persons from Seattle and the reservation pooled their efforts to provide the chief a monument suitable to his rank. Beams were suspended above the tomb to symbolize canoes and to suggest the power to command that was the perogative of the chief. Prior to his death Chief Seattle was converted to Roman Catholicism.

(*Source:* (A) courtesy the Photo Division of the University of Washington, unknown photographer; (B) Peter T. Jacobchuk, 1981.)

through Congress, to deprive Amerindians of what they were granted by treaty and what they have retained of the land and its resources.

The frustration of the Amerindians finally came to a climax in the Battle of Wounded Knee in 1973 when more than 300 of them took up arms and occupied a small South Dakota village—71 days later, 2 people were dead and all of the natives had been arrested. Fought in the glare of television cameras, Wounded Knee was the highwater mark of the American Indian movement. Since then, the U.S. government has moved to rectify some of the inequities that led to the uprising. The Sioux, for example, were awarded $105 million as compensation for the white seizure of their Black Hills; 2 Maine tribes were given $82 million in their land dispute with the state and, in the western states, 25 tribes now control an estimated 40 percent of the country's uranium deposits, a third of its low-sulphur coal, and large deposits of oil, natural gas, shale rock, and geothermal energy through a recognition of Indian treaty rights. Still, in the 1980s, severe cutbacks in many social programs in the United States struck hard at the reservations, cuts said to be ten times greater than those affecting non-Indian Americans (Josephy, 1982).

HOMELAND GHETTOS: APARTHEID IN SOUTH AFRICA

1976 estimates of South Africa's population of about 26 million revealed that only about 17.5 percent of the total was white; Bantus or blacks accounted for about 70 percent, Coloured for 9.4 percent, and Asians, mostly Indians, for 2.9 percent. Dutch settlers, the ancestors of the *Afrikaners,* had reached South Africa early in the seventeenth century. Calvinist in belief, they were fiercely independent and freedom loving.

English settlers arrived in Cape Town after the colony had been ceded to Great Britain in 1806. The Coloured, found principally near the Cape, are of mixed origin: native Bushmen-Hottentot, Malay, and European. The Asians followed the British into East and South Africa to play an important economic role as shopkeepers and middlemen. In the nineteenth century, the Dutch farmers trekked northward from the Cape to escape British influence and founded new inland settlements, but in their migration they came in contact—often violent—with the Bantu peoples pushing southward through eastern Africa. The tensions and fears that arose from the historic interplay of these diverse races and cultures have created a highly segregated society and a world of complex social spaces.

Apartheid is an *Afrikaans* word used to describe the policies adopted since 1948 by the ruling whites in South Africa to separate the republic's races. The word itself literally means separateness (Lemon, 1978). Unofficial segregation had been a characteristic of South African white society, but the 1948 victory of the Afrikaner Nationalists made the separateness official. Although English-speaking South Africans retained control of the economy, it is the Afrikaner Nationalists who assumed political responsibility for the repressive system that came into existence.

The legal basis of apartheid was established by a series of legislative acts beginning in 1949–1950 that, first of all, outlawed marriage and sexual relations between the races. This prohibition was followed by the 1950 Group Area Act. This divided the land into segregated areas in each of which only members of a designated race could live or own property. A 1953 act prevented persons of different races from using the same public facilities or amenities. With slight modifications, these regulations have remained in force ever since.

The most extreme form of separation came, however, with the policy to establish separate homelands, or *Bantustans,* for the Bantu peoples (Fig. 10–10). At the core of this decision was a desire to get black Africans to revert to a tribal environment, one which many had fore-

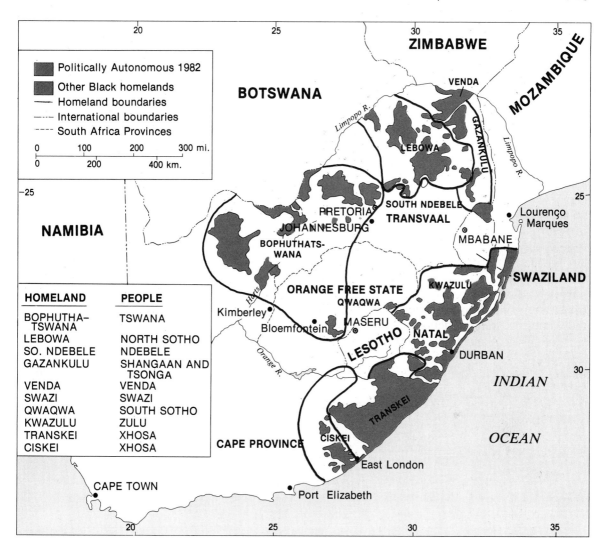

The legend and table on the map:

Politically Autonomous 1982
Other Black homelands
— Homeland boundaries
—·— International boundaries
---- South Africa Provinces

0   100   200   300 mi.
0   200   400 km.

HOMELAND	PEOPLE
BOPHUTHA-TSWANA	TSWANA
LEBOWA	NORTH SOTHO
SO. NDEBELE	NDEBELE
GAZANKULU	SHANGAAN AND TSONGA
VENDA	VENDA
SWAZI	SWAZI
QWAQWA	SOUTH SOTHO
KWAZULU	ZULU
TRANSKEI	XHOSA
CISKEI	XHOSA

Figure 10–10

The Bantu homelands are located primarily in the eastern half of South Africa. Some, like Bophuthatswana, are fragmented into several components. Swaziland and Lesotho, also shown, are former British territories that have gained their "independence," but even these black states are closely associated, for obvious geographic reasons, with South Africa. Lesotho has a population of over 1 million, 70 percent of the men work in South Africa. Swaziland, with a stronger economy based on timber, minerals, and agriculture, has a population of slightly under half a million. Botswana (formerly Bechuanaland) is also closely tied to South Africa. Wheat is its chief export, and migrant labor crosses the border to work in the republic of the south.

saken decades ago for jobs in the white cities and the white-owned mines. Migration to the cities, however, had resulted in the creation of large shantytowns, like Soweto, an African township that served the employment area of Johannesburg and where a large segment of the population was compelled to live below the poverty line.

There have been 10 homelands created since 1959, of which 4—Transkei, Bophuthatswana, Venda, and Lebowa—have been declared "independent." These fragmented tribal reserves contain about 15 percent of the total land area of South Africa, but much of it is inferior land— dry, eroded, and densely settled. Transkei, Bophuthatswana, Venda, and Lebowa have no real independence, remaining economically linked to the republic and serving as labor reservoirs for it. The Transkei in particular is a re-cruiting ground for the South African sugar in-dustry. With their husbands away, Transkei women work as gardeners, farmers, or roadworkers. "You can't work in Venda," one South African service worker is reported as saying, "there is nothing there but rocks and sand." Moreover, although physically "sepa-rated" from South Africa, any oases of fertility or beauty within the Bantu homelands have been reserved for whites (Fig. 10–11).

The drought that struck in 1983 intensified the problems facing the homelands. With crops failing, the inhabitants were faced with malnu-trition, which, by weakening resistance, opened the possibility of incurring a variety of illnesses. Deaths from starvation were reported among young black children at the rate of one every 20 minutes (*Guardian*, May 29, 1983). The lack of doctors and an appropriate health philosophy—

Figure 10–11

Transkei: a black homeland. The black homelands cre-ated within the South African Republic for blacks usu-ally include the most dessicated parts of the country. Densities of population may, however, be very high. Al-though Transkei is nominally autonomous, as of 1972, most of the men must work in the mines and factories of white South Africa in order to support their families who remain in the homeland.

Here, Transkei women work to erect round huts, or *rondavels,* for their families.

Source: Photo Researchers, Inc.

one that is oriented toward nonexistent hospitals rather than toward a community-based system designed to meet the needs of the poor in remote areas—are said to be part of the problem enhancing the plight of homelanders

South Africa's economy has developed on the basis of black labor, but blacks have been relegated to unskilled jobs. Freedom to move or to travel, moreover, is strictly supervised under pass laws. That the incomes of South Africa's blacks are higher than those in the independent black republics of Africa to the north does not soften the sense of deprivation blacks experience under apartheid. Off the reserves, the blacks are made to feel that they are aliens or intruders. As "citizens" of the "independent" homelands, moreover, blacks lose their status as South Africans nationals.

Efforts on the part of the government to induce industries to locate plants near the borders of the homelands have not had much success. So, whether in the homelands or the suburban shantytowns, South African blacks are inevitably linked with the white economy. The present system of job reservations is wasteful of human talent and resources, and white employers are aware of this fact. Yet so long as the whites in authority remain insensitive to the racial question, the overall social and political structure of South Africa will remain frozen.

EPILOGUE

Throughout history, organized society has found ways of dealing with those groups of people it has considered to be unacceptable to the mainstream. Hinduism gave birth to the term outcaste, pariah, and institutionalized—to an incredible degree for over two thousand years—a system that segregated peoples on the basis of their social status and occupation. It was also the great Indian social reformer Mahatma Gandhi (1869–1948) who renamed India's untouchables, or outcastes, harijans (meaning Children of God) to lend moral support to the enormous tasks of reducing the impact of the stigma attached to their historic caste status.

In other societies, whatever their cultural or socioeconomic basis, the creation of pariah landscapes, as spatial evidence of social segregation, has taken many forms, each designed to serve different purposes and to achieve different results. The labor camps, which also served as extermination camps, in Nazi Germany were one of the most extreme forms of banishment, but Soviet Russia has created a structure of incarceration based on "crimes against the state," which is equally monstrous. Ghettos, reservations, and apartheid carry with them the mark of injustice, social degradation, and rejection. They are the creation of fear, hate, and intolerance. Inevitably, they carry within themselves the seeds of their own destruction.

APPLICATION OF IDEAS

1. If the concept of pariah or outcast is as old as civilization itself, is it possible that one day society will no longer have need of it?

2. The Gulag archipelago and concentration camps are extreme forms of man's inhumanity to his fellow man. (Karl Marx once wrote that the exploitation of man by his fellow man would end only with the achievement of socialism.) Do you think that genuine human equality can ever be achieved?

3. The desire to brush aside the elderly and the infirm is in part because of the postwar baby-boom, which brought into the marketplace a supply of youthful laborers and youthful consumer tastes. Do you think that this desire or tendency to isolate the elderly and infirm is now being slowed or even reversed?

4. What is happening to the American population demographically that may require greater use of senior citizens in the future?

5. The black subculture in American life is a

reality, but to what extent can we continue to tolerate inequality of opportunity for all citizens? What can be done to bring blacks more fully into the labor market?

6. The Jewish Pale has disappeared and so have a large percentage of Europe's Jews, but there is evidence that anti-Semitism lingers both in Europe and in the United States.

7. Apartheid is an extreme form of physical segregation based on race, but one wonders how long the policy can survive in view of the emergence of predominantly black and independent Africa. The government of South Africa continues to adhere to its policy in view of the liberation movement that has swept Africa since World War II.

KEY WORDS AND PHRASES

Afrikaans	Jewish Pale
Afrikaner	leper
apartheid	Pale of Settlement
Bantustans	pariah
Bedlam	pariah landscape
color bar	Permanent Indian
concentration camp	Boundary
enclave	pogrom
ghetto	reservation
Gulag archipelago	

QUESTIONS FOR FURTHER DISCUSSION

1. Why has it been necessary for society to create pariahs or outcasts? If geographic relocation of such peoples is necessary, where has society sought to place them?

2. Why do totalitarian regimes, such as that created in Soviet Russia, and dictatorships, such as that established in Nazi Germany, find it necessary to create camps and institutions to which large numbers of people are confined?

3. How did societies that lacked an understanding of the cause of disease and illness generally regard the ill? How did they treat the mentally ill?

4. Do the retirement and convalescent homes of the modern American city suggest to you that certain select groups are isolated from society? Have you ever visited a retirement or a convalescent home?

5. Why were Jews made the scapegoats when calamities struck Europe in the medieval period? Why did Hitler use the Jews as scapegoats for German problems?

6. How extensive was the Pale of Settlement? Why was it necessary to establish it?

7. What is the origin of the term ghetto? Have you lived in one or visited one? What impressions do you have from that experience?

8. Why have black ghettos persisted in American cities when virtually all the European immigrants to the United States in the nineteenth century moved in successive waves through the city?

9. How do you account for the differences in the policies pursued by the French and English in North America toward the Amerindians? What were the consequences of these differences?

10. Explain why the "independent" homelands of the Bantu peoples of South Africa are not truly independent. Why have the four that have been declared independent not been given seats in the U.N. General Assembly?

REFERENCES AND ADDITIONAL READINGS

Billington, Ray A. *Westward Expansion. A History of the American Frontier.* New York: Macmillan, 1950.

Broek, Jan O. M., and Webb, John W. *A Geography of Mankind,* 3rd ed. New York: McGraw-Hill, 1978.

Chief Seattle's Testimony. London: Pax Christi and Friends of the Earth, 1976.

Ernst, Robert T., and Hugg, Lawrence, eds. *Black America. Geographic Perspectives.* Garden City, N.Y.: Doubleday 1976. (Anchor Books)

Francaviglia, Richard V. "The Cemetery as an Evolving Cultural Landscape." *Annals of the Association of American Geographers* 61 (1971): 501–590.

Gilbert, Martin. *Atlas of the Holocaust.* London: Michael Joseph, 1982.

Harmer, Ruth Mulvey. *The High Cost of Dying.* New York: Macmillan, 1963. (Collier Books)

Harrison, Bennet. "Education and Underemployment in the Urban Ghetto." *American Economic Review* 62 (1972): 796–812.

Hart, John Fraser, "The Changing Distribution of the American Negro." *Annals of the Association of American Geographers* 50 (1960): 242–266.

Harvey, David. *Social Justice and the City.* Baltimore: Johns Hopkins University Press, 1975.

Jackson, Peter, and Smith, Susan J., eds. *Social Interaction and Ethnic Segregation.* London: Academic Press, 1981.

Josephy, Jr., Alvin M. *Now That the Buffalo's Gone. A Study of Today's American Indians.* New York: Alfred A. Knopf, 1982.

Kellogg, John. "Negro Urban Clusters in the Postbellum South." *Geographical Review* 67 (1977): 310–321.

Lemon, Anthony. *Apartheid.* Westmead, Eng.: Saxon House, 1978.

Mitford, Jessica. *The American Way of Death.* New York: Simon & Schuster, 1963.

Morrill, Richard L. "The Negro Ghetto: Problems and Alternatives." *Geographical Review* 55 (1965): 339–361.

Morrill, Richard L., and Donaldson, O. F. "Geographical Perspectives on the History of Black America." *Economic Geography* 48 (1972): 1–23.

Pifer, Alan. *Black Progress: Achievement, Failure and an Uncertain Future.* New York: Carnegie Corporation, 1977.

Rose, Harold M. *The Black Ghetto. A Spatial Behavioral Perspective.* New York: McGraw-Hill, 1971.

————, ed. *Geography of the Ghetto: Perceptions, Problems, and Alternatives.* DeKalb: Northern Illinois University Press, 1972.

Solzhenitsyn, Aleksandr I. *The Gulag Archipelago, 1918–1956: An Experiment in Literary Investigation* (3 vols.). (Trans. Thomas P. Whitney.) New York: Harper & Row, 1974–1975.

Ward, David. "The Emergence of Central Immigrant Ghettos in American Cities, 1840–1920." *Annals of the Association of American Geographers* 58 (1968): 343–351.

Zelinsky, Wilbur. "Unearthly Delights: Cemetery Names and the Map of the Changing American Afterworld," pp. 171–195. In *Geographies of the Mind. Essays in Historical Geography in Honor of John Kirtland Wright.* David Lowenthal and Martyn J. Bowden, eds. New York: Oxford University Press, 1976.

11

The Political Partitioning of Earthspace

The distinctiveness of cultures and groups depends upon closure and cannot be conceived as a stable feature of human life without it.

Peter G. Brown and Henry Shue, eds.
Boundaries, 1981.

A State, I said, arises, as I conceive it, out of the needs of mankind; no one is self-sufficing, but all of us have many wants. Can any other origin of a State be imagined?

Plato, *Republic,* Book II (c. 380 B.C.)

Key Ideas

1. The political partitioning of earthspace has always been a complicated affair owing both to human motivations and the highly differentiated endowment of the earth's surface.

2. There are today some 150 sovereign independent states—some very large and some as small as island clusters in the Indian Ocean or the Caribbean.

3. The nation as the basis of the state is a concept that came out of the eighteenth century, receiving its most dramatic exposition in the French Revolution of 1789.

4. The term nation means community—a group of people bound together by common origins, language, beliefs, and occupying a common territory.

5. The formation of a nation-state means implicitly that the state exists to promote the goals of the community, which in some instances may be no more than the preservation of national identity.

6. Where state territory is large and the peoples are regionally diverse, the integration of the territory is often made difficult.

7. A well-defined communications network is necessary to nation building and state preservation, whether these linkages are expressed in roads, railroads, or air and telegraph services.

8. Each state, too, seeks to develop a capital city that is geographically central to the territory or finds acceptance by the people.

9. State rivalries over lands and territories have been a recurrent theme in history.

10. Control of airspace is also a problem of the modern age. Passage over a neighboring airspace requires the negotiation of rights. Control in space, however, remains an open question.

THE STATE AND THE POLITICAL GEOGRAPHIC LANDSCAPE

The state has traditionally been the focus of interest of geographers because they have regarded it as the most important phenomenon in the political geographic landscape. But the way in which geographers have dealt with the state has changed significantly over the past half century. Friedrich Ratzel (1844–1904) was the first to stimulate interest in the state with his monumental study, *Politische Geographie,* published in 1897. For many years, in part through Ratzel's influence, the German school of political geography tended to view the state as akin to an organism that passes through stages of growth from infancy to old age.

This notion of the state as a living organism contributed to the emergence of a related field known as *geopolitics,* which did much to influence thinking about state relationships right up to World War II. Geopolitics was specifically interested in the relationship between state power and a variety of geographic elements, such as size of territory, location, population, resources, and so on; its goal was to seek ways wherein state power could be enhanced.

In recent years, political geographers, although never abandoning their primary interest in the state, have sought new avenues of approach and study. One approach, which had much influence on academic thinking in the 1950s, sought both to define how a state functions and to balance the forces that make for state integration with those that threaten to weaken the state (Hartshorne, 1950). Another approach, borrowed from political science, attempted to conceive of states in terms of *core-periphery relationships* (Burnett and Taylor, 1981; Rokkan, 1975). Dissatisfaction with previous efforts and the long tradition of regional description characteristic of many textbooks, have led some geographers, notably in Great Britain, to move in other directions, including the direction that sees the state only as

an essential part of the capitalist mode of production (Johnston, 1982).

Whatever the perspective, the political landscape intrigues the geographer because of its complexity and importance.

The Spatial Process and Territory

Because there is a spatial as well as a social dimension to collective human activity, the political spatial process is closely associated with territory. A great deal of political behavior is directed toward the partitioning of earthspace and toward maintaining the boundaries thus created. Because of the importance of territory, geographers have been led to review the findings of *ethologists,* or students of animal behavior (Soja, 1971). The concept of *territoriality* is one that intrigues ethologists, who define it as the behavior by which an organism or an animal instinctively lays claim to an area and defends it against members of its own species.

The urge to territory is a strategy that is apparent in human behavior; other parallels have also been found between animal and human activity patterns. But whether human groups possess an instinctual or biologic urge for territory has not been demonstrated. Still, the claiming and defending of territory by humans has led not only to the partitioning of the earth's surface, but also to a sharp awareness of group differences.

POLITICAL PARTITIONING OF EARTHSPACE

Because the earth's surface is irregularly differentiated in terms of land forms, of terrain, and of climate and resource endowment, the political partitioning of earthspace has always been a complicated affair (Gottmann, 1952). Throughout history, territory has been claimed and fought over, not once but many times. The current quiltlike pattern of states—large and small, rich and poor—is the product of the ebb and flow of history. It may not be the same in 100 years, or even 50, because the political process is a dynamic one.

In 1982, the United Nations counted a membership of 157 sovereign independent states. Some of these, like Denmark, Hungary, Italy, and Poland, are based, by definition, on the *nation*. Some, like the USSR and the People's Republic of China, are *multinational* in their composition. Still others, like Zaire, have strong tribal components, and some are, as yet, little more than territorial constructs, successors of former colonies. Namibia falls into this latter category, although it has not been granted independence by the Republic of South Africa, which received the territory, known as South West Africa, as a mandate of the League of Nations after World War I.

Classic examples of *nation-states* are found principally in Europe. Each is built around essentially one "people," as, for example, the Danes, the Hungarians, and the Italians. The United States has become a unique nation-state through the assimilation of its diverse immigrant peoples culturally and economically to form a new group, the Americans. Canada, on the other hand, is binational, organized on the basis of two separate cultures, English and French. South Africa is also binational, that is it consists principally of Afrikaners (Dutch) and people of British descent, if the inhabitants of European stock *only* are considered. But South Africa's political structure largely excludes the African (Bantu) population—which outnumbers the whites—a Coloured or "mixed" population, and an Asian immigrant population.

One of the most diverse states in population composition is the USSR, containing over 100 different ethnic groups distributed in peripheral *oblasts,* or provinces, and subordinate territories around the historic core of the Russian Muscovite state. The USSR embraces a sixth of the earth's surface, and its administration is highly centralized in Moscow. Equally *pluralistic* is Singapore, a *city-state* on an island at the southern end of the Malay Peninsula, which gained its independence from the Federation of Malaysia in 1956. Its population, totaling only 2.5 million, consists of overseas Chinese (75 percent), Malaysians (14 percent), and Indo-Pakistanis and others (11 percent).

Many of the states of Africa, whose populations often are more closely identified with tribal relationships than with a national idea, are still little more than legitimized independent territorial units. When the European powers partitioned Africa in the nineteenth century, they paid scant heed to the dictates of tribal relationships or even geography. The great task facing these states today is integration, both of territory and peoples.

THE NATION-STATE

Foundations

Monarchical absolutism reached its peak in Europe during the early part of the eighteenth century. It then began to be replaced by nationalism as the principal political organizing force. In Britain, the monarch's powers were eroded gradually, after an abortive attempt at revolution and republican rule in the seventeenth century, but the early Stuart monarchs of England and Scotland had never been as absolute in their power as the Bourbons of France. Constitutional limitations were imposed on the British monarch. These were achieved with the restoration of the monarchy in 1660; the Bill of Rights of 1688; the coming to power of the German-speaking Hanoverians in 1714; and, finally, the recurring illness of George III (which contributed to the loss of the Thirteen English Colonies in America).

In France, absolutism survived until the Revolution of 1789, but the foundations of monarchical power had been undermined by corruption, the internal weakness of the court, and the dissemination of the critical writings of such thinkers as Voltaire (1694–1778), Rousseau (1712–1778), Montesquieu (1689–1755), and other representatives of the intellectual movement known as *the Enlightenment.*

For centuries, the chief creative force in European civilization had been Christianity. Then, about 1730, it seemed to lose its influence. In the intellectual life of the period, it practically disappeared, leaving a vacuum. Thinking people, who were unable to get along without a belief in something outside themselves, plunged into a new religion, a belief in the *divinity of nature.*

This belief in nature's divinity was accompanied by the emergence of social and political theories based on the notion of the *natural man.* The most articulate spokesman of these new ideas was Jean Jacques Rousseau (Fig. 11–1). Louis XIV (1638–1715) had declared, "L'état, c'est moi" (I am the state), but Rousseau argued that sovereignty resides in the people, not the monarch. He laid the foundation for the intellectual and spiritual devotion to the concept of the state as the people, a notion that was to influence the framers of the American Constitution. This idea was revolutionary and, in time, it would greatly alter the spatial organization of the state.

Rousseau believed that man in a state of nature is essentially good. Man had been corrupted, however, by society, particularly as it then existed in Europe. Moral redemption, he thought, could be achieved by participation in politics and the creation of a new society where all citizens were identified with the will of the majority as expressed in constitutional government, which would take the form of a *social contract* binding citizens together.

The French Revolution, designed to usher in a reign of liberty and a government of and for the people, also gave birth to the French nation. "The principle of all sovereignty resides essentially in the nation," states the Declaration of the Rights of Man proclaimed by the French

Figure 11–1

Perhaps more than any other European thinker in the eighteenth century, Jean-Jacques Rousseau prepared the soil for the growth of nationalism—and especially French nationalism—by his stress on popular sovereignty, which is the notion that the people in a state are sovereign and not the monarch.

Source: Mary Evans Picture Library/Photo Researchers, Inc.

National Assembly in 1789, "no body nor individual may exercise any authority that does not proceed directly from the nation." This concept was exported from France to the rest of Europe with the wars (1796–1815) of Napoleon I (1769–1821). In the turmoil, ancient principalities disappeared, national passions were aroused, which weakened the imperial monarchies of central and eastern Europe, and nation-states began to emerge.

The political movement that may be called nationalism had begun as a means of limiting autocratic power and securing civil rights for the people. But, as the English economist, John Stuart Mill (1806–1873), complained, it was a movement that made people indifferent to the rights and interests "of any portion of the human species, save that which is called by the same name and speaks the same language."

By the middle of the nineteenth century, the nature of nationalism underwent change. Instead of liberating the people from absolute rulers, it came to be a means of enhancing state power over the individual. As nationalism spread throughout Europe and crossed the seas to other continents, it entered the age of *realpolitik* (Kristof, 1960). State policies were based primarily on *national self-interest*. This kind of nationalism provoked the world wars of the twentieth century, toppled many of the monarchies of Europe, and led to the collapse of the worldwide empires of the past century. It is out of these conflicts that the present political delineation of earthspace has emerged (Box 11–1).

The Formation of a Nation

The term *nation* means *community*—a group of people bound together by a common denominator, such as common origins, language, or beliefs—and occupying a common territory (Deutsch, 1953a). The immediate goal of emerging national communities is freedom to govern themselves. Among European nations, this goal has been realized with few exceptions, for example, the Basques and the Celtic-speaking peoples of Brittany, Wales, and Scotland. Whether these or other minority ethnic groups will demand more of their respective governments in the future remains to be seen.

Karl W. Deutsch, an analyst of the political process, has identified stages in the evolution of a nation community from a simple cluster of settlements to the nation-state. His descriptive model, based on empirical observations of European data, is essentially spatial and, for that reason, is of importance to the geographer (Deutsch, 1953a).

BOX 11–1

Dynastic States: Forerunners of the European Nation-state

Dynastic states have existed since the union of Upper and Lower Egypt about 3000 B.C. What distinguishes a dynastic state from a nation-state is that the former is ruled by a dynasty, or a succession of rulers who are of the same family. The dynastic state that dominated European political life from the fifteenth to the twentieth centuries A.D. represented a type of state that, in effect, laid the foundations of the modern nation-state that we know today.

There had been dynasties on the thrones of European states earlier than the fifteenth century, but the rulers who arose then out of the remnants of feudal Europe represented a degree of centralized control not found among their predecessors: they were absolute monarchs. Moreover, they gave themselves a degree of moral sanctity by claiming to rule by *divine right,* that is, that their authority came from God.

Such a concentration of power was necessary to compete with the *universalism* of the Roman Catholic Church and its political counterpart, the Holy Roman Empire. At the same time, the monarchs had to contend at home with the opposition of lesser nobles and petty princes.

France, England, and Spain were the first of the new post feudal states. Their pattern of spatial organization was copied by other aspiring rulers in Europe, so, absolutism, in the form of the centralized dynastic state, spread eastward across the continent.

This type of dynastic state was essentially a creation from above. Its base was not in the nation or the people. Neither geography, nor religion, nor language played a decisive role in its formation. Rather, the state was the product of imposed monarchical authority, and it was strengthened and expanded through dynastic marriages and alliances. Once established, however, common rule over territory often brought the usage of a common language, some uniformity in religion, and even a common pride. In this

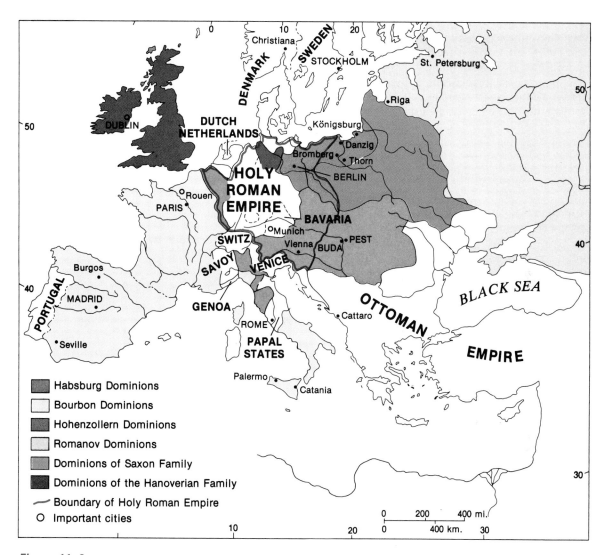

Figure 11–2

European dynasties in 1775. The dynastic (or family) histories of the European states and empires are complex. At the time of the American Revolution, the Hanoverian family, linked to petty principalities in Germany, ruled the United Kingdom. On the French and Spanish thrones sat members of the Bourbon family, which also controlled the kingdoms of Naples and Sicily. The Habsburgs, dominant in central Europe, also held territories in Italy as well as the Austrian Netherlands (Belgium).

Poland, about to be carved up between Prussia, Russia, and Austria, had been united for a period (1697–1763) under Saxon kings. In the east, the Romanovs sat on the imperial throne of Russia. In the nineteenth century, with the union of Victoria (Hanover) and Albert (Saxe-Coburg, a minor German house), the British royal family came to be the central focus of many of the Protestant ruling houses in Europe.

337

Box 11–1 (*continued*)

way, the monarchies contributed (both directly and indirectly) to the growth of the nation idea and a sense of national identity.

The growth of absolutism, however, led to dynastic rivalries that often plunged Europe into conflict, the causes of which are sometimes difficult to comprehend today. Among the more widespread were the Thirty Years War (1618–1648), which had strong religious overtones and tore central Europe apart; the War of the Spanish Succession (1702–1714); and the War of the Austrian Succession (1740–1748). Through the Peace of Utrecht (1713), which ended the War of the Spanish Succession, Great Britain obtained Gibraltar, Minorca, extensive territories in North America, and a dominant role in the African slave trade. Of equal importance at the time, Louis XIV of France (a Catholic) recognized the Protestant succession in Great Britain, and Charles VI (1685–1740), the Emperor of Austria, acknowledged Philip V (1700–1746) as King of Spain. The Seven Years War (1756–1763) spread from Europe to the overseas empires, and its conclusion saw the bulk of the French colonial empire ceded to Britain, making the latter both the chief colonial power in the world and mistress of the seas.

Through such wars and through exchanges, territories were shifted from one family to another (Fig. 11–2). Under Louis XIV, the Sun King, France sought to realize her *natural limits* by expanding—at the expense of weaker neighbors—to the Pyrenees, the Alps, the Rhine, and the sea. The kingdom of Poland, on the other hand, disappeared from the map of Europe altogether in 1795 through a series of partitions engineered by powerful imperial neighbors.

The dynastic state produced some significant political theorists. Niccolo Machiavelli (1469–1527), a Florentine, laid the basis for a new realism in political life in *The Prince* and other works, by giving advice to a monarch on how to found a state and maintain himself in power. Jean Bodin (1530–1596) also helped clarify and strengthen royal authority. It was he who laid the theoretical foundations for the concept that the sovereign is the state. The jurist Hugo Grotius (1583–1645) compiled the earliest work on international law, which reviewed the whole of human political history and development.

Historically, the initial step in the formation of a nation, according to Deutsch, was a farming community's shift from subsistence agriculture to production for exchange. The creation of a surplus of foodstuffs permitted people to leave the land and move into *core areas* of denser settlement where food could be exchanged for the handcrafted articles of town workshops.

A continued influx of people together with a rise in socioeconomic mobility within the towns fostered still greater population concentrations and the rudimentary formation of an elite. With the growth of trade between town and countryside as well as with other regions, lines of communication by land and water were made secure, facilitating both the flow of goods and people. Trading relations and other patterns of interaction encouraged the diffusion of ideas and skills that tended to raise the economic and cultural level of the peoples outside the towns. This development, in turn, contributed to the building of a larger sense of community and of community awareness.

If a region were subject to a degree of isolation from other significant population clusters—whether owing to the presence of intervening mountains (as was often the case in Europe), to vast stretches of empty territory, or to some other geographic barrier—a culture area tended to take shape with a high degree of homogeneity. This entailed the usage of a common dialect or language and the common acceptance of myths and legends about historic origins together with other beliefs and perspectives. Symbols were invented and gained acceptance, and the continued occupancy of the same territory yielded a kind of symbiosis between the people and their land, as popularly expressed, for example, in a national anthem.

At this stage of evolution, a national community tended to mobilize itself, to lay claim to what, by the late eighteenth century, came to be considered *natural rights*—the right to independence from an imperial power and to self-government.

The Deutsch model makes it possible to examine the extent to which nation building today has proceeded in many of the new and largely nonnational states of the world. From such a review, it is possible to suggest what steps leaders must take to further strengthen the process. In some instances, it may be necessary for them to relocate the capital to a more central location; in others, new population clusters may have to be formed through the development of cities and industrialization. Attention may have to be given to the adoption of a common language other than that surviving from a colonial period. The institution and standardization of compulsory education may be necessary to speed the socialization process. Even symbols of statehood may have to be found to gain allegiance and advance national pride. In these and countless other ways, the new countries may strive to create viable national entities.

Core-Periphery Relationships in the Formation of European Nation-states

In historic perspective, it may be seen that Europe consisted of two principal geographic axes: a north-south center-culture axis and a west-east center-economy axis (Rokkan, 1975). The north-south axis extending from Italy to the Baltic occupied much of the old Roman Empire and corresponded closely to the extent of the Holy Roman Empire. This axis was dominated for much of its medieval history by a large number of independent trading cities. Examples of these proud, powerful cities may be found in the loosely knit Hanseatic League and the cities of central Europe and of northern Italy. Although linked to the sea, these cities benefited from the trade that ran through Europe from the Baltic to the Mediterranean.

Cutting across the central cluster of cities was a west-east center-economy axis, which in its western and eastern extremities lay on the periphery of much of the north-south trade and the influence of the powerful trading cities (see Chapter 16).

Stein Rokkan, a political scientist, noticed that the major thrusts in the formation of nation-states came first at the edges of the old empire. As he put it: "Paradoxically the history of Europe is one of *center* formation at the *periphery* of a network of strong and independent cities" (italics added) (Rokkan, 1975, p. 576). As assortment of short-term city alliances, leagues, and confederations took place in the trade-route belt. But, the cities themselves were powerful enough to thwart any efforts on the part of princes or kings to create national territorial entities. Unification did not come to Germany and Italy until the 1870s. Even at that, it was Prussia on the eastern periphery that took the lead in German unification.

On the other hand, the early aggressive efforts at state building took place on the fringes of Europe, on the periphery of Europe's economic center. England, France, the Scandinavian states, Spain, and Portugal were unified at a relatively early date. In the East, Russia, emerging out of the Muscovite core, moved rapidly to consolidate state power and to proceed to the next stage, the creation of a vast land-based empire stretching deep into Asia.

This model of a two-axes Europe (see Table 11–1) affords a basis for understanding the differences that contributed to an early consolidation of state power in peripheral western Europe and a later consolidation in central Europe, the traditional commercial core. Rokkan identified "four dimensions" that he believed were especially significant. These were:

1. Geopolitical distance from Rome, the fountainhead of the old empire and the focus of the drive for Catholic unity in Europe.

2. Geopolitical distance westwards or eastwards from the central belt of trading cities.

3. The concentration of landholding, making possible territorial consolidation around cores forming on the periphery of the central belt.

4. Ethnic unity and linguistic standardiza-

Table 11-1
A Schematic Geopolitical Map of Europe

	◄ WEST-EAST CENTER-ECONOMY AXIS ►				
Strength of Cities	Weaker	Stronger	Stronger	Weaker	Weaker
Strength of Conquest Centers	Weaker	Stronger	Weaker	Stronger	Weaker
Geopolitical Type	Seaward peripheries	Seaward empire-nations	City-state consociations	Landward empire-nations	Landward peripheries
Beyond Reach of Rome: Protestant	*Iceland:* Republic tenth century, later under Norway, Denmark	**Viking Empires** Later reduced to ethnically homogeneous nation-states: *Norway:* later under Denmark *Denmark* ►		◄ *Sweden* State-building 16th century, major empire 17th century	*Finland* Province of Sweden, 1809; Grand Duchy of Russia
Territories Once Under Roman Empire and/or Influenced by Roman Law: Protestant	*Scotland* Monarchy; united with England 1707 *Wales* Subjected 13th century	*England* Consolidated eleventh century, major overseas empire 17th to 18th century	**Hanseatic League** Loose federation of cities around Baltic and North Seas 13th to 16th centuries	*Prussia* State-building 17th century, empire 18th century; nucleus for unification of Germany	

NORTH-SOUTH CENTER-CULTURE AXIS
(Independent Cities, City-States, or Loose Associations)

Religiously mixed	*Ireland*		*Netherlands* Northern provinces united in fight against Habsburgs; independence 1648	*Switzerland* Confederation 1291; major city-states added 14th century	*Bohemia* Subjected by Habsburgs 1620

Table 11–1 (*continued*)

Catholic	Brittany Subjected 16th century	France Consolidated 16th century; empire-building Indo-China, Africa	Belgium Indepen- dent 1830 *Aragon- Catalonia United with Cas- tile 1474; revolt 1640*	Savoy- Piedmont: *Indepen- dent nucleus for unifi- cation of city-state Italy*	Bavaria	Aristocratic Border Empires	
						Poland *Divided* *18th* *century*	*Hungary* *Overrun* *by Turks* *16th* *century;* *with* *Habsburgs* *17th* *century*
Counter-Reformation Territories		**Crusading Empires** Built-up in fight against Muslims; major overseas em- pires: *Portugal* *Spain*				**Crusading Empires** Built-up on dynastic claims and wars against Otto- mans: *Austria*	

Source: After Stein Rokkan, "Dimensions of State Formation and Nation-Building: A Possible Paradigm for Research on Variations Within Europe," in *The Formation of National States in Western Europe*, Charles Tilly, ed. (Princeton, N.J.: Princeton University Press, 1975), pp. 578–579.

tion on the periphery that made for an early, as opposed to a later, national development.

The Nation-state as an Expression of the Capitalist Mode of Production

Whatever historians were recording about European dynasties, Karl Marx had a concept of the state, as it emerged in the nineteenth century, that was identified with one stage in societal evolution, namely, the transition to industrial capitalism.

This transition involved the formation of a new political, social, and economic landscape that, above all, reflected the changes taking place in the ownership of the means of production. The two principal forces shaping this new landscape were the factory system, which brought inanimate energy and labor together, and the spatial concentration of workers in cities. The transition to capitalism also encouraged the growth of an investment-production-accumulation cycle, dependent largely on the growth of trade and commerce as the means whereby needed resources could be obtained and markets could be created as outlets for the products of labor (Johnston, 1982).

The growth of capital obviously was not independent of the growth of a class that owned and controlled capital, namely, the *bourgeoisie*. What this class needed, above all, was political and economic stability, which could only be provided by the state. The state existed, then, primarily to promote the interests, individually and collectively, of the bourgeois class. The state was required, therefore, to legitimize the activities of the capitalists and to administer affairs in a way most beneficial to their interests.

As capitalism evolved, however, Marx believed a series of crises would emerge. Territorial aggrandisement, colonialism and competition for resources would, on the one hand, lead to conflicts between states, whereas inside the state, the growth of monopolies would further alienate the workers from the entire system. The Marxist expectation was that these stresses, generated both within and beyond the state, would bring down both the capitalist system and the state. The revolt of the working class, or *proletariat,* would play a decisive role in this upheaval; victory would lead to the creation of a new class-free state and society in which the means of production would be owned and controlled by the one element capable of redeeming society, namely, the proletariat. Success of the revolution, which would usher in the new socialist mode of production, however, depended on the oppressed workers of all capitalist countries joining together to break the socioeconomic chains that bound them.

The Organization of the Nation-state

Every organization has its purpose, and this is true also of the state. Friedrich Ratzel, a nineteenth-century German geographer, believed that every state is organized according to a distinctive *state idea.* Richard Hartshorne, an American geographer, used the French term *raison d'être* to capture this notion, suggesting quite literally that every state has a reason for existence (Hartshorne, 1950).

In modern times, the reason for creating a state, ideally, has been to give political expression to ethnic or national community. The goals of the state, therefore, tend to be expressed in terms of the aspirations and values of that particular culture group. Often such goals are outlined in the constitution of the state and are reflected in the national anthem or in similar ways. One of the loftiest expressions of the goals that people seek in forming states may be found in the Preamble to the Constitution of the

United States. The Thirteen Colonies came together, it proclaims, "in order to form a more perfect union, establish justice, insure domestic tranquility, provide for the common defense, promote the general welfare, and secure the blessings of liberty."

Not every state has expressed its goals in an elaborate document such as the U.S. Constitution. For example, there is no single document to convey the goals of the United Kingdom; these must be inferred from the historic record. The granting of independence to colonies in Africa and elsewhere simply gave, in many instances, a legitimacy to a somewhat arbitrarily created entity and these new states have yet to enunciate goals that all of their people can accept.

State Structures

Some scholars have come to see the modern state as a system, not unlike a giant cobweb (Easton, 1965b). Each thread of the web represents a specific link in the total pattern of human behavioral and societal spatial relationships. It is this web or system that provides the means whereby decisions made at the center are transmitted to all portions of the political space.

There are variations in the way this is accomplished because each state has its own peculiar potential, behavioral, and perceptual environments. Each state, too, will decide what kind of machinery of government is best suited to its territory, population, location, and so on.

Some modern states are highly centralized, with political administrative authority concentrated in the capital. This is particularly true in France, where the provincial units, created by Napoleon I and known as *départements,* are only responsible for local matters (Fig. 11–3). Such centralized governments are said to be *unitary* in form. On the other hand, when gov-

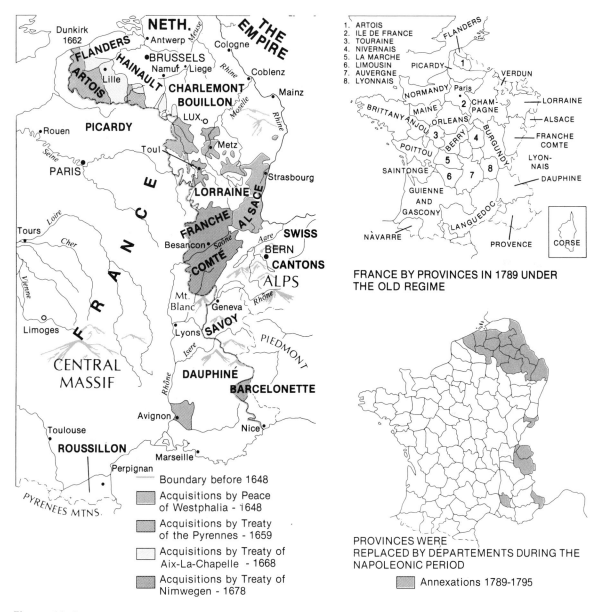

FRANCE BY PROVINCES IN 1789 UNDER THE OLD REGIME

Legend (left map):
- Boundary before 1648
- Acquisitions by Peace of Westphalia - 1648
- Acquisitions by Treaty of the Pyrennes - 1659
- Acquisitions by Treaty of Aix-La-Chapelle - 1668
- Acquisitions by Treaty of Nimwegen - 1678

Province index (right map):
1. ARTOIS
2. ILE DE FRANCE
3. TOURAINE
4. NIVERNAIS
5. LA MARCHE
6. LIMOUSIN
7. AUVERGNE
8. LYONNAIS

PROVINCES WERE REPLACED BY DÉPARTEMENTS DURING THE NAPOLEONIC PERIOD

- Annexations 1789-1795

Figure 11–3

France and internal reorganization. One of the most significant features of the Napoleonic period in France was the concentration of political power. The ancient provinces of France were replaced by *départements,* whose officers were appointed by Napoleon. Thus, France became a highly centralized state in which political power was passed from the top down, not from the people up. In addition, Napoleon was able to gain broad political support through his appointments.

ernment powers are shared between the central government and regional governing bodies, the form of organization is *federal,* as in Canada, Australia, the United States, and India. The USSR, by definition, is said to be a *federative state:* although on paper it subscribes to the federal form, in practice it functions only as a tightly controlled unitary state. On the other hand, the United Kingdom has concentrated great power in London, but Northern Ireland had until the early 1970s its own legislative assembly and separate officials are appointed to look after Scottish affairs. In this way, the United Kingdom, although basically unitary in form, has made concessions to the federal principle, a devolution of authority that may be extended further in the future.

The earliest and one of the most successful experiments in federalism is that afforded by the United States even though there has been constant concern on the part of the states that their rights have been usurped by the central government in Washington, D.C. The Confederation of Canada, which was established in 1867, drew on the American federal system for much of its inspiration. However, Canada represented a different set of geographic circumstances that resulted in a different distribution of powers between the federal and provincial governments. In an attempt to calm the fears of the French-speaking population of Quebec, Canada's constitution gave very specific powers to the provinces, leaving an undefined residue of authority in Ottawa's hands. Canada's second constitution, proclaimed in 1982, reaffirms the powers of the provinces, and at the same time seeks to guarantee specific rights to all Canadians wherever they live. Thus, unlike the states of the American union, Canada's provinces have a firm constitutional basis for confronting federal power, and they have often chosen to exercise this right. The most extreme demonstration of provincial authority would take place if Quebec elected to secede from Canada altogether.

State Characteristics

Equilibrium

There are certain features of function and organization that are characteristic to all states. One feature is to provide within state boundaries equilibrium, peace, and stability. This task is obviously more difficult for large and diverse states than for small ones. Throughout history, the achievement of equilibrium (or balance) and stability has been a goal of those states that had aspirations to political spatial universalism or *imperialism.* For example, the *Pax Romana* was imposed by Rome on its territories and made coincident with Rome's imperial boundaries. Balance and stability, of course, depended on the presence and strength of Roman legions. The *Pax Britannica* of the nineteenth century was Great Britain's attempt to assure the security of the British Empire. That effort was identified primarily with the range and maneuverability of the British navy. When that was challenged, as it was in the early decades of the twentieth century, worldwide conflict ensued. More than that, the increasing inability of Great Britain to control the seas by World War II encouraged the movement for regional autonomy throughout the empire that culminated ultimately in demands for independence. In the United States, the emergence of the sectional conflict between the agrarian South and the industrializing North in the nineteenth century severely challenged those forces that sought to preserve the union. Indeed, the integrity of the United States was achieved only after a bloody and devastating civil war. The stability of the USSR on the other hand has depended on the penetrating control exercised by the Communist party, the secret police, and ultimately the Red Army. Yet the rise of *dissidence* there, that is an opposition to the main policies of the Soviet regime, has shown that Soviet controls are not total and that the state is vulnerable to pressures, both internal as well as external, making for change.

Centrifugal-Centripetal Forces

The integration of political territory is often made difficult if the state contains peoples of different cultures and civilizations. The presence of strong regional cultural traditions creates barriers to the diffusion of the principal culture, making integration slow, if not impossible. The centralizing or *centripetal forces* of central authority may be offset by the disruptive or *centrifugal forces* that may occur from diversity (Gottmann, 1952). Revolts, civil wars, secessionist movements, and related conflicts may ensue. In Canada, the growth of Québécois nationalism in the 1970s caused concern among many Canadians because they feared that a demand for independence by Quebec would threaten the very existence of Canada. Until 1984, the federalists in Ottawa seemed to have convinced Canadians, especially those of Quebec, that there was more to gain from union than from the separation of Quebec from Canada.

The Importance of Communications

To ensure equilibrium and balance a good transportation and communication network is essential to any state. Imperial Rome recognized the validity of this principle when it undertook to secure the Mediterranean Sea against pirates and to build roads throughout the length and breadth of the empire. Roman artifacts, including roads, walls, and aqueducts, may still be seen anywhere from Syria to southern Scotland (Fig. 11–4).

The great railroads that were constructed in the nineteenth century were an extension of the principle. The railroads that linked St. Petersburg (now Leningrad) to Moscow and that tied the vast Eurasian empire together were Russia's means of asserting tsarist control over a landmass that embraced a sixth of the earth's surface. The British-built railroads in India were designed to promote the integration of the various diverse regions of the Indian subcontinent *and* to ensure British *hegemony,* or domination. In North America, the era of transcontinental railroad construction that followed the end of the Civil War in 1864 facilitated the movement of population westward and promoted economic integration. The Canadian Pacific was completed in 1885. In crossing the northern portion of the continent, it had an additional function. It not only tied the Pacific province of British Columbia to the Great Lakes, but also it contributed to the formation of a distinctly Canadian political space in the West, which might have fallen to the United States had the main lines of transportation and communication developed along north-south lines.

The Capital City

Political authority is usually associated with a capital city, which serves as the seat of government. The choice of a specific site or city as capital may be made for a variety of reasons. In the past, access by land or water was important if the city was to serve as a base of operations for administering a large and expanding territory and to be secure in its food supply. These were considerations in the founding of Alexandria, Constantinople, and Baghdad; they were also important in the growth of Rome, Moscow, and St. Petersburg.

Baghdad, founded by the caliph al-Mansur in A.D. 762 on the banks of the Tigris, is truly a classical example. It had only a short period of ascendancy, but it lived on in memory long after the fall of the Abbasid dynasty. During the eighth and early ninth centuries, Baghdad dominated the overland trade routes of the Middle East; the connections with Central Asia, northern Europe, Spain, and North Africa; and the sea routes to East Africa and Southeast Asia. Therefore, a great deal of wealth was concentrated in the city. Its golden age under the caliph Harun ar-Raschid (A.D. 786–809) and his

Figure 11–4

Ruins of Roman Aqueduct at Segovia, Spain. Rome produced excellent engineers who knit together the empire by a vast network of roads, the remains of which have been uncovered from Britain to Asia Minor. In architecture the Romans generally drew their inspiration from the Greeks, but they showed a native ingenuity in the development and construction of aqueducts, such as the one in Segovia, Spain, which survives to the present. The Segovia aqueduct, which is still in use, is one of the greatest monuments of the Roman world.

Source: Fritz Henle/Photo Researchers, Inc.

successor has been depicted in *The Arabian Nights.*

Historic prestige, too, has been a factor in choosing capitals. Athens and Rome met this criterion when the modern states of Greece and Italy chose capitals in the nineteenth century. Although great meaning is attached to the name Jerusalem, it was for essentially historic religious reasons that the capital of Israel was ultimately established there. Not many foreign governments have located their embassies and legations in that city however, because they are aware that Arab states with whom they maintain political relationships do not accept the political role of Jerusalem in Israel.

A central location is essential, too, if a compromise is sought between sections of the country or between differing cultures. In an age when overland movement was slow, Alexander the Great considered the possibility of two capitals for his large empire, one at Babylon to serve the oriental half of the empire, the other

Figure 11-5

The Fortress of Saints Peter and Paul was erected on an island in the Neva River in 1702 when the city of St. Petersburg (now Leningrad) was founded by Tsar Peter the Great to be his "window on Europe." In 1713 St. Petersburg became the capital of the Russian Empire, replacing Moscow. In 1914, the city was renamed Petrograd and in 1918, following the Revolution, the capital of the new Soviet republic was returned to Moscow.

Source: Tass from Sovfoto

at Alexandria in Egypt to control the western half.

Rome, from its central position in the Mediterranean, achieved a brilliance hitherto unknown in the world. However, the capital of the Roman Empire was moved to Constantinople when it became apparent in the fourth century A.D. that the center of economic gravity had shifted to the eastern Mediterranean. The Emperor Constantine rebuilt the old Greek settlement of Byzantium and made it his capital in A.D. 330. Constantinople was given the additional title of Nova Roma or New Rome.

Capitals have frequently been moved to promote state goals. Peter the Great abandoned historic Moscow, despite its centrality, for a new capital at St. Petersburg, at the mouth of the Neva, which he had founded in 1702 (Fig. 11-5). St. Petersburg was to serve as Russia's window on the Baltic through which would come modernizing trends from western Europe. When the Bolsheviks seized power in the autumn of 1917, they promptly returned the capital to Moscow to reinforce their abandonment of western patterns of socioeconomic development. At the founding of the Republic of Turkey in 1923, Ankara on the Turkish plateau was chosen over Istanbul (Constantinople), in part to disassociate the new republic from both its Byzantine roots and the caliphate that the Turks had established there. In Brazil, the capital was moved in 1960 from Rio de Janiero to the new city of Brasilia a thousand miles inland in an attempt to lure people from the coast and stimulate the economic growth of interior provinces.

The need for compromise was a factor in the siting of Washington, D.C., on the Potomac River midway between the North and the South; of Ottawa on the Ottawa River between the French culture region in Quebec and the English region in Ontario (Fig. 11–6); and of Canberra in Australia, halfway between the population of the Sydney region and that of Melbourne. In South Africa, a different type of compromise was arranged when the union of Boer states and British colonies occurred in 1902. Pretoria in the Transvaal was made the seat of the executive branch of government, Cape Town in Cape Province the seat of the legislative branch, and Bloemfontein in the Orange Free State the seat of the judiciary.

Figure 11–6

The Parliament buildings in Ottawa stand on an impressive bluff 150 feet above the Ottawa River. Ottawa became the capital of the united provinces of Upper (Ontario) and Lower (Quebec) Canada in 1858, and capital of the new Canadian confederation embracing Ontario, Quebec, Nova Scotia, and New Brunswick in 1867.

Source: Canadian Government Travel Bureau, Ottawa.

TERRITORIAL SOVEREIGNTY

Independence implies *de jure* (or sovereign) legal control over a political space, but *de facto* (or actual) jurisdiction may be difficult for a state to achieve. Surrounding states may have claims to territory and peripheral sections or regions of the state may feel a closer affinity with peoples in neighboring states. In addition, a territory may be so large or diverse geographically that integration may exact a high price, if it can be achieved at all.

De facto control of legitimate political space requires an effective network of communication and transportation facilities. Sovereignty must be demonstrated in every corner of the political spatial realm and boundaries must be well defined and defensible (Kristof, 1959). Large territorial states that have sparsely populated regions—like Brazil, Canada, the USSR, and the Chinese People's Republic—have had to make heavy investments in remote areas to ensure the viability of their outer reaches. Indeed, conflicts along the Sino-Soviet boundary have compelled both Moscow and Peking to be concerned about the security of vast empty areas along the Amur River in the Far East and in the grasslands and deserts of Central Asia.

At times, political power, in one form or another, may spill over international boundaries. Such a spillover may take the form of direct military intervention—as was the case when Poland was dissected by Russia and Germany in the early days of World War II and when Afghanistan was invaded by Russia in 1979—or it may be little more than the migration of peoples who settle and remain like a latent thorn in the side of the host country—like the migrations of Kazakh tribes across the Sino-Soviet boundary in Central Asia. A spillover may also occur through international financial investment or cultural incursions that create undue influence. For example, Canadians have been fearful of the political consequences of the penetration of American capital and ownership into Canadian resource and industrial development, and in some cases, they have adopted limits for foreign participation.

Zionism and the Founding of Israel

Europe's expression of nationalism was accompanied late in the nineteenth century by the rise of Zionism. Zionism became for Jews an expression of the age-old dream of a Jewish homeland. The movement took its name from the hill in Jerusalem on which the ancient palace of King David and subsequently the Temple were built. Zionism, thus, became the vehicle whereby the dream was translated into Jewish political space in the Middle East.

To escape persecution, migrants from eastern Europe had begun to resettle in Palestine, then under Ottoman Turkish control. In 1908, the city of Tel Aviv was founded. In 1917, the Balfour Declaration promised worldwide Jewry British support for the creation of a homeland in Palestine in exchange for Jewish support in World War I. After that war, migration increased to Palestine, now a British mandate under the League of Nations. Relations between Jews and Arabs were friendly but uneasy. By 1936, the Jewish population of Palestine reached four hundred thousand, almost 30 percent of the total population.

After World War II, survivors of the Holocaust in Europe moved en masse to Palestine. This rapid influx together with the territorial spread of Jewish settlement alarmed the native Palestinian population. Because of British withdrawal, the United Nations in 1947 resolved on a division of the territory into two parts, one Arab, the other Jewish. Following the partition, the State of Israel on May 14, 1948, proclaimed its independence, a move that was immediately recognized by the United States, the USSR, and many other countries.

Simultaneously, war ensued between Israel and its Arab neighbors. The conflict left several

Figure 11–7

Palestine and the shape of Israel, 1947–1982. The 1947 U.N. partition plan for British-held Palestine envisaged two states, one Arab, the other Jewish, and with an international zone in and around Jerusalem. Following the vote of the United Nations on the plan, the Jewish inhabitants in 1948 moved to establish a state, which they called Israel. In the 1948 war between Israel and the Arab states—Egypt, Jordan, and Syria—Israel succeeded in adding significant portions of the territory originally designated Arab by the United Nations. Much

hundred thousand Palestinian Arabs homeless, many resettling in Transjordan. Jerusalem was left divided, with the site of the historic Temple falling to the jurisdiction of the Jordanians (Fig. 11–7). In 1949, the Jewish population amounted to only 660,000, and Israel contained 150,000 Arabs.

Since 1948, four additional wars between Israel and the Arab states have rocked the Middle East. After the 1956 war, which had seen an Israeli invasion of Sinai, thousands of Jews in the Arab countries, known as *Sephardim* or southern Jews, were forced to migrate to Israel. In the 1967 war, Israel gained control of all Jerusalem and the West Bank of the Jordan. Jerusalem was incorporated into the State of Israel, but the West Bank (and Gaza) are "administered" territories. Thus, the 1967 war increased the number of Arabs under Israeli jurisdiction to 1.2 million. The Jewish population at that time totaled 2.5 million.

After the intense struggle of 1973, Israel occupied additional territories at the expense of Egypt and Syria. A 1979 peace treaty between Egypt and Israel required the latter to return, by stages, the lands taken from Egypt in Sinai (excluding Gaza). By 1982, the Sinai was again in Egyptian possession, but fear of Palestine Liberation Organization (PLO) strikes along the northern border sent Israeli forces in 1982 into southern Lebanon as far as Beirut. The removal of many Palestinians from the refugee camps in Lebanon lessened the immediate tension, but a 1983 treaty provided for an Israeli-maintained security zone in southern Lebanon. Even so,

Israel's 3.4 million Jews remained uneasy because the number of Arabs under Israeli control had climbed to 2.2 million. At the same time, Syria continues to be a major adversary in the north and conflicting communities in Lebanon—Christian, Muslim, and Druze—threaten to divide that country, leading to greater regional instability.

SOVEREIGNTY AND SEASPACE

State rivalries over lands have been a recurrent theme in human history. The modern world, however, also has begun to face problems associated with competition for use and control of the oceans and the resources within them (Prescott, 1975).

The discovery of the sea was among the most significant events in the history of the world. The laying of the first intercontinental maritime cable in 1859, however, was the real beginning of the conquest of the vast distances posed by the sea. Such an innovation ushered in the beginnings of the worldwide transoceanic communication system, which was later completed with the introduction of steam navigation and, subsequently, by air travel.

In past centuries, humankind won many battles with the sea, but the limitations of existing technology prevented a real conquest. Maritime trading empires are as old as civilization itself, but it was not until the fifteenth century A.D. that humankind began to lay the foundations of

Figure 11–7 (continued)

of central Palestine, now referred to as the West Bank, came under Jordanian administration, along with eastern Jerusalem, including the Old City.

A third Arab-Israeli War in 1967 left Israel in possession of the Gaza Strip and the entire Sinai Peninsula as far as the Suez Canal, taken from Egypt; the West Bank and the Old City, taken from Jordan; and the Golan Heights, taken from Syria.

An Egyptian-Israeli agreement in 1975 provided for

Israeli withdrawal from the Canal Zone in return for Israeli right of passage through the canal. The 1978 Camp David Agreement between Egypt and Israel provided for a further Israeli withdrawal in stages from the Sinai in return for a treaty of peace that was signed in 1979. In the early summer of 1982, Israel invaded Lebanon and remained in control of the southern part of that state in 1984.

(*Source:* Day, 1982, p. 188.)

a global system of oceanic linkages that helped shape the modern world. And until the latter part of the nineteenth century, a journey by sea remained an interminable affair.

Traditional use of the sea has been limited to navigation and fishing. Since the earliest times, the earth's major bodies of water have been broad highways that linked peoples, even as they separated them. When technology permitted access to the open sea, the establishment of trade and the planting of colonies were encouraged. But, in the process, the seas were also battlegrounds upon which states pushed their ambitions and pursued their objectives.

In the distant past, little thought was given to the ownership of the water bodies. Although the Romans spoke of the Mediterranean as *mare nostrum* (our sea), this was never translated into any kind of legal doctrine. Merchant ships followed the trade routes, fishing fleets ranged steadily further afield in search of migrating fish, and naval engagements took place with increasing frequency—but ownership of the water was never an issue.

European coastal states began to make claims to offshore waters in the early medieval period, but from the early 1600s, the principle of freedom of the seas, as advanced by the Dutch jurist Hugo Grotius, became the basis of international oceanic law. The principle was supported by all the great maritime powers of Europe, especially by Great Britain.

Each state, however, felt the need to control an immediate offshore area for purposes of defense. Another Dutch jurist, Cornelius van Bynkershoek, argued in his treatise *De domino maris* (1702) that dominion over seas could extend only so far as the maximum range of a land-based cannon. This notion was accepted and for over 200 years, sovereignty was fixed at 3 miles. In recent decades, technological advances in fishing and in offshore mining and drilling methods have pushed states to claim territorial waters to 12 and even 200 miles offshore.

In 1945, the United States, in the Truman Proclamation, claimed sole right to the riches of its *continental shelf,* which is the extension of the continent through shallow seas to where the slope drops sharply to the deep sea floor. In 1952, both Ecuador and Chile, although having little continental shelf, claimed exclusive fishing rights up to 200 miles from shore. Since then, other states have laid claims to the extensive waters surrounding them, leading to conflicts, such as the "cod war" between Iceland and Britain in the North Sea (Box 11–2).

In 1958, the Law of the Sea Conference, meeting in Geneva, Switzerland, supported the extension of political jurisdiction of maritime states over the resources on and beneath the seabed of the continental shelf to a depth of 600 feet or beyond that limit to a depth where exploitation of the seabed is possible. This ruling, however, has not resolved the problem. Since 1958, drilling and mining technologies have advanced rapidly, requiring new regulations and delineations. Moreover, the rights of landlocked states to a share of the oceans' mineral and energy resources have yet to be considered and resolved.

SOVEREIGNTY AND AIRSPACE

However the resources of the seas are divided among the states of the world, ships would probably retain the right of innocent passage through the territorial waters of other states, while enroute. Airlines, on the other hand, have no such right through the air. They must negotiate rights to fly over each state's territory.

The question of how far up national sovereignty extends remains an open question. Although it is generally agreed that national airspace ends at some altitude, that altitude has yet to be determined. Application of the van Bynkershoek principle has been suggested, and the USSR quietly tolerated American U-2 flights over its territory only until it possessed the capability of shooting the planes down.

Many scholars favor the designation of the lowest altitude at which satellites can be put into orbit at least once around the earth as the limit of national sovereignty. That figure ranges between 70 and 100 miles.

Also unresolved is the question of sovereignty in outer space. Rules of jurisdiction such as have been applied to Antarctica, the only permanently uninhabited land area on the planet, may be transferred to the moon and beyond. In a treaty signed in Washington, D.C., in 1959, all nations that had claims to Antarctica (such as those based on the sector theory) placed their claims in abeyance, and the entire Antarctic continent is now open to exploration with complete freedom of access. According to

---

BOX 11–2

Property Rights to the Sea's Resources: The "Cod Wars"

Ocean fishing traditionally has been regarded as a *common property right*, with all fish free for the taking. In the twentieth century, however, international treaties have come into being to clarify fishing rights and privileges, to provide for oceanic research coordination, to determine quotas, and to allow for the management of stock. More may still be required as a result of the rapid development of international fisheries. The extension of territorial waters to 12 or more miles and the establishment of exclusive economic zones out to 200 miles are designed to prevent overfishing, but conflicts of interest have also arisen and tension has grown. The fear is that as jurisdictions are extended outward to 200 miles, nations will exercise their control in a capricious manner. Even where research is the prime goal, nations have become increasingly reticent about granting permission for foreign ships to come within territorial waters. They have even become reluctant for research to be published concerning their waters.

The dispute between Iceland and Great Britain over traditional fisheries is indicative of the kind of tension the world faces with respect to the seas. It represents, specifically, a conflict over a diminishing resource. The "cod wars" began in 1958. The first skirmish lasted until 1961, and after that, there were two additional confrontations in 1972–1973 and in 1975–1976. These conflicts entailed encounters at sea between British frigates and trawlers and Icelandic gunboats, as well as dispute and negotiation through diplomatic channels.

Iceland is highly dependent on the fisheries of its surrounding waters. In 1971, for example, 80 percent of its export revenue came from fish products. In 1972, Iceland extended its jurisdiction over the waters and seabed out to a distance of 50 miles. The British, dependent on the fishery as well, objected, and the second dispute ensued. However, the International Court in 1974 gave judicial recognition to the principle that coastal states have a natural interest in and, hence, a special right to protect fish stocks in areas of the high seas adjacent to their territorial seas. This principle also had had majority support at the Geneva Law of the Sea Conferences in 1958 and 1960.

Since the 1950s, Icelandic fishermen have taken about half of the catch originating in their coastal waters. Britain has taken a fourth. Although Iceland has claimed that the grounds were being overexploited—with some degree of truth—it is clear that, by considering the fish a national resource, Iceland felt it could increase its share by demanding and exercising political jurisdiction over the expanded territory.

Since the "cod wars," there have been other instances of tension over claims to fisheries, notably between the United States and Canada in the Pacific. Unless international agreement is achieved, the exploitation of the mineral resources of the seabed could lead the world into further difficulties in the future.

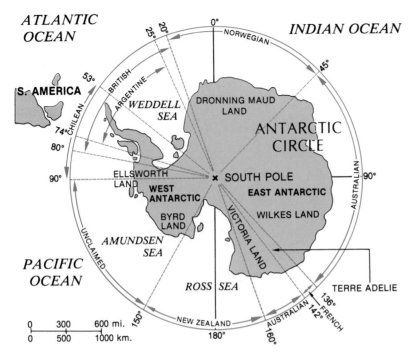

Figure 11–8

Territorial claims in Antarctica. Although first discovered by sealers early in the nineteenth century, Antarctica is a continent that has remained virtually unknown to humankind. About 98 percent of it lies under a huge ice cap. In the two decades prior to World War II, the continent experienced a period of competing national rivalries.

In 1959, the competing states agreed to a treaty that emphasized cooperation for scientific purposes. However, national claims have not been abandoned, only shelved, and they are expected to surface again as the treaty period ends in 1991.

Among the 12 original signers of the treaty were the United States, the Soviet Union, Great Britain, France, Belgium, Norway, and—in the Southern Hemisphere—Chile, Argentina, South Africa, Australia, and New Zealand. Poland, West Germany, Brazil, and India have also been allowed to engage in scientific research on the continent.

Antarctica is suspected to contain deposits of oil, natural gas, iron, coal, and other minerals.

(*Source:* Day, 1983, p. 386.)

---

the treaty, Antarctica must not be militarized, although it is freely accessible for scientific study and research. However, the treaty expires in 1991 and competition may quickly replace cooperation, with claims to Antarctic territory based on sectors (Fig. 11–8).

Although the modern nation-state is the focus of our most intense political loyalties, mankind has never ceased striving to forge even larger political associations. In the past, many territorially vast associations, such as empires, were created by colonization and conquest. Others were formed through alliances and voluntary collaboration. Supranational political associations of the voluntary type, however, have failed to achieve the means of enforcing decisions that are binding on all participants. Nevertheless, the yearning for a world order based on law remains one of the noblest aspirations of humanity.

The League of Nations and the United Nations

The year 1980 marked the 35th anniversary of the United Nations but, like the League of Nations, which preceded it and suffered its greatest defeat with the outbreak of World War II, this newer international association seems still distant from achieving the dream of all peoples—to be allowed to live out their lives on earth in peace. Conflicts between states and civil strife within states leading to armed confrontation are commonplace on almost every continent. As a result of these stresses, the noblest aspirations of the United Nations continue to remain beyond the reach of humankind.

This motive underlay the formation of the United Nations in 1945 as it did that of the League of Nations in 1919. But, the motive is one that has existed throughout history and underlain the creation of all associations designed to promote collective goals. It is probable that in prehistoric times hunting bands larger than the family, although still very small, were formed to ensure food for all and to provide strength against attack from other hunters. To guarantee the group's success, cooperation and some degree of organization and leadership would have been necessary.

In Europe in the past, the great powers frequently banded together in concert to impose stability on the Continent, but when they disagreed, as they frequently did, conflict or war ensued. In addition, Great Britain periodically sought to balance the divisions in Europe by throwing her support to the weaker side, but the success of this *balance of power* required a strong and attentive Britain. The Hague Peace Conferences or the Hague Conventions of 1899 and 1907 were among the first attempts to deal with international problems, such as placing limitations on armaments. The 1899 Convention provided for the establishment of a World Court, or the Permanent Court of International Justice.

The first tangible effort to create a free international association of states came after World War I with the League of Nations, which was housed in Geneva, Switzerland, a neutral country during World War I. The failure of the United States to join the League was a severe blow, but during the late 1920s, the United States participated with League members in discussions on disarmament. The League was a useful forum for discussion; it solved with varying degrees of success a number of political disputes; and it carried out numerous humanitarian projects. It failed, however, to stop Japan's aggression in Manchuria in the early 1930s, to prevent Italy's invasion of Ethiopia in 1935, and to terminate German and Italian intervention in the Spanish Civil War in 1936. Its greatest failure, of course, was its inability to control the forces that led to the outbreak of World War II in 1939.

At the end of World War II, the United Nations came into existence. Although almost all of the world's states are represented, the organization lacks the power or the machinery to enforce decisions. The Security Council is the main repository of power in the United Nations, with primary responsibility for the maintenance of international peace and security, but without unity among its permanent members— the United States, the USSR, the United Kingdom, France, and China—the Council cannot act. The General Assembly, with equal representation for every state, large or small, serves as a rudimentary legislature, but its deliberations are not binding.

More limited associations outside the League or the United Nations have also been formed. Ever since coming to power, the Soviet regime in Russia has tried to develop a world organization under its leadership aimed at promoting its ideological doctrines.

Communist International Organizations

To the end of promoting Marxist-Leninist ideology, the Third Communist International (*Comintern*) was formed in 1919, with the purpose of creating the International Soviet Republic as a transitional stage moving toward the complete abolition of the state. The activities of the Comintern or the Third International came to an end in 1943 when it was necessary for the Soviet regime to gain support from the West during World War II. Following the war, in 1947, a Communist Information Bureau (*Cominform*) was established under Soviet influence. Its objective, more limited than that of the Comintern, was primarily to assist in the consolidation of power in the Eastern European states falling under Soviet domination. It failed to prevent the defection of Yugoslavia under Tito in 1948, and it was subsequently abolished in 1956. In 1949, however, a Council for Mutual Economic Assistance (*COMECON*) was created to adjust economic planning in Soviet-dominated countries to Soviet Russian interests.

The European Community

The European Coal and Steel Community (ECSC) established in Western Europe in 1951, was a supranational authority with powers of regulation over the affected industries. In its administration of the coal, iron, and steel industries of France, West Germany, the Netherlands, Belgium, Luxembourg, and Italy, ECSC did much to speed the economic recovery of war-battered Western Europe. With the Treaty of Rome in 1957, the narrower association was broadened into the *European Economic Community* (*EEC*), or European Common Market.

The immediate goal of EEC was the elimination of restrictions on the free movement of goods, capital, and people within the community; in broader perspective, its aim was the eventual political unification of Europe. By the early 1970s, Denmark, Ireland, and the United Kingdom also sought and gained admission to the Common Market. Close economic ties have also been maintained by EEC with a number of the member nations' former colonial dependencies.

On January 1, 1979, a new European Monetary System (EMS) of linked currencies came into existence, embracing West Germany, France, the Netherlands, Belgium, Luxembourg, and Denmark. Subsequently, the United Kingdom, Italy and Ireland brought their currencies into line with the new monetary system. In the meantime, Greece has been admitted to the EEC and applications for admission from Spain and Portugal are under consideration.

CONTEMPORARY TENSION AREAS

Reference has already been made to a number of problem areas that cause tension in the modern world and challenge regional and international organizations to pressure for mediation and peaceful conflict resolution. Over the past decades since World War II, wars between states, whether declared or undeclared, have claimed millions of lives and forced countless peoples to migrate to other lands. These conflicts involve disputes over territory, over boundaries, over resources, and even over potential resources. Only examples of some of these problems can be presented here.

The Falkland Islands' (Islas Malvinas') Crisis

Despite a checkered history of claims and possession, the Falkland Islands, a group of islands together with dependencies in the South Atlantic came under British sovereignty and occupation in 1833. Basing its claim in part as inheritor of a Spanish legacy, Argentina has challenged the British claim to the islands, which lie 8000 miles from Britain, but only 300 miles from the Argentinean coast. Unable to resolve the dilemma amicably, the Argentinean government elected to invade the islands, which took place on April 2–3, 1982. The conflict that ensued left casualties on both sides, but the Argentineans

Figure 11-9

The Falkland Islands comprise some 200 islands with a total land area of about 4700 square miles. The two main islands are known as East and West Falkland. The capital, Port Stanley, is located on East Falkland. With a climate dominated by prevailing westerly winds, the landscape is bleak and barren, as shown here at a small settlement on New Island. The vegetation, consisting of heather, grasses and low dense shrubby plants, sustains a large sheep population.

Source: George Holton/Photo Researchers, Inc.

were forced to capitulate on June 14 and withdraw to their home base. Since then, the British have taken to strengthening their garrison on the islands in preparation for any future confrontation or negotiation with Argentina.

What has caused this sudden attention to these barren islands, hosts to a native-born British population of less than two thousand whose loyalties are to Britain and whose economy has been based on sheep raising (Fig. 11-9)? The need to refocus Argentinean attention away from domestic pressures, including a galloping inflation, may have been one factor. But, there seem to be other factors more specifically geographic.

An American survey in 1970 of the coastal area around the Falklands described it as one of the most promising in the world for oil. Both Shell and Esso have sunk wells off the Argentine coast that yielded a small but encouraging flow of oil. A 1974 British geologic survey reaffirmed that promise.

If the promise of oil was not the immediate cause of the war, the potential, it is believed, hardened Argentina's resolve to gain the islands and British reaffirmation of a desire to hold them.

In addition, the relationship between the Falklands and the dependencies and the British sector claim to Antarctic territory, must certainly have been a consideration (Fig. 11-10). The British claim to 700,000 miles^2 of Antarctica is based on discovery and sovereignty over the islands to the north. Not only do the seas around the continent contain the largest untapped food resources of the marine world, 150

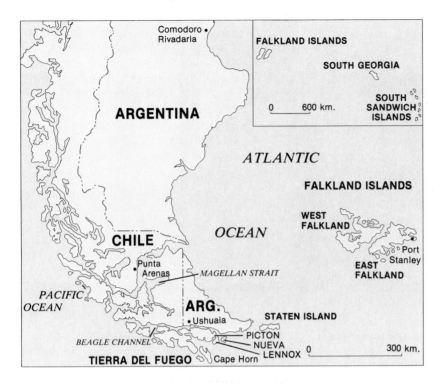

Figure 11–10

The conflict over the Falkland Islands (Islas Malvinas). The British claim to the Falkland Islands and dependencies is based principally on continuous occupance since 1833 and the fact that the islanders, known as kelpers, prefer to remain British. Argentina claims sovereignty over the Islas Malvinas because of short-lived occupance prior to 1833 and because the islands are near the Argentine coastline.

Much of the British claim to a sector of Antarctica ranging from 20° W to 80° W longitude is based on its possession of the Falklands, South Georgia, and the South Sandwich Islands. Argentina's claim to Antarctica, 25° W to 74° W longitude overlaps the claim of Great Britain as well as that of Chile, 53° W to 90° W.

(*Source: Guardian*, May 1, 1983.)

million tons of shrimplike krill, but also the continent itself is believed to possess significant quantities of a variety of minerals.

The Ogaden Crisis and Somalia's Claims

When European powers drew boundaries in Africa, they frequently did so with little regard to tribal or ethnic associations. The drawing of boundaries in the Horn of Africa by Great Britain, Italy, France, and Ethiopia (the sole sur-

viving independent native state in Africa) was an arduous process. And it was not fully complete even by the end of World War II and the granting of independence to a united Somalia in 1960 (Fig. 11–11).

British and Italian possession of the coastal strip along the eastward projection of Africa dates to the end of the nineteenth century. The boundary between British Somaliland and Ethiopia was established in 1897, although the British possession dates from 1884–1886. The boundary between Italian Somaliland and Ethi-

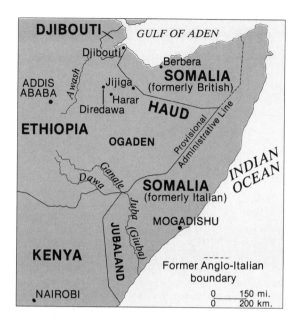

Figure 11-11

The Ogaden crisis. The creation of an independent Somalia out of British and Italian colonial territories in 1960 paved the way for the pressing of Somalia's claims to the Ogaden, a geographically ill-defined region that falls within Ethiopia. Ethiopian control dates from the latter part of the nineteenth century when Great Britain and Italy took possession of the coastal areas that became British and Italian Somaliland. The Ogaden, a dry region, is inhabited by nomadic pastoral tribes that belong ethnically to the Somali family. Somalia's attempt to claim the territory has been rebuffed and thousands of refugees have moved before the advance of the Ethiopian army into Somalia.

Djibouti, formerly French Somaliland, also contains an ethnic Somali population, but its inhabitants in a referendum in 1977, opted for separate independence.

(*Source:* Day, 1982, p. 111.)

opia was more difficult to define, and despite treaties in 1896 and 1908, a definitive line was never agreed on.

At issue is the Ogaden, a desert region inhabited by nomadic pastoralists of Somali ethnicity, but regarded by Ethiopia as part of its eastern provinces. For the Somalis, it is a question of *irredentism*, Western Somalia under foreign domination. The Somalis demand the application of the principle of *self-determination*, the right of all Somalis to live in one, self-governing state.

In 1967, imperial Ethiopia and Somalia agreed to negotiate the issue, but the new republican regime that seized power in Ethiopia in 1974 showed less interest. Somalis in the Ogaden rose in revolt, and by 1977, full-scale war had erupted between the two countries. The USSR, which had initially supported the Somalis, reversed itself and sent military aid to the Ethiopians. Early successes in the field by the Somalis were offset by subsequent Ethiopian gains.

The flood of refugees from Ethiopia has affected the ethnic composition of the Ogaden, which may in the long run lead to a de facto settlement of the problem.

Tension in the Horn of Africa is by no means confined to the Ethiopian-Somalian boundary. Somalia also seeks a rectification of its boundary with Kenya. The latter became independent of Great Britain in 1963, but it inherited the boundary dispute. Britain in 1930 had transferred Jubaland, a territory in northern Kenya with a predominantly Somali population, to Italian Somaliland. However, a number of Somalis remained in northern Kenya.

The Kenyans refuse to recognize Somali claims and have allied themselves with the Ethiopians in a 1979 Treaty of Friendship. There have been a number of border incidents.

Although Somalia also laid claim to French Somaliland, or Djibouti, on the basis that the territory and people belong to the Somali nation, a referendum of 1977 supported Djibouti independence. Somalia subsequently recognized the referendum.

What concerns the West, apart from the tragedy of the refugees, is the growth of Soviet influence in Ethiopia. With its influence over South Yemen intact, the USSR seems to be attempting to encircle the Gulf region and its oil fields.

The Iranian-Iraqi War

Although the Arab-Israeli conflict has been the source of most concern since 1948, it is not the only focal point of Middle East tension. The war between Iran and Iraq has overtones that could threaten the Arab establishment in the Gulf and in Saudi Arabia.

The immediate cause of the war that broke out in 1980 was the long-standing dispute over the Shatt-al-Arab waterway that flows into the Persian, or Arabian, Gulf in the Iraqi-Iranian border area (Fig. 11-12). Negotiations over the western boundary of Iran date back to the seventeenth century when the Ottoman Empire controlled much of the Middle East. However, it was not until 1843 that a boundary was agreed on. The Ottomans secured control over the entire waterway, but Iran was granted the small island of Abadan and anchorage on the left (or eastern) bank of the Shatt.

The discovery of oil in Iran at the turn of the century renewed interest in access to the waterway. At that time, however, Great Britain exercised effective control in the area. Although Abadan had by 1937 become an important oil center, the Iranians moved their main terminals to Kharg Island, lessening dependence on Abadan. Still, Iran depended on the waterway to move supplies to its upstream port at Mohammerah, or Khorramshahr, and found itself paying the bulk of the shipping revenues on the Shatt received by Iraq.

Unable to get a resolution of this issue, the Shah of Iran in 1969 abrogated earlier agreements, whereupon Iraq declared the Shatt-al-Arab solely an Iraqi waterway. Iran, in addition, threw its support behind Iraqi's Kurdish rebels and moved to occupy three small islands claimed by Iraq in the Strait of Hormuz.

However, in 1975, under pressure from the Organization of Petroleum Exporting Countries (OPEC) meeting in Algeria, Iran and Iraq agreed to set up committees to demarcate their land boundary, delimit the river boundary, and prevent border violations. Iran agreed to end its

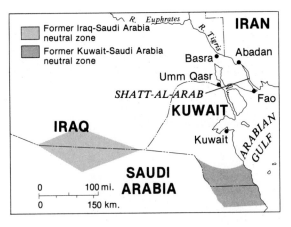

Figure 11-12 (A)

The Shatt-al-Arab—a navigable waterway that drains into the Persian (Arabian) Gulf in the southern border area between Iran and Iraq—has long been a source of conflict between the two countries. In the present century, the importance of the waterway has grown with the expansion of port facilities at Basra (Iraq) and Khorranshahr (Iran). A 1937 treaty offered a compromise formula for use of the waterway and the payment of tolls. In 1969, Iran abrogated the treaty, claiming that it had not received sufficient benefits from the revenues that it paid to maintain the waterway.

Relations between the two countries were further strained by Iran's support for Kurdish rebels fighting against the Iraqi government. However, in 1975, the two

support of the Kurdish rebels, Iraq agreed that the entire waterway should be drawn along the median line of the deepest channel. The overthrow of the Shah in 1979 and the Shiite Muslim revolution aroused the suspicions of the Iraqi government, and it reactivated its claim to the entire waterway. A large-scale offensive was launched against Iran, but by mid-1984, after substantial casualties and extensive damage to Iranian oil facilities, the war had stalemated. What concerns the Gulf states is the fear that should Iraq be defeated in the war, the Shiah revolution might sweep Iraq and the Gulf, which has a large Shiite Muslim population. Such a development would destabilize the Gulf and possibly Saudi Arabia and severely affect

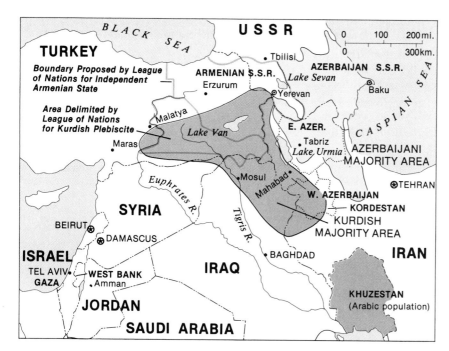

Figure 11–12 (B)

countries agreed to a delimitation of the river boundary, observing the median line principle. The revolution in Iran, which led to the fall of the shah in 1979, led to further tension; finally, in 1980, Iraq claimed sovereignty over the entire waterway. This decision was followed by the outbreak of war.

The neutral zone between Saudia Arabia and Kuwait was divided by agreement in 1969 and between Saudi Arabia and Iraq in 1981.

(*Source:* Day, 1982, p. 215.)

the interests of some of the industrialized countries by disturbing the flow of oil. On the other hand, should Iraq be victorious, there is concerned that this would be the first step in the dismemberment of Iran, affording opportunities for Soviet aggrandizement.

EPILOGUE

Thanks to the development of technology, the land surfaces of the earth have been effectively closed. All the land area has been occupied, in one fashion or another, and modern communication and transportation systems have short-

ened distances and brought all peoples closer together—at least in a physical sense. The creation of a true international economy, despite trade and travel restrictions, is well underway, to the point where crop failures or oil prices in one part of the globe have an almost immediate impact on peoples in another part. Global patterns of interaction on all levels have increased in intensity and in importance.

This high degree of interdependence threatens the existence of the nation-state. Sovereignty continues to be asserted, but the forces shaping the globe as a whole are frequently beyond the control of even such great powers as the United States or the USSR. One of these forces is the influence of large multinational corporations. By almost any reckoning, the role played by Standard Oil or Unilever in the world today is greater than that of most of the states admitted to the United Nations. Often state governments find themselves dealing with corporations as they might with foreign powers and frequently at a greater disadvantage because less is known about the corporations' internal structure or decision-making process.

The new forms of interdependency that have arisen in the twentieth century raise new challenges for humankind. Throughout history, the political organization of earthspace has changed and evolved as cultural and economic factors have altered. Perhaps it is time for the people of the earth to rethink their political situation and transfer their political loyalties to some new form of supranational organization that will better solve the "unsolvable" questions of today.

APPLICATION OF IDEAS

1. The human propensity to form groups or associations entails not only social interaction, but also the process because the very nature of organization is a political one. And, like much of human activity, the process of forming groups has a spatial dimension.

2. One facet of history is the record of humankind's efforts at carving up the earth's surface into units to serve political goals—the promotion of the ambitions, security, and welfare of different groups of people. Indeed, our political territories, our states, are the recipient of our highest loyalties.

3. States are organized to give expression to a national community. Where there is no national community, a state may strive to create one and thereby establish a national basis for securing the loyalty of its people.

4. Because of limited resources and the fact that the earth's surface is not equally endowed, many states lack the resources they deem necessary for a viable economy. This spatial imbalance leads to competition among states and, thus, conflict.

5. One way that states have sought to resolve conflicts and to assure their own security and survival is to form larger associations. This striving for larger association to guarantee the peace often meets with frustration and disappointment. Regional associations usually spring up as an added guarantee of security particularly where larger international associations are seen to be failing.

KEY WORDS AND PHRASES

balance of power
bourgeoisie
centrifugal forces
centripetal forces
city-state
COMECON
Cominform
Comintern
common property
  right
community
continental shelf
core area
core-periphery
  relationship
de facto
de jure
départements
dissidence
divine right
divinity of nature
dynastic state
Enlightenment
ethologist
European Economic
  Community (EEC)
federal
federative state

geopolitics
hegemony
imperialism
irredentism
mare nostrum
monarchical
  absolutism
multinational
nation
national self-interest
nation-state
natural limits
natural man
natural right
oblast
Pax Britannica
Pax Romana
pluralistic
proletariat
raison d'être
realpolitik
self-determination
sephardim
social contract
state idea
territoriality
unitary
universalism

QUESTIONS FOR FURTHER DISCUSSION

1. The concept of territoriality is appropriate to the discussion concerning the partitioning and organization of political space. However, it raises a number of questions pertaining to human motivation. What is the basis for these questions?

2. What is a nation? How does it differ from a nation-state? Give examples of states that are based on the nation. What states are organized on different concepts?

3. What are the origins of the nation? When did the national idea emerge as an important concept in European political history?

4. Compare and contrast the European dynastic state and the nation-states that began to emerge about the middle of the nineteenth century. What was the initial impetus in the formation of nation-states?

5. What was the purpose of Karl W. Deutsch's study of the emergence of the nation and nation-state? Map the historic changes that took place in the occupation and organization of the landscape as nations emerged in Europe.

6. Can the Deutsch model serve any useful purpose in the newly emerging modern states? On the basis of the distribution of population, the transportation network, and the economic development of a selected African state, indicate what recommendations you might deem essential to achieving a greater degree of internal cohesion and economic well-being in that state.

7. Examine the location of the world's great capital cities. What do they have in common? What attempts have been made to achieve specific political goals by moving capital cities? Explain why such moves have been successful in some cases and failed in others.

8. What crucial problems face the world's nations as they confront the possibility of a greater use of the sea's resources? How are these problems to be resolved?

9. What attempts have been made throughout history to achieve world peace and order? Why have such efforts failed in the past? Offer possible suggestions for future efforts.

10. To what extent do regional associations, such as the European Economic Community (EEC), offer a solution to the problem of war and peace? Why has this concept not emerged in the Americas or in other parts of the globe as a viable alternative to competition and confrontation?

REFERENCES AND ADDITIONAL READINGS

Barraclough, Geoffrey, ed. *Times Atlas of World History.* Maplewood, N.J.: Hammond, 1978.

Bennett, D. Gordon, ed. *Tension Areas of the World. A Problem Oriented World Regional Geography.* Delray Beach, Fla.: Park Press, 1982.

Burnett, Alan D., and Taylor, Peter J., eds. *Political Studies from Spatial Perspectives.* New York: John Wiley, 1981.

Cohen, Saul B. *Geography and Politics in a World Divided,* 2nd ed. New York: Oxford University Press, 1973.

Cohen, Saul B., and Rosenthal, L. D. "A Geographical Model for Political Systems Analysis." *Geographical Review* 61 (1971): 5–31.

Day, Alan J., ed. *Border and Territorial Disputes.* London: Longman, 1982.

Deutsch, Karl W. "The Growth of Nations: Some Recurrent Patterns of Political and Social Integration." *World Politics* 5 (1953): 168–195. (a)

——. *Nationalism and Social Communication. An Inquiry into the Foundations of Nationality.* Cambridge: MIT Press; New York: John Wiley, 1953. (b)

Downing, David. *An Atlas of Territorial and Border Disputes.* London: New English Library, 1980.

Easton, David. *A Framework for Political Analysis.* Englewood Cliffs, N.J.: Prentice-Hall, 1965. (a)

————. *A Systems Analysis of Political Life.* New York: John Wiley, 1965. (b)

Eisenstadt, S. N. *The Political Systems of Empires.* New York: Free Press, 1963.

Eisenstadt, S. N., and Rokkan, Stein, eds. *Building States and Nations* (2 vols.). London: Sage, 1973.

Fisher, C. A., ed. *Essays in Political Geography.* London: Methuen, 1968.

Fitzgerald, C. P. *The Chinese View of Their Place in the World.* London: Oxford University Press, 1969.

Gottmann, Jean. "Geography and International Relations." *World Politics* 3 (1951): 153–173.

————. "The Political Partitioning of Our World: An Attempt at Analysis." *World Politics* 4 (1952): 512–519.

————, ed. *Centre and Periphery. Spatial Variation in Politics.* London: Sage, 1980.

Hartshorne, Richard. "The Functional Approach in Political Geography." *Annals of the Association of American Geographers* 40 (1950): 95–130.

Herz, H. H. "Rise and Demise of the Territorial State." *World Politics* 9 (1957): 473–493.

Jackson, W. A. Douglas, ed. *Politics and Geographic Relationships: Readings on the Nature of Political Geography.* Englewood Cliffs, N.J.: Prentice-Hall, 1964.

Jackson, W. A. Douglas, and Bergman, Edward. *A Geography of Politics.* Dubuque, Iowa: William C. Brown, 1973.

Jackson, W. A. Douglas, and Samuels, Marwyn S., eds. *Politics and Geographic Relationships. Toward a New Focus.* Englewood Cliffs, N.J.: Prentice-Hall, 1971.

Johnston, R. J., *Geography and the State.* London: Macmillan, 1982.

Jones, Stephen B. "A Unified Field Theory of Political Geography." *Annals of the Association of American Geographers* 44 (1954): 111–123.

Kristof, Ladis K. D. "The Nature of Frontiers and Boundaries." *Annals of the Association of American Geographers* 49 (1959): 269–282.

————. "The Origin and Evolution of Geopolitics." *Journal of Conflict Resolution* 4 (1960): 15–51.

————. "The State-Idea, the National Idea and the Image of the Fatherland." *Orbis* 9 (1967): 238–255.

Lattimer, Owen. "Origins of the Great Wall of China: A Frontier Concept in Theory and Practice." *Geographical Review* 27 (1937): 529–549.

Mackinder, Halford J. "The Physical Bases of Political Geography." *Scottish Geographical Magazine* 6 (1890): 78–83.

————. *Democratic Ideals and Reality.* New York: Holt, Rinehart & Winston, 1942. (Originally published, 1919)

Martines, Lauro. *Power and Imagination. City-States in Renaissance Italy.* New York: Alfred A. Knopf, 1979.

Minghi, Julian, and Kasperson, Roger, eds. *The Structure of Political Geography.* Chicago: Aldine, 1969.

Prescott, J. R. V. *The Political Geography of the Oceans.* New York: John Wiley, 1975.

Ratzel, Friedrich. *Politische Geographie.* Munich: R. Oldenbourg Verlag, 1897.

Rokkan, Stein. "Dimensions of State Formation and Nation-Building: A Possible Paradigm for Research of Variations Within Europe," pp. 562–600. In *The Formation of National States in Western Europe.* Charles Tilly, ed. Princeton, N.J.: Princeton University Press, 1975.

Soja, Edward W. *The Political Organization of Space.* Resource Paper No. 8. Washington, D.C.: Commission on College Geography, Association of American Geographers, 1971.

Sprout, Harold, and Sprout, Margaret. *Toward a Politics of the Planet Earth.* New York: Van Nostrand, 1971.

Wolfe, Roy I. *Transportation and Politics.* Princeton, N.J.: Van Nostrand, 1963.

12
Settlement and Land Tenure

It is not too soon to provide by every possible means that as few as possible shall be without a little portion of land. The small landholders are the most precious part of a state.

Thomas Jefferson, October 28, 1785,
Letters to Reverend James Madison

[The word *agriculture*] means "cultivation of land." And *cultivation* is at the root of the sense both of *culture* and of *cult.* The ideas of tillage and worship are thus joined in culture. And these words all come from an Indo-European root meaning both "to revolve" and "to dwell." To live, to survive on the earth, to care for the soil, and to worship, all are bound at the root to the idea of a cycle.

Wendell Berry,
The Unsettling of America, 1977

Key Ideas

1. Land possesses many attributes and the human relationship to it needs to be seen not only in terms of settlement, but also in terms of how the land is held.

2. The settlement of western frontier lands took shape after the American Revolution when Congress took up the land question. The implementation of a grid system favored a widespread pattern of dispersed settlement.

3. The Homestead Act of 1862 carried the rectangular survey further across the prairies and plains, allowing for individual title to 160 acres.

4. The U.S. census of 1880 revealed that about a fourth of all farms were operated by tenants.

5. After World War II, tenancy declined, especially in the southern states and among the black population.

6. Land reform was carried out in Japan after World War II.

7. In Taiwan, a reform was carried out by the Nationalists in 1949 under a "land-to-the-tiller" program.

8. In Russia, serfdom was abolished in 1861, but the land was transferred to village communal organizations, which leased land to the villagers.

9. In 1928, the peasants were forced to surrender their holdings to collective farms, where the land was consolidated into large fields.

10. In China, the land reform under the communists after 1949 took a different course. Large landholdings were seized and redistributed among tenant farmers and small landowners. The next stage was the creation of agricultural cooperatives, not unlike Soviet collective farms.

THE SIGNIFICANCE OF LAND

Land possesses many attributes. It may serve as a factor of production, a source of wealth, a symbol of status in the society, and a basis for social and political influence. Thus, settlement on the land is an especially important theme in human geography and one to which geographers have given considerable attention. But, settlement patterns are only one facet of human occupancy of the earth's surface. How land is owned or held is an equally important geographic consideration because it suggests the relationship between a society and the land. The relationship to the land, too, may be an important determination of how land is used and how it is managed.

Governments have a vital interest in this relationship because it serves as a basis of the society over which they seek to govern. Land reform has been the means generally by which the relationship can be modified. The most common objective of land reform within the past few hundred years has been to abolish the legacy of the past, that is, eliminate the feudal land forms that evolved during the medieval period. This act has meant the overthrowing of the gentry or landlord class that owned and controlled the land. A second goal has been to increase social and economic stability by eliminating some of the causes of rural discontent. Land hunger, poverty, and despair were to be replaced by a rural society of individual farmers, people who had direct and vested interest in the land they worked. In short, this meant the creation of family farms.

In the USSR and many (but not all) countries adopting the Soviet model for restructuring the society and the economy, the goal has been (1) to overthrow what were deemed to be feudal and capitalist elements in the relationship of farmers and the land and (2) to create a class of people in the countryside who are not attached to the land but function with respect to the land just as workers relate to a factory.

This chapter focuses on these two fundamental themes: land settlement and land tenure.

SETTLEMENT IS HUMANKIND ADAPTING

Settlement, the geographer knows, is humankind's first step toward adapting to the environment and the formation of a home. The patterns that settlers have created in the process of occupying the land have differed considerably over the surface of the earth because the adaptation has not been uniform. Culture has played a role in how people have taken up the land, and the occupance, in turn, has helped shape culture. But the local physical characteristics of the earth's surface, too, have been influential in molding the patterns of human settlement. Still, for all the manifold variations, there are some basic forms that seem common to all humankind, whether in Japan, western Europe, El Salvador, the USSR, or the United States.

The patterns on the land, particularly where free of urban encroachment and the freeway, are to a large degree a reflection of earlier forms and usages. In many parts of the globe—even in North America—settlements were established in periods when human needs and requirements were dissimilar to those of the present, when the material basis of society was unlike that prevailing in the twentieth century. One cause of much unrest in Meso-America, South America, and in Southeast Asia has been the unwillingness of governments, supported by the military and landowning class, to recognize and accept the need for land reform. Opposition from landowners, however, is not the only reason why reforms, when introduced, have failed. Provision for peasants to have access to markets, credit, and other related necessities have often been ignored, making it virtually impossible for the transition from self-sufficient farming to market-oriented production to take place.

INDIVIDUALISM AND THE FAMILY FARM

Although there were attempts at group settlement in North America leading to the formation of agglomerated or nucleated communities, the occupance of the land was for the most part dispersed. Associated with dispersal was the notion of individual tenure, or right to the land, and a family farmstead. Little of the feudal structure then extant in Europe was transferred to the colonies. Yet to understand the true significance of what took place in the North American wilderness, it is necessary to review briefly the patterns in Europe on the eve of New World colonization.

Settlement and Tenure in Medieval Europe

In Europe, settlement dates back several thousands of years and to understand the evolution of patterns there one would have to investigate the lengthy record (Everson and Fitzgerald, 1969). What seems clear is that initially questions of physical security or preservation of the community must have occupied the minds of settlers.

The process was not a simple one. The early settlers of Europe must have made many attempts at permanent occupance, of which a number surely must have failed. And, moreover, they even occupied less desirable sites when even better locations could be found nearby. This description seems suited to much of the North American experience, although we tend to be reminded only of the successes. In any event, Europeans tended to live together in villages or *nucleated settlements* and go out to work their fields allotted them around the village.

Within the village itself, cottages, animal pens, and storage sheds were clustered about a green or commons, to which all persons had access, and which sometimes contained a pond for geese or ducks (Fig. 12–1). The arrival of Christianity from Rome or Constantinople added a church to the village community (Fig. 12–2).

European village settlements tended to remain stable over long periods of time. Although farming techniques remained crude, such communities tended to achieve a balance with the resources at their disposal. Rural community values also tended to remain relatively constant. Village life achieved social cohesion and awareness, especially through the presence of the church. And, the church graveyard gave a sense of continuity between past and present. Deaths as well as births and marriages were occasions for communal gatherings, whether for mourning or rejoicing and merrymaking. Over centuries, countless numbers of people—adhering to the faith, folkways, and traditions of ancestors—lived out their lives in such settlements. Nevertheless, change occurred, often imperceptibly; but epidemics, wars, religious divisions or ethnic diversification together with population increases in some centuries also from time to time rocked the basis of age-old patterns. France, from the eleventh through the thirteenth centuries, underwent a significant growth in village population that pushed families from overcrowded, long-settled areas onto virgin lands where new settlements were founded.

Although a clustered settlement was a common European phenomenon, it manifested itself in various forms (Box 12–1). The *line, or linear, settlement* is very old and seems to have been widespread even in early times. Most likely, linear settlement was a feature of the initial penetration of forests, with dwellings sitting on individual clearings facing the forest road. Such a cutting up of forestland may have been the forerunner of the *long lot* or *rang* that appeared in France. Such linear settlements appeared also along a river that served as the main artery of transportation (Jordan and Rowntree, 1979).

Throughout medieval Europe, much of the land was held by a relatively small number of

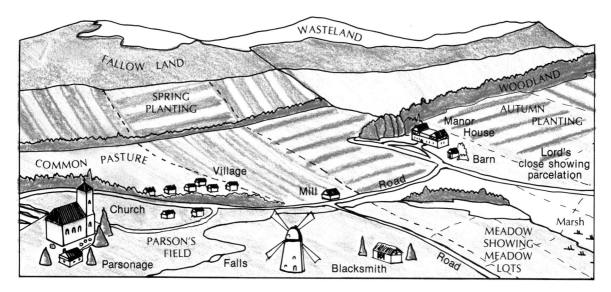

Figure 12–1

The medieval European village economy was dominated by the manor house, which stood some distance from the village proper, sometimes on a hill. The lands of the manor usually were divided into three large fields, which, in turn, were subdivided into strips that the peasants worked for the lord of the manor, for the church, and in a more restricted area, for themselves. Near the center of the village lay the common pastures and meadows where village cattle were allowed to graze. Woodlots, providing fuel and some game, often bounded the manorial estate.

gentry families who functioned as landlords, collecting rent or income from the people who, in their villages, were attached to the estates. Land was worked in common under a *three-field rotation system*. Each villager was allotted strips or plots of land to work for his own purpose, but he was also required to work the fields of the manor house. The three-field rotation imposed a regularized work pattern: one field ordinarily was given over to a spring crop, the second to a fall crop, and the third remained for a year in fallow. Rotation ensured that each field was fallowed every three years, the fallowing being regarded as essential to the preservation of production. In addition to their private or individual plots, the peasants had access to pasturelands and woodlots.

Reaction and Reform in France and England

In France, feudal relationships on the land remained intact until the revolutionary upheaval of 1789. Under the *ancien régime,* which had planted the first colonies in the New World, French society was polarized. Landed gentry and church officials stood over a mass of peasants. By the middle of the eighteenth century, a middle class had taken shape, but its numbers were small, especially in the countryside.

The majority of French country people, then, were hereditary tenants who paid a fixed money rent (*censiers*) for the land they worked or were serfs (*mainmortables*) who paid for the use of the land by *corvée,* or by laboring on the

Figure 12–2A

The Soviet collective farm is built around the village and the private plots of the villagers. Many of these villages, where the number of inhabitants has not grown through village consolidation, are settlements of the linear or line type, as shown here in the open countryside of the southwestern part of the Soviet Union. The private plots behind the cottage are particularly noticeable.

Source: Sovfoto.

Figure 12–2B

A village north of Moscow still shows the influence of the past, although the church, as a result of the Soviet antireligious campaign, in all likelihood is not used for religious purposes but rather for storage. There is a cluster of farmers' houses made of wood and logs, and at the center of the village, there is a duck pond where the women frequently come to wash the family clothing.

(Photo by W. A. Douglas Jackson, 1968.)

BOX 12-1

Central European
Settlement Types

In West Germany, rural settlements of the clustered type were called *haufendorfs,* and they are still visible in the landscape today (Fig. 12–3). Some German religious communities in North America opted for a settlement pattern such as this, although the fields of the villagers were usually of greater acreage.

In addition to settlements of clustered dwellings, nucleated settlement in Europe also took a straight-line form. Such line or linear settlements consisted of two rows of cottages facing a road; they were common in the English Midlands where the road was called a high street. Today, High Street is usually the main street of many English villages and towns. Line settlements were common also in France, Germany, and Russia. The Germans referred to such a village as a *strassendorf.* Barns, sheds, fields and other village lands stretched back from the dwelling, frequently as far as the outer reaches of a neighboring *strassendorf* (Fig. 12–3).

Feudal relations on the land survived in Central Europe until well into the middle of the nineteenth century. It was the revolutionary upheaval of 1848 that freed the peasants and led to land redistribution.

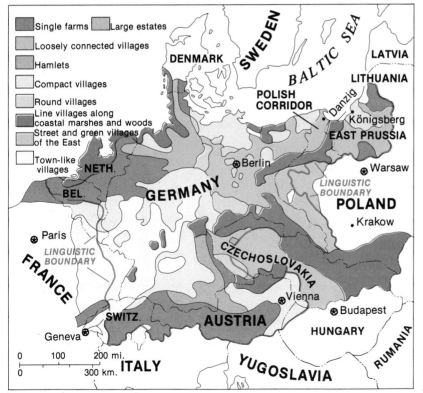

Figure 12-3

Village settlements, although common, were by no means universal in Europe. Townlike villages, compact villages, hamlets, and loosely connected villages were the decisive pattern in prewar western Germany, including the Rhineland, and in Austria and Denmark. In eastern Germany, especially in Prussia bordering the Baltic, large estates were predominant.

(*Source:* Pfeifer, 1956, p. 264.)

gentry estate. The *corvée* entailed about three days work per week. There were other dues and taxes that the peasantry were required to pay as well. In the creation of the *seigneurial system* in New France, the *corvée* was instituted, but it was not strictly adhered to.

Eighteenth-century France had seen the growth of the idea of agricultural individualism and of the concept of private ownership of land. When the *ancien régime* was overthrown, a land reform based on these principles was introduced, making it possible for tenants and serfs to become landowners. Although a new class of large landholders had come into existence with the Napoleonic era, France was set on the path of small family farms. These remain even today the basis of French rural society and agricultural production.

In England, the process of liquidating the feudal pattern began as early as the fifteenth century but was not completed until the nineteenth century. The means whereby this was

accomplished was the *enclosure movement.* Enclosure benefited the large landholders, it made possible the consolidation of their lands, the introduction of large-scale operations, and, of course, it preserved private ownership. However, it drove tenants and small operators off the land, leading to the emptying or abandonment of many small village settlements. Without land, the dispossessed were forced to work on the estates as laborers or to migrate to towns in search of work.

Whereas fifteenth-century enclosure was designed in part to underwrite the development of sheep raising and the production of wool for continental markets, enclosure in the eighteenth and nineteenth centuries was designed to satisfy other needs. A rising demand for foodstuffs in the growing towns together with the modernization of farming methods made enclosure of the remaining tenant-occupied open fields necessary (Fig. 12–4). Enclosure was one cause of migration to the New World.

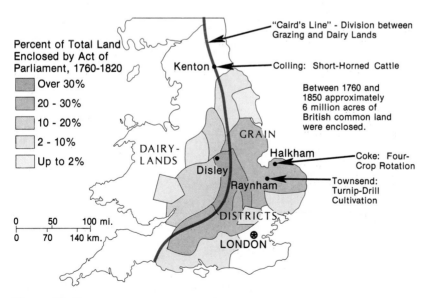

Figure 12–4

Eighteenth- and nineteenth century enclosure of commonly held or open fields was achieved by acts of Parliament. The effect was strongly felt in the central and eastern counties of England, including the Midlands. The tempo of change in the English countryside became quite rapid, especially after 1760, and the last vestiges of the medieval landscape were all but removed.

In the eighteenth and early nineteenth centuries, the possession of a large amount of land carried with it social prestige and political clout. It was a source of considerable wealth. As the nineteenth century progressed, the influence of the landed gentry was felt less and less as that of the commercial interests and industrial capitalists grew. At the same time, parliamentary reforms steadily admitted more members of society to the political process. Finally, the Reform Act of 1867 came close to creating universal male suffrage, which significantly weakened the older aristocratic order and the power of traditional agrarian interests.

NORTH AMERICAN SETTLEMENT AND TENURE

Throughout much of the vast interior of the United States and Canada, the land was framed in the nineteenth century by the imposition of the rectangular grid. The geometry is much in evidence, as any air traveler from the Appalachian Mountains and Great Lakes to the Rockies knows. The rectangular grid had been used elsewhere in the world, but for very different reasons and on a considerably smaller scale (Box 12–2). But, one of the main goals of settling the interior was to disperse settlement on individual homesteads in a massive way, simply because there was a lot of land and a lot of potential productive capacity to absorb. However, life in a homestead on the western frontier was a real test of endurance in the early years. Many are the tales of tragedy, of isolation, loneliness, fear, and despair that pioneers recorded in their journals or in the letters sent to relatives back home (Schlissel, 1982).

Before the United States and, at a later date, Canada undertook to settle the interior, colonies had already, long before, been established on their Atlantic shores. The forms of settlement that were attempted reflect strongly the patterns of Old World settlement, especially those prevailing in Europe at the time of migra-

BOX 12–2
The Rectangular Survey in the Old World

There is widespread evidence of the imposition of the rectangular grid in various parts of the Old World dating from earliest times. The street plan of Mohenjo-Daro, a prehistoric city in the Indus Valley, seems to have been based on straight lines and right angles. Some of China's early cities were also square-shaped, divided into two halves by a central axis that served as a main route from the palace in the north to the gate in the south. The rectangular survey that is still evident in parts of the Po Valley in northern Italy seems to have originated with the Etruscans, the predecessors of the Romans, and initially may have been associated with an art practiced by priests. These priests, or augurs, may not have been unlike the geomancers of ancient China, whose task was to determine the most favorable location for a city or a house.

In the Roman world, however, the use of the rectangular survey, or *centuriatio,* had limited application (Kish, 1962). It seems to have been restricted to more or less planned settlements in newly conquered lands. When Carthage in North Africa was destroyed by Rome in 146 B.C., for example, it was decreed that the site be surveyed and divided according to a grid.

The basis of the Roman rectangular survey was the *centuria,* which was further divided into one hundred *heredia* (homesteads). The *centuria* had an area of 132 acres. The center of the survey was the *umbilicus,* literally the navel, which was the intersection of the principal streets (known as the *decumanus* and *cardo*). In classical Rome, the *centuria* and its coordinates were applied only to limited areas and bore no relationship to the earth itself.

Like the rectangular form of settlements, Roman fields were laid out in square or rectangular lots of approximately 776 yards. Farmers, if they were Roman citizens, had absolute ownership of their land by law, but they could use slaves for all or a portion of the fieldwork. What the imposition

---

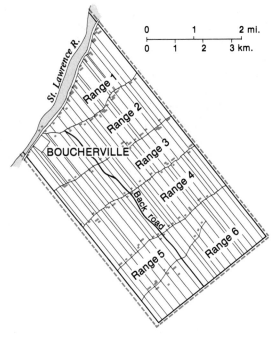

Figure 12–5

The system of land settlement in New France was well suited to the banks of the St. Lawrence where long-distance travel depended on the river. However, although farmhouses were closely spaced, few nucleated settlements emerged. Settlers farther from the river were often isolated. As settlement proceeded beyond the front or river range of lots, roads were extended inland at right angles to the river. These back roads linked the range roads that ran parallel to the river and served as the starting lines of new ranges of lots.

(*Source:* Searfe et al., 1963, p. 138.)

---

tion. Although modifications were introduced to meet the entirely new conditions of North America, it is worth remembering that these forms were derived from the land experience of the Old World, especially of France and England (R. H. Jackson, 1980).

Acadia and New France: French Forms in the New World

Although Spain was the first of the European powers to establish a settlement in what is now the United States (Florida), it is to the French that the honor goes for planting the first successful colony in North America. French colonization was to stand in sharp contrast to that of the English who followed soon after (Fig. 12–5). French settlement tended to reflect rigid French geometry (Harris and Warkentin, 1974). The application of this geometry was particularly evident in Canada along the banks of the St. Lawrence below Montreal and, to a lesser degree, around the Bay of Fundy in Acadia. The pattern was evident also in later French or French-inspired settlements in Louisiana, Wisconsin, Illinois (Vincennes), Michigan (near Detroit, see Fig. 12–6), Manitoba (along the Red River), in Saskatchewan, and in Texas (Jordan and Rowntree, 1979). Only the settlement of French Canada, however, occurred within the context of the medieval manorial or

seigneurial system; in Acadia the latter was only weakly evidenced.

The French initially made large grants of land to seigneurs who had a responsibility for settling their *seigneurie* and who exercised certain feudal rights over the *habitants,* their tenants. In the 1630s, the *seigneuries* along the St. Lawrence were surveyed into long narrow lots, about 400 to 500 feet in width, stretching for nearly a mile back from the river, which was the

Figure 12–6

Long lots characterized French settlement on the Detroit River. They are still evident in the vicinity of Windsor, Canada, today, where they stand in sharp contrast
to the rectangular survey of the later British period (Lajeunesse, 1960).

(Courtesy Ontario Ministry of Natural Resources.)

main artery of movement through New France.
Habitant cottages, normally one to a lot, were
distributed evenly along the river for miles. In
time, sturdy farmhouses replaced the pioneer
dwellings and these can still be seen extending
along the St. Lawrence.

What was particularly unusual about French
settlement was that there were few village nuclei. In Acadia, apart from Port Royal near the
mouth of the Annapolis River, there were none
(Fig. 12–7). In Canada, even as late as 1759
when New France fell to an attacking British-
American army, there were only six villages
and four hamlets between Montreal and the
mouth of the St. Lawrence in addition to Quebec, Trois-Rivières, and Montreal itself. Moreover, each of the last three had been founded to
serve the needs of the fur trade and not those of
the *habitants.* Lacking a system of nucleated
settlements, French Canada found its sense of

community largely through the parish church
and the family.

Although the feudal system was transferred
to New France, it was considerably changed
and liberalized in the process. The demands of
the wilderness environment simply called for
adjustment. In Acadia, feudalism did not adapt
at all; it simply disappeared. In any event, the
French *habitant,* or settler, was never impoverished by feudal demands and seigneurial taxes.
Despite the English conquest in 1759, with the
fall of the Quebec fortress, the seigneurial system, on paper at least, survived until 1854 when
it was abolished legally.

New England Nucleated Settlement

Early seventeenth-century English settlement
in New England adhered to the nucleated form.
A basic land unit was the town, about 36 miles^2,

Figure 12–7

Despite exile in the English colonies of the Atlantic sea-board in 1755, those Acadians who returned to Canada after 1763 continued to form settlements in the traditional French pattern. Caraquet, New Brunswick, established on the south shore of the Chaleur Bay consisted of a single street along which stretched the long lots of the farms. The settlement shown here was photographed in 1910.

(Photo by Father Joseph Courtois. Courtesy Historical Resources Administration. Village Historique Acadien, Caraquet, New Brunswick.)

which contained at its center an organized village community. Initially, the early settlers lived in the *town center* and worked, in a somewhat communal fashion, the surrounding fields allotted them (Fig. 12–8B). Grants of land could be made by the English or colonial authorities to individual settlers but the practice was to convey a large tract to one person who was required to plant a town and bring in settlers.

When the countryside around the town center had been parceled out, a new town would be formed in another part of the colony. Portsmouth, Massachusetts (now Rhode Island), was established in 1638, for example, but in 1639 a group broke away to found Newport and later Warwick (1642) at other points along Narragansett Bay.

The laying out of fields tended not to be done in any strict geometric fashion, although much later surveys became more regularized. At first, however, a system of *metes and bounds*—employed in England in the past—produced irregularly shaped fields whose boundaries were determined by natural features in the landscape, such as a tall tree, a large glacial boulder, or a creek. In time, fields came to be marked by lines of rocks gathered by the farmers to delineate holdings. Such rock dividers may still be seen stretching across the New England countryside.

Although the more southerly parts of New England had undergone extensive clearing as settlement progressed and the Amerindians were driven back, the forest was ever ready to reclaim the land. Because small fields on difficult terrain and poor soil ultimately proved an economic disaster, land abandonment had already gotten underway by the time of the Revolution. Still, by the early decades of the nineteenth century, the New England countryside possessed an open appearance, save for orchards and small woodlots. After the Civil War, the decline of the well-cultivated New England landscape had become striking and second-

Figure 12–8A

The plantations that took root and flourished in the South were often centered on splendid houses such as Shirley Plantation, on the James River below Richmond, Virginia, shown here. Imposing colonades and verandas usually dominated the front of the house, while at the rear were quarters for slaves.

Source: Joseph J. Schomon/Photo Researchers

growth forests were overrunning farmlands, creating a totally different kind of scenery.

The function and purpose of the early New England town had been to afford the pioneers some semblance of community life, an opportunity to practice their religion and preserve the strict Calvinist code of behavior, participation in the regulation of town affairs and, when necessary at first, security against Indian attack. Gradually, assertive individualism led town center dwellers to move out onto their own lands so that settlement became increasingly dispersed. However, after the Revolution, the lure of more fertile western lands steadily drew New Englanders into the Ohio Valley, into Upper Canada (Ontario), and into the prairies beyond.

Indiscriminate Location in the Southern Colonies

The tendency in England had been to envisage and support group settlement in the colonies. This was particularly true when it came to planting settlers along the Tidewater south of Pennsylvania. This policy was reflected in the founding of the Jamestown settlement in 1607. Grants, called hundreds or particular plantations, were to be made to large companies or groups who would undertake to organize the migration to, and resettlement in, America. In the 1970s, a lost settlement of this type, known as Martin's Hundred located on the James River, was excavated. It was found to consist of a twenty-thousand-acre grant that showed the

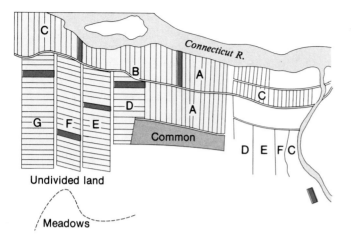

A. House lots
B. Village green
C. Meadow land
D. First division
E. Second division
F. Third division
G. Fourth division
▬▬ Allotments to typical family

Figure 12–8B

Not all of the early New England settlements conformed to a rigid model, but the orderliness of land division that generally prevailed was in sharp contrast to that which prevailed in the southern colonies. As the settlement grew and additional land was cleared, further divisions of land were necessary. When much of the land had been occupied, new towns were founded deeper in the forest and farther from the coast.

(*Source:* After Billington, 1950, p. 69.)

construction of a rudimentary palisaded fort and a fledgling community known as Wolstenholme Towne (Hume, 1982).

Out of many of these early grants to individuals emerged the plantation, a system of land organization under family ownership but dependent on poor-white, indentured, or black-slave labor. Tobacco had become a cash crop, so, by right of early location and to facilitate export to England, plantations tended to front on navigable rivers and waterways (12–8A).

Individual ownership of land also became possible in the 1620s, in response to the demands of colonists. In this case, they were simply granted a warrant by the colonial authorities, which permitted them to occupy and use a specified number of acres. If no one contested the claim, the settler received title based on a simple description (R. H. Jackson, 1981).

Because tobacco as a crop quickly exhausted soil nutrients, requiring the clearing of additional land, new settlers to the southern Tidewater were increasingly required to locate further upstream and inland. There was no preconceived organization of land occupance, with the result that in subsequent years this *indiscriminate* (*location*) often led to confusion over boundaries and titles (Box 12–3).

Spanish *Encomiendas, Rancherias, and Missions*

Although Spain never played a very active nor extensive role in settling its possessions in what is now the southern part of the United States, its efforts, nevertheless, are of interest. On the one hand, the style was reminiscent of Old Spain; on the other hand, Spain showed an awareness of New World conditions that neither France nor England demonstrated.

The Spanish system for settling the New World was derived from Roman principles, with guidelines drawn from the work of the Roman architect, Vitruvius, whose work, written about 27 B.C., had been rediscovered in the fifteenth century A.D. (R. H. Jackson, 1981). In

BOX 12-3

Chesapeake Settlement

In the novel *Chesapeake,* James A. Michener vividly describes the form that early settlement took in the Chesapeake watershed of Maryland and Virginia (Michener, 1978, 200–201). Indiscriminate location proceeded as follows. First, for many decades, Michener writes, there were few towns or villages, unlike New England, where nucleated communities took shape from the beginning of settlement.

In the Chesapeake watershed, a microcosm of the submerged Atlantic coast of the United States, early migrants took up lands first at the ends of the innumerable peninsulas. Because these early settlers were largely self-sufficient farmers, they had no need for trading or service centers. Each family more or less lived unto itself, in isolation, separated from neighbors by swamps, deep woods, broad creeks, and other water bodies.

In time, of course, the nucleus of a village or town began to form, often at the head of a bay for protection against Atlantic storms. Some sites were often soon abandoned for more preferred locations. In any event, nucleated settlements did begin to materialize, and wise settlers were those who laid claim to the land before others arrived.

As coastal lands were patented, other lands were settled and cleared in the interior.

In the early seventeenth century, this meant the dispossession of the native Americans of their traditional hunting grounds. The conflict that ensued diminished the natives, both in terms of numbers as well as in territory, but the decades saw more and more European settlers pushing ever inland.

After the Civil War, which was to destroy the slave-plantation system, plantation lands were subdivided for private farms and sharecropping. The demise of the plantation center, however, was a loss, but it was replaced by crossroads communities. The general store soon became a favorite meeting place for talking, sitting, or just looking.

Florida, towns such as St. Augustine (founded 1565), were laid out as colonial outposts. A regular grid system was imposed on the land, with individual lots emanating from a central square. Beyond such settlement, large tracts of land were granted under the *encomienda* system, the grantee being responsible for development of the tract (Hart, 1975).

In Texas by 1821, when Mexico gained its independence, the Spanish did not have much to show for their occupance. A thin scattering of missions with military support (*presidios*) was the most tangible evidence of Spain's presence. However, there was a recognition that in the droughty climate of much of the region, more land was needed for grazing than for crop cultivation. Thus, grants of land to individual settlers consisted of 4428.4 acres for grazing and only 177.1 acres for farming (Miller, 1972). The ranches, or *rancherias,* that were established were simplistic, consisting of a cluster of buildings around which fields were drawn.

Anglo-American colonization gained impetus after the transfer of the Louisiana Territory from France to the United States in 1803. Moses Austin, (1761–1821), an American, secured permission to settle 300 families on a grant of approximately two hundred thousand acres, a project that his son, Stephen Austin (1793–1836), undertook to carry out when Mexico became independent (Fig. 12–9). Other *empresarios,* or grantees, also contracted to bring in settlers, but only a few lived up to their obligations under their grant.

Individual settlers from the United States also found their way to Texas in the 1820s lured by the price of cheap land. Theoretically, one could obtain land in Texas for $0.38 an acre compared with $1.25 per acre cash for a minimum purchase of 80 acres in the United States.

After Texas became independent, streams of migrants entered the republic from the United States on promises of four thousand acres per family in exchange for small fees. Migrants from Germany, Ireland, Scandinavia, and central Europe also reached the southern frontier.

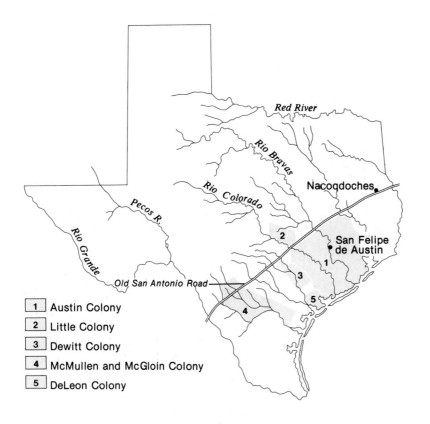

Figure 12–9
Altogether 25 *empresario* contracts for the settlement of the Texas coast were signed, only 5 led to the actual planting of settlers on the land. These contracts lost their validity when Texas declared its independence on March 2, 1836.

(*Source:* Miller, 1972, p. 20.)

1	Austin Colony
2	Little Colony
3	Dewitt Colony
4	McMullen and McGloin Colony
5	DeLeon Colony

Variations on European Settlement Forms

The Dutch, who held the New York region for a time, instituted the practice of making large land grants, particularly in the Hudson River Valley, to private individuals, known as *patroons*. Such grants were not unlike the seigneurial grants in New France. Farm work on these estates was usually done by landless laborers who lived in village communities. Even after the end of Dutch colonial administration, the practice of awarding large grants was continued by the English in the Hudson valley as well as along the tributary Mohawk River. Moreover, after the Revolution, New York State relied on individual colonizers, through grants of substantial tracts of land, to settle the

townships created along the St. Lawrence River below its source in Lake Ontario.

Germans from the Palatinate in the Rhineland were encouraged to migrate to the colonies, especially as regiments had served British military interests in Europe. Early arrivals located in New York and along the Hudson River. However, William Penn (1644–1718), who had received a charter in 1681 to found a colony on the Delaware River as a haven for fellow Quakers, invited the Germans to Pennsylvania, and by the third decade of the eighteenth century, the trickle of immigrants had become a flood. Penn had anticipated that the Germans would settle in nucleated communities as was characteristic of Rhineland settlement, but the immigrants were opposed. They quickly dispersed up the river valleys, especially the

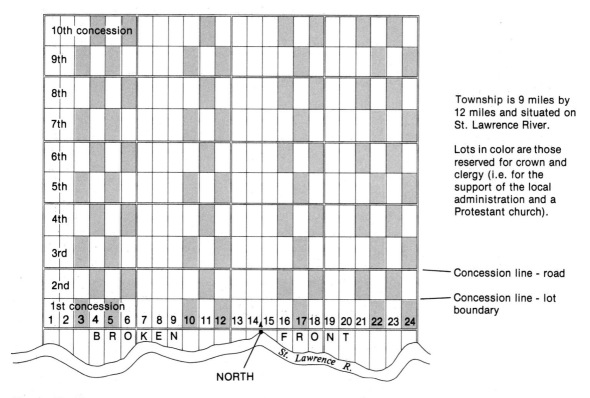

Figure 12–10

This hypothetical model of a rectangular township in Upper Canada shows the broken front, concessions, and concession lots. In this model, allowances are made for concession roads, and the checkered plan of distribution of Crown and Clergy Reserves is indicated.

(Courtesy Archives of Ontario, Toronto.)

Susquehanna, into the Appalachians where they occupied farmsteads of from 100 to 200 acres each. The *dispersed settlement* farm pattern of these Pennsylvania Dutch, as they came to be called, is still evident in the landscape.

The Germans were followed soon after by a strong wave of Protestant Scotch-Irish from Ulster, the northern province of Ireland. Too poor to buy land, the Scotch-Irish reached the Appalachian valleys and, pushing southward through Pennsylvania, Virginia, and into the Carolinas, they squatted on any available land.

Tory Settlement in Upper Canada

Because and in spite of their experience in the Thirteen Colonies, British plans for land settlement in British North America after the American Revolution possessed components that were reminiscent of both French and New England experiences. But, the settlement form that was to be instituted had as its goal, at least on paper, the creation of a stable, somewhat aristocratic but manageable, society on what was left of the British North American frontier.

Figure 12–11A

The first dwelling of a settler's family in the Great Lakes region in Canada or in the United States was usually a one-room log house set in the middle of a forest clearing. Unless supplies of food, clothing and implements were available from some nearby trading center, pioneers were forced to be self-sufficient in every way possible.

After a period of time, assuming the family had been able to endure the hardships of the place, a second house, often of frame construction, but sometimes of stone or brick, replaced the first which became in turn a shed for field equipment or livestock.

The family shown here homesteaded in the extreme northeastern part of Minnesota in the late 1880's, but their attempts to survive in the forest lasted only a few years when they moved back to Duluth and the comforts of civilization.

Source: Nancy Pierce/Photo Researchers

The Revolutionary War did not have the support of all Americans. After independence, these Americans, known as British Americans, Tories, or United Empire Loyalists, were compelled to resettle either in British colonial territory or in Great Britain. Hence, in 1784, shiploads carried them to Halifax, the British fortress in Nova Scotia, or to St. John in the new colony of New Brunswick. Thousands more moved overland to the eastern townships of Quebec (south of Montreal), and still others settled in the virgin territory above Montreal where a new colony or province was created in 1791 known as Upper Canada. The colony of Quebec downstream was reorganized as Lower Canada (12–11A).

Along the St. Lawrence and the Ottawa rivers as well as the waterways to the southwest, townships measuring 9 by 12 miles were laid out. They were then divided into ranges or *concessions,* the concession lines paralleling the "*broken front*," or the baseline that was drawn along the waterway (Fig. 12–10). The concessions, in turn, were subdivided into twenty-four 200-acre lots. A grant of land would normally represent one 200-acre lot, although many grants exceeded that, depending on the military rank or status of the applicant. Inland townships were intended to be 12 miles^2, and they, too, were subdivided into concessions and lots.

The original township plan, however, required that each township have at its center a town, measuring one mile square, with town lots each representing one acre in size as well as squares and streets of specific dimensions (Fig. 12–11B). Surrounding the two were town parks

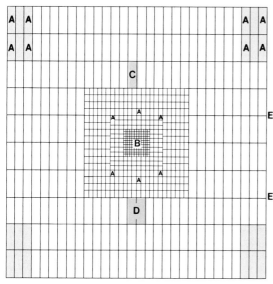

Plan of a Town and Township
Ten Miles Square, 1789

A. Reserves for the crown

B. Town site

C. For the school

D. For the church

E. Concession lines

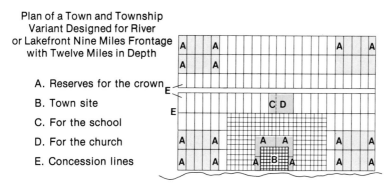

Plan of a Town and Township
Variant Designed for River
or Lakefront Nine Miles Frontage
with Twelve Miles in Depth

A. Reserves for the crown

B. Town site

C. For the school

D. For the church

E. Concession lines

Figure 12–11B

This hypothetical model shows an Upper Canadian township designed for an inland location. At the center of the township, land was set aside for a town, which, in turn, was surrounded by lands set aside for defense (military reservations) and gentry estates. Lots were also reserved for the local clergy and the schoolmaster.

(Courtesy Archives of Ontario, Toronto.)

and other lots reserved as estates for town dwellers. Such a plan was devised by the British to combine settlement in a dispersed orderly fashion throughout the township *with* a nucleated community in the hope of creating a stable society and a loyal one as well (Box 12-4).

In the decades that followed, few of the projected town sites, other than Cornwall on the St. Lawrence, materialized as permanent villages. Nucleated settlements came into existence, but these tended to be spontaneous in origin—at a falls or a ford on a river, a crossroads, or near a mill. Many of the rural roads,

today, however, still adhere to the early survey lines and are known as concession roads.

Even though many features of British land policy pertaining to the Canadian frontier failed to materialize in the fashion initially intended, certain Tory values were nonetheless implanted. These contributed to the growth of an elitist tradition, evident in politics and education, that has survived in parts of Ontario as well as in Nova Scotia and New Brúnswick to the present.

During the period from 1791 to the outbreak of the War of 1812, large numbers of Ameri-

BOX 12–4

The Checkered Plan for Creating a Land Revenue

Beginning in 1791 two sevenths of the land in each township was to be withheld from individual settlement and set aside as a reserve. Known as the *Crown and Clergy Reserves,* the purpose of these lands was to serve as an endowment for a Protestant church and to create an independent source of revenue for the colonial executive (Wilson, 1968). See Fig. 12–10 on p. 383.

In the distribution of these reserves throughout an unsettled township, the original plan called for a checkered pattern. Almost every other lot, in effect, was to be a reserved lot. Many grants of land, however, had already been made by the British government between 1784 and 1791 to British Americans and members of loyalist regiments, especially in the townships along the upper St. Lawrence. The result was that the checkered plan could not be uniformly imposed on some townships. Therefore, large blocks of concession lots (equal to two sevenths of the land area of the township) were set aside at the rear of the township or even consolidated in adjacent townships. The net result was to withdraw significant tracts of land from settlement or immediate occupancy. Because the influx of settlers at first was not sufficiently large enough to generate any great demand for the leasing of these reserves, the revenue that was hoped for failed to materialize; worse, the reserves impeded economic growth by making contiguous farm settlement impossible. It was difficult even for any group of isolated farmers to maintain roads or any good link through the brush with more settled parts of the township.

These reserves survived until the 1830s when the provincial governments undertook to open them up for settlement. Clearly few pioneers had wanted to create farmsteads on leased land when they could obtain private title elsewhere at reasonable cost.

cans, whose main concern was cheap land, took up lands in Upper Canada so that by the second decade of the nineteenth century, the colony seemed destined to become "American." The war ended that possibility and thereafter migrants from England, Scotland, and Ireland assured the British connection. However, to speed up settlement in the province, large grants were made to individuals and to land companies whose responsibility it was to encourage migration and resettlement. The township established in the late eighteenth century remained the format by which order was imposed on all of southern Ontario.

Western Lands Policies and the Settlement of the Interior Prairies and Plains

The settlement of the western frontier lands in the United States was shaped by Congress through land policies adopted in 1785 and in subsequent years (Pattison, 1957). These policies favored a widespread pattern of dispersed settlement, and they supported a strong agrarian individualism that became a characteristic feature of the myth and reality that came out of western frontier experience.

In the Ordinance of 1785, an attempt was made to effect a compromise between New England and southern settlement forms. Publicly owned land was to be divided into townships six miles square, delineated by lines running on the cardinal points of the compass. The townships, in turn, were to be divided into 36 numbered sections, each one mile square or 640 acres in area (Fig. 12–12). Alternate townships were to be sold as a whole and in sections, at a minimum price of $1.00 per acre, thus satisfying those who wanted to obtain large units of land for group settlement, and Southerners, in particular, who preferred smaller individual holdings. The ordinance tended to encourage land speculation however. Because rapid sales were essential if there were to be any revenue to the state, and this would occur if holdings were

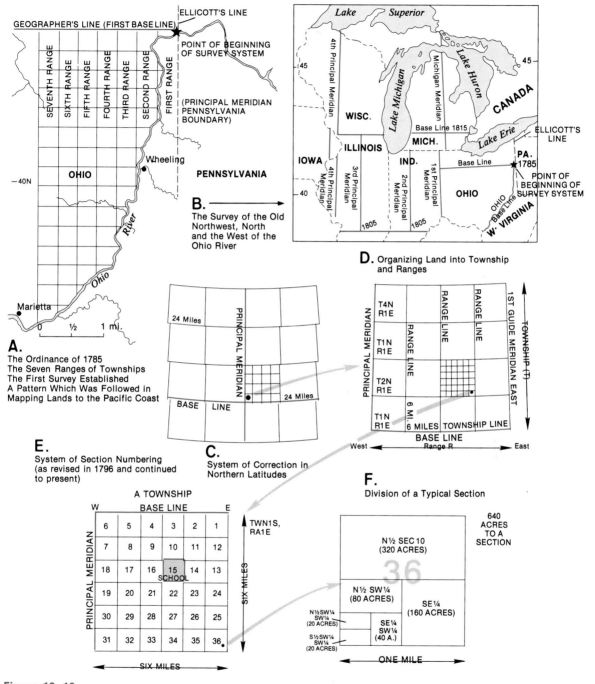

Figure 12–12

The Ordinance of 1785 resulted in the division of all government owned lands into townships six miles square. The townships, in turn, were divided into 36 sections, each one mile square. The first seven ranges of townships were surveyed from a baseline that was drawn due west from the point where the Pennsylvania boundary crossed the Ohio River. It was basically through this grid system that the trans-Appalachian West was surveyed and settled.

(*Source:* Billington, 1950, p. 208.)

smaller, Congress subsequently reduced the minimum size of an individual purchase from 640 acres to 320 acres in 1800, to 160 in 1804, to 80 in 1820, and to 40 in 1832. Whatever the minimum, the rectangular system—through the shape and size of farms and through road patterns—was deeply incised into the western American landscape. The Preemption Act of 1841 and the Homestead Act of 1862 carried the rectangular survey further across the prairies and plains, attaching a residence requirement before title to 160 acres could be transferred to individual possession.

Despite speculation and fraudulent land practices, the net effect of congressional policies was to ensure, especially through the Homestead Act, that widely dispersed individual settlement would result and, in turn, would help preserve that characteristically American phenomenon, the large family farm (Johnson, 1957).

After the vast northwestern interior—once the domain of native hunters and trappers from Canada and the Hudson's Bay Company—had been transferred to the fledgling Dominion of Canada in 1869, the homestead concept took shape as the vehicle for a rapid settlement of the Canadian prairies. However, there were matters that had first to be dealt with.

An immediate problem was the *métis*. The *métis* nation had taken shape along the Red and Assiniboine rivers in what was to become in 1870 the province of Manitoba (Fig. 12–13) (Stanley, 1961). The *métis,* a product of the union of native peoples and French- or English-speaking trappers, were struggling to hang onto their long lots along the rivers and to preserve some of their freedom to hunt the buffalo. Conflict with the Ottawa authorities, who feared a *métis* state, led some of the *métis* to resettle on the South Saskatchewan River to the northwest. There in 1885, the Canadian frontier advance once again caught up with them in the form of Canadian Pacific Railway land grants and the rectangular survey. The *métis* had no alternative but to acquiesce in Canadian nation

building and retreat to the fringes of western Canadian social life.

The Amerindians were also of concern to Canadian authorities. Treaties were signed with resident tribes and inalienable reserves were set up in that part of the country to which they belonged. A police force, the Northwest Mounted Police, was there to protect the natives and to preserve law and order.

Parallel to these concerns was the felt urgency of connecting the far Pacific colony of British Columbia to Canada. A railway linking Canada from coast to coast had become a national dream. To achieve it and to populate the west, the Canadian government agreed to grant the railway blocks of land along a direct line between Winnipeg and the Rocky Mountains. These lands, however, lay within the drier part of the prairie, known as the *Palliser Triangle* (Box 12–5). The railway directors refused to accept anything but the best prairie land, which lay to the north in the slightly better watered fertile central parkland belt. As a result, vast tracts of good land were removed from the reach of the homesteader who was forced into other parts of the prairie. Still, after 1885, the Canadian Pacific attracted migrants from various parts of Europe, but those who opted for railway land found themselves mortgaged to the corporation.

FARM OWNERSHIP AND TENANCY IN THE UNITED STATES

The demand for land was a motivating force that drew many settlers to North America (R. H. Jackson, 1981). In the colonial period, it very quickly became an article of commerce, giving rise to substantial speculation. The basis of the wealth of many prominent patriots was land and the Revolution opened up the possibilities for more extensive gain once the British

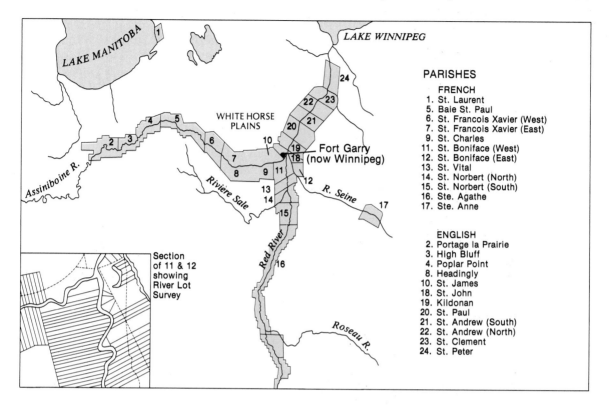

PARISHES

FRENCH
1. St. Laurent
5. Baie St. Paul
6. St. Francois Xavier (West)
7. St. Francois Xavier (East)
9. St. Charles
11. St. Boniface (West)
12. St. Boniface (East)
13. St. Vital
14. St. Norbert (North)
15. St. Norbert (South)
16. Ste. Agathe
17. Ste. Anne

ENGLISH
2. Portage la Prairie
3. High Bluff
4. Poplar Point
8. Headingly
10. St. James
18. St. John
19. Kildonan
20. St. Paul
21. St. Andrew (South)
22. St. Andrew (North)
23. St. Clement
24. St. Peter

Figure 12–13

The first attempt to found a settlement in what was to become the Canadian west occurred in 1812 under Lord Selkirk (1771–1820). Of Scottish origin, Selkirk secured a large grant from the Hudson's Bay Company and undertook to bring people to the Red River. However, the colony never flourished. Still, the population of the region grew, although the number of European and Canadian residents declined. By 1871, according to the census of Canada, there were over 10,000 people living in the region. Of these, more than half were French-speaking half-breeds, a small number were English-speaking half-breeds.

(*Source:* Stanley, 1961, p. 15.)

(and French) presence had been removed from the trans-Appalachian West.

With the passage of the Ordinance of 1785, speculators gained significant blocks of land especially in the Ohio Valley, often under questionable circumstances. However, much of the new public domain was parceled out to individuals and corporations under the terms both of the ordinance and subsequent nineteenth-century legislation. The regulations introduced by Congress laid the legal foundations of the private family farm.

Prior to 1880, there are no statistics available on the question of farm proprietorship in the United States. The census of 1880, however, revealed that about three fourths of all farms were operated by full or part ownership. What came as a surprise and a matter of concern to government officials and land economists of the period was the fact that in a country where private ownership of land was so highly prized, a fourth of all farms was cultivated by tenants. By 1900, one in three farms was tenant operated. Farm tenancy, with sharecropping in various forms, was particularly high in the South, especially among the rural black population.

Because of the high national ratio, some observers feared that it implied (among the white population at least) a *loss* of ownership and, if not halted would, in time, become more widespread (Taylor and Taylor, 1952). On the other

---

BOX 12–5

The Palliser Expedition

The quality of the land in what are now the prairie provinces of Canada was generally known when plans were drawn to build a railroad from Ontario to British Columbia. The Hind-Dawson expeditions of 1857–1858, financed by the colony of Canada, collected much helpful information. However, the expedition of 1857–1860 financed by the British government and led by Captain John Palliser (1834–1907) had a more lasting impact. Palliser and his party undertook an extensive survey of the region between Lake Superior and the Rockies, which at that time was still the domain of the Hudson's Bay Company. (It remained so until 1869 when it was transferred to the Dominion of Canada, formed in 1867).

Palliser classified the territory he mapped into two large areas: the fertile belt and the semiarid region. It was Palliser's evaluation of the latter, subsequently known as the Palliser Triangle, that left an impression on outsiders as to the relatively low agricultural worth of the area. The triangle considered unfit for settlement because of its treelessness and low precipitation extended along the 49th parallel between 100° and 114° W longitude, reaching an apex near 52° N latitude. The Canadian Pacific Railway followed a route that led across the southern prairies, through the broader part of the triangle, but the corporation rejected thousands of acres initially granted it there (west of Moose Jaw, Saskatchewan) in a bid for superior land in the more fertile belt to the north where precipitation was slightly higher and the soils were richer in organic matter.

---

hand, there were those who believed that it simply represented a stage, a rung on the ladder, toward full land ownership. At the turn of the century, a term that was much in use was the agricultural ladder. It held that a young man would first learn the rudiments of farming as an unpaid worker on a home farm (Fig. 12–14). The next rung of the ladder saw him operating as a hired laborer. On the third rung, he advanced to a tenant farmer, reaching ownership on the fourth rung (presumably after much thrift and hard work), leaving him free of mortgage indebtedness.

During the decades that followed, a farm tenure in the United States underwent a number of changes. In 1950, farm tenancy still affected some 27 percent of U.S. farms. The ratio reached 34 percent in the southern states, with a high of 65.5 percent among black farmers. By 1969, however, tenant operations had declined to about a fifth of all farms and to only 13 percent by 1978. In the South, farm tenancy among blacks experienced a sharp drop, falling to only 16.2 percent in 1978, in large part because blacks had abandoned farming altogether for life in the city.

These changes were part of major transformation in the U.S. agricultural sector. From 1969 to 1980, the overall farm population declined from 15.7 million to 7.2 million. This exodus from the land was reflected further in a substantial increase in the size of farms and in corporate holdings but in a decline in the small family farm.

LAND REFORM
IN OTHER PARTS OF THE GLOBE

In many parts of the globe, feudal relationships on the land have survived right up to modern times. Indeed, one of the basic problems facing the developing countries is that land reform is vital to the other programs of economic development that are planned or are underway. In

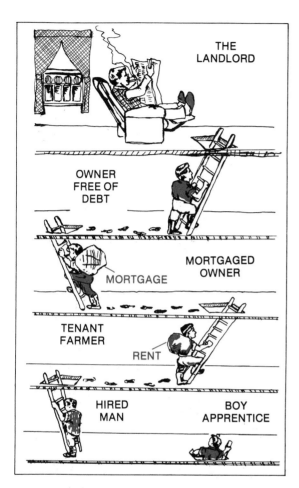

Figure 12–14

The agricultural ladder. Reflecting an era of optimism, the assumption was that the road to farm success lay through hard work. As the boy apprentice matured, he became the hired man, saving his earnings so as to take on the responsibilities of a tenant farmer. Although the payment of rent proved to be a burden that the tenant farmer had to bear, he acquired a piece of farmland, turning rental payments into a heavier burden, a mortgage. Still, his energy and thrift paid dividends because, in time, he eliminated the mortgage, and enjoyed his new debt-free status. The final rung on the ladder saw him enjoying the benefits of a landowner and, ultimately landlord, as he, in turn, leased land to another younger man engaged in a similar ascent on the agricultural ladder.

(*Source:* Taylor and Taylor, 1952, p. 821.)

such countries, much of the land (70 percent or more) still tends to be owned or controlled by a few persons. The rural masses work the land as tenants or as landless farmhands. The problem is especially acute in Latin America, and it is a cause of much of the misery in Meso-America (Box 12–6).

LAND REFORM IN JAPAN AND TAIWAN

Before World War II, agriculture was the backbone of the economy of Japan and of its colony, Formosa (now Taiwan). The Meiji restoration of 1868 had freed the peasants from serfdom, although many of them quickly became tenants. Their holdings were small and extremely fragmented, and the rents they paid were exorbitant. In the decades that followed 1868, the situation worsened. By the beginning of World War II, some 70 percent of all Japanese cultivators were tenants. In some prefectures, or counties, well over 50 percent of the cultivated land was operated by tenants (Fig. 12–15). By 1946, concentration of land in the hands of the few had reached extreme proportions: about 7.5 percent of the landowners owned 50 percent of the land; some 50 percent of the landowners owned less than 10 percent of the land.

Postwar Japanese land reform occurred as a result of a law passed by the Japanese Diet under the supervision of the Supreme Commander of the Allied Powers (Trewartha, 1950). It was unique in the history of land reform, in that it was carried out in 1947–1949 under the pressure of an occupation army. Moreover, the circumstances were unusual, in that Japanese society was characterized by a high degree of literacy and the country possessed a major industrial base—however damaged it was by the war. These conditions certainly facilitated the reform and contributed to its immediate success.

Reform transferred more than 27 million tracts of land, or a third of all the agricultural

BOX 12-6

Landless Peasants and the Threat of Revolution

In nine countries that underwent revolutions in the twentieth century, the number of landless peasants reached 30 percent or more of the total population. When revolution occurred in Mexico in 1911, 62 percent of the population was landless. The ratio ranged from 32 to 47 percent in Russia in 1917 and to about 40 percent in Spain in 1936. In the 1940s, China had a landless population in the rice-growing region of from 35 to 45 percent; in Bolivia in 1952, it amounted to 60 percent; in Cuba in 1959, to 39 percent; in South Vietnam in 1961, from 42 to 58 percent; in Ethiopia in 1975, 38 percent; and in Nicaragua in 1979, 40 percent. In many of these countries the revolution had a Marxist bias.

Today, there are still many countries left with a large landless peasantry. Among these countries are India (41 percent); Pakistan (38 percent); Bangladesh (54 percent); the Philippines (36 percent); Indonesia, that is, the Island of Java (44 percent); El Salvador (39 percent); and Honduras (37 percent).

Roy Prosterman, Professor of Law at the University of Washington and a specialist in writing land reform legislation, believes that unless the landless peasants of the world are given a greater stake in their own society, there will be massive revolutionary violence. He believes that, where the landless peasantry represent about 30 percent of the population, the problem is especially acute. He points out, for example, that El Salvador, the scene of considerable violence and terror today, has the highest ratio of landlessness in Latin America and the lowest per capita gross national product (GNP). Although the population of El Salvador totals only 4.8 million, its density is higher than that of India. On the other hand, until the land redistribution program of 1980 was drafted, a few hundred families owned tens of thousands of acres of prime farmland. With the reform, some 15 percent of the country's cropland was transferred to about 80,000 families who had little or no land.

In Iran, a land reform program was instituted by the shah in the 1950s, but the transfer of land from the large landholders to the landless or small peasants satisfied neither group. The loss of land alienated many of the gentry, whereas the transfers failed to satisfy the needs of the growing population. At the time of the overthrow of the shah, the number of landless peasants had been reduced to about 20 percent of the total peasantry, suggesting that revolutionary turmoil need not be related entirely to the size of the peasant population that is without land.

In Mexico, where annual population growth is about 2.5 percent, the rapid increase in population offsets the benefits of land redistribution. Since 1911, landholdings have been redistributed regularly, yet there are 1 million more landless peasants today than before redistribution began. And this development ignores the overflow of millions into the United States. The problem is clearly a highly complex one.

(*Source: Christian Science Monitor*, September 9, 1981.)

land of Japan, to those who worked it (Eyre, 1955). Owner-operated land expanded from 66.5 percent to over 90 percent, whereas tenant-farmer land declined by 34 percent. On the other hand, because of the large size of the rural population and the limited amount of cropland in Japan, the reform reduced the average size of a farm to about two acres per family, thus increasing the number of tiny holdings. The reform, therefore, did little to solve the question of fragmentation, in fact, it intensified the problem in many cases.

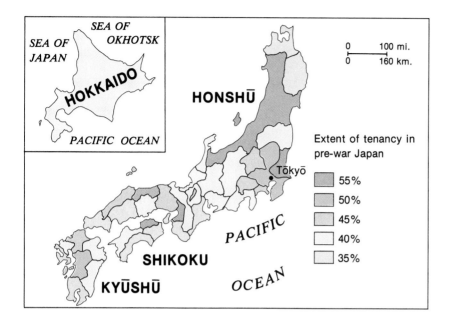

Figure 12-5

In Japan, because the archipelago is dominated by a mountainous spine, cropland comprises only a small portion of the country. Lands with slope gradients of less than 15° occupy only about a fourth of the total area. Hence, the growth of farm tenancy after the Meiji restoration became a serious problem, especially be-cause farmlands were fragmented into patches of highly irregular size and shape. Tenancy on cultivated land, which stood at 30 percent in 1865, reached almost 50 percent by 1930 and was especially high in the paddies (or wetlands) where the basic rice crop was produced. (*Source:* Trewartha, 1950, p. 385.)

Despite subsequent substantial increases in agricultural output, the persistence of land problems associated with small holdings and the opportunities for work in cities have pushed many Japanese farmers off the land. Thousands have left upland areas for Pacific coastal cities. Many of those remaining on the land have been forced to pool their land and labor with neighbors to make possible farm specialization. The small size of farms, however, remains a critical problem in Japan even today. At the same time, urban settlement has spread over the lowland areas, thus reducing the total amount of land available for crop production.

In Taiwan, land reform was introduced by the Nationalist Chinese who established themselves on the island in 1949 after evacuating the mainland in the face of the Communist advance (Cheng, 1961). Under a *"land-to-the-tiller"* program, that is, transferring the land to owner-operators, tenancy was reduced from 39 percent of farm families in 1949 to 15 percent in 1960. Owner-farmers increased from 57 to 88 percent of the total, working some 81 percent of the farmland. One ingenious aspect of the Taiwan reform was the nature of the compensation that landlords received. In exchange for the lands surrendered, the landlords received land bonds and stocks in government-owned industry. Thus, the former landlords had an immediate stake in seeing agriculture prosper and the industrial economy grow, and they threw their support behind the island's economic expansion. On the other hand, the landowners lost much of their former political power. In the last two decades, the improvement in farming techniques together with the expansion of manufacturing have contributed to a substantial rural-urban migration, and the development of rural industries has led to an increasing urbanization of the countryside, as it has in Japan.

Prerevolution Russia and the USSR

On the eve of the abolition of serfdom in 1861, fewer than one thousand gentry families owned about 175 million acres of land from which they received rents and dues. The reforms freed the serfs, but at bottom there were basic flaws in the new land tenure. Allotment land was distributed among the peasantry, but they did not receive individual title. Instead, title was transferred to the village land organization, the *obshchina*, which parceled out the strips of land to the villagers. In exchange for use, the peasants were required to make redemption payments. By the end of the century, it was clear that, with the explosive growth of the rural population, the peasantry as a whole were economically worse off than before. And the redemption payments had become increasingly burdensome.

Rural unrest resulted in the Revolution of 1905, and it prompted P. A. Stolypin (1862–1911), a minister of the tsar, to introduce further reforms. These made possible the creation of consolidated farmsteads under private ownership. However, the outbreak of World War I brought the transition to family farming to a halt. In 1914, of 12.5 million peasant households in European Russia, only a tenth had received individual title (Fig. 12–16). Peasant village or communal lands still embraced some 70 percent of the agricultural area. Large landowners, although declining in number and importance, continued to possess a fourth of the land.

The Bolshevik Revolution in 1917 led first to the nationalization of all land. Still, from 1921 to 1928, the peasants were permitted to work their lands as if they owned them. Alongside these farmsteads, four new types of rural land organization appeared: the *state farm*, the *commune*, the *artel* and the *TOZ (Society for Joint Land Cultivation)*. The state farm was an enterprise owned by the state, but operated by paid workers and employees. The commune, on which daily life and work were shared, left neither land, livestock, nor equipment in the hands of its members. The *artel* permitted the retention of private gardens in back of a worker's cottage, but it also required the sharing of land, livestock, and labor. The TOZ, more loosely organized than the others, was based simply on the principle of cooperation in the cultivation of crops and the raising of livestock.

During the 1920s, these organizations had never seemed attractive to the peasantry, so, fewer than 2 percent of the farm families had ever joined them. In the meantime, the decision had been made to push ahead rapidly with industrialization. As a result of the desire to impose firm control on the countryside, the regime, led by Josef Stalin (1879–1953), called for all-out collectivization of all farmland. The more progressive farmers, whom the regime termed *kulaks*, were forced into Siberian exile or shot. The communes and the TOZ cooperatives disappeared, leaving the *artel* (or collective farm) and the state farm as the only forms of farm organization. During the 1930s, the number of *artels* steadily increased. By 1937, there were more than 240 thousand, containing some 287 million acres of farmland, and 4000 state farms.

By 1980, after a 25-year period of collective-farm consolidation in the USSR, there remained about twenty-six thousand collectives and, after a period of considerable farm expansion in Siberia and Kazakhstan, over twenty thousand state farms. The modern collective farm averages about eighteen thousand acres in size and contains approximately five hundred farm families living in several villages. State farms, traditionally larger than collectives, now average about forty thousand acres, but are usually run by fewer workers.

The 1861 reform had permitted the peasants to hold their cottage gardens as hereditary property. In 1934, because of the opposition of the

Figure 12–16

Transfer in land ownership in Russia was accelerated by reforms introduced in 1906. By 1916, the trend toward private farming was pronounced in the Baltic regions, where the peasants had turned to cattle raising and dairying, and in the grasslands, where commercial grain production had grown in importance with the building of railroads that tied the interior with Black Sea ports. In the northern and eastern provinces, fewer peasants were involved and the movement was slower.

peasantry to collectivization, the Soviet regime was compelled to confirm peasant ownership. These cottage gardens of *private plots*, although never more than a small fraction of the total agricultural area, have been responsible for producing up to 65 percent of Russia's foodstuffs.

China

In Communist China the postrevolutionary reforms in the countryside took a course that differed from that adopted in the USSR. Up until 1950, more than half of China's cropland had been owned by a relatively small percentage of the rural population. Following the revolution, these holdings were seized by the new government and redistributed among the country's tenant farmers, poor peasants, and small landholders. In all, some 116 million acres of land were distributed among 65 million small farmers.

Redistribution alone, however, could not solve the economic problems of the countryside because many peasants lacked the means to work the land efficiently. Cooperation was essential and mutual-aid groups were formed to do the work. The next stage in rural reorganization was the creation of agricultural cooperatives, similar to the Soviet collective farms. By mid-1956, about 90 percent of the cropland had been transferred to cooperatives, which were operated by nearly all of the farm families in China. The move toward cooperatives involved the consolidation of small fields into larger units. In general, each of these cooperatives embraced between 200 to 250 families, united under a single command. As in the USSR, each family also was permitted a piece of land near its cottage for the production of domestic needs.

The agricultural cooperatives changed the appearance of the landscape, but the reorganization failed to open up new land for crops (Kolb, 1971). Where the latter occurred, as in Sinkiang (Xinjiang) and northern Manchuria (Heilongjiang)—some 10 million acres became productive between 1952 and 1957—the expansion came through the efforts of state farms rather than cooperatives.

In August 1958, the Communist regime began to transform the agricultural cooperatives into people's communes, large enterprises that usually contained from ten to thirty thousand people. Moreover, the activities of the farm were enlarged to include craft enterprises, local factories, and social services. The commune workers were organized into brigades to do the work required.

The Chinese Communists have claimed that their communes represent a more advanced stage in the development of socialism than do the Soviet *artels* and state farms, but this notion has been ridiculed by Soviet leaders. Indeed, the ideological antagonism engendered by these different paths contributed to the Sino-Soviet split in the early 1960s.

EPILOGUE

Early land policies affecting the settlement of the North American wilderness reflected the values and cultures of England, France, and Spain. However, the frontier experience greatly modified the original intent and gave rise to those features that came to characterize "European man on the land" in North America. One of these features was the dispersal of settlement, another was the desire for private land ownership. Settlers simply preferred to live on their own farmsteads rather than reside in nucleated population centers. This was true even in New France and Acadia where, despite the strong Old World heritage, French settlers were settled on long lots strung out along a water body. What sense of community they had was preserved not through village organization but by their culture and above all through the influence of the church.

The nature of North American settlement was conducive to the emergence of the family farm and the mystique of private farm ownership, whose praises were constantly sung by men like Thomas Jefferson. Imposed on the landscape, this structure provided the framework within which a continent could be occupied and settled.

The fields, the farm houses, and the transportation links created what one observer calls "a distinctive American style," and it was found throughout most of Anglo-America (J. B. Jackson, 1972). This style gave substance to the landscape and from it sprang values that helped preserve it.

APPLICATION OF IDEAS

1. Settlement is man's first step toward adapting to the environment. This pattern of human settlement throughout the world has varied because the process of adaptation has varied.

2. One important facet of human occupancy of the land is, in the final anlysis, legal: the system that binds people to the land and defines human relationships.

3. In North America, settlement was, for the most part, dispersed. Early New England settlement was by towns and communities, but in the southern colonies as well as among the French in the Bay of Fundy and along the St. Lawrence, the first settlers were not or chose not to cluster in nucleated villages.

4. Dispersed settlement was conducive to the growth of the family farm, which has been part of the North American heritage.

5. In Europe, until relatively modern times, most of the land was held by a few families but worked by the bulk of the peasants.

6. This traditional feudal relationship to the land survives in much of the developing world.

7. Major land reforms were carried out in Japan and Taiwan after World War II, strengthening the role of the independent farmer and laying the basis for rapid economic recovery and expansion.

8. In Communist states, like the USSR, the land has been nationalized and, wherever possible, people have been made to work on collective enterprises. This solution to the land question was a drastic one.

KEY WORDS AND PHRASES

artel	*mainmortable*
"broken front"	metes and bounds
censier	*métis*
commune	nucleated settlement
concession	*obshchina*
corvée	Palliser Triangle
Crown and Clergy	*patroon*
Reserves	*presidio*
dispersed settlement	private plot
enclosure movement	*rancheria*
empresario	*rang*
encomienda	seigneurial system
habitant	*seigneurie*
haufendorf	state farm
indiscriminate	*strassendorf*
location	three-field rotation
kulaks	system
"land-to-the-tiller"	town center
line or linear	TOZ (Society for
settlement	Joint Land
long lot	Cultivation)

QUESTIONS FOR FURTHER DISCUSSION

1. What does the statement that "settlement is humankind's first step toward adapting to the environment" mean to you? Does it apply to your own experience? If so, how?

2. In what ways do you see cultural values expressed in the form that human settlement takes. Can you identify some of these values?

3. Why was the nucleated, or village, settlement so widespread in Europe? Why didn't people choose to live on their own farmsteads? Could they have done so even if their lives were made physically secure?

4. What problems are created when the bulk of the agricultural land is held by a few families? Can you identify countries in the Western Hemisphere where even today this remains a crucial problem?

5. Why was the settlement of New England so carefully controlled in the beginning? What did these early settlers want to preserve? Of what were they afraid?

6. In what way did the settlement of the southern colonies differ from New England? How did the immigrants settling the respective regions differ in culture?

7. Why did France elect the long lot as the basis for settlement in Canada? What were its advantages? Disadvantages?

8. In what way did the United States hope to combine the best features of New England and southern colonial experience in the settling of the West? What were those features respectively?

9. In what way did the Canadian plan for the settlement of the West differ from the American? Why did the railroad fare so much better in the Canadian West?

10. What advantages are to be found in dispersed settlement? Disadvantages? In what way, do you think, did dispersed settlement affect the development of American activity patterns? What might have been the consequences had the West been settled by nucleated communities?

REFERENCES AND ADDITIONAL READINGS

Berry, Wendell. *The Unsettling of America. Culture and Agriculture.* San Francisco: Sierra Club Books, 1977.

Billington, Ray Allen. *Westward Expansion. A History of the American Frontier.* New York: Macmillan, 1950.

Bogue, Donald J. "The Geography of Recent Population Trends in the United States." *Annals of the Association of American Geographers* 44 (1954): 124–134.

Brown, Ralph H. *Historical Geography of the United States.* New York: Harcourt, Brace & World, 1948.

Cheng, Chen. *Land Reform in Taiwan,* Taipei: China Publishing Co., 1961.

Cherry, Gordon E., ed. *Rural Planning Problems.* New York: Barnes & Noble, 1977.

Chisholm, Michael. *Rural Settlement and Land Use: An Essay in Location.* London: Hutchinson, 1979.

Clark, Andrew Hill. *Acadia. The Geography of Early Nova Scotia to 1760.* Madison: University of Wisconsin Press, 1968.

Evans, C. Estyn. "The Personality of Ulster." *Transactions of the Institute of British Geographers* 51 (1970): 1–20.

Everson, J. A., and Fitzgerald, B. P. *Settlement Patterns. Concepts in Geography 1.* London: Longman, 1969.

Eyre, John D. "The Changing Role of the Former Japanese Landlord." *Land Economics* 31 (1955): 35–46.

Fuller, Heather A. "Landownership and the Lindsey Landscape." *Annals of the Association of American Geographers* 66 (1976): 14–24.

Gates, Lillian F. *Land Policies of Upper Canada.* Toronto, Can.: University of Toronto Press, 1968.

Gonner, E. C. K. *Common Land and Inclosure,* 2nd ed. London: Augustus M. Kelley, Publishers, 1966.

Harris, R. Cole, and Warkentin, John. *Canada Before Confederation. A Study in Historical Geography.* New York: Oxford University Press, 1974.

Hart, John Fraser. *The Look of the Land.* Englewood Cliffs, N.J.: Prentice-Hall, 1975.

Hedges, James B. *Building the Canadian West. The Land and Colonization Policies of the Canadian Pacific Railway.* New York: Macmillan, 1939.

Hume, Ivor Noël. *Martin's Hundred.* New York: Alfred A. Knopf, 1982.

Jackson, J. B. "Metamorphosis." *Annals of the Association of American Geographers* 62 (1972): 155–184.

Jackson, Richard H. *Land Use in America.* New York: John Wiley, 1981.

Johnson, Hildegard Binder. "Rational and Ecological Aspects of the Quarter Section. An Example from Minnesota." *Geographical Review* 47 (1957): 330–348.

———. *Order upon the Land.* New York: Oxford University Press, 1976.

Jordan, Terry G., and Rowntree, Lester. *The Human Mosaic. A Thematic Introduction to Cultural Geography,* 2nd ed. New York: Harper & Row, 1979.

Kish, George. "Centuriatio: The Roman Rectangular Land Survey." *Surveying and Mapping* 22 (1962): 233–244.

Kolb, Albert. *East Asia; China, Japan, Korea, Vietnam; Geography of a Cultural Region.* London: Methuen, 1971.

Lajeunesse, Ernest J., ed. *The Windsor Border Region. Canada's Southernmost Frontier.* Toronto, Can.: University of Totonto Press, 1960.

Lawton, R. "Rural Depopulation in Nineteenth Century England," pp. 195–219. In *English Rural Communities: The Impact of a Specialized Economy,* Dennis R. Mills, ed. London: Macmillan, 1973.

Lowenthal, David. "The American Scene." *Geographical Review* 58 (1968): 61–88.

Mayhew, Alan. *Rural Settlement and Farming in Germany.* London: Batsford, 1973.

Michener, James A. *Chesapeake.* New York: Fawcett, 1978 (Crest Books).

Miller, Thomas Lloyd. *The Public Lands of Texas 1519–1970.* Norman: University of Oklahoma Press, 1972.

Pattison, William D. *Beginnings of the American Rectangular Land Survey System, 1784–1800.* Research Paper No. 50, Department of Geography, University of Chicago, 1957.

Pfeifer, Gottfried, "The Quality of Peasant Living in Central Europe, " pp. 240–277. *Man's Role in Changing the Face of the Earth.* William Thomas, ed. Chicago: University of Chicago Press, 1956.

Powell, David E. "The Rural Exodus." *Problems of Communism* 23 (1974): 1–13.

Riegel, Robert E. *America Moves West,* Rev. ed. New York: Henry Holt, 1947.

Saville, J. *Rural Depopulation in England and Wales, 1851–1951.* London: Routledge & Kegan Paul, 1957.

Scarfe, Neville V. et al. *A New Geography of Canada.* Toronto, Can.: W. J. Gage, 1963.

Schlissel, Lillian. *Women's Diaries of the Westward Journey.* New York: Schocken Books, 1982.

Stanley, George F. G. *The Birth of Western Canada. A History of the Riel Rebellions.* Toronto, Can.: University of Toronto Press, 1961.

Taylor, Henry C., and Taylor, Anne D. *The Story of Agricultural Economics in the United States, 1840–1932.* Ames: Iowa State College Press, 1952.

Trewartha, Glenn T. "Land Reform and Land Reclamation in Japan." *Geographical Review* 40 (1950): 376–396.

Tuma, Elias H. *Twenty-Six Centuries of Agrarian Reform. A Comparative Analysis.* Berkeley and Los Angeles: University of California Press, 1965.

Wilson, Alan. *The Clergy Reserves of Upper Canada. A Canadian Mortmain.* Toronto, Can.: University of Toronto Press, 1968.

13
Spatial Structure of World Agriculture

God provides enough and to spare for every creature he sends into the world; but the conditions are often not in accord. Where the food is, the people are not; and where the people are, the food is not. It is, however, . . . within the power of man to adjust these things.

Thomas S. Mort (1875)
cited in James T. Critchell and
Joseph Raymond,
A History of the Frozen Meat Trade, 1912

Key Ideas

1. Activity patterns take shape in response to human needs and wants. Patterns, however, may vary with culture group and through time.

2. The modern network of activity patterns that stretches over the earth's surface is a product of structural changes in regional economies that became pronounced in the eighteenth and nineteenth centuries, and is especially evident in world agricultural activities.

3. Output of foodstuffs must be in balance with, and responsive to, requirements. Throughout history, there are many instances where this was not the case, and the result was starvation and population dislocation.

4. One of the earliest forms of agriculture is known as shifting cultivation, a system based on a keen knowledge of the ecology of the area. But, it can operate only where population densities are low and land is relatively abundant.

5. Nomadic pastoralism, another form of wresting a living from the land, is based on domesticated animals. The system survives in parts of Asia and Africa.

6. Aquatic farming is native to South and East Asia, and it entails the cultivation of rice in paddies.

7. One feature of the agricultural revolution was the introduction into Europe of many foodstuffs from the Americas.

8. The growth of Europe's population in the seventeenth and eighteenth centuries led to a sharp rise in the demand for foodstuffs; this, in turn, led to an increase in land values.

9. Throughout Europe there were changes in land organization and ownership as peasants turned into farmers in the modern sense.

10. The opening of new lands in the Americas and elsewhere had a profound effect on European agriculture.

11. The work of Johann Heinrich von Thünen (1783–1850) affords a basis for understanding the spatial patterns of world agriculture.

12. Population growth poses a real challenge to the world, in that the question of global food resources is essentially one that is based on the ratio of food to population.

13. With land areas suitable for crop cultivation already utilized, the question of how to feed future populations remains an enigma. How is the world to obtain more food and at the same time provide a better balanced diet for its inhabitants?

THE SPATIAL RELATIONSHIP OF HUMAN ACTIVITIES

A basic principle of geographic study recognizes that the patterns of human activity that have evolved over the surface of the earth are not without form or purpose. Indeed, the underlying order in nature has been described by one scientist as "the grain in the stone" (Bronowski, 1973). This reference to inherent orderliness is not confined to nature, it underlies the spatial organization of human activities as well.

As the record of human experience suggests, activity patterns—the way in which people migrate and settle, organize space, and use the land to make a living—take shape in response to human needs and wants. These patterns vary from culture group to culture group over the earth, but they change also from generation to generation. Innovation, or the advent of new technology, and its acceptance are fundamental in the development or evolution of activity patterns.

Many years ago, Derwent Whittlesey coined the term *sequent occupance* to describe the way in which human occupancy and use of a given region change over time (Whittlesey, 1929). Whittlesey knew that the study of any region entails a consideration of the "infinite interplay of many elements of the natural and the cultural landscape." However, he argued that a recognition of the concept of sequent occupance makes it possible to place any given region in proper relationship to what came before and what will come after. In this sense, his attempt to conceptualize the underlying order in the landscape possessed a dynamic quality.

Preston James (1929) employed the concept of sequent occupance in his study of the Blackstone Valley in Massachusetts to highlight and contrast the way in which native Americans, the English colonists, and later generations of Americans utilized the valley differently, each occupancy, in sequence, reflecting different cultures and levels of technological equipment.

What this concept attests is that human activities are not arrived at haphazardly. There is underlying meaning. Occupancy patterns at any given time may not determine the structure of subsequent patterns, although there probably will be relics in the landscape of earlier use, but they do bear a relationship to the larger environment, to the larger culture, and to the needs of the society. Moreover, it cannot be forgotten that activity patterns that have developed in one part of the globe are affected by events, developments, and societal pressures elsewhere. Obviously, we are more aware of this phenomenon today than ever before in history because the diffusion of technology has been accelerated and the means of communication have undergone a revolution within the last 100 years.

THE GROWTH OF REGIONAL INTERDEPENDENCE

The impact on world land use by the rapid population increase in Europe during the second half of the eighteenth century and throughout the nineteenth century affords a good illustration of interdependence. With the growth and mobility of the European population, which was concurrent with, and integrally related to, the quickening tempo of industrialization and urbanization, the use of the earth's natural wealth underwent profound changes. These changes were especially striking in the production of foodstuffs and other crops (such as rubber), and they were evident both in Europe and in other parts of the globe settled by, or under the influence of, Europeans. In Europe, the utilization of the agricultural land became steadily more intensive. On other continents—especially North America, Australia, Africa, and South America—as well as in Asiatic Siberia, vast areas hitherto untouched by the plow were brought under cultivation. In certain tropical areas, Europeans created oases of specialized commercial production (plantations) to meet their needs for raw materials. These commercial estates employed techniques of cultivation vastly different from those used by local peoples engaged in satisfying their daily requirements.

In time, a global network of agricultural regions was formed that continued to grow and expand as the Industrial Revolution spread and the pace of urbanization quickened. Where the impact of the new urban-industrial way of life was not immediately felt, the use of the land remained little changed, but these self-sufficient activity patterns came to be increasingly confined to the more remote or less desirable parts of the globe. Today, few regions and culture groups remain outside the worldwide network of supply and demand.

THE DANGER OF IMBALANCE

Needless to say, the nature of man's relationship to the environment must be balanced in such a way as to ensure human survival. For example, the output of foodstuffs must be responsive to population requirements. When this is not the case, malnutrition and even starvation result (Cohen, 1977). In the medieval period, the lack of foodstuffs in various regions around the globe because of crop failures—notably in India and China—often led to widespread misery and death. Food distribution systems were inadequate to the task of feeding large numbers of people at a distance from surplus supplies. Rapid population growth beyond the capacity of the land to sustain the numbers often triggered the kinds of imbalance that created severe dislocation. But, other factors may have been operative as well: religious or cultural taboos against the use of certain foods, the structure of land tenure, the methods of farming, and so on. At the same time, the elements of the natural environment—temperature, precipita-

tion, the quality of the soils, and the presence of supplemental water supplies—were instrumental in assuring or upsetting food balances. Whatever the association of causes, the human record contains many examples where the balance between a population and its food supply was disrupted (Cohen, 1977).

The Irish Famine

The problem as evidenced in mid-nineteenth century Ireland was especially tragic and had far-reaching implications. During the first four decades of that century, the Irish population doubled, reaching over 8 million by the early 1840s. The structure of land tenure retained many of the features of the medieval manorial system. Large estates were held by absentee Anglo-Irish landlords. Masses of Irish cultivators were reduced to the level of subsistence tenants. Three hundred thousand families lived on farms of less than five acres and one hundred thousand families held seasonal leases to plots of less than an acre. They had also become highly dependent on a single crop, the potato. When the potato blight reached Ireland from the continent in 1845, it devastated the harvests for three years in a row. The result was what is known as the Irish potato famine. Thousands died of starvation and from other diseases induced by malnutrition. Soup kitchens were set up by the government and other forms of support were made available, but these were totally inadequate to the crisis. Many people, the number ranging ultimately in the millions, began an exodus from Ireland that led to resettlement in other parts of Great Britain, in North America, and elsewhere. Decades later, in 1903, an Irish Land Purchase Act finally was passed by the British Parliament; it made possible the transfer of land titles to the cultivators. At the same time, the terrible dependence on the potato was reduced when Irish agriculture turned to dairying and the production of other cash crops. Until then, the Irish economy had endured decades of stagnation, a factor that further intensified the struggle for Irish *Home Rule,* or self-government, and encouraged migration abroad. By 1921, the population of Ireland had fallen to about 4.3 million, roughly one-half of what it had been in the 1840s.

HUNTING, FISHING, AND GATHERING

For the greatest part of its time on earth, the human population survived solely through the activity patterns of hunting, fishing, and gathering. Until the Neolithic period, there was little knowledge of agriculture nor much need to practice it. Existence entailed a dependence on fruits, nuts, roots, and other wild plant foods, whereas hunting and fishing increased the portion of protein in the diet. The extent to which meat or fish formed a portion of the diet obviously varied between communities and regions. Eskimo groups, for example, lived almost entirely on meat, some still do, although the numbers that do are steadily declining. Natives of the Northwest Pacific Coast built their diet and culture around fishing. Still other groups, found in southern Africa or in Amazonia, live almost entirely on plants or roots; animal protein is not a regular part of their food intake. Most likely, the tendency among the prehistoric hunting communities was to gorge on meat when it was available and to go without until another kill was made.

By the standards of civilized humanity, hunting, fishing, and gathering peoples have traditionally been regarded as primitive. Their way of life and their mode of economy have usually been placed at the bottom of the pyramid of progress. However, the early peoples who lived by hunting, fishing, and gathering seldom wanted for food (Sauer, 1947). When they did, some members of the group moved on to other areas. Old Stone Age hunters may have lived for only about 40 years because of an inability to care for the sick or severely injured, but their diet was on the whole balanced and nutritious. Only with the advance of the farmer, the growth of industrial cities, and the advent of sport and commercial fishing and hunting has the fare available to the practitioners of the oldest way of life tended to diminish—and these survivors have been pushed into the most inhospitable areas of the globe.

By the beginning of the Christian era, only about half the world's population (it has been estimated) existed by hunting, fishing, and gathering. By A.D. 1500, perhaps no more than 1 percent of the globe's population was sustained by life-styles within this broad pattern of activity. Today, only a handful of groups scattered in marginally habitable areas survive. And their days are numbered.

In recent decades, some of these relic peoples have been studied extensively by anthropologists. This discovery of the Tasaday people in the dense forests of the Philippines in 1971 has afforded an opportunity to peer through time at a prehistoric pattern of life. The gentle Tasaday gatherers seemingly have survived unchanged from the Old Stone Age!

Among other groups that have aroused interest are the Bushmen of southern Africa (Fig. 13–1). Their way of life in the Kalahari, although lacking in modern comfort, seems not to be wanting in many essentials. Their diet is balanced, they have a goodly amount of leisure time after they have gathered their provisions, and the quality of their community life is high. Above all, their foraging existence seems surprisingly secure.

Such peoples as the Bushmen, the Tasaday, the Amazon natives, the Eskimo, and others have learned to live in their environments. In the process, they have evolved activity patterns that ensure their survival. Yet, in the course of history, many groups who lived by hunting, fishing, and gathering replaced these social patterns in many areas of the world with crop cultivation or herding.

Figure 13–1

The Bushmen of Kalahari desert of south-central Africa are traditionally hunters and gatherers. Usually they travel together in bands, each consisting of 5 to 16 families united by bonds of kinship and friendship. Today, about six thousand Bushmen follow their traditional pattern of hunting and gathering, the rest, some eleven thousand, work at cattle posts for Bantu pastoralists. Few Bushmen, however, are free of European influence, as evident in their clothing and smoking habits.

Source: Botswana Information Services

THE TRANSITION TO AGRICULTURE

How and Why Did the Change Occur?

The transition to what we know as agriculture—cultivating crops and raising livestock—was made some ten thousand to twelve thousand years ago. Exactly what brought this transition about, however, remains in the realm of speculation (Cohen, 1977).

The traditional view of agricultural origins was that the initial transition took place, probably through experimentation, in only one or two centers in Asia. From there, it was thought, agriculture was diffused into other parts of Asia and to other continents. However, recent field and laboratory research refutes this hypothesis. Now, it is recognized that the practice of agriculture had its origins in many centers, occurring independently in each. Among the major Old World agricultural hearths are the Middle East, Southeast Asia, and East Asia. From there and possibly other less well-defined centers, agriculture spread into adjacent parts of the Old World. At a later date and independently, agriculture originated in the New World, particularly in Peru and Mexico. Nor was the adoption of crop cultivation a revolution; it was a slow evolutionary process.

Some scholars have also advanced the notion that it was an imbalance between population growth and food resources that touched off

Figure 13-2

Slash-and burn agriculture, or shifting cultivation, is a method of cultivation found today principally in the humid tropics. Areas are selected for cutting and then the tropical vegetation is fired; this releases nutrients that fertilize the soil. After two years of cultivation, fertility declines and weed infestation increases. The field is then abandoned and allowed to return to forest. Most of the crops grown by this method are usually root crops, which are high in carbohydrates.

Source: Omikron/Photo Researchers, Inc.

the beginnings of agriculture. If true, this would mean that in Asia at least there had to have been a significant increase in population, especially in a southern band stretching from the Middle East to the Far East. Such population pressure, it is believed, would have caused several hunting groups to turn to agriculture at about the same time. But, for such pressure to build, populations would have had to have been at least partially sedentary. When their regional numbers exceeded the capacity of their existing food resources to sustain them, the hunters would then have been forced *by need* to the cultivation of the soil.

What this theory suggests is that ancient peoples knew how to draw food from the soil. What had hitherto been lacking was the need for them to do so. So long as population numbers remained small and scattered, there was enough wildlife for all. When, however, the numbers reached a level where the food balance was disturbed, the hunters and gatherers were compelled to resort to other food sources. Climatic changes, resulting from the retreat of the glaciers into northern Eurasia, may also have been a factor inducing the development of farming. Certainly, the Neolithic period was characterized, at least in the Middle East, by a drier, warmer climate than earlier eras had experienced.

Initially, the search for new foods had been sporadic and haphazard. Some passages of time undoubtedly occurred between the simple harvesting of wild grasses or roots and the actual planting of crops for annual harvest. Whatever the course it took to become mankind's dominant activity pattern, crop cultivation provides more calories per unit of time and energy than the hunt does. Thus, agriculture is capable of supporting larger and denser populations than hunting or gathering. What the practice requires, however, are new social relationships and, above all, a new relationship to the land as a productive unit.

Systems and Methods

Shifting Cultivation

One of the earliest of agricultural systems to be employed was *shifting cultivation,* a practice that survives today principally in the tropics where perhaps up to 50 million people depend on it for their livelihood (Fig. 13–2).

Long thought to be a primitive system, shifting cultivation or slash-and-burn agriculture entails a keen knowledge of the ecology of the area. Karl Pelzer described shifting cultivation as "an economy of which the main characteristics are rotation of fields rather than crops; clearing by means of fire; absence of draught animals and manuring; use of human labor only; employment of the dibble stick or hoe; and short periods of soil occupancy alternating with long fallow periods" (K. Pelzer, 1945).

Where land is plentiful and population density low, shifting cultivation is a desirable system (Harris, 1972). In the lush tropics, the employment of long fallow periods during which the natural vegetation is allowed to return is an efficient system of rebuilding the nutrients that will ultimately be transferred to the soil when the vegetative cover is cut and burned. If shifting cultivation was truly a widespread phenomenon in early times, it would have had to be abandoned as population densities increased to a point where the system could not operate. Large amounts of land per capita must be available for use; thus, settlements cannot remain permanently in one place or the villages must resort to clearing land at ever greater distances from their dwellings. Moreover, in temperate lands, the vegetative cover is slow to restore itself so that it can at best sustain only very small communities.

Nomadic Pastoralism

Dependence on domesticated animals forms the basis of the pastoral existence that evolved quite early in the history of humankind. In this pattern of activity, animals satisfy human needs for food, clothing, shelter, and transportation. Traditionally, *nomadic pastoralism* was a self-sufficient way of life based on a wide knowledge of an extensive geographic region. Today, however, the survivors of this ancient form of animal husbandry may barter with sedentary peoples for some of the food and manufactured goods they need on their migrations. Crop cultivation may not be totally excluded from the life of the pastoralist, but ordinarily it has not played more than a supplementary role in sustaining true nomadic groups. If practiced, it is usually the women and children who sow and harvest the crops.

In the modern world, there may not be more than 15 million people who engage in some form of pastoralism, whether truly nomadic or only seminomadic. This way of life is well adapted to the dry subtropical and temperate regions that include North Africa, the uplands of East Africa, the Middle East, and the interior of Asia that extends from the Ural River and the Caucasus Mountains to the Mongolian Plateau (Fig. 13–3). The animals kept vary with the region, but they consist generally of combinations of cattle, sheep, goats, camels, and horses (Figs. 13–4A, 13–4B). The Mongol pastoralists, although no longer migratory to the degree that they were in the nineteenth century, raise all these animals in addition to the yak. The latter (*Bos grunniens*), a cross between common cattle and a wild, horned, and hairy animal, is a sturdy animal that is exceptionally well adapted to endure the cold. Yak butter provides Tibetans and Mongols with an essential fat. The Yak supplies meat and yak hides also make good rugs and tent coverings.

Nomadic pastoralists are not aimless wanderers. These peoples not only lead their flocks (or follow them, as the Lapps do with the reindeer), but also retain a link to a specific place, usually their winter quarters. During the rest of the year, the pastoralists generally follow fixed cycles of migration over the same general territory year after year. A common form of migration is the ascent from a protected lowland win-

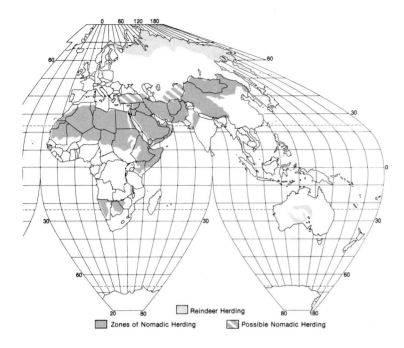

Reindeer Herding
Zones of Nomadic Herding
Possible Nomadic Herding

Figure 13-3
The principal areas of pastoral activity of a nomadic or seminomadic type are found in the Old World, mostly on the drier margins of settled agriculture. From the Atlantic coast of Africa, they stretch across North Africa through the Middle East into Central Asia, reaching as far east as Mongolia.

ter residence to upland summer pastures and back again. This simple pattern of movement is known as *transhumance*.

Although pastoral nomadism was widespread in past centuries, it has undergone considerable territorial contraction in the decades since World War I. The pressures of modern state formation have severely constrained nomadic movements. In the Soviet Union, Mongolia, and China, the physical collectivization of the herds reduced the numbers of pastoralists and almost converted the practice of animal husbandry to ranching (Dienes, 1975). The encroachment of farming communities on the grasslands, too, has severely reduced the patrimony of the nomad. The nomadic pastoral way

of life hangs in the balance, and its days most likely are numbered.

Aquatic Farming

The development of a rice culture in South and East Asia was a phenomenon historically unique to that vast area. Rice has played a role there not unlike that of wheat or barley in Southwest Asia and the Mediterranean basin and not unlike that of corn in the New World. Possessing a high food value, rice has constituted a staple for the majority of the inhabitants living in the lands that stretch from Sri Lanka to Japan. Even today, a high proportion of the inhabitants of these Asian countries—perhaps

Figure 13–4A

The Mongols have traditionally been a nomadic people, raising herds of sheep, goats, yaks, and camels. Their horses were sturdy-legged creatures that, in the thirteenth century, carried them out of Mongolia into Central Asia and ultimately into the Russian grasslands. Since the Communist takeover in 1921, the Mongols have remained essentially livestock raisers, but their movements from pasture to pasture are limited and restricted. The camel herd is a common sight in modern Mongolia.

Source: W. A. Douglas Jackson.

Figure 13–4B

Although Mesopotamia (modern Iraq) is one of the early agricultural hearths—not only where the cultivation of grain evolved, but also where irrigation farming developed—the raising of sheep and goats on dry lowland pastures has remained a feature of the landscape to the present. This shepherd girl in Iraq watches over her father's flock.

Source: W. A. Douglas Jackson.

Figure 13–5

The single most important crop of Taiwan is rice, which is sown in about half the total cultivated area. Virtually all the irrigated land is sown to rice. Because the amount of lowland is restricted to the western third of the island by the mountain range that forms the eastern spine, the hillsides have been terraced to make use of all available land. The ploughing is generally done by buffalo.

Source: W. A. Douglas Jackson.

half the total population of the world—are primarily dependent on rice for food.

Rice was first cultivated as a dry crop, part of a pattern of shifting cultivation, in the uplands of Southeast Asia. In North China, according to local records, it dates to at least 3000 B.C. The wild ancestor of rice in the lowlands, however, is thought to be *Oryza sativa,* a perennial semi-aquatic marsh grass native to humid, tropical Asia. Where it was domesticated first, however, remains unknown. Some researchers think that *aquatic farming* of rice originated in Indochina and was thereafter diffused southwestward into Malaya and Indonesia and northward into China. Still others believe it began in India and spread eastward from there. Whatever its origins, wet rice was a later development than the cultivation of either wheat or barley.

Needless to say, wet rice cultivation requires careful and controlled use of water. In Japan, for example, rice is transplanted from seedbeds to the inundated field. This technique makes it possible to extend the growing season and maintains better care and control of the rice seedlings during early growth. Perhaps more than any other farming culture, the production of rice has left a distinctive imprint on the landscape (Fig. 13–5). The use of the permanent *paddy* is one of the truly great inventions of agriculture (Grigg, 1974). In the humid tropics, river flooding and heavy precipitation provide the necessary water. Elsewhere, especially in Japan, Taiwan, China, and Korea, the farmers have for centuries dug the necessary reservoirs, canals, and ditches and constructed the devices for lifting water to the fields. They have also built levees against destructive flooding and terraced steep slopes.

Of all the agricultural systems in the world,

the aquatic farming of rice in South and East Asia has been based on the most intensive use of both land and labor. In southern Japan after the rice crop is harvested, the field is usually sown to a dry winter crop, after which a third crop may be interplanted between the rows. In parts of central and southern China, two crops of rice per year are common. Work animals, particularly water buffalo, supplement human labor, generally in the preparation of the soil; in Japan and Taiwan increasing use is being made of small machinery.

THE AGRICULTURAL REVOLUTION

Factors Promoting Change

The substantial changes that were manifest in the European agricultural patterns on the threshhold of the Industrial Revolution have been referred to earlier. In reality, these changes—which had brought about an increase in output and, concomitantly, a slow but steady improvement in diet—had been underway for many centuries (Dovring, 1965). England led the way in this Agricultural Revolution, but significant changes were underway on the Continent as well.

The beginning of this transformation might be said to date from the discovery of the New World at the end of the fifteenth century (Wallerstein, 1974). The penetration by Europeans of overseas lands led to the introduction and diffusion of many new crops, some of which were to alter basic European farm patterns by offering important alternatives to existing usage. Following that, the transformation in traditional patterns of land tenure (stimulated in England by the enclosure movement) encouraged the commercialization of food production, which, in turn, was enhanced by new systems and methods for both crop cultivation and livestock raising. An expansion of the knowledge of

agronomy and an increasing availability of machines and fertilizers was a direct outcome of industrialization. At the same time, the gradual expansion of farming in the colonies not only transformed colonial landscapes, but also contributed significantly to a reshaping of land use in Europe. Finally, the growth of markets spurred by improvements in maritime transportation created a new phenomenon—a worldwide pattern of supply-and-demand relationships in food and agricultural products. Altogether these accumulative changes made it possible, in all but a few regions, such as Ireland, for the Europeans in the nineteenth century to escape the dire predictions, made by Thomas Malthus (1766–1834), of an inevitable famine caused by overpopulation. In the process, the foundations of a global network of agricultural regions were laid (Wallerstein, 1974).

New Plants and Foodstuffs

The discovery of the New World presented Europeans with many unfamiliar plants and animals native to the Americas. From the sixteenth to the eighteenth centuries, many of these new foodstuffs were adopted by European farmers, among the most important of which were the potato, corn, and the turkey (Fig. 13–6). The latter, for example, was brought to Spain from Mexico about 1520; within a century, it had become common fare at Christmas time in many parts of Europe. Tobacco was another important new crop, but its cultivation remained somewhat restricted by climate to southern and eastern Europe. In addition, the arrival in Europe of such beverages as coffee (from Africa), tea (from East Asia), and cocoa (from Meso-America and South America) altered drinking habits and, in turn, encouraged the consumption of imported sugar.

Of all these new crops, without doubt, the potato was the most important addition to European farming, although it took a full three centuries for it to win widespread acceptance and use. The Spaniards had found a wide variety of potatoes under cultivation when they penetrated the Americas. Among the Amerindians of what is now Chile and Bolivia, the potato was a staple, which the natives called *pappas*. Sometime before 1560, the potato reached Spain and Portugal, where is was known as *batates* or *patates*. Under cultivation in Spain before the end of the century, the potato was then taken to Italy and the Low Countries. Within a short time, it also had penetrated Austria, Germany, Switzerland, and France. England probably experienced an independent introduction, possibly before 1586. The potato revolutionized the Irish diet in the seventeenth century. Sweden and Prussia also began to cultivate the potato at about that time, after which it spread eastward into Poland and northern Russia (Laufer, 1938).

Acceptance, of course, was a different matter from introduction. Promotion was successful in northern Italy, but it took strong pressure from Frederick the Great to get widespread adoption of the potato in Prussia. Among the peasants of northern Russia, there was little interest at first in cultivating the new crop, and as late as 1793, prejudice against the potato in France inhibited widespread consumption (although the grain shortage in that year seems to have brought a sudden change in taste). In any event, by about 1800, the potato had become an important crop in the gardens and fields of most of the countries of Europe. Moreover, the potato proved to be a good fodder crop for livestock, and by the 1880s, it was used as a principal ingredient in Central European whisky production. Its adaptability to a wide range of soil and climatic conditions, its storability, its greater per unit area yield over the cereals, not to mention its human nutritional advantages, made the potato a staple from Ireland to Russia during the nineteenth century.

It is believed that the native peoples served corn (or maize) to Columbus on his first visit to the West Indies. Shortly thereafter, it was carried back to Spain; however, its diffusion was slow. It took a century to cross the Iberian Peninsula from the Atlantic to the Mediterranean. From Spain, corn spread through southern France and into Italy; by the eighteenth century, it had reached the Balkans, from whence it penetrated southern Russia. Where corn was grown for human consumption, as in the Caucasus, it was eaten as porridge. Generally, though, it proved a nutritious livestock feed, yielding twice as much per acre as any other cereal.

Columbus also witnessed the smoking of tobacco when he reached America. In 1519, the Spaniards found it under cultivation in Mexico, where it was believed to have curative powers for respiratory diseases. However, France was the first European country to grow tobacco (in 1556)—from seed transported from Brazil. Spain and Portugal soon followed, after which it was taken to the Low Countries and to Italy, from whence it reached the Balkans, Turkey, and Russia. By the end of the sixteenth century, tobacco had already become a cash crop in some regions.

Pipe smoking was introduced into England about 1585, and it was to the colonies of the American seaboard that England turned for its supply of tobacco. The first cultivation of tobacco by English colonists was in 1612 at Jamestown, Virginia, from seed brought up from Meso-America. The crop flourished in the southern colonies, particularly as settlers moved inland from the coast. In 1619, 20,000 pounds of tobacco were shipped to England; by 1700 the trade had climbed to 18 million pounds. The British Navigation Acts prohibited the cultivation of tobacco in England but protected the output of the Virginia planters. As a result, by 1750, some 40 million pounds per annum were sent to the mother country.

Such crops as potatoes, corn, and tobacco not only had an effect on European life, but also these and other crops native to the Americas were widely diffused throughout the world. In the sixteenth century, corn, cassava, sweet potato, groundnuts, and tobacco reached Africa; during the seventeenth century, the native peoples of West Africa developed a taste for to-

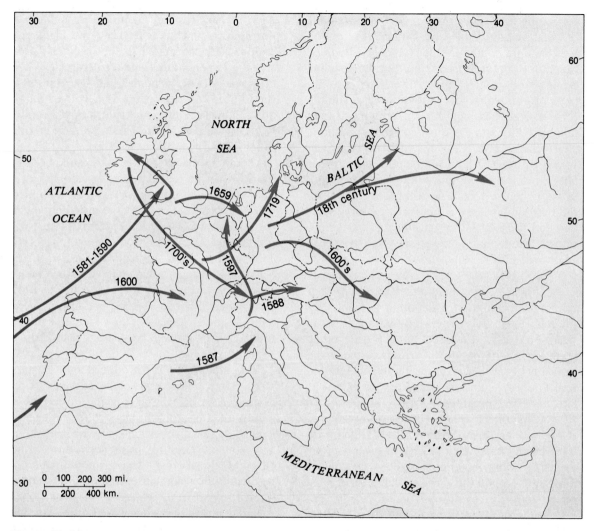

Figure 13–6A

The new crops that were introduced into Europe from the New World were diffused throughout that continent slowly. In some instances, it took almost 200 years before a new crop gained acceptance. (A) the potato, for example, introduced into France from Spain about 1600, was not widely consumed until 1793. (B) Maize or corn moved just as slowly. It took about 100 years for the crop to spread from the Atlantic coast of Spain, where it was first introduced, to the Mediterranean world.

bacco. Corn, tobacco, sweet potato, and groundnuts reached China in the sixteenth century, at about the same time that tobacco reached India, Persia (Iran), and other nearby countries. The potato, which had enhanced European diets, was, in turn, carried by Europeans to the far-flung reaches of their empires. New Zealand received the tuber in 1773, the Guinea coast of Africa in 1776, and by 1880 it had found its way through the Himalayan passes into Tibet.

The introduction in Europe of beverages

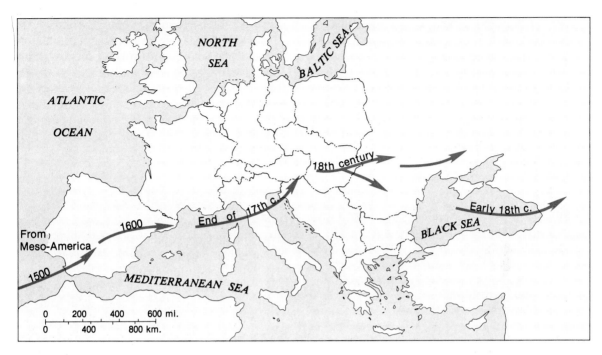

Figure 13–6B

from other parts of the world also had significant effects. Tea was never grown in Europe; with its importation in 1609 by the Dutch East India Company, it quickly became a popular beverage. The coffee bean reached Europe from Africa via the Middle East as an item in the Venetian trade. By 1643, it was being drunk in the coffeehouses of Paris. Cocoa, a native of the Americas, arrived in Spain in 1520; during the following century, as chocolate and as a beverage, it sweetened the tastes of the Low Countries and Italy. By 1657, cocoa also was known to, and appreciated by, the English.

The European demand for sweetness was also satisfied by Genoese and Venetian traders who brought sugar from Egypt and the eastern Mediterranean. Sugarcane was subsequently introduced to Madeira and the Canary Islands. From there, it crossed the Atlantic where it was grown in the West Indies. During the seventeenth and eighteenth centuries, the West India sugar plantations, worked by slave labor, were the main source of Europe's sugar supply.

Evolution to the Modern Pattern

European farming in the seventeenth century was characterized by a heavy emphasis on cereals, with following an essential part of the cropping system. Animal husbandry was poorly developed because of the generally poor fodder base. The upward curve in Europe's population, evident from 1650 and pronounced after 1750, however, led to a sharp rise in the demand for foodstuffs. Food prices rose; grain prices skyrocketed; and the inflationary pressure not only contributed to an increase in farm output, but also led to struggles for control over farmland. Throughout Western Europe, the traditional village system came under attack and the historic patterns of land utilization were altered.

In England, the enclosure movement led to the increasing concentration of land in the hands of the gentry, a trend that continued until the early decades of the nineteenth century. In

Denmark, land consolidation was officially enacted after 1750. Village lands were reorganized and parceled out as consolidated units, a development that required that new houses be built on individual holdings. Elsewhere in Europe, there was also a stirring among the peasantry for the abolition of communal property rights and the creation of individual land ownership, but advances toward this goal varied greatly in tempo. In Russia, this transformation really did not get underway until 1906. In the areas where the move toward land consolidation and individual tenure did begin in the eighteenth and nineteenth centuries, it was accompanied by a significant change in mentality (Blum, 1978). The medieval peasant was passing from the European scene and the modern farmer was beginning to come into focus.

Along with the new patterns of land tenure came efforts to improve and expand crop cultivation. In Scandinavia, vast forested areas were cleared for farming; in the Netherlands, expansion took the form of accelerated reclamation of land from the sea; and in France, extensive areas of wasteland were gradually turned into productive farmland. Alongside these developments, the growth of animal husbandry finally led to the replacement of the three-field system. Root crops—particularly turnips—clover, and grasses were sown in the fields that had been left fallow. Not only did these crops have value as animal fodder, but also they contributed to soil improvement. In England, the *Norfolk system,* based on a wheat-turnip-barley-and-clover field rotation, became the basis of the new farming and the model most widely heralded on the Continent. The use of previously fallow land in this manner represented a significant advance. Not only did it further stimulate livestock raising, but also it assured a larger supply of animal manure for the fields.

The changes in the areas of land tenure and cultivation systems were accompanied by new agricultural methods as well. Innovation followed innovation. Tradition had dictated that seed be sown broadcast. Then in 1701, Jethro Tull (1674–1741), an English agriculturalist, invented a horse-drawn drill, which revolutionized seeding by placing the seed in rows. Tull also demonstrated (in practice as well as in his writings) the value of good plowing and the use of fertilizer. In this way, the foundations of modern British farming were laid, and in time, these new methods were adopted on the Continent.

The Opening of the New Lands

As population continued to increase, Europe was increasingly compelled to turn to the world beyond its immediate boundaries to provide for the needs of its domestic population (Youngson, 1965) (Box 13–1). Much of those peripheral regions had already been delineated and designated colonial or dependent. Central Europe, without the advantage of a maritime exposure, turned to southern and eastern Europe, whose grasslands were rapidly being transformed into grainfields. Western Europe, on the other hand, developed close trading links with the new lands beyond the seas. By the middle of the nineteenth century, it had become clear that the vast interior of North America in particular, parts of temperate South America, and Australia and New Zealand possessed substantial food-producing areas. Europe, increasingly urban, had been compelled to intensify the use of its own agricultural resources; the new lands, by contrast, assured a high yield per acre with a minimum of human guidance.

Australia and New Zealand

In Australia, the frontier pushed inland and northward from the original colonial settlement hearth on the southeastern coast. Restricted by an unreliable precipitation regime, early settlers in Australia turned to sheep raising. In the early decades of the nineteenth century, vast quantities of wool, the volume of which reached 39 million pounds per annum by the end of the 1840s, were exported to Great Britain. As set-

BOX 13-1
The Shaping of the World's Cultivated Areas

In 1750, the European demand for cereals (on the whole) exceeded local supply. Initially, England met this challenge by exporting enough grain to feed 1 million people. However, as grain cultivation improved in Europe, the region of surplus production shifted eastward. By 1800, industrialized England had become a net importer, whereas the grain farmers of Germany and Poland were the chief producers, their exports being channeled through Baltic ports. By 1850, Hungary's grasslands had come under cultivation and thousands of migrating Russian and Ukrainian peasants had settled the Black Sea provinces known as New Russia. Between 1800 and 1850, European Russia added no less than 50 million acres to its grain area. Following the emancipation of the serfs in 1861, the fertile lowlands of the North Caucasus were opened up, to be followed by the colonization of the West Siberian lowlands; in the decade of the 1870s, railroads began to link these grainfields to the Baltic and Black Sea ports. Thus, at the turn of the century, Russia was well on its way to becoming the world's leading grain exporter.

Throughout the first half of the nineteenth century, British agriculture was protected by the corn laws, which generally prohibited grain imports (although grain from Canada was admitted as if it were domestic produce). The protection that the estates and farms enjoyed was withdrawn after 1846; the collapse of government support weakened the foundations of gentry wealth. Many of the gentry class sold their lands to the newly enriched commercial and industrial families. With the opening of the grainlands of the North American West by the 1870s, British agriculture was further threatened. Between 1875 and 1885, the wheat-growing area in England was reduced by nearly 1 million acres. The general tendency to replace wheat with grasses, however, did not result in a corresponding increase in livestock numbers because frozen meat shipments from Australia, New Zealand, and Argentina (inaugurated in the late 1870s) successfully competed with domestic output. These developments gradually turned British farmers toward the cultivation of fresh vegetables for the urban market, and the patterns of the modern world system took shape.

A big factor in the shaping of the world's agriculture, of course, was the reduction of transport costs during the latter part of the nineteenth century. The shipping costs of wheat from Chicago to Liverpool, for example, fell by more than half between the 1860s and the 1890s. This development facilitated the flooding of the British market with North American wheat. Progress in refrigeration had a similar effect on the shipment of animal products. A pioneer in this field, T. S. Mort, set up the first facilities for freezing meat in the world at Sydney, Australia, in 1861.

tlers pushed inland, however, the sheep ranchers were forced into interior stations where the dry pastures were conducive to a system best described as seminomadic (Box 13–2). The more temperature areas—notably of Victoria, New South Wales, and later Western Australia—were devoted to crop cultivation, particularly the production of wheat. Cotton and sugarcane were grown in the subtropical and tropical lands to the north. The growth of railroads in the 1870s and the development of refrigerated shipping expanded Australian potential, opening the British market to shipments of mutton and beef. New Zealand benefited as well, with an economy based mainly on sheep (mutton and wool) and cattle (dairy products).

TEMPERATE SOUTH AMERICA

Temperate South America had been colonized by Europeans since the sixteenth century, but until the nineteenth century, settlements had remained predominantly coastal and restricted. The nineteenth century brought a flood of Europeans to these areas, but the regions of compact settlement remained coastal. The interior, from the Amazon basin of Brazil to the southern *pampas* (or grasslands) of Argentina remained sparsely settled as vast areas were turned into estates controlled by a few persons.

The growth of an agriculture geared to export occurred primarily after 1850, following political stabilization, the pacification of the Amerindians of Argentina's southern frontier, and the coming of the railroad. Brazil's economy rapidly came to focus on coffee as an export crop. Wool and hides had been important to Argentina's export market for decades, and the building of a railroad system in the 1880s opened up the pampas to wheat cultivation. The coming of refrigerated meat shipments late in the 1870s demonstrated, too, the profitability of cattle raising.

NORTH AMERICA

As colonial territories, the French and English settlements in North America from the first were producers of important items—such as fish, furs, and forest products—for their respective mother countries. Tobacco, too, quickly became a valuable commodity item. The in-

---

BOX 13–2

New World Methods of Livestock Raising

Pastoral nomadism is a phenomenon of the drier, less accessible areas of the Old World. In the New World, European settlers with no experience of nomadism were forced to create systems for livestock raising that were suited to the prevailing natural conditions.

Sheep herding, for example, has been adapted to the range areas of Australia and the United States. The animals are grouped into flocks that total several thousand head, and they are grazed on areas that frequently include many thousands of acres. In the Rocky Mountain states of North America, adaptations of the traditional transhumance practiced in Asia have been achieved. On these western ranges, sheep are herded on high mountain ranges in summer and driven to foothill levels in winter. During the spring and fall, they are kept at intermediate elevations. In the interior of Australia, which is too dry for crop cultivation

and cattle raising, vast sheep stations have been created in the midst of areas of controlled grazing. It is at these stations that the shearing of the sheep (for wool) takes place.

In Soviet Central Asia and Kazakhstan, the Soviet regime decided that it would not tolerate the traditional pattern of livestock raising, which was nomadic or seminomadic. Hence, following the collectivization of the herds, the Soviet regime in the mid-1930s instituted a system of herding not unlike that which developed on New World rangelands known as *otgonnoye* (literally movement away from). The new system represents a form of controlled, but extensive, livestock raising. The movements of livestock are directed from central points. These central points serve as villages for the families of the herders, with schools for children and veterinarian services for livestock. Supplemental feeding of livestock is organized around these points, much as it is done at the Australian sheep stations or on the American range. The *otgonnoye* system, which deprives the nomadic pastoralists of their historic right of freedom, nevertheless has led to a higher productivity in Central Asian-Kazakh livestock raising.

vention of the cotton gin by Eli Whitney (1765–1825) at the close of the eighteenth century resulted in the expansion of cotton cultivation, particularly along the southern seaboard, and by the middle of the nineteenth century, the United States had become the world's leading producer and exporter of cotton. Even Russia imported cotton grown in the United States. However, the soils of the seaboard states soon deteriorated under cotton, and the crop migrated westward; by 1860, the major cotton-producing states were Mississippi, Alabama, Louisiana, and Texas.

From colonial times also, stock raising had been part of the economy of the American settlements. The Ohio Valley was particularly suited to livestock. The growing of corn was well adapted to the valley's climate and soil conditions. Because corn provided a nutritious feed for pigs and cattle, its cultivation proved to be a profitable enterprise. By 1830, therefore, a corn-livestock economy had taken shape throughout the valley.

Cotton had penetrated Texas, but climate and range conditions there proved conducive to livestock raising as well. Sheepherding had been introduced to Texas under the Spanish regime, as it was throughout the Southwest. In the latter region, the Spanish missions had come to rule over 1.5 million acres of fine pastoral land by the 1820s. The missions in California alone had over 300,000 head of sheep at the peak of their prosperity. Sheep raising in Texas barely survived the colonial period; in California, the great mission herds declined with the transfer of the territory to the United States in 1848 and the subsequent discovery of gold. Still the demand for meat in California had to be satisfied and long drives from New Mexico, Oregon, and even the Midwest were instituted. By the 1860s, however, the directions were reversed and the sheep were driven eastward to the Rockies. By the 1880s, sheep were being fattened in Nebraska and Colorado for the eastern market.

Although sheep did not remain unimportant

in Texas, cattle had significant impact there. The 1840s witnessed the opening of the cattle drives—the first in 1842 from Texas to New Orleans, which became the chief market for Texas cattle (L. Pelzer, 1936). With the 1850s came the long drives northward into the Ohio Valley where the animals were fattened and to Chicago where the foundations of a meat-packing industry were laid. Within a decade, the American Midwest was attempting to supply refrigerated meat to Europe. The movement was not entirely one-way however. European breeds, such as Aberdeen Angus and Herefords, were introduced to help improve the quality of American range stock. The establishment of Abilene, Kansas, on the Kansas Pacific Railroad as a shipping point to the east in the late 1860s altered the patterns of reaching the market. The extension of the Atchison, Topeka & Santa Fe Railroad across southern Kansas rerouted the drives to Newton, Wichita, and Dodge City, the last center becoming the greatest of all shipping points. By the 1880s, between 250,000 and 300,000 head of cattle had moved north to the railhead (Fig.13–7). With the reduction of the great buffalo herds in the northern plains and the movement of the native Americans to reservations, the stocking of the northern ranges (into Montana) ensued. By the mid 1880s some 45 million head of cattle were grazing on the range from Texas to the Canadian border. The filling up of the range with stock, the Kansas Quarantine Act, and the construction of rail lines into Texas finally brought the great cattle drives to an end. The movement of cattle to the corn-producing states continued, however, although by the end of the century there was a growing tendency to fatten in Texas.

The railroads that doomed the cattle drives also opened up the prairies and plains to the farmers. The Homestead Act (1862), the completion of the Union Pacific Railroad (1869), and the increasing availability of large machinery—that is, reaping and threshing machines—brought millions of acres of new cropland into

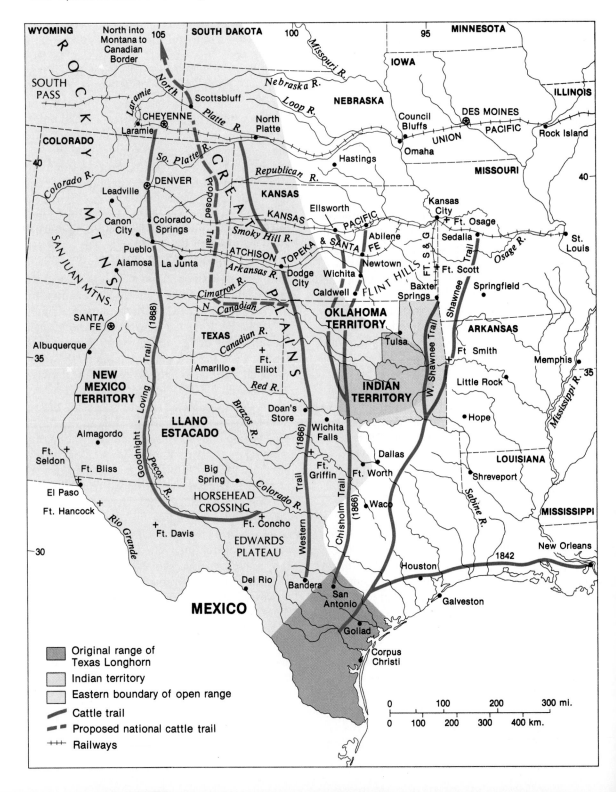

Original range of Texas Longhorn

Indian territory

Eastern boundary of open range

Cattle trail

Proposed national cattle trail

Railways

production. Wheat from Kansas and Nebraska and later from the Dakotas was hauled to elevators to serve the growing American and overseas markets.

The prairies of Canada are physically separated from the eastern provinces by a huge granitic region known as the Canadian Shield. Its existence together with the fact that since the seventeenth century much of the vast western territory had been the fur-trapping grounds of the Hudson Bay Company had hindered settlement. In 1856, there were probably less than two thousand European inhabitants between Lake Superior and the Rocky Mountains, with an additional five thousand of mixed origin (*métis*). The transfer of the Hudson Bay Company's domain to Canada in 1869 opened some 2 million square miles of territory to settlement from eastern Canada. However, until the completion of the Canadian Pacific Railway in 1885, transportation into the region remained a problem. By 1885, however, the quality of western Canadian wheat gained recognition when Manitoba spring wheat was exported to Great Britain. After the opening of the railroad, the Canadian government turned to Europe for its prairie settlers, and by the turn of the century the Canadian prairie began to thrive as new railway spurs were built and the western lands were settled.

The Export of Capital and the Plantation System

An important feature of European agricultural economic development was the emergence of the *plantation system* (Grigg, 1974). Tropical regions, unlike the temperate, did not attract European immigrants, but the tropics, because of their climatic conditions, were capable of supplying crops that could not be produced elsewhere and that became increasingly essential to the industrialized world. To ensure a supply of these commodities, the Europeans transferred capital, management, and technology to far-flung areas of the world.

The plantation, therefore, was an agricultural holding that contained a fairly large area under protection and operated under European supervision, but it relied on large quantities of local or imported labor. The output was predominantly for export. Although extensive land clearing and crop introduction and adaptation were associated with the creation of plantations, the benefits were reaped almost entirely by the foreign owners. The labor force—frequently uprooted, without familial ties, and dependent on the plantation for survival—was often pushed to the limit of endurance. Although the techniques of plantation production became increasingly scientific, the local population per-

Figure 13–7

The cattlemen's frontier lasted from about 1864 to 1887 and was one of the major episodes in the conquest of the West.

The giant cattle industry had its origins in Texas, the cattle having been first introduced there by the Spaniards in the eighteenth century. It was not until 1864–1865, however, that Texas cattlemen became aware of the profits to be made through the sale of their cattle in the upper Mississippi Valley. At the same time, the railroads had begun to penetrate the prairies west of the Mississippi. In 1865, for example, the Missouri Pacific Railroad reached Sedalia, Missouri, which could be used as a shipping point to markets in the East.

The result was the Long Drive of 1865–1866. Although not entirely successful, this cattle drive was followed by others. Soon Abilene, Kansas, replaced Sedalia as the terminus of the Long Drive, and in 1867, some thirty-five thousand Texas steers passed through the bustling town. The Chisholm Trail from San Antonio northward quickly became the major trail with seventy-five thousand head moving northward in 1868. By 1875, Dodge City had become the major railhead for transshipment of cattle. Ultimately, the long drive proved unsound, especially because the northern prairies and plains built their own herds.

sisted in traditional patterns of farming that entailed rice or shifting cultivation. Thus, the plantations represented oases of foreign endeavor, isolated from, although in the midst of, native self-sufficiency. Still, it must be acknowledged that the plantations undertook what small farmers could not. Most plantation crops require a period of initial gestation before harvest can begin (tea requires five to seven years; sisal, three to four years; arabica coffee, from three to four years). Small farmers would not be able to wait that long.

The plantation system had its roots in the seventeenth and eighteenth centuries when the sugar plantations of the West Indies and the tobacco plantations of Virginia were initiated. Both enterprises grew on the basis of slave labor imported from Africa. In time, however, slave labor proved to be both costly and inefficient. When, in the early nineteenth century, the reliance on slave labor in the Caribbean gradually came to an end, the plantation owners turned to indentured or contract labor. The labor was Asian, mostly from the Indian subcontinent.

Rubber, a commodity much in demand in Europe from the 1860s onward, was suited to plantation cultivation, but up until 1910, virtually all the rubber marketed came from the wild rubber trees of the Amazon basin of Brazil. *Hevea brasiliensis*, the principal rubber-producing species in Brazil, grew mainly in the lowlands. During high water, the lowlands flooded so that the trees could only be tapped during the dry periods. After 1910, the sharp rise in European and, subsequently, North American demand led to a dramatic expansion in rubber extraction. Whereas 10 million pounds of raw rubber were taken from Brazil's trees in 1910, some 40 years later, Brazil exported 93 million pounds. The get-rich-quick fever that sprouted in Amazonia drew scores of foreign companies to come and exploit both the area and its people. Although the use of native labor to tap the rubber trees reflected some of the worst features of the plantation system, the Brazilian industry never

took to plantation cultivation. Indeed, it was the rubber from the plantations established in Southeast Asia that provided the competition that led to the collapse of the Brazilian industry.

Although European trading companies had operated in South and Southeast Asia from the seventeenth century, there were no real plantations before the nineteenth century. In the Indies, the Dutch government in the 1820s and 1830s encouraged the development of privately owned European plantations for export production. Then the demand for tropical Asian produce increased dramatically with the opening of the Suez Canal in 1869, which greatly shortened the distance between Europe and Asia. In 1877, the rubber tree was introduced to Malaya, and it rapidly became the predominant agricultural crop of the peninsula. Somewhat later, African palm oil plantations were created there as well, using Chinese and then Indian labor. So extensive were the Malayan plantations that in the early decades of the twentieth century, Malaya turned to other lands for its foodstuffs. Although to a much lesser degree, a similar pattern evolved in the Dutch East Indies and in French Indochina. In the Indian subcontinent, tea, principally from Assam, became the principal plantation crop and India's most important export. Under Japanese domination, tea plantations were created on Taiwan. (Fig. 13–8).

In Africa, where the plantation system developed at a slightly later date, its role varied among the different colonial powers. In West Africa, the British were not inclined to lend their support to the establishment of plantations. On the other hand, in the highlands of Kenya and Uganda, plantations that produced tea, sisal, and coffee were important. In the Ivory Coast, Guinea, and the Cameroons, bananas and coffee were grown for export. In the Congo, the Belgian government was supportive of the plantation system and hundreds of thousands of acres were put into palm oil trees and coffee. Liberia encouraged the raising of rubber trees, an enterprise dominated today by the Firestone Corporation of the United States.

Figure 13–8

Rice, sugarcane, and tea are among the more important crops grown on Taiwan. The tea plantations on Sri Lanka, like Taiwan, are found in the uplands that form the eastern backbone of the island. There the tea is grown in extensive plantations that cover well-drained hillsides.

Source: Bernard Pierre Wolff/Photo Researchers, Inc.

THE THÜNEN HYPOTHESIS

The spatial expansion of commercial agriculture throughout the world in the nineteenth century has long attracted the interest of geographers and economists. In their attempts to analyze and explain the processes whereby this world network took shape, scholars and stu-

dents have turned to the stimulating work of a German landowner named Johann Heinrich von Thünen (1783–1850). In a remarkable study, *The Isolated State* (written in 1826, but only translated into English in 1966), Thünen used the parameters of a hypothetical isolated state to develop theories of agricultural intensity and of the location of agricultural systems (Thünen, 1966). Thünen assumed that within an environment made essentially simplistic, reasonable men would act in a predictable manner.

He imagined, in Part I of his book, a large city in the middle of a fertile plain that is not crossed either by a navigable river or a canal. The soil of the plain is uniformly fertile and capable of cultivation. At some considerable distance from the city, the plain is terminated on all sides by an uncultivated wilderness that isolates the state from the outside world. Because there are no other towns on the plain, the central city must obtain all its supplies from the surrounding countryside in exchange for the manufactured goods it produces. Access to this market would take the form of straight-line wagon movements, and the costs of transportation would be the same in all directions.

Given such a situation and assuming that farmers would seek to maximize their profit or *economic rent* (i.e., the difference between their revenues and their costs of production), Thünen raised two principal questions: What patterns of cultivation will take shape under these conditions? How will the farming systems and the production of crops be affected by the distance from their market?

First of all, Thünen wrote, it is obvious that sharply differentiated concentric rings or belts would take shape around the city. Each ring would be characterized by its own staple product and completely different farming systems would be found from ring to ring (Fig. 13–9). To be produced near the market, a crop would have to yield a high profit. Thus, in the ring nearest the city, farm output would be characterized by highly perishable products that could not stand much transport and would require im-

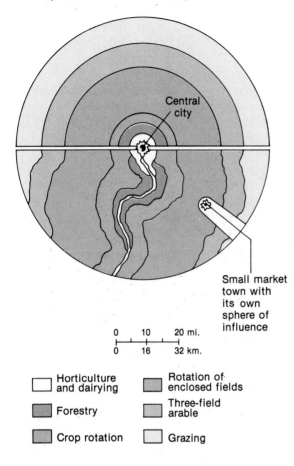

Central
city

Small market
town with
its own
sphere of
influence

| 0 | 10 | 20 mi. |
| 0 | 16 | 32 km. |

☐ Horticulture
and dairying

▨ Rotation of
enclosed fields

■ Forestry

▨ Three-field
arable

▨ Crop rotation

☐ Grazing

Figure 13–9

Thünen's original hypothesis envisaged a series of concentric circle around a central market. The introduction into the model of river transportation a second market town substantially alters the original hypothesis.

mediate use or by heavy or bulky products where costs of transport would preclude their being hauled from some distance.

Application of the Thünen hypothesis can contribute to an understanding of the spatial patterns of world land utilization and crop production that emerged in the nineteenth century. J. R. Peet (1969) has proposed that the urban-industrial areas that appeared first in Great Britain, western Europe, and the northeastern

United States in that century be regarded as a Thünen World City. Like the city in *The Isolated State,* this World City came to be surrounded by a series of large agricultural zones (Fig. 13–10). As the demand for food and raw materials progressed during the century, the zones of agricultural production were pushed further from the core. Gradually, the demands of the World City led to the opening up of the little-used lands of the New World. In this way, Peet stated, the frontier was merely the outer boundary of a dynamic system, and the expansion of the frontier and the changes in agricultural production that took place behind it may be explained through a study of the changes in supply-and-demand conditions throughout the entire world system.

Peet's notion of a Thünen World City is a useful one. There is, however, the danger of oversimplification. In the real world, of course, there is not one center of demand or consumption, as suggested by the Thünen concept, but many. And this factor has become even more significant in the twentieth century as other parts of the globe have industrialized and urbanized. Moreover, technology has vastly altered transportation systems that, in turn, have affected the use of the land in many parts of the globe. Nevertheless, the presence of accessible markets remains important in determining how land is used. Despite its drawbacks, the Thünen hypothesis is helpful in focusing our attention on the question of world interrelationships and how they determine human activity patterns.

MEETING
FUTURE CHALLENGES

Altering Natural Factors

As we have seen, world agriculture has undergone marked changes in recent centuries and similar changes are ongoing. Agriculture is dependent on a number of natural factors—such as climate, soil, and the biologic processes of

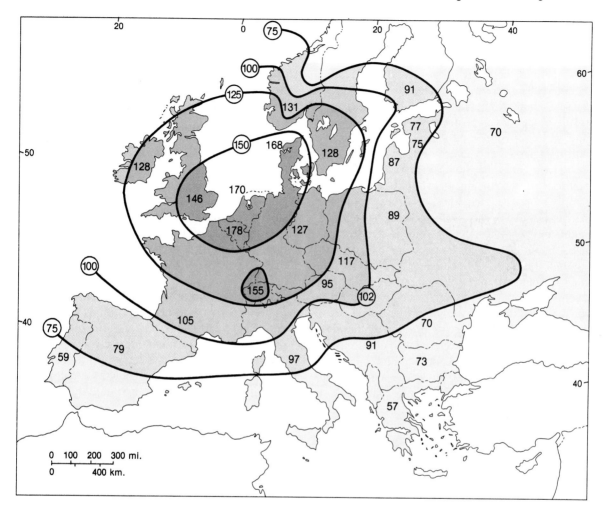

Figure 13–10

Agricultural production in Europe in the mid 1930's reflected some aspects of the Thünen hypothesis. Crop output per acre was highest in northwestern Europe near the great industrial cities, and lowest in the southern and eastern parts of the continents. The index of 100 is based on the average yield of 8 main crops: wheat, rye, barley, oats, corn, potatoes, sugar beets and hay. The boundaries shown are post World War II.

plants and animals. Since the beginning of crop cultivation, humankind has sought to control, or at least lessen the effects of, these factors to be assured a reliable and steady output of foodstuffs.

Despite modern technological advances, people are still not able to control climate, although they have altered, usually unwittingly,

local weather conditions. Attempts have been made to seed clouds when rain is needed, with varied results; but by and large, farmers react to weather rather than affect it. Farmers have learned to place smudge pots around vines and other valuable crops when frost threatens. Growers also have built greenhouses and hotframes to lengthen the growing season. But, to a very high degree, agricultural land remains subject to nature's decree.

People can affect the nature of soils more readily than they can purposely alter climate. People can improve the quality and productivity of soils with applications of peat, lime, and fertilizers; they can protect the soil against wind and water erosion; and they can rotate crops and irrigate. At the same time, people can adversely affect soils by indiscriminate cutting of trees, by overplowing in droughty areas, and simply by poor management. Moreover, the expansion of urban areas into the countryside has taken much good farmland out of agricultural use.

Over the past ten thousand years, humankind also has attempted to intervene in the life cycles of plants and animals. People have domesticated them, have improved on them through feeding, and have practiced selective breeding and plant improvement to obtain more food value per unit of output. The interventions, however, have not always brought beneficial results. The elimination of one plant pest or animal predator, for example, has permitted other pests and predators to get out of hand. In the current century, the use of chemical pesticides, insecticides, and herbicides has reduced the danger to plants and animals of disease and pestilence, but it has also had harmful repercussions for those who consume the treated products. Nevertheless, world requirements for crops continue to grow, taxing humankind's ingenuity, and humans continue to try to meet the challenge by altering nature.

Global Food Requirements

Because of the rapid growth of global population, especially evident in the Third World, the world as a whole faces increasingly complex challenges in supplying the necessary agricultural provisions to feed humankind's expanding numbers (Knight and Wilcox, 1976).

The question of global food resources is essentially one that is based on the ratio of food to population. To maintain present per capita food consumption over the next 20 to 25 years, when the world population is expected to reach 6 billion, will require, it has been estimated, a doubling of world food output. This means that ever larger amounts of food, grain in particular, will be necessary to feed the countries with rapidly growing populations. At the same time, rising affluence also leads to greater consumption levels.

When consumed directly, grains provide 52 percent of humankind's food supply. Consumed indirectly in the form of livestock products, grains also represent a sizeable share of the remainder. At present, grains occupy more than 70 percent of the world's crop area. In the heavily populated countries, such as India, Bangladesh, and others, the annual availability of grain per person averages about 400 pounds per year. Nearly all of this amount must be consumed directly to meet minimal needs. Little can be spared for conversion into livestock products (even assuming that the local culture permits it). In the United States and Canada, only 150 pounds of grain per person are consumed directly each year, but up to 1850 pounds are consumed indirectly in the form of meat, milk, and eggs. Such a level of consumption requires, however, nearly five times more agricultural resources (i.e., land, water, and fertilizers) than are used to support the average peasant in Asia, Africa, or Latin America. Indeed, it takes five times as much water to produce the daily food supply of one person in the United States as in India. Clearly, as income rises so also do per capita grain requirements. Measured in terms of beef consumption, this trend may be seen in the fact that annual per capita consumption in the United States rose from 55 pounds in 1940 to 117 pounds in 1972. Poultry consumption correspondingly increased from 18 to 51 pounds. Obviously, the pressure placed on world grain production derives not only from those countries that depend on grain for survival, but also from those countries whose diets are more varied owing to their affluence. The countries of northern Europe, the Soviet Union, and Japan have dietary habits more or less like those of the United States and Canada. To meet these needs, Japan depends heavily on imports, both of grains and meats. The Soviet Union, despite its massive crop area, in recent years has imported large quantities of grain (for human and animal consumption) from North America, mainly because of the regime's massive effort to upgrade the diet of its people and provide more animal products.

Expanding the Output of Foodstuffs

How are these ever-increasing needs going to be met? There are two ways to expand the output of foodstuffs (Jennings, 1976). One is to increase cropland; the other is to raise output per unit area.

Of the earth's 33 billion acres of land area, some 3.5 billion, or a little over 10 percent, are now cultivated (Tables 13–1, 13–2). Pastures account for about 23 percent, forests occupy 30 percent, and land in other uses, or unused amounts to about 36 percent. Some experts believe that the amount of land used for crop production can be doubled, but it is clear that an

Table 13–1
World Land Categories

	Billion Acres	Percentage
Total Land Area (excluding Antarctica)	33.0	100.0
Cropland	3.5	10.3
Pastures	7.6	23.0
Forests	9.9	30.0
Deserts, Wastelands, Urban Areas, Etc.	12.0	36.7

Source: Production Yearbook, 1971, Vol. 25 (Rome: Food and Agricultural Organization of the United Nations, 1972), pp. 3–8.

enormous investment per unit acre would be required. More than half the earth's pasture lands are used for grazing, but if these lands were cultivated, they would not yield substantial additional amounts of food because of adverse terrain or climatic factors. Because most of the world's great frontier regions were settled and occupied by the end of the nineteenth and the beginning of the twentieth centuries, additional cropland expansion would have to come in marginal areas, which are, for the most part, found on the colder, drier boundaries of present crop areas. More intensive land use

Table 13–2
World Land Categories by Areas (in million acres)

Continental Areas	Total Land Area	Cropland	Pastures	Forests	Other
Europe (excluding USSR)	1,218	363	230	346	279
USSR	5,533	576	924	2,248	1,786
North and Central America	5,535	630	919	2,013	1,974
South America	4,404	207	1,020	2,243	934
Asia (excluding USSR)	6,800	1,139	1,233	1,319	3,108
(China only)	(2,361)	(272)	(437)	(188)	(1,462)
Africa	7,484	506	2,085	1,578	3,315
Oceania	2,102	116	1,146	200	640
Total	33,076	3,537	7,557	9,947	12,036

Source: Production Yearbook, 1971, Vol. 25 (Rome: Food and Agricultural Organization of the United Nations, 1972), pp. 3–8.

there would significantly reduce the habitat of the remaining hunting and nomadic cultures. Elsewhere, the drainage of marshlands, the irrigation of drylands, and the improvement of poor soil areas are possible, but at an exceedingly high cost.

In the past, good free land was available—as in North America, Siberia-Kazakhstan, and Australia—so that it was economically feasible to convert more land to cultivation. In recent decades, the necessary gains in food output have been achieved primarily through intensification—the raising of yields of valuable crops on lands already under cultivation.

Since the end of World War II, the United States has achieved noteworthy success in increasing the output of its land. Over the past quarter century, the production of corn, for example, has risen by about 4 percent per year. In 1954, the average yield per harvested acre was 39.1 bushels, but it reached 83.9 in 1969. The yield of wheat also rose, from 17.7 bushels in 1954 to 30.7 in 1969, and the yield of rice has almost doubled. Along with these improvements, there has been a sharp rise in the output of poultry, eggs, and milk. The average American cow yields about 10,000 pounds of milk per year, although in some states, notably Wisconsin and Washington, individual cows have given 40,000 pounds. These achievements represent major changes in American farm practices and reflect the use of improved seed, fertilizers, better animal fodder, and so on. By contrast, in India, the average yield of milk per cow is only about 600 pounds.

The intensification of the use of the land also has contributed materially to global crop gains since 1950. By the 1970s, intensification rather than cropland expansion accounted for four fifths of the annual increase in output. Much of this improvement has come about as a result of the *Green Revolution*, particularly where it has had its impact on Third World countries. The term Green Revolution refers to the technological breakthrough achieved in the 1950s in the development of new high-yielding varieties of

Table 13–3
The Spatial Diffusion of New High-Yielding Varieties of Grain, Wheat and Rice (1964–1973)[a]

Years	Acres
1964–1965	200
1965–1966	145,000
1966–1967	4,200,000
1967–1968	16,500,000
1968–1969	31,000,000
1969–1970	41,300,000
1970–1971	53,100,000
1971–1972	67,900,000
1972–1973	80,000,000

[a] In Asia and North Africa, non-Communist countries only.

Source: Dana G. Dalrymple, *Development and Spread of High-Yielding Varieties of Wheat and Rice in the Less Developed Nations* (Washington, D.C.: U.S. Department of Agriculture, Foreign Development Division, Economics Research Service, 1974).

wheat (first achieved in Mexico) and rice (in the Philippines).

In 1964–1965 some 200 acres of land were planted to the new, high-yielding varieties of grain in Asia outside the communist bloc. By 1972–1973, the area sown to such varieties had reached 80 million acres (Table 13–3). The development was not a universal success, although it was impressive. By 1968–1969, 40 percent of the wheat sown in Pakistan was of the new varieties; in Nepal, it was 36 percent; in India, it was 27 percent. At the same time, the cultivation of "miracle" rice in the Philippines reached 32 percent of sowings; in Malaysia, 16 percent of sowings. In Mexico, 90 percent of the wheat sown consisted of the new varieties.

Sowings were matched by impressive output figures. In India, grain production between 1947 and 1966 grew from 50 to 80 million tons. By 1970, output had climbed another 10.5 million tons; in 1970–1971 output had climbed an additional 5 million tons. In Bangladesh, steady progress paid off in a bumper harvest in 1979 of 13 million tons (although good weather helped substantially). Despite this phenomenal improvement, global population increase continues to outstrip the growth in the output of foodstuffs. The threat of Malthus's prophecy continues to hover over the peoples of the earth.

Continued success in the current Green Revolution depends on an adequate and controlled water supply, on fertilizer applications, and on pesticides. Good management and sociopolitical stability are obviously essential as well. The sharp rise in the price of natural gas and the consequent rise in nitrogenous fertilizer prices, social unrest, and political instability—all have tended to lessen the full impact of the revolution's promise. Moreover, the increase in the output of rice and wheat, although desirable from one point of view, may have disturbing consequences as well. Other valuable crops may be neglected (such as legumes), and this development may reduce the intake of protein and needed vitamins. In Bangladesh, the cultivation and production of jute in place of food must continue because it helps provide the currency to buy additional supplies of grain and other commodities.

Clearly, new complexities emerge even as new solutions are found to problems. Never before has humankind faced the dilemma that confronts it daily on so vast a scale: how to bring its numbers into balance with its food supply. On the resolution of that question will lie the future security of the globe.

EPILOGUE

No phenomenon better reflects the concept of spatial relationships than does agriculture. Present patterns of crop cultivation and livestock raising are the product of spatial economic changes set in motion by the industrialization and urbanization of the nineteenth century. Although physical geographic factors are important in determining the ecological requirements and conditions of agricultural production, the impact of the World City has been substantial.

The Thünen hypothesis is useful in attempting to understand how these world patterns have come into existence and in explaining present-day relationships. As the developing countries further industrialize, the hypothesis may be useful in attempting to foresee how these relationships will be modified in the future.

The domestication of plants and animals may be dated back about some ten to twelve thousand years. For centuries, agricultural activities were geared to satisfying local needs. When, however, population and food supply fell out of balance, the records show, adjustments occurred—although not without some considerable hardship. The world today is confronted with a rapidly growing population, especially in the developing countries. Crop innovations, under the Green Revolution, have led to substantial increases in food output. Not only must the world sustain its population numbers, but also it must find ways of getting the food to regions where it is badly needed. Changes in crop and harvest patterns and changes in food tastes and levels of consumption warrant attention as they are clues to how the world of the future feeds itself.

APPLICATION OF IDEAS

1. Underlying all geographic inquiry is a fundamental assumption: the patterns of human activity that have evolved over the surface of the earth are not without form or purpose; these patterns have taken shape in response to human needs and wants.

2. Rapid population increase, mobility, industrialization, and urbanization—all of which occurred in Europe in the eighteenth and nineteenth centuries—led to European domination of the world and a growth in world interdependence. The European impact on the rest of the world was simply to bring all parts together in one world system.

3. In no area of activity was this development of European domination more pronounced than in world agriculture. In effect, northwestern Europe together subsequently with the northeastern United States came to form a World City around which broad agricultural zones began to take shape.

4. Gradually, the demands of the World City led to intensification in agriculture near the core, which was surrounded by zones that became progressively less intensively worked as they were further from the core. The frontier was merely the outer boundary of a dynamic system.

5. The World City conceptualization of the spatial patterns of world agriculture is a useful one, but the regularity of zonation is not always easy to see because of the differentiation of the earth surface itself.

6. The continued growth of population and the expansion of industrialization in Third World countries may have further impact on agricultural patterns. In any event, the challenge of feeding the world remains.

KEY WORDS AND PHRASES

aquatic farming	pampas
batates	pappas
economic rent	patates
Green Revolution	plantation system
Hevea brasiliensis	sequent occupance
Home Rule	shifting cultivation
métis	slash-and-burn
nomadic pastoralism	agriculture
Norfolk system	transhumance
paddy	

QUESTIONS FOR FURTHER DISCUSSION

1. Cite examples of landscape change with which you are familiar that fall within the definition of sequent occupance. For example, what has been the nature of occupancy in your own region?

2. Although tangible proof may be difficult to obtain, indicate regions where, historically, food supply and population numbers have suffered imbalance. Some research into available statistical data together with some understanding of the development of these regions might provide some clues.

3. In what regions of the earth do you still find peoples who engage in hunting, fishing, or gathering as a way of life? What do these peoples have in common?

4. Why is shifting cultivation an ecologically sound system of food production? What is essential to ensure success? Why did shifting cultivation yield to regularized field cropping in temperate regions?

5. Why has rice culture been so important to the history of the peoples of Asia? Why do you think it was more valuable in these regions than wheat farming?

6. Consider ways in which crops native to the Americas altered European living (and eating) habits. What, on the other hand, has Europe sent to the Americas that helped transform agriculture in the New World?

7. Technology has frequently altered patterns of human relationships on earth. Consider the implications of steam navigation and refrigeration on the use of lands at great distances from the growing European market.

8. Why was the plantation system important to European industry, but less so to European agriculture? What did it entail?

9. Explain the relationship between the patterns of land utilization that Thünen theorized would develop around a central market city and the patterns that took shape in the nineteenth century in the world at large. What innovations have occurred that make a strict application of the Thünen model to the modern world agricultural network difficult?

10. What is the Green Revolution? Why is it so important today? What is required to ensure a high level of agricultural performance under the Green Revolution?

REFERENCES AND ADDITIONAL READINGS

Ashworth, William. *A Short History of the International Economy 1850–1950*. London: Longmans, Green, 1952.

Asian Development Bank. *Asian Agricultural Survey*. Tokyo: University of Tokyo Press, 1969.

Association of Japanese Agricultural Scientific Societies, ed. *Rice in Asia*. Tokyo: University of Tokyo Press, 1975.

Blum, Jerome. *The End of the Old Order in Rural Europe*. Princeton, N.J.: Princeton University Press, 1978.

Boserup, Esther. *The Conditions of Agricultural Growth: The Economics of Agrarian Change Under Population Pressure*. London: Allen & Unwin, 1965.

Brenner, Y. S. *A Short History of Economic Progress*. London: Frank Cass, 1969.

Bronowski, J. *The Ascent of Man*. Boston: Little, Brown, 1973.

Brown, Lester R. *The Politics and Responsibility of the North American Breadbasket*. Worldwatch Paper 2. Washington, D.C.: Worldwatch Institute, October, 1975.

Chang, Jen-Hu. "Tropical Agriculture: Crop Diversity and Crop Yields." *Economic Geography* 53 (1977): 241–254.

Clark, Colin. *Population Growth and Land Use*, 2nd ed. London: Macmillan, 1977.

Clark, Colin, and Haswell, Margaret. *The Economics of Subsistence Agriculture*. London: St. Martin's, 1964.

Cohen, Mark Nathan. *The Food Crisis in Prehistory. Overpopulation and the Origins of Agriculture*. New Haven, Conn.: Yale University Press, 1977.

Dahlberg, Kenneth A. *Beyond the Green Revolution. The Ecology and Politics of Global Agricultural Development*. New York: Plenum, 1979.

Dalrymple, Dana G. *Development and Spread of High-yielding Varieties of Wheat and Rice in the Less Developed Nations*. Washington, D.C., U.S. Department of Agriculture, Foreign Development Division; Economics Research Service, 1974.

Dienes, Leslie. "Pastoralism in Turkestan: Its Decline and Its Persistence." *Soviet Studies* 27 (1975): 343–365.

Dovring, Folke. "The Transformation of European Agriculture," pp. 604–672. In *The Cambridge Economic History of Europe*, Vol. VI, Pt. II. H. J. Habakkuk et al., eds. Cambridge: Cambridge University Press, 1965.

Duckham, A. N., and Masefield, G. B. *Farming Systems of the World*. London: Chatto & Windus, 1970.

Dunn, Edgar S., Jr. *The Location of Agriculture Production*. Gainesville: University of Florida Press, 1954.

Eckholm, Erik, and Brown, Lester R. *Spreading Deserts—The Hand of Man*. Worldwatch Paper 13. Washington D.C.: Worldwatch Institute, August 1977.

Ekvall, Robert B. *Fields on the Hoof. Nexus of Tibetan Nomadic Pastoralism*. New York: Holt, Rinehart & Winston, 1968.

Farmer, B. H., ed. *Green Revolution? Technology and Change in Rice-Growing Areas of Tamil Nadu and Sri Lanka*. London: Macmillan, 1977.

Forde, C. Daryll. *Habitat, Economy and Society*. New York: E. P. Dutton, 1963.

Grigg, D. B. *The Agricultural Systems of the World. An Evolutionary Approach*. London: Cambridge University Press, 1974.

———. "Population Pressure and Agricultural Change," pp. 133–176. In *Progress In Geography*, Vol. 8. Christopher Board et al., eds. London: Edward Arnold, 1976.

Harlan, Jack R. "The Plants and Animals that Nourish Man." *Scientific American* 235 (1976): 88–97.

Harris, David R. "Swidden Systems and Settlements," pp. 1–18. In *Man, Settlement and Urbanism*, Peter J. Ucko, Ruth Tringham, and G. W. Dimbley, eds. London: Duckworth, 1972.

Heady, Earl O. "The Agriculture of the U.S." *Scientific American* 235 (1976): 106–127.

Hodgson, Harlow J. "Forage Crops." *Scientific American* 234 (1976): 60–75.

Hopper, W. David. "The Development of Agriculture in Developing Countries." *Scientific American* 235 (1976): 196–205.

Jackson, W. A. Douglas, ed. *Agrarian Policies and Problems in Communist and Non-Communist Countries.* Seattle: University of Washington Press, 1971.

James, Preston. "The Blackstone Valley. A Study in Chorography in Southern New England." *Annals of the Association of American Geographers* 19 (1929): 67–109.

Jennings, Peter R. "The Amplification of Agricultural Production." *Scientific American* 235 (1976): 180–195.

Johnson, Douglas L. *The Nature of Nomadism; A Comparative Study of Pastoral Migrations in Southwest Asia and Northern Africa.* Research Paper No. 118, Department of Geography, University of Chicago, 1969.

Johnson, Hildegard Bender. "A Note on Thünen's Circles." *Annals of the Association of American Geographers* 52 (1962): 213–220.

Johnston, Bruce F., and Kilby, Peter. *Agriculture and Structural Transformation. Economic Strategies in Late-Developing Countries.* New York: Oxford University Press, 1975.

Kellerman, Aharov. "The Pertinence of the Macro-Thünian Analysis." *Economic Geography* 53 (1977): 255–264.

Knight, C. Gregory, and Wilcox, R. Paul. *Triumph or Triage? The World Food Problem in Geographical Perspective.* Resource Paper No. 75-3. Washington D.C.: Commission on College Geography, Association of American Geographers, 1976.

Laufer, Berthold. *The American Plant Migration. Part I: The Potato.* Anthropological Series, Publication 418. Chicago: Field Museum of Natural History., 1938.

Loomis, Robert S. "Agricultural Systems." *Scientific American* 235 (1976): 98–105.

Manshard, Walther. *Tropical Agriculture. A Geographical Introduction and Appraisal.* London: Longman, 1974.

Mayer, Jean. "The Dimensions of Human Hunger." *Scientific American* 235 (1976): 40–49.

Mellor, John W. "The Agriculture of India." *Scientific American* 235 (1976): 154–163.

Murray, Jacqueline. *The First European Agriculture. A Study of the Osteological and Botanical Evidence Until 2000 B.C.* Edinburgh: University of Edinburgh Press, 1970.

Orr, David W., and Soroos, Marvin S. *The Global Predicament. Ecological Perspectives on World Order.* Chapel Hill: University of North Carolina Press, 1979.

Peet, J. R. "The Spatial Expansion of Commercial Agriculture in the Nineteenth Century: A von Thünen Interpretation." *Economic Geography* 45 (October 1969): 283–301.

Pelzer, Karl. *Pioneer Settlement in the Asiatic Tropics; Studies in Land Utilization and Agricultural Colonization in Southeastern Asia* (Special Publication No. 29). New York: American Geographical Society, 1945.

Pelzer, Louis. *The Cattlemen's Frontier.* Glendale, Calif.: Arthur H. Clark, 1936.

Perelman, Michael. *Farming for Profit in a Hungry World. Capital and the Crisis in Agriculture.* Montclair, N.J.: Allanheld, Osmun, 1977.

Production Yearbook, 1971, Vol. 25. Rome: Food and Agricultural Organization of the United Nations, 1972.

Revelle, Roger. "The Resources Available for Agriculture." *Scientific American* 235 (1976): 164–179.

Russell, Howard S. *A Long, Deep Furrow. Three Centuries of Farming in New England.* Hanover, N.H.: University Press of New England, 1976.

Sauer, Carl O. "Early Relations of Man to Plants." *Geographical Review* 37 (1947): 1–25.

Scrimshaw, Nevin S., and Young, Vernon R. "The Requirements of Human Nutrition." *Scientific American* 235 (1976): 50–73.

Struever, Stuart, ed. *Prehistoric Agriculture.* Garden City, N.Y.: Natural History Press, 1971.

Symons, Leslie, *Agricultural Geography,* Rev. ed. Boulder, Colo.: Westview Press, 1979.

Tarrant, John R. *Agricultural Geography.* New York: John Wiley, 1974.

Vayda, Andrew P. *Environment and Cultural Behavior.* Garden City, N.Y.: Natural History Press, 1969.

von Thünen, Johann Heinrich. *Der isolierte Staat in Beziehung auf Landwirthchaft und Nationalökonornie.* Carla M. Wartenburg, Trans.; Peter Hall, ed. *Von Thünen's Isolated State.* Oxford: Pergamon Press, 1966. (Originally published, 1826).

Wallerstein, Immanuel. *The Modern World-System. Capitalist Agriculture and the Origins of the European World-Economy in the Sixteenth Century.* New York: Academic Press, 1974.

Wellhausen, Edwin J. "The Agriculture of Mexico." *Scientific American* 235 (1976): 128–153.

Whittlesey, Derwent. "Sequent Occupance." *Annals of the Association of American Geographers* 19 (1929): 162–165.

Wortman, Sterling, "Food and Agriculture." *Scientific American* 235 (1976): 30–39.

Youngson, A. J. "The Opening Up of the New Territories," pp. 139–211. In *The Cambridge Economic History of Europe,* Vol. 6, Pt. 1. H. J. Habakkuk et al., eds. Cambridge: Cambridge University Press, 1965.

14

The Rural Countryside in Transition

E'n now, me thinks, as pondering here I
    stand,
I see the rural virtues leave the land

Oliver Goldsmith,
The Deserted Village, 1769

Woe to those who add house to house
    and join field to field
    until everywhere belongs to them
and they are the sole inhabitants of the land.

Isaiah 5:8,
Jerusalem Bible, 1966

And so it appears that the failure of so many
small farmers over so many years is really a
kind of justice: it is their own fault; they
ought to have been more efficient; if they
had to get bigger in order to be more efficient, then they ought to have got bigger.

Wendell Berry
The Unsettling of America, 1977

Key Ideas

1. There is a long tradition in the United States dating back to Thomas Jefferson, if not before, that sees essential virtues embracing hard work, honesty, integrity, thrift, and naturalness, associated with the countryside.

2. Although there is a collective image of the countryside, individually people differ as to how land in the countryside should be used.

3. There is no one satisfactory definition of rural.

4. Depopulation of rural areas has been a phenomenon in every industrialized country.

5. Repopulation and urban encroachment on rural land is a cause of much concern. Some even see it as a threat to farmland and food production.

6. In a number of the 50 states, legislation has been introduced in an effort to control land use. Most legislation, however, lacks effective means of enforcement.

7. Extensive controls have been placed on rural land use in Great Britain, but many groups remain concerned about effective planning.

8. In the United States, the farm sector has been characterized by a declining population and work force and a declining number of farms *but* an increase in the size of farms and enormous changes in farm operations.

9. Accompanying these changes, there has been a sharp rise in land values and, in the early 1980s, a decline in farm income. High interest rates have contributed to farm indebtedness.

10. Repopulation is placing strains on the rural way of life and blurring further the distinctions between rural and urban.

11. Walter Christaller (whose work was translated from German and published in English in 1966) saw markets as inherent in a landscape and hypothesized that they developed on the basis of centrality.

THE COUNTRYSIDE AS A FOCUS OF GEOGRAPHIC INTEREST

In recent years, geographers in the United States have shown little interest in the countryside, that spatial domain that lies outside metropolitan and urban areas. When expressed, it has taken the form of studies of settlement types, land utilization and the spatial structure of crop and livestock production, and rural-urban migration. For that reason, there is little agreement today as to what constitutes the countryside; nor is there any accepted format as to how to deal with its complexity. This lack of interest on the part of American geographers is not matched in Great Britain where a major attempt has been made in the past decade to draw into focus the forces that are changing countryside landscape. Moreover, as a result of population changes, especially where areas have been significantly depopulated, attention has been directed at facets of rural life that have suffered, namely, the decline in service facilities and the loss of traditional values as well as problems associated with changes in the agricultural sector.

In the industrialized world, up to 40 percent of the population many live in nonurban areas, but only a relatively small fraction are engaged full time in farming. Enormous increases in farm output, evident particularly in the United States and Canada, have made it possible for barely a handful of people, relying on machinery and chemistry, to feed large numbers of people at home as well as abroad. But, in that success, some critical problems have emerged that raise questions about the future of agriculture. At the same time, pressures on agricultural land and on the countryside as a whole by nonfarm interests suggest that some forms of protection are needed if future generations are not to be deprived of an environment that has been part of our culture and heritage.

On the other hand, although rural farm population has declined, that loss has been offset by a turnaround that has brought an influx from metropolitan areas together with the values ordinarily associated with cities. All of these developments are part of the massive changes underway in the United States and in the industrialized world as a whole that are reshaping the total landscape.

THE COUNTRYSIDE AS THE REPOSITORY OF TRADITIONAL VALUES

Beginning with Thomas Jefferson (1743–1826), a founder of the Republic and the third president of the United States, many American writers, thinkers, and politicians have possessed a negative attitude toward the city. Jefferson, who believed that "cultivators of the earth are the most valuable citizens," also wrote, "when we get piled up one upon another in large cities, as in Europe, we shall become corrupt as in Europe, and go on eating one another as they do there" (Padover, 1939, p. 70). Jefferson knew that Europeans were not cannibals, but he thought, as did many eighteenth-century liberals, that urban civilization had a harmful effect on people and that civic virtues resided in the countryside.

Throughout the century and a half since, the virtues associated with the countryside have been cherished because they are seen to embody hard work, honesty, integrity, thrift, and naturalness. These traits are the essence of the character of Abe Lincoln of Illinois. Somehow, too, there seems to be goodness in whatever has sprung from the soil, such as a grassroots political movement as compared to boss-managed politics of large city wards.

This nostalgia for a more innocent past, exemplified by life in the countryside, is not a new phenomenon. It has been effected in every generation by the impact of material change. Such writers as Nathaniel Hawthorne (1804–1864), Henry David Thoreau (1817–1862), and Walt

Whitman (1819–1892), lamented the passing of their New England way of life.

Nor has this lamentation been confined to North America. In Great Britain, the rapid pace of industrialization of the nineteenth century tended to foster the notion that human character, shaped by experience in the countryside, especially on the farm, was somehow vital to development of a healthy nation (Davidson and Wibberley, 1977). Of all the English romantic writers to feel a deep sense of loss at the passing of one landscape and the formation of another, William Wordsworth (1770–1850) was undoubtedly the most expressive.

. . . At social Industry's command,
How quick, how vast an increase! From the
  germ
Of some poor hamlet, rapidly produced
Here a huge town, continuous and compact,
Hiding the fact of the earth for leagues—and
  there,
Where not a habitation stood before,
Abodes of men irregularly massed

The Excursion, Book 8

Even in prerevolutionary Russia, there was a non-Marxist, intellectual movement that looked to the peasantry for inspiration (Box 14–1). The novelist, Leo Tolstoy (1828–1910), in *War and Peace*, a story of upper-class life in Russia in

---

BOX 14–1

Populism: Two Avenues of Approach

During the latter part of the nineteenth century, populist movements whose goals were to obtain reforms that would benefit the rural farm population, took shape both in the United States and in Russia.

In the United States, political action groups grew up among farmers hurt by crop failures, declining farm prices, poor marketing and credit facilities, and general insecurity. These action groups took the shape of Farmers' Alliances, and they were especially important in the South and the West. In the 1890s, these groups came together to form the Populist (People's) party with the aim of exerting direct influence on the government in Washington. For a variety of reasons, the new party met defeat in the national election in 1896 and thereafter the movement died away. Except for wielding considerable influence in some state governments, the Populists have never regained the influence they once had.

What is interesting about American populism is that it represented one of the most powerful protest movements in the United States since the

secession of the South. It was, above all, a grass roots movement that grew out of general farm discontent.

In Russia, on the other hand, the populist movement grew up among the *narodniki,* intellectuals who believed that social transformation in Russia was dependent on the peasantry. They were called *narodniki,* from the Russian word *narod,* meaning people. These populists argued that a modern (non-Marxist) socialist society could be constructed on the basis of the *mir,* the peasants' traditional village communal organization. The movement got started in the 1860s following the emancipation of the serfs in 1861.

In the early 1870s, the *narodniki* took their ideas to the countryside and mingled with peasants, attempting to educate them and inciting them to rebellion. Some *narodniki* were arrested and imprisoned by the tsarist government. Some formed a more secretive organization known as *Zemlya i Volya* (Land and Freedom) in 1876 and even settled among the peasantry in the villages.

The peasantry, recently freed from serfdom, were not responsive. They remained deaf to political action. Impatient with peasant conservatism and stupidity, some *narodniki* embraced Marxism and shifted their attention to the cities and to the urban proletariat.

the early nineteenth century, creates a central figure named Count Pierre Bezukhov. The name Bezukhov is derived from a Russian word *bezukhiy,* meaning earless. Bezukhov's life is without meaning, (Tolstoy shows) simply because he is unaware of the world around him; his life is without purpose; he is without ears to hear, or as we would say "he has blinders on." However, during Napoleon's occupation of Moscow in 1812. Bezukhov is confined to a Kremlin prison where he meets a peasant, Platon Karatayev. It is Karatayev who literally helps Bezukhov to hear, or remove the blinders. Karatayev's life in the countryside seems to be so close to nature that, to Bezukhov, Karatayev is part of it. It is this image of rural sturdiness and virtue that at last inspires the count, awakens him, and reforms his life.

What seems to be different today in much of the industrialized world—from Japan to Western Europe—is that decades of rapid material change have cut deeply into both a way of life and a landscape. The unusually large attendence at annual fairs in the United States, altogether some twenty-three hundred state and county fairs, is strong evidence of the hold that countryside images have on the American consciousness.

PARTICULARIST VIEWS OF THE COUNTRYSIDE

There may be a collective view of the heritage of the countryside, yet individual interpretations of what the countryside actually means and how land in the countryside should be used in the future find no universal consensus.

Farmers are concerned with their economic investment in land and how they, and other primary producers, such as lumbermen, will fare under the rising costs of operation. Mining and energy groups have specific interests in getting at a resource and developing facilities for the production of energy. Land developers are alert

to possibilities of creating new housing projects, including recreational areas and retirement communities. Young people see the countryside as a haven from "the system" or a place to raise a family free of dangers and frustrations of city living. Some turn to the countryside in search of community or naturalness. And, the conservationists, or preservationists, would guard countryside space against overuse, misuse, or in some instances any use.

DEFINING RURAL

What exactly is meant by *rural*—for example, in rural countryside, rural values, rural population? Unfortunately, there is no one satisfactory definition (Clout, 1972). Any land not officially classified as urban may be said to be, ipso facto, rural. Such a division between rural and urban is acceptable so long as the *discontinuities* between rural land use and urban land use are clear.

Traditionally, a rural population was one that engaged directly in gaining a livelihood from the land (or sea). Thus, farming, lumbering, and to a certain extent, fishing—all primary activites—were considered essentially rural activities. A rural population a century ago, for example, might have provided for most, if not all, its own needs. Since World War II, however, the rapid modernization of agriculture, increasing mobility of the population, and the *metropolitan spillover* have led to great changes in the rural landscape, in rural populations, and in so-called rural values. Much of the countryside that might still be officially designated rural on closer inspection carries an urban brand (Fig. 14–1).

In some industrialized countries, notably England, the once obviously rural countryside has become little more than a series of transitional landscape zones with subtly changing land uses: from varying degrees of agricultural, recreational, and other nonurban land uses to a

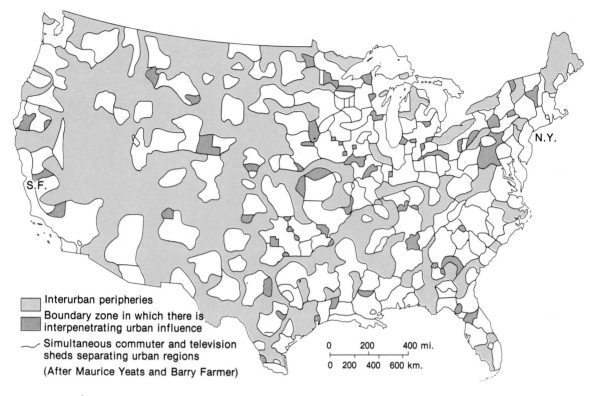

Interurban peripheries

Boundary zone in which there is interpenetrating urban influence

Simultaneous commuter and television sheds separating urban regions

(After Maurice Yeats and Barry Farmer)

0　200　400 mi.

0　200　400　600 km.

Figure 14–1

The decline of rural space is evident in many industrialized countries. In the United States, geographers have mapped the expansion of the cities, metropolitan areas, and daily urban systems—or patterns of daily movement to and from the cities. The converse of this development—the passing of rural areas—is equally significant. Nowhere has this occurred to such a degree as along the Atlantic seaboard of the United States from Boston to Washington, D.C.

(*Source:* Adapted from Brian J. L. Berry and Quentin Gillard, *The Changing Shape of Metropolitan America: Commuting Patterns, Urban Fields, and Decentralization Processes*, [Cambridge, Mass.: Balinger, 1977], Figure 2–7 p. 37.)

rural-urban (or suburban) belt reaching finally the city itself (Fig. 14–2).

One widely accepted British attempt to define rural landscape is, therefore, understandably based on land use. Thus, that which is rural

> describes those parts of a country which show unmistakable signs of being dominated by extensive uses of land. . . . This allows us to look at settlements which to the eye still appear to be rural but which, in practise, are mainly an extension of the city resulting from the development of the commuter train and the private car. (Wibberley cited in Lewis, 1979, p. 22.)

DEPOPULATION OF THE RURAL COUNTRYSIDE

Industrialization, the pull of the city, and the modernization of farming methods have led over past decades to a major exodus of people from the land. *Depopulation* of rural areas has been a phenomenon that may be observed in every industrial country. In some countries in Eastern Europe, it continues even to this day. This exodus is one factor that characterizes rural landscapes.

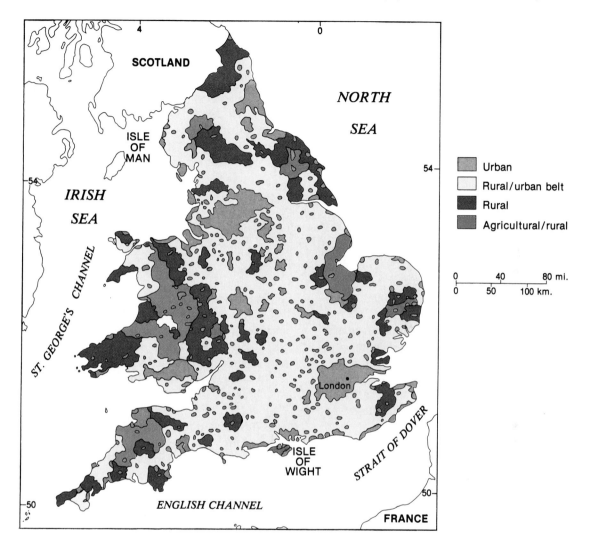

Figure 14–2

In England, the spread of the city has been as pervasive as any on earth. Not only is this true in the London region, but it is also a characteristic of the old industrial district in the Midlands and the west coast ports. In England, grades of administrative areas have been deter-mined, ranging from urban through rural-urban to rural and thence to agricultural-rural. Many rural areas are in transition to urban as housing spreads through the countryside.

Depopulation in Western Europe

The outward migration of the rural population of western Europe has been underway for some time. In England, the first country to industrial-ize, the number of inhabitants classified as ur-ban had already by 1851 exceeded the rural. The drift to towns and cities in search of eco-nomic betterment became even more pro-nounced in later decades of the century (Table

Table 14–1
Rural Depopulation in England and Wales, 1801–1981

	Total Population (million)	Urban		Rural	
		(million)	(percent)	(million)	(percent)
1801	8.9	3.1	(34.8)	5.8	(65.2)
1851	17.9	9.0	(50.2)	8.9	(49.8)
1901	32.6	25.1	(77.0)	7.5	(23.0)
1921	37.9	30.0	(79.3)	7.9	(20.7)
1951	43.7	35.3	(80.8)	8.4	(19.2)
1971	48.6	38.0	(78.2)	10.6	(21.8)
1981	49.0	37.7	(76.9)	11.3	(23.1)

Source: After R. Lawton, "Rural Depopulation in Nineteenth Century England," in *English Rural Communities: The Impact of a Specialized Economy,* Dennis R. Mills, ed. (London: Macmillan, 1973), p. 195.

14–1). By 1900, three fourths of the population of England (and Wales) were classified as inhabitants of cities.

In France, rural depopulation took place at a much slower pace during the nineteenth century owing to the growth of private farming and delays in industrialization. By 1851, only a tenth of the French population lived in towns and cities of over ten thousand inhabitants. As late as 1914, three fourths of the population of France were still classified as rural.

Rural depopulation on the Continent tended to speed up after 1870, especially in Germany, as the demand for labor at specific locations, such as cities and mines, began to expand. At the same time rural communities began to weaken as improvements in transportation facilities increasingly linked rural populations to the growing city markets. This development had the effect of reducing the extent of local services and indeed the abandonment of some.

The depopulation of rural Europe continued at a stable pace until after World War I (Saville, 1957). Two factors then modified it. First, the steady urban expansion was accompanied by a spillover of population from the city into the rural zone around the city. The growth of suburbs led to a blurring of distinctions between city scape and countryscape.

The second major factor affecting population movement was the Great Depression of the 1930s, which led to a drop in the rural exodus because of unemployment in the cities (Lewis, 1983). However, some of the more remote, more marginally productive farm areas, continued to lose population to other areas, both rural as well as urban.

Since World War II, the overspill from the cities has tended to balance the losses from the farm sector. The counter movement has resulted in a statistical balance that masks the continued decline of those areas given over to primary activities.

Rural Depopulations in Soviet Bloc Countries

Although the Soviet Union and much of Eastern Europe trails Western Europe in the tempo of rural depopulation, the process has been underway there also.

The collectivization and mechanization of agriculture in the Soviet Union from 1928 to 1937 pushed millions of peasants and farm laborers off the land. The rapid expansion of the industrial base under the three prewar five-year plans pulled the surplus population into the cities, workers' settlements, and mining communities. Between 1931 and 1940, it is estimated, some 13.7 million rural inhabitants were uprooted. Over the next 20 years, an additional 24.6 million left the collective farms for the city. The phenomenal flow was accompanied by a significant geographic displacement into the developing regions of the country, the Urals, Siberia, Central Asia, and the Soviet Far East. Despite this incredible migration, some 37 percent of the Soviet population were still classified as rural in 1984, with up to 24 percent of the total engaged in agriculture. Women, moreover, constitute about 65 percent of the rural population, and it is from their ranks that the labor force must be drawn.

Declining birthrates in the countryside, especially among the purely Russian component, attest as well to an aging population. Studies of the Soviet Union show that young people are contemptuous of farming and life in the villages. Hence, the bulk of contemporary migrants from the countryside are between the ages of 15 and 35. There are few attractions in the village to hold the ambitious and the energetic; even so, the motives of the young migrants are probably more complex than appear on the surface. Cities—Moscow above all—can offer better living and working conditions, more varied and attractive forms of employment, opportunities for education, contacts with the foreign population, and entertainment. Those who remain in the village retain negative attitudes toward the collective farm system, posing problems for Soviet planners and bureaucrats. Unable to stop the outflow, the Soviet regime has taken steps to channel it. And, an effort has been made to improve the quality of life in the villages.

Elsewhere in Eastern Europe, the exodus from the countryside varies with each country. Where collectivization was introduced—in East Germany, Czechoslovakia, and Hungary—the exodus has left an aging population on the farms. Even in Poland, whose farming remains, for the most part, in private hands, the trend has been comparable. The population loss

has been offset in part by improved farming practices, but the rural farm population seems unable to replace itself. This question has implications for the future of Polish agriculture.

Rural Depopulation in the United States

The United States in the nineteenth century was a young country laying claim to, and settling a land area of, continental proportions. In 1800, the rural population, understandably, amounted to almost 94 percent of the total population. Numerical growth continued through the century as the frontier was settled. In 1870 three fourths of all Americans still lived in rural areas. After 1900, however, the population residing in the countryside continued to increase but at a declining rate. By World War I, the trend was definitely downward, both absolutely as well as relatively. War's end saw the rural population dropping below 50 percent of the total.

In the United States, the exodus from the farms and from rural areas generally continued through the depression of the 1930s. On the prairies and plains, farmers were forced to abandon the land by the prolonged drought and by mortgage forclosures. In the South, many blacks began increasingly to forsake sharecropping to migrate to the northern cities, a trend stimulated further by the outbreak of World War II. By 1971, the rural population represented a fourth of the total population, with the farming segment totaling 9.4 million.

POPULATION TURNAROUND

Despite the pervasive movement from the land, rural-urban migration in much of the industrialized world no longer is evident in statistical summaries. Beginning in the 1960s in the United States—and at varying dates in Canada,

Figure 14–3

In Japan, the encroachment of the city on farmland has been rapid, even in many prefectures away from the main industrial areas. Fukuoka, on the island of Kyushu, is a typical example of the modern transformation of agricultural land into urban, residential. Because the best sites for modern housing are on the level paddies, productive farmland is fast disappearing.

Source: Georg Gerster/Photo Researchers, Inc.

9.8 percent for metropolitan areas (Brewer, 1981). During the 1960s, almost 3 million more people had left the countryside than had moved in. In the 1970s, the balance was 4 million in favor of the countryside.

This turnaround does not mean a growth in the farm population, but rather in the rural nonfarm component of it (Cherry, 1976; Lewis, 1983). This phenomenon has been expressed geographically in a variety of ways. Even in the Soviet Union, there is evidence of such a trend, despite the continued loss of the collective farm population.

What seems to be involved here is a movement from large metropolitan areas back to the countryside (Fig. 14–3). It is expressed in the Free World as:

1. A continual spillover from the city into suburban and rural communities adjacent to metropolitan counties.

2. A migration of senior citizens into retirement communities constructed in the countryside, expressed in the United States in part in the Sunbelt migration.

3. A migration of various peoples in search of alternative lifestyles and quality of life.

4. A migration to work, following the construction of high-technology industries, as in the Silicon Valley in California, and a decentralization of manufacturing operations.

5. A migration to new mining sites and centers of nuclear-power generation and other energy-related facilities.

Whereas the historic rural-urban movement prior to the 1960s was motivated primarily by economic considerations, the motives behind *repopulation,* although not without an economic element in some instances, reflect generally the importance of values associated with the good life, enjoying nature, and personal fulfillment.

Australia, Great Britain, and Japan—a *population turnaround* began to take place. From 1970 to 1980, the rural and small-town population outside metropolitan counties grew by 15.9 percent in the United States, compared with only

Turnaround in the Soviet Union

The turnaround in the Soviet Union is predominantly of a temporary or seasonal nature, yet, its impact is evident in the landscape of the countryside.

Even though up to 24 percent of the Soviet labor force works in agriculture, additional labor is required at harvest time. Thousands of students, pensioners, and urban workers are drafted or enticed, with promises of cash or food, into the countryside to provide temporary help on farms.

The drain of population from the villages to the cities has given rise to a new phenomenon—namely, the empty village or the so-called *futureless village*. The exodus has left cottages empty and garden plots neglected. In the Russian Republic alone there are up to four hundred thousand acres of abandoned *private plots*. Population turnaround in the Soviet Union has taken shape through the purchase by city persons of the abandoned cottages for use as summer houses. Because these urbanites give less attention to gardening, other than to satisfy their own needs, the Soviet press has raised the question as to whether this intrusion into the villages may not hinder the fuller development of the countryside. Because the output on the cottage plots does not go into the city markets, the role of the plots is thereby weakened. In 1978, 42.8 million private plots represented about 3 percent of total Soviet cropland, but accounted for a fourth of total agricultural output. However, in providing foodstuffs to the free markets in the cities, the private plots accounted for only 12 percent of the meat, 5 percent of the milk, and 7 percent of the eggs. The overall decline in the contribution of the plots to the country's food supply is not enhanced by the takeover of village plots because of the urban demand for summer cottages.

In addition to the urban presence in the village, the countryside also shows evidence of urban impact. For over a decade, urban dwellers have been permitted to work plots of land in the countryside. On them, they have built attractive but small sheds, known as *dachnikis* or little *dachas*. These tend to be concentrated on the land much like a nucleated village settlement.

PRESERVING THE RURAL LANDSCAPE

Repopulation is not a universal blessing however. In whatever form it is expressed, it has increasingly demonstrated a capacity to erase the remaining traces of rural landscape and also to threaten good farmland.

According to former Secretary of Agriculture, Bob Bergland (Carter administration, 1976–1980), the United States is losing 1 million acres of "the world's best and flattest agricultural land each year to urban sprawl." In his lifetime, Bergland noted, "we've paved over the equivalent of all the cropland in Ohio. Before this century is out, we will pave over an area the size of Indiana" (*Christian Science Monitor,* June 9, 1980). Mr. Bergland was referring only to prime farmland, which suggests the loss of all agricultural land annually may reach 3 million acres. A similar problem has been reported in the Soviet Union as well as in smaller countries, such as Japan and Great Britain (Champion, 1983). In Japan, even the construction of domestic airfields can occasion widespread conflict.

Although the loss of prime farmland in the United States is to be regretted, the area given over to other uses is relatively small. According to some agricultural experts, the United States is in no danger of running out of food because of disappearing farmland (*Christian Science Monitor,* August 31, 1981). Only 3 percent of the total land area of the country is in urban and built-up uses; much of 1 billion acres remains in agricultural or other extensive uses (Jackson, 1981). Moreover, a National Agricultural Lands

Study in 1981 revealed that the widely publicized loss figures are misleading because they include land that was neither farmland nor land that could be used for agricultural purposes (Brewer, 1981). The loss figure has been given at 875,000 acres per year, and it is expected to decline by the end of the century. Such reassurances assuage concern, but the perception of the loss of prime farmland has prompted a change of attitude toward land, especially at the state level.

In Wisconsin, an important dairy state, nearly 150,000 acres of productive farmland are converted each year to nonfarm uses (Jackson, 1981). In Illinois, strip mining has disrupted the usage of some 172,000 acres. In California, it is estimated that from the end of World War II to 1960, some 3 million acres were taken out of agricultural use. For every thousand immigrants, 238 acres of good farmland were built on or paved over. Between 1950 and 1975, productive Orange County alone lost 100,000 acres of farmland.

These developments have prompted many of the states to seek ways of controlling land use. However, legislation at the state level tends to lack effective enforcement provisions, a problem compounded by overlapping jurisdictions of state agencies. Only Hawaii, the first state to enact a land-use control program in 1961, has been able to implement a program that stands as a model. Its island structure facilitated the application of the legislation, but the pressures of population growth and tourism are especially intense on Oahu, the one island most subject to change (Jackson, 1981).

In Canada, losses of high-quality rural land have prompted a change in the way of viewing land—from commodity to resource (Pierce, 1981). In Ontario, the urban spillover in the Toronto area is especially dramatic, but British Columbia (1973) and Quebec (1978) were the first provinces to protect agricultural land through restrictive zoning.

In Great Britain, extensive controls have been placed on the use of rural land ever since

World War II. *Greenbelts* have been maintained around London and other cities to control urban sprawl; and considerable attention has been given both in academic and government circles to rural planning. Still, agriculture continues to occupy 80 percent of the land surface of Britain (Cherry, 1976). Moreover, the expansion of farming after 1947 on land withheld from urban encroachment made it possible for British farmers to increase their share of the domestic market to over 50 percent of the total (Davidson and Wibberley, 1977).

In other parts of Europe, efforts to maintain the agricultural land fund have taken several directions. In Switzerland, over seventy-eight hundred farms were lost between 1975 and 1980 as farmers sold their property and moved to cities (*Christian Science Monitor,* August 14, 1981). In most cases, the farmland went to accommodate new highways or suburban housing. To counteract the trend, organizations, like the Association for the Protection of Small and Medium-sized Farmers, grew up to urge their respective European governments to aid their survival.

In some countries, like West Germany, Spain, Portugal, and to some extent Italy, fragmentation of farm holdings remains extensive owing in part to inheritance laws (Fig. 14–4). Fragmentation reduces opportunities for agricultural modernization, specialization, and weighs heavily on the use of time and energy. Consolidation authorities have been set up to deal with the problem by encouraging a rearrangement or reallocation of plots through purchase or exchange. Consolidation leads to the formation of more compact holdings, with each holding as near as possible to the owner's existing area of land, main farm, or farmstead. The pace of consolidation, however, varies from country to country.

In Great Britain, where land costs have risen—as elsewhere in the Western industrialized world—there has been a tendency toward farm enlargement, but the result has been to fragment operations if not ownership. Prefer-

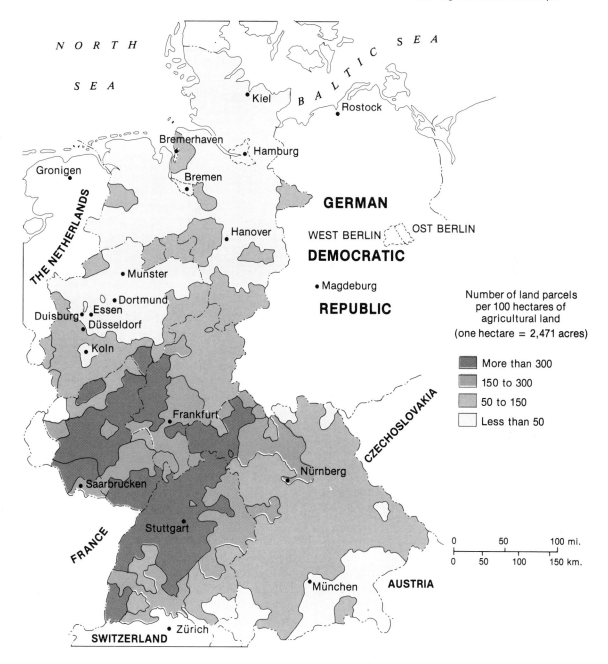

Figure 14–4

The fragmentation of agricultural land remains especially pronounced in West Germany, particularly in the southwestern part of the republic. Investment in the land, in the form of farm machinery, has reached high levels, but enlargement of farm size is necessary for further increases in real family income.

ring to rent land, some farmers have assumed the use of fields that do not necessarily adjoin the main farm. Thus, although ownership of farmland on the Continent may be moving toward consolidation, the leasing of land in Britain tends to disperse farm activities.

In addition to consolidation, efforts have been made, especially in the Netherlands and Italy, to reclaim land. In the Netherlands, where land is scarce and overall population density is high, three categories of land have been created: large-scale agricultural, agricultural-recreational, and rural-urban. In the large-scale agricultural areas, attempts to consolidate land have been pushed and more land has been made available through the reclamation of *polders,* notably in the IJsselmeer. In areas that offer attractive scenery along with agricultural use, the recreational function is established through planting of parks and greenbelts. Finally, in rural-urban zones, buffers are established against urban sprawl and ensure the preservation of open spaces. Such zones obviously must serve as reservoirs of land for further urban development, but the controls are strict. Various types of employment in these zones are made possible by allowing the establishment of agricultural processing and light or service industries. These enterprises can support the local inhabitants and preserve the rural community, but their density is low.

RECENT TRENDS IN THE FARM SECTOR

Many changes have taken place in farming in recent decades. Not only has there been pressure on farmlands for conversion to other uses, but also modern agriculture, whether in the United States, Great Britain, or West Germany, has required modifications in farm methods, even in farm layouts. New technology has not only revolutionized agricultural production, but it has placed strains on the traditional rural

community as well as on local market relationships. Modern farmers are aware of these changes and are conscious of the need to keep abreast of improvements in machinery, seed, and stock. Whatever the nationality, farmers face common problems, that differ only in degree and kind.

The United States

Nowhere have the changes in the farm sector been more pronounced than in the United States. Despite the vagaries of nature, agriculture remains a highly productive enterprise. One American farmer is able to feed himself and 56 other people (Berry, 1977). This high productivity has been achieved even as farm population has dropped—from 25 percent of the total or 30.5 million in 1930 to 2.6 percent or 5.8 million in 1981.

The classical period of American farm life involved most of the years prior to World War I. The family farm ideal was strong and the farmer's political influence was substantial. Thereafter, the farm sector began to be confronted by new circumstances. The number of farms in the United States peaked in the early 1930s at about 6.5 million. By 1970, the number had fallen to less than half or about 2.9 million. Farm abandonment or consolidation with other farms, not to mention the losses to urbanization, were the chief causes of the decline.

Parallel to the decline in numbers was an increase in average size. In 1930, an average farmstead embraced 151 acres; by 1940 on the eve of World War II, it had grown to 175 acres. Thirty years later, it was more than twice that size, expanding to about 440 acres in 1974, but sliding back to 428 in 1981 (Box 14–2).

The drop in the number of farms, especially family-operated farms, was accompanied by a growth in mechanization and a decline in the hired labor force. Hired hands of several generations ago were pretty much a part of a family operation; they often lived at the farmhouse. Hired labor in 1960 totaled 1.9 million, by 1980 the number had slipped to 1.3 million. In the Far West, where specialty crops require a good deal of hand labor, Chicano or Mexican fieldworkers now fill this role.

The rising value of farmland in the United States has also had its impact. From 1971 to 1981, the value quadrupled. The average price of land per acre in 1970 was $176, but by 1981, it had soared to $790. The high cost of land, of fertilizers, and of machinery together discourage many young people who might otherwise choose a farm life. High interest rates, too, have bolstered farm indebtedness. When grain prices are high, for example, farmers have been tempted to increase the size of their farms, through leasing agreements or purchase, to harvest a larger crop. When, however, grain prices decline and the return to the farmer is drastically cut, they then face a serious dilemma. They must borrow to cover seed and other costs for the next year. Should prices remain low or should the weather turn bad, causing a reduction in the harvest, then farmers may not only go deeper into debt, but also may find a foreclosure on their mortgages leading to farm loss. In 1982, farm failures reached their highest level in the United States since the 1930s, with about 34,000 family-run farms being sold, auctioned off, or abandoned.

In recent years, the decline in farm prices in

BOX 14-2

Willamette Valley Farms: A Case Study

According to Professor Van Otten (1980) of Northern Arizona University, farm-size characteristics in the Willamette Valley in Oregon bear a close resemblance to the trends for the United States as a whole. For the valley, he found the there was both a decreasing number of farms and a declining farm population from World War II onward. At the same time, the farm units became larger.

However, he noted that in recent years there has been a reversal of this trend in the valley. The number of farms has increased, but their acreage size has decreased. After a careful study involving sample farms, he found that a number of conflicting forces were shaping the present farm landscape:

1. Commercial farmers have increased the area extent of their operations. Economies of scale have influenced the shift toward larger farm units because technology has made it possible for one person to farm more land.

2. However, as prices that farmers receive relative to the costs of operation have declined, farmers have been faced with some hard choices: (a) sell their farm, (b) farm on a part-time basis and supplement their income with employment elsewhere, or (c) expand their farm operations, when and where possible.

Those who have chosen to expand their operations have increasingly relied on renting or leasing land. What this decision means is that farm operations have become scattered, requiring farmers to move their machinery on public roads for considerable distances. Such scattering of energies has raised costs of farming so that further choices are being forced on farmers: either to secure parcels of land nearer the main farm or to give up farming altogether.

Repopulation of the Willamette Valley has brought about a conversion of farmland to non-farm uses, reflecting national patterns. Such demand for land has further raised its price, making it difficult for farmers to compete for additional farm parcels. Thus, Van Otten concludes, the economic viability of commercial farming, especially of the family farm type in the valley, is threatened.

Is it not time in the United States to direct national energies to tackling this crucial problem?

BOX 14–3

Business Administration Comes to the American Farm

As in a factory, life on a big farm goes by the time clock.

Christian Science Monitor, July 19, 1983

Most farms in the United State are family owned and family run. But, according to Robert M. Press, staff correspondent of the *Christian Science Monitor,* on some of the country's large farms, there is a trend toward increased absentee ownership. Managers who are placed in charge, then, keep time clocks to help keep track of workers' hours. Shades of the Soviet state farm! One major difference is that in the Soviet Union all land is owned by the state and the state farm is operated as a state enterprise.

Press describes a relatively new phenomenon that has appeared on the farm landscape. First Land Management is a new privately owned firm that manages some eighty thousand acres of crops and timber/hunting land. The owners of the land, most of whom are absentee, are wealthy American and foreign investors. However, although increasing in numbers, absentee landowners are not yet a major factor in American agriculture.

Nevertheless, the land-management firm reflects many of the new trends in agriculture. Its offices are equipped with computers, a telex machine, and a number of service personnel. About 125 hired hands work the eighty thousand acres. In 1982, gross sales from the managed land totaled $15 million, or about $500 per acre. Even so, because of the high cost of operation, the firm barely broke even.

If land values remain high, investors have an incentive to put their money in farms; if values decline, the low profit margin lessens the attractiveness of the investment.

But where does all this leave the small farm operator?

the United States has been due to the enormous surpluses produced in 1981 and 1982. Stocks have remained high since the overseas market has been sluggish. The 1980 grain embargo against the Soviet Union harmed Soviet livestock producers, but it equally hurt American grain producers. At the same time, the strength of the American dollar has made exports costly. Because of the desperate straits in which many farmers find themselves, the federal government has expanded its support or subsidy programs. The programs that cost only $4 billion in 1981 soared to $21 billion in 1983. In addition, the federal government has instituted a new payment-in-kind program (PIK). Under this program, the government returns to those farmers who sign up the surplus crops held in government storage in return for leaving some of their land idle—a kind of soil bank program.

The total costs of all these programs exceeds the 1982–1983 total net farm income of only $20 billion. The danger of a political backlash grows because such financial support represents a truly enormous subsidy of a relatively small segment of the population.

Those farmers who possess the highest level of business acumen are the ones who may endure more readily the sharp fluctuations in prices paid and the weather. Possessed with great managerial skill, they have pushed out the limits of their operations and have intensified farming with huge amounts of capital. But, such farmers now find that their capital structure is so large that their sons cannot finance a takeover of the family farm.

An alternative has been to create a family corporation in which all hold shares. In 1980, there were over fifty thousand corporate farms in the United States of which some forty-five thousand were family held. The average size of these and nonfamily corporate or *agribusiness* enterprises is about twenty-five hundred acres. Absentee ownership is also a characteristic of agribusiness or large-scale commercial farming (Box 14–3).

Western Europe

In the 1980s, farming remains the single most important occupation in rural Europe, but agriculture as a whole accounts for a relatively low proportion of the gross national product (GNP) of each country. The size of the work force on farms tends to be relatively small, although it varies from country to country. In Great Britain, only 2 percent of the work force is employed in agriculture; there, in particular, mechanization is well advanced, with tractor densities among the highest in the world. The average size of the full-time farm tends to be about 160 acres, although consolidation has led to an increase in the number of farms working 300 acres or more. In Britain, half the farms are operated as a part-time business, with the farmers also taking jobs in town.

In France, the number of persons employed in farming reaches up to 15 percent, in Italy to 22 percent. The average size of farms in Western Europe, as a whole, is about 30 acres, but two thirds of the farms are smaller than 25 acres. Without supplemental income, the latter are hardly able to support a farm family. Because of their small size, up to 80 percent of the farms are judged to be marginal. Obviously, farm consolidation, not to mention the consolidation of holdings referred to earlier, is a solution.

CONVERGENCE OF RURAL AND URBAN MODES OF LIFE

Farmstead and rural population, in general, have become more citified, and farm operations have become more mechanized and more businesslike. These developments are profound and cannot, as is so often the case, be considered in a vacuum. They must be dealt with only in terms of a larger continuum that includes the growth and expansion of urban populations.

Above all, they are part of a major reshaping of the landscape that is now well underway.

Repopulation has led to a modification of the traditional social structure of the countryside, even though, it should be remembered, the pressures and social forces at work are not homogeneous. Taxing schemes in Europe have encouraged the transfer of old estates and large landed holdings to those who work the land (Dovring, 1965). But, in addition, the countryside has attracted new land holders who want land but do not want to farm. Commuter traffic and the affluence of the middle class have increased the demand for the weekend cottage or a second home. The *dachniki* and small garden plots in the countryside of urban dwellers in the Soviet Union and in Eastern Europe are not dissimilar (Fig. 14–5).

Thus, many rural communities are no longer part of a diversified local economy but exist as a convenience for an urban and mobile population—and often a self-indulgent one. Robert M. Press (*Christian Science Monitor,* June 11, 1979) describes the impact of urban tastes on a once-rural community. "In the village of Jericho, Vermont," he wrote, "a local grocer now stocks marinated artichokes, creamed herring, and imported chocolate to cater to the tastes of the newcomers living in expensive subdivisions where cows once grazed." Fast-growing rural settlements, villages, and towns are not able to keep up with the increasing demands for services, and this new situation has subjected local elected officials to an entirely different political arena.

THE DECLINING SERVICES —RURAL DEPRIVATION

The intrusions by urban populations accentuate difficulties already being experienced by rural residents.

In the 1920s, many rural communities fed off

Figure 14-5

A settlement of *dachnikis* on the steppe, or grasslands, south of Moscow. These little cottages are made by people from the city who are entitled to work small plots of land, what we might call peapatches. Ordinarily, the cot- tages are large enough to store garden tools and permit a small family to stay overnight.

Source: Jacek I. Romanowski.

themselves. When the automobile arrived, a service station or garage became an added feature to the hamlet or village nucleus. But the automobile also made people more mobile. It was no longer necessary for the farmer to obtain needed supplies in the nearest hamlet on a regular basis. He could travel to a larger center, a county seat, or even the city, which offered not only a greater range of goods but, if buying in bulk, lower prices. No other phenomenon in the modern world has constituted such an all-pervasive symbol of ultimate change in the rural landscape than the automobile.

Improved transportation and the decline in farm population have been accompanied by a reduction in the importance of market towns and villages. In truly marginal areas, persistent depopulation has often led to the abandonment of whole centers, reminiscent of the ghost towns of the American mining frontier. In any event, the changes have threatened the survival of village centers as economic and social cen- ters—and this has been repeated throughout rural Europe as well as in North America.

Central Place Theory and Service Centers

Major factors in structuring agricultural activities on the land are the forces of the market, that is, supply and demand (B. J. L. Berry, 1960). These forces not only have an impact on the use of the land, but also have a bearing on farm size and landownership.

An attempt to provide a comprehensive theory pertaining to markets or service centers was developed by Walter Christaller (1893–1969) in the early 1930s. Unfortunately, his *central place theory* was not fully recognized in the United States until later—when a translation from the German was published in English (Christaller, 1966). Whereas Thünen, another German, was concerned with land use and crop and livestock production around a central mar-

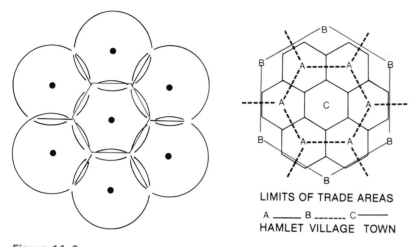

LIMITS OF TRADE AREAS

A ——— B ------- C ———
HAMLET VILLAGE TOWN

Figure 14–6

The diagrams represent a theoretical distribution of trade centers and trade areas according to the classical work by Walter Christaller, *Die zentralen Orte in Süd-* *deutschland [Central Places in Southern Germany]*, published in 1932, translated and published in English in the United States in 1966.

ket (see Chap. 13), Christaller was most interested in finding an explanation for the size, number, and distribution of service places.

In an ideal uniform landscape, Christaller hypothesized that the forces of the market would operate on the principle of *centrality*. Thus, he believed that the main characteristic of a service center or market town is that it is a central point within an area. Accordingly, the exchange patterns of the surrounding inhabitants are bound to it. The status and success of the central point (place) depends on the range and scope of the functions it performs. The immediate or lowest rank center will offer a limited range of services or goods. A wider range of opportunities will be afforded by a higher rank center, but the distance between the higher rank centers will be correspondingly greater. Each center, thus, will have its own trade area, but its status (ranking) in an overall hierarchy of centers will be determined by the number and variety of services each can offer (Fig. 14–6).

It is interesting that high altitude aerial photography has revealed a placing of archeological sites in southern Iraq that tend to fit the Chris-

taller hypothesis (Fig. 14–7). This evidence suggests that there is an essential universality to the placing of service centers that defies time, place, and local culture.

However, in the United States, the first geographer to test the hypothesis was Professor John Brush, who in the early 1950s examined 234 agglomerated settlements in Wisconsin (Brush, 1953). Although the terrain of the study area is highly differentiated because of geologic and physiographic phenomena, Brush's research revealed that there was a hierarchy of places. These ranged in function from tiny hamlets to large towns, each with its own trade areas. It was clear that the functions of these centers, the range of services they offered, and the spatial patterns they formed were controlled by the requirements of the local farm market (Fig. 14–8).

Brush observed that the most rudimentary form of trading center, the hamlet, possessed only a few houses with a grocery store, a tavern, and a service station. A larger center, the village, was characterized by at least 10 retail and service facilities. This type of center re-

URUK COUNTRYSIDE
(SUMER)

Expected settlement lattice
(After Christaller hypothesis)

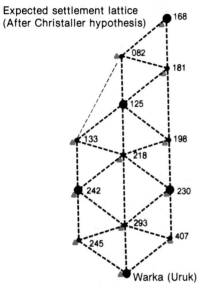

Observed settlement lattice based
on archeological sites (numbered)

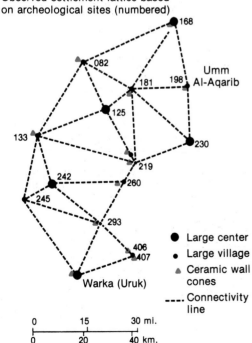

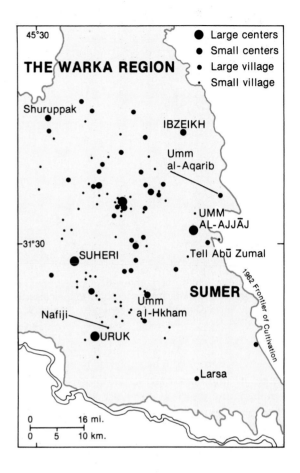

Figure 14–7

High-altitude aerial photography has revealed patterns
in the landscape that were hitherto unsuspected. Survey
maps of the area near Uruk in what is now southern Iraq
suggest a pattern of village and town locations that is
remarkably hexagonal.

(*Source:* John E. Pfeiffer, *The Emergence of Society. A Prehistory of the
Establishment* [New York: McGraw-Hill, 1977], pp. 160–161; Robert McC.
Adams and Hans J. Nissen, *The Uruk Countryside. The Natural Setting of
Urban Societies* [Chicago: University of Chicago Press, 1972], pp. 2–3.)

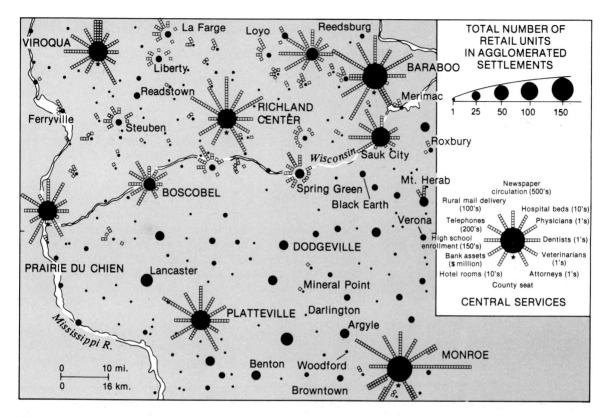

Figure 14-8

John Brush was one of the first geographers in the United States to test the Christaller hypothesis in an American setting. His study, undertaken in the early 1950s, focused on the trade centers of southern Wisconsin, and he employed an unusual graphic technique to identify service offered by each trade center.

(Source: John E. Brush, "The Hierarchy of Central Places in Southwestern Wisconsin," *Geographical Review* 43 (1953), p. 388.)

quired the possession of the above 3 service facilities plus an auto repair facility, a bank, a telephone exchange as well as 4 of the following: a retail auto sales outlet, a farm implements dealership, an appliance store, a lumber mill, and a hardware and feed store. In the hierarchy of places, the town ranked above the village, with a wider array of goods and services. Its place in the rural scheme of things was assured if it served as the seat of county administration (Box 14-4).

A study of central places in Iowa also concluded that, where intervillage competition was intense, the success of an early trading center was assured if the center had some additional attribute serving its surrounding population, such as a gristmill (B. J. L. Berry, 1960). In forested areas settled in the early nineteenth century, such as Ontario, it was not only a gristmill that could give one center an advantage over another, but also a sawmill. That the center was subsequently chosen as county seat was an important sustaining factor as well.

In the American West, the formation of nucleated settlements was almost wholly experiential. When the railroad crossed the continent, many of the villages and hamlets were bypassed, and they subsequently declined. Those reached by rail survived and grew. In the twentieth century, the advent of the automobile and the subsequent improvement of roads increased the distances farmers would go to trade or for services. This increased mobility also doomed many hamlets and villages, whereas those that were easily accessible became nodal points in a larger market network. Since World War II, the freeway has enhanced these tendencies, dealing a severe blow to almost all but the most ideally located market centers.

EPILOGUE

Testing of Christaller's central place theory has shown that it is particularly relevant to the evolution of the pattern of agglomerated or nucleated settlement in much of North America. Because the occupance of the interior of the continent entailed a fairly evenly dispersed farm population, there grew up, spontaneously, trading centers to serve them. Competition between these places, modified through the decades by changing modes of transportation, produced a hierarchical and largely regular pattern of hamlets, villages, and small towns. What is surprising is that research in other areas, such as ancient Mesopotamia (Iraq) and China, have suggested a similar spacing of central places.

The changes that have been occurring in the rural landscape have modified this historic pattern in the United States, in Western Europe, and elsewhere. In many instances, lower rank centers have declined or been abandoned with rural depopulation. This loss has also deprived peoples of many local basic services and community relationships.

It is interesting to speculate on what repopulation means for many of the countryside's hamlets, villages, and towns. Can they recapture something of what they have lost? Will the intruding urban values of the newcomers further lessen the traditional way of life; will the revitalized communities become little more than enclaves of the city planted, like colonies, in an alien setting? If the future landscape can not be

---

BOX 14–4
Central Places in Premodern China

Professor G. William Skinner, who lived in China in 1949–1950, had an opportunity to study the landscape of the province of Sichuan (Szechuan) and found a hierarchy of market centers that accords with the Christaller model (Skinner, 1964, 1965).

The Chinese peasants lived in villages, some of which were minor markets. At a level above the village, however, there was a standard market that met all the normal needs of the peasant households. At a still higher level, embracing a larger region, was an intermediate market and above that was a central market, the region's central place. The latter was normally located at a strategic site in the transport network and had important wholesaling functions.

Rural markets in China, Skinner observed, were normally periodic rather than continuous. It was necessary for the household to go to market every day; because port facilities and rural roads were poorly developed, it would have been difficult to go to the same market daily. What is most interesting in Skinner's study is the fact that each market town had a definite and mappable area (Fig. 14–9).

---

clearly envisaged, certainly there is widespread agreement that many forces are at work reshaping the countryside and steadily eroding the image of the rural setting that appeals to many people.

APPLICATION OF IDEAS

1. In the industrialized countries with their rapid urban growth, the rural countryside has been subjected to severe pressures. Not only is

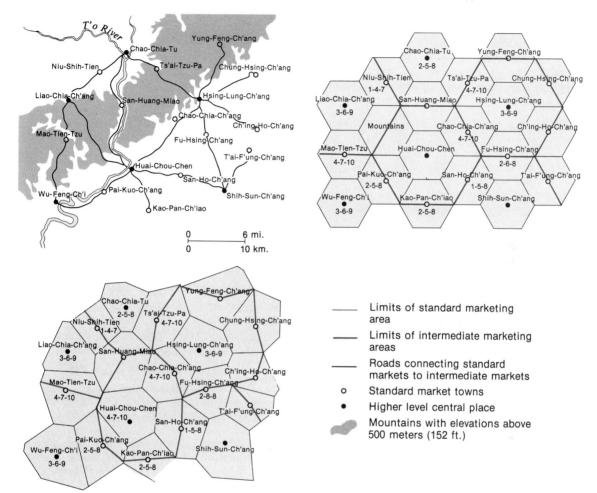

Figure 14–9

The landscape of Sichuan (Szechwan) province is not uniform, but even so the trade areas around the market centers are not greatly distorted from an idealized hexagon network. Such studies as this of Sichuan confirm

the fundamental notion of geographic research that there is an underlying order in human activity patterns.

(*Source:* G. William Skinner, "Marketing and Social Structure in Rural China, Part I," *Journal of Asian Studies*, 1964, p. 22.)

this phenomenon due to the spread of the city and the changing use of land, but also, in the period since 1970 (in the United States at least), there has been a major transfer of urban values to the countryside.

2. This urbanization of the countryside, whether in land use or human values, has been accompanied by a nostalgia for an older, simpler life-style.

3. The changes that have occurred in the rural countryside have caused a blending of the rural and the urban and have made the question of defining rural a difficult one.

4. In Europe generally, farm size is small, and many farmers near cities work in industry as well. Urban dwellers seeking relief from the city have found second homes in the countryside. What these developments have achieved is a loss of open spaces, the decline of family farms, and changes in the appearance of the rural landscape.

5. The phenomenon is known also in the Soviet Union and Eastern Europe, where even the mechanism of central planning is unable to stop rural population drain and the expansion of the urban way of life. At the same time, repopulation, if only seasonal, has become a phenomenon of the Soviet landscape.

6. Major changes have occurred in the farm sector. Farm size has increased as the number of farms have declined.

7. Central place theory affords a conceptual basis for understanding the role and function of service or market centers.

KEY WORDS AND PHRASES

agribusiness	discontinuities
centrality	futureless villages
central place theory	greenbelts
dacha	metropolitan
dachniki	spillover
depopulation	*polders*
population turnaround	repopulation
private plot	rural

QUESTIONS FOR FURTHER DISCUSSION

1. What is the phenomenon known as the countryside? How would you define or describe it?

2. What images do you have when you think about the rural landscape? Are they based on a real knowledge of life there or on such things as Christmas-card art and calendar photos?

3. What pressures and changes have led to the crumbling or destruction of traditional rural values? Is it a search for these values that has led Americans since the 1960s to leave metropolitan areas for small cities or rural areas? Do you think the values can be recovered?

4. Why is urban pressure on rural land a matter for public concern? Is this concern justified in North America? In Europe?

5. How does the average size of a farm in Europe compare with that in the United States? In the Soviet Union? What is a solution to the problem of small size or fragmentation of holdings?

6. What impact has the freeway had on the rural landscape? Why has it drawn city people to the countryside?

7. How extensive is rural-urban migration in the Soviet Union and Eastern Europe? What impact has this migration had on the cities? On the countryside itself?

8. Why did the Great Depression of the 1930s stimulate the movement from the countryside to the city? Was this migration accompanied by a decline in farm ownership? What implications did this trend have?

9. How do you account for such a small percentage of farmers in the United States compared to the Soviet Union? What has made the differences in their productivity?

10. What steps are countries in Europe taking to preserve the rural landscape? Are comparable steps necessary in North America?

11. What role has the market or service center played in shaping the historic rural landscape? How has the rural-urban migration and increased mobility affected the central place hierarchy?

REFERENCES AND ADDITIONAL READINGS

Adams, Robert McC., and Nissan, Hans J. *The Uruk Countryside. The Natural Setting of Urban Societies.* Chicago: University of Chicago Press, 1972.

Bandini, Mario. "National Policies for Rural Development in Advanced Countries," pp. 39–56. In *Rural Development in a Changing World.* Raanan Weitz, ed. Cambridge, Mass.: MIT Press, 1971.

Bates, Robert H. *Rural Responses to Industrialization: A Study of a Village in Zambia.* New Haven, Conn.: Yale University Press, 1976.

Berry Brian J. L. "The Impact of Expanding Metropolitan Communities upon the Central Place Hierarchy." *Annals of the Association of American Geographers* 50 (1960): 112–116.

Berry, Brian J. L., and Gillard, Quentin. *The Changing Shape of Metropolitan America: Commuting Patterns, Urban Fields, and Decentralization Processes, 1960–1970.* Cambridge, Mass.: Ballinger, 1977.

Berry, Brian J. L., and Prakasa Rao, V. L. S. *Urban-Rural Duality in the Regional Structure of Andhra Pradesh: A Challenge to Regional Planning and Development.* Wiesbaden, W. Ger.: F. Steiner Verlag, 1968.

Berry, Wendell. *The Unsettling of America. Culture and Agriculture.* San Francisco: Sierra Club Books, 1977.

Best, Robin H., and Coppock, J. T. *The Changing Use of Land in Britain.* London: Faber & Faber, 1972.

Blunden, J. R. "Rural Land Use," pp. 9–32. In *Spatial Aspects of Society.* Walton Hall, Eng.: Open University Press, 1971.

———. "The Size and Spacing of Settlements," pp. 87–115. In *Spatial Aspects of Society.* Walton Hall, Eng.: Open University Press, 1971.

Brewer, Michael. "The Changing U.S. Farmland Scene." *Population Bulletin* 36 (December 1981): 3–36.

Brush, John E. "The Hierarchy of Central Places in Southwestern Wisconsin." *Geographical Review* 43 (1953): 380–402.

Champion, A. G. "Land Use and Competition," pp. 21–45. In *Progress in Human Geography.* Michael Pacione, ed. London: Croom Helm, 1983.

Cherry, Gorden E., ed. *Rural Planning Problems.* New York: Barnes & Noble, 1977.

Christaller, Walter. *Central Places in Southern Germany.* C. W. Baskin, trans. Englewood Cliffs, N.J.: Prentice-Hall, 1966.

Christensen, David E. *Rural Occupance in Transition: Lee and Sumter Counties, Georgia.* Research Paper No. 43, Department of Geography, University of Chicago, 1956.

Clarke, John I. *Population Geography and the Developing Countries.* Oxford: Pergamon Press, 1971.

Clout, Hugh D. *Rural Geography; An Introductory Survey.* Oxford: Pergamon Press, 1972.

Davidson, Joan, and Wibberley, Gerald. *Planning and Rural Environment.* Oxford: Pergamon Press, 1977.

Davis, Lenwood G. *Rural Population Trends: A Survey.* Monticello, Ill.: Council of Planning Librarians, 1977.

Dovring, Folke. *Land and Labor in Europe in the Twentieth Century: A Comparative Study of Recent Agrarian History,* 3rd Rev. ed. The Hague: M. Nijhoff, 1965.

Eberhard, Wolfram. *Settlement and Social Change in Asia,* Vol. 1. Hong Kong: University of Hong Kong Press, 1967.

Enyedi, Gyorgy. "The Changing Face of Agriculture in Eastern Europe." *Geographical Review* 57 (1967): 358–372.

Freeman, T. W. *Geography and Planning*. London: Hutchinson, 1976.

Friedmann, John, and Wulff, Robert. "The Urban Transition: Comparative Studies of Newly Industrializing Societies." *Progress in Geography* 8 (1976): 1–94.

Heggs, John, ed. *People in the Countryside. Studies in Rural Social Development*. London: National Council of Social Service, 1966.

Hoselitz, Bert F. "Rural-Urban Relationships and the Development of Rural Areas in Developing Countries," pp. 172–185. In *Rural Development in a Changing World*, Raanan Weitz, ed. Cambridge, Mass.: MIT Press, 1971.

Houston, James M. *A Social Geography of Europe*. London: Duckworth, 1953.

Jackson, Richard H. *Land Use in America*. New York: John Wiley, 1981.

Jackson, W. A. Douglas, ed. *Agrarian Policies and Problems in Communist and Non-Communist Countries*. Seattle: University of Washington Press, 1971.

Kolb, Albert. *East Asia*. London: Methuen, 1971.

Kostrowicki, Jerzy, and Tyszkiewicz, Wiestawa, eds. *Transformation of Rural Areas*. Proceedings of the First Polish-Yugoslav Geographical Seminar, May 24–29, 1975. Warsaw: Institute of Geography and Spatial Organization, Polish Academy of Sciences, 1978.

Lamb, Richard. *Metropolitan Impacts on Rural America*. Research Paper No. 162, Department of Geography, University of Chicago, 1975.

Lawton, R. "Rural Depopulation in Nineteenth Century England." In *English Rural Communities: The Impact of a Specialized Ecomony*. Dennis R. Mills, ed., London: Macmillan, 1973.

Lewis, G. J. *Rural Communities*. London: David & Charles, 1979.

———. *Rural Communities*," pp. 149–172. In *Progress in Rural Geography*, Michael Pacione, ed. London: Croom Helm, 1983.

Lowenthal, David, and Prince, Hugh C. "The English Landscape." *Geographical Review* 54 (1964): 309–346.

Malgavkar, P. D. "Industrialization of Rural Areas in Developing Countries," pp. 124–134. In *Rural Development in a Changing World*, Raanan

Weitz, ed. Cambridge, Mass.: MIT Press, 1971.

Mayhew, Alan. "Structural Reform and the Future of West German Agriculture." *Geographical Review* 60 (1970): 54–68.

Mills, Dennis R., ed. *English Rural Communities: The Impact of a Specialized Economy*. London: Macmillan, 1973.

Nove, Alec. "The Decision to Collectivize," pp. 69–97. In *Agrarian Policies and Problems in Communist and Non-Communist Countries*. W. A. Douglas Jackson, ed. Seattle: University of Washington Press, 1971.

Pacione, Michael, ed. *Progress in Rural Geography*. London: Croom Helm, 1983.

Padover, Saul K., ed. *Thomas Jefferson on Democracy*. New York: Appleton-Century, 1939.

Pahl, R. E. "Trends in Social Geography," pp. 81–100. In *Frontiers in Geographical Teaching*. R. J. Chorley and P. Haggett, eds. London: Methuen, 1965.

Perpillou, Aime Vincent. *Human Geography*. New York: John Wiley, 1966.

Pfeiffer, John E. *The Emergence of Society. A Prehistory of the Establishment*. New York: McGraw-Hill, 1977.

Pierce, John T. "Conversion of Rural Land to Urban: A Canadian Profile." *Professional Geographer* 33 (May 1981): 163–173.

Roberts, Brian K. *Rural Settlement in Britain*. Folkestone, Eng.: Dawson, 1977.

Saville, John. *Rural Depopulation in England and Wales, 1851–1951*. London: Routledge & Kegan Paul, 1952.

Schickele, Rainer. "National Policies for Rural Development in Developing Countries," pp. 57–72. In *Rural Development in a Changing World*. Raanan Weitz, ed. Cambridge, Mass.: MIT Press, 1971.

Simmons, Ian Gordon. *Rural Recreation in the Industrial World*. New York: John Wiley, 1975.

Skinner, G. William. "Marketing and Social Structure in Rural China, Part I." *Journal of Asian Studies* (1964): 3–44.

———. "Marketing and Social Structure in Rural China, Part II." *Journal of Asian Studies* (1965): 195–228.

Thijsse, Jac. P. "Changing Patterns of the Rural Space in Western Europe," pp. 156–171. In *Rural Development in a Changing World*. Raanan Weitz, ed. Cambridge, Mass.: MIT Press, 1971.

Tidswell, Vincent. *Pattern and Process in Human Geography*. London: University Tutorial Press, 1976.

Van Otten, George A. "Changing Spatial Characteristics of Willamette Valley Farms." *The Professional Geographer* 32 (Feb. 1980): 63–71.

Weitz, Raanan, ed. *Rural Development in a Changing World*. Cambridge, Mass.: MIT Press, 1971.

15

Humanizing the Environment: Classical Cities and Cityscapes

The building of cities is one of man's greatest achievements. The form of the city always has been and always will be a pitiless indicator of the state of his civilization.

Edmund N. Bacon, *Design of Cities*, 1967

Key Ideas

1. The process of urbanization—that is, the coming together of peoples to form organized communities of large spatial concentrations—is a process that is as old as civilization itself.

2. Although the forms of cities have varied from culture to culture, the city itself remained largely unchanged until the Industrial Revolution in the late eighteenth century turned them into growing beehives of human activity.

3. The city is a complex phenomenon for which no one definition is entirely satisfactory.

4. The city is a dynamic society of human beings. Its structural orderliness is reflected in the patterns of relationships that develop among its inhabitants.

5. Among the reasons for the formation of cities, the ceremonial reason may have been the earliest and possibly the most important. Certainly, early cities without exception had ceremonial cores.

6. However important the ceremonial functions of cities, they could not have survived without drawing on the foodstuffs of the surrounding countryside. This was true in Mesopotamia; it was true in Egypt; and it was true in China, although the circumstances around which food was obtained there may have differed from other regions.

7. Cities, whatever their ceremonial or economic functions, were also fortified places. A wall was a characteristic of these early settlement forms.

8. The *polis* is used interchangeably for a Greek city, but the *polis* referred more to the area controlled by the city than to the entity of the city proper

9. Many cities in the Mediterranean world as well as in Western Europe owe their origins to Roman settlements.

10. Many early Chinese and Japanese cities were square shaped. The geomancer played an important role in determining the site and layout of the city, the public buildings, and the private dwellings.

URBANIZATION

Urbanization—the coming together of peoples to form communities of ever larger spatial concentrations—is a process that is as old as civilization itself (Vance, 1977) and one that has had profound implications for both humankind and the landscape. Not only have large segments of the globe been transformed through the course of human history by urbanization, but also the human psyche has been greatly affected by the adjustments that living in close physical association has required.

Cities have existed for more than 5000 years. Settlements may even have come into existence well before 3500 B.C., but these were essentially farming villages. From the beginning, the establishment of cities has constituted an expression of human adaptability. For a wide variety of reasons, a portion of humankind has found itself able to dwell in places that have been set apart from nature. Through this act, this choice, humans have disassociated themselves from much of nature's realm and have taken—and in ever-increasing numbers continue to take—a major step toward fashioning their own synthetic living space.

Throughout the millennia following their birth, cities have remained essentially the same kind of places, although variations in form have occurred from culture to culture. Until the Industrial Revolution transformed the historic city, the number of people who came to live in these urban environments was never more than a handful. Nevertheless, an understanding of the traditional, preindustrial city affords some insights into the nature of this type of human imprint on the landscape. Moreover, it enables us to comprehend the radical transformation in urban life that industrialization later achieved.

DEFINING THE CITY

The city is the most complex and concentrated of humankind's artifacts, and there is probably no one definition of the term city that would satisfy all students of the urban phenomenon (Vance, 1977). Certainly a city is a conglomeration of houses, streets, and activity centers, but it is not just a random grouping of manufactured alterations on the land lacking any semblance of order. As a product of human invention, the city is a symbol of intentionality. It reflects human will, and the use of its space within given limits is determined. The notion of orderliness has always been inherent to the city; both Plato (c. 428–348? B.C.) and Aristotle (384–322 B.C.) in classical times were conscious of this quality. The latter, in his *Politics,* described the city as a perfect and absolute assembly or communion of many towns or streets in one. Or, as one writer has described it: Civilization is the art of living in towns of such size that everyone does not know everyone else (Jaynes 1976).

The city is also an indicator of the civilization it represents; how the city appears and is structured is determined by the people who live within its boundaries and participate in its life. For example, the peoples of ancient Mesopotamia held a somewhat static view of the cosmos, and this was symbolized in their cities by the fixed central location of palaces and temples. The rectangular grid plans, decaying urban cores, and sprawling suburbs of the modern American city perhaps reflect beliefs in technical progress, human mobility, and a commitment to private ownership of property.

The city, of course, is a dynamic society of human beings. It represents an elaborate pattern of social and economic transactions as it is a center for the exchange of goods, services, and ideas. Its streets, boulevards, and avenues are the web that keep it all together physically. Within this web, the inhabitants of the city, associated in neighborhoods and communities of various types, participate in the decisions that enable them to live together, to work, to create, to govern themselves, and, in some instances, to grow wealthy and powerful.

The city, too, is a state of mind. Perhaps it is this characteristic as much as anything that has separated the people who live in cities from those who live in rural areas. The differences between town and country, as noted in Chapter 14, were a great divisive force in the history of humankind for thousands of years. Those who regulated their lives according to the seasons of the year found those who lived in communities and who did not have to labor in the fields to survive a different breed of people, and they remained suspicious of, if not hostile to, them.

THE EARLIEST CITIES

Ceremonial Origins

The performance of ceremonial rituals was undoubtedly an important, if not necessarily the initial, cause for the founding of a city because people were attracted from surrounding areas into a more concentrated settlement to take part in the ceremonies. Rituals of a religious nature are clearly suggested by archeological research at the site of the ancient Sumerian city of Uruk in southern Mesopotamia (Pfeiffer, 1977). Indeed, each Sumerian city was considered the actual property of its main god; hence, there was a close and real identification of god and city, this notion being basic to Sumerian culture (Box 15–1).

Uruk seems to have embraced an area of about 2 miles². At its center, there was a ceremonial district that contained temples and ziggurats. Archeological evidence suggests that an outer wall of sun-baked bricks rose to 20 feet and extended for some 6 miles. Uruk probably had a population of some twenty thousand persons, as did Ur and other major Mesopotamian cities.

The early city form, in particular the ceremonial district planted at its core, was civilized man's way of revealing a new perception of humankind's relationship to the universe. As Professor Paul Wheatley (1969) has noted, the representative capitals were "*axes mundi* [central

---

BOX 15–1
Authority and the Evolution of the City

With few exceptions, writes Julian Jaynes (1976), the plan of human group habitation from the end of the Mesolithic up to relatively recent periods is of a god-house surrounded by man-houses. What Jaynes means is that the center of almost every organized settlement was dominated by a splendid structure, either the magnificent dwelling of a prince or a king or of his tomb, which represented the focus of authority (pp. 150 ff). It was equally surrounded by ordinary houses and buildings, the dwellings of the populace.

At Eridu (in Mesopotamia), Jaynes notes that the god-houses were set on mud-brick platforms (the stuff of which the city walls were made) and these were the origins of the ziggurats. Small in scale at first, these central structures, which represented the ultimate authority in the community, became increasingly larger in dimension and elaborateness. To stand even today under such mountainous ziggurats, as that of Ur, says Jaynes, is to feel the grip such architecture alone must have had on early mentality, inspiring obedience in all the citizenry.

---

pivots] where it was possible to effect an ontological transition" between the sacred world and the everyday world, "quintessentially sacred enclaves within which man could proclaim the knowledge that he shared with the gods and dramatize the cosmic truth that had been revealed to him" (p. 16). The notion of a ceremonial core seems to have been a consistent phenomenon of the ancient city. It was exemplified in the location of Solomon's Temple in Jerusalem, the Kaaba in Mecca, the ceremonial temples in Mayan cities, and the Orthodox cathedrals in the medieval Moscow kremlin.

Economic Origins

However important their ceremonial functions, these early sites of human concentration would have failed to endure if they had not also had an essential base in agriculture and trade. Cities grew up in areas where farming was already well established and capable of supporting a population whose energies were not principally engaged in producing foodstuffs. To reverse this postulate, it has been suggested that cities could not have grown up had there not been

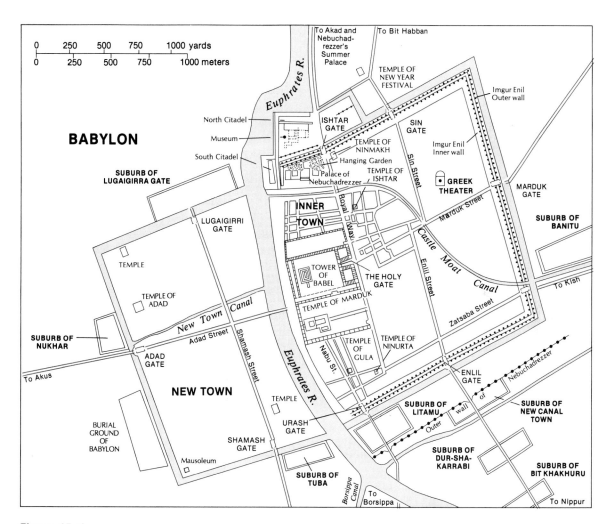

Figure 15–1

At the peak of its power under Nebuchadnezzar II (c. 630–562 B.C.), who ruled from c. 605–562 B.C., Babylon was an impressive center. Much of the city lay along the east bank of the Euphrates River, the main entrance to the city being through the Ishtar Gate and the Royal Way, which paralleled the river and must have been the setting of many royal processions. The shifting of the river to the west may have contributed to the city's decline. (It was Nebuchadnezzar II who destroyed Jerusalem in 586 B.C., carrying its inhabitants into Babylonian exile.)

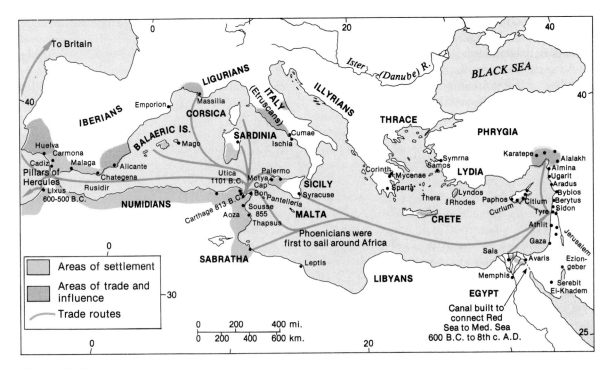

Figure 15–2

Settlements on the Levantine coast probably date back to 2500 B.C. or even earlier. However, about 1200 B.C., these coastal peoples suddenly gained a knowledge that made it possible for them to sail far and wide over the Mediterranean. It is believed that a migration into the area of Sea Peoples from Greece, who possessed a fund of technical maritime information, led to the growth of Phoenician skills and economic power. Subsequently, the Phoenician city-states planted colonies throughout the western Mediterranean, exercising considerable influence on the European coast.

agricultural surpluses and, to a degree, this may have been true. In many instances, it even appears that city walls enclosed farming lands. Walls discovered at Uruk and Ur not only enclosed official structures and dwellings, but also fields, gardens, and grazing areas. According to Aristotle (*Politics*), the city of Babylon had such a "vast circuit" that the city "had been taken [by invaders] for three days before some part of the inhabitants became aware of the fact" (Fig. 15–1). By contemporary standards, the circumferences of these early cities were not large, and from the beginning, each city probably had to draw on the productivity of the lands outside the walls to sustain itself (Fig. 15–2).

In China, early cities were primarily administrative centers, and they grew up on an agricultural base that was still predominantly at the subsistence level. Chinese peasant agriculture could not provide the volume of foodstuffs needed by the city in a spontaneous or voluntary way. However, as Professor Joseph Whitney (1970) suggests, the supplies were collected from the countryside by the strength and power emanating from the urban administration. Each city exercised powerful controls over its immediate support base.

Many of earth's early cities were founded beside rivers or bodies of water. Water transport facilitated the flow of trade, which widened in scope as the populace of the land felt more secure. Recent discoveries indicate that as early as 2500 B.C. an exchange of goods was carried on between Sumer and the Indus Valley via the Persian Gulf (Jaynes, 1976) (Box 15–2).

Fortified Places

To survive and to thrive, early cities had to be defended against marauders. A city's grain and water supply together with its trade had to be protected. Some urban specialists argue that it was the need for protection that brought people into city settlements in the first place. Certainly from the earliest times, cities had elaborate fortifications.[1] Ancient Uruk's walls were dominated by numerous watchtowers with gates opening to the north and to the south. Jericho, we are told in the Old Testament, had walls that collapsed before the trumpets of the invading Israelites led by Joshua. If Jericho's walls fell on that occasion, they were not the first to surround the city. The evidence suggests that they had been erected on older foundations, reportedly made of stone and dating back to about 8000 B.C. when Jericho was still an agricultural settlement.

That the need for protection was an almost universal requirement is evident from ancient Chinese cities as well. Professor Sen-dou Chang (1970) has noted that although the erection of walls was a common phenomenon in the Chinese culture realm—from the high walls enclosing houses to the completion of the Great Wall at the end of the third century B.C.—the most important walls were those surrounding cities. Like walled cities elsewhere, Chinese

---

[1] Recent archeological excavations indicate that the earliest towns or cities in Sumer may not have had walls, the latter developing only after contact had been established between cities (Jaynes, 1976, p. 218).

BOX 15-2
The Minoans and Phoenicians

The Minoans on Crete are credited with establishing the first known *thalassocracy,* or maritime empire. Its basis lay in trade and commerce. The Egyptians, it is recorded, reached Spain as early as 2500 B.C., but the Minoans, after 2400 B.C., were undisputed trading masters of the eastern Mediterranean for almost a thousand years. Fragments of Minoan pottery have been found in many archeological sites between the Black Sea and Spain, suggesting that the Minoan traders were wide-ranging. They also must have possessed considerable navigational skills; although the Mediterranean is virtually tideless, storms and strong winds make even coastal navigation hazardous, especially in winter.

As masters of the sea, the Minoans were succeeded by the Phoenicians (who may have learned the art of navigation from the Egyptians). Sidon and Tyre on the Levantine coast were the chief Phoenician ports; both possessed considerable natural advantages, but Tyre was especially favored. Founded on an island a short distance offshore, Tyre was immune from attack by land. Its island base, moreover, boasted not one but two ports, one facing north and the other facing south (Fig. 15–3). Only Carthage in North Africa could subsequently rival Tyre, and it was a Tyrian colony. Tyre also had direct access to the caravan routes that crossed the Fertile Crescent and, thus, could draw on many Orient-inspired items of commerce. It could also command the timber and metal output of the mountains of Lebanon as well as products of the sea, such as murex, a shellfish from which a purple dye was made.

The Tyrians after 1200 B.C. colonized Cyprus, the copper island, and, drifting with the northwest tradewinds, founded settlements along the African coast. In the tenth century B.C., according to the Old Testament, Hiram, King of Tyre, and Solomon, King of Israel, launched a joint maritime expedition from the Gulf of Aqaba to the legendary Ophir in search of gold, precious stones, and

Box 15-2 (*continued*)

special woods. Ophir is believed to have been in Arabia, but some authorities suggest it might have been as far away as the coast of India.

By the seventh century B.C., Carthage, a Tyrian colony, displaced Tyre in the commerce and fisheries of the western Mediterranean. Sometime around 600 B.C., according to Herodotus (484?–

?425 B.C.), Carthagenian sailors circumnavigated Africa from the Red Sea to Gibraltar. In the following century, frequent contact occurred with both West Africa and Britain. Much of the trade generated within the Mediterranean region during these early centuries was principally in raw materials, metals and grain.

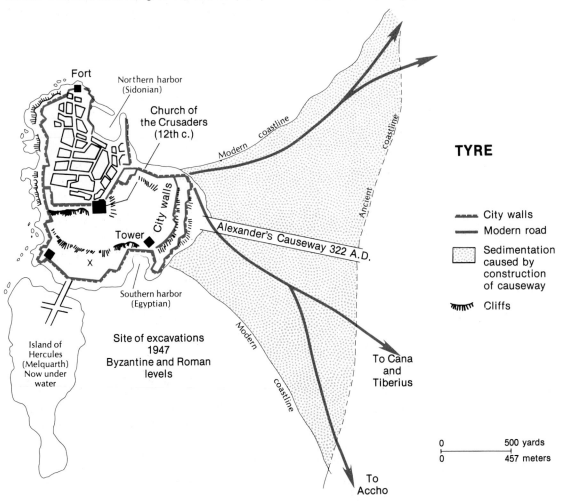

Figure 15-3

Tyre, located on an island off the Levantine coast, had the distinct advantage of having two ports: Port Sidon facing north and the Port of Egypt facing south. Enemy forces on the mainland laid siege to Tyre on several occasions without success. Alexander the Great believed that he could not conquer the Middle East without subduing the Phoenicians, so, he had a causeway built out to the island. He massed an assault, entered the harbors, scaled the walls, and brought the proud city to its feet; with that assault Phoenicia's dominance came to an end.

Source: After de Camp, 1972, p. 109.

cities had towers at the corners and over the gates. Such walls, according to Chang, had symbolic as well as functional significance. They not only provided shelter and protection, but also symbolized the "indisputable local authority of the ruling group who lived inside the city" (pp. 63–64). So essential were walls to the Chinese concept of the city that the traditional Chinese words for city and walls were identical.

GREEK CITIES

Greek Urban Origins

The motives that underlay the founding of the earliest cities were undoubtedly varied and complex, and the form of each city was a reflection of the culture in which it grew up. As one might expect, there were important contrasts between Middle Eastern and Chinese cities, and even Greek and Roman cities exhibited striking differences in design and in their organization of space.

In the Greek world, city development began first on Crete during the Minoan Age, sometime around 3000 B.C. Cretan prosperity was based on maritime trade and because the sea served as a guarantor of security, Cretan communities, unlike those in Mesopotamia, had no need of walls. Palaces and other royal or civil structures, including those at Knossos, the capital, were open to the landscape (Fig. 15-4).

With the transfer of Greek civilization to the mainland after 1600 B.C., however, the fortified site, or citadel, enclosing palaces, temples, granaries, dwellings, and graves became common. The city of Mycenae, which gave its name to this period of Greek civilization, had a fortified core, or *acropolis*, that hugged a limestone piedmont overlooking the Argive plain in the Peloponnesus. Entrance to the acropolis was through a monumental gate known as the Lion Gate.

Greek *genius loci*

From the seventh century B.C. onward, Greek cities began to reflect humankind's potential for creating aesthetically pleasing urban environments. It is not an exaggeration to say that as Greek culture matured and the conciousness of an ideal emerged, city forms began to reflect this ideal. The Greeks possessed a feeling for harmony, symmetry, balance, and reason that was revealed in their art, philosophy, and mathematics, expressed particularly in their use of urban space and in their architecture. They possessed, too, a *genius loci*, an ability to recognize the potentialities for human use of any given natural site.

The Polis

The term *polis* is sometimes used interchangeably for city when describing the early Greek urban experience. However, *polis* referred less to the geographic entity of the city proper than to the area controlled or dominated by the city; the *polis* was more precisely a city-state. It has been suggested that in the fifth century B.C. there may have been as many as 600 *poleis* in Greece and the Aegean region. Naturally, the size of many of these *poleis* was small, nor were many of them sovereign (Pounds, 1969).

The *polis* originated, according to Aristotle, in the coming together of a number of small, rural settlements. "When several villages are united in a single complex community, large enough to be nearly or quite self-sufficient," he wrote in *Politics*, "the state (*polis*) comes into existence." The Greek *polis*, therefore, can be viewed as containing an urban focus, dominated by a fortified core, or acropolis, and including the surrounding land used for agricultural purposes.

Athens

About 700 B.C., the triangular-shaped peninsula of southeastern Greece known as Attica was

Figure 15-4

The site of the city of Knossos on Crete was occupied well before 3000 B.C.; artifacts of the Neolithic period dating to 6500 B.C. have been found there. Excavations begun at Knossos in A.D. 1900 revealed the great palace of the legendary King Minos, which may have been constructed as early as 2000 B.C. The city's principal importance was as the center of a sophisticated Bronze Age culture extending from about 1600 to 1400 B.C.

About the middle of the fifteenth century B.C., fire destroyed many Minoan sites in Crete, including much of Knossos. The palace was destroyed by fire as well, but probably at a later date. Despite the destruction, many of the frescoes on the palace walls remain to this day.

Source: Press and Information Office, Embassy of Greece.

unified under the central control of the *polis* of Athens. All of the rights possessed by the free citizens of Athens were conferred on Attica so that all free Atticans were Athenians. By 500 B.C., the entire population of Attica (including slaves) may have totaled no more than one hundred fifty thousand, even though Athenian Attica was one of the largest city-states in the Greek world.

No Greek city expressed *genius loci* better than did fifth-century Athens, the cultural center of the Aegean world. Atop a steep limestone outcropping at the heart of a plain stood the Acropolis (Fig. 15–5). Originally the site of a royal fortress, it subsequently became the site of a sanctuary to Athena, the Greek goddess of wisdom. Below the rock on the northwest side lay the *agora,* or public square, with its panoply of public buildings. The private dwellings of the Athenians were small, made of baked mud, and strung out along narrow winding streets, but even in ruins, the temples, theaters, and other stone structures that remain seem the embodiment of all that is balanced and creative.

Town Planting and Planning

When the Greeks planted colonies elsewhere in the regions around the Black and Mediterranean seas, they did so by first establishing an

Figure 15–5A

The earliest buildings in Athens date from about 1500–1200 B.C. (the period of the Middle and Late Bronze Age). At that time, the Acropolis was the citadel, which must have exercized an enormous influence on the minds of the Athenians who lived at the southern base of the hill.

Around the top of the Acropolis was a massive wall of huge stone blocks. The handsome stone temples and public structures whose ruins remain today date from the sixth century B.C. The temple in honor of Athena was built about 530 B.C., and its presence turned the Acropolis into a sanctuary. About this time, the broad ramp leading up to the Acropolis from the west (which remains today) was created.

Source: J. Allan Cash/Rapho/Photo Researchers, Inc.

urban focus for each new settlement. Thus, the Greeks brought the city phenomenon to Bulgaria, Africa, Italy, Spain, and France. Syracuse in Sicily, Naples in mainland Italy, and Marseilles in France were founded by Greeks.

Intellectual town planning, as opposed to the following of traditional intuitive forms, may have begun with the laying out of Miletus in Asia Minor by the Greek planner Hippodamus in the fourth century B.C. (Newton, 1976). The plan of Miletus adopted the rigid discipline of the rectangular grid, but it also retained the principle of free-flowing space characteristic of earlier Greek cities (Fig. 15–6). Hippodamus's design for Miletus may have been one of the most splendid city plans ever devised. It met with the approval of Aristotle, who preferred that straight lines be combined with askew ones because "the antiquated mode of building [nongrid] . . . made it difficult for strangers to get out of a town and for assailants to find their way in." Hippodamus was also responsible for the plan of Piraeus, the port that was linked to Athens by walls.

Figure 15–5B

The temple of Athena Parthenos (Athena the virgin), known as the Parthenon, stands on the Acropolis in Athens, Greece, a strong reminder of the brilliance of ancient Greek culture. Built between 447–432 B.C., the Parthenon contained a number of renowned statues that were used in Greek festivals for over eight-hundred years. In the fifth century A.D., the Parthenon was converted into a Christian church, and after the Turks had overrun the area in the fifteenth century, it served as a mosque.

Source: John Veltri/Rapho/Photo Researchers, Inc.

THE ROMAN URBAN EXPERIENCE

If most Greek cities were a spontaneous expression of the spirit and unity of Greek culture, the Romans achieved their urban goals in a more conscious, orderly way. They inherited their concept of planning from the Greeks, but the intuitive, instinctive, sensitive impulses that produced the Greek urban world were largely missing from the Roman experience. On the other hand, the Romans were masters of the art of city planning and engineering. From the extant handbook on architecture by Vitruvius, a Roman architect who flourished in the first century B.C., it is clear that the Romans were eminently practical.

The extensive growth of the Roman Empire, particularly in northern Europe, required the creation of military outposts to guard and protect the frontiers, especially along the Rhine and Danube rivers. As military requirements changed, many of these camps grew into small cities. Castra Regina on the Danube was the origin of what is now Regensburg; Devana Castra in southern Britain was laid out on the site of the future Chester on the Dee. Cities, such as Trier, Augsburg, and Vienna, also had their origin in Roman fortified posts.

The Romans understood that urbanization, that is, the imposition of the forms of Roman civilization, was the key to the pacification of the conquered but restless tribes. Tribal regions, therefore, became *civitates,* or provinces; in time, their centers were granted various municipal rights. Finally, towns known as *coloniae,* that is, colonies of Roman citizens, were founded, notably in Germany and Britain.

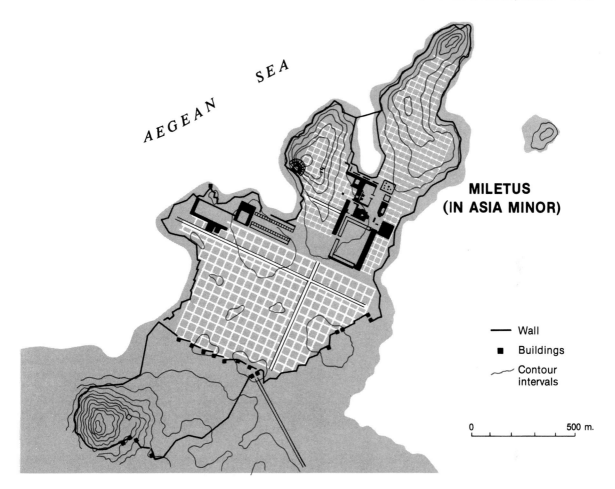

AEGEAN SEA

**MILETUS
(IN ASIA MINOR)**

—— Wall

■ Buildings

⌒ Contour
intervals

0 _____ 500 m.

Figure 15–6

Miletus was one of the greatest Greek cities on the eastern side of the Aegean Sea. Its early prosperity was due to its commerce and its role in the founding of additional Greek colonies on the Black Sea coast to the east. The city was also a center of learning, for it was here in the sixth century B.C., that Thales (c. 636–c. 546 B.C.) and his followers began their empirical study of natural phenomena, laying the foundations of Greek science.

During the Graeco-Persian Wars, which began about

499 B.C., Miletus was destroyed by the Persians. Its rebuilding in the years thereafter, according to a plan devised by Hippodamus, marks the birth of a new style. The configuration of the coast permitted Miletus to have four harbors, but the land between was laid out in a grid system, with streets crossing at right angles. Allowances were made for local topography, with public buildings and private dwellings set within the squares of the grid.

(*Source:* After Hewton, 1976, p. 7)

Colonia Agrippinensis was established on the Rhine during the reign of the Emperor Claudius (A.D. 41–54); it subsequently grew into the city of Cologne. Colchester (Camulodunum) in eastern Britain was established in A.D. 49 near a native settlement. Life in these outposts of the Roman Empire, however, was undoubtedly no richer in a cultural sense than it might be in remote settlements today.

Roman camps and cities, which usually did

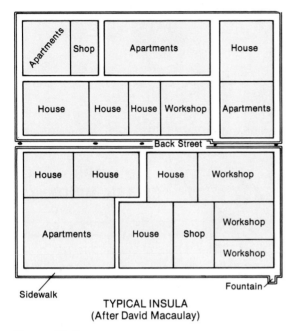

TYPICAL INSULA
(After David Macaulay)

Figure 15-7

The Romans differed from the Greeks in their layout of towns and settlements, in that the former had a love of order and logic. Perhaps nowhere was this better expressed than in the settlements that Rome erected throughout the empire, not only as outposts of Roman culture, but also as guardians of Roman rule. Many of these settlements grew out of a quite simple design.

The plan of a hypothetical Roman fortified settlement shows the intersecting *cardo* and *decumanus*. The area within this settlement was divided into blocks, known as *insulae*, each about 80 yards square. Each *insula* consisted of houses, apartments, and workshops. Spaces were set aside for public buildings, baths, and markets.

not encompass large areas, were organized around the intersection of two roads: the *cardo*, which ran north-south, and the *decumanus*, which intersected the *cardo* at right angles (Macaulay, 1974) (Fig. 15-7). These roads divided the settlement into four areas, all of which were surrounded by walls. In the case of a city, the marketplace and public forum, representing economics and government, were located near the center, but a general feature of Roman urban

spaces was the fragmentation of functions into separate units.

The Romans imposed themselves on the landscape in a very real sense, as the remnants of their roads and aqueducts suggest today. They revealed this tendency even when seeking enjoyment away from the city in the countryside. Beginning with the reign of Augustus Caesar (44 B.C.–A.D. 14), the architectural design of rural villas, was quite elaborate, especially that of the Emperor Hadrian in Tivoli, built between A.D. 117 and 138.

Oriental Cities

Unlike the Romans, the Chinese chose not to dominate nature, but to ally themselves with what they perceived nature to be. This characteristic was as true in the form and layout of their cities generally as it was in their art and philosophy. The square, the basic shape of classical Chinese settlement, was a representation of the belief that although heaven was round, the earth was square (Wheatley, 1971).

The site of a town as well as the location of a single house was chosen according to the practice of *geomancy*. This ensured that the new town or building would not be troubled by evil influences. Once the location was chosen, however, the town was laid out by geometry and strict convention.

During the Han dynasty (202 B.C.–A.D. 220), towns were inhabited primarily by farmers who lived in enclosures and went out to work in the fields during the day. Moreover, the towns themselves were divided into a number of "quarters," each consisting of a number of wards. In Ch'ang-an in Han times, each ward was enclosed by a wall within which lived about 100 households, whose movement out of the ward was controlled by a single gate. Both ward and town gates were closed at night. In this manner, life for the inhabitants was strictly regimented.

Under succeeding dynasties, notably the

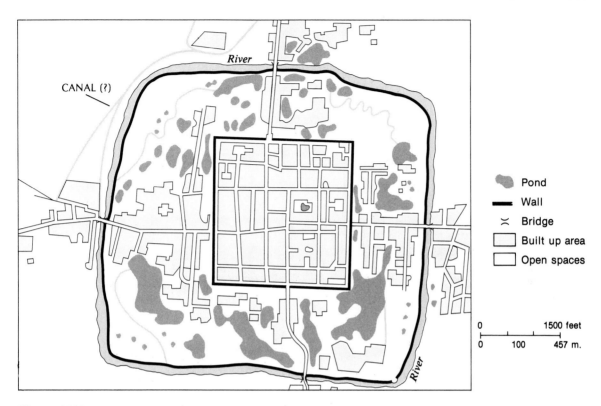

Figure 15–8

Although the earliest towns in North China may have been places of refuge against the raids of nomadic peoples from the interior, these same settlements also tended to be laid out in keeping with natural and divine laws.

During Han times, the towns were generally square-shaped, but at a later date, the town itself seems to have been dominated by temples, and the military and the general populace were forced to live outside the walls. During later dynasties, the rules of geomancy seemed to have played a leading role not only in the siting of a town, but also in the location and construction of public buildings and private dwellings. The general rule governing the layout of the town was called *pei-shan-mien-shui,* meaning mountains to the north, water to the south.

Within this context, important public buildings tended to be located in the north center, facing south. There was usually a north-south thoroughfare, but modifications of this rule occurred. The east and west gates, however, were connected by a straight avenue.

T'ang (A.D. 618–907), some relaxation of control occurred, but the traditional city structure remained (Fig. 15–8). In Ch'ang-an, the central and northern sections were occupied by the imperial palace, other administrative buildings, and the houses of officials. In most historic cities, temples held the central site, but in Chinese cities, administrative buildings or palaces were at the core. On the western and northern side of Ch'ang-an lived the artisans, and the dwellings of the rest of the population were confined largely to the east. Cutting through the city, connecting the palace in the north to the southern city gate, there was the main boulevard. Its north-south alignment made it a significant and meaningful axis. Along this thoroughfare were a

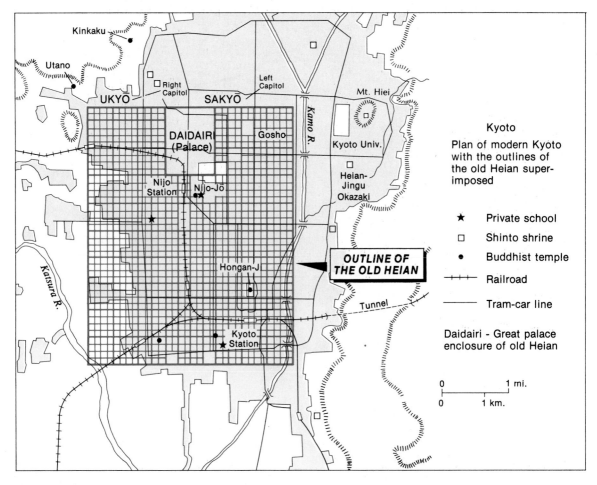

Figure 15-9

Early towns in Japan developed principally after the arrival of Buddhism from China in the sixth century A.D.; in their layout, they clearly reflected the Chinese prototype.

Kyoto founded in A.D. 792, was not the first Japanese town, but it was inspired by Chinese town planning. The original city measured 3.3 by 3.0 miles and was laid out in a regular chessboard pattern. Although some features of the old city, known as Heian-Kyō, are still visible in the modern landscape, its plan has been obscured by the modern city. The Kamo River still flows through the eastern side of the city and Mt. Hiei, as intended by the priests and geomancers, guards the approaches on the northeast. The ancient palace grounds remain in the north, facing southward.

series of markets, each integrated into the corresponding segment of the city.

Many of the principles of Chinese town planning, especially as evolved under the T'ang dynasty, were carried into Japan. The best expressions of this cultural import were to be found in the ancient Japanese capitals of Nara and Heian-Kyō (Kyoto). Both Nara and Kyoto were based on the Ch'ang-an model. Nara, founded in A.D. 710, and Kyoto, dating from A.D. 792, were laid out on sites selected according to the calculations of geomancers. In Nara, great care was taken to select terrain that would afford the city the most favorable arrangement of hills. In Kyoto, the influence of evil spirits that were believed to come from the northeast, was reduced both by the presence of the Kamo River and the temple on Mt. Hiei (Fig. 15–9).

In both Nara and Kyoto, a broad thoroughfare divided the city and linked the royal palace in the north to the main gate in the south. Although walls surrounded the palaces, the cities themselves were not walled. The plans of both cities were rectangular, reflecting a Chinese-inspired rather than a Japanese-inspired taste for symmetry.

EPILOGUE

Scholars disagree as to the exact causes of initial city formation, but it seems reasonable to assume that cities at various times had ceremonial functions that drew people to them. They were usually fortified places, offering protection to the people of the community both within the city and without. And, they were sustained by drawing on the foodstuffs of the surrounding terrain.

The variations that occurred in early city forms were probably not as striking as the similarities. The coming together of peoples to form cities was a matter of choice and a response to a universal need. What is equally surprising is that throughout the ancient and classical eras down to the fall of the Roman Empire, a period of some 4000 years, cities changed so little.

APPLICATION OF IDEAS

1. The formation of the first cities (urbanization) in Mesopotamia reflected a significant change in human outlook or in human consciousness. After hundreds of thousands of years, humans finally took a step that would revolutionize their relationship to one another and to nature, and in the final analysis, a step that would change their culture as well.

2. Definitions are always difficult. But the city from earliest times has always been a place of orderliness, a fact even Aristotle noted over two thousand years ago.

3. The ceremonial or religious function of the early city was an important one, but the city also had roots in the surrounding countryside, from which it drew essential foodstuffs and to which it offered security in time of stress.

4. There were variations in form in cities, reflecting regional, cultural, and natural characteristics, but the city, as such, remained little changed from earliest times down to the Industrial Revolution, which began about the middle of the eighteenth century in England.

KEY WORDS AND PHRASES

acropolis	*decumanus*
agora	*genius loci*
axes mundi	geomancy
cardo	*polis* (plural: *poleis*)
civitates	thalassocracy
colonia (plural: *coloniae*)	urbanization

QUESTIONS FOR FURTHER DISCUSSION

1. What was the difference between the earliest human settlements that sprang up in river valleys of the Middle East and those that were later categorized as urban? What is a city?

2. What are the various explanations for the origin of cities? Could there be others? If so, describe them.

3. Why did cities arise about 3500 B.C. in

Mesopotamia? What economic development was required for their emergence?

4. What was the significance of an *axis mundi* in the early city? Are there *axes mundi* in modern cities? If so, do they have the same meaning and function?

5. If the Greek city, planned or otherwise, was unique, what made it so? What was the nature of the *polis?* Give some examples of American cities that have names ending in *polis*.

6. In what ways did the Romans differ from the Greeks in their planning of settlements? What do the differences in the use of lands in general tell us about both Greek and Roman cultures?

7. Many European cities are built on Roman foundations. How do you account for the persistence of cities on these Roman sites?

8. Why was the square such a common feature of many early Oriental cities? Was the basis for choosing the square in the Orient the same as in the Roman world? How do you account for the differences?

9. Whatever the origins of the city, it is clear that the ceremonial function was an important one. In what way does the modern city retain this ceremonial function? Is it important? Why?

10. In what ways did the earliest New World cities in Mexico resemble the Old? In what ways did they differ?

REFERENCES AND ADDITIONAL READINGS

Adams, Robert McC., and Nissen, Hans J. *The Uruk Countryside. The Natural Setting of Urban Societies.* Chicago: University of Chicago Press, 1972.

Andrews, George F. *Maya Cities. Placemaking and Urbanization.* Norman: University of Oklahoma Press, 1975.

Bacon, Edmund N. *Design of Cities,* Rev. ed. London: Thames & Hudson, 1974.

Chang, Sen-dou. "Some Observations on the Morphology of Chinese Walled Cities." *Annals of the Association of American Geographers* 60 (1970): 63–91.

Christaller, Walter. *Central Places in Southern Germany.* (trans. C. W. Baskin.) Englewood Cliffs, N.J.: Prentice-Hall, 1966.

Davidson, Basil. *The Lost Cities of Africa,* Rev. ed. Boston: Little, Brown, 1970.

de Camp, L. Sprague. *Great Cities of the Ancient World.* Garden City, N.Y.: Doubleday, 1972.

Doxiadis, C. A. "Ancient Greek Settlement." *Ekistics* 31 (1971): 4–21.

Jaynes, Julian. *The Origin of Consciousness in the Breakdown of the Bicameral Mind.* Boston: Houghton Mifflin, 1976.

Jellicoe, Geoffrey, and Jellicoe, Susan. *The Landscape of Man. Shaping the Environment from Prehistory to the Present Day.* London: Thames & Hudson, 1975.

Macaulay, David. *City. A Story of Roman Planning and Construction.* Boston: Houghton Mifflin, 1974.

Newton, Norman T. *Design on the Land. The Development of Landscape Architecture.* Cambridge: Harvard University Press, 1976.

Oppenheim, A. Leo. *Ancient Mesopotamia. Portrait of a Dead Civilization.* Chicago: University of Chicago Press, 1964.

Pfeiffer, John E. *The Emergence of Society. A Prehistory of the Establishment.* New York: McGraw-Hill, 1977.

Pounds, Norman J. G. "The Urbanization of the Classical World." *Annals of the Association of American Geographers* 59 (1969): 135–157.

Schild, Romuald. "The Final Paleolithic Settlements of the European Plain." *Scientific American* 234 (1976): 88–100.

Scullard, H. H. *Roman Britain. Outpost of the Empire.* London: Thames & Hudson, 1979.

Vance, James E., Jr. *This Scene of Man. The Role and Structure of the City in the Geography of Western Civilization.* New York: Harper & Row, 1977.

Wheatley, Paul. "City as Symbol." Inaugural lecture delivered at University College, London, November 20, 1967. London: H. K. Lewis, 1969.

————. *The Pivot of the Four Quarters: A Preliminary Enquiry into the Origins and Character of the Ancient Chinese City*. Chicago: Aldine, 1971.

Whitney, Joseph B. *China: Area, Administration and Nation Building*. Research Paper No. 123, Department of Geography, University of Chicago, 1970.

16
Urban Settlements: Medieval to Industrial

"Town air makes men free," the citizens said.

Morris Bishop, *The Middle Ages,* 1970

Key Ideas

1. The medieval European city or bourg, was invariably fortified.

2. In England, new settlements were known as boroughs. In France, a number of fortified towns were built, known as *bastides.* Fortified places or rundlings marked the advance of the Germanic peoples eastward into Slavic territory.

3. One of the most powerful associations of merchant cities was the Hanseatic League, which came to dominate the trade of the Baltic and the Black seas.

4. In the Mediterranean basin, Venice and Genoa were among the more important Italian commercial cities.

5. Although early Slavic settlers in eastern Europe had a tendency to form nucleated settlements, the founding of cities in Russia is usually attributed to the arrival of Scandinavian adventurers and traders.

6. The early Rus cities were known as *gorods,* small in area, and not unlike the *bourgs* of western Europe.

7. From the very beginning, the basic tenets of Islam were at home in an urban setting. Since water is a scarce commodity in the Dry World, many Islamic cities grew up on the sites of older cities where water was available.

8. Many problems faced the European city in the sixteenth century. There was, first of all, the question of food supply.

9. The sixteenth through the eighteenth centuries were characterized by major urban changes which entailed the building of splendid palaces, gardens and boulevards.

10. The new feeling for space demonstrated in the royal cities of Europe was not confined to Europe; under the direction of the French engineer L'Enfant (1754–1825), the first comprehensive city plan of Washington, D.C., was drawn up, and it reflected the European eighteenth-century model.

THE CITY IN MEDIEVAL EUROPE

"Avignon . . . that disgusting city."

In her detailed account of life in Western Europe in the fourteenth century, Barbara Tuchman (1978) quotes Petrarch (1304–1374), perhaps the greatest scholar of the age, as describing Avignon, a city in what is now France, as "that disgusting city" (p. 29). What was there about Avignon that troubled Petrarch?

First of all, the kings of France had literally held the papacy hostage in Avignon, a *Babylonian captivity* that lasted from 1309 to 1378. This removal from Rome to Avignon weakened the papacy, a development that may have contributed to the Protestant Reformation, the roots of which were to be found in church reformist trends in the fourteenth century. In any event, to Petrarch, Avignon was "Babylon," an ostentatious city where prelates rode white horses "decked in gold, fed on gold, soon to be shod in gold." Moreover, Tuchman writes, "the town was crammed with merchants, artisans, ambassadors, adventurers, astrologers, thieves, prostitutes, and no less than 43 Italian banking houses" (p. 29). Meanwhile, the stench from the town's open sewers caused Petrarch to take refuge in a nearby town.

Avignon attracted people from all over the Christian world because of its papal court, but life there was probably little different from that of any medieval town of note. It had arisen on the ruins of the Roman Empire, but had not advanced very far. Several centuries would pass before the medieval city truly gave way to the full exuberance of the Renaissance and the engineering achievements that would relieve urban settlements of some of their most disgusting attributes.

The Decline of Roman Imperium

A network of splendid roads was the lifeline of the Roman Empire, facilitating the movement of *legions,* the principal units of the army, between lands as far removed from Rome as Britain in the northwest and Mesopotamia in the southeast. However, as the imperial military presence in western Europe weakened under the invasions of tribes from central and eastern Europe and as the roads and outposts had to be vacated in the fifth and sixth centuries, the political unity of the empire collapsed. The Carolingian and Holy Roman empires from the ninth century onward were attempts to preserve some semblance of that unity, but the divisive forces were strong. Out of the disarray evolved the social, economic, and political structures that were to prevail for at least five centuries (Pirenne, 1969).

The thread of urban continuity began to weaken in western Europe as early as the fourth century. The weaknesses in Rome's imperial facade together with the disruption of trade led to an emptying of many of the cities Rome had founded. Moreover, no new cities were established. Early medieval European civilization was predominantly rural, with the urban residues acting as defensive outposts. Cities that were strategically sited on an important waterway or a historic route survived, although it was local authority that preserved and strengthened their fortifications. Such fortified places, like the castles that often sprung up on nearby hills, provided the populace of the surrounding countryside some protection against new invasions from central Europe or Scandinavia. But, like the western frontier forts of ninteenth-century America, they seemed to stand in an alien environment.

The Ecclesiastical City

The ecclesiastical cities were an exception to the general urban decline. The church had patterned its provinces, or *dioceses,* after the administrative units of the Roman Empire, with which it had merged from the third and fourth centuries onward. The collapse of Roman civil authority left ecclesiastical jurisdiction intact, and the Latin church did not retreat. Indeed, it

Figure 16–1

Worcester is a cathedral town situated on the east bank of the Severn River in England. Originally a Roman *castra,* Worcester even as early as the Norman Conquest (A.D. 1066) possessed a cathedral. The present building was begun in 1084, but over the centuries many changes have taken place in its appearance. The tower, for example, was not added until 1374.

Source: J. Allan Cash/Rapho/Photo Researchers, Inc.

Mainz, Trier, Cologne, Rouen, Tours, and Bourges were among such episcopal cities.

The Image of Jerusalem as the Holy City

An urban image that continued to inspire early medieval Christians was that of Jerusalem, the Holy City. Jerusalem was believed to possess both earthly and celestial attributes, just as Babylon was seen to be the opposite. Jerusalem was considered the center of the universe around which everything evolved, even including the planets. In addition, the symbolism associated with Jerusalem and Christianity was widely used in the planning of churches and monasteries throughout Europe, all of which helped give meaning in a time of need.

Jerusalem was lodged in the medieval European mind as the birthplace of Christianity. Concern for the sanctity of the places and artifacts linked to Jesus' life and crucifixion prompted many thousands of Christians in 1095 to set off for the Holy Land on the First Crusade (1095–1099). A few years later, Jerusalem itself was wrested by the Crusaders from its Muslim overlords, and the Latin kingdom of Jerusalem (1099–1291) was created.

THE RESURGENCE OF THE CITY IN THE HIGH MIDDLE AGES

Causes

The Renaissance, the awakening of Europe to its classical origins, is usually dated from about 1400, but for nearly four centuries before that, the pace of economic life had been quickening. Beginning with the eleventh century, western Europe experienced a substantial upsurge in population, an increase in agricultural productivity, and, above all, a swelling tide of trade. Life on the manors was subjected to severe demographic and social pressures. On the one

became expansive, carrying Christianity into parts of eastern Europe that had lain outside Roman imperial jurisdiction. In any case, historic administrative centers that had become seats of high-ranking clergy survived. The presence of the bishop's church or cathedral brought a prestige to such settlements that they would otherwise not have had (Fig. 16–1).

hand, the growth in village population placed a strain on the traditional system of land holding and land utilization. On the other hand, in some regions, there was a relatively high level of agricultural enterprise—evident in the drainage of fenlands and marshes, the terracing of hills, and the clearing of forests—that helped contribute to the surpluses that fed the growth of towns and cities. The stimulation of trade, through the increase in urban demand, led to the growth of capital and the emergence of a class of merchants and traders. This new-found prosperity, in turn, acted as a magnet to draw serfs and the poor from the countryside. Thus, from the eleventh century to (at least) the middle of the fourteenth century, western Europe experienced a substantial exodus from the land.

The Nature of the City

The medieval city in Europe was invariably walled. Lying in the shadow of a castle, these fortified places—known as *bourgs* in French, *burgs* in German, *burghs* in Gaelic, and *burhs* in Anglo-Saxon—were cramped and small in area. In England, the Saxons built *burhs* where the local populace could take refuge from the invading Danes. In some instances, these *burhs* were on the site of Roman settlements. London, for example, had Roman walls that were repaired in A.D. 886.

On the European mainland, the core of the *bourg* or *burg* was dominated by the church and marketplace. Winding streets, framed by squalid dwellings, overhanging balconies, and stalls, linked the square to the city gates. If the *bourg* were of Roman origin, little remained by the eleventh century of the Roman street pavement. The stones and bricks with which the empire had fashioned its streets had been long since removed for other uses. Paving, which began in Germany in the twelfth century, was used sparingly and streets were usually dusty or muddy and rutted. The daily refuse was thrown into these ruts from windows. In time, scavengers with shovels were employed to keep passages free, but an inadequate water supply and poor drainage intensified pollution.

Disease and pestilence found favorable breeding grounds in medieval cities and epidemics were common. In the fourteenth century, plague severely decimated urban populations. Fire, too, was a constant menace because few buildings were made of stone or brick. Even the dwellings of merchants were generally of timber, wattle, plaster, and thatch.

As population continued its upward course in the twelfth and thirteenth centuries, new settlements sprang up outside the walls of the cities. These settlements—known in France as *faux-bourgs* or *faubourgs*—gradually merged to form suburbs. In time, they, too, came to be ringed with walls. However, the *faubourgs* tended to have no "hard edges" or recognizable gateways, and the lack of these visual reference points may have given rise, as Lionel Brett (1971) suggests, to the negative image that suburbia has had ever since.

By the middle of the fourteenth century, Paris with its *faubourgs* was one of the largest cities in Europe, with about one-hundred thousand inhabitants (Fig. 16–2).

London, which dates from pre-Roman times, remained a fortified town at an important Thames crossing throughout the medieval period, drawing migrants from the eastern and southeastern districts of England. The Tower of London was built by the first Norman King, William I, about 1078 (Fig. 16–3). Despite its continuing pattern of growth, London may have had no more than fifty thousand inhabitants by the middle of the fourteenth century when the plague struck.

New Towns, *Bastides*, and *Rundlings*

Medieval Europe was overwhelmingly rural, yet, as W. G. Hoskins (1970) points out, towns were an "important and enduring element in the landscape" (p. 45). (Of course, Hoskins was

Figure 16–2

This medieval representation of Paris shows the central position of Notre Dame cathedral, the congestion of housing, the walls, and a main gate. The inscription (translated) reads: "One thousand five hundred and forty-nine years after the Deluge, the noble King Paris, the eighteenth of his name, founded with great pomp the fine town and city of Paris, anterior to the foundation of Rome, which took place, as I think, 658 years before Jesus Christ."

(*Source:* Paul Lacroix, *The Arts in the Middle Ages and the Period of the Renaissance* [London: Chapman & Hall, 1875]. Courtesy Rare Book Collection, University of Washington Libraries.)

referring specifically to England.) For two centuries following the Norman Conquest in 1066, many new towns came into existence as a result of a "fever of *borough* creation." In the course of the thirteenth century, at least 65 new towns were planted in England where no previous settlements had existed (Fox, 1970). The monarchy played an important role in the creation of boroughs, both on old and new sites, but a large proportion of the new establishments were the work of church and lay overlords who owned the land that was settled. Places like Portsmouth on the channel coast and Liverpool on the Mersey River came into being at this time. Portsmouth was founded in 1194; Liverpool received its first borough charter in 1207.

The steady growth in population together with the opening up to settlement of hitherto forested or unreclaimed land made possible the planting of new towns in sparsely inhabited regions in continental Europe as well as in England. Because of England's insular security after 1066, the new towns were open to the landscape; on the Continent they were usually fortified.

In France, town planting occurred particu-

Figure 16–3

The present Tower of London was built by William the Conqueror between about 1078-1090 just outside the then-existing walls of Saxon London. It was not a large structure, but the thickness of its walls (15-feet thick at the base) was intimidating. Almost every monarch since William I has added some feature to the Tower so that today it reflects several periods of English architecture. Up until the early seventeenth century, the Tower served as a royal residence and, on frequent occasions, a royal prison.

Source: Britton-Logan/Photo Researchers, Inc.

lary in the basin of Aquitaine, which was claimed by both the kings of France and England during the medieval period. Both parties engaged in settling their respective domains in the region, and these *bastides,* or new towns, became an important feature of the landscape of western and southern France (Vance, 1977) (Fig. 16–4).

The *bastides,* unlike many medieval *bourgs,* were the result of conscious design. For the most part, they consisted of rows of parallel streets with a centrally located market and church. Many French towns and cities still reflect this medieval plan. The *bastides* in Aquitaine were usually fortified only if they lay near the boundary of lands claimed by the rival king.

Elsewhere in Europe, new towns served as a device to control a subservient or conquered population. The Norman kings settled troops in new towns in Wales. Along the Baltic and in eastern Europe, fortified settlements were founded by Germanic peoples as they expanded eastward. In Germany, these fortified sites were known as *rundlings* and they were a tangible symbol of the *Drang nach Osten,* the "drive to the east."

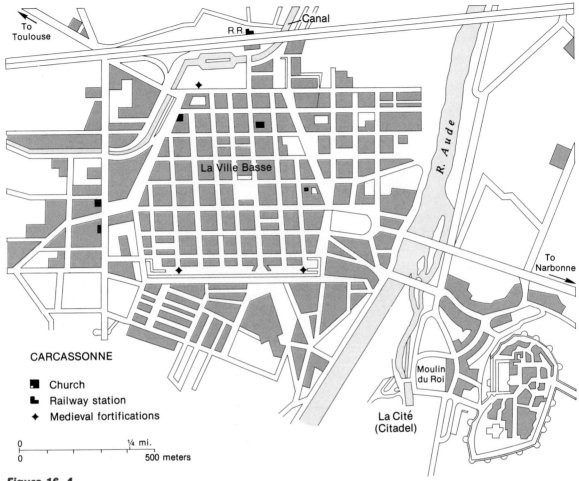

Figure 16–4

Built by Louis IX in 1247, Carcassonne, on the Aude River in southwestern France, is one of the best examples of a *bastide*. The Aude divides the city into two distinct parts: The Cité (citadel), possessing the finest remains of medieval fortifications in Europe, looms over the town; and the Lower Town (Ville Basse), which is pentagonal in shape with a regular street plan. The walls of the Cité are turreted, towered, and crenellated, passage through which is possible only by the Narbonne Gate. The Lower Town, outside the walls, was founded by citizens who were banished from the Cité; the settlement was burned by the English Black Prince, Edward, in 1355 when he found he could not take the citadel. Carcassonne ceased to be a frontier fortress or *bastide* in 1659. Reconstruction of the walls began two centuries later.

(*Source:* Singer et al., 1957, p. 283).

Achieving Status and Privilege

When England was hit by the Black Death in the period 1348 to 1378, the movement to establish new boroughs had run its course. The plague, moreover, wiped out nearly 1.5 million people, or one third of the population of England, so that many boroughs lost inhabitants.

The *rotten boroughs*—the small or vestpocket boroughs that sent representatives to Parliament (even though they had few if any inhabitants)—survived until the eighteenth and nineteenth centuries as a relic of the plethora of towns created at that time.

Most English towns obtained a legal identity in the period between 1150 and 1205. The citizens of London, for example, were given a charter by King Henry I (who reigned from 1100 to 1135) in return for their support of his claims to the throne. In 1191, London received its first mayor.

The granting of a charter was often accompanied or followed by permission to hold a market or a fair (Fox, 1970). During the thirteenth century, between 2500 and 3000 market charters were granted or confirmed in England. Although not all markets were held in towns, these concessions to the towns stimulated their economy and encouraged the professionalization of trades that ultimately led to the growth of guilds.

On the Continent, where political jurisdictions were complex and overlapping, the *bourgs* were in the best position to provide leadership in the struggle of the new mercantile classes for rights from the feudal hierarchy and the church. The increasing wealth of the merchants was expressed in organized associations that demanded greater urban freedom. Venice, at the head of the Adriatic Sea, secured certain trading privileges from the Byzantine emperor late in the tenth century. However, Venice had already begun to command the seas and the trade routes. A similar movement toward the removal of restrictions on trade and economy occurred among the cities of Flanders, such as Bruges and Ghent. By the mid-fourteenth century, both Bruges and Ghent were powerful cities, with populations totalling more than fifty thousand each. A similar development occurred among the cities of northern Italy, where Pisa and Genoa, like Venice, had gained from the lucrative maritime trade.

Maritime Powers
The Hanseatic League Cities

Although the quickening of economic life was widespread, it was especially pronounced in the Baltic and Mediterranean regions. Maritime commerce was the key.

In the Baltic region, the Vikings carried on an active trade with almost all parts of Europe; then as they settled, German merchants assumed an increasing role. Lübeck, founded in 1143 at the base of the Danish peninsula, was the first German town on the Baltic. Shortly thereafter, Germans settled at Visby on the Swedish island of Gotland and, until near the end of the thirteenth century, dominated maritime commerce from the Rhine to the Gulf of Finland. German merchants also established themselves at Danzig around 1200, at Riga in 1201, and at Reval (Tallinn) in 1219. From the middle of the thirteenth century onward, Lübeck's central position became increasingly secure as trade reached westward to the North Sea. Lübeck, in fact, assumed German leadership in the struggle with the Danes over access to the straits linking the North and Baltic seas.

From the eleventh century onward, a trading association began to take shape among the cities of the Baltic and North seas. The "Germanization" of the Baltic was an intergral part of this development, but the term *Hansa,* meaning a commercial confederacy under German leadership, did not come into use until after 1367. At its peak, the *Hanseatic League* included some 52 cities, including Cologne, Groningen, Erfurt, Magdeburg, Bremen, Hamburg, Kiel, Lübeck, Rostock, Danzig, Breslau, Cracow, Königsberg, Riga, Reval (Tallinn), and Stockholm (Fig. 16–5). In addition, the Hansa had control of the trade of London, Bergen, Bruges, and Novgorod. The league not only controlled the trade routes of the Baltic and North seas, but also the lower courses of the rivers emptying into these seas. It monopolized, too, the Baltic herring fisheries.

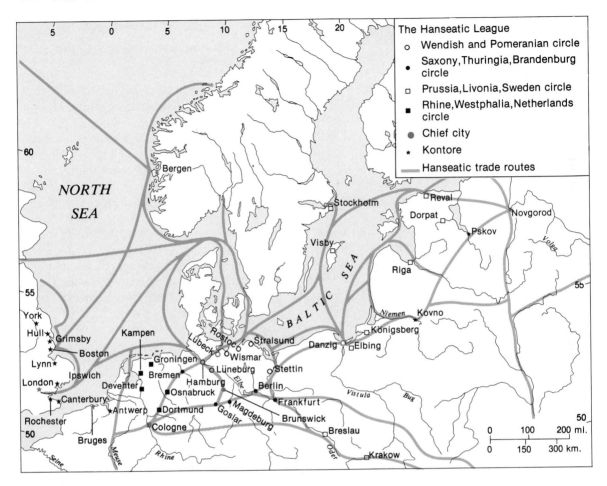

Figure 16-5

Although common political action by the Hanseatic League was impossible, the confederacy—through its commercial and economic wealth and privileges—exercised considerable clout. The Hansa conducted trade wars and claimed free passage through the Baltic. Through its commercial control of northern and north-western Europe, it created a well-integrated economic region. However, by the sixteenth century, the increasing power of new political states had begun to challenge the cities and this together with the silting of historic ports and the disappearance of herring shoals from the Baltic ultimately led to the demise of the league.

The great wealth of the member cities is shown in the gold coinage Lübeck struck in the fourteenth century. Through their wealth, the Hanseatic merchants were able to influence the local heads of state who frequently needed funds for their own purposes (Fig. 16–6). However, the rise of centralized dynastic states together with the collapse of the herring fisheries of the Baltic in the early fifteenth century weakened the Hansa, ultimately securing its demise.

Figure 16–6
Although substantially damaged during World War II, Dantzig (now Gdánsk) was rebuilt by the Polish government in keeping with its medieval architectural design. The size and sturdy appearance of the brick structures, housing dwellings and shops, attest to the past wealth of this former Hanseatic city.

(*Courtesy:* Polska Agencia Interpress.)

The Italian Cities

The Italian cities were even more ideally suited than those on the Baltic to capitalize on the rising demand for trade (Braudel, 1972). Venice, Verona, and Milan benefited from the commerce that came through the passes in the Alps from central Europe. Brindisi, Bari, Rimini, and Ravenna on the Adriatic enjoyed a lucrative trade with the East, although Venice was preeminent in this regard. On the west coast of Italy, Amalfi, Salerno, Naples, and Pisa controlled a substantial traffic.

From the 1150s onward, merchant guilds began to form in the cities, and as they accumulated financial strength, they gained political power at the expense of the older nobility and the church. By about 1200, many specialized guilds had taken shape—bankers, lawyers, artisans of various types, and others.

Pisa, until about 1200, was one of the most prosperous cities in Italy, although its population was only fifteen thousand. In the century following, Florence surged ahead as it began to lay the territorial foundations of a Tuscan city-state. Milan grew in economic power as well, and by 1300, had between fifty and ninety thousand inhabitants, of which an estimated twenty thousand were members of guilds. Both Venice and Genoa benefited from the Crusades, while pursuing an active trade with the Islamic world. By the middle of the fourteenth century, Venice, Genoa, and Florence had populations of about one hundred thousand each.

During the fourteenth century, the Venetian commercial empire was, spatially at least, as great as that of the Hansa (Fig 16–7). Not only were many Adriatic ports, mainland towns, and islands under Venetian domination, but also Venetian galleys dominated the eastern Mediterranean. Moreover, beginning about 1250, the galleys of Venice as well as those of Genoa, Florence, and Catalonia in Spain had reached western Europe, where they provided the Hansa keen competition. Out of this Mediterranean maritime experience came the navigators

Figure 16–7

The historic center of Venice is built on a number of small islands and mudbanks, a total area measuring about 2-miles long and 1-mile across. For almost a thousand years, from A.D. 840 to 1797, its early form of government consisted of a doge, elected by a select portion of the population, and an assembly that gave approval to the doge's decisions. By the early fourteenth century, when Venice became a major commercial power in the Mediterranean, the city-state was governed by a Council of Ten.

Although not a royal city, Venetian wealth was ex-pressed in the architecture and layout of the old city. Many of its public buildings date from the Renaissance—from the doge's palace and the campanile (bell tower) to the square in front of St. Mark's Basilica. The cathedral itself is Byzantine and dates back to the eleventh century. This medieval woodcut affords a view of the cathedral, the doge's palace, and the waterways, or canals.

(*Source:* Buch der Chroniken [Nuremburg Chronicle] 1483. [Leipzig: Hartmann Schedel, fac. 1933], Plate 44. Courtesy Rare Book Collection, University of Washington Libraries.)

who opened up the ocean routes to Africa and North America in the fifteenth century.

THE EMERGENCE OF THE *GOROD* IN RUSSIA

The Coming of the Rus

Roman influence never penetrated into eastern Europe. Outside the Balkans and the Byzantine realm in southeastern Europe, most of the native peoples lived in small nucleated settlements. This was particularly true of the eastern Slavic peoples. Still, it is primarily to the arrival of traders from Scandinavia that the beginnings of urban development in the Russian plain are usually ascribed (Lyashchenko, 1949, p. 73).

In the ninth century, a company of Scandinavian adventurers, known as the Rus established overlordship of both the trade and the peoples of north-central Russia and the Dnieper basin. Wherever they settled as the ruling elite, they erected or rebuilt fortified enclosures, which came to be known in Slavic as *gorods* (Tikhomirov, 1959). Among them were Novgorod (New City) on the Volkhov River, and Smolensk and Kiev on the Dnieper River. These three *gorods* were situated to control the riverine trade route–known as the *Varangian Way*–that linked the Baltic and the Black seas. Kiev, on the high right bank of the middle Dnieper, was the most important of the Rus settlements; Kiev's prince ranked above all other Rus princes. In A.D. 988, the Kievan Rus adopted Byzantine Christianity. Thereafter, Kiev came to be known as the "mother of Russian cities," the key city of all the principalities that formed the Kievan Rus state (Fig. 16–8).

The Nature of the Early *Gorods*

As fortified posts, the early *gorods* occupied very little territory and had few permanent inhabitants. They were initially places of refuge. Gradually, however, settlements became permanent and the cramped space had to be enlarged. Outer walls were built. From the tenth century onward, a new phenomenon emerged. As the towns grew, separate settlements occurred outside the citadel. Ultimately, these settlements merged to form suburbs, or *posads*. The term *gorozhanin* or *grazhdanin,* meaning citizen, also emerged about this time and is the Russian counterpart of the German *burger.*

As early as the tenth century, Kiev contained a palace, a church, and pagan temples. Extensive burial grounds that probably predate the arrival of the Rus were located on the hill outside the early walls. In the eleventh century, the *gorod* was further enlarged by its prince, Yaroslav; the great city of Kiev was given a commanding entrance through its Golden Gate (Tikhomirov, 1959).

Novgorod, near the Baltic terminus of the Varangian Way, was less a princely and more a commercial settlement than Kiev. Not only did it benefit from the trade between Scandinavia and Byzantium, but also it was a center of exchange between northern Europe and the East by means of the Volga River. As the influence of Kiev began to wane under the attacks of successive waves of nomadic invaders from the eastern steppe, Novgorod emerged not only as an independent principality, but also as a kind of commercial republic. Its survival, however, meant dealing with enemies from the northwest and west—the Swedes, Teutonic knights, and Lithuanians—as well as from the grasslands—the Mongols. Until its annexation by Moscow at the end of the fifteenth century, Novgorod controlled an extensive commercial empire throughout northern European Russia.

It is difficult to estimate the size of early Russian cities. It is known that the great fire of Novgorod in 1211 destroyed forty three hundred dwellings and the famine of 1231 took over three thousand lives. As early as 1092, epidemics in Kiev took some seven thousand or more inhabitants. However, Kiev was by far the largest city and most *gorods* probably had no more than one thousand permanent settlers.

The hilltop overlooking the Moskva (Moscow) River in central Russia was not enclosed until about 1148, although there was probably a settlement there long before that time. In any case, the wooden Kremlin, or fortress, of Moscow was a relative latecomer to the Russian urban scene. Its princes were astute, however, and when Kiev and most of the other principalities fell under the Mongol yoke, they were able to seize an advantage in the general misfortune and to secure and strengthen their position. Over the years, Muscovite expansion at the expense of neighboring principalities increased. In 1326–1328, the transfer of the seat of the ecclesiastical primate from Kiev to Moscow was an important factor in enhancing its image. Later (in 1453 when Constantinople fell to the Turks and the Byzantine Empire came to an end), Moscow came to regard itself as the chief center of Orthodox Christianity—the *Third Rome*—a move that greatly strengthened its claim to both Russian and Orthodox Christian continuity and legitimacy.

Figure 16–8

The first Russian state was known as Rus, and it was formed under the leadership of Kiev. In the ninth century A.D., the Slavic peoples of Kievan Rus lived in many small towns and village settlements. One theory holds that the more important towns, especially those along the main trading route from the Baltic to the Black seas, were founded by Scandinavians, a people of Viking origin.

This notion that the urban foundations of the eastern Slavic peoples were laid by Scandinavians is challenged by Soviet historians. They base their argument on the fact that among these early towns there was a total absence of Scandinavian names. Whatever the truth, it seems likely that the sites of the towns commanding the waterways proved especially attractive to ninth-century Scandinavian traders, who on arrival, simply expanded the trading functions of the towns.

EARLY ISLAMIC CITIES

Islam arose in the deserts of Arabia, but from the very beginning, its basic tenets were at home in an urban setting (Hassan, 1969). Mohammed himself had been born in a trading community, and Islam was tailored to the needs of a sedentary commercial society. Moreover, the custom whereby all men in the community would gather at the mosque on Fridays, the Muslim sabbath, to pray both reflected and reinforced the need for an urban environment. The mosque was not only an essential feature of Muslim life, but it was centrally located in the town or city for ease of access.

The presence of water is a major requirement for the establishment of permanent settlements in the region known as the *Dry World*. Consequently, many Islamic cities grew up on the foundations of earlier civilizations—Hellenic, Persian, Roman, and even Semitic. This was true of the major cities of Jerusalem, Damascus, and Alexandria, but it was also the case with Basra at the head of the Arabian Gulf and Seville in Spain.

Baghdad

One of the earliest Islamic cities was Baghdad, which was located on the right bank of the Tigris River. Founded by the Abbasid caliph, al-Mansur, who became ruler in A.D. 754, Baghdad probably was built on the site of an ancient settlement. In 1848, brickwork lining the western bank of the river was unearthed that revealed the name of the Babylonian King Nebuchadnezzar stamped on it. Known initially as Madinat-as-Salam, or the City of Peace, Baghdad was built as a round city, a form that is of ancient origin in Mesopotamia. At the heart of the circle were the caliph's palace and the mosque. Three walls enclosed the circle. Shops and dwellings were confined to the space between the second and innermost walls. The wide central area surrounding the palace and mosque was left for public functions (Box 16–1).

BOX 16–1

Baghdad at the Center of the Earth

With the rise of Islam and the establishment of the caliphate in Baghdad in the middle of the eighth century A.D., a substantial boost was given to trade throughout the Arabian (Persian) Gulf. By the ninth century, Baghdad was the economic heart of the Arabic empire. The city commanded the caravan routes of Mesopotamia, and by virtue of its location on the Tigris River, had water connections with Syria to the north as well as with Basra and the gulf to the south. Under these conditions, the Arabs carried on a flourishing trade with other parts of Asia, with Africa, and with Europe, including the Volga basin. Basra and Siraf on the east coast of the gulf had been important trading centers before Islamic times, but during the Abbasid caliphate in Baghdad, their economies were particularly flourishing. Through Basra came silks from China, tin from Malacca, spices and aromatics from India, and fragrant woods of different varieties—all destined for the bazaars of Baghdad. There, they were exchanged for the produce of northern lands: furs, skins, wax, honey, nuts, swords, falcons, cattle, and fair-headed slaves.

In addition to their dominance of the gulf, the Arabs for a time turned the Mediterranean into a virtual Muslim lake. The conquest of Syria and Egypt and the extension of Islamic control over North Africa (A.D. 698) severely disrupted Byzantine trade. It was centuries before the commercial links between Europe and the Levant reopened; by then, Venice and Genoa vied for economic supremacy of the trade of the east.

The round shape that was Baghdad was a common phenomenon in the Middle East, but when constructed by the Abbasid caliph, al-Mansur, between A.D. 762 and 766–67, it was designed to demonstrate Baghdad's symbolic identity as the navel of the universe (Fig. 16–9). The center of the city was dominated by a palace, a mosque, some administrative buildings, and a wide open space. Walls surrounded the center, which was entered

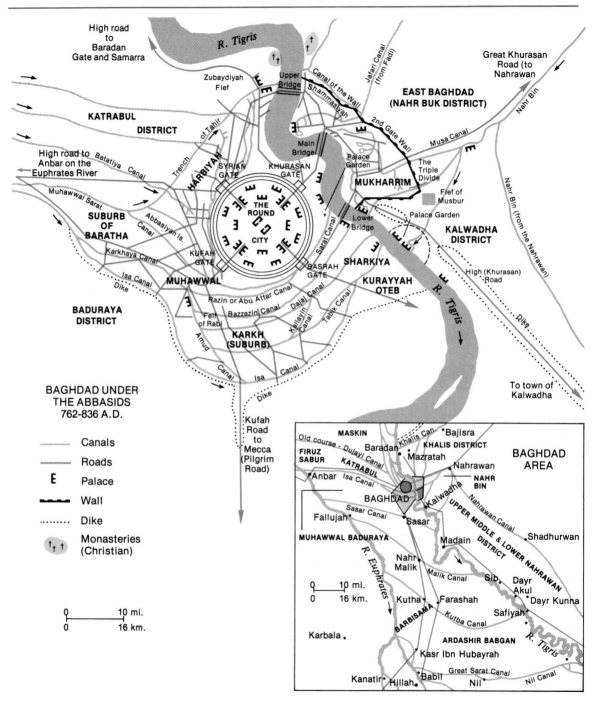

Figure 16–9

At the core of the settlement was the round city located on the right bank of the Tigers River. It was surrounded by farmlands which were served by a network of irrigation canels.

Box 16–1 (continued)

by way of four main gates. Residential quarters were located on either side of the axial streets that connected the outer city with the center.

(*Source:* Adapted from le Strange, [1900] p. 47.)

Baghdad lay at the heart of a productive agricultural region. Its fields were crossed by numerous canals that carried water from both the Tigris and the Euphrates rivers. Outside the outer wall, but accessible from the palace, were elaborate gardens, a phenomenon characteristic of Islamic cities. Baghdad's wealth was based on an extensive trade with the Orient, the Mediterranean, the Baltic, and Africa. Under the reign of Harun-ar-Rashid (A.D. 786–809), the city reached its apogee, contributing to the ninth-century intellectual awakening of the Arabs. However, the subsequent decline of the Abbasid caliphate weakened the base of Baghdad's economy, and the round city was abandoned in 836. Modern Baghdad has grown up largely on the left bank of the Tigris.

Umayyad Spain

Islamic cities tended to decline as the power of a resident caliph waned, but the eclipse of the Abbasid dynasty did not dampen the overall growth of cities in the Muslim world. As the Islamic Empire grew, its urban experience was highlighted by an explosion of artistic and architectural creativity. Mausoleums, *medressas* (universities), palaces, and other public buildings sprang up throughout Islamic society from Inner Asia to Spain.

Spain under the Umayyad dynasty achieved a special brilliance. Between A.D. 755 and 1031, Córdoba, founded on the site of the Roman Colonia Patricia in southern Spain, was the greatest center of Islamic culture in the West. Córdoba's

mosque (now a cathedral) was placed at the center of the city, into which fed narrow winding streets lined with high-backed dwellings that faced onto private courtyards.

As Córdoba declined in the twelfth century, Seville—downstream on the Guadalquivir River—reached its greatest prosperity. The Alcazar in Seville, the palace of the Moorish Kings, remains one of the greatest architectural monuments of Muslim Spain. But of all the artifacts of this age, none is more dramatic than the Alhambra in Granada. Erected between 1238 and 1358, the Alhambra, a citadel of royal residences and structures, stands atop a plateau looking down on the city below (Fig. 16–10).

CITIES OF THE SIXTEENTH THROUGH EIGHTEENTH CENTURIES

Tenuousness of Urban Life

Despite the rapid growth of trade that followed the discovery of America, the Indies, and Africa, urban life in Europe remained somewhat tenuous in the centuries immediately preceding the Industrial Revolution. There was a general growth in towns and cities in the sixteenth century that slackened off in the seventeenth century. Had there not been a continuous in-migration from the countryside, the towns and cities would have had difficulty sustaining themselves.

First of all, there was the continuous problem of providing a city with sufficient food. Many urban residents who retained their links with a village left the city at harvest time, but even so, the urban populace remained a great consumer of grain. When bad weather, such as drought or destructive storms struck the fields, as periodically happened, high prices and severe shortages soon confronted the city. The year 1521 was Portugal's year of great hunger. Southern Spain was drought-stricken in 1525

Figure 16–10

In Arabic, the name Alhambra means The Red, a connotation probably derived from the sun-dried bricks of gravel and clay that formed the outer walls of the palace and fortress of the Moorish monarchs of Granada, Spain.

The Alhambra rises up on a plateau overlooking the city of Granada, which was founded in the early thirteenth century. The palace served several generations of Moorish kings, the walls of which were lavishly decorated by Yusuf I who died in A.D. 1354. However, with the expulsion of the Moors from Spain in 1492, much of the interior of the Alhambra was destroyed. Reconstruction did not begin until the sixteenth century, but then the style was late Renaissance. Some reconstruction of the original structure began in the nineteenth century, this also included the palace itself.

(*Courtesy:* Spanish National Tourist Office.)

and Florence faced famine in 1528. France as a whole experienced 13 general famines in the sixteenth century, 11 in the seventeenth century, and 16 in the eighteenth century, and there were hundreds of local famines as well. Although the cities had warehouses to make provision for such calamities, they were often forced to protect these sources against an invasion of starving country people.

Crowding, filth, and pollution encouraged another great enemy of the city—disease and pestilence. Epidemics of influenza, smallpox, and typhus often took their toll. By the end of the fifteenth century, syphilis had reached Europe from the New World and was quickly diffused by the armies throughout the Continent.

Even more catastrophic was the continued persistence of the Black Death (or the plague). In 1575–1577, Venice lost some fifty thousand inhabitants, or from a fourth to a third of its population. Rome, in 1581, may have been reduced by sixty thousand; Milan in 1630 by eighty-six thousand. After the Thirty Years War in central Europe (1618–1648), the plague spread throughout the Continent, reaching London in the great outbreak of 1665 (Box 16–2). Nor did the dread epidemics end with the seventeenth century. The port of Marseilles in France had the plague in 1720, and as late as 1771, some sixty thousand inhabitants of Moscow succumbed to it. When death struck a city on this scale, the rich generally fled to the countryside until the danger had passed.

A third factor in the tenuousness of urban life was fire. London, having been visited by the plague, was devastated by fire the next year (Fig. 16–11). In five days of September, 1666, 80 percent of the total area—over 300 acres—of the city was destroyed, including thirteen thousand dwellings, numerous churches, and public buildings.

The Commercial Cities

Southern Europe

Despite these serious setbacks, trade and commerce continually stimulated the growth of cities. Sixteenth-century Europe was covered by a network of routes that linked a host of stopping places (Ball, 1977; Braudel, 1972). The routes, some reaching back into the history of the Continent, made extensive exchange possible. Because travel by land and water was slow, frequent stopping places were necessary. If strategically located—on a coast, on a river, or at the junction of routes—these stopping places usually became the great commercial centers of the preindustrial period.

Nowhere in Europe was this network so well developed at this time as in the Mediterranean basin. Numerous cities and towns had grown up to serve the needs of trade. Indeed, the civilization of the Mediterranean region had been essentially urban since earliest times. Because the

Mediterranean itself served as the principal artery of exchange, most of the major cities were ports. Among these were Venice, Genoa, and Naples on the Italian peninsula; Barcelona in Spain; and Algiers in Africa. Florence continued to compete for trade, through the coastal city of Leghorn, but its connections with the outport were poor. Of the inland cities, Milan dominated the overland routes to Europe north and west of the Alps. Seville in southwestern Spain could draw on a rich hinterland, but its ties with the Indies and northwestern Europe were largely responsible for making it one of the great economic centers of the Continent in the seventeenth century. Lisbon in Portugal, hav-

---

BOX 16-2

Samuel Pepys on the London Plague

The plague spread rapidly through the City of London in the summer of 1665. During the week ending June 27, there were 267 deaths owing to the plague. Thereafter, totals rose through July, August, and September, when, during the week ending September 19, the plague carried off 7165 victims. The peak had been reached, and in the weeks following, the numbers steadily declined. By the end of the year, the epidemic had run its course. Altogether 97,506 persons died and were buried in London in 1665, of which the plague claimed 68,596.

The immediacy of the plague was reported by Samuel Pepys (1633–1703), the famous English diarist. In letters dated at the height of the plague, in August and September, 1665, he wrote to friends:

I have been a good while alone here, the rest having to one place or other provided for themselves out of town. The truth is, few but ticketeers and people of

very ordinary errands now come hither, merchants and all persons of better rank with whom we have to deal for provisions and otherwise having left the town.

The absence of the Court and the emptiness of the City take away all occasion of news save only such melancholy stories; . . . I have stayed in the City till above 7,400 died in one week, and of them above 6,000 of the Plague, and little noise heard day or night but tolling of bells; till I could walk Lumber-street and not meet twenty persons from one end to the other, and not fifty upon the Exchange; till whole families, 10 and 12 together, have been swept away; till my very physician, Dr. Burnet, who undertook to secure me against any infection, having survived the month of his own house being shut up, died himself of the Plague; till the nights though much lengthened, are grown too short to conceal the burials of those that died the day before, people being thereby constrained to borrow daylight for that service; lastly, till I could find neither meat nor drink safe, the butcheries being everywhere visited, my brewer's house shut up, and my baker, with his whole family, died of the Plague.

(*Source:* Quote from *The Diary of Samuel Pepys*, Henry B. Wheatley, ed. [New York: Croscup and Sterling], 1894, Vol. 4, Pt. 2.)

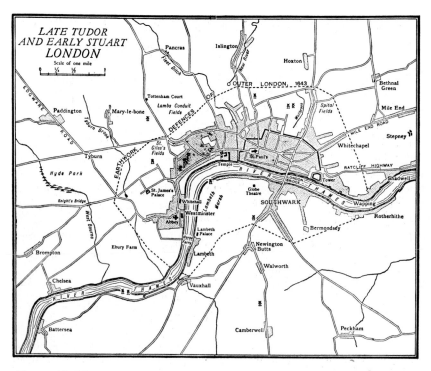

Figure 16–11

London at the time of Samuel Pepys was a city of considerable size. With the City Proper it stretched from the Tower in the east to Westminster in the west. The Great Fire that broke out in the autumn of 1666, however, gutted much of the Old City and left St. Paul's Cathedral in ruins.

The task of rebuilding the cathedral, if not the City itself, was given to Sir Christopher Wren (1632–1723), probably England's most influential architect. The rebuilding of the City was slow to get underway and the plan for St. Paul's was subject to many changes, but work got started in 1675. With its superb dome, still visible on the London skyline, St. Paul's was completed in 1711. The fire had destroyed 87 parish churches as well as St. Paul's, and in the redesigning of some of these, Wren played a role. His style of architecture—simplistic yet elegant—found its way to the colonies to appear in the building of Christ Church, Boston, in 1723.

Source: G. M. Trenelyan, *English Social History* [London: Longmans, Green & Co., 1942].

ing taken the lead in the voyages of discovery, also benefited from its close economic association with Antwerp, Amsterdam, and the growing Dutch trade. Of all the cities of the Mediterranean basin, however, the largest was Constantinople, where European and Asian land and water routes converged. By the seventeenth century, its population totalled about seven hundred thousand, twice the size of Paris.

Northwestern Europe

The rise of northwestern Europe to a leading position in the commercial capitalism of the seventeenth and eighteenth centuries was due to an association of many factors. Certainly the decline of the Hansa opened up opportunities that were quickly seized on by the merchants of England and Holland. By mid-sixteenth century, the English had begun to penetrate the

Muscovite Russian market through the White Sea port of Archangel. Antwerp had been the greatest merchandising city of northwestern Europe until the middle of the century, but the initiative of Protestant merchants and a shift in the direction of trade then brought Amsterdam to the fore. In general, the pattern of European commerce was slowly moving from its long-standing base in the Mediterranean to the ports facing the North Sea and the Atlantic.

Antwerp on the Scheldt River was an important center for trade in spices and metals, its merchants, many of whom were resident foreigners, serving as intermediaries. Cloth and grain also were major components of Antwerp's commercial structure. However, the unsettled nature of its political allegiance left it in a fragile position in the mid-sixteenth century. Thereafter, Amsterdam, whose merchants—like those of the other towns that had grown up around the lower Rhine and Zuider Zee—were independent in spirit, Protestant in religion, and fiercely proud of their new-found wealth, moved rapidly to supplant Antwerp (Fig. 16–12).

Amsterdam was probably the best example of the application of the new philosophy of *mercantilism* to be found in northwestern Europe (Vance, 1977) (Box 16–3). Its site, which afforded access to the Zuider Zee and the North Sea, was not superior to that of Antwerp. Indeed, Amsterdam was built on pilings to prevent it from sinking into marshy ground. It was, however, readily defensible, which was important in a region ransacked by European armies. Having capitalized on local trade and the Baltic fisheries, Amsterdam moved into the commerce of the Orient with the chartering of the United East India Company in 1602 (Barber, 1975).

Evidence of Amsterdam's growth is abundant. Between 1589 and 1611, its customs revenue doubled. Its population at the same time literally exploded, climbing from 30,000 in 1567 to 105,000 in 1622. By 1680, Amsterdam may have passed the 200,000 mark. The growth in population and in wealth led to a vast program of city expansion and beautification. The city

Figure 16–12

Antwerp, situated far inland on the Scheldt River, was already an important trading and shipping center in the thirteenth century. It replaced Bruges as the great mercantile metropolis of western Europe by the end of the fifteenth century and was in a good position to profit from the developing colonial trade. The prospects of further economic development were highly favorable until religious conflict early in the sixteenth century disrupted trading relationships with the interior of the Continent.

The Cathedral of the Holy Virgin shown here dates from the period when Antwerp was a prosperous trading and financial entrepôt. The statue in the foreground is of the great artist Peter Paul Rubens (1579–1640), the greatest of baroque painters.

(*Courtesy of:* The Belgium Institute of Information and Documentation, Brussels.)

was enlarged, canals were dredged, and many impressive public buildings and private dwellings were erected. Amsterdam quicky became the Venice of the north. As a shipping center, commodity market, and as a market for capital, Amsterdam had no equal.

In England, the center of commercial and financial life was the old City of London. In part, this was due to the centralization of national government in nearby Westminster, but the City's merchants played a historic role in regional and overseas trade. The City, too, had very early asserted its independence of royal prerogative and restrictions, clinging tenaciously to its freedom and privileges through the reigns of the Tudors and Stuarts from the fifteenth to the eighteenth centuries (Box 16–4). Indeed, no sovereign would have been welcome within the old City walls unless he was first greeted by the lord mayor at Temple Bar. The latter was an arched gateway designed by Sir Christopher Wren and erected about 1672 between Fleet Street and the Strand, dividing the City from Westminster, where an earlier barrier had been strung.

After the Great Fire, the City was rebuilt, but it remained a merchants' stronghold. The gentry and nobility who were drawn to London set-

---

BOX 16–3

Mercantilism and Its Contribution to the City

Between the sixteenth and eighteenth centuries, a set of economic views prevailed in Europe that the Scottish economist Adam Smith (1723–1790) termed the mercantile system. This philosophy included the belief that the state, or national government, should play a role in regulating commerce and industry (Barbour, 1950). Indeed, an essential notion of the mercantilists was that the economic policies of governments should aim to increase state wealth—that meant an acquisition of precious metals. Gold and silver in particular were believed to constitute basic wealth. They were necessary for the production of coinage, essential to the maintenance of military and naval power, and a key to national power and prestige.

In Spain and Portugal, this goal was achieved by exploiting the metals of the New World. For Holland, England, and other less advantaged colonial powers, such wealth could only be achieved through piracy and smuggling or more honorably through the pursuit of trade. However, to guard against any loss of metal, trading policy had to be so constructed that a country's imports could not exceed exports.

The mercantilists saw the importance of acquiring overseas colonies as markets for home-made manufactures, which they believed should be encouraged. Moreover, the English—through the *Navigation Acts,* the first of which was passed in 1651—sought to ensure that all traffic between the colonies and the mother country be handled by English carriers.

One of the leading contributors to mercantilist thought was the English economist Thomas Mun (1571–1641). In 1615, he became a director of the East India Company. At the time, imports from India exceeded English exports. In a tract published in 1621, "Discourse of Trade, from England unto the East Indies," Mun argued that although trade with India was out of balance, the trade was nevertheless so valuable that it augmented generally the wealth of England. He pointed to the nature of the trade and the advantage the access to Asian goods gave the English trader in the European market. In subsequent tracts, Mun also developed the notion of a favorable balance of trade, which attempted to broaden the rather narrow doctrines of the strict *bullionists,* that is, those who saw wealth only in terms of the accumulation of gold and silver.

tled less in the City itself than in the districts to the west, where squares, parks, and stately rows of houses still memorialize the estates that they laid out in the late seventeenth and eighteenth centuries. Wren was responsible for the rebuilding, although it was not accomplished according to his plan. Among his greatest architectural works was St. Paul's Cathedral.

It was the merchants of London who were largely responsible for the growth of England's commercial empire. As early as 1407, they had taken a role in establishing the Company of Merchant Adventurers, an association of English traders with trading facilities on the Continent similar to those enjoyed (until 1560) by the Hansa in London. Other merchant companies were formed in the sixteenth century to trade in Russia, the Levant, and Africa. London merchants also benefited from the commerce that

was generated when the East India Company was chartered in 1600. London again gained when the Hudson's Bay Company, in 1670, acquired a monopoly of the fur trade in the lands draining into Hudson Bay in the New World.

Bristol, facing Ireland and the Atlantic and some eight miles above the estuary of the Severn on the Avon River, was England's second port. From the fourteenth century onward, its merchants enjoyed considerable prosperity. Bristol's major export was wool and woolen goods; its imports were principally wines and spices. The merchants offset fluctuations in trade by sending out various small expeditions to create new opportunities. Hence, their support of John Cabot (c.1450–c.1499) in his search for a westward route to the Orient in 1497–1498 was totally in character. However, neither the Bristol merchants nor England as a whole at-

---

BOX 16–4

Western European Cities Contrasted with East Asian Cities

Challenge to traditional authority was a characteristic feature of the vital commercial city in western Europe. From medieval times onward, the burghers or burghesses of the cities, grown prosperous on trade, sought to obtain and preserve freedom from princely authority and interference (Murphey, 1954).

In the Orient, and especially in China, the city was basically an administrative center, directed toward controlling and exploiting the surrounding population. Even where domestic trade and manufacturing had developed, as Professor Rhoads Murphey points out in his comparative study of the city in Western Europe and China, there did not emerge an urban society dominated by merchants whe were likely to challenge traditional authority. Where commerce had become a

leading activity of the city as a whole, as in the case of Shanghai near the mouth of the Ch'ang (Yangtze) River, trade alone did not replace the administrative function of most of China's cities. At least this was true until Shanghai and other coastal cities of China became ports under foreign domination.

Because the cities in China were securely in the hands of their administrators, China did not undergo until modern times the "shock" effect that urban areas of western Europe had experienced for centuries. In China, and in much of East Asia as well, the historic city was not a center of change. Unlike the independent merchants of Western Europe, Oriental merchants were both associated with, and regulated by, the political structure.

tempted to capitalize on Cabot's discoveries in North America until over a century later.

The Royal or Boulevard Cities

The consolidation of political power in the hands of the absolute monarchs of Europe during the sixteenth through eighteenth centuries created the desire for tangible and spatial demonstrations of their power. The expansion of commercial activity at that time found expression in the merchant's city; at the same time, the growth in monarchical power came to be symbolized in the construction of splendid palaces and residences, often set amidst elaborate gardens, which helped to adorn the capital cities. Many such royal cities were subjected to substantial faceliftings as well. As the merchants engaged in vigorous competition to enhance the base of their commercial activities, so the monarchs attempted to compete in visual displays of their wealth and majesty. The elaboration of monarchical pomp and circumstance was enhanced by the emergence of a new set of cultural values known as the *baroque*. The baroque began in Italy as an expression of the human spirit and spread in varying degrees throughout central and northern Europe.

In architectural design, baroque meant exuberance, but it was essentially sensual (Jellicoe and Jellicoe, 1975). In some ways, it was anti-Renaissance and anticlassical; it represented a break in a tradition that had been confining and restrictive. As expressed in city planning, the most striking feature of the baroque style was the imposition of the straight boulevard flanked by impressive public buildings and residences. Baroque implied movement, thus the broad boulevard designed for the parade of colorful regiments or the presentation of royal spectacles. This new style was Europe's way of proclaiming its growing economic and political prowess, its developing self-confidence, its intellectual quickening, and its evolving social life.

The new feeling for space may be said to have begun with the work of the Florentine architect and artist, Michelangelo Buonarroti (1475–1564). In Rome about 1544, he began the layout of the ancient Capitol on a scale that clearly surpassed the more limited ordering of buildings of the Renaissance. In his additions to St. Peter's Basilica, he continued to reach for the monumental.

Because the church had both spiritual and temporal authority in Rome, the popes encouraged a restructuring and beautification of the *Eternal City* commensurate with its history and goals. Particularly active was Pope Sixtus V (that was during his reign 1585–1590); he commissioned a new plan for the city, with broad boulevards radiating from a relocated and newly defined center. Through the creativity of the Neopolitan architect Giovanni Bernini (1598–1680), the large colonnaded piazza in from of St. Peter's came into being. One outstanding feature of the plan for Rome was the recognition of the importance of urban reference points, marked by columns or obelisks (Fig. 16–13). These linked the boulevards in such a way as to give the impression of grandeur—a goal of the whole baroque movement.

When European princes found that they could not obtain sufficient space within a city to erect the palace they desired, they took refuge in the suburbs. Versailles, one of the best expressions of baroque, began as a royal hunting lodge. During the reign (1643–1715) of Louis XIV, through the talent of the landscape architect Andre Le Nôtre (1613–1700), Versailles was transformed into a residence whose purpose was to glorify the Sun King. The Italian influence was present in the fountains, stairways, and vistas, but it was Le Nôtre who devised the formal geometric gardens on the palace grounds; they were designed to emphasize the absoluteness of human reason and the power of the king. Clearly, nature was subordinate, like the subjects of the king.

Figure 16–13

The Vatican, although falling within the metropolitan area of Rome, remains a unique independent state of 0.15 miles^2. It is the seat of the Roman Catholic Papacy. Surrounded by medieval and Renaissance walls, the Vatican site contains, in addition to St. Peter's Basilica, St. Peter's Square, the colonnaded piazza, which is thronged on occasions when the pope makes a personal appearance, and numerous other buildings, including palaces, museums, and administrative offices. St. Peter's Basilica is the most impressive structure in the state, dating principally from the sixteenth century.

Source: Karl Gullens/Rapho/Photo Researchers, Inc.

Elsewhere in Europe, other monarchs soon began to imitate the splendors of Versailles. This was true at Potsdam, where Frederick the Great (1712–1786) had founded the German Hohenzollern dynasty. Even in the capitals of small German duchies, such as Karlsruhe and Wilhelmstrohe, the local rulers sought to emulate and outdo Versailles. Through the efforts of the Habsburgs, Vienna was transformed from a fortified medieval trading center into a truly magnificent baroque city. Handsome mansions and townhouses replaced the dwellings of the past, and royal palaces were erected in the suburbs, at Schönbrunn and Favoriten, which reflected the rich tastes of Italian artists.

In Russia, Peter the Great (1672–1725) undertook to build a new city near the mouth of the Neva, which was to be a window through which Western influences could penetrate into Russia. In 1703 a fortress was built on the large Peter Island in the river, and on the mainland to the south the Admiralty was constructed. Initially, it was intended that the islands would form the central core of the city, but site problems associated with high water levels and icing led to a concentration of palaces, gardens, and residences near the Admiralty. Canals were constructed through the marshy terrain so that gradually St. Petersburg gave the impression of a city built around water, like Venice or Amsterdam. A Swiss-Italian architect, Domenico Frezzini (1670–1734) was imported, and it was he who designed the original Cathedral of St. Peter and St. Paul within the fortress walls (where many of Russia's rulers were subsequently buried).

Figure 16–14

L'Enfant's plan for Washington was completed in 1791, and it reflects the landscape design prevalent in Europe at the time. Central to L'Enfant's scheme was the location of the Capitol. The Mall, reminiscent of the broad open boulevards conceived in Europe, and the residence of the president, which came to be called the White House, completed the grand scheme.

Broad boulevards were also intended to radiate outward from the Capitol and the executive mansion to afford long vistas terminated by circular intersections. Some of these features are evident in the modern city today. However, before the cornerstone of the Capitol was laid, L'Enfant was dismissed and in the following century much of what he intended was destroyed.

(*Source:* Jellicoe and Jellicoe, 1975, p. 221)

The accomplishments in laying out the new capital city made during the reign of Peter the Great were substantial, but by the middle of the eighteenth century, the city's facade was sober, reflecting the styles of the Baltic Sea and North Sea region rather than those of the Mediterranean. With the reign (1741–1762), of the Tsarina Elizabeth, however, further development of St. Petersburg passed into the hands of the imaginative Italian architect Bartolomeo Francesco Rastrelli (1675–1744). At Elizabeth's command, he undertook to rebuild many royal palaces, and he also designed residences for the nobility. Among the royal edifices were the Winter Palace facing the Neva, the Palace of Peterhof (Petrodvorets) to the south of the Gulf of Finland, and the Great Palace at Tsarskoe Selo (today called Pushkin). With Rastrelli, the baroque had truly come to Russia. The garden at Tsarskoe Selo with its pavilions and geometric subdivisions was clearly inspired by Versailles.

In England, the baroque influence was muted, mainly because of the influence and talents of Sir Christopher Wren. The formal garden was imported into England, where it provided a setting for Hampton Court Palace, the Tudor palace that Wren rebuilt. The royal hospitals of Chelsea (1682–1692) and Greenwich (about 1696) were other monuments of the baroque. Both were inspired by the Hôtel des Invalides in Paris. However, in seeking a compromise between the monumental and the purely domestic, Wren created something entirely new. It was less flamboyant than European baroque; it was English.

The baroque style was not confined to royalty and Europe. In North America, the newly founded republic of the United States wanted a capital city that would reflect its commitment to all of the principles of the revolution. On July 16, 1790, a capital district along the Potomac River was created by an act of Congress. Thomas Jefferson (1743–1826), Secretary of State in President George Washington's administration and an architect, suggested a simple geometric design for the city that would permit both the president's house and the Capitol to face the river. However, late in 1791 Major Pierre Charles L'Enfant (1754–1825), a French military engineer who had fought in the Revolutionary War, was engaged to survey the site and devise a comprehensive city plan. He rejected Jefferson's grid proposal and offered one that, in its grandiose conception, mirrored Versailles (Fig. 16–14). Its broad avenues, interrupted by circles and public places, were on the scale of Rome. L'Enfant's sensitivity to the site, however, could be seen in his use of spaces in such a way as to bring the land and river together, much as had been achieved in Venice, Amsterdam, and St. Petersburg. The L'Enfant plan for Washington was, indeed, a bold one, a remarkable proposal for a new land founded on the edge of the wilderness.

The cornerstone of the Capitol was laid in 1793, and during much of the nineteenth century, the broad features of the design came into existence, but growth in the fledgling capital, as in other American cities, was haphazard. In 1901, the McMillan Park Commission undertook to continue the orderly development of the main government quarter of the city along the lines of L'Enfant's original plan. This step was the true beginning of the city as it appears today (Fig. 16–15). However, the baroque influence initially associated with L'Enfant's grand design disappeared after 1900 when there was a return to the classical style of architecture, as exemplified in the Supreme Court Building.

EPILOGUE

Medieval Europe was predominantly rural and most medieval towns and cities—even ecclesiastical centers—were probably not unlike Avignon, which Barbara Tuchman describes in detail. The fall of the Roman Empire led to a decline in urban life, but the image of Jerusalem, the Holy City, survived, as did the ecclesi-

Figure 16–15

The capital city of the United States retains some of the original plan for its design, but the latter was lost until 1887. The broad vistas that L'Enfant envisaged were lost, in part through the heavy planting of trees along the streets. More than that, the location of the Lincoln and Jefferson memorials further modified the plan.

By the 1960s, there was some concern that through the construction of many public buildings a city of stone had been created that failed to serve the needs of a resident population. The creation of the President John F. Kennedy Center for the Performing Arts, for example, was an attempt to make the city more functional, serving needs other than administrative.

Source: M. E. Warren/Photo Researchers, Inc.

astical centers that were important in the administration of the Roman Catholic Church.

Although there was no end to economic activity, it was not until about 1400 that the medieval city began to take shape. In part, inspired by the goals of the Renaissance, the city also benefited from the substantial revival of trade and commerce that seems to have begun in the eleventh century. Great trading empires grew up both in the Baltic and Mediterranean regions. And, indeed, it can be argued that the first truly Russian cities, or *gorods,* took shape with the initial coming of the Rus from Scandinavia.

Although material wealth increased in the late medieval period, both through the vigorous commercial life (following the discovery of America) and the growth of royal power, the city on the threshold of the Industrial Revolution was probably nearer its classical origins than to the city that was to emerge as a result of the Industrial Revolution.

APPLICATION OF IDEAS

1. The decline of the Roman Empire was accompanied by a general decay in urban life. In the period between imperial collapse and the emergence of a new feudal order in Europe, the only cities that seemed to survive the transition were the ecclesiastical cities.

2. Owing to an eleventh-century upsurge in population, an increase in agricultural productivity, and an expansion of trade—all largely because of a period of relative calm in Europe after the Viking raids—the city came to life again.

3. Medieval cities had many internal problems, but they did draw people from the land, particularly where there were facilities for trade and where the city itself provided a degree of security not found in the countryside.

4. New towns and cities were founded as well, on frontiers, in sparsely settled regions, or in areas that offered potential for future settlement. To achieve legal identity, it was often necessary for the citizens of the town to secure a charter from the monarch. The monarch gave such charters in return for the support of the towns in the struggle with the nobles and the landed gentry.

5. With the quickening of economic life, the medieval cities in both the Mediterranean basin and in the Baltic region quickly accumulated large fortunes that, in turn, were used to beautify their respective cities.

6. Russian cities, or *gorods,* came into existence largely through the dominance and organizational skills of traders and freebooters from Scandinavia, who laid the foundations of the Kievan Rus state.

7. By the seventeenth century, a number of European cities rose to commercial preeminence in large part owing to their advantageous situation relative to rivers, trade routes, and other waterways.

8. The growth of wealth together with the consolidation of royal power in the hands of the European monarchs led to the creation of royal cities, symbolized by palaces, parks, grand boulevards, and so on.

9. The landscape design that many European monarchs seized on to glorify their capital cities was carried over into the New World and formed the basis of the plan for Washington, D.C.

KEY WORDS AND PHRASES

Babylonian captivity
baroque
bastides
borough
bourg
bullionist
burgher
diocese

Drang nach Osten
Dry World
Eternal City
faubourg
gorod
gorozhanin
  (*grazhdanin*)
Hansa

Hanseatic League
legion
medressa
mercantilism
  (mercantile
  system)

Navigation Acts
posad
rotten borough
rundling
Third Rome
Varangian Way

QUESTIONS FOR FURTHER DISCUSSION

1. What kept cities alive and functioning in early medieval Europe as the Roman Empire declined?

2. What was significant about the ecclesiastical cities? Why did they survive in the face of the general breakdown in civil life?

3. Why was the image of Jerusalem so important? What image, on the other hand, did Babylon convey? Is it evident in Petrarch's statement quoted at the beginning of the chapter?

4. Europe in the eleventh century underwent a substantial economic awakening three centuries before the Renaissance took shape. How do you account for this revival? What effect did it have on cities?

5. What is the relationship between *bourgs, faubourgs, bastides,* and *rundlings*? That is, how did they differ? What did they have in common? How were they expressed in the landscape? Are *faubourgs* evident in the Paris landscape today?

6. What advantage did cities in the medieval period possess that warranted royal charters, royal support, and royal concessions?

7. What made the Hansa cities unique? What evidence of their once-great economic wealth and power is visible today?

8. What made the later royal cities of Europe so different from the medieval cities? In what way did they express the philosophy, political or otherwise, of the age? How did the commercial cities of Europe differ from the royal cities?

9. Account for the differences that emerged in the cities of western Europe and East Asia. Would you have expected such differences?

10. Why did Americans contemplate using the baroque model, characteristic of many European royal cities, for their new capital city of Washington? Would such a model have been chosen in the nineteenth or twentieth centuries? Why or why not?

REFERENCES AND ADDITIONAL READINGS

Ball, J. N. *Merchants and Merchandise. The Expansion of Trade in Europe 1500–1630.* London: Croom Helm, 1977.

Barber, William J. *British Economic Thought and India, 1600–1858. A Study in the History of Development Economics.* Oxford: Clarendon Press, 1975.

Barbour, Violet. *Capitalism in Amsterdam in the Seventeenth Century* (The Johns Hopkins University Studies in Historical and Political Science, Series 67). Baltimore: Johns Hopkins University Press, 1950.

Beckinsale, R. P., and Houston, J. M. *Urbanization and Its Problems. Essays in Honour of E. W. Gilbert.* Oxford: Basil Blackwell, 1968.

Beresford, Maurice. "A Deserted Medieval Village in England." *Scientific American* 235 (1976): 116–128.

Braudel, Fernand. *The Mediterranean and the Mediterranean World in the Age of Philip II* (2 vols.). New York: Harper & Row, 1972.

———. *Capitalism and Material Life 1400–1800.* New York: Harper & Row, 1975.

Brett, Lionel. *Architecture in a Crowded World. Vision and Reality in Planning.* New York: Schocken Books, 1971.

Burckhardt, Jacob. *The Civilization of the Renaissance in Italy* (2 vols.). New York: Harper & Row, 1958.

Cunliffe, Barry. *Rome and Her Empire.* New York: McGraw-Hill, 1979.

Davidson, Marshall B. *Life in America* (2 vols.). Boston: Houghton Mifflin, 1974.

Dickinson, Robert E. *The West European City. A Geographical Interpretation.* London: Routledge & Kegan Paul, 1951.

Fox, H. S. A. "Development of Towns and Market Places: England." *Geographical Magazine* 42 (1970): 658–667.

Geddes, Patrick. *Cities in Evolution.* New York: Oxford University Press, 1950.

Graham, Brian. "The Evolution of Urbanization in Medieval Ireland." *Journal of Historical Geography* 5 (1979): 111–125.

Handlin, Oscar, and Burchard, John, eds. *The Historian and the City.* Cambridge, Mass.: MIT Press, 1963.

Hassan, Riaz. "The Nature of Islamic Urbanization: A Historical Perspective." *Journal of the Pakistan Historical Society* 17 (1969): 77–83.

Hoskins, W. G. *The Making of the English Landscape.* Harmondsworth, Eng.: Penguin Books, 1970.

Jackson, Kenneth T., and Schultz, Stanley K., eds. *Cities in American History.* New York: Alfred A. Knopf, 1972.

Jellicoe, Geoffrey, and Jellicoe, Susan. *The Landscape of Man. Shaping the Environment from Prehistory to the Present Day.* London: Thames & Hudson 1975.

Kornhauser, David. *Urban Japan: Its Foundations and Growth.* London: Longman, 1976.

le Strange, Guy. *Baghdad During the Abbasid Caliphate.* Oxford: Clarendon Press, 1900.

Lyashchenko, Peter I. *History of the National Economy of Russia to the 1917 Revolution.* New York: Macmillan, 1949.

Martines, Lauro. *Power and Imagination. City-States in Renaissance Italy.* New York: Alfred A. Knopf, 1979.

Mumford, Lewis. *The Culture of Cities.* New York: Harcourt, Brace, 1938.

———. *The City in History. Its Origins, Its Transformations, and Its Prospects.* New York: Harcourt, Brace & World, 1961.

Murphey, Rhoads. "The City as a Center of Change: Western Europe and China." *Annals of the As-*

sociation of American Geographers 44 (1954): 349–358.

Pirenne, Henri. *Medieval Cities. Their Origins and the Revival of Trade*. Princeton, N.J.: Princeton University Press, 1969.

Platt, Colin. *Medieval England. A Social History and Archaeology from the Conquest to 1600 A.D.* New York: Charles Scribner's, 1978.

Rose, A. J. *Patterns of Cities*. London: Thomas Nelson, 1967.

Rosenau, Helen. *The Ideal City. Its Architectural Evolution*. New York: Harper & Row, 1972.

Russell, Josiah Cox. *Medieval Regions and Their Cities*. Bloomington: Indiana University Press, 1972.

Singer, Charles et al., eds. *A History of Technology,* Vol. 3. New York: Oxford University Press, 1957.

Sjoberg, Gideon. *The Preindustrial City. Past and Present*. Glencoe, Ill.: Free Press, 1960.

Tikhomirov, M. *The Towns of Ancient Rus*. Moscow: Foreign Languages Publishing House, 1959.

Toynbee, Arnold. *Cities on the Move*. New York: Oxford University Press, 1970.

Tuchman, Barbara W. *A Distant Mirror. The Calamitous 14th Century*. New York: Alfred A. Knopf, 1978.

Vance, James E. *The Scene of Man. The Role and Structure of The City in the Geography of Western Civilization*. New York: Harper & Row, 1977.

Ward, David, ed. *Geographic Perspectives on America's Past. Readings on the Historical Geography of the United States*. New York: Oxford University Press, 1979.

Weber, Adna Ferrin. *The Growth of Cities in the Nineteenth Century. A Study in Statistics* (Columbia University Studies in History, Economics and Public Law, Vol. 11). Ithaca, N.Y.: Cornell University Press, 1969. (Originally published, 1899).

17
The Shaping of the Industrial Landscape

An environment that cannot be changed invites its own destruction. We prefer a world that can be modified progressively, against a background of valued remains, a world in which one can leave a personal mark alongside the marks of history.

Kevin Lynch,
What Time Is This Place?, 1972

Key Ideas

1. The advantage of hindsight is that it permits us to identify turning points in history. By the middle of the nineteenth century, evidence of changes of major importance were clearly visible in the landscape of England.

2. The Industrial Revolution occurred in Great Britain first because of the climate of freedom, the availability and close proximity of resources, the presence of navigable waterways, the increasing productivity of British agriculture as a whole, and a growing worldwide market.

3. Industrialization not only led to new ways of living and working, but also it uprooted vast numbers of people.

4. The employment of steam power to drive the new machines inevitably meant geographic concentration of energy, of machinery, of capital, and above all of labor.

5. Industrialization brought significant changes to the landscape and to the work habits of an industrialized people; to accompany these changes, there had to be a new concept of work, a new sense of purpose, of direction, and of priorities.

6. The materialization of this new milieu required new concepts of time and space.

7. Industrial society could not have developed without the notion of monochronic, or linear, time. Monochronic time emphasizes schedules, the compartmentalization of space, and the periodization of time.

8. Polychronic time is the opposite of monochronic or M-time. P-time is nonlinear and, therefore, not regulated.

9. The growth of the factory town was accompanied by a substantial exodus of people from the countryside.

10. Industrialization, too, gave rise to a whole new dimension of environmental and social problems. Forests were leveled, the air became polluted with smoke, and streams were blackened.

SPATIAL IMPACT OF INDUSTRIALIZATION

The Industrial Revolution, one of the greatest social and economic revolutions in history, introduced some fundamental changes in the landscape. It modified the way in which human beings made a living, altered the conditions of material existence, changed the way in which time was organized and, above all, led to new patterns of settlement and spatial interaction. The revolution affected every aspect of life and its sphere of impact was not confined to a local region. Industrialization laid the basis for a reshaping of the entire human occupance of the globe. As Gregory in a new study of the evolution of the woolen industry in Britain notes: "[the revolution] involved a . . . transition in human experience and social structure which was tied in to much wider congeries of changes in economy, politics, and ideology" (Gregory, 1982).

Geographers have long been interested in a subfield known as industrial geography. They have examined problems in industrial location, linkages between industries and market, between industries and raw-materials supply, and labor.

However, although industrial geography has attracted attention, few geographers have shown an interest in the *industrial landscape* as part of human or cultural landscapes. Geographers speak of the industrial or industrialized countries without reminding their readers of what the transformation from rural to industrial entailed.

FRANKENSTEIN: A PORTENT

Hollywood has so brutally exploited and distorted the story of Dr. Frankenstein and the monster he creates that the novel's original significance is almost lost.

Frankenstein, or the Modern Prometheus

was written by Mary Wollstonecroft Shelley (1797–1851) at the age of 18; she was the wife of the English poet Percy Bysshe Shelley (1792–1822). The novel was first published in 1818 (Shelley, 1818/1965).

Frankenstein tells the story of how a scientist, working in his laboratory, gives life to an ugly monster. The monster spends his time in search of love and, failing that, subsequently turns on and destroys his creator.

In one sense, the novel is a kind of science fiction, yet the author herself says little about science. Nor does she attempt to exploit the *Promethean myth* suggested by the subtitle (Wolf, 1977). Prometheus, it will be remembered, defied the gods to give humankind the knowledge of fire.

What Mary Shelley did in writing *Frankenstein,* however, was to sense the direction in which civilization, in particular the new industrial age, was moving. Above all, she sensed the significance of the enhanced power humankind was achieving over nature and hinted at the possible consequences.

Viewed in this light, *Frankenstein* is not only the remarkable creation of a young Englishwoman, but also it is a testament of concern for the new industrial age that was being born. It rightly has a place in our discussion of the impact of the Industrial Revolution on the world, on the human habitat, and on humankind itself.

THE COMING OF A NEW AGE

The advantage of hindsight is that it permits us to identify specific changes in human activity patterns on the earth's surface that both reflect and portend significant shifts in the way humankind—or a portion of it—lives and works. Evidence of changes of such importance were visible in the English landscape by the middle of the nineteenth century. Indeed, for almost a century, England had been undergoing a transformation that can only be described as revolutionary. This Industrial Revolution was more fundamental in its effect on daily life than were either the American or the French revolutions, which were essentially political.

The Industrial Revolution embraced a complex series of developments that altered traditional relationships significantly. Since its beginnings in England in about 1760, the material culture of humankind as a whole has changed more drastically than it had in the preceding 5000 years. The first phase of industrialization lasted until about 1825, laying the foundations for what was to come. New modes of transportation, technical refinements, and a high degree of prosperity characterized the second phase (in England), which ran its course during the decade of the 1860s.

WHY DID THE INDUSTRIAL REVOLUTION BEGIN IN GREAT BRITAIN?

The revolutionary changes wrought in English industry were not only the accumulative product of practical and often public-spirited people seeking solutions to practical problems. They also were a response to the climate of freedom—political, economic, and social—that prevailed in England relative to that which was characteristic of eighteenth-century absolutist France, Prussia, and the petty kingdoms and principalities of Germany. In addition, England was favored in possessing valuable resources—such as coal, iron ore, tin, copper, stone, and salt—that were necessary for the early development of the metallurgical and other industries. Many of these resources were located in close proximity, their movement facilitated by a network of small but navigable rivers. English agriculture, too, had been greatly altered so that an increase in the output of foodstuffs was accompanied by the freeing of a significant portion of the population for work in the factories. Finally, the kingdom had, at home and abroad, a growing market for its wares. Its merchant ma-

rine was the largest in the world, and English traders handled much of the world's commerce.

What happened in England between 1760 and 1860 subsequently was repeated, but compressed into a shorter time span, in western Europe during the first half of the nineteenth century, in Germany and northern Italy well into the second half of the century, and in Russia in the latter decades of the century. The technological advances began to reach the United States (New England) about the beginning of the nineteenth century, but they were introduced into Japan only toward the end of the century after the political and social reforms of the Meiji Restoration. During the twentieth century, developments associated with the Industrial Revolution have spread to other parts of the globe. After World War II and colonial liberation, many of the world's new countries have seized on industrialization as a necessary component of their regional development and modernization.

Industrialization not only resulted in new ways of living and working, it also was an uprooting and rearranging of population. Mass migrations of people were required. They had to move to the new factories where energy was available to drive the new machines. Such migrations led to the expansion of some old cities and the emergence of many new ones. Major changes in ways of living were imposed on people who had hitherto lived in villages or small settlements.

By 1851—for the first time anywhere on the globe—the number of people in England living in urban agglomerations and engaged in activities that were nonrural exceeded those classified as rural. Although only a small fraction of the total British population had been drawn to the large cities (those of more than one hundred thousand inhabitants), a major turning point in the urbanization of the landscape had been reached (Box 17–1). Rapid urban growth became a significant motif of nineteenth-century life, and it has continued to be so in the twentieth century.

BOX 17–1

The British Sense of Pride

The achievements of the first half of the nineteenth century aroused a great sense of pride in Victorian England, which was expressed rather effusively at mid-century by the then-popular poet, Martin Tupper (1810–1889) (Briggs, 1968):

These twenty years—how full of gain to us,
To common humble multitudinous Man;
How swiftly Providence advances thus
Our flag of progress flaming in the van!

This double decade of the world's short span
Is richer than two centuries of old:
Richer in helps, advantages, and pleasures,
In all things richer—even down to gold—
To all of every class in liberal measures.

The Great Exhibition of the Works of Industry of all Nations that opened in London in the spring of 1851, although designed as an international show, was also an expression of British pride: its

Figure 17–1

The Crystal Palace, because of its size and the fact that it was constructed of glass, was a remarkable structure for its time. It was 1848-feet long, 408-feet wide, and 66-feet high. The walls and roof, consisting of about 1 million feet^2 of glass, were supported by 2300 cast-iron girders and 3300 hundred pillars. So ingenious was the construction of the "wonderhouse" that it contained some of the finest elms growing in Hyde Park.

Source: Mary Evans Picture Library/Photo Researchers, Inc.

Box 17-1 (continued)

prime purpose was to show the extent of British technological and industrial accomplishments over the previous quarter century. The focus of the exhibition was the Crystal Palace, a giant exhibition hall (Fig. 17-1). The palace was truly the symbol of the age, in much the same way the Eiffel Tower (erected at a cost of more than $1 million dollars for the Paris International Exposition in 1889) came to commemorate France's achievements in the latter quarter of the century.

In opening the exhibition—to the preparation of which he had given tirelessly of his energies—Prince Albert, the consort of Queen Victoria, declaimed:

So man is approaching a more complete fulfillment of that great and sacred mission which he has to perform in this world. His reason being created after the image of God, he has to use it to discover the laws by which the Almighty governs His creation, and, by making these laws his standard of action, to conquer nature to his use; himself a divine instrument.

Never before had the future seemed so full of promise nor had Britannia seemed more satisfied with her accomplishments.

(*Source*: Quote from *Principal Speeches and Addresses of H. R. H. the Prince Consort* (London: 1862), pp. 110–112.)

THE EMERGENCE OF THE FACTORY

The Industrial Revolution was rooted in the English countryside, a fact that is often overlooked. It grew up in part out of the *cottage industry,* then prevalent throughout much of Europe (Fig. 17-2). In this system of enterprise (also known as the *putting-out system*), an entrepreneur provided the raw materials to the cottager who, working largely by hand, returned a finished product or a segment of a finished product. Such cottage industries helped spread skills among the rural population without the need of grouping workers together in one structure.

Within this context emerged a group of craftspersons—watchmakers, toolmakers, clothiers, potters, millwrights, gunsmiths, silversmiths, and the like—who designed inventions for everyday use, which served to increase their own output as well as the output of the villagers who worked for them. As population increased during the eighteenth century, there came a growth, however small at first, of market. Further improvements in technique were necessary to meet the demand created by this increasing market, and the imaginations of these practical entrepreneurs rose to meet this challenge.

One of the first stages in the emergence of factories was the use of water power to replace hand labor or animal power. This was especially appropriate in the textile industry (Fig. 17-3). Mills could utilize falling water for energy, so, they were often located in remote river valleys. The first large mills in the English textile industry spread through Yorkshire where mill sites were available in the valleys that drained the eastern flank of the Pennine Mountains.

The application of steam power to the factory, however, was the stage that proved revolutionary. The first steam engine was not invented by James Watt (1736–1819), a Scottish engineer, but his modifications and improvements were of such magnitude that he might rightfully be dubbed the "father of the factory system" (Fig. 17-4). In 1765, the Soho factory near Birmingham in the Midlands began production of steam engines, using Watt's technology. Steam power transformed the textile industry, but mechanization was not really complete until the 1830s and 1840s (Box 17-2).

During the same period, new developments led to an expansion of coal mining and the production of metals. Early in the eighteenth century (1709), Abraham Derby (1678–1717) began

Figure 17–2

From the earliest recorded times, craftspersons had worked individually or in small groups. By the High Middle Ages, these artisans could be found in cottages or small shops. Human energy drove whatever devices were used in the manufacture of household items and clothing. For heavier tasks, animals were sometimes harnessed, but the preference was for human labor because of its greater reliability.

Source: Mary Evans Picture Library/Photo Researchers, Inc.

Figure 17–3

The water mill, with its wheel turned by running water, is a device that has been known since earliest times. In ancient Greece, the water mill was used for grinding grain. Somewhat later, it was modified and used in China to operate bellows in making iron. The earliest known European water mill dates to Roman times, but its diffusion throughout the Continent was slow. From the eighth to the eleventh centuries A.D., it became increasingly specialized.

In the settlement of North America, all mills for grinding grain, lumber mills, and subsequently early textile factories made use of the waterwheel as a principal energy source.

Source: Mary Evans Picture Library/Photo Researchers, Inc.

Figure 17–4

The use of a jet of steam to power simple machines was an idea that was understood quite early, but attempts through the seventeenth century to harness steam failed to yield success. Then, about 1712, steam-powered engines were installed in collieries, or coal mines, in western England, and their use spread rapidly (A).

James Watt (B) began to make significant improve-ments in the existing technology in the 1760s, which he patented in 1769. However, it was not until he developed the rotary steam engine in 1781 that steam power came into general use for driving machinery in manufac-turing.

Source: (A) Mary Evans Picture Library, Photo Researchers, Inc; (B) Culver Pictures, Inc.

smelting iron ore with coke instead of charcoal. The Derby ironworks at Coalbrookdale in Shropshire, northwest of Birmingham, became one of the earliest centers of the new iron age. Gradually the demand for coal grew. The first coal-mining shafts had been sunk in 1700, but the presence of groundwater limited their depth. Thomas Newcomen (1663–1729) invented a steam-driven pump in 1705 to draw off the water, and as improvements were made, the mines tapped deeper layers of coal.

From 1760 on, the practice of smelting iron through the use of coke spread rapidly. However, impurities in pig iron remained until

Henry Cort (1740–1800) devised a method known as puddling (or rolling) to eliminate them. Thereafter, coke-produced iron became the basis of English metallurgy. From 1770 to 1800, the output of iron increased from 50,000 to 130,000 tons, while that of coal grew from 6 to 12 million tons. About the same time, near Sheffield, a process for producing crucible, or cast, steel was devised. The new technology yielded a more durable and uniform metal than any attempted before. Finally, the use of the Watt steam engine at the ironworks to fire the blast led to rapid increases in production.

Steam power and the new inventions inevita-

BOX 17–2

Innovation and Diffusion in the English Textile Industry

The earliest textile industries of England—producing wool and linen goods, and subsequently silk and cotton—were cottage industries. Cotton textiles were made in Lancashire as early as 1601, although the cotton thread was not strong, and for that reason, it was usually blended with linen.

The first significant innovation in the industry came with the development of the "flying shuttle," which John Kay (1704–1764) invented and patented in 1733. The shuttle saved labor and increased the output of the weaver, but handweavers were hostile to the new device.

In the 1760s, James Hargreaves (1720?–1778), a weaver, devised a frame that contained several spindles, substantially increasing the output of the spinner. Hargreaves's hand-operated spinning jenny was also seen as a threat by cottage workers. In 1768, at Nottingham, Richard Arkwright (1732–1792) went a step further and invented a frame that was worked by horses. Then, in 1769, Arkwright devised a water-powered spinning frame, which he installed in a mill (1771) employing almost 600 workers. The advantage of Arkwright's frame was that it produced strong cotton yarn, and with this innovation, the English cotton industry could be said to have truly begun.

Difficulties, however, remained; there were defects in the operation of the jenny. In 1779, Samuel Crompton (1753–1827) produced a hybrid, the spinning mule, which combined the best features of Hargreaves's jenny and Arkwright's frame (Fig. 17–5). This invention made possible manufacture of fine yarn or muslin. The term mus-

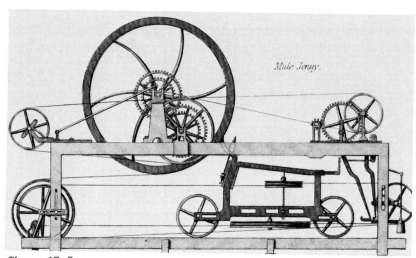

Figure 17–5

The speed with which invention followed invention in the British textile industry in the eighteenth and early nineteenth centuries was phenomenal. Between 1733 and 1779, technology advanced from a simple hand-driven-roller spinning machine to the spinning jenny, through the water-powered spinning frame, to Crompton's more elaborate mule, which could be operated by steam.

Source: Mary Evans Picture Library, Photo Researchers, Inc.

Box 17-2 *(continued)*

lin is derived from the city of Mosul on the Tigris River in Mesopotamia where the cloth is thought to have been originally made.

These advances in the spinning of thread required comparable advances in weaving. Necessity was, indeed, the mother of invention. In 1785, Edmund Cartwright (1743–1823) patented a power loom. In 1789, he adapted the machine to steam power. Still, the awkwardness of the machinery together with opposition from the handweavers delayed its diffusion. Not until the 1830s did power weaving in factories supplant manual labor in cottages. By 1835, there were some 114,000 power looms in operation in Britain, of which 17,531 were in the Scottish Lowlands.

Spinning, too, had continued its march toward mechanization, and by 1812, it was essentially a factory industry, employing no less than seventy thousand people. Lancashire, on the west side of the Pennines, remained the seat of the cotton textile industry.

The year 1836 marks the real beginning of factory production of linen, with Leeds the headquarters of the flax-spinning industry. The woolen industry was a widely scattered cottage industry, but in the nineteenth century, it came to be concentrated in parts of Lancashire and the adjacent West Riding of Yorkshire. Tweed became a specialty cloth of Scotland, whereas North Wales produced flannel. The production of silk had also been widely scattered, but with the development of water power, it had been one of the first to be concentrated in mills.

No summary of innovation in the textile industry would be complete without reference to the development of a machine that had enormous consequences for the English cotton textile industry (and the course of U.S. history). This was the invention of the cotton gin by Eli Whitney (1765–1825) of New England. The gin facilitated the separation of tight-clinging green seeds from the short-staple cotton then grown in the South. As a result of this innovation, the export of raw cotton from the United States to English mills increased rapidly, contributing to the phenomenal growth of English textile towns in the first half of the nineteenth century. By 1800, export of cotton had jumped to 2 million pounds per year. The industry was revolutionized and the demand for slaves on southern plantations grew in response to the rapid development of the British market for cotton.

---

bly meant geographic concentration—of energy, of machinery, of capital, and above all of labor. In the premachine period when industry was confined to the cottage, it grew up where the villagers lived. With the increasing reliance on steam power, industry began to concentrate in factories near the coalfields or near other raw materials that were essential to an enterprise. Hence, by the end of the eighteenth century, there emerged a distinct pattern of regional specialization in specific manufactures (Fig. 17–6). The growth of concentration was also accompanied by specialization within branches of each industry. In any case, the factory or mill had arrived, its machines were operated increasingly by inanimate labor, and this new manufac-turing complex became the focus of new cities, transforming many of the old settlements as well.

TRANSPORTATION

In England, the banks of navigable waterways afforded ideal sites for the location of factories. Not only could the water be tapped as an energy source before the coming of the railroad in the 1830s, but also the waterways made possible the movement of raw materials through the heart of England. Where natural watercourses were lacking, entrepreneurs had canals built. In

Figure 17-6

The development of steam power radically transformed the English landscape. From a pattern of scattered settlement in small towns and villages, the countryside—particularly astride the Pennine range in central England, or the Midlands—became marked by concentrations of people. As industrialization advanced, it was always accompanied by substantial urbanization.

Source: Mary Evans Picture Library/Photo Researchers, Inc.

1760, a canal was built by James Brindley (1716–1772) for Francis Egerton, the third duke of Bridgewater, to connect the rivers Trent and Mersey. The duke wanted a link between his collieries at Worsley and the mills at Manchester. By 1767, there was also a canal between Manchester and the growing seaport of Liverpool. At the turn of the century, all the large industrial centers in central England and the Midlands were connected by canals. London, too, was joined to the coalfields by the Grand Junction Canal. In 1830, there were some twenty-five hundred miles of canal throughout England, which added to the rivers totaled five thousand miles of navigable waters (Fig. 17–7). Aqueducts to carry barges over rivers were in-

genious solutions to problems of canal engineering, as were tunnels through hills (Fig. 17–8).

The iron and stone bridges that began to span the broader rivers, joining new hard-surfaced, or macadamized (after John L. Macadam, 1756–1836), roads, improved overland transportation routes. However, nonmaritime transportation—and the Industrial Revolution—entered a significant new phase with the application of steam to railway locomotion. The first public railway, the Stockton-Darlington line, opened in 1825, but its passenger coaches were initially drawn by horses. In 1829, George Stephenson (1781–1848), a self-made engineer, demonstrated successfully the principle of

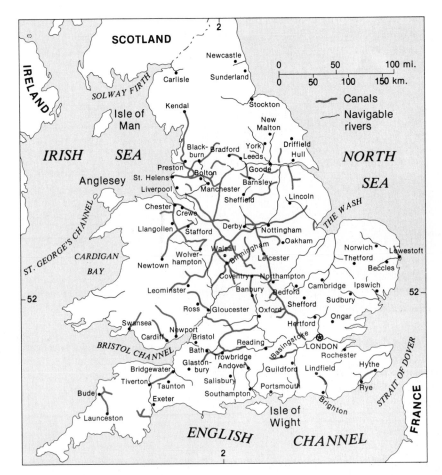

Figure 17–7

The improvements in navigation on the numerous small rivers that drain England and their linkage by canal by the early nineteenth century afforded the industrial areas access to needed raw materials, frequently located only short distances away. The development of this water transportation network facilitated England's march toward industrialization.

steam locomotion when his locomotive the *Rocket* ran between Liverpool and Manchester at speeds ranging up to 16 miles per hour. The Liverpool-Manchester line was officially opened in 1830, an event that marked the real beginning of the railway age in England. By 1838, Great Britain had 500 miles of track, which reached 6,500 miles by 1850 and over 15,000 by 1870 (Fig. 17–9).

OF TIME AND SPACE

To accommodate and adapt to the kind of changes that industrialization brought to the landscape and to the work habits of an industrialized people, there had to emerge not only a new concept of work but also a new sense of purpose, of direction, and of priorities. The ma-

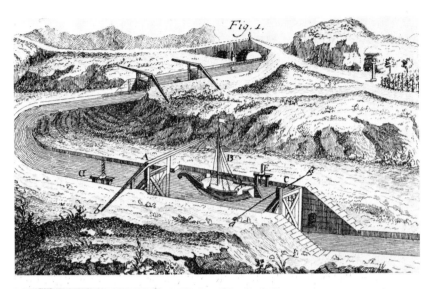

Figure 17–8

The engineering of canals and locks, as shown in these sketches, was widely known throughout Europe. These diagrams are of interest because they appear in a French work first published between 1779 and 1781. The author, Denis Diderot (1713–1784), was probably the best known of the French *philosophes,* a group of French writers and thinkers who sought rational under-

standing of their world. Diderot toiled over an encyclopedia for more than 20 years, a work that culminated in some 35 volumes, and included many plates and tables.

(*Source: Recueil de Planches,* Vol. 1 (1779), Vol. 3 (1781), to accompany *Dictionnaire Raisonné. Courtesy Rare Book Collection, University of Washington Libraries.*)

terialization of this new milieu required, above all, new concepts of time and space (Hall, 1977).

Industrial civilization probably could not

have developed without the notion of *monochronic (M-) time*. M-time is *linear time*. It represents one method of using both time and space as organizing frameworks for human ac-

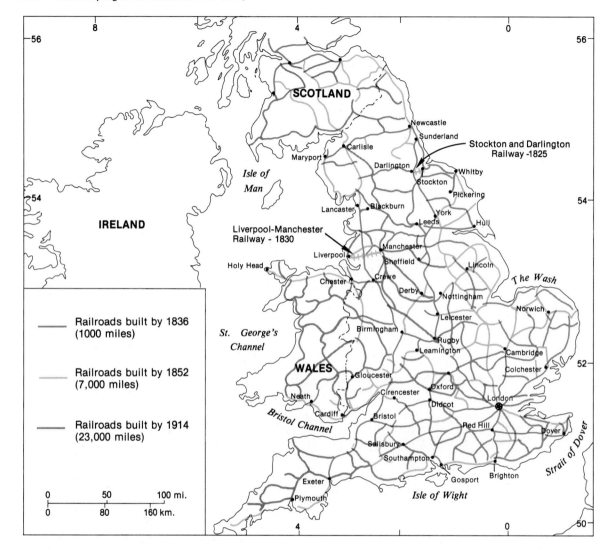

Figure 17–9
Together with the use of steam as an energy source, the construction of the early nineteenth-century railroad network in England was perhaps the most significant phenomenon in remaking the historic landscape. The railroad could penetrate regions that were without navi- gable waterways or canals. Its role in overcoming the problems of distance facilitated the industrialization not only of England, but also continental Europe, Russia, the United States, and Japan.

tivities. It emphasizes schedules, periodization or compartmentalization, and, above all, promptness. It requires and imposes selectivity. People who operate on M-time recognize how important time is. They know that only a limited number of things can be done within a given period of time. They are aware, too, that M-time intensifies personal relationships with a limited number of people, thus sealing them off from others. Adherence to M-time limits, restricts, and enslaves. Priorities and specialization are attributes of linear time.

Organized time, in turn, requires that space be organized. If workers arrive on time, their work space must be prepared for them. Machines must be placed in the sequence where the most efficient use can be made of them. Hence, as industrialization proceeded into the twentieth century, the handling of space came to be a matter of overriding concern. The assembly line, which Henry Ford (1863–1947) introduced into the automobile industry and which was one of the major contributions of the United States to a later stage of industrialization, truly symbolized the highest pursuit of organized time and space.

The adoption of M-time is a learned experience; it is not inherent in the nature of humankind. One of the predicaments of the modern city is undoubtedly the way in which M-time works to cut off people from more varied experiences because they have become slaves to time. As Thomas Carlyle (1795–1881), the Scottish writer, observed of London in 1831, "How men are hurried here; how they are hunted and terrifically chased into double-quick speed; so that in self-defence they *must not* stay to look at one another!" (cited in Williams, 1973, p. 215).

Polychronic (or P-) time is the opposite of M-time. P-time is nonlinear and, therefore, unregulated. Time remains the servant, not the master, of mankind. To groups that adhere to the concept of P-time, human involvement and numerous ongoing transactions—not scheduled and not restricted—are the general rule. Modern Americans are generally uncomfortable when thrust into a culture group that functions on P-time. On the other hand, they often fail to comprehend the anxiety that groups accustomed to P-time have endured in a society dominated by M-time. The Amerindian, for example, has had difficulty adjusting to Anglo-American time and work schedules and for that reason has been accused of being lazy.

The development of the concept of M-time, in northwestern Europe and Anglo-America in particular, was consistent with the belief in progress that arose in the sixteenth century. This belief had its roots in the Judaeo-Christian heritage, and its early focus—at least for the Christian—was salvation. With the Renaissance, that focus began to shift and the notion of progress came to be associated with belief in an irreversible movement forward toward something better on earth. By the seventeenth and eighteenth centuries, reason was seen as the key to this progress. As knowledge grew and technology opened new horizons, progress also came to be associated with material improvement. For the new class of entrepreneurs, whether in Europe or America, material improvement meant capital investment, reliance on the self-regulating forces of the marketplace, freedom from government interference, and individual self-assertiveness.

Geographers have long shown an interest in the question of spatial organization, and there has also been growing interest in the organization of time. One of the most useful studies in this direction is that by Edward L. Ullman (1974). In his study, Ullman concluded that space and time had literally become one and the same thing. "Space," he wrote, "is subsumed under movement, and time under change. Empty or static space or time has no meaning" (p. 136). Because of this development, he saw two implications for the geographer: (1) space can often be substituted for time, or vice versa; (2) modern geography would come to emphasize "a space with movement and change or, in summary, process, which implies change with a forward-moving, developing action from beginning to completion. Process . . . for geography, is more a time than a spatial concept." Ullman argued that by focusing on change and movement, the geographer derives "new significance from time and space; by noting the degree of interrelationship, similarity, and substitution between the two, we stretch space and time into fruitful new, overlapping zones. This should aid us in understanding man and in making better adjustments to changing technology and environments'' (p. 136).

THE GROWTH OF THE FACTORY TOWN

The growth of the factory town was accompanied by a very substantial migration of the British population. During the first half of the eighteenth century, over 60 percent of the population in England was concentrated in the south—in the region stretching from the port of Bristol in the west to London in the east. Beginning with the latter half of the century, population shifts began to take place toward the coalfields, the source of energy in the new machine age. Englishmen from the southern counties poured into the growing ironworks of South Wales. Still others moved to the textile mills of Lancashire and the mines and mills of Yorkshire and the Midlands. Welshmen from the counties of North Wales crossed into England to form a permanent segment of workers in the industrial complex of the Merseyside-Manchester region. Scotsmen abandoned their crafts in the Highlands for the mills and ironworks of Glasgow and the Clydeside, and the Irish crossed the Irish Sea to settle in Wales, parts of Scotland, and Merseyside. The major attractions, however, were the rapidly expanding industries astride the Pennine Mountains. As a result, the center of gravity, apart from London itself, moved toward the central counties of England (Fig. 7–10).

In the United Kingdom in 1800, only London and Dublin had more than one hundred thousand inhabitants (Table 17–1). Five cities ranged upward of fifty thousand inhabitants, the largest being Manchester (including Salford) with over ninety thousand. By 1831, Glasgow, Manchester, Liverpool, Birmingham, and Leeds also had passed the one-hundred-thousand mark. Edinburgh, together with Leith, Scotland's principal port on the North Sea coast and a growing fishing center, had climbed to over one hundred fifty thousand inhabitants. The rapid urbanization continued; by 1850, several cities were well over three hundred thousand in size. Some cities expanded as much as 40 percent in a decade alone. Between mid-century and 1890, the urban population of England

Table 17–1

The Growth of the Major British Cities (1800–1890) (in thousands)

	1800	1831	1850	1890
London	958.8	1400.0	2362.1	4211.7
Manchester (with Salford)	90.4	182.8	388.5	703.5
Glasgow	77.1	202.4	329.1	658.2
Liverpool	82.3	165.7	376.0	518.0
Birmingham	70.7	146.9	232.8	478.1
Bristol	61.0	—	137.0	239.0
Leeds	53.2	123.4	172.3	367.5
Sheffield	45.8	—	135.3	324.2
Edinburgh (with Leith)	81.4	162.4	191.2	329.9
Dublin	165.0	—	272.0	245.0

Source: Adna Ferrin Weber, *The Growth of Cities in the Nineteenth Century. A Study in Statistics.* (Columbia University Studies in History, Economics and Public Law, Vol. 11) (Ithaca, N.Y.: Cornell University Press, 1969), p. 450. [Originally published, 1899]. Data for 1831 from G. P. Jones and A. G. Pool, *A Hundred Years of Economic Development in Great Britain* (London: Duckworth, 1940), pp. 18–19.

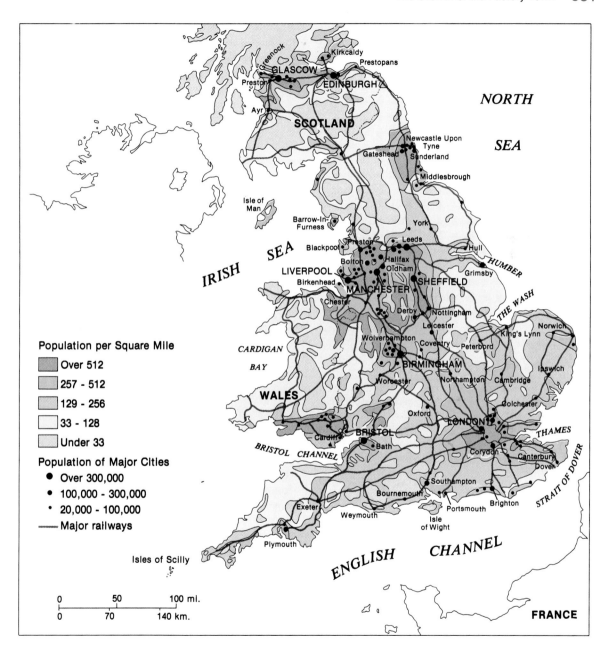

Figure 17–10

Industrialization, first evident in England, has been accompanied by massive transfers of population. In England, during the eighteenth century, the population was predominantly rural and agrarian, the one metropolis was London. During the last two decades of the century as industrial development began to make great strides, the entire geographic basis of the population changed. Migration was toward the new towns and industry, the population growth in the countryside provided the surplus for the factories. By the middle of the nineteenth century, the pattern of population distribution, as evident today, had taken shape.

and Wales (those living in cities of one hundred thousand or more), grew from about 17 or 18 percent to over 31 percent. At the latter date, Glasgow contained almost 20 percent of the population of Scotland.

London, of course, was the political center of the kingdom and the financial hub of a vast industrial empire that was not only spreading over Britain, but also reaching out to Europe, the Americas, and the British Empire as a whole. From less than 1 million inhabitants in 1800, it mushroomed to well over 4 million by the end of the century.

A similar pattern of growth occurred in the smaller industrial and port cities, that is, those with populations over twenty thousand. In 1811, there were 19 such cities, of which 8 were ports, 8 produced textiles, 2 had metal works, and 1 (Bath) was a resort and fashion center. By 1831, the number of cities in this category reached 49 and expanded considerably thereafter. Overall, during the nineteenth century, the urban population of Great Britain increased from about 27 percent to over 60 percent.

BOX 17-3

"Coketown"

Charles Dickens (1812–1870) was especially sensitive to the social problems of the time. In his novel *Hard Times,* written in 1854, he describes the appearance of a Lancashire industrial city:

> It was a town of red brick, or of brick that would have been red if the smoke and ashes had allowed it; but as matters stood it was a town of unnatural red and black like the painted face of a savage. It was a town of machinery and tall chimneys, out of which interminable serpents of smoke trailed themselves forever and ever and never got uncoiled. It had a black canal in it, and a river that ran purple with ill-smelling dye, and vast piles of buildings full of windows where there was a rattling and a trembling all day long, and where the piston of the steam-engine worked monotonously up and down, like the head of an elephant in a state of melancholy madness. It contained several large streets still more like one another, inhabited by people equally like one another, who all went in and out at the same hours, with the same sound upon the same pavements, to do the same work, and to whom every day was the same as yesterday and tomorrow, and every year the counterpart of the last and the next.

Source: Complete Works of Charles Dickens. Vol. 5, *Hard Times* (New York: Fred DuFau & Co., 1904), pp. 238–239.

British Industrial Cityscape

The Industrial Revolution gave rise to a whole new dimension of environmental and social problems (Box 17–3). The application of water power to manufacturing, in itself, created few serious adjustments. When, however, the mill owners converted to steam, the face of the countryside and of society began to change. As early as 1775, the English agriculturalist Arthur Young (1741–1820) noted the destruction of the natural beauty of the landscape and what the industrialists were doing to it. The reliance on coal to generate steam or simply to provide heat had almost immediate and visible consequences. Industries associated with coal mining, factories producing dyes and chemicals, and glassworks yielded wastes in great quantities that soon piled up. A red glow and a pall of smoke hung over the factories as the air became poisoned and workers' cottages blackened with soot. Streams that once ran fresh became clogged and polluted in a "flood of liquid manure."

The industrial city was, by the very nature of its origins and development, bound to be a place of staggering problems. Low-cost worker housing grew up around the factories. Because the land was often low lying, the streets were frequently mired in mud. This condition gave rise about 1820 to the use of the word *slum,* which was derived from *slump,* meaning a wet mire. Because these worker districts were often wet mires, the term was increasingly associated with lower-class or working-class neighborhoods. Today, slum is applied to any area where housing is substandard and where the inhabitants suffer unemployment, low incomes, and poverty.

The rapid in-migration to the factory towns and cities led to overcrowding and filth, especially where dwellings were strung out in rows, back to back. Rents for rooms in these structures took a high proportion of working-class income. Moreover, the most elemental rules of sanitation were forgotten, and water supplies were both inadequate and often unsafe for human consumption.

One of the most depressing urban slums grew up in Nottingham, a town that, until the Industrial Revolution, was described as one of the most beautiful in England. A report dated in 1845 gives some idea of the extent of the squalor (Hoskins, 1970, 280–281):

> Nowhere else shall we find so large a mass of inhabitants crowded into courts, alleys, and lanes as in Nottingham, and those, too, of the worst possible construction. Here they are so clustered upon each other; court within court, yard within yard, and lane within lane, in a manner to defy description. . . . Some parts of Nottingham [are] so very bad as hardly to be surpassed in misery by anything to be found within the entire range of our manufacturing cities.

Not only were workers subjected generally to living and working conditions that were insensate, but also they suffered the fears and loneliness uprooted peoples experience everywhere. The psychologic impact of the Industrial Revolution created problems that the age was either indifferent to, or unable to, resolve (Klingender, 1972).

The concentration of workers near the mills and factories at the core of an urban area reached its peak about mid-century; thereafter, it began to decline. However, the central wards of English cities remained densely occupied

even up to 1885. As housing was torn down, additional factories, warehouses, banks, and office buildings replaced workers' dwellings in the city center, and the workers began pressing outward into areas formerly occupied by the well-to-do and the new middle class, who, in turn, abandoned their neighborhoods in a race toward the suburbs. The very affluent moved to the hills overlooking the industrial valleys or gave up the city altogether. But so rapid was industrial expansion in the latter half of the century as the railway network tightened that suburban villages were soon engulfed by the city. Fields and parish lands were swallowed up, much as in America in recent years the freeway and new shopping plazas have eaten up the countryside.

EPILOGUE

The Industrial Revolution that began in England in the latter half of the eighteenth century was a major force making for landscape change. By promoting the concentration of workers in factories, energized by the steam engine and other forms of machinery, new towns and cities came into existence, and many of the traditional centers of urban activity were greatly altered. At the same time, older rural settlements declined as people migrated to the cities and towns.

The model of development is England's, but it was repeated with only local variation throughout Europe from France to Russia, in Japan, and in the United States. It is a model that is being repeated in many developing countries of the world today, although government initiative may replace individual entrepreneurship in industrial location and expansion. New urban settlements, urban sprawl, and shantytowns are a common enough feature of Third World landscapes. One wonders to what extent local cultures will be altered to reflect the new norms of the industrial age.

APPLICATION OF IDEAS

1. The Industrial Revolution was a major turning point in human history and *Frankenstein,* the novel written by Mary Shelley, hinted at this.

2. The new source of energy, concentrated in the steam engine, made possible the factory system whereby large numbers of people could be employed. The factory system was to spell the end of cottage industry.

3. The use of coal as a source of fuel led to the emergence of modern metallurgical and associated industries. Such industries needed workers, and they were drawn from the countryside. In England in the late eighteenth and early nineteenth centuries, this rural-urban migration resulted in a major shift in population from the south to the Midlands where the coalfields were located.

4. The Industrial Revolution brought a new and dazzling prosperity to England as a whole, although the conditions under which the factory workers toiled left much to be desired. England prospered because of its political stability, its resource base, the ingenuity of its people, and its foreign markets built around a worldwide empire.

5. In time, the Industrial Revolution spread to the Continent and from there to other parts of the world. Its acceptance required, however, new concepts of time and space.

KEY WORDS AND PHRASES

cottage industry
industrial landscape
linear time
monochronic time
  (M-time)
polychronic time

(P-time)
Promethean myth
putting-out system
slum
slump

QUESTIONS FOR FURTHER DISCUSSION

1. In what way is the Promethean myth applicable to the events that took place in the early period of the Industrial Revolution?

2. What were the association of factors that enabled England to take the lead in industrialization at the end of the eighteenth century? What conditions prevailed on the continent of Europe that retarded development in Belgium? In France? In Germany? In Italy? In Russia?

3. What were the implications of industrialization on the distribution of the population of England? Why did the rearrangement take the pattern it did?

4. It is often suggested that cities are centers of change, and yet the Industrial Revolution began in the countryside. How do you account for this phenomenon?

5. What were some of the basic differences between cottage industry and factory production? What was so essential to factory production that it led to concentrations of people in one place as opposed to workers scattered through the villages?

6. In what way was the rapid development of technology in the British textile industry linked to the expansion of slavery in the United States? Suggest other examples of similar interrelationships within the community of nations today.

7. Why was a revolution in transportation necessary to ensure the success of industrial growth? What is implied in the statement that the railroad helped overcome the "friction of space"?

8. What advantages did the railroad offer that the network of English canals could not? Was this equally true of Europe? Of the United States?

9. Although you may have grown up in a

society where M-time is widely accepted, identify some cultures that tend to operate on P-time. How is this phenomenon demonstrated? How would you react to living in such a society?

10. Identify some of the tangible consequences of an acceptance of M-time. Is there a relationship between the assembly line mode of production as developed by Henry Ford and the acceptance of M-time?

REFERENCES AND ADDITIONAL READINGS

Ashworth, William. *A Short History of the International Economy 1850–1950*. London: Longmans, Green, 1952.

Briggs, Asa. *Victorian Cities*. Harmondsworth, Eng.: Penguin Books, 1968.

Freeman, T. W. "Boroughs in England and Wales of the 1830s," pp. 70–91. In *Urbanization and Its Problems*. R. P. Beckinsale and J. M. Houston, eds. Oxford: Basil Blackwell, 1968.

Geddes, Patrick. *Cities in Evolution*. New York: Oxford University Press, 1950.

Gerard, L. "Transport," pp. 212–273. In *The Cambridge Economic History of Europe,* Vol. 6, Pt. 1. H. J. Habakkuk and M. Postan, eds. Cambridge, Cambridge University Press, 1965.

Gregory, Derek. *Regional Transformation and Industrial Revolution*. London: Macmillan, 1982.

Hall, Edward T. *Beyond Culture*. Garden City, N.Y.: Doubleday, 1977. (Anchor Books)

Hoskins, W. G. *The Making of the English Landscape*. Harmondsworth, Eng.: Penguin Books, 1970.

Jones, G. P. and Pool, A. G. *A Hundred Years of Economic Development in Great Britain*. London: Duckworth, 1940.

Klingender, Frances D. *Art and the Industrial Revolution*. London: Paladin, 1972.

Lynch, Kevin. *What Time Is This Place?* Cambridge, Mass.: MIT Press, 1972.

Shelley, Mary. *Frankenstein, or the Modern Prometheus*. New York: New American Library, 1965. (originally published, 1818)

Turnock, David. *Railways in the British Isles*. London: Adam & Charles Black, 1982.

Ullman, Edward L. "Space and/or Time: Opportunity for Substitution and Prediction." *Transactions of the Institute of British Geographers* 63 (1974): 125–139.

Weber, Adna Ferrin. *The Growth of Cities in the Nineteenth Century. A Study in Statistics* (Columbia University Studies in History, Economics and Public Law, Vol. 11). Ithaca, N.Y.: Cornell University Press, 1969. (Originally published, 1899)

Williams, Raymond. *The Country and the City*. New York: Oxford University Press, 1973.

Wolf, Leonard. *The Annotated Frankenstein*. New York: Clarkson N. Potter, 1977.

18

Diffusion of Industrialization and the Remaking of the Landscape

By changing what he knows about the world, man changes the world he knows, and by changing the world in which he lives, man changes himself.

Theodosius Dobzhansky,
Mankind Evolving, 1962

Key Ideas

1. Great Britain had a lead of from 50 to a 100 years over Western Europe in industrialization. There were many factors that delayed the diffusion of the new technology to the Continent.

2. Belgium was the first country on the continent to begin industrialization followed by France.

3. German industrialization came after unification in 1870-1871, and it was not until 1880 that Russia took its first successful step toward creating a base for the manufacture of iron and steel in the Donets basin.

4. Japanese industrialization had to wait on the reforms instituted after 1868 with the Meiji Restoration, but the Japanese government took steps to encourage private initiative.

5. It was English capital and inventiveness that helped inaugurate the Industrial Revolution in the United States. Development came mainly after 1790 with the building of the first textile mills in New England; by the 1830s, factory production had taken over the textile industry.

6. The U.S. seaboard cities, oriented toward trade, were not unlike the commercial cities of Europe. But, the ending of the Civil War (1861–1865) brought many changes.

7. Facilitating the rapid development of industrialization was a dynamic expansion in transportation facilities, which by the end of the Civil War included a program of railroad building that spanned the American continent.

8. As the industrial city in the United States took shape, crowding together led to the construction of mass housing units called tenements.

9. Technical progress, mobility, and urban opportunity led to the rise of large cities and metropolitan areas.

10. The technological revolution, summed up in the phrase high-tech industries, now promises to alter the traditional base of manufacturing in the United States, as it has done in Japan and, to a lesser degree, in Western Europe.

THE DIFFUSION OF THE INDUSTRIAL REVOLUTION

The Industrial Revolution in Britain had entailed small-scale entrepreneurs or manufacturers, their capital primarily based on their own or family wealth. From those early beginnings, however, Britain had come, throughout the first decades of the nineteenth century, to produce more than half the world's industrial output. The achievement of this economic preeminence was accompanied, as we have seen, by significant landscape changes. Above all, mining and metallurgical industries, the geographic core of the revolution, had created a "black country" where serious environmental problems had become evident. The wedding of steam power to "iron horses" had created a network of "iron roads" over which the "horses," the steam locomotives, puffed their way.

Resources and transportation were essential to industrialism, but equally important to humankind were the social consequences of the revolution. Insightful contemporaries saw this revolution as the beginning of a new world, as indeed it was; it inexorably changed the way people behaved both in time and space.

Great Britain had a lead of 50 to 100 years over the other nations of western Europe. Initially, the diffusion of the new technology to the Continent was slow, mainly because of a number of *absorbing barriers,* the least of which was the English Channel (Fig. 18–1).

A British law prohibited the export of machinery to the Continent, a law that remained in effect until 1825, long after the Napoleonic Wars had ended. In addition, there were on the Continent a number of national state barriers to the acceptance of new technology. Some of these barriers were political, others economic and social. After 1825, however, the barriers gradually came down, permitting waves of technological innovation that originated in Great Britain to hit the Continent.

First, British investment on the Continent grew from an estimated 500 million pounds sterling in 1750 to 1000.5 million in 1800, and to 6 billion by 1865. British capital and know-how helped establish factories and lay railways; in addition to that, thousands of British workers crossed the English Channel to work on the Continent (Schaefer et al., 1970).

The Bases of Industrialization

Certain geographic conditions were necessary for industrialization to take place. Following the British model, there had to be (1) an adequate supply of readily accessible resources, especially coal; (2) a transportation network that could move bulk commodities, whether by water or rail; (3) a population that was mobile and free of medieval guild and other work restrictions; and (4) political stability and government support of the new mode of production. These conditions were not readily met in Europe in 1825, and this phenomenon accounts for the pattern that the spread of industrialism took.

Belgium

Belgium was the first to follow the British lead, although that small country was not well endowed in resources. Still, there were coalfields in and to the north of the Meuse Valley and iron deposits lay nearby. Railroad construction began in 1834 only four years after the completion of the first line in England. English émigre workers together with a substantial Belgian rural-urban migration beginning about 1830 provided the labor for the new mines and factories. Thereafter, the tempo of industrialization was rapid. In 1830, Belgium produced a total of 5 million tons of coal; after 1840 it was forced to import additional coal from Britain to meet its expanding needs (Fig. 18–2). The iron ore from the Sambre-Meuse deposit served Belgian needs, but by the latter part of the century, the quality of the ore began to decline. Still, during the century, Belgian industrial output kept pace with that of Great Britain.

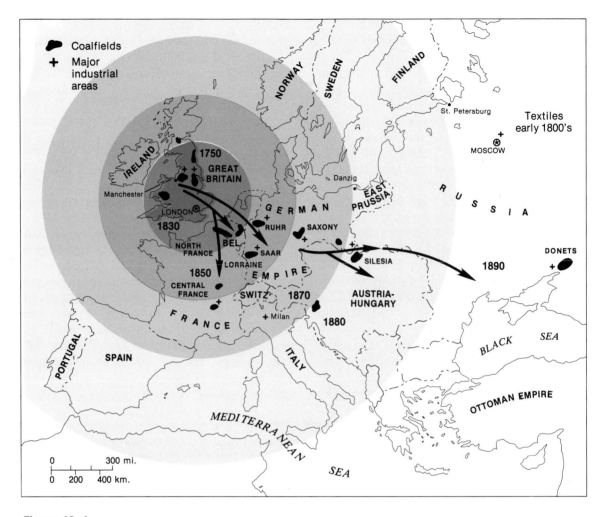

Figure 18–1

From its hearth in the English Midlands, the new technology, especially in the smelting of iron, crossed in time over to Europe. When, after the Napoleonic Wars, the barriers to the spread of the new technology were removed, the Continent began to industrialize. In the decades that followed, the factory system was carried eastward through Europe, reaching Russia in the 1880s.

France

France, in time, followed Belgium but at a considerably slower pace. Owing to the overall impact of the Napoleonic Wars (1800–1815) and the restoration of the French monarchy (1815), it was not until 1830 that the French government showed a favorable disposition toward the use of machinery in manufacturing. It was not until after 1840, however, that the textile industry moved into machine-powered factories. Most of the industrial activity was concentrated in the northeast near the Belgian border; in the east in Alsace-Lorraine, with its rich iron deposits; in Rouen; and in Paris, the capital. But continued French industrial expansion was in-

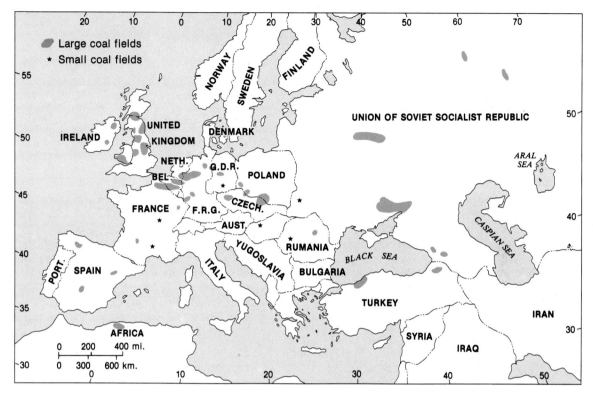

Figure 18–2

Because coal was the source of energy that fueled Europe's developing industries for over a century, the presence of extensive fields that stretched form northeastern France and Belgium diagonally across Europe to southern Russia proved an enormous advantage. Although productivity per worker in many of the European mines has declined, coal today remains an important energy source.

terrupted by the war with Prussia in 1870 and the loss of Alsace-Lorraine to the new Germany united under Prussian leadership.

In some areas of manufacturing, France's performance was outstanding. From 1890 to 1914, for example, France, moving into the new phase of the Industrial Revolution, led the world in the production of automobiles.

However, there was a potentially serious weakness in France's industrialization drive, a weakness rooted in the demographic structure. France, in 1801, was Europe's most populous state, with one sixth of the inhabitants of the Continent. However, a lowering of the birthrate—associated with many factors, including the use of birth control measures—slowed France's rate of population increase. Thus, as Germany, in particular, moved into the industrial era, after 1870 France was faced with a population that was aging coupled with a decline in the work force (Box 18–1). By 1914, France was little more than a semi-industrialized country, lagging behind other countries, such as Great Britain, Belgium and, above all, Germany its competitor and enemy.

Germany

Because of historic political fragmentation, the industrialization of Germany had to wait until its principalities and states were united under

BOX 18–1

France and Its Population Decline

For several centuries, France had been the most powerful state on the Continent. The decline in its rate of population growth, clearly evident in the latter decades of the nineteenth century, had a profound effect both on the tempo of industrialization and on the psychology of the French people. During the same decades, Germany, France's eastern neighbor, was united under Prussia's leadership to become by the turn of the century Europe's leading industrial power.

In 1861, France had a population of 37.4 million compared to Prussia with 19.1 million. By 1886, France had grown to 38.1 million, but the Prussian German state had achieved a population of some 30 million. Following the Franco-Prus-

sian War of 1870, which dealt France a humiliating defeat, the population of France fell to 36.1 million, in part through the loss of resource-rich Alsace-Lorraine to Germany. The German empire, on the other hand, had climbed to 41.1 million. During the first decade of the twentieth century, France numbered about 39.5 million, whereas Germany claimed upwards of 60.3 million.

Despite the Universal Exhibition held in Paris in 1878, which proudly displayed France's economic recovery from the war and its progress in iron and chemical industries in the northeast and in textiles around Rouen, it was becoming evident that Germany was moving to industrial and economic preeminence (Fig. 18–3).

Figure 18–3

The exhibition, which was staged with great care and public interest, drew about 13 million visitors. It was in fact an occasion for national celebration, for it was

France's testament to its recovery from the humiliation of the war with Germany.

Source: Mary Evans Picture Library/Photo Researchers, Inc.

Prussian leadership, an achievement of Prussia's chancellor, Otto von Bismarck (1815–1898). Still, decades earlier, English-made machinery had been smuggled into some of the principalities and railroad construction on a limited scale had begun. A magnificent system of waterways, which reached from the heart of Europe to the North and Baltic seas, however, was strangled by tolls. At the same time, a strong guild organization, which dated from medieval times, opposed the adoption of the factory system because of the fear that it would lead to unemployment.

Thus, the political unification of Germany in 1870 was a first essential step. The railroads were then integrated into a German network, and an industrial base, shaping up in the Ruhr Valley, a tributary of the Rhine, was broadened with the annexation of Alsace-Lorraine. A protective tariff of 1879 as part of a program of state support greatly stimulated German industrial expansion. One feature that was to mark the new era of the Industrial Revolution—evident in Germany as well as in the United States and in Japan—was the formation of industrial corporations that drew on capital reserves greatly exceeding the financing of these corporations. This had not been a characteristic of the first firms of the British revolution.

When, in the latter decades of the century, Germany industrialized, the process encapsulated two industrial revolutions—the first was shared with Great Britain, Belgium, and France and was based on iron and steel; the second witnessed the growth of electrical and chemical industries. By World War I, Germany had become an industrial giant, its output in crude steel double that of Great Britain (Table 18–1)

Table 18–1
Output of Hard Coal, Pig Iron, and Crude Steel Among Major European Industrial Powers (million metric tons)

	1830	1860	1880	1900	1910	1935	1950
Great Britain							
Hard Coal	22.8	81.3	149.3	228.8	268.7	226.5	216.3
Pig Iron	0.7	3.9	7.9	9.1	10.2	6.5	9.8
Crude Steel	—	—	1.3	5.0	6.5	10.0	16.5
Belgium							
Hard Coal	2.3	9.6	16.9	23.5	25.5	26.6	26.9
Pig Iron	—	0.3	0.6	1.0	1.8	3.0	3.7
Crude Steel	—	—	0.1	0.6	1.9	3.0	3.8
France							
Hard Coal	1.9	8.3	19.4	33.4	38.3	46.2	51.7
Pig Iron	0.3	0.9	1.7	2.7	4.0	5.8	7.8
Crude Steel	—	—	0.4	1.6	3.4	6.2	9.8
Germany[a]		(4.4)	(12.1)	(40.3)	(69.5)		
Hard Coal	1.8	12.3	47.0	109.3	152.8	143.0	185.2
Pig Iron	0.1	0.5	2.5	7.5	13.1	12.8	9.5
Crude Steel	—	—	0.7	6.5	13.1	16.4	13.5
Russia							
Hard Coal	—	0.3	3.3	16.1	24.9	103.8	252.0
Pig Iron	0.2	0.3	0.4	2.9	3.0	12.5	19.2
Crude Steel	—	—	0.3	2.2	3.3	12.6	27.3

[a] West Germany only after World War II. Data in parenthesis from 1860 to 1910 show additional output of soft coal or lignite.

Source: B. R. Mitchell, *European Historical Statistics, 1750–1970* (New York: Columbia University Press, 1975), pp. 360–365, 391–396, 399–402.

Russia

Elsewhere in Europe, industrial development was spotty and small scale—and it did not get underway until late in the nineteenth century. Russia had an iron industry in the Urals, which in 1800, produced the bulk of the world's pig iron, but it was achieved through charcoal smelting, drawing on the local forest for its energy source. The textile industry—first linen and then cotton—was largely cottage based. By the 1870s, the textile industry had begun to move into large mills, located principally near Moscow and St. Petersburg, where the market for goods was located (Portal, 1965). However, it was not until the 1880s that Russia took its first successful step toward the creation of a metallurgical base consistent with the latest technology arriving from western Europe (Shaw, 1977).

The rich coal deposits of the Donets region in southern Russia supplied the fuel to smelt the iron ores of Krivoy-Rog to the west. But railroad connection was necessary. Its completion led to the formation of a "miniature Ruhr" in the Donets basin, with its cluster of metal-working and machine-producing cities (Fig. 18–4). The Urals industry produced the iron for the construction of the Trans-Siberian Railway, but industrial modernization came only after 1928–1929.

After the Russian Revolution, the 1920s were a period of economic recovery; the regime then plunged into a program of rapid industrialization, beginning with the first Five-Year Plan in 1928. The Soviet Union is well endowed in natural resources, but distances from mine to factory are great. To overcome this *friction of space,* the Soviet government undertook a massive program of canal building and railway expansion, particularly in European Russia. In addition to expanding the Donets metallurgical base and rebuilding the Urals industry, new industrial centers were created in Siberia, notably in the Kuznetsk basin, rich in coal.

By the 1950s, the Soviet Union had recovered from the devastation of World War II and

had pushed forward to become Europe's major industrial power.

The Urbanization of Europe

Until about 1870, Paris, the Continent's largest city, had also been Europe's political and social center of gravity (Table 18–2). After 1871, though still in the forefront of European culture, Paris had lost something of its prestige. As capital of the new Germany, Berlin replaced Paris as the center of European politics, and London began to play a larger international role. Few of Europe's great cities, however, were industrial; their importance had been rooted in an earlier political era as well as in commerce. Cities, such as St. Petersburg, Russia's capital, Hamburg in Germany, and Amsterdam in the Netherlands, developed a base in manufacturing, primarily because they were great ports as well. Smaller cities, such as Breslau on the Oder River in Germany (today Wroclaw in Poland), served as the gateway to the Silesian industrial region; Milan in the Po Valley of northern Italy became that country's leading manufacturing center after the unification of Italy in 1871. On the whole, the growth of the metallurgical and chemical industries was concentrated in smaller cities located in or near the coalfields and iron-mining areas.

Japan

In the transformation of the traditional landscape of Japan into one similar to that found in any industrializing country of the era, the state played a prominent role—more nearly akin to that characteristic of Germany and tsarist Russia than that of either liberal England at an ear-

Figure 18–4
The basis of Russia's plunge into modern metallurgy was the large deposits of coal in the Donets basin, the reserves of which were estimated in 1900 to be about 15 billion tons. The output provided the energy for creation of Russia's first metallurgical region.

●	Manufacturing areas
○	Steel, iron and metalwork
■	Textiles
⬤	Food manufacturing (mainly sugar)
	Areas with greatest influx of workers from other areas
	Railroads
	The Russian Frontier 1815-1914
<u>REVAL</u>	Ports with flourishing import and export trades by 1900

WHITE SEA

North Divina

Archangel

Sukhona

Kotlas

<u>Reval</u>   Narva   *LAKE LADOGA*
<u>Pernov</u>   ST. PETERSBURG

<u>Libau</u>   <u>Riga</u>   Pskov
<u>Mitau</u>   W. Divina
Koyno   Vitebsk   Yaroslavl   Kostroma
Grodno   Volga   Volga   Perm   Ekaterinburg
Bug   MOSCOW   Kama
Bialystok   Minsk   Simbirsk   Ufa
WARSAW   Tula   Samara
Pripyat   Tambov   Penza   Orenburg
Zhitomir   Kursk   Voronezh   Saratov
KIEV   Poltova   Kharkov   Volga
Dnieper   Yekaterinoslav   Lugansk   Tsaritsyn   Ural
Krivoyo Rog   Don   Emba
Kishinev   Novocherkassk
<u>Odessa</u>   Dnestr   *SEA OF AZOV*   <u>Astrakhan</u>
<u>Nikolaev</u>   Prut
<u>Sevastopol</u>   Kerch   <u>Novorossiysk</u>   *CASPIAN SEA*

BLACK   SEA

Grozny (oil)

CAUCASUS   MTNS.

Poti
Batum

Baku (oil)

0   100   200   300 mi.
0   200   400 km.

Table 18–2

The Growth of Population of Major European Cities in the Nineteenth Century (in thousands)

	1800	1850	1890
Paris	546.9	1,053.3	2,448.0
Berlin	173.4	378.2	1,578.8
Vienna	232.0	431.1	1,341.9
St. Petersburg	180.0 (1764)	668.0(1869)	1,265.0(1897)
Constantinople	300.0–1,000.0?	c.400.0+	873.6
Moscow	271.0 (1811)	336.0(1835)	1,039.0(1897)
Hamburg (Altona)	c.120.0	205.0	711.9
Budapest	61.0	156.5	491.9
Warsaw	c.65.0	c.160.0	485.3
Madrid	156.7	281.2	470.3
Brussels	66.3	188.5	465.5
Naples	c.400.0	c.415.0	463.2
Lyons	109.5	177.2	429.3
Amsterdam	217.0 (1795)	224.0	408.1
Odessa	9.0(1802)	101.3(1856)	404.0(1897)
Marseilles	111.1	195.3	403.7
Copenhagen	101.0	c.143.0	375.7
Leipzig	32.1	62.4	357.1
Munich	40.6	109.5	350.6
Breslau (Wroclaw)	62.9	110.7	335.2
Milan	c.134.5	c.190.0	321.8
Lisbon	350.0	275.0	307.7
Rome	c.153.0	175.9	300.5

Source: Adna Ferrin Weber, *The Growth of Cities in the Nineteenth Century. A Study in Statistics.* (Columbia University Studies in History, Economics and Public Law, Vol. 11) (Ithaca, N.Y.: Cornell University Press, 1969), p. 450. (Originally published, 1899.) Data pertaining to Russian cities derived from several volumes of the *Soviet Historical Encyclopedia* (in Russian).

lier age or of the United States in the latter decades of the nineteenth century.

When Commodore Matthew Perry (1794–1858) visited Japan in 1853–1854, he found a people totaling about 30 million living under conditions reminiscent of medieval Europe. Most of Japan's inhabitants were peasants working small plots of land over which presided a feudal nobility. Population densities in the main islands of the archipelago were high, although the northernmost island, Hokkaido, was all but empty save for the indigenous Ainu. Handicraft industries were widely distributed. Internal trade was sufficient to support the relatively small population (consisting primarily of nobility and artisans) living in the castle and market towns.

Industrialization came only after the Meiji Restoration in 1868, when a number of constitutional reforms laid the foundation for economic change and development. A favorable atmosphere was created by the government for the growth of capital and, subsequently, of the great financial combines (the *zaibatsu*), which remain a feature of the Japanese economy even today. The state, as in Russia, kept close watch over the development of specific industries, such as metallurgy and shipbuilding.

The textile and food-processing industries were among the first to adapt to factory technology—in Okayama, Osaka, and Tokyo on the main island of Honshu. Factory cotton production began in Osaka in 1868 in a mill built by one of the great landlords; but it was not until the

1890s that the industry underwent considerable expansion. By 1914, some 40 percent of Japan's urban workers were concentrated in the textile mills alone. The state, as indicated earlier, took an active interest in the metallurgical industry. In 1880, English enterprise had laid the foundations of an iron industry in Osaka, but it was only at the turn of the century, under military pressure, that the scale of operations underwent impressive expansion. Several early iron works were located near Japan's small deposits of ore in northwestern Honshu, but the Imperial Steel Works established in 1896 on Kyushu (at Yawata), was based on imported ores as well as coal brought from China.

The development of a transportation network accompanied industrialization almost from the beginning. The first rail line, opened in 1872, linked Tokyo with the port of Yokohama to the south. Kobe and Osaka were joined in 1874, with an extension to Kyoto in 1876. These initial developments were to form the nucleus of the Tokaido Line, which was to extend from Tokyo southward paralleling the Pacific coast to Kobe. By 1906, two thirds of the line was in operation, built and maintained by private funding. By 1927, 11,000 miles of railway tied Japan's industrial centers, and this was accompanied by a growth of bulk traffic on the Inland Sea, Japan's great internal waterway.

Japan's population possessed a tradition of workshop discipline going back many centuries, and this factor enabled Japan to organize its labor force with considerable speed (Johnson, 1983). However, territorial expansion was an essential element of Japan's entry into the modern world. Japan's domestic resource base was weak, and there was always a concern for food, but the early growth of the Japanese empire was triggered in large measure by a desire to emulate the European imperial powers.

The underlying concern for food, however, stimulated a program of agricultural expansion. From 1890–1894 to 1910–1914, Japanese production of rice, the basic staple, increased by 30 percent, although cropland remained largely

unchanged at 6 million acres. Because the farm labor force remained constant, despite a strong rural-urban migration, the growth in food output came as a result of increased productivity. Even though Japan's population was trending sharply upward—a 17-million increase between 1875 and 1915—Japan's industrial advance required no food imports. However, there was always a nagging fear that urban population increase would severely strain domestic supply, a nightmare that did begin to manifest itself in the 1920s.

This underlying concern for food together with the knowledge that the country's raw materials base was weak help explain the direction of Japan's military adventures in Asia. The Sino-Japanese conflict of 1894–1895, the Russo-Japanese War of 1904–1905, and the involvement in World War I established Japan as a recognizable industrial, military, and naval power in the Pacific. The subsequent Japanese invasion of resource-rich Manchuria in 1931, which grew into a general war with China in 1935, were all part of a plan to secure control of a broader resource base.

During the early years of industrialization, the historic structure of Japan's cities remained largely unchanged. Much of the new manufacturing took shape in the historic castle towns, *jokamachi,* which were the most important and most widespread urban phenomenon in pre-Meiji Japan. Castle towns, because of their defensive positions, were important centers of regional, political, and administrative control; they also had religious significance, and in time, they had gradually acquired commercial or market functions. A large number of the major industrial cities of Japan today were originally castle towns. Among these centers are Tokyo, Osaka, Nagoya, Hiroshima, and Kitakyushu (Table 18–3). Other cities, such as Yokohama, Kobe, and Kawasaki, grew up near old castle towns. Of the present 46 provincial or prefectural capitals, 34 were castle towns in origin.

During the early decades of the present century, urbanization proceeded at a rapid pace. At

Table 18–3
The Growth of Population in Japan's Principal Industrial Cities (Thousands)

	1750	1850	1900	1930	1960	1975	1982
Tokyo[a]	509	567	1,497	2,070	8,310	8,643	8,139
Osaka	403	373	931	2,453	3,012	2,779	2,542
Yokohama	—	—	245	620	1,376	2,622	2,823
Nagoya	96	100	260	907	1,592	2,080	2,053
Kyoto	362	323	362	765	1,285	1,461	1,458
Kobe	22	22	250	788	1,114	1,361	1,361
Sapporo	—	—	44	168	524	1,241	1,419
Kitakyushu[b]	—	—	—	—	—	1,058	1,055
Kawasaki	—	—	—	104	633	1,015	1,027
Fukuoka	—	—	—	228	647	1,002	1,065
Hiroshima	—	—	—	—	431	853	891

[a] Known as Yedo or Edo in the pre-Meiji era.

[b] Created through the merger of five cities.

Source: Tertius Chandler and Gerald Fox, *3,000 Years of Urban Growth* (New York and London: Academic Press, 1974), pp. 296–299; *The Japan Year Book 1935* (Tokyo: Foreign Affairs Association of Japan, 1935), pp. 73–74; *Japan Statistical Yearbook 1978* (Tokyo: Bureau of Statistics, 1978), pp. 18–23; *Nippon: A Charted Survey of Japan, 1977/78* (Tokyo: 1977) pp. 16–20; *Nihon Kokusei Zue* (Tokyo: Kokusei-sha, 1983), pp. 73–78 (In Japanese).

least four major urban-industrial nodes materialized: (1) Tokyo-Yokohama; (2) Kobe-Osaka-Kyoto; (3) Nagoya, north of Tokyo; and (4) southern Honshu-northern Kyushu (Fig. 18–5).

The United States

The seaboard cities, such as New York, Boston, Philadelphia, Baltimore and, to a much lesser degree, Charleston, were not unlike the preindustrial cities of northwestern Europe (Fig. 18–6). Their economies had been based primarily on commerce. Processed goods passed through these cities from Britain and the European continent in exchange for the raw materials of America (Pred, 1966).

As in Great Britain, however, the Industrial Revolution in the United States began in the countryside.

The first cotton-spinning mill—containing a 24-spindle water frame and two carding machines—was launched in 1790–1791 by Samuel Slater (1768–1835), who had learned the trade as a youth under Richard Arkwright (1732–1792) and associates in Lancashire, England. The mill was erected at the falls (later known as Pawtucket) on the Blackstone River, north of the port of Providence, Rhode Island.

Following the War of 1812, a group of Massachusetts merchants led by Francis Cabot Lowell (1775–1817) organized the Boston Manufacturing Company to carry out all phases of clothmaking in one large mill, which was located in Waltham, near Boston. Subsequently, a new site for a textile mill was found on the Merrimack River near the New Hampshire boundary and the textile center of Lowell was founded (Box 18–2). Because water power was the source of energy, falls on rivers and streams determined the location of the towns built around mills. By the 1830s, the textile industry in the United States had been concentrated in factories.

Not all attempts to establish factory enterprise in the United States in the early period of industrialization succeeded. Some failed in infancy; others survived several decades and then folded leaving few traces on the landscape to-

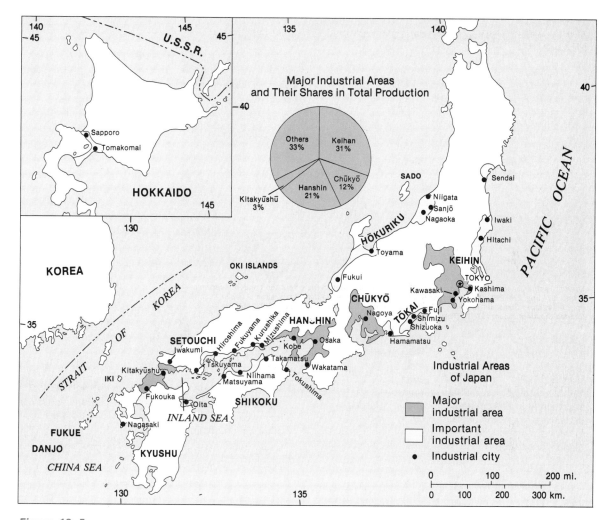

Figure 18–5

Although many of Japan's cities are rooted in the preindustrial period before 1868, the real growth of urban concentrations occurred with industrialization. Enterprises were particularly drawn to the lowlands fronting on the Inland Sea, which remains today one of the most industrialized regions in the world.

day (Wallace, 1978). In southeastern Pennsylvania, for example, a group of enterprising individuals set up seven textile mills along Chester Creek that continued to produce up to and through the Civil War. In the decades following, because of changing conditions in American technology and business and the inability of these mills to compete, production fell off, and they were finally forced to close.

One of the most effective agents of early economic development was the dynamic growth of transportation facilities. During the early decades of the nineteenth century, a substantial effort had gone into the creation of a national

Figure 18–6

Manufacturing first sprang up in southern New England, particularly in coastal settlements that afforded water either for power sites or transportation. From there, the factory system moved northward throughout New England, southward into the mid-Atlantic states, and west-ward into the Ohio Valley. Nevertheless, the major cities of the United States until well into the nineteenth century were seaboard cities whose economies were based primarily on commercial activities.

Source: Museum of the City of New York/Photo Researchers, Inc.

BOX 18–2

Charles Dickens and Lowell, Massachusetts

Charles Dickens came to the United States in 1842. In the course of his journey, he visited Boston, Lowell, Worcester, New Haven, and New York before heading down the coastal plain to Philadelphia and Washington, D.C. He then toured parts of the Midwest. Of Lowell, which he reached by rail from Boston, he wrote the following rather favorable account:

Lowell is a large, populous, thriving place. Those indications of its youth which first attract the eye give it a quaintness and oddity of character which, to a visitor from the old country, is amusing enough. It was a very dirty winter's (January) day, and nothing in the whole town looked old to me, except the mud, which in some parts was almost knee-deep, and might have been deposited there on the subsiding of the waters after the Deluge. . . .

The very river that moves the machinery in the mills (for they are all worked by water power) seems to acquire a new character from the fresh buildings of bright red brick and painted wood among which it takes its course. . . .

Figure 18–7

Lowell, Massachusetts, was not the first factory town in the United States, but it gained fame as "the spindle city" because of its important role in the production of textiles. The Pawtucket Falls of the Merrimack, with a drop of 32 feet, was capable of providing ample power.

For almost a century, Lowell ranked as a major cotton textile center, but many of its mills closed after 1929, relocating in the South.

Source: Randolph Langenbach.

There are several factories in Lowell, each of which belongs to what we should term a Company of Proprietors, but what they call in America a Corporation. I went over several of these, such as a woolen factory, a carpet factory, and a cotton factory: examined them in every part; and saw them in their ordinary working aspect, with no preparation of any kind, or departure from their ordinary everyday proceedings. . . .

I happened to arrive at the first factory just as the dinner hour was over, and the girls were returning to their work; indeed, the stairs of the mill were thronged with them as I ascended. . . .

These girls . . . were all well dressed: and that phrase necessarily includes extreme cleanliness. . . . They were healthy in appearance, many of them remarkably so, and had manners and deportment of young women: not of degraded brutes of burden. . . .

The rooms in which they worked were as well ordered as themselves. In the windows of some there were green plants, which were trained to shade the glass; in all, there was as much fresh air, cleanliness,

and comfort as the nature of the occupation would possibly admit of. . . .

They reside in various boarding-houses near at hand. The owners of the mills are particularly careful to allow no persons to enter upon the possession of these houses, whose characters have not undergone the most searching and thorough inquiry. . . . There are a few children employed in these factories, but not many. The laws of the State (Massachusetts) forbid their working more than nine months in the year, and require that they be educated during the other three.

Despite the inevitable comparisons to be made between the new society and the old, Dickens took pains to assure his readers that he was well acquainted with manufacturing towns in England and had visited many mills in Manchester and elsewhere. Lowell comes off very well in this account (Fig. 18–7).

Source: Quote from Charles Dickens, *American Notes for General Circulation and Pictures from Italy* (London: 1881), p. 75 ff.

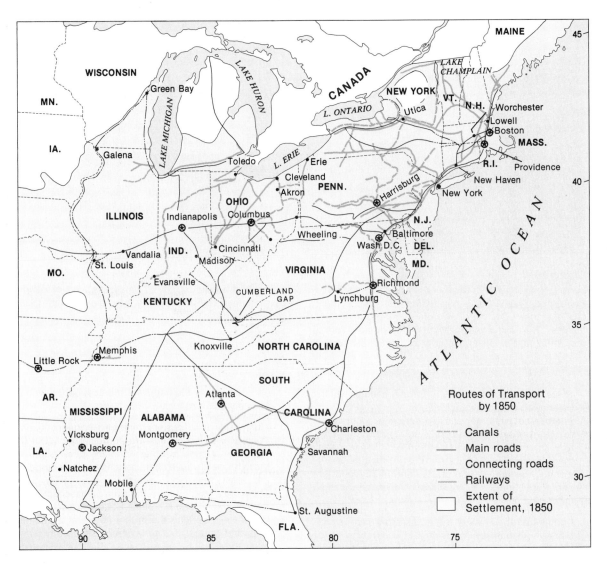

Figure 18–8

Coastal navigation had been an important factor in the rise of the textile industry, but as settlement spread west of the Appalachians, improved inland routes of travel were required. A network of roads built in the years following the War of 1812 facilitated movement into the interior. (The most widely used, perhaps, was the Na-

tional Road built by the government that linked Baltimore with Wheeling, West Virginia, on the Ohio River.) However, the opening of the Erie Canal in 1825 radically improved the means of reaching the West. Thousands of migrants were barged to Buffalo and the Great Lakes.

road system that sought to tie the seaboard cities together and reach into the Appalachians and beyond. Then, when the War of 1812 ended, the canal age began. The first and most

successful system was the Erie Canal (1817–1825), which linked the Great Lakes, via the Mohawk and Hudson valleys, with New York City (Fig. 18–8). The Canadian merchants of

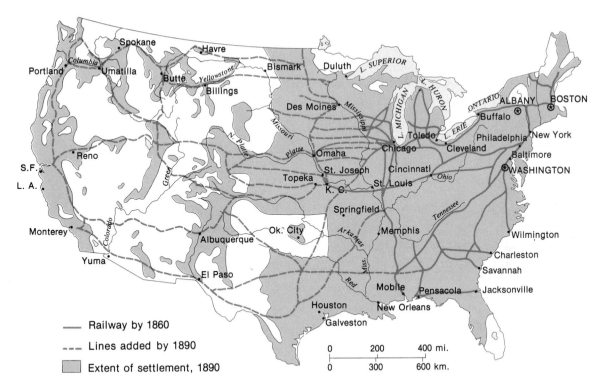

Figure 18-9

As in England and Europe, the railroad opened up areas that were not immediately affected by river or canal navigation. Vying for the commerce of the interior, the seaboard cities sought ways to tap the western trade. By mid-century, a number of rail routes extending westward from the coast had been constructed, including the Western Railroad (linking Boston and Albany in 1842), the Baltimore & Ohio (which reached Wheeling, West Virginia, in 1853), the New York Central (which became a single line between New York and Buffalo in 1852), and the Pennsylvania Railroad (linking Philadelphia and Pittsburgh in 1852). In the decades that followed, the rail density in the states east of the Mississippi increased, to be followed after the Civil War with the great trancontinental lines to the Pacific coast.

Montreal hoped to capture some of the trade with the interior through improvements on the St. Lawrence River at Lachine (where a canal was constructed, 1821–1825) and with the construction of the Welland Canal (opened in 1829) around Niagara Falls, but the Erie Canal gave New York an early advantage. At the same time, the Erie Canal stimulated the growth of Buffalo, its western terminus, and, subsequently, other lake ports. The advent of the steamboat on inland waterways, especially on the Mississippi River system, was another significant factor, not only promoting settlement, but also the growth of manufacturing centers as well.

Canals and steamboats, however, were soon rendered obsolete. The railroad, which had begun to revolutionize the English industrial landscape, now appeared alongside the growth of factories in the United States (Fig. 18–9). By 1840, some twenty-eight hundred miles of disconnected lines had been built. In the next two decades, a well-defined network of over thirty thousand miles had been constructed.

Following the Civil War, the growth of manufacturing west of the Appalachians came on the heels of improvements that opened up new lands and resources and encouraged increasing penetration of the continent by pioneer settlers. The rapid growth in general population increased the demand for manufactured goods.

Expanding routes that reached into the interior not only made possible a speedup in the extension of the American political system, but also enhanced the scale of industrial operations, especially in the Middle West. The value of farm produce continued to exceed that of manufacturing until about 1885, but in the two deades prior to the turn of the century, the United States made the transition to industrial capitalism, took unprecedented strides toward economic independence, and progressed toward assuming the status of the world's leading industrial power.

An economic core, contained within Boston, Minneapolis, St. Louis, and Baltimore came into existence, but at its heart was the metallurgical industries of the Ohio Valley and Great Lakes region, based on the rich resources of Mesabi (iron) and the Midwest (coal).

The years from the Civil War and the turn of the century were also years of feverish invention. They added up, in effect, to a new stage in the Industrial Revolution that was based on the use of electricity, chemicals, and the automobile.

In the 1890s, the number of patents granted anually averaged about twenty-two thousand. In 1916 alone, there were over forty-three thousand patents granted. The development of the gasoline-powered internal combustion engine, from the 1870s onward, led to the appearance by 1900 of the American automobile industry. This innovation in transportation was not only to assure individual mobility, but also was to have enormous consequences on the shaping of the American landscape, both urban and rural.

In 1900, there were only 8000 motor vehicles registered in the United States, but by 1920, there were 7,567,888, and by 1929, 26,501,433! The United States had fast outdistanced France, through the introduction by Henry Ford of the assembly line, and had five sixths of the world's output, with 1 car for every 5 people. The growth in automobile ownership generated an improvement and expansion of the road system; when applied to farm equipment, the new source of motive power revolutionized farming.

Life in America was further altered by the development of the electric light bulb, through the research of Thomas A. Edison (1847–1931), one of the last of the great tinkerers. His major feat was the bringing together of the incandescent lamp and an electrical distributing system, laying the foundation of commercial lighting. The first American commercial central station opened in New York in 1882, a little over a century ago. Almost 20 years later, the Italian inventor Guglielmo Marconi (1874–1937) flashed the first wireless signal across the English Channel from France to Dover, England, and with that a new form of communication came into being—radio. In the United States, radio caught on rapidly, with expenditures rising from $10.6 million in 1920 to $411.6 million in 1929 (Johnson, 1983).

Throughout the United States, population growth and economic development stimulated the expansion of lightly industrialized cities, such as Atlanta; Portland, Maine; Minneapolis; Kansas City, Kansas and Seattle (Fig. 18–10) (Table 18–4), Factories for the mass production of automobiles contributed to Michigan's wealth, especially as Detroit surged ahead. In the Los Angeles basin, light manufacturing, the film industry, and a gentle climate, proved a magnet to a migrating population. Finally, the growth of affluence, especially in the Northeast, began to express itself in the growth of recreational and resort centers outside the region, especially in Florida.

Table 18–4
Growth of Population of Selected Cities of the United States 1830–1980 (in thousands)

	1830	1850	1860	1890	1900	1910	1950	1980
New York	202.5	660.8	1,174.8	2,740.6	3,440.0	4,766.8	7,892	7,071
Chicago	—	30.0	112.2	1,099.9	1,700.0	2,185.2	3,621	3,005
Philadelphia	161.0	408.8	565.5	1,047.0	1,300.0	1,549.0	2,072	1,688
St. Louis	6.7	77.0	160.8	451.8	575.0	687.0	857	453
Boston	61.3	136.9	177.8	448.5	560.0	670.5	801	563
Cleveland	1.1	17.0	43.4	261.3	325.9	560.6	915	574
Baltimore	80.6	169.1	217.0	434.4	510.0	558.4	950	787
Pittsburgh	15.3	37.9	49.2	343.9	450.0	533.9	677	424
Detroit	2.2	21.0	45.6	205.9	285.7	465.7	1,850	1,203
Buffalo	8.6	42.3	81.1	255.7	354.0	423.7	580	358
San Francisco	—	34.8	56.8	298.9	345.0	416.9	775	679
Los Angeles	—	1.6	4.4	50.4	102.0	319.2	1,970	2,967
Seattle	—	—	—	42.8	80.7	237.2	468	494

Source: L. Dudley Stamp and S. Carter Gilmour, *Chisholms' Handbook of Commercial Geography,* 14th ed. (London: Longman's, Green, 1954), pp. 70–71; John S. Adams, ed., *Cities of the Nation's Historic Metropolitan Core,* Contemporary Metropolitan America, 1 (Association of American Geographers Comparative Metropolitan Analysis Project). (Cambridge, Mass.: Ballinger, 1976), pp. 5–12; selected census volumes of the United States (1830–1910); *Statistical Abstract of the United States, 1980, 1981,* U.S. Department of Commerce. Bureau of the Census (Washington, D.C.: 1980, 1981).

THE NEW URBAN AMERICAN LANDSCAPE

The Tenement

Although the population of the United States grew rapidly in the decades leading up to the Civil War (over 30 percent per decade), the population living in urban settlements of twenty-five hundred or more increased by three times the national rate (Table 18–5). This was the era of massive immigration to the United States from the British Isles and from northwestern Europe. In the late 1840s and early 1850s, some 4 million new settlers reached the United States, including large contingents from Ireland and Germany. Many immigrants brought new skills, new techniques, and (in some cases) new industries. This immigrant influx together with rural-urban migration created a rate of urban growth that has never been matched since.

Population numbers continued to move upward. Between 1865 and World War I, more than 25 million immigrants entered the United States. In 1907 alone, 1,199,566 came. These new Americans tended to concentrate in the industrial cities. In the decade 1860–1870, there was one urban inhabitant for every three or four rural inhabitants in the United States. Between 1910 and 1920, the urban population reached and climbed above 50 percent of the total.

By the end of the nineteenth century, 3 out of 4 urban dwellers lived in rented quarters, and the proportion was higher in strictly working-class districts. The demand for living space together with a steep rise in urban land values associated with competition for office space, drove rents up. Those who could afford their own housing moved outward from the center. Those who could not, doubled up, taking in the extended family and lodgers as well, thus adding to the concentration. Land pressures led to the construction of new mass housing units

Figure 18–10(A)

By 1891, Seattle had recovered from the devastating fire that swept the core of the city on June 5, 1889. This wood engraving, with a view facing eastward, shows trolley cars on Yesler Way (formerly Skid Road, so named because logs were skidded down the hill to sawmills on the waterfront of Elliot Bay). The square is Pioneer Square, and although several of the buildings have since been demolished—including the triangular-shaped structure (now a parking garage) and the hotel on the right (which collapsed)—others have been restored, such as the Pioneer, or Yesler, Building, by private investment in a move to revitalize an older section of the city.

(Wood engraving from Northwest Magazine, 1981. Courtesy Historical Photography Collection, University of Washington Libraries.)

called *tenements*. Although they varied in size from city to city and district to district, four-to-six story tenements, housing anywhere from 16 to 24 families or a total of up to 150 people, were not unusual. In New York City alone, the tenement population climbed from 21,000 in 1879 to 1.5 million by 1900. Rooms were small, dimly lit, and poorly ventilated. Tenements, too, seldom had any toilet facilities save for outdoor privies, little if any central heat, and scarcely any individual facilities for cooking (Fig. 18–11).

The City Core

In view of the steep rise in the value of urban real estate, city cores in the 1920s began their upward thrust. Soon, almost every major city could boast a skyscraper or a tower (Fig. 18–12). As the concentration of service activities, such as insurance, banking, and commercial retail functions, increased at the core, surrounding residential areas also underwent changes. The ethnic and racial composition of the inhabitants shifted as wave followed wave of new

Figure 18-10(B)

Seattle was founded in 1851–1852 as part of the westward movement, but settlement initially was slow. By the 1870s, after the city had received its charter, it boasted a population of little more than three thousand. The great fire of 1889 destroyed much of the business center, but recovery was rapid as shown here. In the two decades after 1890, Seattle's growth was marked by the arrival of the railroad and the construction of its first skyscraper, the Smith Tower building built in 1911–1914, as seen in this panoramic view of the city set against the majesty of Mount Rainier rising to 14,410 feet in the background. World War II and the growth of the aircraft industry in the area opened another era in Seattle's history.

(Photo Courtesy of the Historical Photography Collection, University of Washington Libraries. Photograph of panorama by Lawrence Lindsley, 1918.)

Figure 18-10(C)

Seattle's financially-successful World's Fair in the early 1960's contributed a cultural center and a Space Needle, shown here. Soon, other office structures began to dwarf the historic Smith Tower (lower left). The arrival of the Interstate-5 freeway slicing through the heart of the city was hailed as additional evidence of progress and coming of age.

Source: Georg Gerster/Photo Researchers, Inc.

Table 18–5
**The Growth of Urban Population, Industrial Output, and the Railroad
Network in the United States (1860–1920)**

	1860	1870	1880	1890	1900	1910	1920
Total Population (millions)	31.4	39.8	50.1	62.9	76.0	92.0	105.7
Total Urban Population (millions)	6.2	9.9	14.1	22.1	30.2	42.0	54.2
Total Number of Cities over 100,000	9	14	20	28	38	50	69
Total Urban Population in Cities over 100,000 (millions)	2.6	4.1	6.2	9.7	14.2	20.3	27.4
Bituminous Coal Production (million short tons)	9.0	20.5	50.8	111.3	212.3	417.1	568.7
Pig Iron Shipments (thousand short tons)	82	1,665	3,835	9,203	13,789	26,674	35,710
Raw-steel Produced (thousand short tons)	13	77	1,397	4,779	11,227	28,330	46,183
Miles of Railroad (excluding sidings and track yards)	30,626	52,922	93,262	166,703	206,631	226,185	296,836

Source: U.S. Department of Commerce. *Historical Statistics of the United States. Colonial Times to 1970*, (2
Parts). (Washington, D.C.: Bureau of the Census, 1975), pp. 8, 11–12, 589–905, 693–694, 728–731.

Figure 18–11

The Statue of Liberty in New York Harbor, a gift of the
French people and built in 1885, has for nearly a century
welcomed immigrants arriving in the United States by
way of New York. Its open arms beckoned to the masses
of impoverished people who sought a new life in this
country. However, these immigrants, in search of security, wealth, political power, or private dreams of their
own, frequently ended up in tenements in ethnic neighborhoods. There, they were crowded together in small
apartments, frequently lacking the essentials that give
life dignity. During the hot, humid summers, doors and
windows were left open for ventilation, the smell of
cooking permeating the entire building. In time, however, many of these families prospered and moved into
new neighborhoods, their places being taken by hundreds of thousands of new immigrants.

Source: The Bettmann Archive.

Figure 18–12

If the suburb is as American as apple pie, so too is the skyscraper, perhaps one of the most distinctive contributions to architectural design and urban land use. The skyscraper began to take shape at the end of the nineteenth century, but it was in the late 1920s that cities began to grow skyward. As America urbanized, the core of the urban landscape came increasingly to be dominated by the thrusting peaks of the skycrapers.

Source: Georg Gerster/Photo Researchers, Inc.

immigrants, particularly as the stream of blacks from the South grew steadily. By the 1930s the black populations of most eastern and midwestern cities had more than doubled, with blacks usually settling in older neighborhoods near the city center.

The Suburbs

As millions of people from the countryside and from abroad streamed into cities in search of jobs, long-term residents of the city moved out into the suburbs (Fig. 18–13). The proliferation of urban settlements around the fringes of the industrial cities—the refuge of a growing, predominantly white middle class—created a host of new problems. Initially, the cities tended to expand their legal boundaries to take in the new

suburbs, putting a strain on municipal services. However, many suburbanites balked at the annexation of their communities. They remained dependent to a high degree on the city center for employment, but they allowed a patchwork of administrative structures to grow up to collect their taxes and provide the services needed locally.

The Metropolitan District

Because urban networks had begun to form metropolitan clusters, the U.S. Census Bureau in 1910 gave official recognition to the concept (Pred, 1965). By 1920, there were 58 *metropolitan districts* and near-metropolitan districts, containing about two thirds of the urban population of the country. Of this total, actual city

Figure 18–13

Suburbs are as old as the Middle Ages in Europe—if not older—but the modern suburb that emerged in the United States with the increasing mobility of the popula-tion is, perhaps, one of the major contributions of Americans to the forms and patterns of human settlement.

Source: M. E. Warren/Photo Researchers, Inc.

dwellers accounted for 66 percent of the residents of the metropolitan areas, whereas the suburbs accounted for 33 percent. America was coming of age as an urban civilization.

Rapid technological improvements in transportation, incredible industrial expansion, and an exploding urbanization wrought startling and sometimes shocking material and social transformations on the landscape and in people. Cities were places of wonderment, excitement, and opportunity. But they had a negative side, too: poverty, crowding, filth, and social tension. And for many newcomers, there was confusion and loneliness. The turn-of-the-century city was the center of American civilization, but it was also—and clearly has remained—the storm center.

THE NEW TECHNOLOGICAL REVOLUTION

It is widely held that late in the 1960s the economy of the United States began to unravel (Reich, 1983). The two decades of incredible economic and industrial progress following World War II had been characterized by high volume of output and standardization of product. In both areas, American manufacturing was highly successful and largely unchallenged at the international level; American exports dominated world markets. Thus, the 1950s and early 1960s saw a degree of affluence in the United States unparalleled in history. Improvements in transportation through the use of the automobile, the construction of freeways, and the coming of the jet engine were matched by the revolution in communications ushered in by television and stereo sound systems. And, these changes were accompanied by a mobility of population that witnessed the further growth of metropolitan areas, above all, of California.

In the late 1960s, while the United States was embroiled in the war in Vietnam, a new round of technological innovation, precision and quality manufacturing, and customization of products began to assert a new pattern of industrial operation and management that was, in turn, to affect and be effected by the American life-style and consumer tastes.

When technological (and management) innovation was applied to some important sectors of modern industry, as was the case in Japan and, to a lesser degree, in some Western European countries, U.S. firms found they could no longer compete. This inability to compete, owing in large measure to obsolescence in manufacturing procedures and plants, was expressed clearly in the steel industry; in the automobile industry, where consumers were showing a preference for more fuel-efficient, smaller cars; and in the electronics industry. A new technology, involving computerization, was revolutionizing older industries and creating a host of new industries. These new industries—associated with the development of the means whereby information could be stored, transmitted, and made available for future use—were associated with the information, or communications, revolution.

The revolution had not passed the United States by, and certainly, its forms were becoming visible in the American landscape. However, some observers felt that the movement of the U.S. economy into these new fields of endeavor had not proceeded rapidly enough. Bankrupt industrial concerns; the closing of mills and factories, especially in the northeastern and midwestern states; stiff competition from foreign producers had resulted in the expansion of the unemployed work force geared to the old industrial base but had not equipped

them to move into the new base. Still, new centers of research and development had quietly taken shape, the earliest and most impressive being Silicon Valley, California.

Silicon Valley

Silicon Valley, a stretch of land reaching from San Jose to Palo Alto, California, is indicative of the new industrial landscape (Fig. 18–14). There are over a thousand plants devoted to the manufacture of computers, computer games, software programs, and other types of systems designed to process and disseminate information lining U.S. Highway 101. So extensive and impressive has the development been that Silicon Valley has entered the modern vocabulary as a term suggestive of the new landscape. Ultimately, the *industrial park* is expected to stretch about 75 miles along the eastern part of San Francisco Bay southward to about 35 miles south of San Jose. A major factor drawing investment to the area is the presence nearby of Stanford University, the University of Santa Clara, and San Jose State University.

Similar developments, although somewhat less extensive geographically, have occurred in other parts of the country, including New York, Massachusetts, Texas, Florida, Virginia, and the Pacific Northwest (Fig. 18–15). In Virginia, Fairfax County has become a base for high-tech industries that serve and cater to the needs of the federal government. Rapid growth has also occurred in North Carolina, where Research Triangle Park, in the Raleigh-Durham metropolitan area has become the country's largest research park. A highly trained work force and the proximity to universities have been major attractions. The Raleigh-Durham area claims more Ph.D. engineers and scientists per 100,000 population than any other urban-suburban area in the country.

New developments, such as these in the South and West, are not confined to states in these areas. California has the highest number of high-tech workers, but the old Northeast has

Figure 18–14

The patterns formed by research and industrial enterprises, together with access roads, in the new industrial parks are not unlike those of many residential suburbs.

Perhaps Silicon landscape is an apt term for the new high-tech agglomerations.
Source: Robert A. Isaacs/Photo Researchers, Inc.

also advanced with 16.1 percent or more of the high-tech work force.

Japan and Western Europe

The transformation and modernization of the Japanese economy in the postwar period has been nothing less than phenomenal. From the mid-1960s, the Japanese economy grew faster than that of the United States, and by 1982, Japanese workers' real wages almost equaled those of their American counterparts (Reich, 1983). Japan's share of manufactured goods in total world sales rose from 4 to 10 percent in the 1970s, reaching 13 percent by 1980. In the same period the U.S. share declined by 23 percent. Although facing rising labor costs, Japanese manufacturers turned increasingly to the new technology. A $375 million investment in 1980 in the industrial use of robots is expected to grow to more than $2 billion by the end of the decade (Hofheinz and Calder, 1982).

In Europe, in an attempt to keep abreast of developments in the United States and Japan, individual governments have given encouragement and support to new enterprise. At the same time, they have embarked on a cooperative plan of development. In 1982–1983, a program called ESPRIT, European Strategic Program for Research and Information Technology, was created by the 10-nation European Community (EEC). ESPRIT intends to invest in research and development of computer software, information processing, integrated circuits, robots, computerized machine tools, and office automation.

As this trend continues within the industrialized nations of the non-Communist world, one may expect to find a migration of older manufacturing activities, including textiles and clothing (long underway), steel, automobiles, shipbuilding, and others, to industrializing countries. Among these may be South Korea, Taiwan, the Philippines, Indonesia, India, Bra-

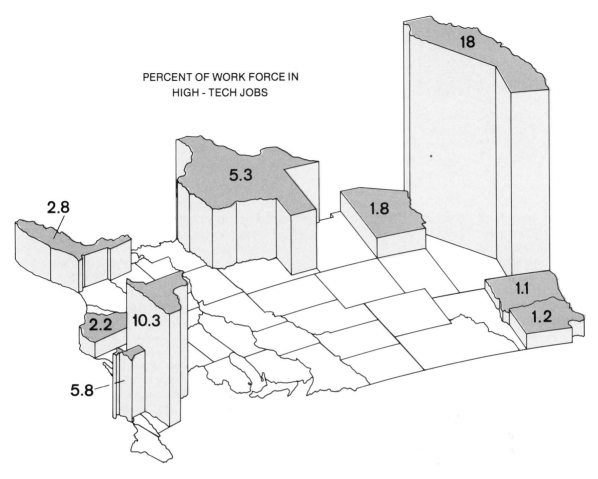

PERCENT OF WORK FORCE IN
HIGH - TECH JOBS

Figure 18–15
Although it is expected that the distribution of high-tech industries will be more widely dispersed throughout the United States in future, coastal states seem to have gained a preemptive lead as of 1984.

zil, Argentina, and several countries in Africa. What this entails, then, is a shift of some traditional *secondary activities* from industrialized to industrializing countries. A whole new set of secondary activities, as we have seen, is coming into existence in the industrialized countries. This development is taking place alongside a further expansion of *tertiary activities* or service activities (Box 18–3).

EPILOGUE

The Industrial Revolution, with all its attendant features, spread from its original hearth in England to the European continent and thence to other parts of the globe, principally the United States and Japan. Although the pattern of industrial development may have varied from country to country—depending on raw material

BOX 18-2

How People Are Employed

In the nonindustrialized (or developing) countries of the world, *primary activities* employ the greater portion of the able-bodied population. That is, farming, herding, clearing the land, fishing, mining, or any activity associated with the extraction of raw materials from the earth claim the attention of the population. *Secondary activities* engage a smaller percentage of the population, although cottage industries for domestic needs are common. Certainly, factory processing engages relatively few people.

This pattern was characteristic of Great Britain and other countries in Europe and North America during the early period of their industrial revolutions. As industrialization continued, the proportion of the population employed in secondary activities increased. Among the latter were initially the textile manufacturers, food processors, and the creators of other consumer goods. As industrialization deepened further, greater attention was given to the production of capital goods. In Great Britain in 1841, for example, light industries occupied 79 percent of the industrial employment, whereas capital goods accounted for only 8 percent. By 1901, industrial employment in consumer goods had declined to 45 percent, whereas that in capital goods had risen to 24 percent. By 1935, the ratios stood at 40 and 33 percent respectively; by 1948, at 32 and 55 percent respectively.

In the United States and Japan, the evolving pattern of employment was comparable to that in Britain. In the USSR—building on the foundations laid during the tsarist period in textiles, glass, food processing, and other related industries—the government, in 1928, embarked on a program of industrialization that mobilized workers into capital goods production at the expense of consumer goods.

Ordinarily, tertiary activities—the provisioning of services, retailing, administration, and the host of other activities that are essential to the maintenance of society—have grown in scope with the maturation of the industrial base and the growth of technology. In advanced industrial societies today, tertiary activities claim anywhere from 40 percent (in Western Europe generally) to 70 percent (in the United States) of the labor force. Manufacturing accounts for one fourth to one third of the working population, and primary activities engage only a small fraction of the work force. In many industrialized countries, the latter represents no more than 4 to 5 percent, although it is higher in the USSR and in France.

In industrially advanced countries, an additional, or *quaternary activity*, has come to be identified. The term quaternary has increasingly been applied to such sectors of employment as insurance, real estate, education, and health.

supply, political organization, and the role of government in aiding economic growth—the industrial landscapes that resulted were similar from country to country.

Associated with industrialization was a pronounced rural-urban migration, which tended to slacken or reverse itself by the 1970s. The city that emerged—the new industrial city—was essentially a new phenomenon. In the United

States, the city was characterized by suburban growth; workers' tenements; and, subsequently, owing to high land values at the core, to the construction of skyscrapers.

The Industrial Revolution, in retrospect, is not one revolution by a series of revolutions, that have shaped and reshaped the landscape over the past century. The high-tech revolution, with its high density of skilled workers and professional and research personnel located in industrial or research parks with access to a freeway, promises to make further changes in the landscape.

to cities and have participated in the modern urban landscape.

APPLICATION OF IDEAS

1. It was inevitable, given the proper circumstances, that the Industrial Revolution would be exported to the Continent. The process of diffusion lagged, but once accepted, industrialization moved through western Europe and eastward into Russia.

2. Although local conditions varied, the countries of Europe passed through stages of economic development and change comparable to that experienced by Great Britain a half century or more earlier.

3. Industrialization came to Japan only after the Meiji Restoration had wiped away many of the last vestiges of the feudal order. With government encouragement Japan made rapid progress.

4. British capital and inventiveness brought the Industrial Revolution to the United States. 1790 may be said to mark the beginning of the textile mill in New England. However, it was not until the early decades of the nineteenth century that the landscape of the northern states began to reveal the impact of industrialization.

5. Following the Civil War, not only did the United States throw rail lines across a continent—which carried settlers into the vast interior—but also industrial progress was of such an order that, by the end of the nineteenth century, the United States (perhaps without realizing it) had become a world industrial power.

6. Industrialization has been the most important factor in the modern world: shaping and reshaping the landscape, altering the face of traditional cities, and compelling major readjustments in the lives of peoples who have migrated

KEY WORDS AND PHRASES

absorbing barrier	quaternary activity
friction of space	secondary activity
industrial park	tenement
metropolitan districts	tertiary activity
primary activity	*zaibatsu*

QUESTIONS FOR FURTHER DISCUSSION

1. Why did it take so long for the Industrial Revolution to reach the Continent from England? What were the barriers that prevented ready acceptance of the new technology in Europe?

2. Why was Belgium the first continental country to undergo industrialization? What advantages did it possess?

3. What were the causes that left France in 1914 in fourth place as an industrial nation after England, Belgium, and Germany?

4. Why did it take so long for Germany to industrialize? When industrialization occurred, why was its tempo so rapid?

5. Russia was the last of the great European empires to industrialize. How do you account for this late entry into industrialization?

6. In what way did the process of industrialization in Japan differ from that in England or the United States? How did the preconditions of industrialization differ?

7. How do you account for the early arrival of the Industrial Revolution in the United States? What part of the country was affected first?

8. What were some of the truly American features of the industrial city that emerged toward the end of the nineteenth century?

9. What form is the new technological revolution taking? Describe how it would appear in the landscape.

10. Why do tertiary activities account for so large a percentage of the work force in industrialized countries?

REFERENCES AND ADDITIONAL READINGS

Abler, Ronald, ed. *Comparative Metropolitan America: Twenty Geographical Vignettes,* Vol. 1. Cambridge, Mass.: Ballinger, 1976.

Adams, John S., ed. *Cities of the Nation's Historic Metropolitan Core.* Contemporary Metropolitan America, 1 (Association of American Geographers Comparative Metropolitan Analysis Project). Cambridge, Mass.: Ballinger, 1976.

Allen, G. C. "The Industrialization of the Far East," pp.875–924. In *The Cambridge Economic History of Europe,* Vol. 6, Pt. 2. H. J. Habakkuk and M. Postan, eds. Cambridge, Cambridge University Press, 1965.

Beckinsale, R. P., and Houston J. M. eds. *Urbanization and Its Problems: Essays in Honour of E. W. Gilbert.* Oxford: Basil Blackwell, 1968.

Berry, Brian J. L. "City Size Distributions and Economic Development." *Economic Development and Cultural Change* 9 (1961): 573–588.

Berry, Brian J. L., et al. "Urban Population Densities: Structure and Change." *Geographical Review* 53 (1963): 389–405.

Chandler, Tertius, and Fox, Gerald. *3,000 Years of Urban Growth.* New York and London: Academic Press, 1974.

Chudacoff, Howard P. *The Evolution of American Urban Society.* Englewood Cliffs, N.J.: Prentice-Hall, 1975.

Cohen, Saul B. *Geography and the American Environment* (Voice of America Forum Lecture). Washington, D.C.: U.S. Information Agency, 1968.

Dempster, Prue. *Japan Advances. A Geographical Study.* London: Methuen, 1967.

Detweiler, Robert, et al. eds. *Environmental Decay in Its Historical Context.* Glenview, Ill.: Scott, Foresman, 1973.

Detwyler, Thomas R. et al. *Urbanization and Environment.* Belmont, Calif.: Duxbury Press, 1972.

French, R. A., and Hamilton F. E. Ian, eds. *The Socialist City. Spatial Structure and Urban Policy.* New York: John Wiley, 1979.

Fuchs, Roland J., and Demko, George J. "The Postwar Mobility Transition in Eastern Europe." *Geographical Review* 68 (1978): 171–182.

Gerschenkron, A. "Agrarian Policies and Industrialization: Russia 1861–1917," pp. 706–800. *The Cambridge Economic History of Europe,* Vol. 6, Part 2. H. J. Habakkuk and M. Postan, eds. Cambridge: Cambridge University Press, 1965.

Gottman, Jean. *Megalopolis. The Urbanized Northeastern Seaboard of the United States.* New York: Twentieth Century Fund, 1961.

Gutnov, Alexei et al. *The Ideal Communist City.* New York: George Braziller, 1968.

Hall, Robert B., Jr. *Japan: Industrial Power of Asia.* Princeton, N.J.: Van Nostrand, 1963.

Hamilton, F. E. Ian. *The Moscow City Region.* London: Oxford University Press, 1976.

Hansen, Niles M., ed. *Human Settlement Systems. International Perspectives on Structure, Change and Public Policy.* Cambridge, Mass.: Ballinger, 1978.

Harris, Chauncy D. *Cities of the Soviet Union.* Association of American Geographers Monograph Series 5. Chicago: Rand McNally, 1970.

Harris, Chauncy D., and Ullman, Edward L. "The Nature of Cities," *Annals of the American Academy of Political and Social Science* 242 (1945): 7–17.

Harris, Walker D., Jr. *The Growth of Latin American Cities.* Athens: Ohio University Press, 1971.

Herbert, D. T. and Johnston, R. J. *Spatial Processes and Form,* Vol. 1. London: John Wiley, 1976.

Hoffman, W. G. *The Growth of Industrial Economies.* New York: Oceana Publications, 1958.

Hofheinz, Roy, Jr., and Calder, Kent E. *The Eastasian Edge.* New York: Basic Books, 1982.

Hoselitz, Bert F. *Sociological Aspects of Economic Growth.* Glencoe, Ill.: Free Press, 1960.

Jackson, Kenneth T., and Schultz, Stanley D., eds. *Cities in American History*. New York: Alfred A. Knopf, 1972.

Jackson, W. A. Douglas. "Urban Expansion." *Problems of Communism* 23 (1974): 14–24.

Japan Statistical Yearbook 1978. Tokyo: Bureau of Statistics, 1978.

The Japan Year Book 1935. Tokyo: Foreign Affairs Association of Japan, 1935.

Johnson, Paul. *A History of the Modern World from 1917 to the 1980s*. London: Weidenfeld and Nicolson, 1983.

Jones, Ronald, ed. *Essays in World Urbanization*. London: George Phillip, 1975.

Kornhauser, David. *Urban Japan. Its Foundations and Growth*. London: Longman, 1976.

Lakshmanan, T. R., and Chatterjee, Lata R. *Urbanization and Environmental Quality*. Resource Papers for College Geography No. 77–1. Washington, D.C.: Association of American Geographers. 1977.

Landes, David S. "Technological Change and Development in Western Europe, 1750–1914," pp. 274–603. In *The Cambridge Economic History of Europe*, Vol. 6, Part 2. H. J. Habakkuk and M. Postan, eds. Cambridge: Cambridge University Press, 1965.

Lerner, Max. *America as a Civilization. Life and Thought in the United States Today*. New York: Simon & Schuster, 1957.

Lockwood, William W. *The Economic Development of Japan. Growth and Structural Change 1868–1938*. Princeton, N.J.: Princeton University Press, 1954.

Lynch, Kevin. *What Time Is This Place?* Cambridge, Mass.: MIT Press, 1972.

Mayer, Harold M. *The Spatial Expression of Urban Growth*. Resource Paper No. 7. Washington, D.C.: Commission on College Geography, Association of American Geographers, 1969.

Mayer, Harold M. and Kohn, Clyde eds. *Readings in Urban Geography*. Chicago: University of Chicago Press, 1959.

Mitchell, B. R. *European Historical Statistics, 1750–1970*. New York: Columbia University Press, 1975.

Mumford, Lewis. *The Culture of Cities*. New York: Harcourt, Brace, 1938.

———. *The City in History. Its Origins, Its Transformations, and Its Prospects*. New York: Harcourt, Brace & World, 1961.

———. *The Urban Prospect: Essays*. New York: Harcourt, Brace & World, 1968.

Nippon. A Charted Survey of Japan, 1977/78. Tokyo: 1977.

North, Douglass. "Industrialization in the United States," pp. 673–705. In *The Cambridge Economic History of Europe*, Vol. 6, Pt. 2. H. J. Habakkuk and M. Postan, eds. Cambridge: Cambridge University Press, 1965.

Orchard, John E. *Japan's Economic Position. The Progress of Industrialization*. New York: McGraw-Hill, 1930.

Portal, Roger. "The Industrialization of Russia," pp. 801–874. In *The Cambridge Economic History of Europe*, Vol. 6, Pt. 2. H. J. Habakkuk and M. Postan, eds. Cambridge: Cambridge University Press, 1965.

Pred, Allan. "Industrialization, Initial Advantage, and American Metropolitan Growth." *Geographical Review* 55 (1965): 158–185.

———. "Manufacturing in the American Mercantile City, 1800–1840." *Annals of the Association of American Geographers* 56 (1966): 307–338.

———. *The Spatial Dynamics of the U.S. Urban-Industrial Growth, 1800–1914*. Cambridge, Mass.: MIT Press, 1966.

Reich, Robert B. *The Next American Frontier*. New York: Times Books, 1983.

Revelle, Roger, and Landsberg, Hans H. *America's Changing Environment*. Boston: Houghton Mifflin, 1970.

Rose, A. J. *Patterns of Cities*. Melbourne, Austral.: Nelson, 1967.

Rosenau, Helen. *The Ideal City. Its Architectural Evolution*. New York: Harper & Row, 1972.

Rugg, Dean S. *Spatial Foundations of Urbanism*, 2nd ed. Dubuque, Iowa: William C. Brown, 1979.

Schaefer, Ludwig, F., et al. *The Shaping of Western Civilization*, Vol. 2. New York: Holt, Rinehart & Winston, 1970.

Shaw, Denis J. B. "Urbanism and Economic Development in a Pre-Industrial Context: The Case of Southern Russia." *Journal of Historical Geography* 3 (1977): 107–122.

Stamp, L. Dudley, and Gilmour, S. Carter. *Chisholm's Handbook of Commercial Geography,* 14th ed. London: Longman's, Green, 1954.

Stavrianos, L. S., ed. *The Epic of Modern Man. A Collection of Readings.* Englewood Cliffs, N.J.: Prentice-Hall, 1966.

Sutton, Horace. "America Falls in Love with Its Cities—Again." *Saturday Review* (August 1978), pp. 16–24.

Tanaka, Kakuei. *Building a New Japan. A Plan for Remodeling in the Japanese Archipelago.* Tokyo: Simul Press, 1973.

Toynbee, Arnold. *Cities on the Move.* New York: Oxford University Press, 1970.

Ullman, Edward L. "A Theory of Location for Cities." *American Journal of Sociology* 46 (1941): 853–864.

———. "The Nature of Cities Reconsidered." *Papers and Proceedings of the Regional Science Association* 9 (1962): 7–23.

Ullman, Edward L., and Dacey, Michael F. "The Minimum Requirements Approach to the Urban Economic Base." *Papers and Proceedings of the Regional Science Association* 6 (1960) 175–194.

U.S. Department of Commerce. *Historical Statistics of the United States. Colonial Times to 1970,* (2 Parts). Washington, D.C.: Bureau of the Census, 1975.

Vance, James E., Jr. *This Scene of Man. The Role and Structure of the City in the Geography of Western Civilization.* New York: Harper & Row, 1977.

Wallace, Anthony F. C. *Rockdale. The Growth of an American Village in the Early Industrial Revolution.* New York: Alfred A. Knopf, 1978.

Ward, David. "The Emergence of Central Immigrant Ghettoes in American Cities, 1840–1920." *Annals of the Association of American Geographers* 58 (1968): 343–351.

———. *Geographic Perspectives on America's Past. Readings on the Historical Geography of the United States.* New York: Oxford University Press, 1979.

Weber, Adna Ferrin. *The Growth of Cities in the Nineteenth Century. A Study in Statistics.* (Columbia University Studies in History, Economics and Public Law, Vol. 11. Ithaca, N.Y.: Cornell University Press, 1969. (Originally published, 1899).

Wright, Frank Lloyd. *The Living City.* New York: Horizon Press, 1958.

19

Landscapes in the Lesser Developed Countries

New environments are often sought as escapes from servitude to the past, even if the freedom found thereby is sometimes less complete than it promised to be, and even if many valuable memories are lost in the severing.

Kevin Lynch, *What Time Is This Place?*
1972

The abject patience of the oppressed is perhaps the most inexplicable, as it is also the most important, fact in all history.

Aldous Huxley, cited in Hugh Thomas,
A History of the World, 1979.

Key Ideas

1. The LDCs, falling primarily within the Subtropical or Tropical zones of the globe, are characterized by a low per capita gross national product (GNP).

2. The World Bank has divided the LDCs into four subcategories: (1) low-income, (2) middle-income, (3) middle-income oil exporters, and (4) middle-income oil importers. A totally different group is represented by the high-income oil exporters.

3. The LDCs contain three fourths of the world population, with a rate of natural increase well above the world average.

4. The model of demographic transition is of Western origin, with social scientists hoping the experience of Western Europe and the United States would be followed in the LDCs.

5. The growth of the urban sector means that urban problems command the attention of local political leaders and that the problems of the countryside are neglected.

6. In one area, considerable progress has been made, namely, the increase in food production under the Green Revolution.

7. The progress registered through the 1970s has been offset by the continued upsurge in population and the increasing number of mouths to feed.

8. Many developmental policies have stimulated an upsurge in disease because of the increase in water surfaces, which has led to a growth in waterborne diseases.

9. In most of the LDCs, the state plays an important role in economic development, especially where private capital is not available or not welcomed.

10. Where foreign capital has been welcomed into the LDCs, it has been provided by multinationals.

DEFINING THE REGION

Since the end of World War II and the subsequent granting of independence to their colonies by the imperial powers, the world's peoples have fallen into two broad categories: one that belongs to the *developed world,* the other to the *underdeveloped or lesser developed world.* The peoples of the developed world are part of the industrialized or economically advanced countries, found principally in the temperate latitudes of the Northern and Southern Hemispheres. Included in this group are the United States, Great Britain and the countries of Western Europe, Japan, the Soviet Union and the associated countries of Eastern Europe together with Canada, Australia, New Zealand, and South Africa (white population only). The peoples of the lesser developed world are found throughout the rest of the world, in varying stages of economic development. They inhabit for the most part the Subtropical and Tropical zones of the globe (Fig. 19–1).

Within the latter camp, the per capita GNP remains well below that of the *developed countries (DCs).* For 143 *lesser underdeveloped countries (LDCs),* the average income in 1983 was $772 (U.S.), far below that of Sweden ($14,500), the United States ($12,530), Japan ($10,330), and the Soviet Union ($4701) (*Christian Science Monitor,* June 30, 1983). However, the range of income within the LDC's is wide, from $156 in Nepal and $185 in Mali to $2250 in Mexico and $2369 in Taiwan.

The *World Development Report 1983,* published for the World Bank, divides the LDCs on the basis of income into: (1) low-income economies with a 1981 GNP per person of less than $410 and (2) middle-income economies with a GNP per person of $410 or more (p. ix). Middle-income economies are further structured into oil exporters and oil importers. Among the former group are Algeria, Egypt, Indonesia, Iran, Iraq, Malaysia, Mexico, and so on. Middle-income importers include the Philippines,

South Korea, and many of the Latin American countries. Low-income countries, the least developed economically, include most of the lands of sub-Saharan Africa and South and East Asia, among which are Nepal, Bangladesh, Mali, Ethiopia, Sudan, and the Yemenite republics. In a totally separate and quite unique category are the high-income oil exporters, such as Bahrain, Kuwait, Qatar, and Saudi Arabia in the Persian Gulf and Libya in North Africa, where the GNP ranges upward to $27,790 (Qatar).

For many of the low-income countries of the world, the economic gains made in the 1960s and the 1970s came to a halt in the early 1980s owing to the recession in the United States and the industrialized West. Africa's per capita growth rate fell, exacerbating many long-standing problems. Investment funds formerly available from the DCs were reduced, and, with fluctuation in world prices for staples produced in the LDCs, their productive capacities and employment levels were severely lowered. On top of that, a prolonged drought in the Sahel, the region along the southern margin of the Sahara Desert, followed by a period of severe aridity in southern Africa, led to a decline in crop and livestock output. Hunger has been a widespread phenomenon, especially in Africa. Thus, many of the poor countries tend to be worse off than ever before, whereas the gap between the high-income and low-income countries widens.

The term *Third World* is sometimes used to refer to the *developing world* or LDCs. The former is political in origin, deriving from an Afro-Asian conference held in 1955 in Bandung, Indonesia. There, some 27 newly independent states in Africa and Asia gathered to discuss issues of mutual concern. In time, Third World began to be adopted for those nations that had experienced colonialism and whose peoples were brown or black, nations that were struggling to find their own identity or were searching for ways to promote economic development, which they all wanted (Fig. 19–2).

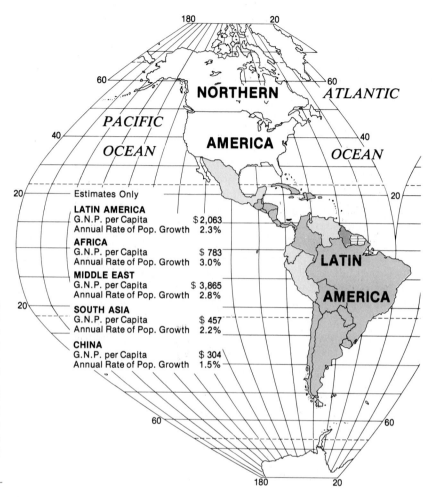

Figure 19–1

World Bank estimates of gross national product per capita clearly emphasize the significant disparities within the lesser developed countries. Even so, almost all, with the possible exception of China, are faced with alarming rates of population growth—a trend that makes it difficult for the poorer countries to achieve any progress in raising living standards.

By contrast, the industrialized and capitalist West together with Japan came to be referred to as the First World and the countries of the Soviet bloc, the Second World. To suggest the great differences in levels of economic development between the "haves" and the "have-nots", the world pattern has also been conceived in terms of a *North-South* dichotomy (North-South, 1980). The geographic imprecision of the latter concept, however, tends to lessen its value for analytical purposes.

THE GEOGRAPHIC INTEREST

Geographers have long been interested in LDCs, but their studies, following a regional or topical format, have tended to focus on individual countries or on specific economic or social geographic problems. As a group, however, geographers have lagged behind sociologists, anthropologists, economists, and political scientists who have striven to provide a framework for studying and analyzing the origins and na-

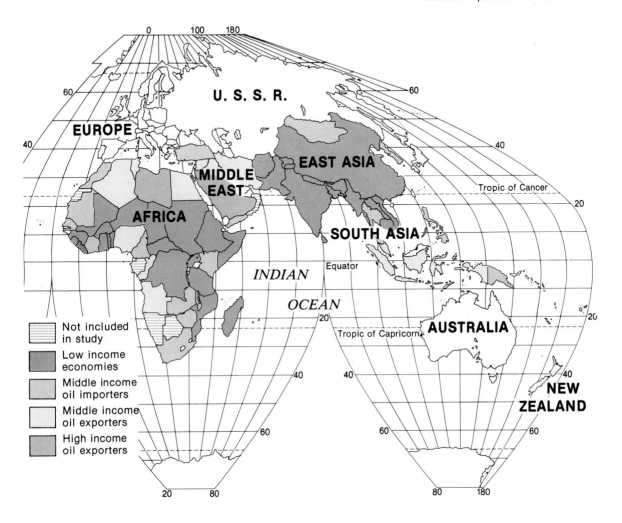

ture of the problems of modernization as they affect LDCs as a whole. This weakness in the geographic literature is one of considerable concern to geographers (Rimmer and Forbes, 1982).

This chapter attempts a discussion of some of the problems facing the people of the LDCs as they seek to promote their economies and transform the landscape. Some of the problems referred to have been touched on elsewhere in preceding chapters, but they are brought to-

gether here because of the need for our understanding.

GENERAL POPULATION TRENDS

Dealing with Population Growth

In 1983 the LDCs contained three fourths of the world population, that is, if China with its estimated 1,023,300,000 inhabitants is included. The average rate of natural increase in such

Antigua - Barbuda (1981)
Barbados (1966)
Cuba (1848)
Dominica (1978)
Dominican Republic (1844)
Grenada (1974)
Jamaica (1962)
Saint Lucia (1979)
St. Vincent and
    the Grenadines (1979)
Trinidad and Tobago (1976)

Argentina (1810-19)
Belize (1981)
Bolivia (1825)
Brazil (1822)
Colombia (1819)
Costa Rica (1821)
Chile (1810-19)
Ecuador (1830)
El Salvador (1821-39)
Guatemala (1839)
Guyana (1966)
Haiti (1804)
Honduras (1821-38)
Mexico (1821)
Nicaragua (1821-38)
Panama (1821-1903)
Paraguay (1811)
Peru (1824)
Suriname (1975)
Uruguay (1825)
Venezuela (1821-30)

| 0 | 1000 | 2000 mi. |
| 0 | 1500 | 3000 km. |

☐ Great Britain ■ France ☐ Italy ■ Spain

Figure 19–2

With the exception of the Spanish and Portuguese colonies in Meso- and South America, the LDCs gained their political independence only after World War II. Problems of political organizations, severe as they have been, have been compounded by the weakness of internal unity and, above all, rapid population growth.

countries greatly exceeds that of the developed world, but there are nevertheless important differences among them. Taiwan's rate of increase has dropped to that of the world average (1.8 percent) through a vigorous effort to lower the birthrate, now standing at 2.3 percent. But, many African countries are experiencing what can only be described as calamitous rates of population increase relative to their stage of economic development and their resource base. Some of the very small countries of Western Africa (e.g., Guinea-Bissau and Gambia) are near the world average; but, throughout the continent, 3.0 percent is more common. Kenya with 4.1 percent has the highest rate of increase of any country in the world.

Through the United Nations, an effort has been made to coordinate a program designed to expand the notion of family planning throughout the LDCs, but funds from government and private sources are hardly adequate to the task. Progress in this area is slow.

By the year 2000, at current rates of increase, the LDCs are expected to comprise almost 80 percent of the world's population. China's population will exceed 1.2 billion; India's should be slightly under 7 billion. Six other countries, however, will have populations ranging from 100 to 200 million, such as Mexico (115.1), Pakistan (141.5), Nigeria (148.2), Bangladesh (149.4), Brazil (187.7), and Indonesia (198.7).

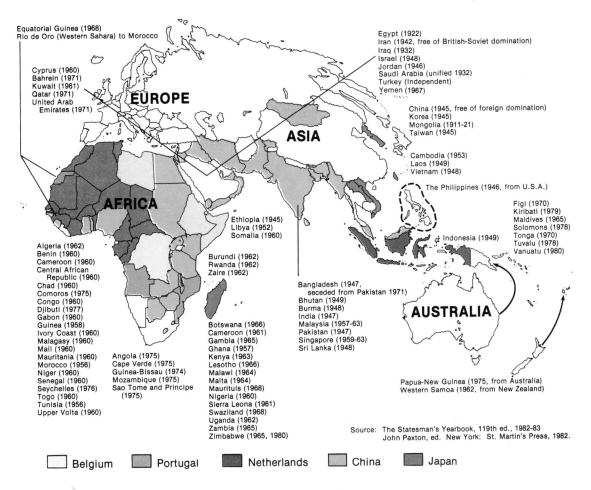

Equatorial Guinea (1968)
Rio de Oro (Western Sahara) to Morocco

Cyprus (1960)
Bahrein (1971)
Kuwait (1961)
Qatar (1971)
United Arab
 Emirates (1971)

Egypt (1922)
Iran (1942, free of British-Soviet domination)
Iraq (1932)
Israel (1948)
Jordan (1946)
Saudi Arabia (unified 1932)
Turkey (Independent)
Yemen (1967)

China (1945, free of foreign domination)
Korea (1945)
Mongolia (1911-21)
Taiwan (1945)

Cambodia (1953)
Laos (1949)
Vietnam (1948)

The Philippines (1946, from U.S.A.)

Figi (1970)
Kiribati (1979)
Maldives (1965)
Solomons (1978)
Tonga (1970)
Tuvalu (1978)
Vanuatu (1980)

Indonesia (1949)

Ethiopia (1945)
Libya (1952)
Somalia (1960)

Algeria (1962)
Benin (1960)
Cameroon (1960)
Central African
 Republic (1960)
Chad (1960)
Comoros (1975)
Congo (1960)
Djibuti (1977)
Gabon (1960)
Guinea (1958)
Ivory Coast (1960)
Malagasy (1960)
Mali (1960)
Mauritania (1960)
Morocco (1956)
Niger (1960)
Senegal (1960)
Seychelles (1976)
Togo (1960)
Tunisia (1956)
Upper Volta (1960)

Burundi (1962)
Rwanda (1962)
Zaire (1962)

Angola (1975)
Cape Verde (1975)
Guinea-Bissau (1974)
Mozambique (1975)
Sao Tome and Principe
 (1975)

Bangladesh (1947,
 seceded from Pakistan 1971)
Bhutan (1949)
Burma (1948)
India (1947)
Malaysia (1957-63)
Pakistan (1947)
Singapore (1959-63)
Sri Lanka (1948)

Botswana (1966)
Cameroon (1961)
Gambia (1965)
Ghana (1957)
Kenya (1963)
Lesotho (1966)
Malawi (1964)
Malta (1964)
Maurituls (1968)
Nigeria (1960)
Sierra Leona (1961)
Swaziland (1968)
Uganda (1962)
Zambia (1965)
Zimbabwe (1965, 1980)

Papua-New Guinea (1975, from Australia)
Western Samoa (1962, from New Zealand)

Source: The Statesman's Yearbook, 119th ed., 1982-83
John Paxton, ed. New York: St. Martin's Press, 1982.

Belgium   Portugal   Netherlands   China   Japan

The Urban Crisis

Equally shocking are the rates of increase in the urban population of the LDCs (Abu-Lughod and Hay, 1977). In 1975 for the first time in history, a majority of the world's urban population was to be found not in the industrialized world but in the LDCs. Urban growth rates in the latter are roughly double the growth rates of their national populations and in some instances reach upwards to 10 percent.

There is no standard definition among the LDCs as to what constitutes a city (Dwyer, 1974). Some settlements in Algeria with populations reaching up to ten to twelve thousand remain rural in function: that is, the basis of their economy is agriculture, including livestock raising. For this reason, despite their size, they are not classified as cities. In Nigeria, settlements containing at least twenty thousand inhabitants, where occupations are *not* predominantly agrarian, are deemed to be cities. Based on this definition, Nigeria in 1983 was 20 percent urbanized. On the other hand, in Kenya, settlements of two thousand or more are described as urban. As of 1983, only 13 percent of Kenya's population could be classified as urban. These are not high percentages, but what they disguise is the fact that the bulk of the urban population is concentrated in the largest or primate cities "Urbanization . . . ," 1983, p. 4).

What is equally disturbing about urban population growth in the LDCs is that at least half continues to be due to natural increase. But this reveals only part of the story. Contributing to high rates of growth is a rural-urban migration of monumental proportions. And, as population mushrooms, previously rural areas adjacent to the cities are reclassified, increasing not only the population base but also the city's geographic area.

The massive movement to the cities throughout most of the LDCs seems determined less by poverty, although that has remained an element, than by the incentive of economic improvement. Moreover, the migrants have tended to be young, predominantly single, with a basic education, and among them there is a rising proportion of women. Zambia in East Africa reflects the trend. Out of a total population of 6.2 million, 1 million are out of work, a very high percentage of which are persons under 21 years of age. Each year thousands of young people finish primary schooling but are turned

---

BOX 19–1

How to Cope with Urban Unemployment?

In Latin American countries, such as Brazil and Argentina, where industrialization has been underway since 1900, the proportion of the population that is urban ranges from 59.5 percent in Brazil to 80 percent in Argentina. The urban proportion tends to be considerably less in most African countries, but there the rates of urban increase are high, greatly dwarfing rates of national growth.

The young, who represent a large proportion of Third World rural-urban migrants, flock to the cities in the hope of finding employment. When frustrated, they have frequently taken to the streets in demonstrations, which can get out of hand. In São Paulo, Brazil's largest industrial city, over 30 percent of the work force were without work in 1983. Their violent street rioting led to deaths, threatening Brazil's shaky new democracy, and forced the government to take steps to find jobs.

In fast-growing Nairobi, about half the population is under 15 years of age. To deflect migrants to the capital, the Kenyan government has attempted to relocate workers by shifting the textile industry to other regional centers, such as Thika and Mombasa.

In Thailand, where 60 percent of the urban population lives in Bangkok (about 15 million), the capital city, the government has sought to lay the foundation for industrial takeoff by creating eight secondary cities to which manufacturing enterprises will be transferred. In this manner, Thailand hopes to cap the population on Bangkok at just over 8 million by 1990.

Can, however, the LDCs solve the problems of their cities on their own? Probably not. If unemployment is a major problem, how is it to be solved? Simply by putting people to work. How can that be done? By selling more goods. To whom? The countries of the First World; but the demand of the latter for goods and materials depends on their own economic health, which in 1983–1984 meant continued recovery from the recession of the early 1980s. Economists suggest that continued economic recovery in the First World depends on maintaining relatively lower interest rates, so that borrowing for industrial growth can be assured. Should the First World falter, then the rest of the world will sink deeper into economic depression with all its attendant social degradation.

Figure 19-3

Despite the presence of colonial commercial and administrative cities, the countries of Asia and Africa did not truly begin to experience the urban rush until after World War II. During the decade of the 1950s, the urban population of the developing countries expanded by about 50 percent; since then, the major cities of Asia, Africa, and Latin America have been doubling in size every decade. As a result of this rapid growth, vast shantytowns, such as this one in India, have appeared around almost every city.

(Photo Courtesy Agency for International Development.)

away from a secondary education because of lack of facilities and lack of openings. The youth tend to drift to Lusaka, the capital. Without income, they may fall victim to malnutrition; some turn to petty crime or worse (Box 19-1).

One factor that tends to encourage migration seems to be the ease of access to the city, particularly where there is an existing social network of friends and relations that can take the country people in. Where this network is weak, the migration places enormous strains on the municipal and national governments. Without funds to provide the basic necessities, the governments are also unable to house the newcomers. As a result shantytowns have grown up both inside city areas as well as in the suburbs. In some LDCs, shantytown inhabitants represent one third or more of the city's population and will easily form a majority in the future, given present trends (Fig. 19-3)

Unable to provide housing, the respective governments, moreover, are unable to check the growth of shantytowns. In many Latin American countries, for example, the problem is acute, even where industrialization has been underway for many decades. Recent rates of increase in squatter populations range from 5.5 percent for Rio de Janeiro, Brazil, to 28 percent for Guatemala City, Guatemala. In parts of Africa and Asia, rates of increase tend to be, on the whole, substantially higher: 17.4 percent for

Bombay, India; 19.1 percent for Amman, Jordan; 22.5 percent for Nairobi, Kenya; and 35.7 percent for Dar es Salaam, Tanzania. Lagos, Nigeria, for example, grew from approximately 100,000 inhabitants in 1950 to 1.5 million in 1980. Some estimates for the Lagos population, possibly reflecting seasonal migration, reach 3 million.

In effect, many cities of the LDCs are bearing the brunt of the population explosion. Urbanization for them is literally an explosion within an explosion. In the 1960s in the major countries of Latin America, almost three fourths of the overall population increase was absorbed by urban areas. By the 1970s, the absorption rate had risen to 85 percent of the total. Despite the high levels of unemployment in the cities, the young continue to be attracted and, since they represent a large and growing proportion of the total national population, urban population increase can be expected to continue throughout this century.

Whether the inevitable process of urbanization will focus on a few urban centers or whether a more dispersed pattern of smaller cities will emerge, remains to be seen. National governments have expressed the need to develop smaller cities. India seems to have achieved a balanced urban growth, despite migration to the big cities. China, on the other hand, has dealt with the problem by banning migration from the countryside to major urban centers. As of the 1980s, however, polarization in a few cities will be the tendency in most LDCs.

There is by no means a consensus as to what path of development would be most effective: To allow central city development, followed by the establishment of subsidiary cities spread throughout the countryside, thus permitting a trickle-down of innovation and wealth? Or, to encourage rural development based on small market centers, thus achieving a bottom-up approach?

In Asia in 1981, there were 81 cities with a population over 1 million. By the year 2000,

nearly 160 cities are expected to top 1 million. Of the world's largest cities, 9 out of 14 will be in Asia.

For the world as a whole, 264 of the million-plus cities are expected to be in the LDCs. It is anticipated that Mexico City will be the world's largest, with 31 million inhabitants (larger than the present population of California). São Paulo, Brazil, with about 26 million (Table 19–1), may compete with Tokyo for second place in the world.

Demographic Transition: Mobility Revolution

Based on the experience of, and the model provided by, the industrialized world, social scientists have tended to expect that with urbanization in the LDCs, birthrates and, thus, rates of natural increase will drop. This is, indeed, a possibility. One may expect, therefore, that the present high urban rates of increase are transitory and associated with early phases of urbanization. However, it should be remembered that urban growth rates will decline only in the very long run when rates of natural increase fall as fertility is reduced.

Zelinsky (1971) has attempted to provide a spatial counterpart of the demographic transition, which he calls *mobility revolution*. Demographic transition, it will be recalled, pertains to the process whereby high deathrates and birthrates move to low deathrates and low birthrates, thereby reducing the rate of natural increase. Reflecting the stages in the demographic transition, Zelinsky has identified five stages in the mobility revolution, the first three of which seem especially appropriate to the present situation in the LDCs.

Stage One (according to Zelinsky) is found in traditional societies, and is a stage that is characterized by both high birthrates and high deathrates, true of Russia and Japan before 1880. A certain balance is preserved in the population, growth is slow, and there is little permanent migration from the countryside to the

Table 19–1
The Growth of Major Cities in the Developing World

	(Thousands) Year		(Millions) Year		
	1850	1900	1950	1975	2000 (Projected)[a]
Mexico City	170	344	2.9	10.9	31.6
Buenos Aires	74	806	4.5	9.3	14.0
São Paulo	—	205	2.5	10.0	26.0
Rio de Janeiro	166	750	2.9	8.8	19.4
Bogota	40	110	0.7	3.4	9.5
Cairo	260	595	2.4	6.9	16.4
Seoul	194	195	1.0	7.3	18.7
Manila	114	190	1.5	4.4	12.7
Kinshasa	—	—	0.2	2.0	9.1
Lagos	—	—	0.3	2.1	9.4
Shanghai	250	837	5.8	10.9	19.2
Peking	1,648	1,100	2.2	8.5	19.1
Jakarta	71	115	1.6	5.6	16.9
Calcutta	413	1,085	4.4	8.1	19.7
Bombay	580	780	2.9	7.1	19.1
Karachi	—	114	1.0	4.5	15.9

[a] By the year 2000, New York is expected to have a population of 22.2 million; London 12.7 million; Paris, 12.3 million; and Tokyo, 26.1 million.

Source: George J. Beier, "Can Third World Cities Cope?" *Population Bulletin* 31, 1976, p. 9. Data for 1850 and 1900 from Tertius Chandler and Gerald Fox, *3,000 Years of Urban Growth* (New York and London: Academic Press, 1974), pp. 328–336.

cities. A number of African countries still meet these criteria, notably Mali and Chad in the Sahel and Malawi and Uganda in East Africa. In those countries, the population remains overwhelmingly rural and engaged in some form of agriculture.

Stage Two is represented by a sharp decline in the deathrate, which stimulates a rapid rise in population. Population growth in rural areas together with the initial stages of industrialization contribute to a massive movement from rural to urban areas. Many of the LDCs, such as India, Kenya, Tanzania, and Zambia, now fall into this category. Egypt and Honduras have reached the transition from Stage Two to Stage Three.

Stage Three, a late transitional stage, is marked both by a decline in fertility leading to a drop in the birthrate *and* a slackening of rural-urban migration. Taiwan, Brazil, and Mexico

together with South Korea and Indonesia may be considered to be moving through Stage Three.

Stages Four and Five, characteristic of the Industrialized World today, are identified by a falling off of rural-urban migration. Rates of natural increase are low. Stage Five, representing superadvanced or postindustrial societies, seems now to reflect a new phenomenon, namely, a reverse flow of people from older metropolitan areas to the countryside. The Soviet Union and the East European states may be considered to be at the end of Stage Four; the United States, Japan, Great Britain, and parts of Western Europe in Stage Five.

However optimistic this schemata, based as it is on a notion of progress common in the Industrialized World, the push that sent people from the villages to the cities may not in the future work itself out in the developing world in this agreeable way. The rural-urban migration has turned many LDC cities into wretched megalopolises where the prospects of immediate improvement seem dim and social conflict may ensue. Thousands of Ghanians, for example, were expelled from Nigerian cities in 1982 because of the economic setback following the decline in the world demand for Nigeria's oil. Ghana could offer no employment to the returnees, so the migrants were forced back into the bush.

The Changing Role of Women

In traditional societies, women have been primarily family oriented by custom and necessity, trained to serve the needs of their husbands and to produce children. The demands placed on them for children have been especially severe, often reinforced by the prevailing socioreligious mores. With a lack of knowledge of family planning, the consequences have been particularly harsh. High maternal mortality rates have been the reward for multiple pregnancies, inadequate medical care, improper diet, and, in many instances, illegal abortions.

The perceived opportunities offered by the city have drawn women from the countryside. The search for a better life, for employment, however, often ends in failure. Where there is an excess of labor, few jobs are available. Moreover, in many societies, particularly the Muslim, men workers are preferred over women. However, in East Asian countries, such as Taiwan and South Korea, where economic growth has been relatively rapid, women have played an increasingly active role in the development process—whether pulled into a factory assembly line or employed at home on a piece-work basis.

Organizations, such as the Cooperative for American Relief Everywhere (*CARE*)—founded in 1946—have moved into programs especially designed to assist women. A CARE urban-renewal program in Lima, Peru, for example, enables women to exchange their labor for food. Elsewhere, women are being taught how to improve and balance home nutrition, to lay out parks and construct health centers, to build classrooms, and to organize preschool feeding programs as well as to undertake heavier work tasks, such as digging ditches and laying out roads. Such programs operate specifically on the premise that women have an extremely important role to play in the economic process (Fig. 19–4).

PROBLEMS OF INTERNAL DIVERSITY

The boundaries that delimit the territories of many of the LDCs, most notably in Africa, are of European origin. When first drawn in the nineteenth century, they marked spheres of European colonial influence, commercial activity, and political control. In many instances the product of accident, they paid scant attention to the diversity of ethnic, linguistic, and religious associations on which they were imposed. The tribal communal conflicts that have broken out since independence—again, especially in Africa—and that have relied on violence for resolution, were to a great degree frozen under colonial control (Fig. 19–5).

The existence of conflict has in many instances been a factor that has drained creative energies and taken lives that might, under happier circumstances, have been directed toward social and economic improvement.

Of all the continents, Africa has probably the greatest diversity. Of its 41 independent states, only Egypt, Tunisia, Morocco, Lesotho, and Somalia seem homogeneous—and even some of these have debatable borders. As a result of internecine tribal conflicts and wars, Africa had, in 1980, 2.7 million U.N. recorded refugees in 17 African countries and an additional 2 million displaced persons.

Among some of Africa's more disruptive conflicts was the Biafran War of Secession in

Figure 19–4

In many of the LDCs, women are playing an increasingly important role in the national economy. Women, for example, are employed at this corned-beef canning factory in Kano, Nigeria.

Source: Diane Rawson/Photo Researchers, Inc.

Nigeria (1967–1969). A great deal was at stake in the war. Great Britain had tried to hold Nigeria together after independence with a federal system of government, but competition between the associated regions flared in 1964. The breakaway of the Eastern Region (Biafra) threatened the future of the Nigerian oil industry. The war that ensued ended in a great loss of life and considerable material destruction. Similarly, in the former Belgian Congo, the conflicts between tribes, regions, and political personalities led to attempts on the part of the copper-rich Katanga province to secede from the new state, now known as Zaire—a move that led to a protracted struggle lasting from 1959 to 1965. There have been, of course, many other disputes in Africa, which have been referred to elsewhere in this book.

But Africa is not alone. India, despite the immense problems of population growth and conflicts with both China and Pakistan, has struggled to preserve unity and a national economy in the face of great linguistic diversity. The cost has been the recognition, in the form of provincial autonomy, of some of its major language families.

Pakistan, formed in 1947–1948 out of British India, was subsequently torn apart by the secession of its eastern Bengali province, which formed Bangladesh.

Sri Lanka, with a population of 15 to 16 million, has been one of the latest to be subjected to communal violence and frenzy. The conflict that broke out in 1983 between the Buddhist Sinhalese (70 percent of the population) and the Hindu Tamils (22 percent) has simmered for

Figure 19–5(A)

A

Because human labor is plentiful in most LDCs, it makes little economic sense to employ machines that consume costly fossil fuels. The use of human power in landscape modification, as shown here in Taiwan, is a phenomenon that is old to many Asian countries. Here, workers move earth for a bridge construction.

Sources: (A) George Holton/Photo Researchers; (B) H. W. Silvester Rapho/Photo Researchers; (C) Carl Frank/Photo Researchers.

many decades because of linguistic and communal differences.

The Tamils, consisting of two groups—the Sri Lankan Tamils who invaded the island from southern India centuries ago and the Indian Tamils who were transported to Ceylon by the British after 1830 to work on the plantations—are concentrated principally in the northern and northeastern parts of Sri Lanka. The Sinhalese, the majority, are older inhabitants of the island, having migrated to the island centuries ago, and Sinhala has been the official language of the state since 1975. Tamil opposition, how-

ever, has led to the use in practice of both the Tamil and Sinhala languages in areas where either group is in a majority. Some Tamils, however, are unwilling to accept *only* that concession and demand a federal union, if not outright separation. It is official opposition to the latter that has provoked violence, destroyed lives and property, and dislocated the economy.

Obviously, the most extreme instance of internal conflict, which quickly took on an international aspect, was the war in Vietnam between North and South, leading also to the invasion of Laos and Cambodia.

B

C

Figure 19–5(B) and (C)

The great variety of cultures that characterize the LDCs is evident, in particular, in costume design. A Peruvian woman in traditional dress (B) at a Cuzco market trans-ports a bundle of straw on her back while supporting a child in front. A Sierra Leone woman (C) in a colorful wrap-around carries wood for the fire on her head.

RURAL ECONOMY

Despite high out-migration rates, most of the LDCs are expected to remain predominantly rural throughout the present century.

The rural-urban flow, on the one hand, reflects pressure on the land and the inability of national governments to improve life in the villages. On the other hand, the growth in the urban population immediately strengthens the power of the urban sector, so that national governments are compelled to direct their resources toward tackling urban problems, including those created by the shantytowns. Still, in countries such as Bangladesh, attempts are being made to stimulate economic development in the countryside by devolving authority to local administrative units to raise and collect taxes and to plan local development.

In one area, however, considerable success has been achieved, and that has been in the raising of crop yields through the Green Revolution. The introduction of high yielding varieties (*HYVs*) has been one of the most significant technological changes taking place in the agriculture of the LDCs. This technological transfer has entailed the diffusion and acceptance of hybrid seeds, fertilizers and pesticides, and special cultivation practices. When properly introduced, the yield potential and the income-generating capacity of the new varieties have been greatly superior to those of tradi-

Figure 19–6

Much of the field work in the LDCs is done by hand and is often tedious and physically tiring. Here, Indonesian women plant rice in Java, using bamboo sticks to align the crop.

Source: Bernard Pierre Wolff/Photo Researchers, Inc.

tional crops (Ruttan and Hayami, 1971) (Fig. 19–6).

From 1950 to 1980, food production within the LDCs increased at an annual rate of 2.9 percent per year, compared with 2.5 percent for the Industrialized World. In a number of LDCs, the annual increase was over 4.0 percent. Such sustained rates were achieved by Mexico, Tai-

wan, and Israel. In individual instances, results were truly remarkable. Significant surpluses have piled up in Taiwan. From 1967 to 1979, India's wheat production tripled to 33 million tons, making India largely self-sufficient. Indonesia doubled its rice output to 22 million tons by 1982.

However, continued population growth in the LDCs reduced the rate of increase of per capita food production to only 0.5 percent (compared to 1.4 percent for the DCs). Indeed, in a number of countries, especially in Africa, per capita food production actually declined. Between 1961 and 1978, overall African food output dropped by more than 20 percent. In the Sahel, where because of drought, overgrazing, and conflict, widespread hunger ensued. In 1983, drought seared southern Africa as well. It is estimated that catastrophic food shortages imperiled 150 million Africans. But, this state of affairs is by no means confined to Africa. In Manila, in the Philippines, the deficiency of food intake among the poorest third of the urban population has been found to be nearly twice that of its rural counterpart. To meet the needs of the urban poor, the government has set up special food stores, known as *kadiwa* (togetherness). Food riots sustained by the poor in the summer of 1983 rocked Rio de Janiero, Brazil, and were followed by riots in Chile.

Clearly, in many LDCs, the problem of ensuring that food is available to the people is enhanced where transportation or distribution facilities are poorly developed.

Where plateaus of production have been reached under existing techniques, there is now a need for a further breakthrough in production, involving continued high inputs of capital and skills that range from the scientific to the technical, managerial, and organizational. In the 1970s, a new global network of 13 agricultural research centers was established to identify and produce new varieties of crops suited to local regions.

Rural electrification is a high priority, as is the development of a network of rural roads.

Figure 19–7

With the recent relaxation of governmental controls on the economy, and especially in agriculture, individual initiative in China has come to the fore. Here, a young farmer waters his plants near Gulin.

Studies in Brazil of the construction of the Belem-Brasilia Highway (1940–1970) have shown the kind of positive impact that road construction can have on agricultural activities, especially in a frontier region. The development of small rural manufacturing enterprises would afford an alternate source of income to rural families, and, where gainfully employed, slow the rural exodus, as has been the case in Taiwan and South Korea. In Taiwan, the agricultural share of the economy has dropped to 7.5 percent, with 92 percent of the rural population in farming on a part-time basis only. A major part of rural income now comes from nonfarming sources.

In some of the LDCs where land still is held by a few owners, reform is needed, so that those who work the land have a direct interest in it as well. The creation of small holdings, however, seems not to be the answer to the farm problem if the future is taken into consideration. In Taiwan, for example, small holdings, resulting from the post-World War II reforms, have proven too small for efficient farming. As a result, the government has encouraged the formation of loose cooperatives or joint-farming ventures where equipment and labor may be shared. Elsewhere, additional incentives are required. In China, to raise the level of farming and output, the government has instituted a "responsibility system," which allows farmers to produce and sell their own crops once they have met government production quotas. Chinese farmers have been quick to respond to the new incentives (Fig. 19–7). Similarly, in the southern half of Vietnam, the

Figure 19–8

In the tropics, pressure is mounting to clear the forests for export of timber and for agricultural purposes. Widespread clearing, however, will have devastating conse- quences on the ecological system. Here, slash-and-burn is being practiced as the forest is cleared to construct the Trans-Amazon Highway near Belém in Brazil.

Hanoi government has permitted the farmers to keep their surplus production (for sale) afer fixing and meeting their quotas with local coopera- tives.

The 1970s saw the closing of the frontier in most of Southeast Asia. In Africa and Latin America, the opening of new areas for produc- tion awaits the development of the means to control disease and pests. At the same time, techniques must be adopted to manage fragile tropical soils to prevent loss of fertility and soil erosion. But the further clearing of forested lands threatens the habitat of the wildlife that shares the planet with humankind; their further loss would represent a major tragedy (Fig. 19–8).

DISEASE

Disease, where 1 person in 10 is disabled, is part of the landscape of developing countries (Desowitz, 1981). Smallpox was eradicated dur- ing the 1960s and 1970s but many diseases spread by water have fought back as the envi- ronment that supports the dissemination of dis- eases has been enhanced by economic devel- opment.

Malaria, which drains intellectual and physi- cal energies, has been taking 1 million lives each year in Africa, and many million more cases are reported annually in India (Fig. 19–9). The major potential carrier of malaria is the mosquito (*Anopheles aquasalis*), against which

Figure 19–9

Despite the rapid growth in population, the number of medical facilities per person throughout most LDCs remains low. Clinics have been established by various international agencies to help the local authorities stem the tide of tropical disease. In Africa, as shown here, children are tested for schistosomiasis, an especially debilitating disease.

vaccines are under development. However, the expansion of tropical water surfaces, owing in part to the creation of dams for hydroelectric-power production, in part to the expansion of irrigated rice culture, and in part to forest leveling that allows the sun to penetrate to rivers and lakes of the earth's surface have encouraged the breeding of mosquitoes. Such open-water surfaces in tropical areas provide an ideal habitat for the mosquito, and breeding is prolific. Mass immunization is necessary but difficult to achieve; some vaccines are often effective only against one strain of malaria.

Second only to the human devastation caused by malaria is the debility caused by *schistosomiasis*. Like malaria, schistosomiasis is water associated, but this intestinal illness is transmitted by fresh-water snails. Water, poverty, and unsanitary habitats are the basic ingredients for schistosomal epidemics (Desowitz, 1981). The impact of the disease is believed to be expanding, especially in Africa, as projects associated with water impounding—like Lake Volta in Ghana—and hydraulic agriculture increase. Because the poor, especially in rural areas, use water bodies for a variety of purposes, including bathing and as a toilet, they become a target for the parasites that are borne by the snails and that penetrate human skin. The immune system is attacked, and inflammation of the bladder results.

Among other diseases that are endemic to the tropics is *trypanosomiasis* (sleeping sickness), an infection transmitted by the tsetse fly. Tsetse flies inhabit Africa south of the Sahara, but varieties of flies have their own particular geographic or ecologic setting. The latter may range from the humid riverine forests of West and Central Africa to the dry savanna woodlands of East and Central Africa. The most serious form of sleeping sickness occurs when people settle in the savanna to hunt wild game or to graze cattle. The presence of wild game reserves, for example, encourages the presence of infected flies. Nomadic and seminomadic cattle-owning tribes, such as those who inhabit Mali and Chad, have been forced to pasture their animals in fly-free zones in and near the Sahel. The trek into more humid regions during the dry season encourages the flies. One way to control the disease is to control game by use of insecticides and vaccines, but, to date measures have not proven successful. Although the prevalence of sleeping sickness is low, it nevertheless remains a disease of the African environment.

To reduce debilitating diseases of the tropics will require changes in the environment that breed the diseases as well as in the habits and ways of life of countless people. Most countries are too poor to undertake programs of control without massive aid from outside.

THE ROLE OF THE STATE IN ECONOMIC DEVELOPMENT

On granting independence, most European colonial powers attempted to provide political constitutions for their former colonies. Based on European experience, however, few at-

Figure 19–10

The leaders of many of the LDCs have often had little experience at government or administration, a phenomenon of course that is not restricted to LDCs. Palace coups have in many instances replaced democratically-elected governments with one-party dictatorships or military rule. General Joseph Désiré Mobutu, the ruler of Zaire, Africa, shown here, is representative of the military leaders that have seized power since independence.

tempts to build democratic societies succeeded. With the exception of such new countries as the Ivory Coast (formerly French) and India (formerly British), most countries quickly fell under one-party rule and opted for various degrees of state involvement in economic development. Much of Latin America had had some experience with democratic institutions, but the middle class was not sufficiently large to counter the tendencies toward government by generals (Fig. 19–10).

Some newly independent countries welcomed economic aid and investment from Europe and the United States; others, on the other hand, were attracted to the socialist model and sought guidance from the Soviet Union or one or other of its satellites. Adoption of the socialist model, however, was triggered less by ideology than by the problems arising from economies traditionally dependent on world markets. In the Caribbean area, for example, small countries moved to control their economies, not necessarily because of any left-wing influence from Cuba, but because leaders could find little alternative. Even in conservative Trinidad, an oil-exporting, middle-income country, the government has become an active participant and investor in a wide range of developmental projects.

Many of the newly independent states were not only weak economically, but also unbalanced in social structure. The new bureaucracy as well as the leadership, for example, has come not from the traditional and classic entrepreneurial middle class (as was the case in Europe), but from a small educated group—lawyers, teachers, doctors, dentists, trade union leaders, or simply professional politicians educated in Europe of the United States and with little practical experience and no experience in planning or administration. Invariably, such a domestic leadership mix has led to error. Overspending has produced chronic inflation, weakened purchasing power, and led to further impoverishment—intensified by the economic problems of the industrialized world.

THE MULTINATIONALS

Many of the income-generating enterprises in the developing countries, such as the mining of bauxite in Jamaica, the production of aluminum in Ghana, and the output of manganese, copper, and chromite in southern Africa, have remained foreign owned, falling under the control of multinational or transnational corporations. Stability is essential to multinational operations, but the allegiance of the latter is not to local governments. On the other hand, the latter as a group are unable to exert any significant influence on the global giants because they have so little stake in their operations. Thus, a dangerous separation sometimes develops between the form and substance of national state power. This separation has been expressed in demands for an increase in the national share of the income, that is, higher royalties for the extraction of the mineral wealth and, failing that, in threats to take over or nationalize the corporation's holdings.

ECONOMIC DEVELOPMENT: THE SEARCH FOR CAUSES AND EFFECTS

Although the poor in the LDCs cannot eat theories, social scientists have offered many explanations as to why many of them remain poor.

Modernization Theory

Prior to the granting of independence to the colonies, the uneven economic development of the diverse peoples of the globe was not regarded as a problem. Indeed, the difficulties facing the tropical regions were regarded as natural, their peoples generally incapable of self-government and advancement.

A major change in thinking about economic development occurred in the 1960s after Rostow (1960) published a thesis outlining stages in economic growth. Rostow assumed that in the process of development or *modernization,* all societies begin at the bottom of the ladder, with a *traditional economy* based primarily in agriculture. Then, through a series of stages, one following logically on the other, a transition takes place—from traditional economy to industrial *takeoff.* Takeoff involves industrial expansion and urbanization, leading to maturity, and, subsequently, to a fully industrialized society based on high mass consumption (Rostow, 1960).

Underlying this evolutionary, progressive upward path is the historic model afforded by the Western World's experience in the nineteenth and early twentieth centuries. In Rostow's opinion, therefore, a theoretical model derived from the developed world should have meaning and value for the LDCs.

This impulse toward economic development, however, was thought to lie within the native society. Growth, then, was believed to be sparked by domestic initiatives. At the heart of modernization was a belief in the beneficial effects of spatial diffusion. Waves of modern innovation were seen to filter down from the urban core to the countryside, in a kind of operation bootstrap. Indeed, the developing city was envisaged as a *growth pole* that would provide the initiative for development and change through time as well as over earth space (Gould, 1970). Where a fully fledged urban populace was not in place, then some external stimulant would be required to initiate development.

This notion of modernization very much reflected the American geographer's belief in progress and in a rational world order. It was the path of sure-fire success.

Should growth not occur, it was believed that the problems "experienced by those living in less developed areas are largely of their own making and . . . the solution to such problems are likewise to be found within the confines of the less developed areas themselves" (Browett, 1980, vol. 4, pp. 64–65).

This concept of a "similar path" modernization was widely hailed by geographers (Soja, 1968; Gould, 1970; Haggett, 1983; Berry et al., 1976; and others). However, the increasing evidence of differences in income within the LDCs and between the LDCs and the developed world led other social scientists to question the validity of modernization theory. These critics came to feel the economic development could not be measured against some historic model. They began to believe that the variations in degrees of development over the surface of the earth were part of the larger world system and could not be isolated from worldwide patterns of economic organization and control. This line of reasoning drew social scientists to review and examine, above all, the relationships between the industrialized cores and the rest of the world.

Core-Periphery Relationships

One way to visualize the modern world, social scientists have hypothesized, is to consider the industrialized countries collectively as representing the global economic core; the rest, then, is peripheral to it. Most of the countries of the core have broadly based economies. Whether capitalist or socialist, the core countries have experienced to date many of the phases of the Industrial Revolution, possess capital resources, and are capable of providing economic and financial assistance to the periphery on which they are dependent for many industrial and agricultural resources.

The periphery is represented by the LDCs, with all the attendant and pressing problems referred to earlier. In various stages of economic growth, unevenly endowed in industrial or agricultural resources, most of the LDCs are highly dependent on export earnings to finance needed imports.

The *core-periphery* relationship may be understood simply as a geographic conceptualization without the attachment of any value. However, not all geographers or social scientists would treat the relationship in this manner. Some, including contemporary students of the writings of Karl Marx, called neo-Marxists, would see the relationship as exploitative or as one of conflict. They see the capitalist members of the economic core pitted against the LDCs, much as they believe capitalist entrepreneurs were pitted against labor during the period of industrialization in the nineteenth century—in England, in France, in Germany and in the United States.

Dependency Theory

In attempting to explain what they see as the true nature of core-periphery relationships, social scientists have coined the term *dependency*. Dependency studies may include a variety of perspectives however. They may range from suggestions as to how the countries of the core may assist economically the LDCs to explanations as to how the countries of the core have contributed to the many developmental problems facing the periphery.

In a severly critical form, dependency theory sees the LDCs as being *forced* into a subordinate economic position. Through economic domination of the periphery, the core, or *metropolitan state,* extracts the surplus from each stage of peripheral activity, from mining or cultivation to the semiprocessing of the raw material, the surplus being returned in the form of profit to stockholders at the core. In this exchange, *class stratification* results, which forces the LDCs to provide the labor that supports the consumption patterns of the social classes at the core.

The implication of this thesis is that if only LDCs had been spared inclusion in the capitalist-dominated international economic system, they would have—could have—undergone development or modernization on their own terms. There is, however, no evidence to suggest that this thesis is true. Countries like Taiwan, on the other hand, have become very closely integrated into the world economy and

have grown faster than others that have attempted a separate—or a socialist—path of development.

In some Third World countries, dependency is translated into *neocolonialism.* By neocolonialism is meant that the newly independent countries of the periphery are independent, with all the outward trappings of international sovereignty, but that in reality their economic—and, thus, their political systems—are directed from abroad. Political independence is, thus, only a sham.

Neocolonialism has become a powerful slogan, and it is one that Soviet bloc countries in particular have employed to criticize the policies of the capitalist core (Box 19–2). However, such a simplistic interpretation of historical events tends to ignore reality. The Indian textile industry, for example, provided severe competition for the British textile industry in the early decades of the twentieth century, but it was the British themselves who stimulated the growth and development of the Indian industry so as to expand opportunities for employment in India. As far as Karl Marx was concerned, British colonialism had been necessary to awaken India from the social and economic stagnation it had fallen into in the nineteenth century.

Dependency theory, moreover, cannot account for the experience of the *Overseas Chinese* in many countries, especially in Southeast Asia, which were subject to European or American political domination. The Chinese often began life in a Southeast Asian country as penniless laborers who worked and saved until they had enough money to begin businesses of their own. The presence of the Chinese brought economic vitality to the tradition-bound peasant folk cultures of Southeast Asia (Sowell, 1983). The skills and entrepreneurship of the Overseas Chinese raised their living standards as well as those of the native peoples themselves. The essential weakness of dependency theory or of the neocolonialist bias is that one or the other robs the people of the LDCs of their own history or integrity, making them little more than

BOX 19–2

Colonialism, Imperialism, and the Developing Countries

Neocolonialism is derived from the notion of capitalist exploitation of the kind that is said to have prevailed in the relationships between Western Europe and its historic colonial holdings. Associated with this relationship is the concept of imperialism. Empires have existed since early times. But throughout much of the nineteenth century the term *imperialism* had various meanings, all of which were neutral in application.

Imperialism, as a value-laden term implying exploitation, dates from the end of the nineteenth century, particularly following the scramble for colonies that was part of European history after 1870. Some Europeans attributed Britain's wealth to its colonies. Others argued that colonies would provide living space for Europe's overcrowded population—or at least drain off its unemployed. In reality, however, colonies at that time were more valued for political glory than for any real economic motive.

The publication in 1902 of a book entitled *Imperialism,* by John A. Hobson, added a new dimension to the concept. Hobson argued that imperialism was, in effect, an act of wickedness, led by "finance-capital," often Jewish. It was stimulated by the need to find markets for domestic production and to obtain high returns on the export of capital. The only persons, according to Hobson, who benefited from this arrangement were the "finance-capitalists"; everyone else suffered, including both the populations of the colonies as well as of the colonizing nations. Hobson, therefore, defined imperialism as the use of the machinery of government by private interests, mainly capitalists, to secure for themselves economic gains outside the country.

Such views were developed further by later European writers, including V. I. Lenin, the leader of the Russian revolution, who adapted the theme in his influential work *Imperialism: The Highest Stage of Capitalism* (1917/c1939).

Other writers—including economic historians—however, have questioned the assumption that colonies played a major role in capitalist development. After 1870, by far the greater part of European investments flowed not into the colonial periphery, but into areas undergoing industrialization—in Europe, in North America, in South Africa, and in Australia. Britain, for example, was more likely to invest in Argentina or the Dutch East Indies than in its own empire. Trade between the mother countries and their colonial acquisitions was usually only a small fraction of their foreign trade. Raw materials were important in the case of some colonial acquisitions, but their share in the raw materials market as a whole was not large. And the bulk of European migration at the turn of the century was not to the colonies, but to the United States. Finally, big business exerted very little influence on colonial or foreign policy at the time.

Although the exploitative interpretation of imperialism appeals to neo-Marxists, who use it in association with neocolonialism, such slogans distort the facts of history and do little more than to straightjacket creative thinking about LDC problems.

local actors or pawns in a larger chess game. The role that local culture, tradition, and community have played before or after independence is rejected. Each people has its own response to core capitalism, imperialism, or colonialism.

EPILOGUE

The enthusiasm that greeted political independence throughout the colonial world has been tempered by the experience of time. Political independence transferred the reins of government but did not provide a formula for steady economic growth. Economic progress achieved in the 1970s has been offset by the worldwide recession of the early 1980s. Investment projects have fallen idle for want of foreign capital. Population continues to grow, the rural surplus spilling over into the cities, forming shantytown communities that offer their inhabitants little hope for the future. Where agricultural expansion was achieved, leading to a greater output of foodstuffs, it has been offset by more mouths to feed. Drought in many parts of the tropical and subtropical regions has compounded the misery.

Increasingly, the economic and social strains that Third World countries experience are proving too great for existing often *oligarchical* political structures, governments dominated by a few of the historically wealthy landed families. The stress is triggering upheavals, acts of terrorism, and revolution—from Vietnam to Nicaragua.

APPLICATION OF IDEAS

1. The world has fallen into two camps, each based on income; the differences between the two camps appear to be widening.

2. The problems facing the LDCs seem overwhelming, not the least of which is the difficulty of slowing population growth by a reduction in birth rates.

3. Population growth is glaringly demonstrated in Third World cities. The world watches and wonders how the LDCs will be able to cope with exploding urban size and numbers.

4. Related to population growth in cities is the need to find housing and employment, especially for the young who are migrating from the countryside in large numbers.

5. Most of the LDCs are rural, the bulk of their populations are engaged in agriculture;

this pattern will endure for most countries through the end of this century.

6. However, because of the political clout wielded by the cities, national governments have had difficulty deciding on priorities. Generally, they have tended to focus on urban problems.

7. One great area of success has been in the use and spread of high-yielding varieties, (HYVs) of wheat and rice. But more needs to be done to ensure that food production remains ahead of population increase.

8. Social scientists have been attracted to the plight of the LDCs and have attempted to find the causes of their low level of economic development and what must be done to stimulate their economic development. However, there is no easy explanation for the causes, nor is there any easy formula for economic growth.

KEY WORDS AND PHRASES

class stratification	mobility revolution
core-periphery	modernization
dependency	neocolonialism
developed countries	North-South
(DCs)	overseas Chinese
developed world	schistosomiasis
developing world	takeoff
growth pole	Third World
high-yielding	traditional economy
varieties (HYVs)	trypanosomiasis
lesser developed	underdeveloped
countries (LDCs)	world
metropolitan state	

QUESTIONS FOR FURTHER DISCUSSION

1. What is the origin of the term *Third World*? Is it a satisfactory term? Is there another term that seems preferable?

2. What percentage of world population is to be found in the Third World? What are the demographic characteristics of Third World countries?

3. Why are the cities of the LDCs growing so rapidly? How does their rate of increase compare with that of their respective countries generally?

4. What problems face both governments and populations in those countries experiencing urban explosion?

5. Why have social scientists been optimistic about population growth and economic development in the LDCs? What has tended to erode that optimism?

6. Why do many of the LDCs face problems of integrating their populations into national communities? What is the nature of the problems?

7. What policies must the LDCs adopt to ensure that more and more people remain on the land and do not migrate to the cities?

8. What is the relationship between economic development and the expansion of disease in the LDCs? Was this a matter of concern in the industrialized countries as they underwent economic development in the past? Why? Why not?

9. Why has modernization theory been rejected by many social scientists as an inadequate framework for economic growth in the LDCs?

10. Does dependency theory offer a more realistic assessment of core-periphery relationships than any theory hitherto advanced?

REFERENCES AND ADDITIONAL READINGS

Abu-Lughod, Janet, and Hay, Richard, Jr. *Third World Urbanization*. Chicago: Maaroufa Press, 1977.

Asia Urbanizing. Population Growth and Concentration and the Problems Thereof. Social Science Research Institute, International Christian University. Tokyo: Simul Press, 1976.

Beier, George J. "Can Third World Cities Cope?" *Population Bulletin* 31 December (1976).

Bergesen, Albert, ed. *Studies of the Modern World-System*. New York: Academic Press, 1980.

Bergesen, Albert. "The Emerging Science of the World System." *International Social Science Journal* 24 (January 1982).

Berry, Brian et al. *The Geography of Economic Systems*. Englewood Cliffs, N.J.: Prentice-Hall 1976.

Browett, John. "Development, The Diffusionist Paradigm and Geography."*Progress in Human Geography* Vol 4 (1980): 57–79.

Chandler, Tertius and Fox, Gerald. *3,000 Years of Urban Growth*. New York and London: Academic Press, 1974.

Cross, Malcom. *Urbanization and Urban Growth in the Caribbean. An Essay on Social Change in Dependent Societies*. Cambridge: Cambridge University Press, 1979.

"Crowded Cities, Unemployment are Threatening Latin America." *Popline* 4 (December 1982).

deSouza, Anthony R., and Porter, Philip W. *The Underdevelopment and Modernization of the Third World*. Resource Paper No. 28. Washington, D.C.: Commission on College Geography, Association of American Geographers, 1974.

Desowitz, Robert S. *New Guinea Tapeworms and Jewish Grandmothers*. New York: Avon Books, 1981.

Dwyer, D. J. *The City in the Third World*. New York: Harper & Row, 1974.

Gould, Peter R. "The Spatial Impress of the Modernization Process: Tanzania 1920–1963." *World Politics* 22 (1970): 149–170. Reprinted in *Ekistics* 30 (1970): 356–362.

Hagett, H. P. *Geography: A Modern Synthesis*. New York: Harper & Row, 1983.

Hansen, Dean. "Geography and Development." Unpublished paper. Department of Geography, University of Washington, Seattle, 1983.

Hobson, John A. *Imperialism, A Study,* 3rd rev. ed. London: Allen & Unwin, 1938.

Katzman, Martin T. "The von Thünen Paradigm, the Industrial-Urban Hypothesis, and the Spatial Structure of Agriculture." *American Journal of Agricultural Economics* 56 (November 1974): 683–696.

Katzman, Martin T. "Regional Development Policy in Brazil: The Role of Growth Poles and Development Highways in Goias," *Economic Development and Cultural Change* 24 (October 1975): 75–107.

Lenin, Vladimir I. *Imperialism: The Highest Stage of Capitalism; A Popular Outline*. New York: International Publishers, 1939. (Originally published, 1917.)

Mountjoy, Alan B. *The Third World: Problems and Perspectives*. London: Macmillan, 1978.

Myint, Hla. "The 'Classical Theory' of International Trade and the Underdeveloped Countries." *Economic Journal* 68 (June 1958): 317–337.

Nicholls, William H. "The Transformation of Agriculture in a Semi-Industrialized Country: The Case of Brazil, pp. 311–378. In *The Role of Agriculture in Economic Development*. Erik Thorbecke, ed. New York: Columbia University Press, 1969.

North-South. A Program for Survival. (Introduction by Willy Brandt.) Cambridge, Mass.: MIT Press, 1980.

Poethig, R. P. "The Squatters of Southeast Asia." *Impact* 5 (1970): 4–10. Reprinted in *Ekistics* 31 (1971): 121–124.

Reitsma, Hendrik-Jan A. "Development Geography, Dependency Relations, and the Capitalist Scapegoat," *Professional Geographer* 34 (May 1982): 125–130.

Reitsma, Hendrik-Jan A. "A Constellation of Core-Periphery Relations." *Professional Geographer* 35 (February 1983): 84–86.

Rimmer, Peter J. and Forbes, Dean K. "Underdevelopment Theory: A Geographical Review." *Australian Geographer* 15 (November 1982): 197–211.

Robinson, Joan. *Aspects of Development and Underdevelopment*. New York: Cambridge University Press, 1979.

Rogers, Andrei. "Sources of Urban Population Growth and Urbanization, 1950–2000: A Demographic Accounting." *Economic Development and Cultural Change* 30 (April 1982): 483–506.

Rogers, Andrei and Williamson, Jeffrey G. "Migration, Urbanization and Third World Development: An Overview." *Economic Development and Cultural Change* 30 (April 1982): 463–482.

Rostow, W. W. *The Stages of Economic Growth: A Non-Communist Manifesto*. Cambridge: University Press, 1960.

Ruttan, Vernon and Hayami, Yujiro. *Agricultural Development. An International Perspective*. Baltimore: Johns Hopkins University Press, 1971.

Smith, Anthony D. *Theories of Nationalism,* 2nd ed. London: Duckworth, 1983.

Soja, Edward W. *The Geography of Modernization in Kenya: A Spatial Analysis of Social Economic and Political Change*. Syracuse N.Y.: Syracuse University Press, 1968.

World Bank. *World Development Report 1983*. New York: Oxford University Press, 1983.

Sowell, Thomas, *The Economics and Politics of Race. An International Perspective*. New York: William Morrow, 1983.

"Urbanization Is Called Dominant Problem." *Popline* 5 (April 1983).

Whyte, R. O. *The Spatial Geography of Rural Economies*. Delhi, India: Oxford University Press, 1982.

Wolf, Eric R. *Europe and the People Without History*. Berkeley and Los Angeles: University of California Press, 1982.

Zelinsky, Wilbur. "The Hypothesis of the Mobility Transition." *Geographical Review* 61 (1971): 219–249.

Epilogue

Do not imagine that the exploration
Ends, that she has yielded all her mystery
Or that the man you hold
Cancels further discovery
I tell you her uncovering takes years,
Takes centuries, and when you find her
    naked
Look again,
Admit there is something else you cannot
    name,
A veil, a coating just above the flesh
Which you cannot remove by your mere wish
When you see the land naked, look again
(Burn you maps, that is not what I mean),
I mean the moment when it seems most plain
Is the moment when you must begin again.

Gwendolyn Macewen, *The Discovery,* 1970

These chapters have attempted to show that throughout history humankind has arranged and rearranged the patterns of occupance of the earth to suit particular human needs and wants. As these needs and wants have changed, occupance patterns have undergone modification to reflect new land uses, variations in types of settlement, in ways of making a living, and so on. As technical capacity to effect change has grown, the human species has strived increasingly to alter the natural environment to create a habitat that is expected to meet those needs and wants to an ever greater degree.

The historical record contains ample evidence of humankind's strivings, of creative and engineering skills, of achievements, and of failures. The folly of many human decisions relative to achieving certain goals is often very obvious. And the rapid growth of the human population, especially in recent centuries, has endowed the entire change process with an ever greater complexity leading to a mix of patterns and unresolved problems.

Of one thing we can be certain—the geography of humankind is subject to a continuous process of change. However different in degree the evidence of human occupance at various stages in history may be, there are certain constants underlying all, as this text has attempted to show, rooted as they are in the natural environment, in the culture, in human behavior, and in the residuals of preceding times. The residuals of the past pose a special problem for the geographer, for their identification and understanding require an historical insight that is difficult to grasp. This is, of course, the basic challenge of history: it is not whether the past is to be studied, but whether the search reveals the evidence for which we are digging and whether the discovery sheds any light on the present.

History suggests that we can only know a little about the past and about the people who preceded us, who contributed to the world they knew, building on what went before. Memory has a way of simplifying the record, erasing important details. Because only so much can be drawn from the past, in an attempt to understand the present, the geographer must guess and speculate.

Sadly, much of geography is written as if only the immediate present matters. The instant is dealt with and time is ignored, just as the camera shutter closes on an image. This tendency to focus solely on the present, ignoring the process whereby the world as we know it has come into existence, leaves us with a one-dimensional kind of geography. What is it then, students ask, that can give us perspective on our world? How can we comprehend it?

If a sense of time is sometimes lacking, the space with which geographers must deal, on the other hand, has expanded. Interchange—trade, transportation, travel, investment, wars, and migration—has opened up areas of the world that were once remote in imagination. Geographers have been forced, therefore, to a command of earth space—both in macrocosm and microcosm—that would have amazed past scholars, but in attempting to see the whole, as if from an encircling satellite, a lack of intimacy, or closeness, has forced them to remain somewhat dissociated from it.

Objective analysis, where presumably only the "facts" are involved, can, however, proceed without hindrance and geographers can become masters to a degree. But such competence is achieved when subtle—intuitive, subjective—forces are generally not permitted to intrude on and complicate the analysis. The moment geography attempts to evaluate the world subjectively, divergences occur. Interpretations of the world "out there," of what the geographer comprehends, vary because perspectives differ. Subjectively has flowered, freedom has been exercised, the word images of our world may enrich, but they may also confuse. What we have learned, however, by probing into the landscapes of humankind is not only the possibilities for doing different things on earth. We have also learned of the possibilities for making sense of human life.

GLOSSARY

absolutism In government it pertains to a system of unlimited power held by the ruler, such as a monarch or a dictator.

absorbing barrier In the broadest sense, any phenomenon that prevents the spread of ideas or knowledge. An absorbing barrier may be compared to a sponge that is used to soak up a fluid and thus inhibit free flow.

acropolis Literally, the highest part of the city. In the ancient Greek city-states, the highest point in the city was usually fortified. The best-known example is the Acropolis in Athens.

adaptive capacity The ability to adjust to new ideas, techniques, and so forth.

Afrikaans A language spoken in South Africa, derived from seventeenth-century Dutch.

Afrikaner A South African of Dutch or Boer descent.

agora The *agora* in an ancient Greek city, often the marketplace, was a place of assembly; the word itself means assembly.

agribusiness An agricultural enterprise run along business lines.

agrogorod Literally, agricultural city (Russian term). During the 1950s there were some attempts made to replace old villages with new settlements that were supposed to have some of the basic amenities of the city.

ahimsa A traditional prohibition against killing, which is prevalent in India. The word itself is of Sanskrit origin and means noninjury.

alienation Separation from: the state of being detached or estranged from society or from other members of the community.

amenities Qualities of attractiveness that offer particular blessings or rewards

Ameslan The sign language of the deaf.

anadromous Pertains to fish that ascend rivers from the sea or ocean at certain periods of the year to spawn.

animism A type of religious belief holding that all natural phenomena possess spirits or souls.

anthropomorphic Pertaining to humankind; ascribing human characteristics to nonhuman forms of life.

apartheid An Afrikaans word meaning apartness. It pertains to the policy of strict racial segregation developed in the Republic of South Africa to separate black peoples from the ruling whites.

aquatic farming Essentially, farming in water. The cultivation of rice in paddies constitutes a historic form of aquatic farming.

arable land Land suitable for cultivation.

artel A Russian term for a type of collective farm. The artel, which first appeared in the Russian landscape early in the 1920s, became the prototype of the collective farm established in the 1930s, for which a charter of rights and obligations was created (1934).

artifact Literally, any object made by humans. The artifacts of history are the tangible remains of human creativity—the pottery, body adornments, houses, roads, and so on.

atrium The principal room in a Roman house, where visitors were received. Usually square or rectangular, it was covered by a roof, except for the central section. This was left open so that rain fell into a shallow pool sunk into the floor.

Australopithecines The term given to forms of life believed by anthropologists to represent the forebears of humankind. To these apelike creatures, whose fossil skulls and skeletons have been found, the name *Australopithecus* was given.

axis mundi Literally, axis of the earth, meaning the axis on which the earth spins and suggesting a central focus around which life evolves.

Babylonian captivity Term designating the exile of the papacy in Avignon, France.

Baha'i A religion that arose in India based on the doctrines of Gautama Buddha.

balance of power Among European powers, an equilibrium betwen antagonistic states so that no one state could dominate another.

Bantu line A linguistic boundary extending across north-central Africa, separating the Bantu-speaking peoples to the south from those speaking the Arabic, Chari-Nile, and Hamitic languages to the north.

Bantustans The homelands that the South African government is creating for its black, predominantly Bantu peoples.

baroque A term applied to the period in European history (about A.D. 1550 to 1700) during which ornamentation was characteristic of art forms and expression.

bastides New towns, usully fortified, that were created in France, especially in the western and southern provinces, from the fourteenth century onward.

batates A Spanish word for potatoes.

Bedlam A term derived from the Bethlehem Royal Hospital for the insane, in London. Colloquially, it means an uproar.

bedouin The nomadic people of the Arab world of North Africa and the Middle East.

behavioralists Students of human behavior who seek an empirical basis for understanding.

belief in progress The origins of science in the Western World date to the sixth century B.C. (Greece), and the concept of an unfolding of the historical drama may be said to originate with the Bible. But the modern belief in material betterment is of relatively recent origin, dating to the sixteenth century at least.

bilingual Literally, of two languages; a person capable of speaking two languages may be described as bilingual.

Officially, Canada is a bilingual country; English and French have both been given legal status.

biological evolution Pertains to the unfolding of life; the development of species from early forms to their present state.

biome An association of natural phenomena, as found, for example, in the tundra, the evergreen forest zone, or the grasslands.

birthrate The number of births per unit of population at any given time.

borough A term for a town that was in common usage in medieval England. In time, the inhabitants of boroughs sent representatives to Parliament.

bourg (burg) A town; originally, a fortified settlement.

bourgeoisie Literally, the people who inhabit a burg or bourg; in the Marxist usage pertains to the moneyed or propertied class.

broken front In Upper Canada (now Ontario), the baseline that was laid out along a waterfront. Subsequent surveys of the land into concessions, lots, and townships were made on this baseline.

bullionist A term applied to economic thinkers, government leaders, and commercial groups in the sixteenth century who measured the wealth of a state in terms of the possession of bullion, or gold and silver.

burgher A citizen of a burg or a townsperson.

caliphate The office of the caliph, a title taken by the successors of Mohammed, who served not only as heads of Islam, but also of the lands under their control.

cardo The road in a Roman settlement that was extended from north to south.

carnivorousness The eating of meat or flesh.

carrying capacity The ability of a region or territory to support its population from its own resources.

cascade diffusion A process whereby ideas or techniques are disseminated throughout a society from the center, much as water cascades downward from a mountain slope.

caste A distinct or exclusive hereditary class in Hindu society.

censier The rents required of peasants for the land they held and worked under the pre-revolutionary French land system.

central place theory The theory that recognizes a hierarchy of service centers in the landscape.

centrality A term that helps us understand patterns of human thought and endeavor, for example, the differentiation between core (or center) and periphery in spatial organization.

centripetal force The force that tends to direct toward the center, used in political geography to suggest the pressures that might bring the peoples of a state together.

centrifugal force The force that tends to impel outward, used in political geography to suggest the pressures that might disrupt the unity of the state or political entity.

centuria A unit in the Roman land survey that consisted of 132 acres.

challenge and response A concept of history that, as used by the historian Arnold Toynbee, sees the course and differentiation of civilization as entailing a series of encounters or challenges. The nature of the response to the encounter constitutes a vital factor in the ability of the civilization to survive.

Chartists Supporters of a movement for democratic reform in England in the period 1836–1848. The movement was based on principles laid down in the People's Charter of 1838.

Christaller hypothesis Walter Christaller hypothesized that under free market conditions over a uniform surface a hierarchy of service centers takes shape. Each center offers the same level of service; each is spaced at an equal distance from the other, and each has a hexagonal service area.

city-state A historic form of political organization that consists of a city, its population, and the territory immediately controlled by it, as in ancient Greece.

civilization From the Latin *civilis,* pertaining to citizens, implying a community of civilians. Civilization is seen to occur when people are made civil, or enlightened, such a condition being associated with the formation of a state, a sedentary population, and the keeping of records.

civitates Provinces, derived from tribal territories, in the Roman Empire.

class stratification The socioeconomic divisions within society; in Marxist usage pertains to the hardening of those divisions.

class struggle An essential element of the Marxist concept of history prior to the emergence of socialism or communism.

Cod War The term given to the dispute that broke out (first in 1958) between Iceland and Great Britain over the fishery resources of the waters of the North Atlantic surrounding Iceland.

cognitive mapping A representation of the world as we see it. Science has increasingly made possible ever more precise measurements of the earth's surface, but humans carry about in their heads images or mental maps of the world around them.

collectivization In the Soviet Union, the process whereby individual peasant land holdings were merged into large farms. Widespread collectivization began in the Soviet Union in 1928 and 1929, and was adopted in some East European countries after World War II and in China after 1949.

colonia A Roman town inhabited by citizens of the empire.

color bar A term used to suggest discrimination based on skin color.

Comecon The Council for Mutual Economic Assistance, founded in 1949 to integrate the planning policies of the Soviet Union and East European States.

Cominform (Communist Information Bureau) Formed in 1947 in Eastern Europe, an organization of Communist party representatives whose goal is to spread communism throughout the world. It was abolished in 1956.

Comintern (Communist International) An association of international socialist organizations, first formed in London in 1864–1876. A Second International was created in Paris in 1884. A Third International was formed in Moscow in 1919 under Russian leadership; it came to an end in 1943.

common property right A right to the use of property or a resource that is shared by all, such as the use of the village commons of the past, which belonged to the citizens of the village at large.

communalism Pertains to the grouping of people in communities, differentiated by philosophy, religion, or way of life.

commune A type of collective farm first established in the Soviet Union, in which the inhabitants share the land, their labor, their livestock, and their housing. The commune disappeared in the Soviet Union in 1928 and 1929 during the collectivization drive. Subsequently, the commune reappeared in China after the Communists siezed power.

community A social grouping possessing shared attributes or characteristics.

complementarity A condition of being complemented. Karl Deutsch has used the term as a key to determining the degree to which people can communicate with and understand each other.

concentration camp A detention camp for political or military prisoners.

concession A division of the land survey established in Upper Canada, now Ontario, after 1784.

concert (of Europe) In the nineteenth century, a group of European powers that agreed to work together for their common interests, which, at that time, meant the putting down of revolutionary movements.

Confucianism The ethical teachings of Confucius, the Chinese sage of the sixth century B.C.

contagious diffusion The dissemination or spreading of disease (or ideas) through personal contact or from person to person.

continental shelf The shelf of land or submarine plain that borders the continents and descends to the ocean depths. The shelf varies in width from a few miles to several hundred miles.

Copernican revolution The transformation brought about in medieval European thinking by the ideas advanced by Copernicus, notably that the sun, not the earth, was at the center of the universe.

core area A focal or central region.

core-periphery A geographic perspective that recognizes a socioeconomic division between a focal point or region and the surrounding territory.

corvée The labor required of peasants under the pre-revolutionary French land system.

cosmic cross The term implies a grand design within the universe that is based on the human concept of the cross. Christians made the cross the central fact of their religion.

cosmogony From the Greek word *kosmogonia*, pertaining to the origin of the universe. *Cosmogony*, then, represents the human attempt to explain, understand, or come to terms with origins.

cosmos Literally meaning the universe, the word connotes harmony and order as well. The antithesis to cosmic harmony is chaos.

cottage industry An enterprise, such as weaving or leather-making, conducted in workers' cottages as opposed to a factory.

Creole The origins of the word are not clear, but a Creole is essentially a person of French or Spanish descent born in the New World.

creolized language Technically, a language that has grown out of a mixture of languages as, for example, the mixed French-Spanish-English dialects of groups of people in the Caribbean area or in Louisiana.

Cro-Magnon The name of a cave near Dordogne, France, where the remains of an early representative of *Homo sapiens* were first found, that is Cro-Magnon man.

Crown and Clergy Reserves Reserves of land set aside in the townships created by the British government after 1791 in Upper Canada (Ontario) for the support of the local administration and a Protestant clergy.

cultural change The temporal and spatial sequence whereby components of culture undergo transformation, and religions, habits of speech, and institutions are changed.

cultural ecology The term used to embrace that branch of learning that seeks to understand the relationship between human groups, their material resources, and the cultural patterns that emerge as a consequence.

cultural landscape The imprint of human occupance on the land.

culture The sum total of the learned experience of human groups, that is, their knowledge, concepts, skills, arts, crafts, languages, religions, institutions, and so on.

culture area An extent of territory characterized by a common culture, or common trust, that is, language, religion, or any common practice.

culture hearth A term used to denote a place or region where certain facets of human experience are believed to have occurred first, for example, the domestication of animals and plants.

culture lag The gap that emerges when humans fail to keep up with, or adjust to, the changes that occur in their larger world, for example, the perseverance of a politically structured world based on uncontrolled nationalism and national competition despite evidence of the enormous destructive capability of modern weaponry.

culture traits Characteristics shared by a community of people in a given area or territory.

culture transfers The movement of a trait or characteristic from one people to another; the adoption of new ideas, techniques, or practices held by other peoples.

dacha A Russian word that means vacation residence.

dachniki Literally, a small summer residence; in reality, the small wooden sheds erected by urban workers on their individual garden plots in the countryside.

deathrate The number of deaths per unit of population at any given time.

decumanus In a Roman settlement, the road that was run from east to west to intersect the north-to-south *cardo*.

de facto A Latin phrase meaning in reality.

de jure A Latin phrase meaning legal.

demersal Pertains to fish that feed off the bottom of the seabed.

demographic Pertains to the statistical characteristics of a population.

demographic transition Demographic transition describes the process whereby the deathrate of a population falls and is subsequently accompanied by a decline in the birthrate, thus lowering the rate of natural increase.

départements Internal political subdivisions of France after the Revolution.

dependency A territory that is subordinate to another.

depopulation The loss of population.

desertification The drying up of areas together with their misuse, leading to an expansion of desertlike conditions.

determinism A theory that everything is based on a sequence of cause-and-effect relationships. Acceptance of the concept in human activity patterns rules out the possibility of freedom of choice.

developed countries See *developed world*.

developed world Essentially, the industrialized world.

developing world The countries undergoing economic growth or industrial development.

dialect A subdivision of a language, or variations from a standard expression in word usage or intonation.

diaspora Literally, a dispersion; used primarily in the context of Jewish dispersion outside the original homeland.

diffusion A term that means spreading or dissemination, as in the spreading of ideas through communication, travel, trade, or other forms of contact.

diglossia From the Greek meaning two languages. The term is used specifically where two or more varieties of the same language are used by a group, as among Slavic peoples who speak a Slavic language and use as the language of worship Old Church Slavonic.

diocese A division of territory under the jurisdiction of a bishop, as in the Roman Catholic Church.

discontinuities Literally, interruptions.

dispersed settlement Literally, scattered settlement, as in the rural American West.

dissidence Disagreement; lack of harmony.

distance decay See *time-distance decay*.

divine right In medieval times, the notion that the king ruled by the authority of God.

divinity of nature Pertains to the special quality of nature that draws people to its worship.

doctrine of the tao See *Taoism*.

domestication Literally, the act of makng something domestic. The term is used for the historic process of taming wild animals and the modification for human use of both animals and plants.

Drang nach Osten A German phrase meaning drive to the east, which described the pressure exerted by Germanic peoples against the Slavic peoples in eastern Europe and which was demonstrated not only in colonization but also in imperial expansion.

Druze (Druse) A religious belief or sect that grew out of Islam.

Dry World Pertains primarily to the belt of territory stretching from Mongolia through Central Asia to the Atlantic shores of North Africa.

dynastic state A political state where the line of succession is determined by family, for example, Tudor or Stuart England, Bourbon France, Romanov Russia.

Eastern Christianity The term used to denote the Eastern branch of Christianity led by Constantinople, as opposed to the Western branch led by Rome.

ecology The branch of biology that pertains to the relationships between living organisms and their environment.

economic rent Profit, being the net return on investment.

economic zone Some states had in the past unilaterally extended their jurisdiction out to a distance of 200 miles from their coasts to control the fisheries. By 1975, world pressure led to the widespread acceptance of a 200-mile "exclusive economic zone" that would give the coastal state virtually complete control over the resources of the ocean and the seabed within that distance. The existence of such a zone does not, however, preclude the right of free navigation on the high seas and transit through international straits.

ecosystem The term coined for the pattern of interlocking relationships that exist between living organisms and their environment.

effective environment A term that attempts to emphasize those components of the environment that have recognizable bearing on human activities.

emancipation of the peasantry In Russia in 1861 the Edict of Emancipation freed the serfs of their traditional obligations to the landlord.

empresario A grantee of a large tract of land in Texas under Mexican authority who undertook to bring in settlers.

enclave A territory enclosed within a foreign state, for example, Lesotho within the Republic of South Africa.

enclosure The process whereby the small holdings of peasants are consolidated into a larger farm unit, which excludes them.

encomienda A system of landholding not unlike the seigneurial system in New France, where grantees were responsible for the development of their individual grants.

Enlightenment The term given to the period in European thought (eighteenth century) that was characterized by a drive for learning, for rational understanding, and skepticism.

environing factors Those elements in the world, of both natural and human origin, believed to have an influence on human behavior or activity.

environment Traditionally thought to consist primarily of the physical world, the concept has been broadened to include all the phenomena that surround an organism.

environmentalism The doctrine that the development of humans (or of any organism) is affected or determined by surrounding conditions, influences, or circumstances.

Eternal City Literally, the City of God; sometimes used in reference to Jerusalem or Rome or both.

ethnic Pertains to a community sharing common traits, especially language.

ethnic space The space or territory occupied by an ethnic community aware of its separateness from other like groups.

ethnicity Pertaining to the formation of a community of people sharing a common culture and sociocultural values.

ethnologist A student of animal behavior.

European Economic Community An association of European states, created in 1957 and known as the Common Market.

excommunication A means of censuring a member of a community; a process of casting out a member.

existentialist writers The name given to many modern writers whose concern is with the central focus of human life as they see it, namely, the attempt to find meaning in a universe that seems to hold no meaning and that can be given meaning only through a decisive exercise of individual human will.

expansion diffusion The spread or dissemination of ideas or techniques from a point of origin or from one place to another.

experienced space A term that suggests the process whereby humans augment the spaces they inhabit through their imagination, their dreams, their memories, and their reflections.

fall line A break between a lowland and an upland often demonstrated by the presence of waterfalls on descending rivers.

faubourg A suburb of a French city. As the city grew, the suburbs became, in effect, quarters of the expanded urban area.

federal A system of government whereby powers are shared between a central government and associated provincial or state governments, as in the United States, Canada, Australia, and India.

federative state The term *federative* means pertaining to a federation, but does not necessarily guarantee a true sharing of power. The Soviet constitution describes the structure of the Russian republic as a federative one, that is, Russian Soviet Federative Socialist Republic.

feudal tenure A system of landholding that prevailed in medieval Europe whereby land was held at the pleasure of a higher authority, traced ultimately back to the liege lord or king.

friction of space See *tyranny of space.*

Frostbelt A term that pertains to the northeastern states of the United States generally characterized by severe winters.

fundamentalist A person who adheres to basic or essential beliefs.

futureless villages In the Soviet Union, villages that have been abandoned or are not included in future rural development planning.

genius loci Literally, genius or spirit of a place. The Greeks had a special sensitivity to landscape, possessing a gift for creating a structure that seemed admirably and harmoniously suited to its site.

genus A class of phenomena that is usually divided into species or subtypes.

geographic disinvestment A policy sometimes employed by banks or lending institutions to discourage investment in specific areas.

geomancer Literally, one who practices geomancy, the practice of discovering hidden meaning through auguries, omens.

geopolitics The use of geography, that is, location primarily, to gain access to resources and to strengthen the state's power base.

ghetto The section or quarter of a city to which specific groups have been confined or in which they are concentrated, as the Jewish ghettos in pre-World War II East European cities or the black ghettos in American cities.

glaciation The process whereby the earth's surface is shaped by the action of glaciers.

glossalalia The phenomenon found among Christian groups that entails the speaking, through inspiration and spontaneously, in languages other than one's own.

gorod A Russian term for city, as in Novgorod, meaning new city; or shortened to *grad,* as in Leningrad, meaning Lenin's city.

goroshanin A Russian term meaning citizen of a *gorod* or city.

Great Siberian Migration The colonization of Asiatic Russia by Slavic peoples from European Russia, which got underway in the last decade of the nineteenth century and came to a close by World War I, has been termed the Great Siberian Migration.

Great Vehicle See *Mahayana Buddhism.*

Greek rite The ritual used in the services of the Orthodox Church, as compared with that used in Roman Catholic churches known as the Roman rite.

Green Revolution The term given to the development and spread in the past two decades of new high-yielding varieties of grain that have done much to increase world food output.

greenbelts Extensive plantings of trees in urban areas to reduce noise pollution and to serve as aesthetic breaks.

gross national product The sum total of goods and services produced by a country.

growth pole A center of focus of economic activity from which development is expected to radiate.

Gulag Archipelago A term used to describe the vast network of penal institutions and forced labor camps in the Soviet Union.

habitants A French term used to denote the rank-and-file settlers of New France.

hajj The pilgrimage to Mecca required of the Muslim faithful.

Hansa See *Hanseatic League.*

Hanseatic League An association of north European cities that dominated the economic life of the Baltic region in medieval times.

haufendorf Literally, a rural settlement containing a cluster of houses, which is common in Germany.

hegemony A term meaning predominance or leadership.

Hejira (also Hegira) The flight of Mohmmed from Mecca to Medina in A.D. 622, which is taken as the first year of the Muslim era.

heliocentric universe The concept of the universe that places the sun at the center (Copernicus), as opposed to the geocentric universe, which conceives of the earth as the center.

Hellenistic thought The thought of the Greeks, especially after the reign of Alexander the Great.

Hevea brasiliensis The botanical name of Brazilian rubber.

hierarchic diffusion The process whereby new ideas or techniques may be disseminated throughout a society either from the top downward or from the broad base upward to the top.

hieroglyphic A form of writing involving characters.

high-yielding varieties See *miracle wheat.*

Hinayana Buddhism Known also as the Little Vehicle, it is the more conservative of the two major divisions of Buddhism.

home rule A term meaning self-government.

hominid A term that embraces humanlike creatures.

hominization The stage or process in which humanlike creatures appeared.

Homo erectus The genus that includes creatures who walked in an upright or erect position and from which *Homo sapiens* is said to have evolved. Among members of the genus are Peking man and Java man.

Homo sapiens The genus that includes all humans, from Neanderthal and Cro-Magnon types to the present.

Huguenot A term by which a French Protestant in the sixteenth and seventeenth centuries was known.

human ecology The term that was applied in geography by Harlan Barrows to the study of the relationships between humans and their environment.

imageability A vivid representation of some phenomenon that stimulates mental activity and promotes the formation of images.

imperialism A term that pertains to the creation of an empire or domination of one territory by another.

indiscriminate location The term given to the haphazard manner in which the land in the southern colonies along the Atlantic seaboard was occupied.

industrial landscape A segment of the earth's surface that has undergone industrialization.

industrial park A large tract of land in which are concentrated a large number of industrial enterprises.

Industrial Revolution The complex series of developments beginning in England about 1760 that ushered in the modern world and transformed the landscape. It was based on a dramatic change in the way in which nonanimate energy was harnessed.

innovation The process of creating something new—an invention or a discovery. This is an important concept in cultural geography.

innovation diffusion The widespread acceptance of a new idea or technique.

innovation waves A term used by the Swedish geographer Torsten Hägerstrand to characterize the process whereby new ideas or techniques spread from one place to another. He likened this process to the waves that roll in on a beach.

irredentism A policy or movement that seeks to bring all territories occupied by common nationals under one government.

Islam A monotheistic religion that preaches that Mohammed is the messenger or prophet of God.

Isolated State The hypothetical situation devised by Thünen, a nineteenth-century German estate owner, to demonstrate his hypotheses concerning the distribution of crops and farming activities around a central market town.

Jewish Pale The territory to which Jews were confined in Eastern Europe by a 1791 decree of Catherine the Great of Russia.

Judaism The religion (doctrine, rites, and practices) of the Jews.

khutora (khutors) A Russian term for a farmstead whose fields were detached from village communal lands and on which the farmer himself might live, as opposed to living in the village.

Kremlin A Russian word meaning fortress, the most renowned being the Kremlin of Moscow.

kulaki (kulaks) A Russian term derived from the word for fist, implying that the class of farmers, described by Communist writers as kulaks, were capitalistic, landgrabbing people.

laissez-faire A French phrase meaning let do; in economics, the principle of noninterference by government in human affairs.

land tenure The system whereby land is held.

"land-to-the-tiller" A land reform program carried out in Taiwan by the controlling Nationalist Chinese government after 1950 wherein the central principle was to turn over ownership of the land to those who actually worked it. The concept, in its Chinese context, originated with Sun Yat-sen (1866–1925), the father of the revolution that led to the establishment of the Chinese Republic.

Latin rite The ritual employed in the Roman Catholic Church (as distinct from the Orthodox Church), wherein the pope is recognized as both bishop of Rome and patriarch (that is, patriarch of the West).

Latter-Day Saints Also referred to as Mormons, members of one of the major new religious movements whose headquarters lie in the United States.

lebensraum A German word meaning literally living room or living space. Prior to World War II, the Nazis argued that Germany had insufficient territory for its people, hence, the demand for additional lebensraum.

legion A body of infantry in the Roman army, whose numbers ranged from 3000 to 6000, usually with cavalry.

leper A person affected with leprosy, a disease that slowly eats away the body.

less developed countries Countries that have not undergone industrialization or are in the process of industrialization.

life expectancy The number of years, usually an average, that a person at birth would be expected to live given existing mortality trends.

line or linear settlement A straight or street settlement.

linear time A one-dimensional measurement of time.

lingua franca Literally, language of the Franks. Today a lingua franca is any language that has wide usage over an area, such as Swahili in East Africa.

Little Vehicle See *Hinayana Buddhism*.

living space See *lebensraum*.

long lot In the New World in particular, the land surveys conducted by the French and to some degree by the Spanish that led to the subdivision of the land in long, narrow lots. The long lots surveyed along the St. Lawrence River are especially noticeable even today.

magic Historically, a realm of thought and activity that seeks to influence or control natural events through the use of charms, spells, and incantations.

Mahayana Buddhism Known also as the Great Vehicle, this is the form of Buddhism that predominates in Southeast Asia; it tends to emphasize temple worship, mythology, and abstract philosophy.

mainmortable A French term referring to a serf as the permanent property of the manor lord.

Malthusian One who believes that unless some restraint is placed on population growth, poverty, starvation, or conflict will result.

mandala Essentially, a religious symbolization of the earth or the universe. Although such symbolization has been found among different cultures, it is most commonly a sacred art form among Oriental religions, in particular among Buddhists.

mare nostrum A Latin phrase meaning our sea. The Roman Empire came to embrace virtually all the lands washed by the Mediterranean Sea, with the result that the sea came to be seen by Romans as theirs.

Marxian Pertains to the socialist principles of Karl Marx.

medressa A center of learning in the Muslim world, comparable to a college or university.

Meiji Restoration The overthrow of the Tokugawa shogunate, which was the military dictatorship that had ruled Japan from the early seventeenth century. This led to the resurgence of the power of the Meiji emperor. In 1890, the Meiji constitution named the emperor the highest authority in the land.

melting pot A term used to describe the mingling of peoples to form a new people, as was believed to have happened in the social experience of the United States in the nineteenth and early twentieth centuries.

mental maps Literally, the maps of the mind; the images of places carried in the mind.

mentifact A term that is used to refer to the products of mental activity. They lie within the realm of beliefs, ideas, attitudes, and so on.

mercantilist policy (mercantilism) A policy based on a system of public economy that emerged in Europe at the end of the medieval period. It envisaged considerable government control and regulation of foreign trade, domestic economy, and colonization.

metes and bounds A system of surveying based on boundary stones or some prominent object in the landscape.

métis A people that emerged in western Canada through the union of native peoples and Canadians, of predominantly French origin.

metropolitan Pertaining to a large city or metropolis.

metropolitan district A large urbanized region, identified by the U.S. Census Bureau.

metropolitan spillover The impact of activities of large urban areas on the surrounding countryside.

metropolitan state A term that denotes a political-economical core area, on which the periphery is dependent.

middle passage The term applied to that portion of the three-way trade between Great Britain, Africa, and the American colonies that involved the shipment of blacks as slaves to work in the fields of the New World.

Millet system A system of local self-government that permitted religious communities to order their own affairs under the Ottoman Empire.

miracle wheat A high-yielding variety of wheat that gained widespread acceptance in the less developed countries in the 1950s and 1960s.

mirror image Used in the context given to suggest the tendency to see others in terms of preconceived notions and to ignore basic differences.

misery and vice Thomas Malthus believed that certain controls would become operative should population growth exceed the capacity of the land to feed. These controls he called 'misery,'' meaning starvation and sickness, and ''vice,'' meaning war, social conflict, and so on.

mobility revolution A term that associates demographic transition with spatial mobility within a state.

mode of production The manner in which resources are owned, developed, and processed.

modernization A process of development that sees the emergence of improved living standards; associated with economic growth.

monarchical absolutism Unquestioned authority vested in a king.

monarchical centralism The condition whereby all power is concentrated within the state in the hands of the monarch. In Europe, the great age of monarchical centralism occurred between the sixteenth and twentieth centuries.

monasticism A movement that developed early in the history of the Christian Church that entailed a retreat from the world. St. Augustine in the fourth century A.D. was one of the earliest known monastics.

monochronic time (M-time) Linear time, implying an organization of time whose purpose is to permit movement forward, promptness, and efficiency.

monotheism Literally, belief in one God. Judaism, Christianity, and Islam are monotheistic religions.

Mormons See *Latter-Day Saints*.

Mormon Corridor The stretch of territory leading from the main cluster of Mormon settlements in Utah southwestward toward California.

mosque An Islamic place of worship.

Mousterian From Le Moustier a cave in southwestern France that gives its name to a stage of Paleolithic culture, identified with *Homo neanderthalensis*.

mullah A Muslim religious leader, found particularly in the Shiite sect of Islam.

multilingual Literally, of many languages. A person capable of speaking many languages may be described as multilingual, just as a people, like the Swiss, represented by groups speaking at least four different languages, may be said to be multilingual.

multinational Transnational, embracing many countries, as in the operation of a multinational business corporation.

nation A group of people or a community bound together by a common culture, common history, and a common sense of destiny, ordinarily occupying a common territory.

nation-state The independent, politically organized territory occupied by a nation.

national self-interest A policy that seeks to secure or enhance the status and welfare of a state.

nationality A term that implies association with or belonging to a nation.

nationalism Pertaining to the nation. It entails devotion to the nation, but it may also be characterized by exclusivity, excessive self-interest, and jingoism.

natural environment See *physical environment*.

natural limits Delineation of a territory based on physical features in the landscape.

natural man The notion of a human who is unspoiled or uncorrupted by civilization.

natural right The right that was believed to be part of the human endowment by virtue of the very nature of humankind, as opposed to that which was granted by a superior political authority.

natural selection See *theory of natural selection*.

nature In geography, a term that usually refers to the world system outside of humans, in which all other phenomena are interrelated.

Navigation Acts A series of acts of the English Parliament, beginning in 1645, that regulated shipping between Britain and her colonies; finally repealed in 1849.

Neanderthalensis A subgenus of *Homo sapiens*, first identified from remains found in the valley of the Neander River in Germany.

neocolonialism Pertains to a new form of colonialism, as in economic control.

Neolithic period The period of culture following the Paleolithic, identified as the New Stone Age.

Neolithic revolution The transformation during which early man in the Old World came to use polished stone tools and weapons.

neo-Malthusian Malthusianism, as revived or modified by modern students of population and resources.

new towns See *bastides*.

noble savage The image that emerged in Europe of the natives of the New World—savages who were thought to possess a natural dignity uncorrupted by the Old World lust for power and prestige.

nomadic pastoralism See *pastoral nomad*.

Norfolk system A system of land utilization developed in England that entailed the cultivation of root crops for livestock as part of the rotation system.

North-South A division of the globe into the developed or industrial countries of the temperate lands and the less developed countries of the subtropics and tropics.

nucleated settlement A pattern of settlement that entails the clustering of village dwellings.

nurture Implies nourishment and the process of training and upbringing as opposed to nature and the role of heredity in human development.

oblast A political-territorial subdivision in the Soviet Union, comparable to an American county.

obshchina A Russian term for the village organization that controlled the distribution of land to members of the village prior to the Bolshevik Revolution.

operational environment See *effective environment*.

Oriental despotism A form of government entailing the concentration of absolute power in the hands of a leader or leaders whose authority is used in an arbitrary or capricious manner.

Orthodox Christianity The dominant form of Christianity that emerged in the Eastern Mediterranean and spread into adjacent lands, notably into southwest Asia, eastern Europe, and Russia.

Orwellian nightmare The term *Orwellian nightmare* refers to the image of the future (1984) as conceived by the English novelist George Orwell, where the state has the means to dominate all facets of life and many traditional values are inverted.

otgonnoye A Russian term literally meaning movement away from. It implies a controlled structure of livestock raising, not unlike American ranching, where grazing patterns are predetermined, thus preventing the free movement of livestock raisers or pastoralists.

otruby (otrubs) A Russian term for a farmstead whose fields were detached from village communal lands but where the farmer himself continued to live in the village rather than on the farmstead. (See *khutora*.)

overseas Chinese Ethnic Chinese who have resettled outside China.

paddy A field flooded for the purpose of growing rice.

pagus The Latin word for countryside. Initially, a pagan was a person who lived in the countryside. In early Christian times the term became synonymous with heathen. Thus, a pagan was a heathen, or non-Christian.

Pale of Settlement See *Jewish Pale*.

Paleolithic Refers to the Old Stone Age, specifically the culture that entailed the making of crude stone tools.

Palliser Triangle The triangular-shaped region in the Canadian prairies that was explored by Captain John Palliser and initially believed to be infertile because of drought.

pampas The term given to the vast grassland of southern South America.

papacy The office or position of the pope.

Paradise Originally a garden surrounded by a wall, hence the Biblical Garden of Eden, paradise came to be associated in Christian times with a place or condition of peace and happiness. Ultimately, for followers of Christ, it came to mean the Kingdom of Heaven.

pariah A term, of Indian origin, that means social outcast.

pariah landscape A landscape, characterized by lands set aside for the outcasts of society.

pastoral nomad A migratory person whose livelihood is based on the raising and herding of animals. Pastoral nomads today are found largely in semiarid or arid regions of the earth.

patates See *batates.*

patroon Used in connection with the Dutch landholders of New York and the Hudson River Valley.

Pavlovian dogs The Russian physiologist, Ivan Petrovich Pavlov (1849–1936) trained dogs to respond to external stimuli. The term has been applied somewhat derisively to people who respond to command with a corresponding loss of their own initiative and individualism.

Pax Britannica Literally, British peace, established in the nineteenth century, particularly where Britain dominated the seas.

Pax Romana Literally, Roman peace, designating the peace imposed on the peoples Rome subjugated throughout the Mediterranean Basin.

Peking man The name given to the fossil remains of *Homo erectus,* found in the cave at Zhoukoudian near Peking (Beijing), China.

pelagic fish That category of fish who live near the surface of the sea.

Pentecostal movement An evangelical movement that had a great impact on religious thinking in the United States in the nineteenth and twentieth centuries.

perceptual or perceived environment Increasingly, geographers and students of human behavior have come to recognize that people may respond not only to the conditions of the environment in which they live, but may also respond to the way in which they themselves look out at the world and, therefore, in the context of their own experience, they may act on what they see or perceive.

peristyle The name given to the columns surrounding an open space. In the Roman house, the peristyle was not unlike the atrium, but it was open to the sky.

Permanent Indian Boundary A line drawn parallel to the 95th meridian, south of the Missouri River, beyond which the Amerindians of the United States were to be confined.

permeable barrier A boundary or zone that fails to halt the penetration of new ideas or techniques.

personal space The space an individual requires to live, often defined in terms of one's psychologic requirements rather than strictly physical space.

physical environment The term used for the world outside humankind, composed of the components of physical geography, that is, land forms, climate, and so on.

pidgin A mixed language developed primarily for the purposes of trade. Pidgin English is a common form used in Oceania by the native population when dealing with outsiders.

Pithecanthropecines A genus of human forebears, who walked in an upright position (*Homo erectus*) and to which Peking and Java fossils belong.

place A recognizable or particular space on the earth's surface, giving additional meaning to an individual through his or her experience.

plantation system A system of agriculture developed by the European powers in overseas colonies entailing investment in specialty or cash crops.

Pleistocene epoch A term designating the earlier period of the Quaternary, beginning about two million years ago.

pluralistic A term used to denote the presence of peoples of diverse cultures, languages, or religions within a given society.

pogrom An organized massacre, used with respect to the massacre of Jews in Russia before the Revolution.

polders Reclaimed, low-lying land, protected by dikes, as in the Netherlands.

polis The area, with its inhabitants, controlled by the city-state in ancient Greece.

polychronic time (P-time) Literally, pluralistic, nonlinear time, implying unregulated usage of time.

polytheism Literally, belief in many gods or divinities. Hinduism, the religion of most of the inhabitants of India, is an excellent illustration of a polytheistic religion.

population explosion An expression used to describe a rapid increase in population; widely used today with reference to many countries of the Third World.

population profile Pertains to the age and sex structures of a population.

population turnaround A reverse flow of people, as in the migration from city to countryside.

populist movement A movement whose origins lay in doctrines, with goals said to reflect the wishes and needs of the people.

posad A Russian term meaning suburb; employed in the medieval period.

possibilists A school of geographers, originating principally in France, who recognized that the physical environment imposed constraints on human activities but believed that humans, given certain technological equipment, could make choices as to how they might utilize the resources at their disposal.

potential environment Even though our knowledge of the world around us has grown, there remains much in the larger environment about which we have yet to learn and understand.

presecular man A term that has been given by some writers to humankind living in a state of nature, that is, whose existence is rooted in nature.

presidio A fortified Spanish mission in the southern part of the United States.

primary activities Activities associated with the extraction of raw materials from the earth, such as mining, farming, and fishing.

primate The order of mammals that includes humankind and the apes.

primate city Literally, first city; the city whose position in the country is so commanding that it sets the pattern of culture, styles, and so on, such as New York in the United States.

principal language family A main division of the world's languages, such as, Indo-European, Sino-Tibetan, Dravidian.

private garden or plot A phenomenon characteristic of contemporary land-holding in the Soviet Union. Whereas most of the farmland is relegated to state or collective farms, farm workers (and some industrial workers as well) are permitted to tend plots of land (not unlike the American peapatch) for their own use. Such plots are usually located near a cottage.

proletariat In Marxist usage, a term that pertains to the working class.

Protestant Reformation The break with the Roman Catholic Church that occurred in sixteenth-century Europe. Many Christians, principally in northern Europe, professed a different interpretation of Christian experience from that of the Roman Catholic Church.

Ptolemaic system A theory of the universe devised by Ptolemy (Claudius Ptolemaeus)—a second century A.D. astronomer, geographer, and mathematician—according to which the earth was the central, fixed point of the universe, around which the heavenly bodies or planets moved.

purdah A term meaning veil, connoting the seclusion of women behind a screen, a practice of Islam where women have been kept in purdah.

push-pull mechanism A concept devised to explain the causes of migration.

putting-out system The practice of assigning work to individuals employed in their own dwellings or cottages.

quality of life A term that has been used to describe the condition of human existence, implying the possibility of improvement.

quaternary activity An economic activity that pertains to research-oriented enterprises, to education, and to similar endeavors.

raison d'être A French phrase meaning reason for being or reason for existing. It is employed in political geography.

rancheria An individual grant of land in Spanish Texas, often consisting of several thousand acres.

rang See *long lot*.

rate of natural increase The rate at which population is changing (increasing or decreasing) in any given year owing to the relationship between births and deaths.

Realpolitik Literally, realist politics, a term that falls within the realm of geopolitics.

redlining See *geographic disinvestment*.

regional geography An important branch of geography that is devoted to the study of regions or places. Regional geography, because of its focus on synthesizers—components of regions—is contrasted with systematic geography, the aim of which is the development of laws or principles that underlie the patterns of human activity over the surface of the earth.

relocation diffusion A term used to identify and describe the process whereby a new idea or technique undergoing dissemination leaves its center of origin.

Renaissance Literally, rebirth. The Renaissance in European history (fourteenth to sixteenth centuries) marked a period of rediscovery of the classics; thus it was a period of transition between the medieval and modern ages.

repopulation The addition of population, largely through resettlement.

reservation Territory set aside or reserved, as in the Indian reservations of North America.

right to self-determination The notion that peoples, especially nations, have the right to determine their own future within their own independent, self-governing state.

rite A religious custom or procedure in a religious service.

Romantic gardens The Romantic Movement in Europe sought to recapture the traditions of the past other than classical traditions. It found expression in literature, art, music, and (in England in particular) in the layout of gardens.

Romantic Movement A reaction to classical modes of artistic expression in Europe. It entailed an assertion of the imagination, sentiment, and nostalgia for the non-classical past.

rotten borough A borough within England that retained the privilege of sending a representative to Parliament, but contained few if any voters. The abuse was rectified in the Reform Act of 1832.

rundling A radial form of settlement, common in Germany.

rural Pertaining to the country, as distinguished from the city or town. As a result of growth of suburbs, the dividing line is often difficult to determine.

Sahel The African territory bordering the Sahara desert on the south.

Sanskrit The ancient language of India, belonging to the Indo-European linguistic family.

schistosomiasis An intestinal disease of the tropics transmitted by freshwater snails where water bodies are used for bathing and toilet purposes.

secondary activities Activities that pertain to the processing of raw materials and their reconstitution in a new form.

sectarianism Adherences to a particular sect, particularly in religion.

seigneurial system A social system based on the preeminent landholding position of the lord or seigneur.

seigneurie A French term for a large grant of land to a lord or seigneur.

self-determination The act of making oneself judge or arbiter, as in the process whereby a community seeks to govern itself.

Semitic A language family to which belong Hebrew, Arabic, and a number of other languages of southwest Asia and northern Africa.

sensory deprivation The loss of the use of one's senses.

Sephardim The Jews of southern Europe, identified principally with Spain and Portugal, as distinguished from the Jews of central and eastern Europe, known as the Ashkenazim.

sequent occupance   A succession of human-use patterns over time within a given region or territory—a term coined by Derwent Whittlesey.

serf   A peasant in servitude to a lord through his or her attachment to the land.

shah   A Persian or Iranian title equivalent to king.

shakkei   A Japanese term meaning borrowed landscape, that is, the use of a natural setting to enhance the background of a garden.

shamanism   The native religion of many North American and Eurasian tribes, in which the good and evil spirits in the world are believed to be influenced by the practices of a shaman, or religious man.

Shia   See *Shiite faith.*

shifting cultivation   The practice of cultivating a plot of land until its fertility is reduced or exhausted and then moving on to another. It is usually found today in the tropics and in association with slash-and-burn agriculture.

Shiite faith   A branch of Islam whose followers reject the first three caliphs and consider Mohammed's son-in-law, Ali, as the rightful successor of Mohammed.

Shintō   A system of beliefs, largely derived from nature worship, that emerged in Japan. The term Shintō was coined in the sixth century A.D.

shock city   An industrial town or city where the living conditions of the workers are severe because of poverty, overcrowding, filth, and despair—most applicable to the nineteenth century in Great Britain.

slash-and-burn agriculture   The practice of clearing the land and burning the vegetation for the purpose of raising crops—still practiced widely in tropical lands.

slum   Any depressed area where living conditions are poor because of substandard housing, low incomes, unemployment, and filth.

slump   An English term meaning a bog or a wet mire on which workers' houses were built; the origin of the word *slum.*

Snowbelt   See *Frostbelt.*

Social contract   The notion, developed in a book by Jean Jacques Rousseau, that society was based on a contract voluntarily agreed to by its members.

Social Darwinism   A transfer of Darwin's hypothesis concerning natural selection designed to account for the evolution of plants and animals into the realm of society and social conflict.

socialization   The process whereby people are integrated into or fitted together in a society through the educational role of institutions, schools, newspapers, and the like. The term has also come to mean the taking over of ownership by a government.

sociofact   A term used to designate those components of human culture that pertain essentially to the institutions and institutional structures of a group.

spatial interaction   The movement of goods, services, or ideas over the surface of the earth.

squatter settlements   Spontaneous occupance and settlement of land, title to which is held by others.

state farm   A type of farm first established in the 1920s in the Soviet Union where all the land, implements, livestock, and seed are owned by the state.

state idea   A term used in political geography to denote the key idea around which the state was formed.

steppe versus sown   Steppe means grassland and suggests a way of life that is nonsedentary; sown implies a sedentary agricultural existence. History records many examples of conflict between the peoples who live on the move and those who are fixed in permanent settlements.

struggle for existence   A term probably coined by the British philosopher Herbert Spencer to explain the forces at work in nature that lead to the extermination of life even as life struggles to survive.

strassendorf   Literally, a street village, with housing fronting a single street—a linear settlement pattern.

stupa   A dome-shaped architectural form found in India, designed to represent the cosmos, or universe.

subsistence farming   A type of farming that for the most part provides only for the needs of farmers and their families.

Sunbelt   A term used to describe the Southern and Southwestern states of the United States.

Sunnite faith   The major sect in Islam, which acknowledges the historic succession to the caliphate as correct. In belief, the Sunnis tend to be orthodox or conservative.

supranatural   Meaning literally above nature.

suq   Arabic word, meaning market.

survival of the fittest   A term probably coined by the British philosopher Herbert Spencer to explain the fact that in nature some forms of life survive struggle, whereas others are exterminated.

Swahili   A language spoken widely in East Africa, it is a Bantu language modified by the introduction of Arabic words. It is an excellent example of a lingua franca.

swidden farming   Essentially, slash-and-burn farming. *Swidden* is an Old English word meaning burn.

syncretic   Pertains to the mixing of different beliefs, systems, or practices.

takeoff   The point at which modern economic development begins; the transition from traditional economy to a modern one.

Taoism   A system of belief that emerged in China in the sixth century B.C. The word *Tao* means The Way.

tenement   A several-storied dwelling divided into separate apartments.

tertiary activities   Those activities that fall within the service category, for example, banking, administration, and education.

territoriality   Literally, possessing territorial status. The term today is used to ascribe to animals (and humans) an inherent identification with territory, leading to a willingness to fight to protect one's own territory.

thalassocracy   Of Greek origin, a word that means rule of the sea, or maritime supremacy.

theory of natural selection The theory states that species with characteristics that enable them to adapt and survive in their environment transmit those characteristics, whereas those less able to adapt die out. In the course of time, there evolves a species possessing a greater degree of adaptation.

Theravada Buddhism See *Hinayana Buddhism*.

three-field system A system of land utilization prevalent in medieval Europe in which village holdings were divided into three fields, one sown to a winter grain, the second to a spring crop, and the third left in fallow. Each year the fields were rotated.

Third Rome Literally, Moscow. In historic Russian Orthodoxy, the doctrine that Moscow is the successor to Rome and Constantinople as the center of Christian faith.

Third World A term that pertains to the less developed or underdeveloped world.

time-distance decay The length of time required to accept a new idea or technique that is being disseminated at ever greater distances from a point of origin.

toponymy The study of place names.

topophilia A term, derived from the Greek, that may be translated as love of place.

torii The gate at the entrance of a Shintō shrine.

totemism A system of beliefs, derived from nature worship, that sees underlying relationships between humans and other forms of life, real or spiritual. It is often demonstrated in the creation of symbols, such as carved poles.

town center In New England, the nucleated center of a township.

TOZ An abbreviation of a Russian word meaning Society for Joint Land Cultivation. It connotes a type of collective enterprise that emerged in Russia after the Bolshevik Revolution.

traditional economy An economy that conforms to tradition; historically, a preindustrialized economy, depending on human or animal labor.

transcendentalists A group who assert the primacy of the spiritual and subjective in life. Transcendentalism flourished in New England in the early nineteenth century.

transhumance The system of livestock raising that entails the guided movement from winter to summer pasture and vice versa.

transmigration of souls A belief entailing the passage of the soul from life to death.

trypanosomiasis (sleeping sickness) A disease of the tropics, transmitted by the tsetse fly.

tsunami A great sea wave produced by submarine earthquake or volcanic eruption.

tundra The treeless region of the Arctic islands and northern coastal areas of North America and Eurasia. The tundra is also found on the upper slopes of higher mountains.

tyranny of space A concept that emphasizes the problems associated with overcoming or bridging vast distances.

underdeveloped world See *developing world*.

unitary Pertaining to a single unit. In government, it implies consolidation of power in one central administration as opposed to a federal form that implies division of power.

universalism Literally, all encompassing; embracing the entire globe.

universality Pertains to widespread acceptance or distribution; without exception.

untouchables In the Indian caste system, those persons at the bottom of the socioeconomic hierarchy.

Upanishads Metaphysical books that form part of the Vedic literature of ancient India.

urbanization The process of becoming urban; in geography, the transformation of a rural landscape into an urban one.

utopia Essentially, an imaginary place or an island described as having a perfect society.

Varangian Way The trade route followed by Scandinavians through western Russia to the Black Sea.

Vedas The sacred books of ancient India.

villein Initially, a free peasant, but later (c. thirteenth century A.D.) an unfree peasant or serf.

Weltansichten A German word meaning world views or world perspectives.

world view A perspective on, or an image of, the world—particularly in terms of the dynamic relationships between peoples or states.

zaibatsu Large Japanese financial organizations.

zero population growth A demographic situation achieved when births equal deaths, resulting in a growth rate of zero.

ziggurat A pyramidlike structure found in many ancient Mesopotamian cities.

Zion Historically, a hill in Jerusalem on which stood Solomon's Temple and David's royal palace. Zion has come to be regarded by Jews generally as the symbol of their socioreligious life.

INDEX